Houghton Mifflin Reading

Teacher's Edition

Grade 6

Triumphs

Back to School
Theme 1 **Courage**
Focus on **Poetry**

Theme 2 **What Really Happened?**
Focus on **Plays**

Theme 3 **Growing Up**

Theme 4 **Discovering Ancient Cultures**
Focus on **Myths**

Theme 5 **Doers and Dreamers**
Focus on **Speeches**

Theme 6 **New Frontiers: Oceans and Space**

Senior Authors J. David Cooper, John J. Pikulski

Authors David J. Chard, Gilbert G. Garcia, Claude N. Goldenberg,
Phyllis C. Hunter, Marjorie Y. Lipson, Shane Templeton,
Sheila W. Valencia, MaryEllen Vogt

Consultants Linda H. Butler, Linnea C. Ehri, Carla B. Ford

 HOUGHTON MIFFLIN BOSTON

LITERATURE REVIEWERS

Consultants: Dr. Adela Artola Allen, Associate Dean, Graduate College, Associate Vice President for Inter-American Relations, University of Arizona, Tucson, AZ; **Dr. Manley Begay,** Co-director of the Harvard Project on American Indian Economic Development, Director of the National Executive Education Program for Native Americans, Harvard University, John F. Kennedy School of Government, Cambridge, MA; **Dr. Nicholas Kannellos,** Director, Arte Publico Press, Director, Recovering the U.S. Hispanic Literacy Heritage Project, University of Houston, TX; **Mildred Lee,** author and former head of Library Services for Sonoma County, Santa Rosa, CA; **Dr. Barbara Moy,** Director of the Office of Communication Arts, Detroit Public Schools, MI; **Norma Naranjo,** Clark County School District, Las Vegas, NV; **Dr. Arlette Ingram Willis,** Associate Professor, Department of Curriculum and Instruction, Division of Language and Literacy, University of Illinois at Urbana-Champaign, IL

Teachers: Sylvia Brown, Lawrence Middle School, Lawrence, NY; **Debbie Carr,** Comanche Middle School, Comanche, OK; **Nancy Chin,** Justice Thurgood Marshall Middle School, Marion, IN; **Daniel Lee,** Alisal Community School, Los Angeles, CA; **Patricia Olsen,** Memorial Middle School, Las Vegas, NM; **Ronald E. Owings,** Jones Middle School, Marion, IN

PROGRAM REVIEWERS

Linda Bayer, Jonesboro, GA; **Sheri Blair,** Warner Robins, GA; **Faye Blake,** Jacksonville, FL; **Suzi Boyett,** Sarasota, FL; **Carol Brockhouse,** Madison Schools, Wayne Westland Schools, MI; **Patti Brustad,** Sarasota, FL; **Jan Buckelew,** Venice, FL; **Maureen Carlton,** Barstow, CA; **Karen Cedar,** Gold River, CA; **Karen Ciraulo,** Folsom, CA; **Marcia M. Clark,** Griffin, GA; **Kim S. Coady,** Covington, GA; **Eva Jean Conway,** Valley View School District, IL; **Marilyn Crownover,** Tustin, CA; **Carol Daley,** Sioux Falls, SD; **Jennifer Davison,** West Palm Beach, FL; **Lynne M. DiNardo,** Covington, GA; **Kathy Dover,** Lake City, GA; **Cheryl Dultz,** Citrus Heights, CA; **Debbie Friedman,** Fort Lauderdale, FL; **Anne Gaitor,** Lakeland, GA; **Rebecca S. Gillette,** Saint Marys, GA; **Buffy C. Gray,** Peachtree City, GA; **Merry Guest,** Homestead, FL; **Jo Nan Holbrook,** Lakeland, GA; **Beth Holguin,** San Jose, CA; **Coleen Howard-Whals,** St. Petersburg, FL; **Beverly Hurst,** Jacksonville, FL; **Debra Jackson,** St. Petersburg, FL; **Vickie Jordan,** Centerville, GA; **Cheryl Kellogg,** Panama City, FL; **Karen Landers,** Talladega County, AL; **Barb LeFerrier,** Port Orchard, WA; **Sandi Maness,** Modesto, CA; **Ileana Masud,** Miami, FL; **David Miller,** Cooper City, FL; **Muriel Miller,** Simi Valley, CA; **Walsetta W. Miller,** Macon, GA; **Jean Nielson,** Simi Valley, CA; **Sue Patton,** Brea, CA; **Debbie Peale,** Miami, FL; **Loretta Piggee,** Gary, IN; **Jennifer Rader,** Huntington, CA; **April Raiford,** Columbus, GA; **Cheryl Remash,** Manchester, NH; **Francis Rivera,** Orlando, FL; **Marina Rodriguez,** Hialeah, FL; **Marilynn Rose,** MI; **Kathy Scholtz,** Amesbury, MA; **Kimberly Moulton Schorr,** Columbus, GA; **Linda Schrum,** Orlando, FL; **Sharon Searcy,** Mandarin, FL; **Melba Sims,** Orlando, FL; **Judy Smith,** Titusville, FL; **Bea Tamo,** Huntington, CA; **Dottie Thompson,** Jefferson County, AL; **Dana Vassar,** Winston-Salem, NC; **Beverly Wakefield,** Tarpon Springs, FL; **Joy Walls,** Winston-Salem, NC; **Elaine Warwick,** Williamson County, TN; **Audrey N. Watkins,** Atlanta, GA; **Marti Watson,** Sarasota, FL

Supervisors: Judy Artz, Butler County, OH; **James Bennett,** Elkhart, IN; **Kay Buckner-Seal,** Wayne County, MI; **Charlotte Carr,** Seattle, WA; **Sister Marion Christi,** Archdiocese of Philadelphia, PA; **Alvina Crouse,** Denver, CO; **Peggy DeLapp,** Minneapolis, MN; **Carol Erlandson,** Wayne Township Schools, IN; **Brenda Feeney,** North Kansas City School District, MO; **Winnie Huebsch,** Sheboygan, WI; **Brenda Mickey,** Winston-Salem, NC; **Audrey Miller,** Camden, NJ; **JoAnne Piccolo,** Westminster, CO; **Sarah Rentz,** Baton Rouge, LA; **Kathy Sullivan,** Omaha, NE; **Rosie Washington,** Gary, IN; **Theresa Wishart,** Knox County Public Schools, TN

English Language Learners Reviewers: Maria Arevalos, Pomona, CA; **Lucy Blood,** NV; **Manuel Brenes,** Kalamazoo, MI; **Delight Diehn,** AZ; **Susan Dunlap,** Richmond, CA; **Tim Fornier,** Grand Rapids, MI; **Connie Jimenez,** Los Angeles, CA; **Diane Bonilla Lether,** Pasadena, CA; **Anna Lugo,** Chicago, IL; **Marcos Martel,** Hayward, CA; **Carolyn Mason,** Yakima, WA; **Jackie Pinson,** Moorpark, CA; **Jenaro Rivas,** NJ; **Jerilyn Smith,** Salinas, CA; **Noemi Velazquez,** Jersey City, NJ; **JoAnna Veloz,** NJ; **Dr. Santiago Veve,** Las Vegas, NV

ISBN-13: 978-0-618-85179-9
ISBN-10: 0-618-85179-8

2 3 4 5 6 7 8 9 10 L 12 11 10 09 08 07

CREDITS

Cover
Cover Illustration Copyright © 2005 by Leo & Diane Dillon.

Photography
BTS1 © Jim Cummins/CORBIS. **BTS2** © Bill Bachman/Midwest Stock. **Theme Opener** © Jim Cummins/Taxi/Getty Images. **BTS11** © Eric Lessing/Art Resource, NY. **39** © CORBIS. **50** Hemera Technologies, Inc. **55** Joe Atlas/Brand X Pictures/PictureQuest. **91** © CORBIS. **93AA** U.S. Navy. **106** © Getty Images. **117K** © ImageState.

Assignment Photography
i, ii, iii, iv, v © HMCo./Michael Indresano.

Illustration
All kid art by Morgan-Cain & Associates.

ACKNOWLEDGMENTS

Grateful acknowledgment is made for permission to reprint copyrighted material as follows:

Theme 1
"The Great Figure," by William Carlos Williams from *Collected Poems: 1909–1939, Volume I.* Copyright 1938 by New Directions Publishing Corp. Reprinted by permission of New Directions Publishing Corp.

"Invention," by Billy Collins from *The Atlantic Monthly,* December 1998, Volume 282, No. 6. Copyright © 1998 by Billy Collins. Reprinted by permission of the author.

"Courage is something everyone has inside them," by Son Ca Lam from *The Courage of Boston's Children: Award-Winning Essays.* Copyright © 1999 by The Max Warburg Courage Curriculum, Inc. Reprinted by permission of The Max Warburg Courage Curriculum, Inc.

"The Rescuer from Lime Rock," by Stephen Currie from *Cricket* Magazine, January 1998 issue, Vol. 25, No. 5. Text copyright © 1998 by Stephen Currie. Cover copyright © 1998 by Carus Publishing Company. Text reprinted by permission of the author. Cover reprinted by permission of Cricket Magazine.

"Storm at Tempest Cove," by Margaret Underwood from *Highlights for Children* Magazine, March 1999 issue, Vol. 54, No. 3. Copyright © 1999 by Highlights for Children, Inc., Columbus, Ohio. Reprinted by permission.

STUDENT WRITING MODEL FEATURE

Special thanks to the following teachers whose students' compositions appear as Student Writing Models: **Cindy Cheatwood,** Florida; **Diana Davis,** North Carolina; **Kathy Driscoll,** Massachusetts; **Linda Evers,** Florida; **Heidi Harrison,** Michigan; **Eileen Hoffman,** Massachusetts; **Julia Kraftsow,** Florida; **Bonnie Lewison,** Florida; **Kanetha McCord,** Michigan

Back to School

Use this section to get to know your students at the beginning of the school year and to get them off to a good start with reading strategies. Also use the overview of assessment tools to help you plan for student evaluation and differentiated instruction.

Getting to Know Your Students

Strategy Workshop

In the first few weeks of school, you will want to get acquainted with the unique individuals who make up your class. Back to School presents the first opportunity for informal screening of students in the Strategy Workshop. Use the workshop to—

- introduce the reading strategies students will use throughout the year,
- observe and evaluate skill development and instructional strengths and needs,
- evaluate students' understanding of reading strategies,
- evaluate how well they express their thoughts in writing.

Other Suggestions for Informal Evaluation

- Have a short conference with each student. Ask about interests and attitudes toward reading and writing.
- Review student portfolios from the previous year.
- To check for fluency, have each student read aloud.
- Ask each student for a writing sample on a topic of his or her choice.
- Observe students as they work together on a small-group activity.

For more information on instructional planning and placement, see the *Teacher's Assessment Handbook*.

Initial Screening

In addition to your own informal observation and evaluation, the *Baseline Group Test* will help you to estimate the amount of support students are likely to need with the level of reading materials you are using with them.

Use the *Baseline Group Test* for screening at the beginning of the year to assess your students' reading level, writing, and comprehension skills. Analysis of the test results will help you to evaluate your students' needs and to customize your teaching to help them achieve their full potential.

The following schematic shows the suggested sequence for evaluation, starting at the beginning of the school year with the Strategy Workshop.

BACK TO SCHOOL

Evaluating Your Students

Strategy Workshop

Baseline Group Test

Phonics/Decoding Screening Test

For further evaluation, use the **Leveled Reading Passages Assessment Kit** and each theme's **Reading-Writing Workshop**.

To further evaluate students' skills, use the **Lexia Quick Phonics Assessment CD-ROM**.

Refer to pages BTS20–BTS22 at the end of Back to School for other resources available for differentiating student instruction.

Getting Started with Reading Strategies

READING STRATEGIES

Predict/Infer

Phonics/Decoding

Monitor/Clarify

Question

Evaluate

Summarize

The reading strategies covered in the Strategy Workshop are the same ones students will work with throughout the year. Students will learn that they should usually apply *all* the reading strategies to *every* selection they read. However, for instructional purposes, starting with Theme 1, students will focus on an individual reading strategy with each selection of the Anthology. In this way, all the strategies are modeled and scaffolded in a systematic way through the year.

In the Strategy Workshop, a different strategy will be introduced and taught with each segment of the story *A Mummy Mystery*. This Read Aloud selection is intended to be read in six segments, with one segment and one strategy presented each day.

Strategy Workshop Steps

Use these steps with each reading strategy in the workshop to help students become successful readers.

1. **Introduce the Strategy.**

2. **Read Aloud.**

3. **Try It Out.**

4. **Discussion/Modeling**

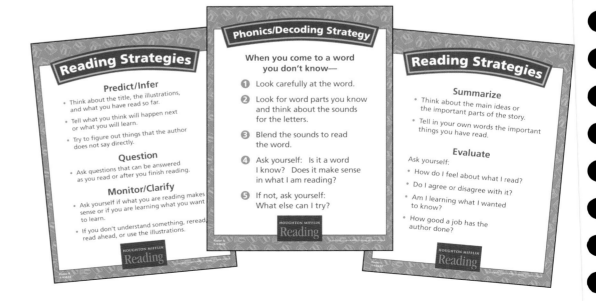

Reading Strategies

Predict/Infer
- Think about the title, the illustrations, and what you have read so far.
- Tell what you think will happen next or what you will learn.
- Try to figure out things that the author does not say directly.

Question
- Ask questions that can be answered as you read or after you finish reading.

Monitor/Clarify
- Ask yourself if what you are reading makes sense or if you are learning what you want to learn.
- If you don't understand something, reread, read ahead, or use the illustrations.

Phonics/Decoding Strategy

When you come to a word you don't know—
1. Look carefully at the word.
2. Look for word parts you know and think about the sounds for the letters.
3. Blend the sounds to read the word.
4. Ask yourself: Is it a word I know? Does it make sense in what I am reading?
5. If not, ask yourself: What else can I try?

Reading Strategies

Summarize
- Think about the main ideas or the important parts of the story.
- Tell in your own words the important things you have read.

Evaluate
Ask yourself:
- How do I feel about what I read?
- Do I agree or disagree with it?
- Am I learning what I wanted to know?
- How good a job has the author done?

Introducing the Strategy Workshop

Discuss with students what good readers do when they read. Talk about the following points:

- Good readers use strategies whenever they read.
- Different strategies are used before, during, and after reading.
- As readers learn to use strategies, they must think about how each strategy will help them.

Then display the strategies, using either the **Strategy Posters** or **Transparencies BTS–1** through **BTS–3.** Tell students that you will review with them each of the strategies that will help them be successful readers.

Explain that you will read aloud the story *A Mummy Mystery* and help students use a different strategy with each segment of the story. Students will respond in their **Practice Books** to each strategy. Then you will help students as needed to model use of this strategy and discuss how it is helpful. **Transparencies BTS–4** through **BTS–25** will enable you to display the appropriate passages of text for modeling. Students can refer to **Practice Book** page 1 throughout the workshop as a reminder of how the strategies will be of use to them.

Remind students that all of the reading strategies together are meant to be used when they read, but that in this workshop, they will study each strategy separately during the reading of the story. One or more strategies may be presented each day, depending on the needs of your students.

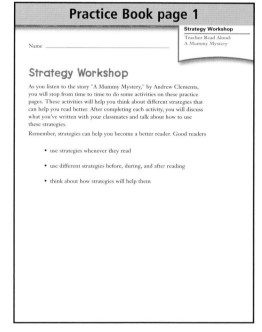

Practice Book page 1

Strategy Workshop
Teacher Read Aloud:
A Mummy Mystery

Name _____

Strategy Workshop

As you listen to the story "A Mummy Mystery," by Andrew Clements, you will stop from time to time to do some activities on these practice pages. These activities will help you think about different strategies that can help you read better. After completing each activity, you will discuss what you've written with your classmates and talk about how to use these strategies.

Remember, strategies can help you become a better reader. Good readers

- use strategies whenever they read
- use different strategies before, during, and after reading
- think about how strategies will help them

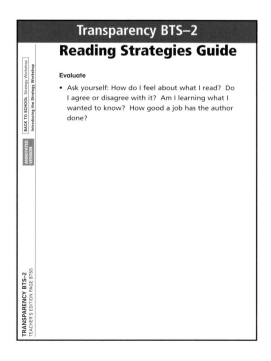

Transparency BTS–1

Reading Strategies Guide

Use these strategies. Be a better reader!

Predict/Infer

- Think about the title, the illustrations, and what you have read so far.
- Tell what you think will happen next or what you will learn.
- Try to figure out things that the author does not say directly.

Question

- Ask questions that can be answered as you read or after you finish reading.

Monitor/Clarify

- Ask yourself if what you are reading makes sense or if you are learning what you want to learn.
- If you don't understand something, reread, read ahead, or use the illustrations.

Summarize

- Think about the main ideas or the important parts of the story.
- Tell in your own words the important things you have read.

Transparency BTS–2

Reading Strategies Guide

Evaluate

- Ask yourself: How do I feel about what I read? Do I agree or disagree with it? Am I learning what I wanted to know? How good a job has the author done?

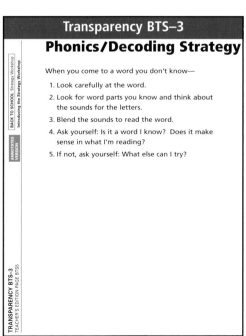

Transparency BTS–3

Phonics/Decoding Strategy

When you come to a word you don't know—

1. Look carefully at the word.
2. Look for word parts you know and think about the sounds for the letters.
3. Blend the sounds to read the word.
4. Ask yourself: Is it a word I know? Does it make sense in what I'm reading?
5. If not, ask yourself: What else can I try?

Strategy Workshop

STRATEGY
Predict/Infer

1. **Introduce the Strategy** Use **Practice Book** page 2 and **Transparency BTS–6,** and together with students, read and discuss the steps of the Predict/Infer strategy.

2. **Read Aloud** Invite students to listen as you read aloud the title and the first three paragraphs of *A Mummy Mystery*. Continue reading Segment 1 after you have discussed the Predict/Infer strategy with students.

3. **Try It Out** Have students turn to **Practice Book** page 2 and write what they think.

Teacher Read Aloud

A Mummy Mystery
by Andrew Clements
SEGMENT 1

"You know what we are?" Molly asked Lena.

Lena wasn't listening. She was reading the placard next to the leg bone of a brontosaurus.

Molly repeated, "Do you know what we are? We're lost, that's what we are."

For the past twenty minutes Molly had forgotten about Mr. Gardiner and the rest of the class as she followed Lena from room to room on the first floor of the Natural Science Museum. Now they stood in the center of a room called The Great Hall. Antique airplanes and ancient battle flags hung from the ceiling. The skeleton of a Tyrannosaurus rex loomed in the distance, towering above a stuffed African elephant. Near a reconstructed castle wall, six knights in armor stood next to their war horses, and forty yards away there was a whole house from a Japanese fishing village.

But Molly saw none of it. "We're lost, Lena—and it's all your fault. Mr. Gardiner will be furious with us!"

Transparency BTS–4
Predict / Infer

A Mummy Mystery
Segment 1

"You know what we are?" Molly asked Lena.
Lena wasn't listening. She was reading the placard next to the leg bone of a brontosaurus.
Molly repeated, "Do you know what we are? We're lost, that's what we are."
For the past twenty minutes, Molly had forgotten about Mr. Gardiner and the rest of the class as she followed Lena from room to room on the first floor of the Natural Science Museum. Now they stood in the center of a room called The Great Hall. Antique airplanes and ancient battle flags hung from the ceiling. The skeleton of a Tyrannosaurus rex loomed in the distance, towering above a stuffed African elephant. Near a reconstructed castle wall, six knights in armor stood next to their war horses, and forty yards away there was a whole house from a Japanese fishing village.
But Molly saw none of it. "We're lost, Lena — and it's all your fault. Mr. Gardiner will be furious with us!"
Lena turned to Molly and shrugged. "You worry too much. Besides, we're *not* lost. We're just on our own for a little while. In another hour it'll be lunch."

BACK TO SCHOOL Strategy Workshop
Strategy: Predict/Infer

ANNOTATED VERSION

TRANSPARENCY BTS–4
TEACHER'S EDITION PAGE BTS6

Transparency BTS–5
Phonics/Decoding

A Mummy Mystery
Segment 1, continued

time, and then all we have to do is go to the cafeteria with everyone else. No one will even realize we've been gone."
Molly didn't look reassured, so Lena shrugged again and looked past her friend at a sweeping gold banner at the far side of The Great Hall. It had red letters three feet tall that said VALLEY OF THE KINGS. It was a visiting exhibit, and it had just opened three days ago.
Ancient Egypt was one of Lena's major interests; it was all she could do to keep from running toward the banner. But Molly still looked as tense as a cat about to spring on a mouse. So Lena pointed and said soothingly, "I don't think we've looked over there yet, over by that big banner? Maybe that's where they are. Want to go see?"
Molly said, "I guess . . . You must think I'm a big baby."
Lena smiled at her. "Not really. I mean, you *are* right. As far as Mr. Gardiner's concerned, we *are* lost, and he could be really worried. So we should keep trying to find them . . . but we can still look at stuff, too, don't you think?"
Molly nodded. "Sure."

BACK TO SCHOOL Strategy Workshop
Strategy: Phonics/Decoding

ANNOTATED VERSION

TRANSPARENCY BTS–5
TEACHER'S EDITION PAGE BTS6

Lena turned to Molly and shrugged. "You worry too much. Besides, we're *not* lost. We're just on our own for a little while. In another hour it'll be lunchtime, and then all we have to do is go to the cafeteria with everyone else. No one will even realize we've been gone."

Molly didn't look reassured, so Lena shrugged again and looked past her friend at a sweeping gold banner at the far side of The Great Hall. It had red letters three feet tall that said VALLEY OF THE KINGS. It was a visiting exhibit, and it had just opened three days ago.

Ancient Egypt was one of Lena's major interests; it was all she could do to keep from running toward the banner. But Molly still looked as tense as a cat about to spring on a mouse. So Lena pointed and said soothingly, "I don't think we've looked over there yet, over by that big banner? Maybe that's where they are. Want to go see?"

Molly said, "I guess … You must think I'm a big baby."

Lena smiled at her. "Not really. I mean, you *are* right. As far as Mr. Gardiner's concerned, we *are* lost, and he could be really worried. So we should keep trying to find them … but we can still look at stuff, too, don't you think?"

Molly nodded. "Sure."

STRATEGY
Predict/Infer

4. **Discussion/Modeling** Have students model how to use the Predict/Infer strategy. Have them discuss their predictions and whether or not their predictions are based on what you have read so far and on their own background information. If students need help with the strategy, use the Think Aloud.

Think Aloud *I can see from the title this story will be about a mystery and will have something to do with a mummy. The character Molly says the two girls are lost. That may play a part in the story too. I'll start reading to see if I'm right.*

Transparency BTS–6

Predict / Infer

A Mummy Mystery
Segment 1, continued

Use these strategies. Be a better reader!
Predict/Infer Strategy

- Think about the title, the illustrations, and what you have read so far.
- Tell what you think will happen next or what you will learn.
- Try to figure out things that the author does not say directly.

TRANSPARENCY BTS–6
TEACHER'S EDITION PAGE BTS7

ANNOTATED VERSION   BACK TO SCHOOL Strategy Workshop   Strategy: Predict/Infer

---

Practice Book page 2

Back to School
Practice Book Page 2

Name _____

Strategy 1: Predict / Infer
Use this strategy before and during reading to help make predictions about what happens next or what you're going to learn.
Here's how to use the Predict/Infer Strategy:
1. Think about the title, the illustrations, and what you have read so far.
2. Tell what you think will happen next—or what you will learn.
3. Thinking about what you already know on the topic may help.
4. Try to figure out things the author does not say directly.
Listen as your teacher begins "A Mummy Mystery." When your teacher stops, complete the activity to show that you understand how to predict what the story might be about and what the mystery might be.

Think about the story and respond to the question below.
What do you think the story is about, and what might the mystery be?

_____
_____
_____
_____

As you continue listening to the story, think about whether your prediction was right. You might want to change your prediction or write a new one below.

_____
_____
_____
_____

Monitoring Student Progress

If . . .	Then . . .
students have difficulty making reasonable predictions,	guide them in looking for clues in the title and in the beginning text. Tell them that thinking about what they have just read and about any background knowledge they have will help them think about what will happen next.

Phonics/Decoding

1. **Introduce the Strategy** Tell students that as they are reading they will use the Phonics/Decoding Strategy to help them read new words. Use **Practice Book** page 3 and **Transparency BTS–10,** and together with students, read and discuss the steps of the Phonics/Decoding Strategy.

2. **Read Aloud** Continue reading the story, stopping at the word *Dynasty*. Then print the word *Dynasty* on the chalkboard. After you have completed discussion of the Phonics/Decoding Strategy with students, finish reading Segment 2.

3. **Try It Out** Now have students turn to **Practice Book** page 3 and write the words in the blanks to complete the steps of the Phonics/Decoding Strategy. Discuss the steps.

Teacher Read Aloud

A Mummy Mystery
SEGMENT 2

Two minutes later Lena and Molly walked under the banner and into a maze of enormous stone blocks. The whole north wing of the museum's first floor had been transformed to look and feel like the inside of an ancient Egyptian tomb. The stone walls were covered with hiero-glyphics, little carved and painted pictures that told stories from four thousand years ago. Dim light filtered down from fixtures that looked like torches, and flute music floated in the still air.

The stone passageway led to a wide central area. A dozen large display cases held objects and artifacts from tombs in the Valley of the Kings, the part of Egypt where many pharaohs had been buried, including King Tutankhamen. Lena had seen pictures of things like this in her books and on the Internet, but this was the real deal.

There was no one else in the area except a small group of high school students. Molly said, "I don't see *our* class. We'd better go ask at the security desk."

"Good idea," Lena said. "But let's look around first, okay?" Then she pointed at a case ten feet away near a wall. "Look—a mummy!" She ran over, and Molly trailed behind her.

Lena read the placard aloud. "Egyptian boy, probably a prince during the Twentieth **Dynasty**. Estimated to be twelve years old at the time of his death."

Transparency BTS–7
Phonics/Decoding

A Mummy Mystery
Segment 2

Two minutes later Lena and Molly walked under the banner and into a maze of enormous stone blocks. The whole north wing of the museum's first floor had been transformed to look and feel like the inside of an ancient Egyptian tomb. The stone walls were covered with hieroglyphics, little carved and painted pictures that told stories from four thousand years ago. Dim light filtered down from fixtures that looked like torches, and flute music floated in the still air.

The stone passageway led to a wide central area. A dozen large display cases held objects and artifacts from tombs in the Valley of the Kings, the part of Egypt where many pharaohs had been buried, including King Tutankhamen. Lena had seen pictures of things like this in her books and on the Internet, but this was the real deal.

There was no one else in the area except a small group of high school students. Molly said, "I don't see *our* class. We'd better go ask at the security desk."

Transparency BTS–8
Phonics/Decoding

A Mummy Mystery
Segment 2, continued

"Good idea," Lena said. "But let's look around first, okay?" Then she pointed at a case ten feet away near a wall. "Look — a mummy!" She ran over, and Molly trailed behind her.

Lena read the placard aloud. "Egyptian boy, probably a prince during the Twentieth **Dynasty**. Estimated to be twelve years old at the time of his death."

Molly said, "What are those jars?"

Lena didn't have to read the placard. She knew all about the jars. "Those are called canopic jars," she said. "In that big one is probably his heart or his stomach, and in the smaller one could be his tongue or his liver."

"Gross!" said Molly.

"Maybe so," said Lena, "but the Egyptians thought that after people got to the afterlife, they'd kind of get put back together and keep on living. So they sent all the important parts along for the journey."

Transparency BTS–9
Phonics/Decoding

A Mummy Mystery
Segment 2, continued

The face of the mummy had been partly unwrapped and peered out between the strips of coarse, discolored cloth. His dried skin was the color of brown shoe leather, and his nose had settled back into the face so it was almost flat. He looked as if he was grinning, with his rows of brown and black and white teeth. His arms were laid across his chest, and one of his hands was turned with the palm up. Bony fingertips poked out of the end of the wrapping.

Molly said, "I know this is history and everything, but it's still creepy, don't you think?"

Lena nodded and said, "But what gets me is that this was a real kid, just like us. He probably wore one of those gold necklaces, and one of those fancy things on his head, too. And those fingers were probably loaded with . . ."

Molly said, "What are those jars?"

Lena didn't have to read the placard. She knew all about the jars. "Those are called canopic jars," she said. "In that big one is probably his heart or his stomach, and in the smaller one could be his tongue or his liver."

"Gross!" said Molly.

"Maybe so," said Lena, "but the Egyptians thought that after people got to the afterlife, they'd kind of get put back together and keep on living. So they sent all the important parts along for the journey."

The face of the mummy had been partly unwrapped and peered out between the strips of coarse, discolored cloth. His dried skin was the color of brown shoe leather, and his nose had settled back into the face so it was almost flat. He looked as if he was grinning, with his rows of brown and black and white teeth. His arms were laid across his chest, and one of his hands was turned with the palm up. Bony fingertips poked out of the end of the wrapping.

Molly said, "I know this is history and everything, but it's still creepy, don't you think?"

Lena nodded and said, "But what gets me is that this was a real kid, just like us. He probably wore one of those gold necklaces, and one of those fancy things on his head, too. And those fingers were probably loaded with …"

STRATEGY
Phonics/Decoding

4. **Discussion/Modeling** Have students model how to use the Phonics/Decoding Strategy to decode the word *Dynasty*. Have them discuss the steps they find most helpful as they read. If students need help with the strategy, use the Think Aloud.

Think Aloud *First, I look carefully at the word to see if there are any word parts I know. I see an entire word I know—nasty. I know that the sounds for* dy *at the beginning of a word are* d *plus the long* i *sound, as in* dynamite. *I'll blend the sounds together: /die-NASTY/. That can't be right. Maybe the* a *has the schwa sound. I'll put the stress on the first syllable: /DIE-nuhsty/. The word is* dynasty. *I think that's the right word because a dynasty is a long line of rulers, which they had in Egypt. It makes sense in the sentence.*

Transparency BTS–10
Phonics/Decoding

A Mummy Mystery
Segment 2, continued

Phonics/Decoding Strategy

When you come to a word you don't know—

1. Look carefully at the word.

2. Look for word parts you know and think about the sounds for the letters.

3. Blend the sounds to read the word.

4. Ask yourself: Is it a word I know? Does it make sense in what I'm reading?

5. If not, ask yourself: What else can I try?

Practice Book page 3

Back to School
Practice Book Page 3

Name _____

Strategy 2: Phonics/Decoding
Use this strategy during reading when you come across a word you don't know.

Here's how to use the Phonics/Decoding Strategy:
1. Look carefully at the word.
2. Look for word parts you know and think about the sounds for the letters.
3. Blend the sounds to read the words.
4. Ask yourself: is this a word I know? Does it make sense in what I am reading?
5. If not, ask yourself what else can I try? Should I look in a dictionary?

Listen as your teacher continues the story. When your teacher stops, use the Phonics/Decoding Strategy.

Now write down the steps you used to decode the word *Dynasty*.

_____
_____
_____
_____
_____
_____
_____
_____

Remember to use this strategy whenever you are reading and come across a word that you don't know.

Monitoring Student Progress

If . . .	Then . . .
students have difficulty using the decoding strategy in their reading,	review the steps with them. Remind them that some words are made up of smaller words they know.

STRATEGY
Monitor/Clarify

1. **Introduce the Strategy** Remind students that good readers ask themselves if what they are reading makes sense. Tell them that when they are confused by what they are reading they can reread or read ahead. Use **Practice Book** page 4 and **Transparency BTS–13,** and together with students, read and discuss the Monitor/Clarify strategy.

2. **Read Aloud** Invite students to listen as you read aloud Segment 3 of *A Mummy Mystery*.

3. **Try It Out** Now have students turn to **Practice Book** page 4 and answer the questions about the mummy mystery.

   1. Describe what happened with the mummy's hand.
   2. Can you tell from listening to the story how everyone reacts to the mummy's hand moving? Why or why not?
   3. How can you find out what made the mummy's hand move?

Teacher Read Aloud

A Mummy Mystery
SEGMENT 3

Lena stared, her mouth open. She reached over and grabbed Molly's arm. Breathing hard, she pointed.

And Molly saw it too. The mummy's hand. It *moved*.

"Oh!" Molly whispered, "Oh! … it … it … C'mon, let's get out of here!"

Lena gulped and said, "Wait … wait a second." They both stared at the wrapped hand, and it lay still. "I mean we both saw that, right? It really moved, right?"

Molly was loud and shrill. "I don't care! Let's go!"

Suddenly a deep voice said, "Is there a problem here?"

Both girls jumped, and Molly gave a little yelp.

The security guard smiled. "It's all right, girls. I didn't mean to startle you. Is everything okay?" He was a big man with kind eyes. The badge on his uniform shirt said Officer Johnson.

Molly forced a smile and said, "Fine. Everything's fine. We were just going. Down to the cafeteria. For lunch. Our class is waiting for us." And she took Lena's hand and started pulling her toward the exit.

But Lena stayed put, and Molly had to stop. Lena said, "We were looking at the display here, and … and the hand there … it … it moved a little." The guard's face broke into a big smile, and right away Lena wished she hadn't said it.

Transparency BTS–11
Monitor/Clarify

A Mummy Mystery
Segment 3

Lena stared, her mouth open. She reached over and grabbed Molly's arm. Breathing hard, she pointed.

And Molly saw it too. The mummy's hand. It *moved.*

"Oh!" Molly whispered, "Oh! . . . it . . . it . . . C'mon, let's get out of here!"

Lena gulped and said, "Wait . . . wait a second." They both stared at the wrapped hand, and it lay still. "I mean we both saw that, right? It really moved, right?"

Molly was loud and shrill, "I don't care! Let's go!"

Suddenly a deep voice said, "Is there a problem here?"

Both girls jumped, and Molly gave a little yelp.

The security guard smiled. "It's all right, girls. I didn't mean to startle you. Is everything okay?" He was a big man with kind eyes. The badge on his uniform shirt said Officer Johnson.

Molly forced a smile and said, "Fine. Everything's fine. We were just going. Down to the cafeteria. For lunch. Our class is waiting for us." And she took Lena's hand and started pulling her toward the exit.

TRANSPARENCY BTS-11
TEACHER'S EDITION PAGE BTS10

BACK TO SCHOOL Strategy Workshop
Strategy: Monitor/Clarify

ANNOTATED VERSION

Transparency BTS–12
Monitor/Clarify

A Mummy Mystery
Segment 3, continued

But Lena stayed put, and Molly had to stop. Lena said, "We were looking at the display here, and . . . and the hand there . . . it . . . it moved a little." The guard's face broke into a big smile, and right away Lena wished she hadn't said it.

Still smiling, Officer Johnson said, "Well, you have to remember, kids, this isn't a theme park. This is a natural history museum, and our exhibits just sit still. Mummies always seem to get folks stirred up, but . . ."

Lena wasn't listening to the guard. She was staring at the case again, and the look on her face stopped him in the middle of his sentence. So he looked too. "Whoa!" he said, and he took a quick step backward. "It moved! It moved, just like you said." Then the guard's eyes narrowed, and a big silly grin spread across his face. "Hey," he said. He looked at Lena, and then at Molly, and then he did a slow turn all the way around, still grinning. He said, "This is a T.V. show, right? You've got a camera hidden somewhere! I bet I'm on T.V. right now. Hi, Mom!"

Lena said, "I hate to disappoint you, but we're just here on a field trip."

TRANSPARENCY BTS-12
TEACHER'S EDITION PAGE BTS10

BACK TO SCHOOL Strategy Workshop
Strategy: Monitor/Clarify

ANNOTATED VERSION

Still smiling, Officer Johnson said, "Well, you have to remember, kids, this isn't a theme park. This is a natural history museum, and our exhibits just sit still. Mummies always seem to get folks stirred up, but … "

Lena wasn't listening to the guard. She was staring at the case again, and the look on her face stopped him in the middle of his sentence. So he looked too. "Whoa!" he said, and he took a quick step backward. "It moved! It moved, just like you said." Then the guard's eyes narrowed, and a big silly grin spread across his face. "Hey," he said. He looked at Lena, and then at Molly, and then he did a slow turn all the way around, still grinning. He said, "This is a T.V. show, right? You've got a camera hidden somewhere! I bet I'm on T.V. right now. Hi, Mom!"

Lena said, "I hate to disappoint you, but we're just here on a field trip."

"Well, then something's not right," said Officer Johnson, "and I'm going to call someone. Now don't either of you go anywhere, you hear?"

Molly said, "But we have to go to the cafeteria and find our class now. You don't want us to get into trouble, do you?"

STRATEGY
Monitor/Clarify

4. **Discussion/Modeling** Have students model how to use the Monitor/Clarify strategy and discuss how it helps them understand what they are reading. Remind them that when they're confused by what they're reading, they can reread or read ahead. If students need help with the strategy, use the Think Aloud.

Think Aloud *After I read the part about the mummy's hand moving, I was a little confused. How could the hand move? After all, mummies are dead! For centuries! I thought I'd read it incorrectly. I reread the last few paragraphs to see if I had missed something, but I hadn't. So I read ahead and found that I had read it correctly—the mummy's hand had in fact moved. Then I remembered that this is a mystery story. I guess this is the beginning of the mystery.*

Transparency BTS–13

Monitor/Clarify

A Mummy Mystery
Segment 3, continued

"Well, then something's not right," said Officer Johnson, "and I'm going to call someone. Now don't either of you go anywhere, you hear?"
Molly said, "But we have to go to the cafeteria and find our class now. You don't want us to get into trouble, do you?"

Monitor/Clarify Strategy
• Ask yourself if what you are reading makes sense or if you are learning what you want to learn.
• If you don't understand something, reread, read ahead, or use the illustrations.

Practice Book page 4

Back to School
Practice Book Page 4

Name _____

Strategy 3: Monitor/Clarify
Use this strategy during reading whenever you're confused about what you are reading.

Here's how to use the Monitor/Clarify Strategy:
• Ask yourself if what you're reading makes sense—or if you are learning what you need to learn.
• If you don't understand something, reread, use the illustrations, or read ahead to see if that helps.

Listen as your teacher continues the story. When your teacher stops, complete the activity to show that you understand what's happening in the story.

Think about the mummy and respond below.
1. Describe what happened with the mummy's hand.

_____
_____
_____

2. Can you tell from listening to the story how everyone reacts to the mummy's hand moving? Why or why not?

_____
_____
_____

3. How can you find out what made the mummy's hand move?

_____
_____
_____

Monitoring Student Progress

If . . .	Then . . .
students have difficulty monitoring as they read,	tell them to stop and think about what they are reading. This will help them understand the meaning.

Question

1. **Introduce the Strategy** Remind students that good readers ask themselves questions about important ideas as they read. Tell them that by asking questions they will understand and enjoy the story more. Use **Practice Book** page 5 and **Transparency BTS–16,** and together with students, read and discuss the Question strategy.

2. **Read Aloud** Invite students to listen as you read aloud Segment 4 of *A Mummy Mystery.*

3. **Try It Out** Now have students turn to **Practice Book** page 5 and write down a question they might ask themselves at this point.

Teacher Read Aloud

A Mummy Mystery
SEGMENT 4

"Well, you'll be in trouble with me if you leave. When I tell my boss that I saw a mummy move his hand, I want witnesses to say 'We did too!' You stay put, both of you," said Officer Johnson, and then he was gone.

Molly gulped and said, "I think we should just leave. He can't make us stay here if we don't want to."

But it was too late. Officer Johnson hurried toward them from one of the passageways, accompanied by a white-haired man wearing a lab coat. "Girls, Dr. Martin Trevor is the museum's chief Egyptologist." To Dr. Trevor he said, "These girls are going to tell you what we *all* saw."

As the three witnesses told their story, Dr. Trevor nodded thoughtfully, his bushy white eyebrows bunched together above his round glasses. Then, speaking with a British accent, he said, "I think we'd better get some technicians in here so we can take a closer look at the mummy." He pulled a phone out of his pocket and punched a number. "Dr. Hines," he said, "could you and your team please come down to the Valley of the Kings room?"

While they waited, Lena said, "Dr. Trevor, why do you think the hand moved?"

Dr. Trevor smiled slightly. "I have been responsible for six different archaeological expeditions in the Valley of the Kings. And the one thing I have learned is this: never to make guesses about the ancient Egyptians. Just when you

---

Transparency BTS–14

Question

A Mummy Mystery
Segment 4

"Well, you'll be in trouble with me if you leave. When I tell my boss that I saw a mummy move his hand, I want witnesses to say 'We did too!' You stay put, both of you," said Officer Johnson, and then he was gone.

Molly gulped and said, "I think we should just leave. He can't make us stay here if we don't want to."

But it was too late. Officer Johnson hurried toward them from one of the passageways, accompanied by a white-haired man wearing a lab coat. "Girls, Dr. Martin Trevor is the museum's chief Egyptologist." To Dr. Trevor he said, "These girls are going to tell you what we *all* saw."

As the three witnesses told their story, Dr. Trevor nodded thoughtfully, his bushy white eyebrows bunched together above his round glasses. Then, speaking with a British accent, he said, "I think we'd better get some technicians in here so we can take a closer look at the mummy." He pulled a phone out of his pocket and punched a number. "Dr. Hines," he said, "could you and your team please come down to the Valley of the Kings room?"

Transparency BTS–15

Question

A Mummy Mystery
Segment 4, continued

While they waited, Lena said, "Dr. Trevor, why do you think the hand moved?"

Dr. Trevor smiled slightly. "I have been responsible for six different archaeological expeditions in the Valley of the Kings. And the one thing I have learned is this: never to make guesses about the ancient Egyptians. Just when you think you know something for sure, that's when you need to pay even closer attention. We shall wait to examine the evidence."

Dr. Clara Hines came into the room followed by two men and another woman. The men each carried large plastic tool boxes, and the woman pushed a rolling cart with a long flat top.

Standing off to one side, Molly nudged Lena. "Aren't you hungry?" she whispered. "We should really go to the cafeteria now."

Lena looked at Molly the way that Abraham Lincoln would have looked at an astronaut. "Are you crazy?" Lena said. "I'm not going anywhere."

Molly pouted. "I'm not crazy, I'm just hungry . . . and we're still in big trouble, you know."

think you know something for sure, that's when you need to pay even closer attention. We shall wait to examine the evidence."

Dr. Clara Hines came into the room followed by two men and another woman. The men each carried large plastic tool boxes, and the woman pushed a rolling cart with a long flat top.

Standing off to one side, Molly nudged Lena. "Aren't you hungry?" she whispered. "We should really go to the cafeteria now."

Lena looked at Molly the way that Abraham Lincoln would have looked at an astronaut. "Are you crazy?" Lena said. "I'm not going anywhere."

Molly pouted. "I'm not crazy, I'm just hungry … and we're still in big trouble, you know."

Ignoring Molly, Lena stepped to one side so she could see better. Under the watchful eyes of Drs. Trevor and Hines, the technicians attached suction-cup devices to three sides of the glass case that protected the mummy. Dr. Hines counted, "One, two, three—" and they lifted the case straight up, took four steps back, and gently placed it on the floor.

Dr. Hines said, "I think we'd better move the mummy before it's examined. Our loan agreement with the museum in London says that the mummy must not be exposed to any moisture, and it's too humid in here today. I'd feel better if we took him to the lab."

The technicians carefully lifted the mummy and set it gently on the wheeled cart. The mummy looked like a patient on a rolling bed at a hospital. They began to wheel the mummy toward the lab.

STRATEGY
Question

4. **Discussion/Modeling** Have students model how to use the Question strategy, and discuss how asking about something they want to know more about will help them understand what they are reading. Have students discuss the questions they've written. If students need help with the strategy, use the Think Aloud.

Think Aloud *At this point in the story I have to ask myself this question: How could the mummy's hand move? There has to be a reasonable explanation that is not that the mummy is still alive. I'll have to read on to get that explanation.*

Transparency BTS–16

Question

A Mummy Mystery
Segment 4, continued

Ignoring Molly, Lena stepped to one side so she could see better. Under the watchful eyes of Drs. Trevor and Hines, the technicians attached suction-cup devices to three sides of the glass case that protected the mummy. Dr. Hines counted, "One, two, three—" and they lifted the case straight up, took four steps back, and gently placed it on the floor.

Dr. Hines said, "I think we'd better move the mummy before it's examined. Our loan agreement with the museum in London says that the mummy must not be exposed to any moisture, and it's too humid in here today. I'd feel better if we took him to the lab."

The technicians carefully lifted the mummy and set it gently on the wheeled cart. The mummy looked like a patient on a rolling bed at a hospital. They began to wheel the mummy toward the lab.

Question Strategy
• Ask questions that can be answered as you read or after you finish reading.

TRANSPARENCY BTS–16
TEACHER'S EDITION PAGE BTS13

BACK TO SCHOOL Strategy Workshop
Strategy: Question

ANNOTATED VERSION

Practice Book page 5

Back to School
Practice Book Page 5

Name _____

Strategy 4: Question
Use this strategy during and after reading to ask questions about important ideas in the story.
Here's how to use the Question Strategy:
• Ask yourself questions about important ideas in the story.
• Ask yourself if you can answer these questions.
• If you can't answer the questions, reread and look for answers in the text. Thinking about what you already know and what you've read in the story may help you.
Listen as your teacher continues the story. Then complete the activity to show that you understand how to ask yourself questions about important ideas in the story.
Think about the story and respond below.
Write a question you might ask yourself at this point in the story.

_____
_____
_____
_____

If you can't answer your question now, think about it while you listen to the rest of the story.

Monitoring Student Progress

If . . .	Then . . .
students have difficulty coming up with questions,	have them discuss things in the story that they want to know more about. Model for them how to formulate questions.

STRATEGY
Evaluate

1. **Introduce the Strategy** Remind students that good readers should always think about their reaction to what they are reading and why they are reacting that way.

   Tell them that they can *evaluate* a story in many different ways:
   - by how well the author writes
   - by what the story is about
   - by their reaction to the story

   Use **Practice Book** page 6 and **Transparency BTS–19,** and together with students, read and discuss the Evaluate strategy.

2. **Read Aloud** Read aloud the next segment of *A Mummy Mystery*.

3. **Try It Out** Now have students turn to **Practice Book** page 6 and respond to one of the prompts on that page:

   1. Tell whether or not you think this story is entertaining and why.
   2. Is the writing clear and easy to understand?
   3. This is a mystery story. Did the author make the characters interesting and believable?

Teacher Read Aloud
A Mummy Mystery
SEGMENT 5

Lena darted around Officer Johnson and Dr. Hines and put a hand on Dr. Trevor's arm. He looked down at her, and she said, "Can I come too … and Molly?"

He smiled and said, "By all means. You two are part of the team now."

In the lab, the technicians lifted the mummy onto a table, and Dr. Hines leaned over the body. Molly whispered, "It seemed a lot scarier downstairs, don't you think? Up here it's more like a squirrel that's been hit by a car or something." Lena nodded and moved a little closer. Molly stayed right by her side.

Dr. Trevor said, "Dr. Hines, is there a stethoscope handy? I've got a theory, and as mad as it may seem, I'd like to test it."

Lena looked at Molly and whispered, "A stethoscope— that's what a doctor uses to listen for a … for a heartbeat."

Molly edged closer to Lena and said, "But it's … it's *dead* … right?"

Lena shrugged and kept her eyes on Dr. Trevor.

Dr. Trevor put the ends of the stethoscope into his ears and leaned over the mummy, gently pressing the flat metal end of the device onto the mummy's hand. The room was quiet as a tomb.

Transparency BTS–17
Evaluate

A Mummy Mystery
Segment 5

Lena darted around Officer Johnson and Dr. Hines and put a hand on Dr. Trevor's arm. He looked down at her, and she said, "Can I come too . . . and Molly?"

He smiled and said, "By all means. You two are part of the team now."

In the lab, the technicians lifted the mummy onto a table, and Dr. Hines leaned over the body. Molly whispered, "It seemed a lot scarier downstairs, don't you think? Up here it's more like a squirrel that's been hit by a car or something." Lena nodded, and moved a little closer. Molly stayed right by her side.

Dr. Trevor said, "Dr. Hines, is there a stethoscope handy? I've got a theory, and as mad as it may seem, I'd like to test it."

Lena looked at Molly and whispered, "A stethoscope — that's what a doctor uses to listen for a . . . for a heartbeat."

Molly edged closer to Lena and said, "But it's . . . it's *dead* . . . right?"

Lena shrugged and kept her eyes on Dr. Trevor.

Dr. Trevor put the ends of the stethoscope into his ears and leaned over the mummy, gently pressing the flat metal end of the device onto the mummy's hand. The room was quiet as a tomb.

TRANSPARENCY BTS–17
TEACHER'S EDITION PAGE BTS14

ANNOTATED VERSION
BACK TO SCHOOL Strategy Workshop
Strategy: Evaluate

Transparency BTS–18
Evaluate

A Mummy Mystery
Segment 5, continued

Dr. Trevor slowly nodded. Pulling the ends from his ears, he turned to Lena. "Care to have a listen?"

Lena was surprised, but said, "Sure," and stepped forward quickly. He helped her put it on, and then put the flat end back on the mummy's hand. At first, Lena heard only the scratching sound as the end of the stethoscope moved slightly over the mummy's wrappings. But then . . . no, it couldn't be. But wait . . . it was . . . and there it was again! Lena felt the hairs on the back of her neck prickle, and she shivered.

"Well?" said Dr. Trevor. "Hear anything?"

Lena pulled the ends of the stethoscope from her ears. Dr. Trevor stood there, his eyebrows up above his glasses, waiting for Lena to say something.

"I know this sounds crazy," she began, "but I heard . . . *snoring!*"

"Exactly," said Dr. Trevor, and a hushed wave of surprised exclamations rippled around the room. Dr. Trevor said, "I have to call Phillip Cowan at the museum in London. This mummy belongs to them, so we need permission before we can take any action. It's already past closing time in London, but as I recall, Phillip tends to work late."

TRANSPARENCY BTS–18
TEACHER'S EDITION PAGE BTS14

ANNOTATED VERSION
BACK TO SCHOOL Strategy Workshop
Strategy: Evaluate

Dr. Trevor slowly nodded. Pulling the ends from his ears, he turned to Lena. "Care to have a listen?"

Lena was surprised, but said, "Sure," and stepped forward quickly. He helped her put it on, and then put the flat end back on the mummy's hand. At first, Lena heard only the scratching sound as the end of the stethoscope moved slightly over the mummy's wrappings. But then … no, it couldn't be. But wait … it was … and there it was again! Lena felt the hairs on the back of her neck prickle, and she shivered.

"Well?" said Dr. Trevor. "Hear anything?"

Lena pulled the ends of the stethoscope from her ears, and Dr. Trevor stood there, his eyebrows up above his glasses, waiting for Lena to say something.

"I know this sounds crazy," she began, "but I heard … *snoring!*"

"Exactly," said Dr. Trevor, and a hushed wave of surprised exclamations rippled around the room. Dr. Trevor said, "I have to call Phillip Cowan at the museum in London. This mummy belongs to them, so we need permission before we can take any action. It's already past closing time in London, but as I recall, Phillip tends to work late."

Dr. Trevor pulled a small black notebook from the pocket of his tweed jacket, flipped past a few pages, adjusted his glasses, and then punched in a twelve-digit number. The room was quiet except for the rustling of paper. Lena turned toward the sound and saw Molly unwrapping a candy bar. Molly smiled and shrugged as she took a bite.

STRATEGY
Evaluate

4. **Discussion/Modeling** Have students model how to use the Evaluate strategy and discuss how following the steps can help them understand the story. If students need help with the strategy, use the Think Aloud.

Think Aloud *The author gets me interested in the story from the very start. The author did a good job with the characters, especially Molly and Lena, who seem like kids I know. I like the humor, too: the way Molly is so hungry the whole time is funny. And I couldn't guess the answer to the mystery, which is good; it made me want to keep reading.*

Transparency BTS–19
Evaluate

A Mummy Mystery
Segment 5, continued

Dr. Trevor pulled a small black notebook from the pocket of his tweed jacket, flipped past a few pages, adjusted his glasses, and then punched in a twelve-digit number. The room was quiet except for the rustling of paper. Lena turned toward the sound and saw Molly unwrapping a candy bar. Molly smiled and shrugged as she took a bite.

Evaluate Strategy
- Ask yourself: How do I feel about what I read? Do I agree or disagree with it? Am I learning what I wanted to know? How good a job has the author done?

Practice Book page 6

Back to School
Practice Book Page 6

Name _____

Strategy 5: Evaluate
Use this strategy during and after reading to help you form an opinion about what you read.
Here's how to use the Evaluate Strategy:
- Tell whether or not you think this story is entertaining and why.
- Is the writing clear and easy to understand?
- This is a mystery story. Did the author make the characters believable and interesting?

Listen as your teacher continues the story. When your teacher stops, complete the activity to show that you are thinking of how you feel about what you are reading and why you feel that way.

Think about the story and respond below.

1. Tell whether or not you think this story is entertaining and why.
_____
_____
_____

2. Is the writing clear and easy to understand?
_____
_____
_____

3. This is a mystery story. Did the author make the characters interesting and believable?
_____
_____
_____

Monitoring Student Progress

If . . .	Then . . .
students have difficulty evaluating the story,	guide them with questions that require students to give opinions about the story. Explain that when giving opinions, they are evaluating the story.

STRATEGY
Summarize

1. **Introduce the Strategy** Explain to students that summarizing means briefly telling the most important parts of a story in a quick way. Remind students that thinking about the following story elements can help them summarize a story:

   - who the main character is
   - where the story takes place
   - what the problem is
   - what happens in the beginning, middle, and end

   Use **Practice Book** page 7 and **Transparency BTS–25,** and together with students, read and discuss the Summarize strategy.

2. **Read Aloud** Read aloud Segment 6 of *A Mummy Mystery* on pages BTS16–BTS19.

3. **Try It Out** Now have students turn to **Practice Book** page 7 and respond to the three prompts on that page.

   1. Who is the main character?
   2. Where does the story take place?
   3. What is the problem and how is it resolved?

Teacher Read Aloud

A Mummy Mystery
SEGMENT 6

"Phillip? This is Martin Trevor.... Yes, I'm just fine, couldn't be better, really.... Yes, well I've called on museum business, Phillip. It's about that Twentieth Dynasty mummy you've loaned to us. We've found something, shall we say, irregular, and I may have to tamper a bit to set things right.... Of course I shall.... Yes.... Oh yes, a full report. And you know I shall exercise the utmost care.... Splendid.... Thank you, Phillip. Good-bye now."

Putting away his phone, Dr. Trevor was all business. "Dr. Hines, I'm going to need some forceps, a small sprayer filled with some textile solvent, and a piece of plastic sheeting about a half meter square. We also need a 500-milliliter glass beaker, and of course I'll need some gloves."

Less than a minute later, Dr. Hines had supplied the needed equipment. The spray bottle looked like the kind Lena had seen the custodians use at her school, except there was a long plastic tube that went from the neck of the bottle to the sprayer head. Dr. Trevor sprayed the mummy's hand. Looking at it again, he said, "This liquid will temporarily soften the wrappings so we can move them a little without doing any serious damage."

Bending low over the mummy, Dr. Trevor carefully began to loosen the cloth covering the hand. He held the forceps with his right hand, and used his left hand to

---

Transparency BTS–20
Summarize

A Mummy Mystery
Segment 6

"Phillip? This is Martin Trevor. . . . Yes, I'm just fine, couldn't be better, really. . . . Yes, well I've called on museum business, Phillip. It's about that Twentieth Dynasty mummy you've loaned to us. We've found something, shall we say, irregular, and I may have to tamper a bit to set things right. . . . Of course I shall. . . . Yes. . . . Oh yes, a full report. And you know I shall exercise the utmost care. . . . Splendid. . . . Thank you, Phillip. Good-bye now."

Putting away his phone, Dr. Trevor was all business. "Dr. Hines, I'm going to need some forceps, a small sprayer filled with some textile solvent, and a piece of plastic sheeting about a half meter square. We also need a 500-milliliter glass beaker, and of course I'll need some gloves."

Less than a minute later, Dr. Hines had supplied the needed equipment. The spray bottle looked like the kind Lena had seen the custodians use at her school, except there was a long plastic tube that went from the neck of the bottle to the sprayer head. Dr. Trevor sprayed the mummy's hand. Looking at it again, he said, "This liquid will temporarily soften the wrappings so we can move them a little without doing any serious damage."

TRANSPARENCY BTS–20
TEACHER'S EDITION PAGE BTS16

Transparency BTS–21
Summarize

A Mummy Mystery
Segment 6, continued

Bending low over the mummy, Dr. Trevor carefully began to loosen the cloth covering the hand. He held the forceps with his right hand, and used his left hand to support the mummy's long bony fingers. Lena edged forward. The wrapping that had covered the mummy's hand had been pushed toward his fingertips, and Dr. Trevor was squinting as he peered into the hollow of the boy's cupped palm.

Suddenly lifting his face to look at Lena, Dr. Trevor said, "Come here."

Lena stepped to the edge of the table, and Dr. Trevor handed her a pair of gloves. "Put these on." Lena did. "Take these." He handed her the forceps. "Now, as I pull the wrapping back another centimeter or two, I want you to look into the palm of his hand, then reach in there with the forceps — very, very, gently. You may not like what you find in there. Do you think you can do this?"

Lena gulped. Reading about mummies was a lot different than shaking hands with one. But she nodded and said, "Yes."

TRANSPARENCY BTS–21
TEACHER'S EDITION PAGE BTS16

Transparency BTS–22
Summarize

A Mummy Mystery
Segment 6, continued

Dr. Trevor pulled back the wrapping, and Lena bent over the mummy's hand. She strained to see beneath the cloth coverings. Then she gasped, and quickly looked up at Dr. Trevor. He nodded to encourage her, so Lena took a deep breath and slid the end of the forceps into the opening. She spread her fingers slightly to open the jaws of the forceps. Then her fingers closed, and she slowly pulled the slender silver tool out of the mummy's hand. Lena straightened up and held up the forceps to show the others what she'd found. Everyone stared, amazed.

Dr. Trevor made the announcement. "Ladies and gentlemen, what you see before you is one of the greatest dangers a mummy can ever face. This is *Mus musculus* — otherwise known as the common mouse!" Hanging gently by its tail, a sleepy-looking brown mouse peered around the room and wiggled its small pink nose. Lena quickly lowered the mouse into the glass beaker and let go of its tail. The mouse immediately sat up on its back legs and began to rub its ears and whiskers with its front paws.

Dr. Trevor grinned at Lena and said, "I declare this mystery to be solved." Everyone applauded.

TRANSPARENCY BTS–22
TEACHER'S EDITION PAGE BTS16

---

support the mummy's long bony fingers. Lena edged forward. The wrapping that had covered the mummy's hand had been pushed toward his fingertips, and Dr. Trevor was squinting as he peered into the hollow of the boy's cupped palm.

Suddenly lifting his face to look at Lena, Dr. Trevor said, "Come here."

Lena stepped to the edge of the table, and Dr. Trevor handed her a pair of gloves. "Put these on." Lena did. "Take these." He handed her the forceps. "Now, as I pull the wrapping back another centimeter or two, I want you to look into the palm of his hand, then reach in there with the forceps—very, very gently. You may not like what you find in there. Do you think you can do this?"

Lena gulped. Reading about mummies was a lot different than shaking hands with one. But she nodded and said, "Yes."

Dr. Trevor pulled back the wrapping, and Lena bent over the mummy's hand. She strained to see beneath the cloth coverings. Then she gasped, and quickly looked up at Dr. Trevor. He nodded to encourage her, so Lena took a deep breath and slid the end of the forceps into the opening. She spread her fingers slightly to open the jaws of the forceps. Then her fingers closed, and she slowly pulled the slender silver tool out of the mummy's hand. Lena straightened up and held up the forceps to show the others what she'd found. Everyone stared, amazed.

(Segment 6 *continues on next page.*)

STRATEGY
Summarize

4. **Discussion/Modeling** Have students model how to use the Summarize strategy by telling the following in their own words:

- who the main character is
- what the problem is
- how the problem is solved

If students need help with the strategy, use the Think Aloud.

Think Aloud *The main characters in the story are two girls, Molly and Lena. On a field trip to a museum, they are looking at a mummy when they see its hand move. The museum guard calls the museum's Egyptologist, who, along with some technicians, unwraps the mummy's hand to uncover the source of the movement: a mouse that had crawled into the wrapping in search of food.*

Transparency BTS–23
Summarize

A Mummy Mystery
Segment 6, continued

Ten minutes later, Dr. Trevor walked down the main staircase from the second floor with Lena and Molly. He had volunteered to help them find their class. Talking about the mouse, Dr. Trevor said, "I imagine it got into the middle of things sometime during the shipping. The Egyptians always sent along food for the trip to the afterlife, so the mouse may have found an ancient piece of corn or wheat somewhere. If the little fellow hadn't made that mummy wave at you girls, in another day or so he'd have become a permanent part of the exhibit — mummified mouse. Or he could have started chewing on the mummy and done some serious damage. Either way, I want to thank you both for being so observant and so brave."

As they reached the basement level and entered the cafeteria, Molly said, "There's Mr. Gardiner! We're really going to catch it now."

But Dr. Trevor saved them. He introduced himself to Mr. Gardiner and said, "I hope you don't mind that we borrowed these two students for a while. They've been a great help; you must ask them to tell you all about it."

Transparency BTS–24
Summarize

A Mummy Mystery
Segment 6, continued

Dr. Trevor shook hands with Molly. She said a quick "Good-bye," and then rushed over to get in line for food.

Taking Lena's hand, Dr. Trevor said, "It's been a pleasure to work with you, Lena." He handed her his business card and said, "Please feel free to call me here at the museum. I'd be honored to take you and your parents on a tour of the entire Egyptian collection. We have rooms and rooms full of things that the public rarely gets to see."

Lena's eyes sparkled as she said, "That would be super! Thank you!" Then she said, "By the way, Dr. Trevor, when did you know for sure that it was a mouse that moved the mummy's hand?"

With a twinkle in his eye, he said, "When did I know for sure? When my assistant picked it up by its long pink tail. Until then, it was just a theory. Good-bye, Lena. And come back to visit us often."

Lena smiled and said, "I will. You can count on it."

Monitoring Student Progress

If . . .	Then . . .
students have difficulty summarizing the story,	use a Graphic Organizer to chart the story setting, the main characters, the main events, the problem, and the solution of the problem. Then have students use this information to summarize the story.

Strategy Workshop

Segment 6 *continued*

Continue reading the story to the end of Segment 6 on page BTS19.

A Mummy Mystery

SEGMENT 6 continued

Dr. Trevor made the announcement. "Ladies and gentle-men, what you see before you is one of the greatest dangers a mummy can ever face. This is *Mus musculus*—otherwise known as the common mouse!" Hanging gently by its tail, a sleepy-looking brown mouse peered around the room and wiggled its small pink nose. Lena quickly lowered the mouse into the glass beaker and let go of its tail. The mouse immediately sat up on its back legs and began to rub its ears and whiskers with its front paws.

Dr. Trevor grinned at Lena and said, "I declare this mys-tery to be solved." Everyone applauded.

Ten minutes later, Dr. Trevor walked down the main staircase from the second floor with Lena and Molly. He had volunteered to help them find their class. Talking about the mouse, Dr. Trevor said, "I imagine it got into the middle of things sometime during the shipping. The Egyptians always sent along food for the trip to the afterlife, so the mouse may have found an ancient piece of corn or wheat somewhere. If the little fellow hadn't made that mummy wave at you girls, in another day or so he'd have become a permanent part of the exhibit—mummified mouse. Or he could have started chewing on the mummy and done some serious damage. Either way, I want to thank you both for being so observant and so brave."

Transparency BTS–25

Summarize

A Mummy Mystery

Segment 6, continued

Summarize Strategy

- Think about the main ideas or the important parts of the story.
- Tell in your own words the important things you have read.

BACK TO SCHOOL Strategy Workshop
Strategy: Summarize

ANNOTATED VERSION

TRANSPARENCY BTS–25
TEACHER'S EDITION PAGE BTS18

Practice Book page 7

Back to School
Practice Book Page 7

Name _____

Strategy 6: Summarize

Use this strategy after reading to summarize what you read.

Here's how to use the Summarize Strategy:

- Think about the characters.
- Think about where the story takes place.
- Think about the problem in the story and how the characters solve it.
- Think about what happens in the beginning, middle, and end of the story.

Think about the story you just listened to. Complete the activity to show that you understand how to identify important story parts that will help you summarize the story.

Think about the story and respond to the questions below:

1. Who is the main character?

_____

_____

2. Where does the story take place?

_____

_____

_____

3. What is the problem and how is it resolved?

_____

_____

_____

Now use this information to summarize the story for a partner.

As they reached the basement level and entered the cafeteria, Molly said, "There's Mr. Gardiner! We're really going to catch it now."

But Dr. Trevor saved them. He introduced himself to Mr. Gardiner and said, "I hope you don't mind that we borrowed these two students for a while. They've been a great help; you must ask them to tell you all about it."

Dr. Trevor shook hands with Molly. She said a quick "Good-bye," and then rushed over to get in line for food.

Taking Lena's hand, Dr. Trevor said, "It's been a pleasure to work with you, Lena." He handed her his business card and said, "Please feel free to call me here at the museum. I'd be honored to take you and your parents on a tour of the entire Egyptian collection. We have rooms and rooms full of things that the public rarely gets to see."

Lena's eyes sparkled as she said, "That would be super! Thank you!" Then she said, "By the way, Dr. Trevor, when did you know for sure that it was a mouse that moved the mummy's hand?"

With a twinkle in his eye, he said, "When did I know for sure? When my assistant picked it up by its long pink tail. Until then, it was just a theory. Good-bye, Lena. And come back to visit us often."

Lena smiled and said, "I will. You can count on it."

Comprehension: Story Response

1. Why does Molly want to get back to the class? (She's afraid that she and Lena will get in trouble, and she's hungry.)

2. Why does Officer Johnson insist that the girls stay? (He wants them to tell about the mummy with him, so he'll be believed.)

3. How did food get into the mummy's wrapping? (It was probably buried with it, as part of the ancient Egyptian ceremony.)

4. Do you think that Dr. Trevor's theory probably had something to do with a mouse or other creature? Why or why not? (Answers will vary.)

Evaluating Reading Strategies

Discuss with students the strategies that they have used in listening to this story. Have students respond to the following prompts:

1. What strategies were the most helpful to you in understanding this story?

2. What strategies do you use when you are reading? Why do you find them helpful?

Encourage students to be strategic readers as they begin reading this year. Discuss from time to time which strategies students are using and which strategies would be helpful to use. Remind students that the opening page of their **Practice Book** provides a quick reference to using strategies.

Learning More About Your Students

Now that you have had a chance to observe your class at work, you probably have an idea about which students will need extra support. In addition to ongoing informal assessment, you may wish to use one or more diagnostic instruments to assess certain students' strengths and needs. Your diagnosis can help in planning instruction and customizing your teaching to meet students' individual needs.

Diagnosing Needs

Once you have administered the *Baseline Group Test* for initial screening, you can use the *Leveled Reading Passages Assessment Kit* to take an Oral Reading Record. This individual assessment can give a more detailed diagnosis, providing information about the individual student's reading level, phonics and decoding skills, comprehension, use of strategies, and fluency. See the chart at left for additional assessment instruments that you can use.

Test	Assesses
Baseline Group Test (Group Administration)	Comprehension Reading Level Writing
Leveled Reading Passages Assessment Kit (Individual Administration)	Reading Level Decoding Comprehension Strategies Oral Reading Fluency
Phonics/Decoding Screening Test (Individual Administration)	Phonics Structural Analysis
Lexia Quick Phonics Assessment CD-ROM (Individual Administration, with Computer)	Phonics

Monitoring Student Progress

As students begin work in Theme 1, you may want to make some of the informal observations listed below. Additional suggestions for informal assessment are in Planning for Assessment at the start of each theme.

- Listen to students read aloud to observe fluency, decoding, and expression.

- To note students' comprehension of Anthology selections, check answers to Comprehension/Critical Thinking and Think About the Selection questions in the *Teacher's Edition,* or use the Selection Tests in the *Teacher's Resource Blackline Masters*.

- Use the suggestions in the Monitoring Student Progress boxes provided throughout the theme to evaluate student performance and to differentiate further instruction or practice.

- Observe students' writing in the Reading-Writing Workshop writing lessons or in Quick Writes, Practice Book pages, Journals, or other writing assignments.

- Note students' interest in and motivation for reading.

Planning for Instruction

Results of diagnostic assessment can be used to help plan appropriate instruction for each student. Instructional support to meet a variety of individual needs is included in this *Teacher's Edition* and in other components of *Houghton Mifflin Reading*. The chart below suggests the appropriate instructional emphasis and resources for students with different individual needs.

Differentiating Instruction

Student Performance Shows	Modifications to Consider
Difficulty with Decoding or Word Skills	• **Emphasis:** Word skills, phonics, reading for fluency, check for phonemic awareness • **Resources:** Teacher's Edition: *Phonics Review, Structural Analysis Reteaching lessons;* Leveled Readers; Lexia Phonics CD-ROM: Intermediate Intervention; Get Set for Reading CD-ROM
Difficulty with Oral Fluency	• **Emphasis:** Reading and rereading of independent level text; vocabulary development • **Resources:** Teacher's Edition: *Fluency Practice;* Leveled Readers; Theme Paperbacks; Reader's Library; Get Set for Reading CD-ROM and Selection Summary Masters; Book Adventure® website
Difficulty with Comprehension	• **Emphasis:** Oral comprehension; strategy development; story comprehension; vocabulary development • **Resources:** Teacher's Edition: *Teacher Read Alouds, Strategies, Extra Support notes, Comprehension Reteaching lessons, Vocabulary Skills;* Leveled Readers; Get Set for Reading CD-ROM; Extra Support Handbook
Overall High Performance	• **Emphasis:** Independent reading and writing; vocabulary development; critical thinking • **Resources:** Teacher's Edition: *Think About the Selection questions, Challenge notes, Challenge/Extension Activities, Assignment Cards;* Leveled Readers; Theme Paperbacks; Book Adventure® website; Education Place® website; Challenge Handbook

Managing Instruction

Throughout *Houghton Mifflin Reading,* you will find support for differentiating and managing instruction in the following features and components:

Reaching All Learners

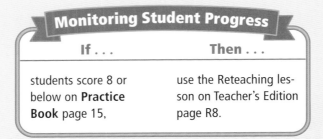

Monitoring Student Progress

If . . .	Then . . .
students score 8 or below on **Practice Book** page 15,	use the Reteaching lesson on Teacher's Edition page R8.

Use these notes to help you evaluate student performance and to differentiate further instruction or practice.

Extra Support / Intervention

On Level   Challenge

Challenge

English Language Learners

Use the suggestions in these boxes to provide differentiated instruction for students at all levels of ability.

Classroom Management

Managing Flexible Groups

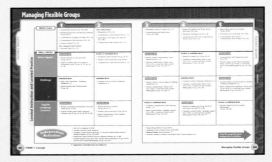

Plan your reading block with these suggested grouping options.

Ready-Made Small Group Activities

Assign these independent cross-curricular activities while you work with small groups.

Small Group Independent Activities Kit

Use this kit to manage small group activities. Included in the kit are ready-made manipulatives for Reading, Writing, Word Work, and Cross-Curricular practice.

Assessment Management and Reporting

HOUGHTON MIFFLIN **Assessment System**

Create tests and practice online, get instant results online or by scan-and-score, report performance on your state standards, and run prescriptions to differentiate instruction.

COURAGE

Theme 1

OBJECTIVES

Reading Strategies summarize; evaluate; predict/infer; monitor/clarify; phonics/decoding

Comprehension noting details; making judgments; sequence of events; predicting outcomes

Decoding Longer Words suffixes *-ful, -less,* and *-ly;* syllabication; prefixes *un-* and *re-;* possessives and contractions; short vowels; long vowels; more vowel spellings; /ou/, /o͞o/, /ô/, and /oi/ sounds

Vocabulary using context; dictionary: alphabetical order and guide words; dictionary: parts of an entry; word families

Spelling short vowels; long vowels; more vowel spellings; /ou/, /o͞o/, /ô/, and /oi/ sounds

Grammar kinds of sentences; subjects and predicates; conjunctions; compound sentences; complex sentences; correcting fragments and run-on sentences; common and proper nouns; singular and plural nouns

Writing instructions; memo; friendly letter; opinion; process writing: personal narrative

Listening/Speaking/Viewing retelling a story; speaking on the telephone; literature discussion; directions

Information and Study Skills print and electronic card catalogs; print and electronic reference sources; parts of a book/index; graphic aids: maps, globes, graphs, tables, captions, charts

COURAGE

CONTENTS

Vocabulary Reader

Nonfiction

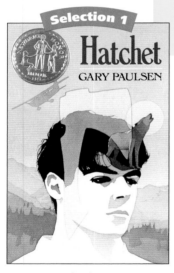

Fiction

Below Level

On Level

Above Level

Language Support

Leveled Readers

Writing Process ▶

Nonfiction

Selection 4

Historical Fiction

Below Level   On Level   Above Level   Language Support

Leveled Readers

Theme Wrap-Up

Monitoring Student Progress

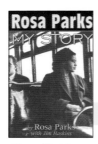

Nonfiction

Realistic fiction

Focus on Genre POETRY

Vocabulary Reader

Nonfiction

POETRY

Below Level   *On Level*   *Above Level*   *Language Support*

Leveled Readers

Leveled Theme Paperbacks

Leveled Bibliography

BOOKS FOR INDEPENDENT READING AND FLUENCY BUILDING

 To build vocabulary and fluency, choose books from this list for students to read outside of class. Suggest that students read for at least thirty minutes a day, either independently or with an adult who provides modeling and guidance.

Key

 Science

Social Studies

Multicultural

Music

Math

 Classic

Art

Career

Classroom Bookshelf

WELL BELOW LEVEL

Fireboat: The Heroic Adventures of the *John J. Harvey*
by Maira Kalman
Putnam 2002 (32p)

Launched in New York in 1931, the fireboat John J. Harvey came out of retirement to help fight flames in New York's harbor on September 11, 2001.

A Picture Book of Anne Frank
by David A. Adler
Holiday 1993 (32p)
The author introduces readers to the well-known World War II heroine.

Black Whiteness: Admiral Byrd Alone in the Antarctic
by Robert Burleigh
Simon 1998 (32p)

Byrd must summon all of his courage when he becomes seriously ill.

Crocodiles, Camels, and Dugout Canoes
by Bo Zaunders
Dutton 1998 (48p)
Eight explorers who overcame fear and danger are profiled.

New York's Bravest
by Mary Pope Osborne
Knopf 2002 (32p)
In a tribute to the New York firefighters who lost their lives on 9/11, Osborne tells the story of the 1840s New York firefighter Mose Humphrey, whose bravery became legendary.

BELOW LEVEL

Teammates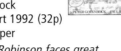
by Peter Golenbock
Harcourt 1992 (32p) also paper
Jackie Robinson faces great hostility, but gets support from teammate Pee Wee Reese.

Through My Eyes
by Ruby Bridges
Scholastic 1999 (64p)
Bridges recalls her experience as a six-year-old integrating a school in Louisiana in 1960.

Dear Mrs. Parks
by Rosa Parks and Gregory Reed
Lee & Low 1997 (121p)
Parks reveals her thoughts on courage and wisdom.

Talkin' About Bessie
by Nikki Grimes
Orchard 2002 (144p)

This award-winning fictionalized account of Bessie Coleman's life is told through the words of twenty-one friends and relatives who have gathered to mourn Coleman's death.

The Top of the World: Climbing Mount Everest
by Steve Jenkins
Houghton 1999 (32p)
Brave the harsh conditions and terrain of Mount Everest.

ON LEVEL

Number the Stars ∗
by Lois Lowry
Houghton 1989 (160p)
Annemarie must save the life of her best friend, threatened by the Nazis. **Available in Spanish as** *¿Quién cuenta las estrellas?*

I Am Lavina Cumming
by Susan Lowell
Milkweed 1992 (200p) also paper

Lavina shows courage when she leaves her home in Arizona to live with her aunt in Santa Cruz, California.

Over the Edge
by K. C. Tessendorf
Atheneum 1998 (112p)
Several explorers have tried to conquer the North Pole by air travel.

Stowaway
by Karen Hesse
Simon 2000 (318p)
When eleven-year-old Nicholas Young stows away on the H.M.S. Endeavor, he unknowingly becomes part of Captain James Cook's crew on the historic voyage around the world.

∗Included in Classroom Bookshelf, Level 6

Island of the Blue Dolphins

by Scott O'Dell
Houghton 1960
(192p)
Karana survives by herself for eighteen years on a deserted island. **Available in Spanish as** *La isla de los delfines azules.*

Titanic Crossing

by Barbara Williams
Dial 1995 (160p) also paper
Albert wonders if he can save his sister's life—and his own.

Courage at Indian Deep *

by Jane Resh Thomas
Clarion 1983 (128p)
When a ship sinks during a blizzard on Lake Superior, Cass and his dog are the only ones who can help the survivors.

 Red-Tail Angels

by Patricia and Fredrick McKissack
Walker 1995 (144p)
The Tuskegee Airmen were the first squadron of African American fighter pilots of World War II.

Shipwreck Season *

by Donna Hill
Clarion 1998 (215p)
Daniel's work at a lifeguard station is both dangerous and exciting.

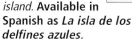 **ABOVE LEVEL**

The Wild Colorado

by Richard Mauer
Crown 1999 (120p)
A seventeen-year-old boy realizes his dream when he accompanies John Wesley Powell down the Colorado River.

*Included in Classroom Bookshelf, Level 6

Waiting for Anya

by Michael Morpurgo
Viking 1991 (172p) also paper
When Jo discovers Widow Hordada is hiding Jewish children from the Germans, he helps her smuggle them to safety in Spain.

 Redwall

by Brian Jacques
Philomel 1987 (334p) also paper
In this well-loved fantasy, Matthias and his friends fight to save Redwall Abbey from their enemies. See others in series.

 The Endless Steppe

by Esther Hautzig
Harper 1968 (243p) also paper
The author recounts her experiences as a young prisoner in a Russian forced-labor camp in Siberia during World War II.

BOOKS FOR TEACHER READ ALOUD

Beyond the Western Sea, Books 1 and 2

by Avi
Orchard 1996 (304p)
An Irish brother and sister and their landlord's son head for Liverpool to sail to America.

 The Upstairs Room

by Johanna Reiss
Crowell 1972 (196p) also paper
The author describes her life hiding from the Nazis for over two years in an upstairs room on a Dutch family's farm. **Available in Spanish as** *La habitación de arriba.*

 **Technology**

Computer Software Resources

- **Get Set for Reading CD-ROM**
- **Courage**
  Provides background building, vocabulary support, and selection summaries in English and Spanish.
- **Number the Stars CD-ROM** *by Lois Lowry. Recorded Books*

Video Cassettes

- **Island of the Blue Dolphins** *by Scott O'Dell. Library Video*
- **Call It Courage** *by Armstrong Sperry. Media Basics*
- **Hatchet** *by Gary Paulsen. Media Basics*

Audio

- **Redwall** *by Brian Jacques. Listening Library*
- **Brian's Return** *by Gary Paulsen. BDD*
- **Hatchet** *by Gary Paulsen. BDD*
- **The True Confessions of Charlotte Doyle** *by Avi. Recorded Books*
- **Number the Stars** *by Lois Lowry. Recorded Books*
- **The Endless Steppe** *by Esther Hautzig. Recorded Books*
- **Island of the Blue Dolphins** *by Scott O'Dell. Recorded Books*
- **I Am Lavina Cumming** *by Susan Lowell. Recorded Books*
- **Out of the Dust** *by Karen Hesse. Listening Library*
- **CD–ROM for** *Courage. Houghton Mifflin Company*

Technology Resources addresses are on page R37.

Education Place®

www.eduplace.com *Log on to Education Place for more activities relating to* Courage, *including vocabulary support—*
  e • **Glossary**
  e • **WordGame**

Book Adventure®

www.bookadventure.org *This Internet reading incentive program provides thousands of titles for students to read.*

Accelerated Reader® Universal CD-ROM

This popular CD-ROM provides practice quizzes for Anthology selections and for many popular children's books.

Theme Skills Overview

	Selection 1	Selection 2	Selection 3
Pacing Approximately 6 weeks	**Hatchet** Realistic Fiction pp. 24A–47R	**Passage to Freedom** Biography pp. 49I–71R	**Climb or Die** Realistic Fiction pp. 71S–93R
Reading Comprehension Information and Study Skills Vocabulary Readers Leveled Readers • Fluency Practice • Independent Reading	**Guiding Comprehension** 🌀 **Noting Details** T 🌀 **Summarize** **Media Link** How to Read a News Article Using Library Catalogs **Vocabulary Reader** **Leveled Readers** *River of No Return* *Weathering the Storm* *An Unexpected Hero* *Fear of White Water* Lessons and Leveled Practice	**Guiding Comprehension** 🌀 **Making Judgments** T 🌀 **Evaluate** **Social Studies Link** How to Read Primary Sources Using Reference Sources **Vocabulary Reader** **Leveled Readers** *Corrie's Secret* *Cesar Chavez* *The Story of Oskar Schindler* *Corrie's Important Decision* Lessons and Leveled Practice	**Guiding Comprehension** 🌀 **Sequence of Events** T 🌀 **Predict/Infer** T **Social Studies Link** How to Read a Social Studies Article Using Parts of a Book T **Vocabulary Reader** **Leveled Readers** *I Double Dare You* *Underground Rescue* *Hurricane Music* *Double Trouble* Lessons and Leveled Practice
Word Work Decoding Phonics Review Vocabulary Spelling	🌀 **Suffixes -ful, -less, and -ly** T **Short Vowels** 🌀 **Using Context** T Short Vowels T	🌀 **Syllabication** T **Long Vowels** 🌀 **Dictionary Guide Words** T Long Vowels T	🌀 **Prefixes un- and re-** T **More Vowel Spellings** 🌀 **Parts of a Dictionary Entry** T More Vowel Spellings T
Writing and Oral Language Writing Grammar Listening/Speaking/Viewing	✏️ **Writing Instructions** Sequence Words T Kinds of Sentences T Subjects and Predicates T Retelling a Story	✏️ **Writing a Memo** Capitalization and Punctuation T Conjunctions T Compound Sentences T Speaking on the Telephone	✏️ **Writing a Friendly Letter** Voice Complex Sentences T Fragments and Run-ons T Hold a Literature Discussion
Cross-Curricular Activities	Responding: Science, Health, Internet Classroom Management Activities	Responding: Social Studies, Art, Internet Classroom Management Activities	Responding: Vocabulary, Listening and Speaking, Internet Classroom Management Activities

T Skill tested on Weekly or Theme Skills Test and/or Integrated Theme Test

Target Skills

Phonics
Comprehension
Vocabulary
Fluency

 **Vocabulary Readers**

Nonfiction

Selection 4	Monitoring Student Progress	Focus on Genre
The True Confessions of Charlotte Doyle  Historical Fiction pp. 93S–115R	**Check Your Progress**  Rosa Parks: My Story Nonfiction **Making a Difference** Realistic Fiction pp. M1–M43	**Poetry**  pp. 117A–135R
Guiding Comprehension ⓖ **Predicting Outcomes** T ⓖ **Monitor/Clarify** T **Social Studies Link** How to Take Notes Using Graphic Aids T	**Guiding Comprehension** Theme Connections ⓖ **Comprehension Skills Review** T ⓖ **Predict/Infer** T **Taking Tests: Choosing the Best Answer**	**Guiding Comprehension** ⓖ **Understanding Poetry** ⓖ **Evaluate** Specialized Dictionaries
Vocabulary Reader **Leveled Readers**  *Riding with the Vaqueros* *Johnny Kelley's Tale* *Hannah Brown, Union Army Spy* *Yao's Wild Ride* Lessons and Leveled Practice	**Connecting Leveled Readers** 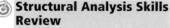	**Vocabulary Reader** **Leveled Readers**  *Robert Frost: The Journey of a Poet* *The Images of Nikki Grimes Gary Soto* *Robert Frost, New England Poet* Lessons and Leveled Practice
ⓖ **Possessives and Contractions** T **The /ou/, /o͞o/, /ô/, and /oi/ Sounds** T ⓖ **Word Families** T /ou/, /o͞o/, /ô/, and /oi/ T	ⓖ **Structural Analysis Skills Review** T **Silent Consonants** ⓖ **Vocabulary Skills Review** T Spelling Skills Review T	ⓖ **Prefixes and Suffixes** *un-, re-, -ful, -less,* and *-ly* **Silent Consonants** ⓖ **Connotation** Consonant Changes
✎ **Writing an Opinion Paragraph** Combining Sentences T Common/Proper Nouns T Singular/Plural Nouns T Giving and Listening to Directions	✎ **Writing Skills Review** Grammar Skills Review T	✎ **Writing a Poem** Sensory Language Using Subordinate Clauses Compound-Complex Sentences Read a Poem Aloud
Responding: Math, Listening and Speaking, Internet Classroom Management Activities	Cross-Curricular Activities Classroom Management Activities	Responding: Internet Classroom Management Activities

Combination Classroom

See the **Combination Classroom Planning Guide** for lesson planning and management support.

Writing Process ▶

Reading-Writing Workshop: Personal Narrative
• Student Writing Model
• Writing Process Instruction
• Writing Traits Focus

Additional Theme Resources

• Leveled Theme Paperbacks Lessons
• Reteaching Lessons
• Challenge/Extension Activities

 **Technology**

Education Place®
www.eduplace.com

Log on to Education Place for more activities relating to *Courage*.

Lesson Planner CD-ROM
Customize your planning for *Courage* with the Lesson Planner CD-ROM.

Cross-Curricular Activities

Independent Activities

Assign these activities at any time during the theme while you work with small groups.

Additional Independent Activities

- Challenge/Extension Activities, Theme Resources, pp. R9, R11, R13, R15

- Theme 1 Assignment Cards 1–17, **Teacher's Resource Blackline Masters**, pp. 47–55

- Ready-Made Small Group Activities, pp. 25E–25F, 49Q–49R, 71AA–71BB, 93AA–93BB

- Language Center Activities, pp. 47M–47N, 71M–71N, 93M–93N

- **Classroom Management Handbook,** Activity Masters CM1-1–CM1-16

- **Challenge Handbook,** Challenge Masters CH1-1–CH1-8

Drama

Common Courage

 Groups	🕐 45 minutes
Objective	Dramatize a courageous act.

Write a dramatic scene that presents ordinary people acting courageously in everyday life. You might dramatize a situation such as

- dealing with a bully
- rescuing a pet
- standing up for a belief

Brainstorm a situation that you would like to dramatize and decide who the characters will be. Divide writing and editing tasks among the group.

After the scene has been written, give it a title, make a cover for it, and publish it in the class reading center. The group may want to perform it for the class on another occasion.

Music

Songs of Bravery

👥 Pairs	🕐 30 minutes
Objective	Research and perform songs about courage.
Materials	Music books, Internet

Work with a partner to use music books and the Internet to find the words and histories of folk songs, ballads, and other of songs that describe heroes or courageous actions. Present the song to the class in one of these ways:

- Provide a copy of the song lyrics.
- Offer background information about the people and events described in the song.
- Sing the song with or without musical instruments.

The Star Spangled Banner

♪ Oh, say, can you see,
   by the dawn's early light,
What so proudly we hail'd
   at the twilight's last gleaming?
Whose broad stripes and bright stars,
   thro' the perilous fight,
O'er the ramparts we watch'd,
   were so gallantly streaming?
And the rockets' red glare,
   the bombs bursting in air,
Gave proof thro' the night
   that our flag was still there.
O say, does that star-spangled
   banner yet wave
O'er the land of the free
   and the home of the brave?

Consider copying and laminating these activities for use in centers.

Science

Make a Timeline

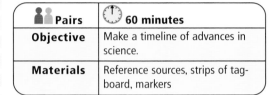

Pairs	🕐 60 minutes
Objective	Make a timeline of advances in science.
Materials	Reference sources, strips of tagboard, markers

Many advances in science have been made possible because of courageous people. Work with a partner to create a timeline that lists at least three scientific advances. Use encyclopedias, science books, and the Internet to do your research. Here are some areas of science you might research:

- medicine
- aviation and aeronautics
- space travel

Social Studies

Acts of Courage

👤 Singles	🕐 60 minutes
Objective	Write a description of an act of bravery.
Materials	Reference sources, Internet

Research a historical figure who showed outstanding courage. Choose an incident from that person's life that illustrates his or her courage. Write a brief description of the event and the individual's courageous deed. Look for information in sources such as these:

- social studies textbooks
- encyclopedias
- nonfiction books
- Internet

Language Arts

How to Have What It Takes

👤 Singles	🕐 45 minutes
Objective	Write instructions for how to be courageous.

What does it take to act courageously? What suggestions would you give someone about being courageous in everyday life? Write a set of how-to instructions on being courageous. Think about ideas such as these:

- the meaning of courage
- how to overcome fears and self-doubt
- the character traits of courageous people you know or have read about

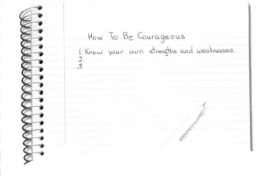

Planning for Assessment

During the first few weeks of school . . .

1 SCREENING

To obtain information about all students' instructional levels and to identify students in need of further diagnostic assessment, administer the **Baseline Group Test.**

If performance is	Then use these teaching resources:
■ **ABOVE LEVEL**	• Systematic instruction in the Teacher's Edition • Practice Book • Challenge Handbook • Leveled Readers and Leveled Practice
▲ **ON LEVEL**	• Systematic instruction in the Teacher's Edition • Classroom Management Handbook • Practice Book • Leveled Readers and Leveled Practice
● **BELOW LEVEL** If below level, further diagnose student needs.	• Systematic instruction in the Teacher's Edition • Practice Book • Extra Support Handbook • Vocabulary Readers • Leveled Readers and Leveled Practice

2 DIAGNOSIS

To determine individual students' specific instructional needs and to plan instruction, you may wish to administer the following tests:

- **Leveled Reading Passages Assessment Kit**
- **Phonics/Decoding Screening Test**
- **Lexia Quick Phonics Assessment CD-ROM**

Once you have begun your instructional plan . . .

3 MONITORING PROGRESS

To ensure that students are making adequate progress throughout this theme, you may wish to use the following resources:

- **Monitoring Student Progress boxes**
- **Theme 1: Selection Tests**
- **End-of-Theme Monitoring Student Progress**
- **Assessing Student Progress**
- **Theme 1: Weekly Skills Tests, Integrated Theme Test, Theme Skills Test**

4 MANAGING AND REPORTING

HOUGHTON MIFFLIN Assessment System

Create tests and practice online, get instant results online or by scan-and-score, report performance on your state standards, and run prescriptions to differentiate instruction.

National Test Correlation
Documenting Adequate Yearly Progress

SKILLS for *Courage*	ITBS	Terra Nova (CTBS)	CAT	SAT	MAT
Comprehension Strategies and Skills					
• Strategies: Predict/Infer, Summarize*, Evaluate*	O	O	O	O	O
• Skills: Noting Details, Sequence of Events, Predicting Outcomes, Making Judgments, Cause and Effect*, Propaganda*, Story Structure*, Fact and Opinion*, Making Generalizations*	O	O	O	O	O
Structural Analysis					
• Suffixes *-ful, -less, -ly*; Prefixes *un-, re-*	O	O	O	O	O
• Syllabication					
• Possessives and Contractions	O	O		O	
Vocabulary/Dictionary					
• Using Context	O	O	O	O	O
• Alphabetical Order/Entry and Guide Words	O		O	O	O
• Parts of an Entry	O		O	O	
• Word Families					
Information and Study Skills					
• Using Graphic Aids: Maps, Globes, Graphs, Tables, Captions, Charts*	O	O	O	O	O
• Using Parts of a Book/Index	O		O	O	O
Spelling					
• Short Vowels; Long Vowels; /ou/, /o͞o/, /ô/, /oi/	O	O	O	O	O
Grammar					
• Kinds of Sentences	O	O			O
• Subjects and Predicates	O	O	O	O	O
• Conjunctions	O	O	O	O	
• Nouns: Common and Proper, Singular and Plural	O	O	O	O	O
• Correcting Fragments and Run-ons	O	O	O	O	O
Writing					
• Formats: Instructions, Memo, Friendly Letter, Opinion					
• Using Time Words and Phrases					
• Capitalizing and Punctuating Sentences					
• Combining Sentences with Appositives					
• Reading-Writing Workshop: Personal Narrative					

*These skills are taught, but not tested, in this theme.

 KEY

ITBS Iowa Tests of Basic Skills

Terra Nova (CTBS) Comprehensive Tests of Basic Skills

CAT California Achievement Tests

SAT Stanford Achievement Tests

MAT Metropolitan Achievement Tests

Launching the Theme

Theme **1**

COURAGE

"You must do
the thing you think
you cannot do."

— *Eleanor Roosevelt*

20   21

Introducing the Theme: Discussion Options

Read aloud the theme title and quote on Anthology page 21. Ask:

1 What is courage?
(the ability to face danger or hardship with confidence and control; being brave)

2 What does Mrs. Roosevelt seem to be saying?
(You must try to do things even if they seem impossible.)

3 Based on the photograph and the quote, what will the stories in this theme be about?
(common people demonstrating unusual and notable acts of courage)

4 Name someone you think is courageous and explain why.
(Sample answer: My aunt is a police officer. She is courageous because she risks her life every day.)

Combination Classroom

See the **Combination Classroom Planning Guide** for lesson planning and management support.

COURAGE

with Avi

What qualities make a person courageous? Read this letter, and discover how author Avi defines courage. Take a chance, compare ideas, and find out what courage means to you.

THE NEWS

Firefighters to the Rescue!!!!

22

Dear Reader,

Courage is often used to describe larger than life actions. It might be a soldier's actions on the battlefield. It might refer to the rescue of someone from a life–threatening situation. Such actions make headlines.

I suspect, however, that most acts of courage go unnoticed by the public. Acts of courage — in my opinion — have to be noticed by *someone*, because I believe courage is *a moral action performed with the awareness that the result may well be failure.*

What do I mean by "moral action"? It is an act that is based on the desire to do good.

The soldier, for example, who acts *mindlessly* to save a comrade from harm may be acting heroically, but it is not courage if he or she isn't aware of the danger involved. If that same soldier *does* realize the danger and risk involved in saving a comrade, yes, that is courage.

It is an act of courage to speak publicly about your ideas and feelings when you *know* other people will not like what you have to say. It is an act of courage for a publisher to issue books knowing that some people might not approve. It is an act of courage to walk down a school hallway and say a big public "hello" to someone who is thought to be different from the majority. It is even an act of courage to cut your hair in the way you like, even though you know others might make fun of you.

23

Building Theme Connections

Read Aloud Anthology page 22. Tell students that Avi wrote *The True Confessions of Charlotte Doyle,* a selection that they will read in this theme. (See Teacher's Edition page 96 for more information on Avi.)

Ask volunteers to read aloud the author's letter on Anthology pages 23–24. Use the following questions to prompt discussion:

1 When was the last time you did something courageous?
(Sample answer: Last week I helped someone who was being picked on gather up his books that had been knocked to the floor.)

2 How do you think people feel when they do something courageous?
(Sample answer: a little nervous at first, but overall, proud)

3 Why is it sometimes hard to do courageous things?
(Sample answer: Sometimes doing the right thing is not popular.)

It Takes Courage

Theme Connections

Compare Avi's ideas about courage with your own. When you think of a courageous action, what comes to mind? Who, in your opinion, has performed an act of courage?

Look at the selections shown below. In what ways do you think the characters in these selections will show courage? As you read, think about each character's bravery. Compare how the characters change as they find ways to solve their problems. Discover the many different ways people learn to be courageous.

In all of society there is tremendous pressure to look, act, talk, and think the same. But it is particularly hard for young people to show courage. Kids want so much to be accepted that they more often than not reject what may be different. If one breaks "the rules," kids can and will inflict extraordinary pain and rejection on those who are different.

Think about your classmates. Who struggles (often loudly) to be the same as everyone else? Who is quietly different?

Why is this important? It is important because every person alive has unique thoughts and ideas. Having a unique idea is not unusual. Acting upon those ideas is.

So, if courage is acting in a moral way that has the potential for risk and failure, ask yourself this hard question: "When did I last do a courageous thing?"

Sincerely,

Avi

Internet To learn about the authors in this theme, visit Education Place. www.eduplace.com/kids

24 / 25

Building Theme Connections, continued

Read aloud the first paragraph on Anthology page 25.

- Have students brainstorm ideas, images, and words they associate with the word *courage*. Record their thoughts.

- Discuss how students' ideas compare with Avi's.

Have students finish reading Anthology page 25.

- Explain that the books in the photo are the selections students will read in the theme *Courage*.

- Ask students to predict in what ways the selections will show courage. (Answers will vary.)

- Allow students time to look ahead at the selections and illustrations. Have them revise their original predictions as necessary.

Home Connection

Send home the theme letter for *Courage* to introduce the theme and suggest home activities. (See the **Teacher's Resource Blackline Masters.**)

For other suggestions relating to *Courage*, see **Home/ Community Connections.**

Making Selection Connections

Introduce Selection Connections in the Practice Book.

- Preview the **Graphic Organizers** on pages 9 and 10. Read aloud the directions, column heads, and selection titles. Explain that as they finish reading each selection, students will add to the chart to deepen their understanding of the theme *Courage*.

Classroom Management

At any time during the theme you can assign the independent cross-curricular activities on Teacher's Edition pages 23K–23L while you give differentiated instruction to small groups. For additional independent activities related to specific selections, see the Teacher's Edition pages listed below.

- Week 1: pages 25E–25F, 47M–47N
- Week 2: pages 49Q–49R, 71M–71N
- Week 3: pages 71AA–71BB, 93M–93N
- Week 4: pages 93AA–93BB, 115M–115N
- Week 5: pages M6–M7, M24–M25, M26–M27, M42–M43

Monitoring Student Progress

Monitoring Progress

Throughout the theme, monitor your students' progress by using the following program features in the Teacher's Edition:

- Guiding Comprehension questions
- Literature discussion groups
- Skill lesson applications
- Monitoring Student Progress boxes

Wrapping Up and Reviewing the Theme

Use the two selections and support material in **Monitoring Student Progress** on pages M1–M43 to review theme skills, connect and compare theme literature, and prepare students for the Integrated Theme Test as well as for standardized tests measuring adequate yearly progress.

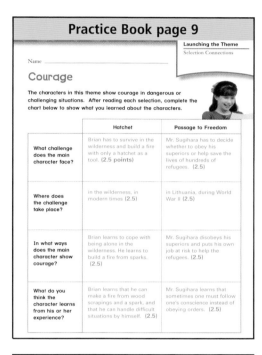

Lesson Overview

Literature

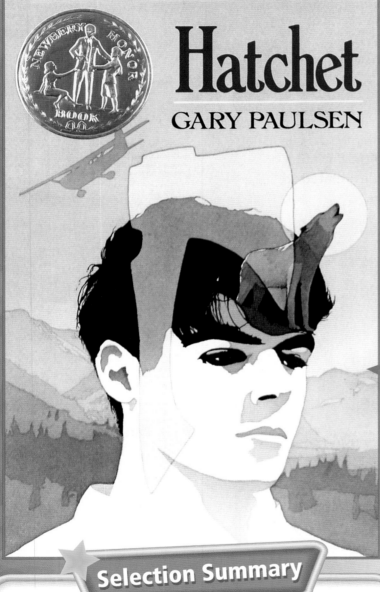

Hatchet
GARY PAULSEN

NEWBERY HONOR BOOK

Selection Summary

After a plane crash, Brian struggles to survive alone in the Canadian wilderness with only the aid of his hatchet.

1 Background and Vocabulary

Nonfiction

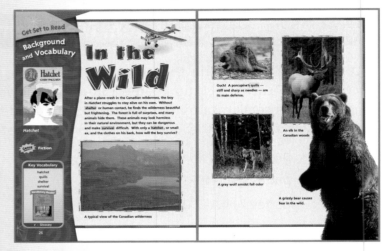

2 Main Selection

Hatchet
Genre: Fiction

3 Media Link

Instructional Support

Planning and Practice

Teacher's Edition

Practice Book

Teacher's Resources

Transparencies

Differentiated Instruction

Intervention Strategies
for Extra Support

Instructional Activities
for Challenge

Instructional Strategies for
English Language Learners

Ready-Made Centers

Building Vocabulary Flip Chart
- center activities
- word skills practice

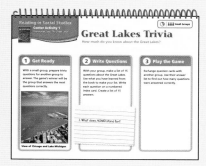

Reading in Science and Social Studies Flip Chart
- books and center activities
- support for state content standards

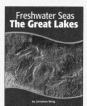

Hands-On Literacy Centers for *Hatchet*
- activities
- manipulatives
- routines

Technology

Audio Selection
Hatchet

Get Set for Reading CD-ROM

Accelerated Reader®

www.eduplace.com
- over 1,000 Online Leveled Books

HOUGHTON MIFFLIN
Assessment System
- Test Generator

Leveled Books for Reaching All Learners

Fluency

Increase students' reading fluency using these activities.

● BELOW LEVEL

Have a student listen to the Leveled Reader audio CD while following along in the book. Then have the student read aloud with the audio as you replay it.

▲ ON LEVEL

Model reading with expression. Then have students take turns reading the same passage with expression.

■ ABOVE LEVEL

Model fluent reading. Have students discuss how punctuation affects reading with pauses and expression.

◆ LANGUAGE SUPPORT

Model fluent reading while students follow in the book, pointing to words. Then have students read in unison with you.

Skills Practice

- Topic, comprehension strategy, and vocabulary linked to main selection
- Lessons in Teacher's Edition, pages 47O–47R

● BELOW LEVEL

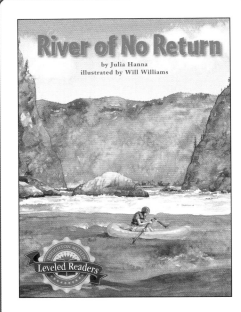

River of No Return
by Julia Hanna
illustrated by Will Williams

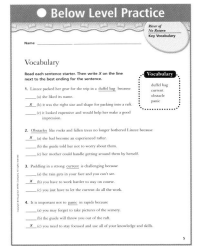

▲ ON LEVEL

Weathering the STORM
by Barbara A. Donovan
illustrated by Rosanne Kaloustian

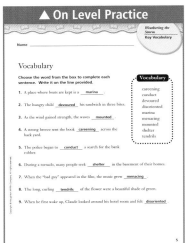

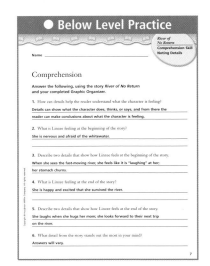

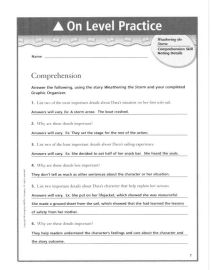

■ ABOVE LEVEL

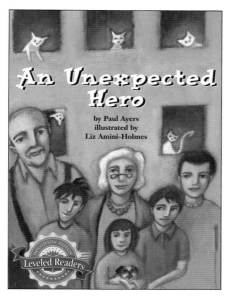

An Unexpected Hero
by Paul Ayers
illustrated by
Liz Amini-Holmes

Leveled Readers

■ Above Level Practice

Name _____

Vocabulary

Choose the term that means the same as the underlined word in each sentence. Write it on the line.

Vocabulary
avert
combustion
condoned
curmudgeonly
evacuated
frustration
kindling
recounted
vigorously

1. David often told the story to his friends. __recounted__

2. The police officer closed off the area of the accident. __condoned__

3. Abby smiled at her bad-tempered neighbor. __curmudgeonly__

4. He would do anything to prevent an argument with his sister. __avert__

5. "I forgot my ticket," Jake said with annoyance. __frustration__

6. They moved out of the science lab when a mouse escaped from its cage. __evacuated__

7. Amy ran energetically the week before her first track meet. __vigorously__

8. The easily ignited material will help us build a fire. __kindling__

9. The sound produced by the explosion could be heard for blocks. __combustion__

5

■ Above Level Practice

Name _____

An Unexpected Hero
Comprehension Skill
Noting Details

Comprehension

Respond to the following, using the story *An Unexpected Hero* and your completed Graphic Organizer.

1. Describe two details that led Rafael to have negative feelings about himself.
He didn't answer the question in science class; he was afraid to meet the bullies.

2. Describe two details that led Rafael to have positive feelings about himself.
He warned Eddie to leave the building; he rescued Mrs. Lavinski's dog.

3. At what point in the story do you think Rafael felt worst about himself?
just before he smelled the gas

4. What details helped you decide when Rafael felt worse?
He didn't face up to the bullies; he was angry that he hadn't given the answer in class; he wanted to lie on his bed and stare at the ceiling.

5. At what point in the story do you think Rafael felt best about himself?
at the dinner table that night

6. What details helped you decide when Rafael felt at his best?
He asked his parents for a kitten; he had realized Eddie wasn't so bad; he knew he wasn't as big a coward as he had thought because everyone called him a hero.

7

◆ LANGUAGE SUPPORT

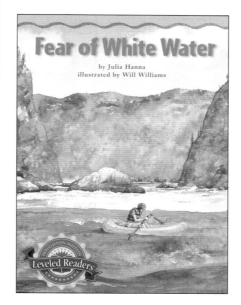

Fear of White Water
by Julia Hanna
illustrated by Will Williams

Leveled Readers

◆ Language Support Practice

Name _____

Fear of White Water
Build Background

Build Background

Draw a picture in each box to go with its heading. Draw as many details as you can. On a separate sheet of paper write a short paragraph to go with each of your drawings.

White-Water Rafting Is Fun!

White-Water Rafting Is Scary!

5

◆ Language Support Practice

Fear of White Water
Key Vocabulary

Name _____

Vocabulary

Write the word from the box that best fits each description.

Vocabulary
current
downstream
overboard
rapids
terrified
white-water rafting

1. This is the path of water in motion.
__current__

2. A person who falls over the side of a boat goes here:
__overboard__

3. This is how someone feels who is filled with fear or terror:
__terrified__

4. You will find these in a river where water flows very fast:
__rapids__

5. This is the direction in which the water current flows:
__downstream__

6. This is what you are doing when you go through rough water in a small boat: __white-water rafting__

6

Leveled Theme Paperbacks

- Extended independent reading in theme-related paperbacks

- Lessons in Teacher's Edition, pages R2–R7

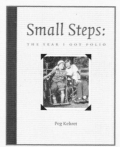

The Little Ships
THE HEROIC RESCUE AT DUNKIRK IN WORLD WAR II
by LOUISE BORDEN
Illustrated by MICHAEL FOREMAN

Small Steps:
THE YEAR I GOT POLIO
Peg Kehret

● **BELOW LEVEL**   ▲ **ON LEVEL**

SHIPWRECK AT THE BOTTOM OF THE WORLD

■ **ABOVE LEVEL**

Technology

HOUGHTON MIFFLIN
Online Leveled Books
www.eduplace.com

- over 1,000 Online Leveled Books

Leveled Readers
Audio available

Daily Lesson Plans

 **Technology**
Lesson Planner CD-ROM allows you to customize the chart below to develop your own lesson plans.

T Skill tested on Weekly or Theme Skills Test and/or Integrated Theme Test

 50–60 minutes

Reading
Comprehension

 Hatchet GARY PAULSEN

Vocabulary Reader

Leveled Readers
• Fluency Practice
• Independent Reading

 20–30 minutes

Word Work
Phonics/Decoding
Vocabulary
Spelling

 20–30 minutes

Writing and Oral Language
Writing
Grammar
Listening/Speaking/Viewing

DAY 1

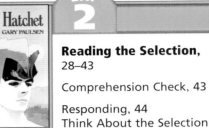 Hatchet GARY PAULSEN

Teacher Read Aloud, 25G–25H
The Rescuer from Lime Rock

Background and Vocabulary, 26

Key Vocabulary, 27
frustration   quills   survival
hatchet   shelter   terrified
kindling   slithering

Vocabulary Reader

Reading the Selection, 28–43

Comprehension Skill, 28
Noting Details **T**

Comprehension Strategy, 28
Summarize

Leveled Readers
River of No Return
Weathering the Storm
An Unexpected Hero
Fear of White Water

Lessons and Leveled Practice, 47O–47R

Phonics/Decoding, 29
Phonics/Decoding Strategy

Vocabulary, 28–43
Selection Vocabulary

Spelling, 47E
Short Vowels **T**

Writing, 47K
Prewriting Instructions

Grammar, 47I
Kinds of Sentences **T**

Daily Language Practice
1. the team of climbers reached the top of the highest clif. (The; cliff.)
2. That player has a really fast pich (pitch.)

Listening/Speaking/Viewing, 25G–25H, 37
Teacher Read Aloud, Stop and Think

DAY 2

 Hatchet GARY PAULSEN

Reading the Selection, 28–43

Comprehension Check, 43

Responding, 44
Think About the Selection

Vocabulary Reader

Comprehension Skill Preview, 33
Noting Details **T**

Leveled Readers
River of No Return
Weathering the Storm
An Unexpected Hero
Fear of White Water

Lessons and Leveled Practice, 47O–47R

Structural Analysis, 47C
Suffixes

Vocabulary, 28–43
Selection Vocabulary

Spelling, 47E
Short Vowels Review and Practice **T**

Writing, 47K
Drafting Instructions

Grammar, 47I
Kinds of Sentences Practice **T**

Daily Language Practice
3. What elce is there to make for our dinner. (else; dinner?)
4. Did you like that filem as much as i did? (film; I)

Listening/Speaking/Viewing, 43, 44
Wrapping Up, Responding

Target Skills of the Week

Phonics	Suffixes -ful, -less, and -ly
Comprehension	Summarize; Noting Details
Vocabulary	Using Context
Fluency	Leveled Readers

DAY 3

Rereading the Selection, 28–43

Rereading for Genre, 31
Realistic Fiction

Vocabulary Reader

Comprehension Skill, 47A–47B
Noting Details T

Leveled Readers
River of No Return
Weathering the Storm
An Unexpected Hero
Fear of White Water

Lessons and Leveled Practice, 47O–47R

Phonics Review, 47D
Short Vowels

Vocabulary, 47G
Using Context T

Spelling, 47F
Vocabulary: Classifying; Short Vowels
Practice T

Writing, 47L
Revising Instructions
Sequence Words T

Grammar, 47J
Subjects and Predicates T

Daily Language Practice
5. my glasses had sunked to the bottom of the pool. (My; sunk)
6. Will you flip the light swich off when we leave the room. (switch; room?)

DAY 4

Reading the Media Link, 46–47
"Boy Wonder"

Skill: How to Read a News Article

Comprehension Skill Review, 35
Propaganda

Leveled Readers
River of No Return
Weathering the Storm
An Unexpected Hero
Fear of White Water

Lessons and Leveled Practice, 47O–47R

Phonics/Decoding, 46–47
Apply Phonics/Decoding Strategy to Link

Vocabulary, 47M
Language Center: Building Vocabulary

Spelling, 47F
Short Vowels Game, Proofreading T

Writing, 47L
Proofreading Instructions

Grammar, 47J
Subjects and Predicates Practice T

Daily Language Practice
7. that bee stug me twice! (That; stung)
8. What an amazing shipwrek? (shipwreck!)

Listening/Speaking/Viewing, 47
Discuss the Link

DAY 5

Rereading for Fluency, 39

Responding Activities, 44–45
Write an Explanation
Cross-Curricular Activities

Information and Study Skills, 47H
Using Library Catalogs

Comprehension Skill Review, 41
Cause and Effect

Leveled Readers
River of No Return
Weathering the Storm
An Unexpected Hero
Fear of White Water

Lessons and Leveled Practice, 47O–47R

Phonics, 47N
Language Center: Character Description

Vocabulary, 47M
Language Center: Vocabulary Game

Spelling, 47F
Test: Short Vowels T

Writing, 47L
Publishing Instructions

Grammar, 47J, 47M
Combining Sentences
Language Center: Sentence Type Challenge

Daily Language Practice
9. Do you know the lenth of this movie. (length; movie?)
10. i plege to get to school on time tomorrow. (I; pledge)

Listening/Speaking/Viewing, 47N
Language Center: Retelling a Story

Managing Flexible Groups

WHOLE CLASS

DAY 1

- Teacher Read Aloud (TE pp. 25G–25H)
- Building Background, Introducing Vocabulary (TE pp. 26–27)
- Comprehension Strategy: Introduce (TE p. 28)
- Comprehension Skill: Introduce (TE p. 28)
- Purpose Setting (TE p. 29)

After reading first half of *Hatchet*
- Stop and Think (TE p. 37)

DAY 2

After reading *Hatchet*
- Wrapping Up (TE p. 43)
- Comprehension Check (Practice Book p. 13)
- Responding: Think About the Selection (TE p. 44)
- Comprehension Skill: Preview (TE p. 33)

SMALL GROUPS

Extra Support

DAY 1

TEACHER-LED
- Preview vocabulary; support reading with Vocabulary Reader.
- Preview *Hatchet* to Stop and Think (TE pp. 28–37).
- Support reading with Extra Support/ Intervention notes (TE pp. 29, 33, 36, 38, 41, 42).

DAY 2

Partner or Individual Work
- Reread first half of *Hatchet* (TE pp. 28–37).
- Preview, read second half (TE pp. 38–43).
- Comprehension Check (Practice Book p. 13)

Challenge

DAY 1

Individual Work
- Begin "Bare Necessities" (Challenge Handbook p. 2).
- Extend reading with Challenge Note (TE pp. 42).

DAY 2

Individual Work
- Continue work on activity (Challenge Handbook p. 2).

English Language Learners

DAY 1

TEACHER-LED
- Preview vocabulary; support reading with Vocabulary Reader.
- Preview *Hatchet* to Stop and Think (TE pp. 28–37).
- Support reading with English Language Learners notes (TE pp. 26, 30, 34, 39, 43, 44).

DAY 2

TEACHER-LED
- Review first half of *Hatchet* (TE pp. 28–37). ✔
- Preview, read second half (TE pp. 38–43).
- Begin Comprehension Check together (Practice Book p. 13).

Independent Activities

- Get Set for Reading CD-ROM
- Journals: selection notes, questions
- Complete, review Practice Book (pp. 11–15) and Leveled Readers Practice Blackline Masters (TE pp. 47O–47R).
- Assignment Cards (Teacher's Resource Blackline Masters pp. 47–48)
- Leveled Readers (TE pp. 47O–47R), Leveled Theme Paperbacks (TE pp. R2–R7), or book from Leveled Bibliography (TE pp. 23E–23F)

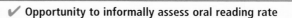 ✔ **Opportunity to informally assess oral reading rate**

DAY 3

- Rereading: Lessons on Genre (TE p. 31)
- Comprehension Skill: Main lesson (TE pp. 47A–47B)

TEACHER-LED

- Reread, review Comprehension Check (Practice Book p. 13).
- Preview Leveled Reader: Below Level (TE p. 47O), or read book from Leveled Bibliography (TE pp. 23E–23F). ✔

TEACHER-LED

- Teacher check-in: Assess progress (Challenge Handbook p. 2).
- Preview Leveled Reader: Above Level (TE p. 47Q), or read book from Leveled Bibliography (TE pp. 23E–23F). ✔

Partner or Individual Work

- Complete Comprehension Check (Practice Book p. 13).
- Begin Leveled Reader: Language Support (TE p. 47R), or read book from Leveled Bibliography (TE pp. 23E–23F).

DAY 4

- Reading the Media Link (TE pp. 46–47): Skill lesson (TE p. 46)
- Rereading the Media Link (TE p. 46)
- Comprehension Skill: First Comprehension Review lesson (TE p. 35)

Partner or Individual Work

- Reread the Media Link (TE pp. 46–47).
- Complete Leveled Reader: Below Level (TE p. 47O), or read book from Leveled Bibliography (TE pp. 23E–23F).

Individual Work

- Complete activity (Challenge Handbook p. 2).
- Complete Leveled Reader: Above Level (TE p. 47Q), or read book from Leveled Bibliography (TE pp. 23E–23F).

TEACHER-LED

- Reread the Media Link (TE pp. 46–47) ✔ and review Link Skill (TE p. 46).
- Complete Leveled Reader: Language Support (TE p. 47R), or read book from Leveled Bibliography (TE pp. 23E–23F). ✔

DAY 5

- Responding: Select from Activities (TE pp. 44–45)
- Information and Study Skills (TE p. 47H)
- Comprehension Skill: Second Comprehension Review lesson (TE p. 41)

TEACHER-LED

- Comprehension Skill: Reteaching lesson (TE p. R8)
- Preview, begin Leveled Theme Paperback: Below Level (TE pp. R2–R3), or read book from Leveled Bibliography (TE pp. 23E–23F). ✔

TEACHER-LED

- Evaluate activity and plan format for sharing (Challenge Handbook p. 2).
- Read Leveled Theme Paperback: Above Level (TE pp. R6–R7), or read book from Leveled Bibliography (TE pp. 23E–23F). ✔

Partner or Individual Work

- Preview, begin book from Leveled Bibliography (TE pp. 23E–23F).

- Responding activities (TE pp. 44–45)
- Language Center activities (TE pp. 47M–47N)
- **Fluency Practice:** Reread *Hatchet*. ✔
- Activities relating to *Hatchet* at Education Place® www.eduplace.com

Turn the page for more independent activities.

FLEXIBLE GROUPS

Hatchet

Ready-Made Small Group Activities

ABC Word Work

Building Vocabulary Center Activity 1
● ▲ ■ *Living off the Land*

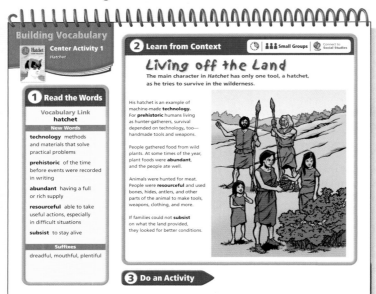

Building Vocabulary
Center Activity 1
Hatchet

2 Learn from Context — Small Groups — Connect to Social Studies

Living off the Land
The main character in *Hatchet* has only one tool, a hatchet, as he tries to survive in the wilderness.

1 Read the Words

Vocabulary Link
hatchet

New Words

technology methods and materials that solve practical problems

prehistoric of the time before events were recorded in writing

abundant having a full or rich supply

resourceful able to take useful actions, especially in difficult situations

subsist to stay alive

Suffixes
dreadful, mouthful, plentiful

His hatchet is an example of machine-made **technology**. For **prehistoric** humans living as hunter-gatherers, survival depended on technology, too—handmade tools and weapons.

People gathered food from wild plants. At some times of the year, plant foods were **abundant**, and the people ate well.

Animals were hunted for meat. People were **resourceful** and used bones, hides, antlers, and other parts of the animal to make tools, weapons, clothing, and more.

If families could not **subsist** on what the land provided, they looked for better conditions.

3 Do an Activity

Leveled Activities on side 2

Game Board 2
● ▲ ■ *Big Word Factory*

Houghton Mifflin Reading
Game Board 2
Suffixes

Big Word Factory
We Build Bigger, Better Words

Base Words

brave	small	bend
love	color	play
joy	safe	danger
laugh	friend	help
good	humor	adjust
thin	ill	thought
comfort	prosper	

ful ness ous ly able

Bigger, Better Words

Key Vocabulary Cards 1–8

frustration

Spelling Word Cards 1–20

depth

Cross Curricular

Reading in Social Studies Independent Book
● *Freshwater Seas: The Great Lakes*

Freshwater Seas The Great Lakes

by Jonathan Wing

Reading in Social Studies Center Activity 1
● ▲ ■ *Great Lakes Trivia*

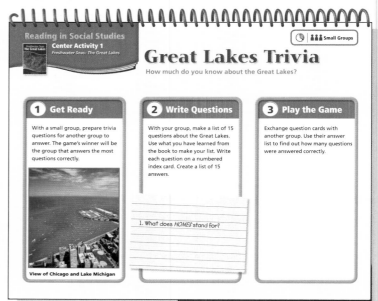

Reading in Social Studies
Center Activity 1
Freshwater Seas: The Great Lakes

Small Groups

Great Lakes Trivia
How much do you know about the Great Lakes?

1 Get Ready
With a small group, prepare trivia questions for another group to answer. The game's winner will be the group that answers the most questions correctly.

View of Chicago and Lake Michigan

2 Write Questions
With your group, make a list of 15 questions about the Great Lakes. Use what you have learned from the book to make your list. Write each question on a numbered index card. Create a list of 15 answers.

1. What does *HOMES* stand for?

3 Play the Game
Exchange question cards with another group. Use their answer list to find out how many questions were answered correctly.

Leveled Activities on side 2

Leveled for ● Below Level, ▲ On Level, ■ Above Level

SMALL GROUP ACTIVITIES

 # Reading

  # Writing

Multiple Tiers of Intervention

Activity Card 3
● ▲ *Hollywood Hatchet*

Hatchet   GRADE 6   THEME 1   WEEK 1
                                      ACTIVITY CARD

3. Hollywood Hatchet

Brian's story will become a major motion picture. As a script writer, write a short scene or a preview to share with the class.

• Change the title for the movie if you want.
• Be creative!
• Highlight interesting details in the preview.

Activity Card 4
▲ ■ *Accomplishments*

Hatchet   GRADE 6   THEME 1   WEEK 1
                                      ACTIVITY CARD

4. Accomplishments

Look through *Hatchet* and choose one of Brian's achievements that you think is significant. Write a paragraph showing how the event affected Brian's mood. List details that make a connection between Brian's actions and how he feels.

Activity Card 6
● *Cave Wall Scrawl*

Hatchet   GRADE 6   THEME 1   WEEK 1
                                      ACTIVITY CARD

6. Cave Wall Scrawl

Write a poem, a letter, or make a drawing from Brian's perspective. Imagine that you have been all alone in the wilderness for several weeks. Sitting by the fire, you find that you can sketch on the cave wall with a shiny white rock. You decide to express your feelings through writing and drawing.

Challenge Card 1–2
■ *What Makes a Hero?*

THEME 1 / *Hatchet*

2. What Makes a Hero?

Goal: Write a short paper about a character's courage

Using *Hatchet* and another book of your choice, write a short paper on one of the following topics.

• Choose a character from each book. Write a dialogue between them as they discuss the most difficult moments of their lives.
• Pretend you are a journalist and write a persuasive article about one of the characters. Convince the reader that the character you've chosen is a hero.

TIPS
• List ideas or events that are similar in the books you've chosen.
• Look up the term *characterization*. Think about the qualities of the characters you are writing about. What details from the story show these qualities?

3. News at Eleven!

Goal: Record a fictional interview between a reporter and Brian from *Hatchet*

Brian has just returned home from two months in the wilderness. Your radio station wants the community to hear about his experience. With a partner, record a six-minute audio or video interview to share with the class.

TIPS
• List initial questions and possible follow-ups.
• Include music or sound effects.
• Avoid simple yes or no questions. Think of questions that give the listener background information and help Brian tell his story.

Gr. 6, Challenge Card **1–2**

Core Program Instruction

• research-based
• systematic
• assessment-driven

Group Support

Daily lessons and activities for differentiated instruction

Intervention Strategies for Extra Support, pages 12–23

Instructional Activities for Challenge, pages x–3

Instructional Strategies for English Learners, pages 16–27

Intervention Program

Proven efficacy for struggling readers

Soar to Success

For these materials and more, see **Small Group Independent Activities Kit.**

Oral Language and Fluency

- Listen to identify important details.

Building Background

Tell students that you are going to read aloud a story about Ida Lewis, a brave woman who was famous for rescuing people from drowning.

- Explain that Ida Lewis was a lighthouse keeper in Newport, Rhode Island, in the middle to late 1800s.

- Have students discuss why a lighthouse would be necessary near a busy harbor.

Fluency Modeling

Explain that as you read aloud, you will be modeling fluent oral reading. Ask students to listen carefully to your phrasing and your expression, or tone of voice and emphasis.

TARGET SKILL

COMPREHENSION SKILL

Noting Details

Explain that details may

- reveal characters' thoughts and feelings;
- reveal why characters act as they do.

Purpose Setting Read the selection aloud, asking students to note important details about Ida Lewis and her rescue work as they listen. Then use the Guiding Comprehension questions to assess students' understanding. Reread the selection for clarification as needed.

Teacher Read Aloud

The Rescuer from Lime Rock

by Stephen Currie

INTRODUCTION

Ida Lewis and her family were lighthouse keepers on the small island of Lime Rock, off the coast of Newport, Rhode Island. Ida, born in 1842, learned safety skills from an early age, and as a young woman she gained fame as a lifesaver.

①

On Lime Rock, a small island near Newport, Ida Lewis had been sneezing and coughing all afternoon. Ida was a lighthouse keeper. Each night she lit the huge lamp that guided ships safely into Newport Harbor. She had just propped her chilly bare feet next to the kitchen oven when she heard a cry. Ida knew what it meant: out in the ocean, a boat had tipped over.

Ida didn't hesitate. "I started right out, just as I was," she recalled years later: no shoes, no jacket, no hat. Ignoring her mother, who begged her to stay inside, Ida ran to the rowboat she kept on the beach. Far from shore, two men were struggling in the icy water. Could she reach them in time?

② Quickly Ida slid her boat into the waves and began to row. It was hard work. The wind made steering almost impossible, and waves splashed over her every few seconds. Luckily Ida was strong and determined, and she never lost sight of her target. Little by little she worked her way through the storm toward the drowning men.

She had steered well. One of the men, nearly unconscious, was within reach. Seizing his hand, she turned him onto his back and pulled him toward her. Then she reached under his shoulders and locked her arms securely around his chest.

Ida balanced as steadily as she could in the rocking surf. With all her might, she heaved the man up and back. She pulled again, drawing more of his body over the side, but it took several lifts before his knees cleared the stern. Ida made sure he was still breathing. Then, leaving him at the bottom of the boat, she fished the other man out of the water, too.

Even now, the rescue was not over. Between the boat and safety lay a hundred yards of wind and waves. Shivering with cold, her strength almost gone, Ida rowed through the blinding spray. Again, her aim was perfect. One last pull on the oars, and she was safely on the beach. Ida had saved the men from certain drowning. Now she *really* had a reason to warm her feet!

Lime Rock saw plenty of boating accidents. Some people forgot to watch for rocks, and others went out when the wind and waves were too strong. Still others couldn't handle a boat properly. But few of the accident victims drowned. During fifty years of keeping the Lime Rock lighthouse, Ida single-handedly rescued seventeen people—and most of the other rescues were just as dangerous as this one.

Living on a tiny island had taught Ida to be resourceful and independent. She rowed her sister and brothers to school in Newport each morning and rowed back to pick them up every afternoon. Her father had been Lime Rock's lighthouse keeper before her, but when he had a stroke and could no longer work, she took over. Not everyone approved. A few people felt that being a lighthouse keeper was unladylike, and some said that women were too weak to do the job properly—even while Ida was busy rescuing one person after another!

3 But Ida never cared what other people thought, nor did she believe that she was unusually brave. Although her rescues made her famous, she disliked the attention. "If there were some people out there who needed help," she told a writer, "I would get into my boat and go to them even if I knew I couldn't get back. Wouldn't you?" Like taking over for her father or rowing to Newport every school day, rescuing people was something that simply had to be done. "I just went," she said, "and that was all there was to it."

CRITICAL THINKING
Guiding Comprehension

1 **NOTING DETAILS** What details tell you how Ida feels at the beginning of the story? (Ida is coughing and sneezing, and her feet are cold. She probably does not feel well.)

2 **NOTING DETAILS** How can you tell that the rescue of the two men was dangerous? (Sample answers: Ida had to row through wind and waves; one of the men was nearly unconscious; Ida's strength was almost gone, but she still had to row back to shore.)

3 **NOTING DETAILS** How can you tell that Ida does not think she is unusually brave? (She says she would help people even if she could not get back to shore. Then she asks, "Wouldn't you?")

Discussion Options

Personal Response Ask students to discuss what qualities Ida had that made her such an outstanding lighthouse keeper.

⭐ **Connecting/Comparing** Remind students of the quote by Eleanor Roosevelt at the beginning of the theme: "You must do the thing you think you cannot do." Have students compare this quote with Ida's words: "I would get into my boat and go to them even if I knew I couldn't get back."

English Language Learners

Language Development

Explain that a *lighthouse* is a building by an ocean or waterway with a very bright light, or *lamp*, at the top that guides ships safely to land. If possible, show students pictures of lighthouses. Invite them to use a flashlight to model how the lighthouse lamp might guide ships to safety.

Background and Vocabulary

Key Concept: Wilderness Survival

Tell students that the selections in this theme are about courage. Explain that the next story is about a boy who must find the courage to survive on his own in the wilderness. Discuss with students the kinds of challenges one might face in the wilderness. Then use "In the Wild" on Anthology pages 26–27 to build background and introduce key vocabulary.

- Have a volunteer read aloud "In the Wild."

- Point out the aerial view of the Canadian wilderness, the story's setting, on page 26. Ask, How would you feel if you found yourself alone there?

- Discuss dangers that the animals shown on page 27 might pose.

Vocabulary Preview

The Vocabulary Reader can be used to preteach or reinforce the key vocabulary.

Vocabulary Reader

Lost in the Wilderness!

Get Set to Read

Background and Vocabulary

In the Wild

Hatchet
GARY PAULSEN

Hatchet

Genre **Fiction**

Key Vocabulary

hatchet
quills
shelter
survival

Vocabulary Reader

e ● Glossary

26

After a plane crash in the Canadian wilderness, the boy in *Hatchet* struggles to stay alive on his own. Without shelter or human contact, he finds the wilderness beautiful but frightening. The forest is full of surprises, and many animals hide there. These animals may look harmless in their natural environment, but they can be dangerous and make survival difficult. With only a hatchet, or small ax, and the clothes on his back, how will the boy survive?

A typical view of the Canadian wilderness

REACHING ALL LEARNERS

English Language Learners

Supporting Comprehension

Beginning/Preproduction Have students listen to the article. Then ask them to draw a picture of a porcupine.

Early Production and Speech Emergence Have students repeat these Key Vocabulary words after you: *shelter, survival, hatchet, kindling,* and *quills.* Use the photographs on pages 26 and 27 to help students understand the meaning of each word. Mime *frustration, terrified,* and *slithering.*

Intermediate and Advanced Fluency In small groups, have students read and then restate in their own words the information provided in the article.

Ouch! A porcupine's quills — stiff and sharp as needles — are its main defense.

An elk in the Canadian woods

A gray wolf amidst fall color

A grizzly bear causes fear in the wild.

Introducing Vocabulary

Key Vocabulary

These words support the Key Concept and appear in the selection.

frustration the discouragement and irritation that comes from not being able to achieve one's goal

hatchet a small, short-handled ax, to be used with only one hand

kindling small pieces of wood or other material used for starting fires

quills a collection of sharp, hollow spines on the back of a porcupine

shelter a place that provides protection from the weather

slithering *n.* a sliding, slipping movement; *adj.* slipping and sliding

survival the preservation of one's life; the continuing of life

terrified extremely frightened

e • Glossary
e • WordGame

See Vocabulary notes on pages 30, 32, 34, 36, 38, and 40 for additional words to preview.

Transparency 1–1
Wilderness Words

Two Teenage Girls Survive Long Night in Wilderness
Daniel Klein of the *Centerburg Times Journal*

Two teenagers were rescued today by park rangers in the Morel Wilderness Area. Sophie Barkley, 16, and her friend Carmina Ramirez, 17, had the good sense to build a shelter from tree branches and their raincoats after they discovered they were lost. They also gathered twigs and leaves to use as kindling for a small fire. They had learned all of these skills in a high school class on wilderness survival.

When asked what caused them the most frustration, the girls said it took hours to start their fire.

Carmina said they wished they had been carrying a small hatchet to chop up firewood more quickly.

Both girls said they got little sleep. At one point, they heard a slithering sound and saw a porcupine with long, sharp quills. They also heard coyotes howling. "I was terrified," Sophie admitted.

The girls say they are relieved to be home again.

ANNOTATED VERSION | COURAGE *Hatchet* Key Vocabulary

Practice Book page 11

Hatchet
Key Vocabulary

Name _____

Words in the Wild

Answer each of the following questions by writing a vocabulary word.

Vocabulary
hatchet
quills
shelter
survival
terrified
frustration
slithering
kindling

1. Which word tells what you should seek in a rainstorm so you won't get wet? shelter **(1 point)**

2. Which word describes what a snake is doing when it moves across the ground? slithering **(1)**

3. Which word names a tool used to chop wood? hatchet **(1)**

4. Which word describes small pieces of wood needed to build a fire? kindling **(1)**

5. Which word means "very frightened"? terrified **(1)**

6. Which word names the sharp spines a porcupine uses to defend itself? quills **(1)**

7. Which word means "the process of staying alive"? survival **(1)**

8. Which word describes a feeling a person has when he or she keeps trying to do something but cannot do it? frustration **(1)**

Write two questions of your own that use vocabulary words from the list above.

9. Accept reasonable answers. **(1)**

10. Accept reasonable answers. **(1)**

Display Transparency 1–1.

- Model how to figure out the meaning of the word *shelter* from context clues.

- Have students use letter sounds and context clues to figure out each remaining Key Vocabulary word. Have students model how they figured out each word.

- Ask students to look for these words as they read and to use them to discuss wilderness survival.

Practice/Homework Assign **Practice Book** page 11.

TARGET SKILL

COMPREHENSION STRATEGY
Summarize

Teacher Modeling Ask a volunteer to read aloud the Strategy Focus. Explain that a summary includes only the main events of a story. Ask students to read aloud the introduction on page 30. Then model the strategy.

Think Aloud *Brian is in his shelter at night. He hears a noise and smells something but can't see where it's coming from. He throws his hatchet toward the smell. Suddenly he feels pain in his leg.*

Test Prep Students can use the Summarize strategy as they read a test passage by stopping periodically to retell key facts or events in their own words. Encourage them to pay attention to the order of facts or events. This will make it easier to find answers to questions later.

TARGET SKILL

COMPREHENSION SKILL
Noting Details

Introduce the Graphic Organizer. Tell students that a Details Chart can help them understand how details show a character's feelings. Explain that as they read, students will fill out the Details Chart on **Practice Book** page 12.

- Display **Transparency 1–2**. Have students read Anthology pages 30–33.
- Model how to fill out the empty box for page 30 and the empty box for pages 32–33. Then monitor students' work.

Meet the Author
Gary Paulsen

"I simply can't not write," says Gary Paulsen. "I tried it when I ran dogs, but I ended up writing in longhand by the campfire when the dogs were sleeping. *Hatchet*, *Dogsong*, and *Woodsong* were all written while I was camping with dogs."

Besides being an award-winning author, Paulsen has also been a teacher, field engineer, magazine editor, soldier, actor, director, farmer, rancher, truck driver, trapper, professional archer, migrant farm worker, singer, sculptor, and sailor.

Meet the Illustrator
Michael Steirnagle

Growing up in El Paso, Texas, Michael Steirnagle played basket ball and baseball when he wasn't drawing and painting. Being around his mother, an artist, may have helped him decide to become an illustrator. He also teaches art at Palomar College in California. His advice to would-be artists or illustrators: "Learn to draw. Draw all the time and also use your imagination."

Internet

To find out more about Gary Paulsen and Michael Steirnagle, visit Education Place. **www.eduplace.com/kids**

28

Transparency 1–2
Details Chart

Page(s)	Brian feels ___.	Details that show how Brian feels
30	terrified	• his nostrils widened and he opened his eyes wider • he thought of every monster he had ever seen • his heart hammered in his throat
32–33	in pain; hurt	• the eight quills in his leg seem like dozens • his pain spreads • catches his breath when he pulls out the quills out
33–34	sorry for himself	• He thinks, "I can't take this" and "I can't do this." • He cries until he is cried out.
34–35	frustrated	• can't understand what his father and Terry are telling him in his dream • thinks "so what" and "I know" when he thinks about the fire in his dream
36–37	motivated; excited; happy	• realizes the hatchet can make sparks • recognizes the message about fire from his dreams • begins to make sparks to start a fire
38–41	determined	• doesn't give up when his first attempts fail to start a fire • takes two hours to gather tree bark • finally succeeds in lighting the fire
43	satisfied	• smiles and calls the fire a good friend

TRANSPARENCY 1–2
TEACHER'S EDITION PAGES 28 AND 47A
COURAGE Hatchet
Graphic Organizer Details Chart
ANNOTATED VERSION

Practice Book page 12

Hatchet
Graphic Organizer
Details Chart

Name _____

Details Chart

Page(s)	Brian feels ___.	Details that show how Brian feels
30	terrified	• his nostrils widened and he opened his eyes wider • he thought of every monster he had ever seen • his heart hammered in his throat (**3 points**)
32–33	in pain; hurt (1)	• the eight quills in his leg seem like dozens • his pain spreads • catches his breath when he pulls the quills out
33–34	sorry for himself (1)	• He thinks, "I can't take this" and "I can't do this." • He cries until he is cried out.
34–35	frustrated	• can't understand what his father and Terry are telling him in his dream • thinks "so what" and "I know" when he thinks about the fire in his dream (2)
36–37	motivated; excited; happy (1)	• realizes the hatchet can make sparks • recognizes the message about fire from his dreams • begins to make sparks to start a fire
38–41	determined	• doesn't give up when his first attempts fail to start a fire • takes two hours to gather tree bark • finally succeeds in lighting the fire (3)
43	satisfied	• smiles and calls the fire a good friend (1)

Hatchet
GARY PAULSEN

Strategy Focus

How does Brian handle being alone in the wilderness? As you read the selection, **summarize** in your own words what happens.

29

Extra Support/Intervention

Selection Preview

pages 29–33 Stranded and alone in the wilderness, Brian is stuck by quills from a porcupine.

pages 34–35 Brian cries until he realizes that crying will do no good. He dreams of his father and his friend Terry.

pages 36–37 Brian realizes that he may be able to use his hatchet to make a fire by striking it against a rock. Do you think this realization makes him feel more hopeful? Why?

pages 37–39 Brian tries unsuccessfully to light grass, twigs, a torn-up twenty-dollar bill, and some papery tree bark. How does this make him feel?

pages 40–43 Brian realizes that he must blow on the sparks until they ignite. Will this work?

Purpose Setting

- Have students read to find out what Brian will do to survive.

- Have students preview the selection by looking at the illustrations. Have them predict whether Brian will learn the skills he needs to survive.

- Ask students to summarize the story as they read.

- Encourage students to pay attention to details that show Brian's feelings.

- You may want to preview with students the Responding questions on Anthology page 44.

Journal ▶ Students can record their predictions, any questions they have about Brian's situation, and their summaries of different parts of the story.

STRATEGY REVIEW

Phonics/Decoding

Remind students to use the Phonics/Decoding Strategy as they read.

Modeling Write this sentence from *Hatchet* on the board: *His leg still hurt, it was still dark, he was still alone and the self-pity had <u>accomplished</u> nothing.* Point to *accomplished*.

Think Aloud *How do I pronounce the first part of this word? I'll try* uh-KOM. *In the second part I recognize the* -ed *ending and the* ish *sound from words like* fish. *When I sound it out, I get* uh-KOM-plihsht. *I'm still not sure what it means from the sentence, so I'll look it up in the dictionary.* Accomplished *means "to have completed something."*

CRITICAL THINKING
Guiding Comprehension

❶ NOTING DETAILS What details show that Brian is nervous? (Brian wakes up and mistakes the sound of the wind for a wild animal.)

❷ STORY STRUCTURE Why do you think the author decided to set this scene in total darkness? (Darkness can be frightening; Brian cannot even see the intruder.)

❸ DRAWING CONCLUSIONS What do you think is causing the pain in Brian's leg? Explain. (Answers will vary, but should include details from the text.)

Thirteen-year-old Brian Robeson is flying to meet his father when the pilot of the plane suffers a heart attack. When the plane crashes into a lake, Brian is stranded and alone in the Canadian wilderness. He builds a shelter near the lake and has a close encounter with a bear. As the days go by, Brian realizes that he must find food to survive.

❶ At first he thought it was a growl. In the still darkness of the shelter in the middle of the night his eyes came open and he was awake and he thought there was a growl. But it was the wind, a medium wind in the pines had made some sound that brought him up, brought him awake. He sat up and was hit with the smell.

❷ It terrified him. The smell was one of rot, some musty rot that made him think only of graves with cobwebs and dust and old death. His nostrils widened and he opened his eyes wider but he could see nothing. It was too dark, too hard dark with clouds covering even the small light from the stars, and he could not see. But the smell was alive, alive and full and in the shelter. He thought of the bear, thought of Bigfoot and every monster he had ever seen in every fright movie he had ever watched, and his heart hammered in his throat.

Then he heard the slithering. A brushing sound, a slithering brushing sound near his feet — and he kicked out as hard as he could, kicked out and threw the hatchet at the sound, a noise coming from his throat. But the hatchet missed, sailed into the wall where it hit the rocks with a shower of **❸** sparks, and his leg was instantly torn with pain, as if a hundred needles had been driven into it. "Unnnngh!"

Now he screamed, with the pain and fear, and skittered on his backside up into the corner of the shelter, breathing through his mouth, straining to see, to hear.

30

Vocabulary

shelter a place that provides protection from the weather

terrified extremely frightened

musty having a stale, moldy smell

slithering *n.* a sliding, slipping movement; *adj.* slipping and sliding

hatchet a small, short-handled ax, to be used with only one hand

English Language Learners

Language Development
Discuss the action verbs the author uses and the feeling he creates with each one.
- Point out and mime *widened, hammered, kicked, threw, sailed, torn, skittered.*
- Encourage students to write these new words in their vocabulary notebooks and to use them in their own writing.

31

Realistic Fiction

Teach

- In realistic fiction, the events, the problem, and the solution could happen in real life.
- The story characters think, feel, and behave as real people do. They have problems that real people might have.
- The setting is a real place. The time may be in the present or in the past.

Practice

- Point out that Brian's problem of having to survive alone in the wilderness is one that could happen in real life.
- Then ask students to identify other realistic details on page 30. (Sample answers: the setting; Brian's fear; the unknown animal)

Apply

- Have students complete a chart like the one below about *Hatchet*. (Sample answers are shown.)

Realistic Events and Details

Problems (needs to survive; needs to make fire)

Actions (throws hatchet; collects tinder; makes fire)

Thoughts and Feelings (is afraid; is lonely; is happy to have fire)

ASSIGNMENT CARD 3

How to Build a Shelter

Writer's Craft

At the beginning of the story, Brian is asleep in the shelter he has made by the lake. As you read the story, look for details in the words and pictures that help you figure out what the shelter is like and how it might have been made. Then write a set of directions for how to make a good shelter. You may write your directions as numbered steps or in several paragraphs. Remember that the only tool Brian has is a hatchet.

Before you begin to write, think about

- where would be the best place to put a shelter
- what materials you would need to gather from the forest
- what steps you would follow to make the shelter

Theme 1: Courage

Teacher's Resource BLM page 48

CRITICAL THINKING

Guiding Comprehension

4 **WRITER'S CRAFT** What words and phrases does the author use to make the porcupine seem like a horrible monster? (*slithering, scraping; bulk in the darkness; a shadow that lived*)

5 **DRAWING CONCLUSIONS** What does the author mean by the phrase *in just a moment it was all different*? (When the porcupine slaps Brian with its quills, Brian's feelings instantly change.)

COMPREHENSION STRATEGY

Summarize

Teacher/Student Modeling Guide students in summarizing what they have read through page 33. Ask the following questions:

- What is the main event in the story so far?

- What was Brian doing just before this event occurred?

- In summarizing these pages, would you include Brian's thoughts about Bigfoot? Why or why not?

Vocabulary

rasping having a rough, scratchy sound

gingerly carefully avoiding harm or danger

quills a collection of sharp, hollow spines on the back of a porcupine

4 The slithering moved again, he thought toward him at first, and terror took him, stopping his breath. He felt he could see a low dark form, a bulk in the darkness, a shadow that lived, but now it moved away, slithering and scraping it moved away and he saw or thought he saw it go out of the door opening.

He lay on his side for a moment, then pulled a rasping breath and held it, listening for the attacker to return. When it was apparent that the shadow wasn't coming back he felt the calf of his leg, where the pain was centered and spreading to fill the whole leg.

His fingers gingerly touched a group of needles that had been driven through his pants and into the fleshy part of his calf. They were stiff and very sharp on the ends that stuck out, and he knew then what the attacker had been. A porcupine had stumbled into his shelter and when he had kicked it the thing had slapped him with its tail of quills.

He touched each quill carefully. The pain made it seem as if dozens of them had been slammed into his leg, but there were only eight, pinning the

32

cloth against his skin. He leaned back against the wall for a minute. He couldn't leave them in, they had to come out, but just touching them made the pain more intense.

So fast, he thought. So fast things change. When he'd gone to sleep he had satisfaction and in just a moment it was all different. He grasped one of the quills, held his breath, and jerked. It sent pain signals to his brain in tight waves, but he grabbed another, pulled it, then another quill. When he had pulled four of them he stopped for a moment. The pain had gone from being a pointed injury pain to spreading in a hot smear up his leg and it made him catch his breath.

Some of the quills were driven in deeper than others and they tore when they came out. He breathed deeply twice, let half of the breath out, and went back to work. Jerk, pause, jerk — and three more times before he lay back in the darkness, done. The pain filled his leg now, and with it came new waves of self-pity. Sitting alone in the dark, his leg aching, some mosquitoes finding him again, he started crying. It was all too much, just too much, and

❺

33

Extra Support/Intervention

Strategy Modeling: Summarize

Use this example to model the strategy.

Brian falls asleep in his shelter. He wakes up suddenly, smells something odd, and hears strange noises. It is a porcupine, and when Brian kicks out and throws his hatchet at it, the porcupine whacks him with its sharp quills. In great pain, Brian pulls them out and begins to cry.

TARGET SKILL 🎯 Noting Details

Teach

- Ask a volunteer to read aloud the second paragraph on page 32.
- Point out *the pain was ... spreading to fill the whole leg.* Explain that this detail describes how Brian is feeling.
- Tell students that authors use details to create pictures of events and characters in readers' minds.

Practice

- Ask partners to reread pages 32–33.
- Have them discuss details that describe Brian's pain.
- Compare answers as a class.

Apply

- Have partners list details that reveal how Brian feels after he pulls the quills out.

Details About Brian's Injury and Pain

- dozens of needles slammed into his leg
- needles stiff and very sharp
- pain signals to his brain in tight waves
- hot smear up his leg

Target Skill Trace	
Preview; Teach	p. 25G, p. 28. p. 33; p. 47A
Reteaching	p. R8
Review	pp. M32–33; p. 85; Theme 2, p. 173; Theme 3, p. 279; Theme 4, p. 393; Theme 5, p. 503

CRITICAL THINKING
Guiding Comprehension

❻ MAKING INFERENCES What does Brian learn about feeling sorry for himself? (Self-pity is a waste of time and accomplishes nothing.)

❼ WRITER'S CRAFT What does the author include in Brian's dream to make it seem like the dreams people have in real life? (includes people Brian knows and things he has been thinking about, details that don't always make sense, parts that fade in and out)

❽ NOTING DETAILS How does the author show Brian's frustration with his dream about Terry? (by having him think *so what?* and having him repeat *I know* three times)

---

he couldn't take it. Not the way it was.

I can't take it this way, alone with no fire and in the dark, and next time it might be something worse, maybe a bear, and it wouldn't be just quills in the leg, it would be worse. I can't do this, he thought, again and again. I can't. Brian pulled himself up until he was sitting upright back in the corner of the cave. He put his head down on his arms across his knees, with stiffness taking his left leg, and cried until he was cried out.

❻ He did not know how long it took, but later he looked back on this time of crying in the corner of the dark cave and thought of it as when he learned the most important rule of survival, which was that feeling sorry for yourself didn't work. It wasn't just that it was wrong to do, or that it was considered incorrect. It was more than that — it didn't work. When he sat alone in the darkness and cried and was done, was all done with it, nothing had changed. His leg still hurt, it was still dark, he was still alone and the self-pity had accomplished nothing.

At last he slept again, but already his patterns were changing and the sleep was light, a resting doze more than a deep sleep, with small sounds awakening him twice in the rest of the night. In the last doze period before daylight, before he awakened finally with the morning light and the clouds of new mosquitoes, he dreamed. This time it was not of his mother, but of his father at first and then of his friend Terry.

In the initial segment of the dream his father was standing at the side of a living room looking at him and it was clear from his expression that he was trying to tell Brian something. His lips moved but there was no sound, not a whisper. He waved his hands at Brian, made gestures in front of his face as if **❼** he were scratching something, and he worked to make a word with his mouth but at first Brian could not see it. Then the lips made an *mmmmm* shape but no sound came. *Mmmmm — maaaa.* Brian could not hear it, could not understand it and he wanted to so badly; it was so important to understand his father, to know what he was saying. He was trying to help, trying so hard, and when Brian couldn't understand he looked cross, the way he did when Brian asked questions more than once, and he faded. Brian's father faded into a fog place Brian could not see and the dream was almost over, or seemed to be, when Terry came.

He was not gesturing to Brian but was sitting in the park at a bench

---

Vocabulary

survival the preservation of one's life; the continuing of life

initial beginning

expression a look on one's face that shows a certain mood or feeling

frustration discouragement and irritation that come from not being able to achieve one's goal

---

 REACHING ALL LEARNERS
English Language Learners

Supporting Comprehension

Check that students understand the second paragraph on page 34.

- Tell students that Brian is feeling sorry for himself when he sits in the corner of the cave and cries.

- Ask volunteers to share a time when they had a problem and felt sorry for themselves.

- Have volunteers explain whether or not feeling sorry for themselves helped solve their problem.

looking at a barbecue pit and for a time nothing happened. Then he got up and poured some charcoal from a bag into the cooker, then some starter fluid, and he took a flick type of lighter and lit the fluid. When it was burning and the charcoal was at last getting hot he turned, noticing Brian for the first time in the dream. He turned and smiled and pointed to the fire as if to say, see, a fire.

But it meant nothing to Brian, except that he wished he had a fire. He saw a grocery sack on the table next to Terry. Brian thought it must contain hot dogs and chips and mustard and he could think only of the food. But Terry shook his head and pointed again to the fire, and twice more he pointed to the fire, made Brian see the flames, and Brian felt his frustration and anger rise and he thought all right, all right, I see the fire but so what? I don't have a fire. I know about fire; I know I need a fire.

I know that.

His eyes opened and there was light in the cave, a grey dim light of morning. He wiped his mouth and tried to move his leg, which had stiffened like wood. There was thirst, and hunger, and he ate some raspberries from the jacket. They had spoiled a bit, seemed softer and mushier, but still had a rich sweetness. He crushed the berries against the roof of his mouth with his tongue and drank the sweet juice as it ran down his throat. A flash of metal caught his eye and he saw his hatchet in the sand where he had thrown it at the porcupine in the dark.

8

35

Propaganda

Review

- Tell students that propaganda is information or ideas used to influence how others think.

- Discuss the following propaganda techniques and examples.

Overgeneralization makes general statements based on few facts: "Boone Boots makes hiking easier for everyone!"

Testimonial uses a celebrity to make a statement supporting a product: "A famous climber says, 'I always wear Boone Boots.'"

Bandwagon claims that everyone else buys this product: "Everyone wears Boone Boots, so you should too!"

Faulty Cause and Effect implies that consumers will be happier simply by using the product: An ad shows a happy family all wearing Boone Boots.

Practice/Apply

- Tell groups to think of a product that Brian could have used in the woods.

- Have each group use at least two different propaganda techniques to present their product.

- Discuss which techniques worked best.

Review Skill Trace	
Teach	Theme 5, p. 473A
Reteaching	Theme 5, p. R8
Review	p. 35

CRITICAL THINKING

Guiding Comprehension

9 MAKING INFERENCES Why should Brian not have thrown his hatchet? (Sample answer: It has a special use, cutting, and it is a tool he would not be able to make himself.)

10 PROBLEM SOLVING AND DECISION MAKING Suppose Brian had not dreamed about Terry and his father. Would Brian still have figured out how to make a fire? Explain. (Sample answer: yes, because seeing the hatchet make sparks is what really gives him the idea)

He scootched up, wincing a bit when he bent his stiff leg, and crawled to where the hatchet lay. He picked it up and examined it and saw a chip in the top of the head.

The nick wasn't large, but the hatchet was important to him, was his only tool, and he should not have thrown it. He should keep it in his hand, and make a tool of some kind to help push an animal away. Make a staff, he thought, or a lance, and save the hatchet. Something came then, a thought as he held the hatchet, something about the dream and his father and Terry, but he couldn't pin it down.

"Ahhh . . ." He scrambled out and stood in the morning sun and stretched his back muscles and his sore leg. The hatchet was still in his hand, and as he stretched and raised it over his head it caught the first rays of the morning sun. The first faint light hit the silver of the hatchet and it flashed a brilliant gold in the light. Like fire. That is it, he thought. What they were trying to tell me.

Fire. The hatchet was the key to it all. When he threw the hatchet at the porcupine in the cave and missed and hit the stone wall it had showered

36

Vocabulary

staff a long stick or cane sometimes used as a weapon

lance a long wooden spear used as a weapon

glancing striking a surface at such an angle as to fly off to one side

REACHING ALL LEARNERS

Extra Support/Intervention

Review (pages 29–37)

Before students who need extra support join the whole class for Stop and Think on the next page, they should

- review their predictions/purpose
- take turns modeling Summarize and other strategies they used
- add to **Transparency 1–2**
- check and revise their Details Chart on **Practice Book** page 12, and use it to summarize

sparks, a golden shower of sparks in the dark, as golden with fire as the sun was now.

The hatchet was the answer. That's what his father and Terry had been trying to tell him. Somehow he could get fire from the hatchet. The sparks would make fire.

Brian went back into the shelter and studied the wall. It was some form of chalky granite, or a sandstone, but imbedded in it were large pieces of a darker stone, a harder and darker stone. It only took him a moment to find where the hatchet had struck. The steel had nicked into the edge of one of the darker stone pieces. Brian turned the head backward so he would strike with the flat rear of the hatchet and hit the black rock gently. Too gently, and nothing happened. He struck harder, a glancing blow, and two or three weak sparks skipped off the rock and died immediately.

He swung harder, held the hatchet so it would hit a longer, sliding blow, and the black rock exploded in fire. Sparks flew so heavily that several of them skittered and jumped on the sand beneath the rock and he smiled and struck again and again.

37

ASSIGNMENT CARD 2

Literature Discussion

Discuss the following questions and questions of your own with a group of your classmates:

- The porcupine is a small, non-threatening animal, especially compared to a bear or a mountain lion. How does the author turn Brian's encounter with the porcupine into a terrifying experience?

- Brian is in a scary situation, all alone in the wilderness. Why do you think that he begins to cry after he has removed the porcupine quills, but not before?

- What are Brian's reasons for thinking that feeling sorry for oneself is a bad idea? What other reasons can you think of to support Brian's opinion?

- The hatchet is the only tool Brian has. With it, he hopes to make a fire. If you were alone in the wilderness and had only one tool, what would you want it to be? Why?

Theme 1: Courage

Teacher's Resource BLM page 47

Stop and Think

Critical Thinking Questions

1. **COMPARE AND CONTRAST** What contrasting feelings does Brian have in the first half of the story? Give examples to support your answer. (self-pity when he cries about his leg; determination when he tries to make a fire)

2. **MAKING GENERALIZATIONS** What does Brian's behavior so far tell you about the way he handles challenges? (Sample answer: He may be discouraged at first, but he eventually faces challenges with intelligence and courage.)

Strategies in Action

Have students take turns modeling Summarize and other strategies they used.

Discussion Options

You may want to bring the entire class together to do one or more of the activities below.

- **Review Predictions/Purpose** Have students share predictions they made about what Brian will do to survive. Ask them if their predictions are accurate so far. Tell students to record any additional predictions or questions they have.

- **Share Group Discussions** Have students share their literature discussions.

- **Summarize** Ask students to use their Details Chart to summarize the story so far.

Monitoring Student Progress

If . . .	Then . . .
students have successfully completed the Extra Support activities on page 36,	have them read the rest of the story cooperatively or independently.

Reading the Selection 37

CRITICAL THINKING

Guiding Comprehension

⑪ MAKING INFERENCES What does the author mean by the sentence *Brian found it was a long way from sparks to fire?* (Brian does not yet know how to turn the sparks into a fire.)

⑫ WRITER'S CRAFT What words or phrases does the author use to make the sparks seem alive? (*must make a home; a perfect home or they won't stay*)

COMPREHENSION STRATEGY

Summarize

Student Modeling Ask students to summarize pages 37–39. If students need help modeling, offer these prompts.

- What main event happens after Brian wakes from his dream?
- What does Brian do after he can't start a fire with grass and twigs?
- Do you need to mention that the wall was made of chalky granite or sandstone? Why or why not?

Vocabulary

ignite to cause to start burning

tinder a material that catches fire easily

kindling small pieces of wood or other material used for starting fires

exasperation the feeling of being extremely annoyed or irritated

tendrils long, slender curling things

painstaking requiring great and careful effort

---

⑪

There could be fire here, he thought. I will have a fire here, he thought, and struck again — I will have fire from the hatchet.

Brian found it was a long way from sparks to fire.

Clearly there had to be something for the sparks to ignite, some kind of tinder or kindling — but what? He brought some dried grass in, tapped sparks into it and watched them die. He tried small twigs, breaking them into little pieces, but that was worse than the grass. Then he tried a combination of the two, grass and twigs.

Nothing. He had no trouble getting sparks, but the tiny bits of hot stone or metal — he couldn't tell which they were — just sputtered and died.

He settled back on his haunches in exasperation, looking at the pitiful clump of grass and twigs.

He needed something finer, something soft and fine and fluffy to catch the bits of fire.

Shredded paper would be nice, but he had no paper.

"So close," he said aloud, "so close . . ."

He put the hatchet back in his belt and went out of the shelter, limping on his sore leg. There had to be something, had to be. Man had made fire. There had been fire for thousands, millions of years. There had to be a way. He dug in his pockets and found a twenty-dollar bill in his wallet. Paper. Worthless paper out here. But if he could get a fire going . . .

He ripped the twenty into tiny pieces, made a pile of pieces, and hit sparks into them. Nothing happened. They just wouldn't take the sparks. But there had to be a way — some way to do it.

Not twenty feet to his right, leaning out over the water were birches and he stood looking at them for a full half-minute before they registered on his mind. They were a beautiful white with bark like clean, slightly speckled paper.

Paper.

He moved to the trees. Where the bark was peeling from the trunks it lifted in tiny tendrils, almost fluffs. Brian plucked some of them loose, rolled them in his fingers. They seemed flammable, dry and nearly powdery. He pulled and twisted bits off the trees, packing them in one hand while he picked them with the other, picking and gathering until he had a wad close to the size of a baseball.

38

Extra Support/Intervention

Strategy Modeling: Phonics/Decoding

combination

KOM-buh-NAY-shuhn

Model the strategy for the word *combination* on page 38.

I see the VCCV pattern in the first part of this word. I can divide the first two syllables between the m and the b, KOM-buh. I know how to pronounce tion. *Is na pronounced* nah *or* nay? *I'll try the long a sound. When I combine all the parts, I get KOM-buh-NAY-shuhn. It sounds familiar. Maybe it has to do with combining. Yes, I'm right. The sentence talks about using grass and twigs together.*

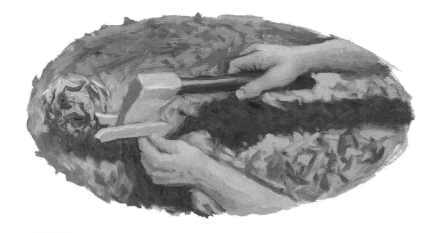

Then he went back into the shelter and arranged the ball of birchbark peelings at the base of the black rock. As an afterthought he threw in the remains of the twenty-dollar bill. He struck and a stream of sparks fell into the bark and quickly died. But this time one spark fell on one small hair of dry bark — almost a thread of bark — and seemed to glow a bit brighter before it died.

The material had to be finer. There had to be a soft and incredibly fine nest for the sparks.

I must make a home for the sparks, he thought. A perfect home or they won't stay, they won't make fire.

He started ripping the bark, using his fingernails at first, and when that didn't work he used the sharp edge of the hatchet, cutting the bark in thin slivers, hairs so fine they were almost not there. It was painstaking work, slow work, and he stayed with it for over two hours. Twice he stopped for a handful of berries and once to go to the lake for a drink. Then back to work, the sun on his back, until at last he had a ball of fluff as big as a grapefruit — dry birchbark fluff.

He positioned his spark nest — as he thought of it — at the base of the rock, used his thumb to make a small depression in the middle, and slammed the back of the hatchet down across the black rock. A cloud of sparks rained down, most of them missing the nest, but some, perhaps thirty or so, hit in the depression and of those six or seven found fuel and grew, smoldered and

12

39

Fluency Practice

Rereading for Fluency Have students choose a favorite passage from *Hatchet* to reread to a partner, or suggest that they read the first three paragraphs on page 39. Encourage students to read with feeling and expression.

English Language Learners

Supporting Comprehension

Read aloud the paragraph at the bottom of page 38. Discuss these descriptive phrases: *with bark like clean, slightly speckled paper; tiny tendrils, almost fluffs; flammable, dry and nearly powdery.* If possible, show real birch bark or a picture of birch bark to explain these descriptive phrases.

Guiding Comprehension

13 **NOTING DETAILS** What details does the author include to show that Brian is hard on himself for his failure to start the fire? (having him think that a cave dweller would have easily started a fire by now)

14 **DRAWING CONCLUSIONS** Why does Brian think the sparks are starving? (Sample answer: He knows they need something more to stay lit, but he can't figure out what that is.)

15 **MAKING JUDGMENTS** How well do you think Brian is coping with the challenges he faces? Give examples. (Sample answer: He is doing well. He builds a shelter; he pulls out porcupine quills; he realizes he can use a hatchet to make a fire; he makes a fire.)

---

caused the bark to take on the red glow.

Then they went out.

Close — he was close. He repositioned the nest, made a new and smaller dent with his thumb, and struck again.

More sparks, a slight glow, then nothing.

13 It's me, he thought. I'm doing something wrong. I do not know this — a cave dweller would have had a fire by now, a Cro-Magnon man would have a fire by now — but I don't know this. I don't know how to make a fire.

Maybe not enough sparks. He settled the nest in place once more and hit the rock with a series of blows, as fast as he could. The sparks poured like a golden waterfall. At first they seemed to take, there were several, many sparks that found life and took briefly, but they all died.

14 Starved.

He leaned back. They are like me. They are starving. It wasn't quantity, there were plenty of sparks, but they needed more.

I would kill, he thought suddenly, for a book of matches. Just one book. Just one match. I would kill.

What makes fire? He thought back to school. To all those science classes. Had he ever learned what made a fire? Did a teacher ever stand up there and say, "This is what makes a fire . . ."

He shook his head, tried to focus his thoughts. What did it take? You have to have fuel, he thought — and he had that. The bark was fuel. Oxygen — there had to be air.

He needed to add air. He had to fan on it, blow on it.

He made the nest ready again, held the hatchet backward, tensed, and struck four quick blows. Sparks came down and he leaned forward as fast as he could and blew.

Too hard. There was a bright, almost intense glow, then it was gone. He had blown it out.

Another set of strikes, more sparks. He leaned and blew, but gently this time, holding back and aiming the stream of air from his mouth to hit the brightest spot. Five or six sparks had fallen in a tight mass of bark hair and Brian centered his efforts there.

15 The sparks grew with his gentle breath. The red glow moved from the sparks themselves into the bark, moved and grew and became worms, glow-

40

Vocabulary

Cro-Magnon a member of a prehistoric race of humans who lived on the European continent, walked upright, and used stone and bone tools

consuming eating up; destroying, as by fire

gratified pleased

take to work as intended; to catch (fire)

ASSIGNMENT CARD 4

*Spark*ling Descriptions

Writer's Craft

The author of *Hatchet* describes the sparks and the fire that Brian makes by comparing them to a hungry or starving person, crawling red worms, and a golden waterfall.

Look back through the selection and make a list of the ways in which the author describes the sparks and fire. Add your own ideas to the list. Choose the images you think are the strongest, and use them to write a one-paragraph description of sparks or fire.

Theme 1: Courage

ing red worms that crawled up the bark hairs and caught other threads of bark and grew until there was a pocket of red as big as a quarter, a glowing red coal of heat.

And when he ran out of breath and paused to inhale, the red ball suddenly burst into flame.

"Fire!" He yelled. "I've got fire! I've got it, I've got it, I've got it . . ."

But the flames were thick and oily and burning fast, consuming the ball of bark as fast as if it were gasoline. He had to feed the flames, keep them going. Working as fast as he could he carefully placed the dried grass and wood pieces he had tried at first on top of the bark and was gratified to see them take.

41

Extra Support/Intervention

Strategy Modeling: Summarize

Use this example to model the strategy.

I want to make sure I understand how Brian figures out how to make fire, so I'll summarize the last few pages. At first Brian can't get the ball of bark to ignite. Then he remembers that fire must have oxygen. Brian realizes that he needs to blow on the sparks. After many tries, the ball of bark finally catches fire.

Cause and Effect

Review

- Define cause as an event that makes something happen and effect as the result of something that happened.

- Have a volunteer read the last paragraph on page 40 through the first full paragraph on page 41. Explain that Brian's breath and the sparks are the cause and that the flame is the effect.

- Tell students that sometimes one event causes another event that causes another event, and so on. Explain that this is called a cause-and-effect chain.

Practice

- Have students record an example of a cause-and-effect chain in *Hatchet*.

- They can use a chart like the one below.

Cause	Effect	Effect
Brian throws his hatchet.	It hits the stone wall.	Sparks appear.

Apply

- Have partners create a cause-and-effect chain for at least three connected story events.

- Tell them to create a chart like the one shown above.

Review Skill Trace	
Teach	Theme 4, p. 407A
Reteaching	Theme 4, p. R10
▶ Review	p. 41; Theme 3, p. 261

CRITICAL THINKING

Guiding Comprehension

16 **NOTING DETAILS** What details does the author include to show that Brian's mood has changed? (saying that he smiles; that he thinks that he now has a friend and is no longer all alone)

17 **MAKING INFERENCES** Why does Brian think of the fire as a good friend? (It will keep him warm; maybe it will keep wild animals away.)

REACHING ALL LEARNERS — Extra Support/Intervention	On Level	Challenge
### Selection Review	### Literature Discussion	

Selection Review

Before students join the whole class for Wrapping Up on page 43, they should

- review their predictions/purpose

- take turns modeling Summarize and other strategies they used

- complete their Details Chart on **Practice Book** page 12 and help you complete **Transparency 1–2**

- use their Details Chart to summarize

Literature Discussion

In mixed-ability groups of five or six, students can discuss the questions they had as they read or the questions in Think About the Selection on page 44 of the Anthology.

But they would go fast. He needed more, and more. He could not let the flames go out.

He ran from the shelter to the pines and started breaking off the low, dead small limbs. These he threw in the shelter, went back for more, threw those in, and squatted to break and feed the hungry flames. When the small wood was going well he went out and found larger wood and did not relax until that was going. Then he leaned back against the wood brace of his door opening and smiled.

16

I have a friend, he thought — I have a friend now. A hungry friend, but a good one. I have a friend named fire.

17

43

Wrapping Up

Critical Thinking Questions

1. **SEQUENCE OF EVENTS** Explain the steps Brian had to take to finally light the fire. (gathered and shredded birch bark; made nest; made sparks with hatchet; blew on sparks; gathered kindling to keep fire going)

2. **DRAWING CONCLUSIONS** Why does it make sense for Brian to rip up the twenty-dollar bill to start the fire? (In the wilderness, Brian's survival depends on fire more than money.)

Strategies in Action

Have students take turns modeling how they used the Summarize strategy.

Discussion Options

Bring the entire class together to do one or more of the activities below.

Review Predictions/Purpose Have students discuss their predictions. Also ask them to share questions they had as they read and explain how they came up with answers.

Share Group Discussions Have students share their literature discussions.

Summarize Ask students to use the completed Details Chart on **Practice Book** page 12 to summarize the story.

Comprehension Check

Use **Practice Book** page 13 to assess students' comprehension of the selection.

English Language Learners

Language Development

Read this line: *I have a friend named fire.* Explain that Brian has started a fire. Ask students, Why would Brian call fire a friend? (Fire is like a friend because the fire helps Brian with cooking and staying warm and keeps away animals.) Explain that he calls the fire a *hungry* friend because he must *feed* it fuel often.

Practice Book page 13

Hatchet
Comprehension Check

Name _____

What Really Happened?

These sentences tell about Brian and the things that happen to him in the story. Write T if the sentence is true. Write F if the sentence is false. If the sentence is false, correct it to make it true.

1. __F__ Brian wakes up when he hears a bear growling outside his shelter.
Brian wakes up when he hears the wind growling outside his shelter. **(1 point)**

2. __F__ Brian's leg gets injured when he kicks out in the darkness and hits the hatchet.
Brian's leg gets injured when he kicks out in the darkness and hits a porcupine. **(1)**

3. __T__ After crying for a long time, Brian realizes that feeling sorry for yourself changes nothing.
__(1)__

4. __F__ Seeing his father and his friend Terry in a dream makes Brian feel happy.
Seeing his father and his friend Terry in a dream makes Brian feel frustrated. **(1)**

5. __F__ In Brian's dream, his friend Terry shows him a path out of the forest.
In Brian's dream, his friend Terry shows him a fire in a barbecue pit. **(1)**

6. __T__ Brian thinks that throwing his hatchet to protect himself from wild animals is a bad idea.
__(1)__

7. __T__ By hitting the hatchet against a hard black rock, Brian is able to make sparks.
__(1)__

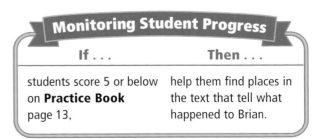

Monitoring Student Progress

If . . .	Then . . .
students score 5 or below on **Practice Book** page 13,	help them find places in the text that tell what happened to Brian.

Responding

Think About the Selection

Have students discuss or write their answers. Sample answers are provided; accept reasonable responses.

1. **PREDICTING OUTCOMES** yes, because his need for warmth would have inspired him to figure out a way to make a fire; no, because he would not have learned that striking a hatchet against rock creates sparks

2. **MAKING JUDGMENTS** Answers will vary.

3. **MAKING GENERALIZATIONS** because he had had several terrible experiences in a row; this shows that Brian is a normal person—most people in a similar situation would feel sorry for themselves

4. **DRAWING CONCLUSIONS** Brian's father must have been saying something like "Make," as in "Make a fire"; his friend Terry showed Brian a fire blazing in a barbecue pit. Brian had seen that the hatchet could make sparks when it struck rock; he connected all of these ideas and began to make a fire.

5. **CONNECTING TO PERSONAL EXPERIENCES** Answers will vary.

6. **DRAWING CONCLUSIONS** The fire had to be constantly fed with fuel in order for it to keep burning; it was also valuable and comforting, like a friend.

7. **Connecting/Comparing** yes, because once he had faced up to the fact that self-pity was not going to help him, he figured out how to make a fire, which helped him to survive in the wilderness

---

Responding

Think About the Selection

1. If the porcupine hadn't entered Brian's shelter, do you think Brian would have discovered a way to make fire? Why or why not?

2. If you were Brian, would you pull the quills out of your leg? Explain.

3. Why does Brian feel sorry for himself? What does this tell you about Brian?

4. Think about the people in Brian's dream. What part do they play in his thinking of using the hatchet to make fire?

5. Brian recalls what he learned in school about what makes a fire. What have you learned in school that has helped you solve a problem or make a decision?

6. Why do you think Brian calls fire "a hungry friend"?

7. **Connecting/Comparing** Do you think Brian's actions alone in the wilderness showed courage? Why or why not?

Explaining

Write an Explanation

To Brian, the most important rule of survival is that feeling sorry for yourself doesn't work. Do you agree? If so, why? If not, what do you think is the most important rule of survival? Why? Write an explanation of your point of view or opinion.

Tips
- Begin by thinking of what you know about survival rules or skills.
- State your point of view clearly in a topic sentence. Support it with details and reasons.

44

English Language Learners

Supporting Comprehension

Beginning/Preproduction Ask students to make drawings of key story events.

Early Production and Speech Emergence Have pairs of students use the illustrations to talk about the key events in the story.

Intermediate and Advanced Fluency Have students work in pairs to write three sentences about how Brian felt at different times during the story.

Science
Design a Poster

With a partner, review the materials Brian gathers and the steps he takes to make a fire. Then make a poster showing the materials and the steps he uses to build the fire.

Health
Chart the Five Senses

Make a chart listing the five senses: touch, taste, smell, sight, hearing. Look back at the selection and list under each sense what Brian experiences.

Bonus Find examples of similes (comparisons using *like* or *as*) that describe what Brian feels with his senses. Add the similes to the five senses chart.

Internet

Post a Review

Write a review of *Hatchet*. Post your review on Education Place.

www.eduplace.com/kids

45

Additional Responses

Personal Response Invite students to share their personal responses to the selection.

Journal ▸ Have students write in their journal about a time when they couldn't do something at first and then succeeded.

Selection Connections Remind students to add to **Practice Book** page 9.

REACHING ALL LEARNERS
Extra Support/ Intervention

Surviving in the Wild

Have mixed groups do Internet or library research to find websites or guidebooks with advice about wilderness survival. Review all the groups' research as a class. Ask, Do you still agree with Brian that the most important rule of survival is not to feel sorry for yourself? Why or why not?

Practice Book page 9

Launching the Theme
Selection Connections

Name _____

Courage

The characters in this theme show courage in dangerous or challenging situations. After reading each selection, complete the chart below to show what you learned about the characters.

	Hatchet	Passage to Freedom
What challenge does the main character face?	Brian has to survive in the wilderness and build a fire with only a hatchet as a tool. (2.5 points)	Mr. Sugihara has to decide whether to obey his superiors or help save the lives of hundreds of refugees. (2.5)
Where does the challenge take place?	in the wilderness, in modern times (2.5)	in Lithuania, during World War II (2.5)
In what ways does the main character show courage?	Brian learns to cope with being alone in the wilderness. He learns to build a fire from sparks. (2.5)	Mr. Sugihara disobeys his superiors and puts his own job at risk to help the refugees. (2.5)
What do you think the character learns from his or her experience?	Brian learns that he can make a fire from wood scrapings and a spark, and that he can handle difficult situations by himself. (2.5)	Mr. Sugihara learns that sometimes one must follow one's conscience instead of obeying orders. (2.5)

Monitoring Student Progress

End-of-Selection Assessment

Selection Test Use the test on page 109 in the **Teacher's Resource Blackline Masters** to assess selection comprehension and vocabulary.

Student Self-Assessment Have students assess their reading with additional questions such as the following:

- What parts of this selection were easy for me to understand?
- What strategies helped me understand the parts that were difficult?
- What new words did I learn?
- Would I like to read the rest of the book *Hatchet?* Why or why not?

Media Link

Skill: How to Read a News Article

- **Introduce** "Boy Wonder," a nonfiction article from the *St. Louis Post-Dispatch* newspaper.

- **Explain** that because the article is non-fiction, students should read it to understand facts and opinions rather than plot and character.

- **Discuss** the Skill Lesson on Anthology page 46.

- **Model** using the headline, photographs, and caption to tell what the article is about.

- **Explain** that a good newspaper article always answers the questions shown on Anthology page 46: Who? What? Where? When? Why? Explain also that journalists—people who write newspaper articles—are trained to ask and answer these questions.

- **Set a purpose** for reading. Have students read the article. Remind them to use Question and other strategies as they read.

Media Link

Genre

Newspaper Article

Skill: How to Read a News Article

1. Look first at the **head-line** to find out what the article is about.

2. Then look for answers to these questions:

   Who is the article about?

   What happened?

   Where and **when** did the event occur?

   Why did it happen?

3. Look at the **photo-graphs** and read the **captions** to help you picture the event.

46

COURAGE in the NEWS

Newspapers are full of stories about courage. As you read the following news article, you may wonder: "What would I do in the same situation?"

Boy Wonder; 5th-Grader Stops Bus After Driver Collapses

Carolyn Bower of the Post-Dispatch Staff

A fifth-grade student became a hero Tuesday when he took control of a runaway school bus on U.S. Highway 40 in St. Louis and stopped it before anyone was badly injured, police and the boy's principal said.

Larry Champagne III, 10, was credited with saving the lives of about 20 fellow students, including his brother, on a Mayflower bus when its driver apparently suffered a stroke.

The students from St. Louis were en route to Bellerive School in the Parkway School District when Larry felt the bus swerve back and forth and saw the driver slump and fall into the stairwell.

Larry ran to the front of the bus, grabbed the wheel and stomped on the brake. A passer-by stopped to help, and Larry opened the door.

Authorities said the driver, Ernestine Blackman, apparently suffered a stroke that temporarily paralyzed the right side of her body. Blackman was reported in serious condition late Tuesday at Barnes Hospital.

Five children suffered minor injuries. Two were treated at St. Louis Children's Hospital and released, and three at Cardinal Glennon Hospital.

Larry was fairly low-key about what had happened. But other

---

children chanted to Ken Russell, principal at Bellerive:

"Larry saved our lives."

Larry Champagne is a hero to his classmates.

Here's the story police and Russell pieced together:

At 8 A.M., about 20 minutes before Blackman's bus normally delivered the voluntary transfer students to Bellerive, Blackman apparently suffered a stroke driving on Highway 40 near Sarah Avenue. Police don't know how fast the bus was traveling.

The bus started swerving, passing cars honked their horns, and Blackman slid from her seat. Larry rushed forward to apply the air brake. Before he got the bus under control, it hit a guardrail, swerved and hit another guardrail, and a pickup hit the bus. Police had no indication whether the truck's driver was injured.

At some point, other students came forward to help. They included Crystal Wright and Gregory McKnight, both third-graders; and Gregory's brother, Angelo McKnight, and Imani Butler, both in fourth grade.

Crystal handed a passer-by Blackman's radio microphone to call Mayflower. Someone with a cellular phone called police.

Gregory, Angelo and Imani were unable to move Blackman. Imani and Angelo were among the children treated for minor injuries, the principal said.

Another bus took the uninjured children to Bellerive. Russell met with them and asked them how they had known what to do.

They told him the bus driver earlier had instructed them what to do in an emergency. And Larry said his grandfather, Lawrence Champagne, had given him some driving tips.

Russell said: "I'm proud our students were able to remain calm and take care of one another. I'm also proud that they listened to the instructions that the driver gave them and remembered those."

The bus company's division manager, Tim Stieber, marveled at Larry's success in stopping the bus.

"Considering how bad it could have been, it was good," Stieber said.

Larry was too nervous to talk to a reporter later Tuesday, his mother, Dawn Little, said. She praised Larry for his fast thinking and said she was especially grateful that he and his brother, Jerrick, 9, were uninjured.

47

Wrapping Up

Critical Thinking Questions

Ask students to use the selection to answer these questions.

1. **MAKING JUDGMENTS** Do you think Larry is a hero? Why or why not? (Sample answer: yes, because he risked his own life when he took the wheel of the bus, and his actions saved lives)

2. **MAKING JUDGMENTS** What questions would you ask Tim Stieber if you could interview him? (Answers will vary.)

3. **MAKING JUDGMENTS** Do you think students Larry's age should be given driving tips? Explain your answer. (Sample answer: Maybe they should be shown the location of important parts of a vehicle, such as the emergency brake, and told how to use them in case of an emergency.)

4. **Connecting/Comparing** How are Larry's actions like those of Brian, the main character in *Hatchet*? How are their actions different? (Same: both boys show intelligence and courage; Different: Larry acts fast to save a busload of people and Brian has more time and only needs to worry about himself)

English Language Learners

Supporting Comprehension

The numerous details in the article, such as the names of various people and hospitals, may confuse some students.

- Explain that newspaper writers include this information to make the article as accurate as possible.

- Have students write these questions on a sheet of paper: Who? What? When? Where? Why? They can jot down the answer to each question as they learn it.

OBJECTIVES

- Use story details to explain events and a character's feelings.
- Identify details that help readers understand a character's motives.

Target Skill Trace

Preview; Teach	p. 25G, p. 26, p. 33; p. 47A
Reteach	p. R8
Review	pp. M32–M33; Theme 2, p. 173; Theme 3, p. 279; Theme 4, p. 393; Theme 5, p. 503
See	*Extra Support Handbook*, pp. 16–17; pp. 22–23

Transparency 1–2

Details Chart

Page(s)	Brian feels	Details that show how Brian feels
30	terrified	• his nostrils widened and he opened his eyes wider • he thought of every monster he had ever seen • his heart hammered in his throat
32–33	in pain; hurt	• the eight quills in his leg seem like dozens • his pain spreads • catches his breath when he pulls the quills out
33–34	sorry for himself	• He thinks, "I can't take this" and "I can't do this." • He cries until he is cried out.
34–35	frustrated	• can't understand what his father and Terry are telling him in his dream • thinks "so what" and "I know" when he thinks about the fire in his dream
36–37	motivated; excited; happy	• realizes the hatchet can make sparks • recognizes the message about fire from his dreams • begins to make sparks to start a fire
38–41	determined	• doesn't give up when his first attempts fail to start a fire • takes two hours to gather tree bark • finally succeeds in lighting the fire
43	satisfied	• smiles and calls the fire a good friend

TRANSPARENCY 1–2
TEACHER'S EDITION PAGES 28 AND 47A

COURAGE: Hatchet
Graphic Organizer Details Chart
ANNOTATED VERSION

Practice Book page 12

Name _____

Hatchet
Graphic Organizer
Details Chart

Details Chart

Page(s)	Brian feels _____	Details that show how Brian feels
30	terrified	• his nostrils widened and he opened his eyes wider • he thought of every monster he had ever seen • his heart hammered in his throat **(3 points)**
32–33	in pain; hurt **(1)**	• the eight quills in his leg seem like dozens • his pain spreads • catches his breath when he pulls the quills out
33–34	sorry for himself **(1)**	• He thinks, "I can't take this" and "I can't do this." • He cries until he is cried out.
34–35	frustrated	• can't understand what his father and Terry are telling him in his dream • thinks "so what" and "I know" when he thinks about the fire in his dream **(2)**
36–37	motivated; excited; happy **(1)**	• realizes the hatchet can make sparks • recognizes the message about fire from his dreams • begins to make sparks to start a fire
38–41	determined	• doesn't give up when his first attempts fail to start a fire • takes two hours to gather tree bark • finally succeeds in lighting the fire **(3)**
43	satisfied	• smiles and calls the fire a good friend **(1)**

TARGET SKILL COMPREHENSION: Noting Details

❶ Teach

Review the details in *Hatchet*. Complete the Graphic Organizer on **Transparency 1–2** with students. (Sample answers are shown.) Have students refer to the selection and to **Practice Book** page 12. Discuss these points.

- Details can show how a character feels.
- Details can help explain why a character acts in a certain way.

Model finding details to identify a character's motive.
Explain that motive is a character's reason for acting in a particular way. Have students turn to the last complete paragraph on page 36 as you think aloud.

Think Aloud *Why does Brian begin to hit the rock with the hatchet? First, the sun's reflection on the hatchet makes Brian think of fire. Then Brian remembers the sparks made when the hatchet hit the rock. These details help explain why he hits the rock with the hatchet: he hopes to make a fire from the sparks.*

❷ Guided Practice

Have students find details that identify a character's motive.
Display the chart below on the board. Complete the Action column. Have small groups find details that help explain these actions. Ask volunteers to list them in the Details column.

Action	Details That Identify Motive
Brian spends two hours ripping tree bark.	The material to start the fire must be very fine.
Brian runs to gather dead tree limbs.	He knows the wood will burn fast and doesn't want the flames to go out.
Brian leans against the opening to his shelter and smiles.	The larger pieces of wood are finally burning well.

❸ Apply

Assign Practice Book pages 14–15. Also have students apply this skill as they read their **Leveled Readers** for this week. You may also select books from the Leveled Bibliography for this theme (pages 23E–23F).

Test Prep Tell students that questions on reading tests usually focus on important details only. Remind students that being able to distinguish more important from less important details will help them do better on reading tests.

Leveled Readers and Leveled Practice

Students at all levels apply the comprehension skill as they read their Leveled Readers. See lessons on pages 47O–47R.

● BELOW LEVEL — River of No Return — by Julia Hanna — illustrated by Will Williams

▲ ON LEVEL — Weathering the STORM — by Barbara A. Donovan — illustrated by Roxanne Kaloustian

■ ABOVE LEVEL — An Unexpected Hero — by Paul Ayers — illustrated by Liz Amini-Holmes

◆ LANGUAGE SUPPORT — Fear of White Water — by Julia Hanna — illustrated by Will Williams

Reading Traits

Teaching students how to note details is one way of encouraging them to "read the lines" of a selection. This comprehension skill supports the reading trait **Establishing Comprehension**.

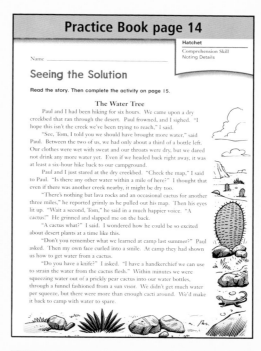

Practice Book page 14

Name _____

Hatchet
Comprehension Skill
Noting Details

Seeing the Solution

Read the story. Then complete the activity on page 15.

The Water Tree

Paul and I had been hiking for six hours. We came upon a dry creekbed that ran through the desert. Paul frowned, and I sighed. "I hope this isn't the creek we've been trying to reach," I said.

"See, Tom, I told you we should have brought more water," said Paul. Between the two of us, we had only about a third of a bottle left. Our clothes were wet with sweat and our throats were dry, but we dared not drink any more water yet. Even if we headed back right away, it was at least a six-hour hike back to our campground.

Paul and I just stared at the dry creekbed. "Check the map," I said to Paul. "Is there any other water within a mile of here?" I thought that even if there was another creek nearby, it might be dry too.

"There's nothing but lava rocks and an occasional cactus for another three miles," he reported grimly as he pulled out his map. Then his eyes lit up. "Wait a second, Tom," he said in a much happier voice. "A cactus!" He grinned and slapped me on the back.

"A cactus what?" I said. I wondered how he could be so excited about desert plants at a time like this.

"Don't you remember what we learned at camp last summer?" Paul asked. Then my own face curled into a smile. At camp they had shown us how to get water from a cactus.

"Do you have a knife?" I asked. "I have a handkerchief we can use to strain the water from the cactus flesh." Within minutes we were squeezing water out of a prickly pear cactus into our water bottles, through a funnel fashioned from a sun visor. We didn't get much water per squeeze, but there were more than enough cacti around. We'd make it back to camp with water to spare.

Practice Book page 15

Name _____

Hatchet
Comprehension Skill
Noting Details

Seeing the Solution *continued*

Answer these questions about the story on page 14.

1. How do Paul and Tom feel when they reach the dry creekbed? Why?
   They feel discouraged because the creek is dry and they are
   almost out of water. (2 points)

2. What details in the first paragraph help you figure out how the boys feel?
   Paul frowns. Tom sighs. (2)

3. What kind of danger are the boys in? What details help you understand the danger?
   They could run out of water. They are in the hot desert with only a
   third of a bottle of water left, and must hike at least six hours back
   to their campground. (2)

4. How does Paul feel when he remembers that they can get water from a cactus? How do you know his feelings change?
   He is suddenly happy. His eyes light up and he says "A cactus!" in
   a happy voice. He then grins and slaps his friend on the back. (2)

5. How do the boys make use of what they have to get water?
   They use a handkerchief to strain the water from the cactus pulp.
   They use a visor to funnel the water into their water bottles. (2)

6. Do you think that the task of filling the water bottles will be a fast one or a slow one? Why?
   It will probably be slow because they don't get very much water
   per squeeze. (2)

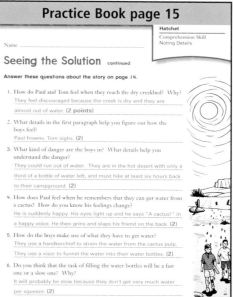

Monitoring Student Progress

If . . .	Then . . .
students score 8 or below on **Practice Book** page 15,	use the Reteaching lesson on Teacher's Edition page R8.
students have successfully met the lesson objectives,	have them do the Challenge/ Extension activities on Teacher's Edition page R9.

OBJECTIVES

- Read words that have suffixes *-ful*, *-less*, and *-ly*.
- Use the Phonics/Decoding Strategy to decode longer words.
- Learn academic language: *suffix, word part, base word.*

Target Skill Trace

Teach	p. 47C
Reteach	p. R16
Review	pp. M34–M35
See	*Handbook for English Language Learners*, p. 19; *Extra Support Handbook*, pp. 14–15; pp. 18–19

Practice Book page 16

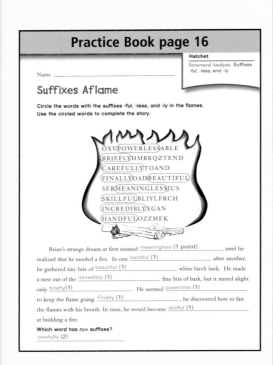

Name _____

Suffixes Aflame

Circle the words with the suffixes *-ful, -less,* and *-ly* in the flames. Use the circled words to complete the story.

Brian's strange dream at first seemed meaningless (1 point) _____, until he realized that he needed a fire. In one handful (1) _____ after another, he gathered tiny bits of beautiful (1) _____ white birch bark. He made a nest out of the incredibly (1) _____ fine bits of bark, but it stayed alight only briefly (1) _____. He seemed powerless (1) _____ to keep the flame going. Finally (1) _____, he discovered how to fan the flames with his breath. In time, he would become skillful (1) _____ at building a fire.

Which word has *two* suffixes?
carefully (2)

Monitoring Student Progress

If . . .	Then . . .
students score 7 or below on **Practice Book** page 16,	use the Reteaching lesson on Teacher's Edition page R16.

STRUCTURAL ANALYSIS/ VOCABULARY: Suffixes *-ful, -less,* and *-ly*

① Teach

Introduce suffixes. Explain that a suffix is a word part that comes after a base word and changes its meaning.

Explain the suffix *-ful*. Write *Brian was <u>careful</u> not to blow too hard on the sparks.*

- The suffix *-ful* means "full of" or "characterized by."
- The base word is *care*. The whole word means "full of care."

Explain the suffix *-less*. Write *The twenty-dollar bill was <u>worthless</u> in the wilderness.*

- The suffix *-less* means "without."
- The base word *worth* means "value." The meaning of the whole word is "without value."

Explain the suffix *-ly*. Write *His leg was <u>instantly</u> torn with pain.*

- The suffix *-ly* often means "like" or "in a way that is."
- The base word *instant* means "immediate." The meaning of the whole word is "in a way that is immediate."

Model the Phonics/Decoding Strategy. Write *The red ball <u>suddenly</u> burst into flame.* Then model decoding *suddenly.*

Think Aloud *I see the suffix -ly, and I know that the y stands for the long e sound. I can pronounce the base word: SUHD-uhn. When I blend the sounds, I get SUHD-uhn-lee, which means "in a way that is sudden."*

② Guided Practice

Have students use suffixes. Display these sentences. Have partners copy the suffix in each underlined word, decode it, and give its meaning. Call on volunteers to model at the board.

1. Sparks died <u>immediately</u>.
2. The bear is a <u>powerful</u> animal.
3. He had another <u>sleepless</u> night.

③ Apply

Assign Practice Book page 16.

PHONICS REVIEW: Short Vowels

OBJECTIVES
- Decode words with short vowels.
- Apply the Phonics/Decoding Strategy.
- Learn academic language: *short vowel*.

❶ Teach

Review short vowels. Discuss these points.

- Short vowel sounds are usually spelled with a vowel followed by a consonant: *can, ran, fan*.

- When a syllable ends with a vowel followed by a consonant, the syllable usually has the short vowel sound: *horn<u>e</u>t, wat<u>e</u>r*.

Model the Phonics/Decoding Strategy. Write *They seemed <u>flammable</u>, dry, and nearly powdery.* Then model decoding *flammable*.

Think Aloud *I see a short vowel pattern in the first syllable,* flam. *This looks like the word* flame, *but that word has a long* a *sound. Which is right? I see the ending* -able. *That usually means "able to do something." I'll try* FLAYM-uh-buhl. *That doesn't sound right, so I'll try* FLAM-uh-buhl. *That sounds right. Maybe it means "able to catch fire." That meaning makes sense.*

Phonics/Decoding Strategy

When you come to a word you don't know—

❶ Look carefully at the word.

❷ Look for word parts you know and think about the sounds for the letters.

❸ Blend the sounds to read the word.

❹ Ask yourself: Is it a word I know? Does it make sense in what I am reading?

❺ If not, ask yourself: What else can I try?

HOUGHTON MIFFLIN
Reading

❷ Guided Practice

Help students identify words with short vowels. Display these sentences. Have partners circle the short vowel pattern in the first syllable of each underlined word, pronounce the word, and see if it makes sense. Ask volunteers to model at the board.

1. His <u>nostrils</u> widened.

2. The bits of hot stone <u>sputtered</u> and died.

3. The pain was <u>centered</u> in his calf.

4. He <u>gingerly</u> touched the needles.

❸ Apply

Have students decode words with short vowels. Ask students to find and decode these words from *Hatchet* and discuss their meanings.

| accomplished | page 34 | finally | page 34 | happened | page 35 |
| hunger | page 35 | heavily | page 37 | imbedded | page 37 |

SPELLING: Short Vowels

OBJECTIVES

- Write Spelling Words with short vowel patterns.
- Learn academic language: *short vowel sound.*

SPELLING WORDS

Basic

depth	prompt
craft	pitch
plunge	else
wreck	cliff
sunk	pledge
film	scrub
wince*	brass
bomb	grill
switch	stung
length	bulk*

Review	**Challenge**
swift	habitat
tense*	cobweb*
bunch	tepid
grasp*	magnetic
ditch	deft

Forms of these words appear in the literature.

Extra Support/Intervention

Basic Word List You may want to use only the left column of Basic Words with students who need extra support.

Challenge

Challenge Word Practice Have students write a sentence for each Challenge Word and then rewrite the sentences with blanks in place of vowels. Tell them to decode one another's sentences.

DAY 1 INSTRUCTION

Short Vowels

Pretest Use the Day 5 Test sentences.

Teach Write *craft, depth, film, bomb,* and *plunge* on the board. Say each word and have students repeat it.

- Underline *a, e, i, o,* and *u.* Explain that each word has a short vowel sound spelled with the short vowel pattern: a single vowel followed by a consonant sound.
- Erase the Spelling Words and write these symbols as column heads: /ă/, /ĕ/, /ĭ/, /ŏ/, /ŭ/. Have students identify the sound each represents.
- Say each Basic Word; ask a student to name its vowel sound. Write it below the symbol.
- With the word *pledge,* underline the *dge* pattern and mention that in one-syllable words with a short vowel sound followed by /j/, the /j/ sound is usually spelled *dge.*

Practice/Homework Assign **Practice Book** page 281.

Practice Book page 281

Take-Home Word List	Take-Home Word List	Take-Home Word List
Passage to Freedom	**Courage** Reading-Writing Workshop	**Hatchet**
Long Vowels	Look for familiar spelling patterns in these words to help you remember their spellings.	**Short Vowels**
/ā/ → gaze, trait		/ă/ → craft
/ē/ → theme, preach, sleeve		/ĕ/ → depth
/ī/ → strive		/ĭ/ → film
/ō/ → quote, roam		/ŏ/ → bomb
/yōō/ → mute		/ŭ/ → plunge

Spelling Words	**Spelling Words**	**Spelling Words**
1. theme 11. strain	1. your 8. wouldn't	1. depth 11. prompt
2. quote 12. fade	2. you're 9. we're	2. craft 12. pitch
3. gaze 13. league	3. their 10. to	3. plunge 13. else
4. pace 14. soak	4. there 11. too	4. wreck 14. cliff
5. preach 15. grease	5. they're 12. that's	5. sunk 15. pledge
6. strive 16. throne	6. its 13. knew	6. film 16. scrub
7. trait 17. fume	7. it's 14. know	7. wince 17. brass
8. mute 18. file		8. bomb 18. grill
9. sleeve 19. toast		9. switch 19. stung
10. roam 20. brake		10. length 20. bulk

Challenge Words	**Challenge Words**	**Challenge Words**
1. microphone	1. pennant	1. habitat
2. emphasize	2. bureau	2. cobweb
3. refugee	3. interpret	3. tepid
4. pertain	4. forfeit	4. magnetic
5. coax	5. perspiration	5. deft

My Study List Add your own spelling words on the back →

DAY 2 REVIEW & PRACTICE

Reviewing the Principle

Go over the spelling principle for short vowels with students.

Practice/Homework Assign **Practice Book** page 17.

Practice Book page 17

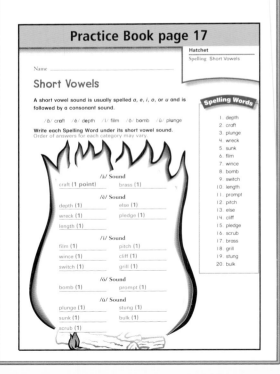

Hatchet
Spelling Short Vowels

Name _____

Short Vowels

A short vowel sound is usually spelled *a, e, i, o,* or *u* and is followed by a consonant sound.

/ă/ craft   /ĕ/ depth   /ĭ/ film   /ŏ/ bomb   /ŭ/ plunge

Write each Spelling Word under its short vowel sound.
Order of answers for each category may vary.

/ă/ Sound
craft (1 point)   brass (1)

/ĕ/ Sound
depth (1)   else (1)
wreck (1)   pledge (1)
length (1)

/ĭ/ Sound
film (1)   pitch (1)
wince (1)   cliff (1)
switch (1)   grill (1)

/ŏ/ Sound
bomb (1)   prompt (1)

/ŭ/ Sound
plunge (1)   stung (1)
sunk (1)   bulk (1)
scrub (1)

Spelling Words
1. depth
2. craft
3. plunge
4. wreck
5. sunk
6. film
7. wince
8. bomb
9. switch
10. length
11. prompt
12. pitch
13. else
14. cliff
15. pledge
16. scrub
17. brass
18. grill
19. stung
20. bulk

Take-Home Word List

DAY 3 VOCABULARY

Classifying

Write the Basic Words on the board.

- Dictate each word group below and tell students to write the Basic Word that belongs with each group.
  - wash, scour, _____ (*scrub*)
  - camera, flash, _____ (*film*)
  - grin, frown, _____ (*wince*)
  - copper, silver, _____ (*brass*)
  - promise, oath, _____ (*pledge*)
  - stove, microwave, _____ (*grill*)
- Have students use each Basic Word from the board orally in a sentence. (Sentences will vary.)

Practice/Homework For spelling practice, assign **Practice Book** page 18.

Practice Book page 18

Name _____

Hatchet
Spelling Short Vowels

Spelling Spree

Change the Word Write a Spelling Word by adding one letter to each word below.

Spelling Words
1. depth
2. craft
3. plunge
4. wreck
5. sunk
6. film
7. wince
8. bomb
9. switch
10. length
11. prompt
12. pitch
13. else
14. cliff
15. pledge
16. scrub
17. brass
18. grill
19. stung
20. bulk

1. ledge pledge (1 point)
2. bass brass (1)
3. sun sunk (1)
4. itch pitch (1)
5. raft craft (1)
6. wine wince (1)
7. lunge plunge (1)
8. gill grill (1)
9. bob bomb (1)
10. sung stung (1)

Word Detective Write a Spelling Word to fit each clue.

11. great size or volume bulk (1)
12. the measure of being long length (1)
13. something used in a camera film (1)
14. an overhanging rock face cliff (1)
15. other or different else (1)
16. what's left after a crash wreck (1)
17. the quality of being deep depth (1)
18. a device used to turn on the power switch (1)
19. to clean very well scrub (1)
20. right on time prompt (1)

DAY 4 PROOFREADING

Game: Word Brainstorm

Have groups of students play a game in which they brainstorm words with short vowel sounds.

- Set a time limit of 2 minutes. Each group member writes down as many short *a* words with the short vowel pattern as he or she can think of.
- When time is called, students make certain, using a dictionary if necessary, that all words are spelled correctly and have the short vowel pattern.
- Group members compare their lists. If 2 or more people have written the same word, they must cross it off their lists. Students score 2 points for each unique word they have written.
- Groups repeat these steps for words with short *e*, short *i*, short *o*, and short *u*.

Practice/Homework For proofreading and writing practice, assign **Practice Book** page 19.

Practice Book page 19

Name _____

Hatchet
Spelling Short Vowels

Proofreading and Writing

Proofreading Circle the five misspelled Spelling Words in this journal entry. Then write each word correctly.

Spelling Words
1. depth
2. craft
3. plunge
4. wreck
5. sunk
6. film
7. wince
8. bomb
9. switch
10. length
11. prompt
12. pitch
13. else
14. cliff
15. pledge
16. scrub
17. brass
18. grill
19. stung
20. bulk

I spent all day today starting a fire. Building a fire is a real craft! I began by trying to light pieces of a torn twenty-dollar bill. Then I decided to swich to strips of birch bark. I gathered some pieces of the right lenth and width and made them into a ball. I lit the ball with the sparks made by striking my hatchet against the rock wall. It was hard work, but I don't know what els I could have used to start the fire. I still winse when I think about another night without one. My next goal is to figure out how to make a gril that I can cook on.

1. switch (1 point)
2. length (1)
3. else (1)
4. wince (1)
5. grill (1)

Write an Opinion What do you think about the way the writer of this journal entry went about building a fire? Was there anything about his or her behavior that you admired? Is there anything you would have done differently?

On a separate piece of paper, write a paragraph in which you give your opinion of the writer's way of doing things. Use Spelling Words from the list. Responses will vary. (5)

DAY 5 ASSESSMENT

Spelling Test

Say each underlined word, read the sentence, and then repeat the word. Have students write only the underlined word.

Basic Words

1. The **depth** of the water is too shallow for diving.
2. I sailed my **craft** into the harbor.
3. Who will **plunge** into the pool?
4. The old car was a **wreck**.
5. The boat was **sunk** by the storm.
6. We need **film** for the camera.
7. I **wince** at the sight of blood.
8. The **bomb** exploded near the city.
9. Will you **switch** places with me?
10. The **length** of the pool is thirty feet.
11. Be **prompt** for school, not late.
12. The batter hit the first **pitch**.
13. Somebody **else** looks like you.
14. Rocks fell from the edge of the **cliff**.
15. I **pledge** to study harder.
16. Please **scrub** the tub until it is clean.
17. The door has a shiny **brass** knob.
18. He will cook on the **grill**.
19. Joe was **stung** by a bee.
20. Lifting weights will add **bulk** to your body.

Challenge Words

21. What is the **habitat** of an owl?
22. The spider spun a beautiful **cobweb**.
23. The water is **tepid**.
24. Steel is a **magnetic** metal.
25. The **deft** basketball player stole the ball.

OBJECTIVES

- Use context clues in a sentence to figure out unfamiliar words.
- Learn academic language: *context, context clues.*

Target Skill Trace

Teach	p. 47G
Review	pp. M36–M37
Extend	Challenge/Extension Activities, p. R17
See	*Handbook for English Language Learners,* p. 23

VOCABULARY: Using Context

TARGET SKILL

❶ Teach

Introduce context. Explain that a word's context is the words and sentences around it that give readers clues to its meaning.

Explain context clues. Write *He wiped his mouth and tried to move his leg, which had <u>stiffened</u> like wood.* Discuss clues to the meaning of *stiffened.*

- The word's position in the sentence, after the word "had," shows it is probably a verb or a word describing an action.
- The phrase *tried to move* shows that the action was difficult.
- The phrase *like wood* shows that the word is being compared to wood. *Stiffened* means "became difficult to bend."

Model how to use context clues. Write *Where the bark was peeling from the trunks it lifted in tiny <u>tendrils</u>, almost fluffs.* Then model using context clues to figure out the meaning of *tendrils.*

Think Aloud *The beginning of the sentence tells me that this word has to do with peeling bark. I know that* tiny *means "little," and the phrase* almost fluffs *makes me think of curly strands of fluffy hair. So* tendrils *must be little curly pieces of bark that stick up in the air.*

❷ Guided Practice

Help students use context clues. Display the words below. Have students locate each word in *Hatchet* and then figure out its meaning. Ask volunteers to explain their thinking.

upright	*page 34*
cross	*page 34*
nicked	*page 37*
registered	*page 38*

❸ Apply

Assign Practice Book page 20.

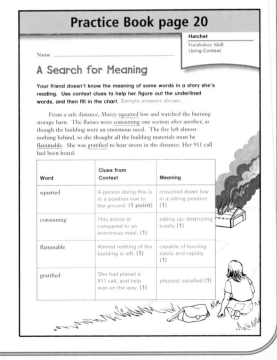

Practice Book page 20

Hatchet
Vocabulary Skill
Using Context

Name _____

A Search for Meaning

Your friend doesn't know the meaning of some words in a story she's reading. Use context clues to help her figure out the underlined words, and then fill in the chart. Sample answers shown.

From a safe distance, Marcy <u>squatted</u> low and watched the burning storage barn. The flames were <u>consuming</u> one section after another, as though the building were an enormous meal. The fire left almost nothing behind, so she thought all the building materials must be <u>flammable</u>. She was <u>gratified</u> to hear sirens in the distance. Her 911 call had been heard.

Word	Clues from Context	Meaning
squatted	A person doing this is in a position low to the ground. **(1 point)**	crouched down low in a sitting position **(1)**
consuming	This action is compared to an enormous meal. **(1)**	eating up; destroying totally **(1)**
flammable	Almost nothing of the building is left. **(1)**	capable of burning easily and rapidly **(1)**
gratified	She had placed a 911 call, and help was on the way. **(1)**	pleased; satisfied **(1)**

Monitoring Student Progress

If . . .	Then . . .
students score 6 or below on **Practice Book** page 20,	have them work with partners to correct the items they missed.

STUDY SKILL: Using Library Catalogs

OBJECTIVES

- Use library catalogs to locate call numbers and other information.
- Use call numbers to locate books.
- Learn academic language: *card catalog, title card, author card, subject card, call number, electronic catalog.*

1 Teach

Explain how to use card catalogs.

- All the books and other materials in a library are listed in either a card catalog or an electronic catalog.
- Card catalogs contain three types of cards—title cards, subject cards, and author cards—filed alphabetically.
- A call number in one corner of a card matches the number on the book's spine. It tells the location of the book in the library.
- Cards may also list suggestions for related titles or subjects.

Explain how to use electronic catalogs.

- Directions for using the electronic catalog usually appear on the first screen. Search for a book by its author, subject, or title.
- When a search finds many books, the screen shows a numbered list of choices. Type in the number of a book and press enter.
- The screen for a particular book shows the same information as in a card catalog. It will also tell whether the book is checked out.

Display Transparency 1–3, and model how to use an electronic catalog.

- Start by showing only the first screen, at the top of the transparency.
- Show the second screen while discussing the subject Survival—Fiction.

Think Aloud *I enjoyed reading* Hatchet, *and I want to know if the library has any similar adventure books. I could type in the subject,* Adventure, *but first I'll look for the entry on* Hatchet *to see how the library defined its subject. It's listed as* Survival—Fiction. *Now I look up that subject. Here it is on the second screen, at the bottom of the transparency. It shows a list of other books about survival and even a video recording,* Abel's Island.

2 Practice/Apply

Have students use library catalogs.

- Have students use a card catalog or an electronic catalog to find a book on wilderness survival or a related topic.
- Have students record how they used the catalog and the call number to locate the book.

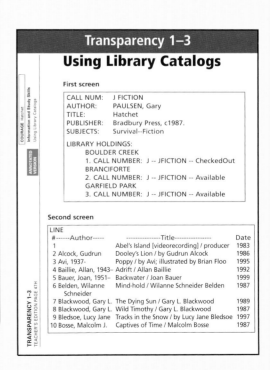

Transparency 1–3

Using Library Catalogs

First screen

CALL NUM:	J FICTION
AUTHOR:	PAULSEN, Gary
TITLE:	Hatchet
PUBLISHER:	Bradbury Press, c1987.
SUBJECTS:	Survival--Fiction

LIBRARY HOLDINGS:
 BOULDER CREEK
  1. CALL NUMBER: J -- JFICTION -- CheckedOut
 BRANCIFORTE
  2. CALL NUMBER: J -- JFICTION -- Available
 GARFIELD PARK
  3. CALL NUMBER: J -- JFICTION -- Available

Second screen

LINE # ------Author-----	----------------Title---------------	Date
1	Abel's Island [videorecording] / producer	1983
2 Alcock, Gudrun	Dooley's Lion / by Gudrun Alcock	1986
3 Avi, 1937-	Poppy / by Avi; illustrated by Brian Floo	1995
4 Baillie, Allan, 1943–	Adrift / Allan Baillie	1992
5 Bauer, Joan, 1951–	Backwater / Joan Bauer	1999
6 Belden, Wilanne Schneider	Mind-hold / Wilanne Schneider Belden	1987
7 Blackwood, Gary L.	The Dying Sun / Gary L. Blackwood	1989
8 Blackwood, Gary L.	Wild Timothy / Gary L. Blackwood	1987
9 Bledsoe, Lucy Jane	Tracks in the Snow / by Lucy Jane Bledsoe	1997
10 Bosse, Malcolm J.	Captives of Time / Malcolm Bosse	1987

GRAMMAR: Sentence Kinds and Parts

OBJECTIVES

- Identify the four kinds of sentences.
- Identify complete and simple subjects and complete and simple predicates.
- Proofread and correct sentences with grammar and spelling errors.
- Combine simple subjects and simple predicates into compound subjects and compound predicates to improve writing.
- Learn academic language: *declarative, interrogative, imperative, exclamatory, subject, complete subject, predicate, complete predicate, compound subject, compound predicate.*

Transparency 1–4
Daily Language Practice

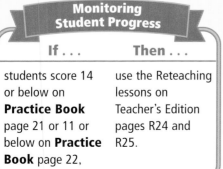

Correct two sentences each day.

1. the team of climbers reached the top of the highest clif.
   The team of climbers reached the top of the highest cliff.
2. That player has a really fast pich
   That player has a really fast pitch.
3. What elce is there to make for our dinner.
   What else is there to make for our dinner?
4. Did you like that filem as much as i did?
   Did you like that film as much as I did?
5. my glasses had sunked to the bottom of the poof.
   My glasses had sunk to the bottom of the pool.
6. Will you flip the light swich off when we leave the room.
   Will you flip the light switch off when we leave the room?
7. that bee stug me twice!
   That bee stung me twice!
8. What an amazing shipwrek?
   What an amazing shipwreck!
9. Do you know the lenth of this movie.
   Do you know the length of this movie?
10. i plege to get to school on time tomorrow.
    I pledge to get to school on time tomorrow.

TRANSPARENCY 1-4
TEACHER'S EDITION PAGE 471

Monitoring Student Progress

If . . .	Then . . .
students score 14 or below on **Practice Book** page 21 or 11 or below on **Practice Book** page 22,	use the Reteaching lessons on Teacher's Edition pages R24 and R25.

DAY 1 INSTRUCTION

Kinds of Sentences

Teach Go over the following:

- A declarative sentence makes a statement. It ends with a period.
- An interrogative sentence asks a question. It ends with a question mark.
- An imperative sentence gives a command or makes a request. It ends with a period. The subject *you* is usually understood.
- An exclamatory sentence shows excitement or strong feeling. It ends with an exclamation point.

- Display the example sentences at the top of **Transparency 1–5,** and identify each sentence type.
- Ask volunteers to write the sentence type for Sentences 1–6.
- Have students find examples of different types of sentences in *Hatchet.*

Daily Language Practice
Have students correct Sentences 1 and 2 on **Transparency 1–4.**

Transparency 1–5
Kinds of Sentences

The setting sun is to our left.
Are we on the right trail?
Hand me the compass.
I've lost my map!

1. We are definitely headed north. declarative sentence
2. We should be headed southeast! exclamatory sentence
3. Shouldn't we retrace our steps? interrogative sentence
4. That's a great idea! exclamatory sentence
5. Watch for a crossroads just beyond the stream. imperative sentence
6. Hooray, we've found the trail back to camp! exclamatory sentence

TRANSPARENCY 1-5
TEACHER'S EDITION PAGE 471

DAY 2 PRACTICE

Independent Work

Practice/Homework Assign **Practice Book** page 21.

Daily Language Practice
Have students correct Sentences 3 and 4 on **Transparency 1–4.**

Practice Book page 21

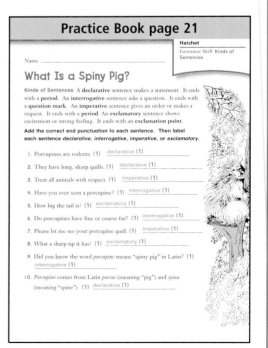

Name _____

Hatchet
Grammar Skill Kinds of Sentences

What Is a Spiny Pig?

Kinds of Sentences A **declarative** sentence makes a statement. It ends with a period. An **interrogative** sentence asks a question. It ends with a **question mark.** An **imperative** sentence gives an order or makes a request. It ends with a **period.** An **exclamatory** sentence shows excitement or strong feeling. It ends with an **exclamation point.**

Add the correct end punctuation to each sentence. Then label each sentence *declarative, interrogative, imperative,* or *exclamatory.*

1. Porcupines are rodents. (1) declarative (1)
2. They have long, sharp quills. (1) declarative (1)
3. Treat all animals with respect. (1) imperative (1)
4. Have you ever seen a porcupine? (1) interrogative (1)
5. How big the tail is! (1) exclamatory (1)
6. Do porcupines have fine or coarse fur? (1) interrogative (1)
7. Please let me see your porcupine quill. (1) imperative (1)
8. What a sharp tip it has! (1) exclamatory (1)
9. Did you know the word *porcupine* means "spiny pig" in Latin? (1) interrogative (1)
10. *Porcupine* comes from Latin *porcus* (meaning "pig") and *spina* (meaning "spine"). (1) declarative (1)

Subjects and Predicates

Teach Go over the following:

- The subject tells whom or what the sentence is about.

- The complete subject includes all the words in the subject. The simple subject is the main word or words in the complete subject.

- The predicate tells what the subject does, is, has, or feels.

- The complete predicate includes all the words in the predicate. The simple predicate is the main word or words in the complete predicate. It is always a verb.

- Display **Transparency 1–6.** Point out the complete and simple subjects and predicates in the example sentence.

- Have students write in the chart the complete and simple subjects and predicates of Sentences 1–10.

Daily Language Practice
Have students correct Sentences 5 and 6 on **Transparency 1–4.**

Independent Work

Practice/Homework Assign **Practice Book** page 22.

Daily Language Practice
Have students correct Sentences 7 and 8 on **Transparency 1–4.**

Combining Sentences

Teach Tell students that if two sentences have the same predicate, the subjects can be combined as a compound subject using *and* or *or.* If two sentences have the same subject, the predicates can be combined as a compound predicate. Model:

- Chipmunks stole food from the table. Blue jays stole food too.

- *Improved:* <u>Chipmunks and blue jays</u> stole food from the table.

- Rita poured water on the coals. She stomped on them.

- *Improved:* Rita <u>poured</u> water on the coals <u>and</u> <u>stomped</u> on them.

- Have students combine subjects or predicates in their own writing.

Practice/Homework Assign **Practice Book** page 23.

Daily Language Practice
Have students correct Sentences 9 and 10 on **Transparency 1–4.**

Transparency 1–6

Subjects and Predicates

COURAGE *Hatchet*
Grammar Skill Subjects and Predicates

ANNOTATED VERSION

The weary hikers will sleep until midmorning.
1. Sam should throw another log on the fire.
2. A noisy bluejay awakened me an hour ago.
3. The large black pan is very hot.
4. Pancakes taste great on a camping trip.
5. This bacon will produce a wonderful smell.
6. The sizzle sounds loud in this quiet spot.
7. I will cook the pancakes in a few minutes.
8. The bubbles are a signal to the chef.
9. Sam flips a pancake high in the air.
10. He catches it expertly in the pan!

Complete Subject	Simple Subject	Complete Predicate	Simple Predicate
Sam	Sam	should throw another log on the fire	should throw
A noisy bluejay	bluejay	awakened me an hour ago	awakened
The large black pan	pan	is very hot	is
Pancakes	Pancakes	taste great on a camping trip	taste
This bacon	bacon	will produce a wonderful smell	will produce
The sizzle	sizzle	sounds loud in this quiet spot	sounds
I	I	will cook the pancakes in a few minutes	will cook
The bubbles	bubbles	are a signal to the chef	are
Sam	Sam	flips a pancake high in the air	flips
He	He	catches it expertly in the pan	catches

TRANSPARENCY 1–6
TEACHER'S EDITION PAGE 47J

Practice Book page 22

Hatchet
Grammar Skill Subjects and Predicates

Name _____

Campfires Need . . .

Subjects and Predicates The **subject** of a sentence tells whom or what the sentence is about. The **complete subject** includes all the words in the subject. The **simple subject** is the main word or words of the complete subject.

The **predicate** tells what the subject does, has, or feels. The **complete predicate** includes all the words in the predicate. The **simple predicate** is the main word or words of the complete predicate.

Draw a line between the complete subject and the complete predicate in each sentence below. Then write the simple subject and the simple predicate on the lines.

1. Brianna | needed kindling for a fire. (1 point)
   Simple subject: Brianna (1)
   Simple predicate: needed (1)

2. A fire | needs oxygen. (1)
   Simple subject: fire (1)
   Simple predicate: needs (1)

3. A roaring fire | will keep them warm. (1)
   Simple subject: fire (1)
   Simple predicate: will keep (1)

4. The first spark | has faded quickly. (1)
   Simple subject: spark (1)
   Simple predicate: has faded (1)

5. I | am learning about building safe campfires. (1)
   Simple subject: I (1)
   Simple predicate: am learning (1)

Practice Book page 23

Hatchet
Grammar Skill Combining Sentences

Name _____

This and That

Combining Sentences A good writer avoids writing too many short, choppy sentences. Combine short sentences by creating **compound subjects** or **compound predicates**.

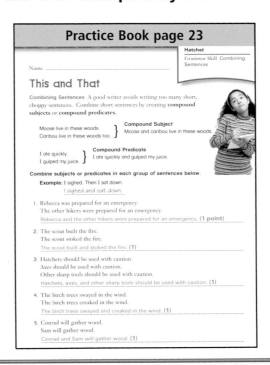

Moose live in these woods.
Caribou live in these woods too.
Compound Subject Moose and caribou live in these woods.

I ate quickly.
I gulped my juice.
Compound Predicate I ate quickly and gulped my juice.

Combine subjects or predicates in each group of sentences below.
Example: I sighed. Then I sat down.
I sighed and sat down.

1. Rebecca was prepared for an emergency.
   The other hikers were prepared for an emergency.
   Rebecca and the other hikers were prepared for an emergency. **(1 point)**

2. The scout built the fire.
   The scout stoked the fire.
   The scout built and stoked the fire. **(1)**

3. Hatchets should be used with caution.
   Axes should be used with caution.
   Other sharp tools should be used with caution.
   Hatchets, axes, and other sharp tools should be used with caution. **(1)**

4. The birch trees swayed in the wind.
   The birch trees creaked in the wind.
   The birch trees swayed and creaked in the wind. **(1)**

5. Conrad will gather wood.
   Sam will gather wood.
   Conrad and Sam will gather wood. **(1)**

WRITING: Instructions

OBJECTIVES

- Identify the characteristics of good written instructions.
- Write instructions.
- Use sequence words and phrases.
- Learn academic language: *sequence words, sequence phrases.*

Writing Traits

Organization As you teach the lesson on Day 2, encourage students to think about their audience as they decide how to order their steps. Ask these questions:

- What do your readers need to know right at the beginning?
- What can you wait to tell your readers? When do they need to know these details?

DAY 1 PREWRITING

Introducing the Format

Define instructions.

- Instructions explain how to make or do something.
- Instructions should be clear, complete, and easy to follow.
- Each step should be written in the correct order.

Start students thinking about instructions.

- Ask students to list three things they know how to make or do.
- Ask students to discuss their ideas with a partner and take notes on whether or not their topics can be explained clearly.
- Have them save their notes.

DAY 2 DRAFTING

Discussing the Model

Display and read Transparency 1–7. Ask:

- What are these instructions for? (making a solar cooker)
- Which part tells what materials are needed? (the second sentence)
- What's the first step? (cutting a circle from cardboard) What's the second step? (cutting the circle in half)
- Which words help you know the order in which you should complete the steps? (*First, Then, Next, Now, Finally*)
- What details make the steps clear? (Sample answers: *about 3 inches from the straight side; shiny side out*)

Display Transparency 1–8 and discuss the guidelines.

Have students draft instructions.

- Have students decide on a topic, using their prewriting notes from Day 1.
- See Writing Traits on this page.
- Assign **Practice Book** page 24 to help students organize their writing.
- Provide support as needed.

Transparency 1–7

Instructions

How to Build a Solar Cooker

A solar cooker is a simple oven that allows campers to cook food using the sun's energy. To make a solar cooker, you need a thick piece of 12-by-12-inch cardboard, scissors, tape, aluminum foil, a thin piece of 18-by-12-inch cardboard, a long skewer, and bricks. Here are a few safety tips. Avoid looking directly into the sun's reflection in the cooker. Be careful with scissors and skewers. Use a potholder to handle hot items.

Follow these steps to make a solar cooker. First, cut an 11-inch diameter circle from the stiff cardboard. Then cut the circle in half, making two half-circles for the sides of the cooker. Make a hole for a skewer in each half-circle, about 3 inches from the straight side.

Next, make a reflector by taping foil to the thin cardboard, shiny side out. Put foil over the half-circles too. Curve the foil-board reflector around the half-circles. Tape the reflector securely in place.

Now you are ready to cook. Put a small piece of food on the skewer. Then put the ends of the skewer into the two half-circles. Rest each outside end of the skewer on bricks. Aim the reflector toward the sun. Turn the skewer as needed until the food is done. Finally, you can eat! Hold the hot skewer carefully to remove the food.

TRANSPARENCY 1–7
TEACHER'S EDITION PAGE 47K

Transparency 1–8

Guidelines for Writing Instructions

- Choose an activity you know well.
- Write a title that describes what the instructions are for.
- List all the materials needed.
- Explain each step. Include details that make each step clear.
- Put the steps in the correct order.
- Number each step, or use sequence words such as *first, next, then, before, after,* and *finally.*
- Include diagrams or pictures if they will help make the steps and details clear.

TRANSPARENCY 1–8
TEACHER'S EDITION PAGE 47K

Practice Book page 24

Hatchet
Writing Skill Instructions

Name _____

Writing Instructions

In *Hatchet*, Brian is stranded alone in the Canadian wilderness. The only tool he has is a hatchet. How could Brian explain to someone else how he used the hatchet to start a fire? **Instructions** tell readers how to do or make something. Good written instructions clearly explain the materials needed and the order in which the steps are to be followed.

Use this page to plan and organize your own written instructions. First, choose a process you would like to explain. Then list the materials that are needed. Finally, write each step in the process, giving details that readers will need to know.

How to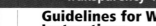

Materials (2 points)		

Steps	Details	
Step 1	(2)	
Step 2	(2)	
Step 3	(2)	
Step 4	(2)	
Step 5	(2)	

Using the information you recorded, write your instructions on a separate sheet of paper. You can either number each step or use sequence words such as *first, next,* **and** *finally.* **Include diagrams or pictures to help readers picture this process.** (10)

47K **THEME 1: Courage**

Improving Writing: Sequence Words

Explain using sequence words.

- Sequence words and phrases help readers keep track of the order of steps.
- This helps readers understand what to do and when to do it.

Display Transparency 1–9.

- Ask volunteers to identify the sequence words and phrases in Passage 1.
- Discuss how these words and phrases help make the order of the steps clear.
- Have students fill in each blank in Passage 2, using words and phrases from the box. Discuss how this improves Passage 2.

Assign Practice Book page 25.

Have students revise their drafts.

- Display **Transparency 1–8** again. Have students use the guidelines to revise their instructions.
- Have partners hold writing conferences.
- Ask students to revise any parts of their instructions that still need work. Have them add sequence words and phrases.

Checking for Errors

Have students proofread for errors in grammar, spelling, punctuation, or usage.

- Students can use the Proofreading Checklist on **Practice Book** page 297 to help them proofread their instructions.
- Students can also use the Proofreading Marks on **Practice Book** page 298.

Sharing Instructions

Consider these publishing options.

- Ask students to read their instructions or some other piece of writing from the Author's Chair.
- Encourage students to make a class how-to activity book.

Portfolio Opportunity

Save students' written instructions as samples of their writing development.

Transparency 1–9

Using Sequence Words and Phrases

COURAGE *Hatchet* Writing Skill Improving Your Writing

ANNOTATED VERSION

first	then	now	before	last
start by	finally	the next step	after that	at this point
again	next	second		

How to Create Static Electricity

Passage 1:

First, blow up a balloon and tie it. Then rub it briskly against a sweater or wool cloth. Next, hold the balloon against a wall and see if it sticks. At this point, blow up another balloon. Now tie a string to each balloon. Before going on to the next step, rub the first balloon again. Then hold both balloons by their strings. What happens? Last, rub both balloons with the sweater or cloth and hold them by their strings again. What happens?

Passage 2:

_____First_____ , rub a piece of wool or silk cloth back and forth very fast along a comb. _____Next_____ tear some tissue paper into small pieces. _____Then_____ hold the comb near the pieces of paper. What happens?

_____At this point_____ you can see if the comb will attract a balloon, so _the next step_ is to blow up a balloon. _____Now_____ hold the comb near the balloon. What happens? If necessary, charge the comb again by rubbing it with the cloth. _____After that_____ see what happens if you rub both the balloon and the comb with the cloth. _____Finally_____ hold the comb and balloon near each other. What happens? Were you surprised?

TRANSPARENCY 1–9
TEACHER'S EDITION PAGE 47L

Practice Book page 25

Name _____

Hatchet
Writing Skill Improving Your Writing

Using Sequence Words and Phrases

Following steps correctly is a matter of life or death for Brian in *Hatchet*. A careful writer gives clear instructions so that a reader can complete the steps in a process. Sequence words and phrases in instructions help readers understand a process and keep track of the order of steps.

The following page is from a first-aid manual. The instructions tell readers how to treat puncture wounds like those Brian suffered from the porcupine quills in his leg. In the blanks provided, add sequence words and phrases from the list to make the connection between steps clearer. Remember to capitalize sequence words as needed.

Sequence Words and Phrases

first	after	by the time
during	prior to	finally
before	then	as soon as possible

First (2 points) _____, you will need to wash your hands with soap and water. _After (2)_ _____ you have washed your hands, remove the object with a pair of tweezers. _Then (2)_ _____ control any bleeding with direct pressure and elevation. Wash the puncture wound thoroughly with soap and water. _Finally (2)_ _____, cover the wound with a sterile dressing.

Check with a doctor to find out whether a tetanus shot is needed. If you see any signs of infection, such as pus, pain, redness around the wound, or a fever, call the doctor back _as soon as possible (2)_

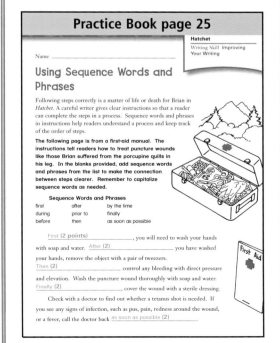

First Aid

Monitoring Student Progress

If . . .	Then . . .
students' writing does not follow the guidelines on **Transparency 1–8**,	work with students to improve specific parts of their writing.

Language Center

VOCABULARY
Easily Confused Words

👥 Pairs	🕐 45 minutes
Objective	Define similarly spelled words.
Materials	Dictionary

Brian used a gentle breath to help start the fire. The words *breath, breadth,* and *breathe* are easily confused because they are spelled similarly. Work with a partner to do the following:

- Identify the meaning of *breath, breadth,* and *breathe.*
- Use your own knowledge and a dictionary to figure out the meaning of each word on the chart below.
- Write a sentence using each word correctly.

adapt	human	loose
adept	humane	lose
adopt	imitate	picture
emerge	intimate	pitcher
immerge	lay	quit
farther	lie	quite
further		

GRAMMAR
Sentence Type Challenge

👤 Singles	🕐 45 minutes
Objective	Write different sentence types.
Materials	Activity Master 1–1, page R32

A declarative sentence makes a statement, an interrogative sentence asks a question, an imperative sentence gives a command, and an exclamatory sentence makes an exclamation.

For each of the situations listed below, write a declarative, an interrogative, an imperative, and an exclamatory sentence. Use Activity Master 1–1.

- Brian and the brushing sound in the shelter
- Brian's dream

Make sure you use the correct pronunciation for each type of sentence. Then repeat the process for these sentences:

- Brian's first efforts to start a fire
- Brian's success in starting a fire

VOCABULARY
Rebus Puzzles

👥 Pairs	🕐 20 minutes
Objective	Solve and create rebus puzzles using vocabulary words.
Materials	Drawing paper, colored pencils or markers

The solution to each rebus below is a Key Vocabulary word.

- Study each rebus and identify the word it represents.
- Create two more rebuses whose solutions are different Key Vocabulary words. (Remember, the clues can be both pictures and phonetic spellings.) Trade papers with a partner and solve the rebuses.

1. 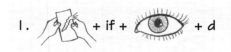 + if + + d

2. kw + 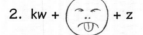 + z

Consider copying and laminating these activities for use in centers.

LISTENING/SPEAKING

Retelling a Story

👤👤👤 Groups	🕐 45 minutes
Objective	Retell a story.
Materials	Anthology or other book

Plan a retelling of *Hatchet* or another story that every member of the group has read.

- Assign one part of the story to each group member.
- Practice retelling the story together.
- Follow the guidelines listed below to be sure your story is complete.
- Present your group retelling to the rest of the class at an appropriate time.

Retelling Guidelines

A good retelling includes these elements.

- Main events in correct sequence (beginning, middle, end)
- Major characters
- Setting, if important to the story
- Story problem and outcome

PHONICS/SPELLING

Character Description

👤 Singles	🕐 30 minutes
Objective	Write sentences using words with short vowels.

Write a paragraph describing the kind of person Brian is.

- In the paragraph, use each of the following short vowel sounds in a different word: *a*, *e*, *i*, *o*, and *u*.
- Trade paragraphs with a partner.
- Underline each short vowel in the paragraph you receive.

Brian i̱s a brave person eve̱n i̱n di̱ffi̱cu̱lt experie̱nces.

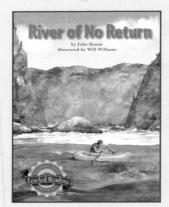

River of No Return

Summary *Linzee is apprehensive when she and her mom go white-water rafting in Idaho. Linzee learns rafting basics, but retains some of her fear of the river. On the third day, Mom falls out of the raft. Using all her strength, Linzee struggles to pull the raft through the rapids and is relieved when her mom successfully emerges from the River of No Return.*

Vocabulary

Introduce the Key Vocabulary and ask students to complete the BLM.

duffel bag a long bag made of fabric, used as a suitcase, *p. 5*

obstacle something that's in the way; a challenge, *p. 9*

current part of a river that moves steadily in a certain direction, *p. 16*

panic act suddenly, often ineffectively, out of fear, *p. 20*

● BELOW LEVEL

Building Background and Vocabulary

Explain to students that this story is about what happens when Linzee and her mother go white-water rafting. Have students share what they know about rafting, boating, or canoeing. Guide students through the text, using some of the vocabulary from the story.

Comprehension Skill: Noting Details

Have students read the Strategy Focus on the book flap. Remind students to use the strategy and to note details as they read the book. (See the Leveled Readers Teacher's Guide for **Vocabulary and Comprehension Practice Masters.**)

Responding

Have partners discuss how to answer the questions on the inside back cover.

Think About the Selection Sample answers:

1. Because the trip provides a way for Linzee's mom to connect with Linzee's dad.
2. The author tells about accidents that have occurred on the river, a bear that rafters saw, and the guide's own healthy fear of the current.
3. Answers will vary.
4. She learned she is stronger and more courageous than she believed.

Making Connections Answers will vary.

Building Fluency

Model Read aloud pages 3–6 and point out that thought speech is shown in italics. Distinguish this from spoken speech (in quotes).

Practice Volunteers can read aloud the examples of thought speech on the other pages of the story.

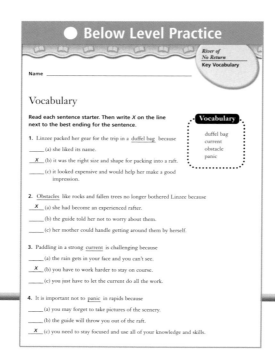

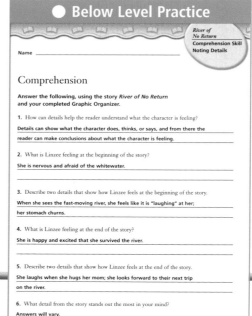

Weathering the Storm

Summary *Dara is out on her first solo sail. A sudden storm forces her to seek shelter on an uninhabited island. She must rely on her own intuition, skills, and knowledge throughout the long night. The next morning she signals a passing patrol boat and is rescued.*

Vocabulary

Introduce the Key Vocabulary and ask students to complete the BLM.

tendrils objects of a long, slender, and curled shape, *p. 3*

careening lurching wildly, *p. 4*

menacing threatening, *p. 4*

mounted grew in size, *p. 6*

marina a place for docking boats, *p. 6*

shelter* a place that provides protection from the weather, *p. 8*

conduct to lead or guide, *p. 12*

disoriented confused about time and place, *p. 13*

devoured consumed quickly and completely, *p. 13*

*Forms of these words are Anthology Key Vocabulary words.

▲ ON LEVEL

Building Background and Vocabulary

Explain to students that this story is about a girl named Dara who weathers a storm on an uninhabited island. Ask students what they know about boating and especially sailing. Discuss the pleasures and dangers of sailing. Guide students through the text, using some of the vocabulary from the story.

Comprehension Skill: Noting Details

Have students read the Strategy Focus on the book flap. Remind students to use the strategy and to note details as they read the book. (See the Leveled Readers Teacher's Guide for **Vocabulary and Comprehension Practice Masters.**)

Responding

Have partners discuss how to answer the questions on the inside back cover.

Think About the Selection Sample answers:

1. The day starts out calm, and the clouds don't look threatening.

2. Dara remembers to stay off the damp ground and to collect fresh water.

3. Possible response: Dara would have continued to try to signal the crew with the whistle, flashlight, and distress signal. If those methods failed, she would have found another boat to help her get home.

4. Answers will vary.

Making Connections Answers will vary.

Building Fluency

Model Read aloud page 3. Define a simile (a comparison using *as* or *like*) and ask students to identify the simile in the passage (*like chocolate sprinkles on an ice cream cone*).

Practice Ask a fluent reader to read page 5. Ask the class to identify the simile (*like a painted horse on a merry-go-round*).

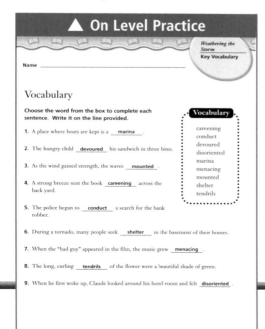

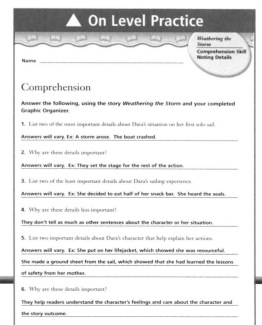

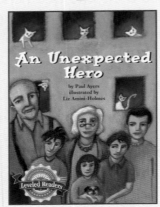

An Unexpected Hero

Summary *Rafael is shy, but when he finds a gas leak in his apartment building, he knows he must be courageous. He notifies the tenants to evacuate the building and in the end is recognized for his heroism.*

Vocabulary

Introduce the Key Vocabulary and ask students to complete the BLM.

combustion the process of burning, *p. 3*

frustration* the discouragement and irritation that come from not being able to achieve one's goal, *p. 3*

curmudgeonly ill-tempered, *p. 5*

vigorously done with force and energy, *p. 6*

kindling easily ignited material for a fire, *p. 11*

cordoned prevented movement in or out of an area, *p. 13*

evacuate to move out of an unsafe location, *p. 13*

avert to prevent, *p. 14*

recounted told a story, *p. 15*

*Forms of these words are Anthology Key Vocabulary words.

■ ABOVE LEVEL

Building Background and Vocabulary

Explain to students that this story is about one boy's heroic actions when he discovers a gas leak in his building. Have students share what they know about the dangers of gas leaks. Guide students through the text, using some of the vocabulary from the story.

Comprehension Skill: Noting Details

Have students read the Strategy Focus on the book flap. Remind students to use the strategy and to note details as they read the book. (See the Leveled Readers Teacher's Guide for **Vocabulary and Comprehension Practice Masters.**)

Responding

Have partners discuss how to answer the questions on the inside back cover.

Think About the Selection Sample answers:

1. He has been afraid to speak up in class even though he knew the answer.
2. Sample answer: Yes. When Eddie realizes that there's a gas leak, he offers to help Rafael tell the neighbors.
3. A sense of confidence, and two new friends: Eddie and Mr. Martinez.
4. Answers will vary.

Making Connections Answers will vary.

Building Fluency

Model Read aloud page 7 with inflection and feeling, showing the different emotions of the characters.

Practice Ask groups of three to take the roles of an interviewer, Rafael, and Eddie. Have the interviewer ask questions about the event and encourage "Rafael" and "Eddie" to answer with inflection and emotion.

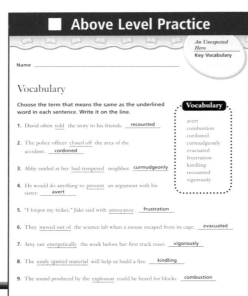

Leveled Readers

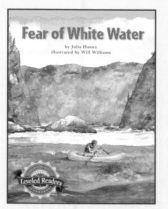

Fear of White Water

Summary *Linda's mother wants to take a white-water rafting trip with her daughter. Her mother is very excited, but Linda is frightened of rafting through white water. As Linda conquers her fear, the two experience a special time together.*

Vocabulary

Introduce the Key Vocabulary and ask students to complete the BLM.

white-water rafting using a small boat in rough water that moves very quickly, *p. 3*

rapids a place in a river where water flows very fast, *p. 3*

current the path of water that is in motion, *p. 8*

downstream in the direction of the current, *p. 10*

overboard over the side of a boat, *p. 11*

terrified* frightened, *p. 11*

*Forms of these words are Anthology Key Vocabulary words.

◆ LANGUAGE SUPPORT

Building Background and Vocabulary

Display the cover of the book and explain that this story is about white-water rafting. Ask students why they think the people are wearing life jackets and helmets. Discuss what might be fun and what might be dangerous about white-water rafting. Then distribute the **Build Background Practice Master** and have students complete it.

Comprehension Skill: Noting Details

Have students read the Strategy Focus on the book flap. Remind students to use the strategy and to note details as they read the book. (See the Leveled Readers Teacher's Guide for **Build Background, Vocabulary,** and **Graphic Organizer Masters.**)

Responding

Have partners discuss how to answer the questions on the inside back cover.

Think About the Selection Sample answers:

1. They're going on a rafting trip to the Salmon River in Idaho.
2. Before Linda's father died, he and her mother went on rafting trips. Now her mother wants to share the experience with Linda.
3. It has rapids, strong currents, and "holes," or whirlpools.
4. Answers will vary.

Making Connections Answers will vary.

Building Fluency

Model Read aloud page 19. Point out that the words in italic type are words that Linda is thinking.

Practice Have partners of mixed ability read together. Partners should read the text three times or until they can read with accuracy and expression.

Reading-Writing Workshop

Personal Narrative

In the Reading-Writing Workshop for Theme 1, *Courage,* students read Megan's personal narrative, "Rappelling in Ocala," on Anthology pages 48–49. Then they follow the five steps of the writing process to write a personal narrative.

Meet the Author

Megan M.
Grade: six
State: Florida
Hobbies: swimmimg and rollerblading
What she'd like to be when she grows up: an actress or a news broadcaster

Theme Skill Trace

Writing
• Using Sequence Words and Phrases, 47L
• Capitalizing and Punctuating Sentences, 71L
• Voice, 93L
• Combining Sentences with Appositives, 115L

Grammar
• Sentence Combining: Compound Subjects and Compound Predicates, 47J
• Sentence Combining: Compound Sentences, 71J
• Avoiding Run-On Sentences, 93J
• Capitalization and Punctuation of People's Titles, 115J

Spelling
• Short Vowels, 47E
• Long Vowels, 71E
• More Vowel Spellings, 93E
• The /ou/, /o͞o/, /ô/, and /oi/ Sounds, 115E

Pacing the Workshop

Here is a suggestion for how you might pace the workshop within one week or on five separate days across the theme.

DAY 1 — PREWRITING

Students
• read the student model, 48–49
• choose a topic, 49A
• explore and plan their personal narrative, 49B
• check that events are arranged in the correct sequence, 49C

Spelling Frequently Misspelled Words, 49F; *Practice Book,* 281

DAY 2 — DRAFTING

Students
• add details that make their narrative more interesting, 49D
• draft their personal narrative, 49D

Spelling *Practice Book,* 28

Focus on Writing Traits: Personal Narrative

The workshop for this theme focuses on the traits of voice and sentence fluency. However, students should think about all of the writing traits during the writing process.

VOICE When a piece of writing has voice, it sounds distinct, even unique. It has personality. Help students develop voice by encouraging them to do the following.

- Write about an experience that matters to them.
- Focus on details that will interest their audience.
- Choose words and phrases that show clearly how they feel.

SENTENCE FLUENCY Students will improve the flow of their writing if they learn to see alternative ways of writing the same sentence. When students revise, encourage them to look for places where they can do the following.

- Include both long and short sentences.
- Use a question or an exclamation instead of a statement.
- Begin each sentence in a different way.

Tips for Teaching the Writing Traits

- Teach one trait at a time.
- Discuss examples of the traits in the literature students are reading.
- Encourage students to talk about the traits during a writing conference.
- Encourage students to revise their writing for one trait at a time.

DAY 3 REVISING

Students
- evaluate their personal narrative, 49E
- revise their narrative, 49E
- have a writing conference, 49E
- improve their writing by varying sentences, 49E

Spelling *Practice Book,* 29

DAY 4 PROOFREADING

Students
- proofread their personal narrative, 49E
- correct frequently misspelled words in their narrative, 49F

Spelling *Practice Book,* 30

DAY 5 PUBLISHING

Students
- publish their personal narrative, 49G
- reflect on their writing experience, 49G

Spelling Assessment, 49F

Personal Narrative

Discussing the Guidelines

Display **Transparency RWW1–1,** and discuss what makes a great personal narrative.

- Remember that students should think about all the writing traits as they write: ideas, organization, voice, word choice, sentence fluency, conventions, and presentation.

Discussing the Model

Have students read the Student Writing Model on Anthology pages 48–49.

- Discuss with students what the writer did to make her personal narrative interesting to read.
- Use the Reading As a Writer questions on the next page.

Student Writing Model

A Personal Narrative

A personal narrative gives a first-person account of a true experience. Use this student's writing as a model when you write a personal narrative of your own.

Rappelling in Ocala

> **Beginning** your narrative with a question helps to hook your reader.

Have you ever gone rappelling? In case you don't know, rappelling is a way to descend from a mountain using a special kind of rope. On January 3, 1999, I went rappelling with my three cousins, my brother, and my two uncles. Wow! Did I learn a lot, and have fun at the same time. I had only been rappelling one other time before that special day. The most awesome part was the zip line. A zip line means that you tie one end of a rope to a tree and the other end of the rope to another tree down low or at a slant, and then you hook your carabiner (a long metal ring with a clip) to the rope and slide down.

> Using careful **sequencing** is essential for clarity.

One of the things I learned this time was to turn upside down while I was rappelling. It took me a couple of tries before I got the hang of it. It was especially exciting because I was given plenty of chances to rappel and also to go down the zip line.

48

I had a great time learning to use some equipment that I hadn't used on my last trip. The barrack and the ascender are two pieces of rappelling equipment I learned to use. The last time I went rappelling, I used an item called a figure eight instead of the barrack, but now that I have used the barrack I am more comfortable with it. A barrack is what the rope slides through to get down to the bottom. The ascender is something you hook onto a rope to help you climb. I only used the ascender when I was trying to get to the top of the cliff. My three cousins used their ascenders to get to the top of the cliff and climb the wall. They had an advantage over me because they had been rappelling more often.

On this rappelling trip, I learned a lot and enjoyed myself at the same time. Because I hope to do a lot more rappelling, I have asked for some equipment for my birthday. I am hoping to get many more opportunities to rappel with my cousins and the rest of my family.

Using specific **details** brings your narrative to life for the reader.

It's important to draw your narrative to a satisfactory **conclusion**.

Meet the Author

Megan M.
Grade: six
State: Florida
Hobbies: swimming and rollerblading
What she'd like to be when she grows up: an actress or a news broadcaster

49

Reading As a Writer

1. What experience is Megan writing about? (rappelling)

2. What clues does the author use to indicate the sequence of events in the personal narrative? (She gives the date; she describes events from previous outings; she describes events from this outing; she discusses future outings.)

3. What details about rappelling does the author provide? (She describes the zip line; the carabiner; upside-down rappelling; the barrack, ascender, and figure eight.)

4. What new information did you learn as a result of reading this personal narrative? (what rappelling is; how to rappel; what equipment you need to rappel)

READING-WRITING WORKSHOP

Choosing a Topic

1 **Explain how to choose a topic for a personal narrative.**
Tell students that they will write a personal narrative about an experience they have had. Have students list at least three ideas for personal narratives they could write. Offer these prompts if students are having trouble getting started.

- What has been your most memorable experience?
- What was the bravest thing you have done lately?
- Thirty years from now what will be your favorite childhood experience?

2 **Have students answer these questions** as they choose a topic, either in a writing journal or on a sheet of paper.

- Who will be your audience: friends your age? adults in your family? adults you don't know?
- What will be your purpose: to entertain? to reveal something about yourself?
- How will you publish your personal narrative: in written form? as a spoken or visual performance? as a multimedia Internet presentation?

3 **Have students discuss their ideas with a partner** and decide which topic would be the best to write about. Then review these tips with students.

Tips for Getting Started with a Topic

- Discuss your topic with a partner. Tell your partner what details you plan to use. Is your idea too broad? Can it be narrowed?
- Think of a one-line advertisement that would describe your personal narrative.
- Imagine your personal narrative as a movie. Make a scene-by-scene description for the preview. Tell the description to your partner. Which events does your partner like best?

Exploring and Planning

1 Explain exploring and planning a personal narrative. Tell students that a good personal narrative vividly recreates an experience.

- Write about only one experience. This experience is your main topic.
- List the main events. Think about causes and effects to help you remember everything that happened.
- List details that tell more about each event.
- Number the events in time order.
- Delete any events and details that do not tell more about this one experience.

2 Display Transparency RWW1–2. Model identifying causes and effects.

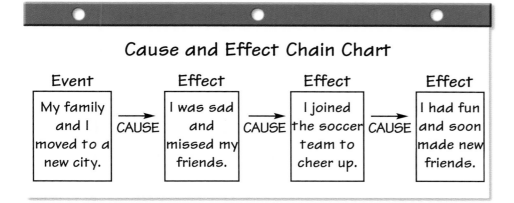

Cause and Effect Chain Chart

Event		Effect		Effect		Effect
My family and I moved to a new city.	→CAUSE	I was sad and missed my friends.	→CAUSE	I joined the soccer team to cheer up.	→CAUSE	I had fun and soon made new friends.

3 Have students identify causes and effects for their personal narratives.

- Distribute copies of **Transparency RWW1–2.**
- Have students complete it, using the topic they chose.

4 Have students explore and plan their narratives.

- Have students list the main events of their narrative. They can use information from their Cause and Effect Chain Chart.
- Have students list related details under each event.

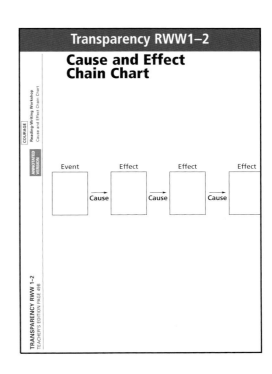

Transparency RWW1–2

Cause and Effect Chain Chart

Sequencing

1 Explain sequence. Remind students that in a good personal narrative, a writer tells events in chronological sequence, the order in which they happened.

2 Discuss sequence words. Explain that sequence words and phrases give clues about when events happened.

- Good writers use sequence words and phrases to guide their readers through the events of the story.

- Discuss the examples of sequence words and phrases in the chart below.

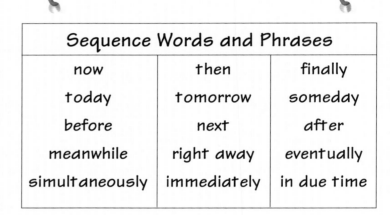

Sequence Words and Phrases		
now	then	finally
today	tomorrow	someday
before	next	after
meanwhile	right away	eventually
simultaneously	immediately	in due time

3 Display Transparency RWW1–3.

- Have volunteers arrange the first group of sentences into the correct sequence.

- Go over the students' solutions in class.

- Then have students arrange the other two groups of sentences in sequence.

- Discuss sequence words and phrases, as well as other kinds of clues that students used to determine sequence.

4 Have students organize events and details in their narrative. Ask students to return to the list of events and details they made.

- Have them number the events in the order they happened.

- Ask partners to brainstorm additional sequence words to use when drafting.

- Remind students to make sure that all events are focused on a single experience.

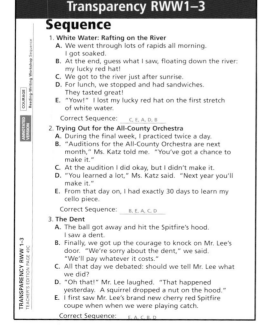

Transparency RWW1–3

Sequence

1. **White Water: Rafting on the River**
   A. We went through lots of rapids all morning. I got soaked.
   B. At the end, guess what I saw, floating down the river: my lucky red hat!
   C. We got to the river just after sunrise.
   D. For lunch, we stopped and had sandwiches. They tasted great!
   E. "Yow!" I lost my lucky red hat on the first stretch of white water.

   Correct Sequence: C, E, A, D, B

2. **Trying Out for the All-County Orchestra**
   A. During the final week, I practiced twice a day.
   B. "Auditions for the All-County Orchestra are next month," Ms. Katz told me. "You've got a chance to make it."
   C. At the audition I did okay, but I didn't make it.
   D. "You learned a lot," Ms. Katz said. "Next year you'll make it."
   E. From that day on, I had exactly 30 days to learn my cello piece.

   Correct Sequence: B, E, A, C, D

3. **The Dent**
   A. The ball got away and hit the Spitfire's hood. I saw a dent.
   B. Finally, we got up the courage to knock on Mr. Lee's door. "We're sorry about the dent," we said. "We'll pay whatever it costs."
   C. All that day we debated: should we tell Mr. Lee what we did?
   D. "Oh that!" Mr. Lee laughed. "That happened yesterday. A squirrel dropped a nut on the hood."
   E. I first saw Mr. Lee's brand new cherry red Spitfire coupe when when we were playing catch.

   Correct Sequence: E, A, C, B, D

Adding Details

1 **Explain the importance of details** in a personal narrative. Discuss with students how the right details bring writing to life.

- Write the first example shown below on the board. Discuss with students how this sentence has almost no detail. It is difficult to picture what the author wishes the reader to see.

- Write the second and third examples shown below on the board. Discuss how details tell us what the writer saw, heard, and tasted.

Without Detail	We ate our dinner.
With Detail	We ate our dinner of baked salmon while watching the sun set over the tundra.
With Detail	We ate our dinner of one stale bread crust.

2 **Display Transparency RWW1–4.**

- Have a volunteer read the first sentence aloud.

- Work as a class to provide details for the sentence, using the directions in parentheses.

- Have the students complete the rest of the sentences.

3 **Have students draft their personal narrative.** Remind them to include specific details that communicate sights, sounds, feelings, tastes, and smells. Encourage them to choose words that help paint a vivid picture.

Writing Traits

VOICE As students start to draft, remind them that voice is especially important in a personal narrative.

- Encourage students to picture their audience as they write.

- Encourage students to ask themselves this question: What can I write to show this audience how I feel about what happened?

Transparency RWW1–4

Adding Details

Responses will vary.

1. Moxie was a good dog who ___liked to eat shoes___ .
   (something Moxie does)

2. We had ___a mushroom and hot pepper___ pizza for
   dinner that ___just melted in your mouth___ .
   (what kind of pizza, how it tasted)

3. I fell down ___on the ice and hurt my ankle___ .
   (where you fell, what happened then)

4. The swamp was ___nasty, dangerous, and full of mosquitoes___ .
   (what the swamp was like: 3 things)

5. The ___double-chocolate orange layer___ cake with
   ___pecans and whipped cream___ was ___heavenly___ !
   (type of cake, topping on cake, how it tasted)

6. My ___brand new___ bike was ___run over by a truck___ .
   (type of bike, what happened to it)

7. The card that said *Do Not Fold, Spindle, or*
   Mutilate was ___bent, twisted, and burned___ .
   (what happened to the card: 3 things)

Practice Book page 26

Name _____

Reading-Writing Workshop

Revising Your Personal Narrative

Revising Your Personal Narrative

Reread your narrative. Put a checkmark in the box for each sentence that describes your paper. Use this page to help you revise.

Loud and Clear!
- [ ] The beginning catches the reader's interest.
- [ ] All events are focused on a single experience. They are also told in order.
- [ ] Many details and exact words bring the story to life.
- [ ] My writing sounds like me. You can tell how I feel.
- [ ] Sentences flow smoothly, and there are few mistakes.

Sounding Stronger
- [ ] The beginning could be more interesting.
- [ ] A few events are out of order, and a few are unrelated.
- [ ] More details and exact words are needed.
- [ ] My voice could be stronger. It doesn't always sound like me.
- [ ] The sentences don't always flow smoothly. There are some mistakes.

Turn Up the Volume
- [ ] The beginning is missing or weak.
- [ ] The story is not focused. The order is unclear.
- [ ] There are no details or exact words.
- [ ] I can't hear my voice at all.
- [ ] Most sentences are choppy. Mistakes make it hard to read.

Practice Book page 27

Name _____

Reading-Writing Workshop

Improving Your Writing

Improving Your Writing

Varying Sentences Rewrite the paragraphs in the spaces provided. Each paragraph should include at least one example of each type of sentence: declarative, interrogative, imperative, and exclamatory. (4 points each)

Backstage Pass NO SENTENCE VARIATION	Backstage Pass SENTENCE VARIATION
I shook hands with Whole New Crew! I was at their concert! I went backstage! I met Jeff! I met Pinky! I met Wanda! I met Therese! At first, I was so excited I could hardly breathe! And guess what — they ignored me! After a while it got boring! So we went home!	

Jalapeño Biscuits NO SENTENCE VARIATION	Jalapeño Biscuits SENTENCE VARIATION
Do I know how to make biscuits? Sort of. Did I put in the flour, butter, and baking powder? I did. Did I add jalapeño peppers? Accidentally. What did it taste like? It was sort of good. Then why did I end up running to get a drink of water? Because it was so HOT.	

Early Start NO SENTENCE VARIATION	Early Start SENTENCE VARIATION
The coach said to meet at 6 A.M. for Saturday's game. Anyone late would not play, the coach said. On Friday, I set my alarm for 5. I went to the field. Everyone was there — except the coach. We finally found her. Her car had broken down. She said, "I guess I don't get to play."	

Transparency RWW1–5

Varying Sentences

Life Without TV No Sentence Variation	Life Without TV Sentence Variation
My family never had a TV. I never minded. I saw TV at the houses of my friends. I liked the commercials better than the shows. Our family got a TV last year. I hardly ever watch it. I think reading is more fun.	I grew up without a TV. Don't feel sorry for me, though. I saw plenty of TV at other kids' houses. And guess what? I liked the commercials more than the shows. Our family finally got a TV last year. Can you believe it? I still never watch it! I prefer reading.

Make-Believe You No Sentence Variation	Make-Believe You Sentence Variation
Pretend to be a new person, just for the day. Join an Internet chat group. Make up a new name. Pretend you're 17 years old. Pretend you have a sports car. Have fun. Just remember: don't believe what anyone on the Internet says. They're probably pretending, just like you.	Sentences will vary.

Foot Heaven Shoes No Sentence Variation	Foot Heaven Shoes Sentence Variation
Were Foot Heaven shoes my mom's favorite shoes? You bet. Why couldn't you find them anymore? No one knew. Did we look everywhere for them? Of course. Did we get the Foot Heaven shoes for my mom? Finally. Was she happy? Absolutely.	Sentences will vary.

TRANSPARENCY RWW 1–5
TEACHER'S EDITION PAGE 49E

ANNOTATED VERSION

COURAGE Reading-Writing Workshop Varying Sentences

Revising

Have students use **Practice Book** page 26 to help them evaluate and then revise their personal narratives. Students should also discuss their drafts in a writing conference with one or more classmates. (Distribute the Conference Master on page R36. Discuss the sample thoughts and questions before students have their conferences.) Remind students to keep in mind their listeners' comments and questions when they revise.

Improving Writing: Varying Sentences

Writing Traits

SENTENCE FLUENCY Explain that good writers vary the sentences they use. Review the different types of sentences: a declarative sentence makes a statement; an interrogative sentence asks a question; a command sentence makes a command; an exclamatory sentence strongly declares.

Display and discuss the first two paragraphs on **Transparency RWW1–5**.

- Read aloud the first paragraph. Point out how repetitive it sounds. Explain that it has only one type of sentence (declarative).
- Read aloud the second paragraph. Point out that it sounds livelier because it uses different types of sentences. The sentences also vary in length.
- Work with students to complete the transparency, using at least one of each type of sentence in each new paragraph.
- Have volunteers read the new paragraphs aloud. Discuss the improvements.

Assign **Practice Book** page 27. Then have students look at their personal narratives to see how they can improve them by varying sentences.

Proofreading

Have students proofread their papers to correct capitalization, punctuation, spelling, and usage. They can use the proofreading checklist and proofreading marks on **Practice Book** pages 297–298.

Frequently Misspelled Words

Write the Spelling Words on the board, or distribute the list on **Practice Book** page 281. Help students identify the part of the word likely to be misspelled.

Spelling Pretest/Test

Basic Words

1. **Your** job is to be a golf caddie.
2. **You're** one of the lucky ones.
3. You help golfers with **their** bags.
4. **There** is no time to waste.
5. **They're** waiting for you.
6. Golf has **its** own logic.
7. **It's** both fun and frustrating.
8. **Wouldn't** you like to try it?
9. **We're** holding a place for you.
10. I'm going **to** Scotland for golf.
11. Golf is big in England, **too**.
12. **That's** where golf was invented.
13. They **knew** a good thing.
14. I **know** I'll never break eighty.

Challenge Words

15. My **pennant** says GOLF IS ALL.
16. I keep it over my **bureau**.
17. I **interpret** its message freely.
18. To play golf is to **forfeit** all else.
19. It takes hard work and **perspiration** to win.

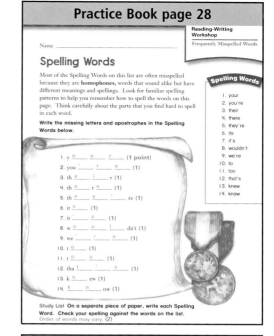

Practice Book page 28

Reading-Writing Workshop
Frequently Misspelled Words

Name _____

Spelling Words

Most of the Spelling Words on this list are often misspelled because they are **homophones**, words that sound alike but have different meanings and spellings. Look for familiar spelling patterns to help you remember how to spell the words on this page. Think carefully about the parts that you find hard to spell in each word.

Write the missing letters and apostrophes in the Spelling Words below.

1. y o u r (1 point)
2. you ' r e (1)
3. th e i r (1)
4. th e r e (1)
5. th e y ' re (1)
6. it s (1)
7. it ' s (1)
8. w o u l dn't (1)
9. we ' r e (1)
10. t o (1)
11. t o o (1)
12. tha t ' s (1)
13. k n ew (1)
14. k n ow (1)

Spelling Words
1. your
2. you're
3. their
4. there
5. they're
6. its
7. it's
8. wouldn't
9. we're
10. to
11. too
12. that's
13. knew
14. know

Study List On a separate piece of paper, write each Spelling Word. Check your spelling against the words on the list.
Order of words may vary. (2)

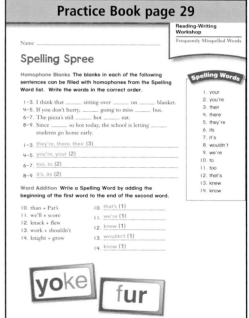

Practice Book page 29

Reading-Writing Workshop
Frequently Misspelled Words

Name _____

Spelling Spree

Homophone Blanks The blanks in each of the following sentences can be filled with homophones from the Spelling Word list. Write the words in the correct order.

1–3. I think that _____ sitting over _____ on _____ blanket.
4–5. If you don't hurry, _____ going to miss _____ bus.
6–7. The pizza's still _____ hot _____ eat.
8–9. Since _____ so hot today, the school is letting _____ students go home early.

1–3. they're, there, their (3)
4–5. you're, your (2)
6–7. too, to (2)
8–9. it's, its (2)

Word Addition Write a Spelling Word by adding the beginning of the first word to the end of the second word.

10. than + Pat's   10. that's (1)
11. we'll + score   11. we're (1)
12. knack + flew   12. knew (1)
13. work + shouldn't   13. wouldn't (1)
14. knight + grow   14. know (1)

Spelling Words
1. your
2. you're
3. their
4. there
5. they're
6. its
7. it's
8. wouldn't
9. we're
10. to
11. too
12. that's
13. knew
14. know

yoke   fur

Practice Book page 30

Reading-Writing Workshop
Frequently Misspelled Words

Name _____

Proofreading and Writing

Proofreading Circle the five misspelled Spelling Words in this poster. Then write each word correctly.

What Is Courage?
Maybe it's sticking to you're beliefs, no matter what. Courage can also mean pushing yourself at times when most people wouldn't. And if you put yourself in danger to help someone, thats courage by any definition. But even if we don't now exactly how to define it, we recognize it when we see it. And were all grateful every time we do.

1. your (2 points)   4. know (2)
2. wouldn't (2)   5. we're (2)
3. that's (2)

Spelling Words
1. your
2. you're
3. their
4. there
5. they're
6. its
7. it's
8. wouldn't
9. we're
10. to
11. too
12. that's
13. knew
14. know

Writing Headlines Suppose that a newspaper were going to write articles covering the events that take place in each of the selections in this theme. What would some good headlines be?

On a separate piece of paper, write a headline for each selection in the theme. Use Spelling Words from the list. Responses will vary. (5)

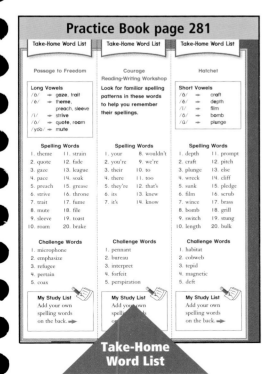

Practice Book page 281

Take-Home Word List   Take-Home Word List   Take-Home Word List

Passage to Freedom	Courage Reading-Writing Workshop	Hatchet
Long Vowels /ā/ ➡ gaze, trait /ē/ ➡ theme, preach, sleeve /ī/ ➡ strive /ō/ ➡ quote, roam /yōō/ ➡ mute	Look for familiar spelling patterns in these words to help you remember their spellings.	**Short Vowels** /ă/ ➡ craft /ĕ/ ➡ depth /ĭ/ ➡ film /ŏ/ ➡ bomb /ŭ/ ➡ plunge

Spelling Words
1. theme   11. strain
2. quote   12. fade
3. gaze   13. league
4. pace   14. soak
5. preach   15. grease
6. strive   16. throne
7. trait   17. fume
8. mute   18. file
9. sleeve   19. toast
10. roam   20. brake

Challenge Words
1. microphone
2. emphasize
3. refugee
4. pertain
5. coax

Spelling Words
1. your   8. wouldn't
2. you're   9. we're
3. their   10. to
4. there   11. too
5. they're   12. that's
6. its   13. knew
7. it's   14. know

Challenge Words
1. pennant
2. bureau
3. interpret
4. forfeit
5. perspiration

Spelling Words
1. depth   11. prompt
2. craft   12. pitch
3. plunge   13. else
4. wreck   14. cliff
5. sunk   15. pledge
6. film   16. scrub
7. wince   17. brass
8. bomb   18. grill
9. switch   19. stung
10. length   20. bulk

Challenge Words
1. habitat
2. cobweb
3. tepid
4. magnetic
5. deft

My Study List Add your own spelling words on the back. ➡

My Study List Add your own spelling words on the back. ➡

My Study List Add your own spelling words on the back. ➡

Take-Home Word List

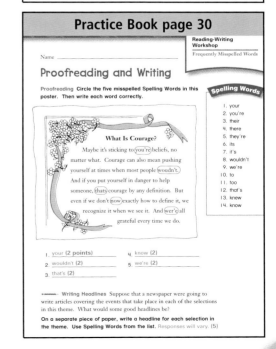

Publishing

Have students publish their personal narratives.

- Ask them to look back at the publishing ideas they noted when they chose a topic. Discuss the Ideas for Sharing box below.
- Then ask students to decide how they want to publish their writing.
- Tell them to make a neat final copy of their description. Remind them to use good penmanship and to be sure that they have fixed all mistakes.

 Portfolio Opportunity

Save students' final copy of their personal narrative as an example of the development of their writing skills.

Ideas for Sharing

Write It
- Make a class book of personal narratives.
- Mail or e-mail your narrative to a friend or a relative.

Say It
- Tape-record your story, and pantomime it for the class.
- Read your narrative aloud in a video "broadcast."

Show It
- Create a collage to display with your narrative. Use photographs, post cards, or souvenirs.
- Draw a picture of your narrative's high point, and tack it with your narrative to the bulletin board.

Tips for Video Broadcasting
- Speak clearly. Don't rush.
- Make eye contact with the camera.
- Have the camera operator use different shots and angles.
- Use props related to your narrative.

Monitoring Student Progress

Student Self-Assessment
- What was your favorite part of your personal narrative?
- Did you meet the goals that you set for yourself when you started this personal narrative?
- What would you change in this personal narrative if you wrote it over again?
- What did you learn from your readers' response to your personal narrative?
- What did you learn about writing from having completed this personal narrative?

Evaluating

Have students write responses to the Student Self-Assessment questions.

Evaluate students' writing, using the Writing Traits Scoring Rubric. This rubric is based on criteria in this workshop and reflects criteria students used in Revising Your Personal Narrative on **Practice Book** page 26.

Personal Narrative

Writing Traits Scoring Rubric

4

IDEAS	The narrative is focused on a single experience. Details tell what the writer saw, heard, tasted, smelled, and felt.
ORGANIZATION	The beginning catches the reader's interest. Events are all told in the order that they happened. The ending ties the narrative together.
VOICE	The writer chooses words and phrases that express his or her personality.
WORD CHOICE	The writer used exact, interesting words.
SENTENCE FLUENCY	Sentences vary in length and structure. They flow smoothly.
CONVENTIONS	There are almost no errors in spelling, capitalization, punctuation, or usage.
PRESENTATION	The final copy is neat and legible.

3

IDEAS	A few more details are needed. One or two events and details may not relate to the experience.
ORGANIZATION	The beginning or ending may be weak. The order of events may not be clear.
VOICE	The writer's thoughts and feelings sometimes do not come through clearly.
WORD CHOICE	More exact words would help the reader create a mental picture of events.
SENTENCE FLUENCY	The paper would benefit from greater sentence variety.
CONVENTIONS	There are a few mistakes, but they do not affect understanding.
PRESENTATION	The final copy is messy in a few places but still legible.

2

IDEAS	More details are needed everywhere. Many events and details do not relate to the experience.
ORGANIZATION	The beginning or ending may be missing. The order of events is confusing.
VOICE	The writer's thoughts and feelings often do not come through clearly.
WORD CHOICE	The writer uses few exact words.
SENTENCE FLUENCY	Many sentences may be short and choppy.
CONVENTIONS	Mistakes sometimes make the essay hard to understand.
PRESENTATION	The final copy is messy. It may be illegible in a few places.

1

IDEAS	The narrative is not focused on a single experience. There are almost no details, and it is hard to understand what happened.
ORGANIZATION	There may be no identifiable beginning, middle, or end.
VOICE	The writer sounds uninterested in the experience.
WORD CHOICE	The writer repeats the same words. Some words are vague or confusing.
SENTENCE FLUENCY	Almost all sentences may be short and choppy.
CONVENTIONS	Many mistakes make the paper hard to understand.
PRESENTATION	The final copy is messy. It may be illegible in many places.

Lesson Overview

Literature

PASSAGE TO FREEDOM
The Sugihara Story

Written by KEN MOCHIZUKI
Illustrated by DOM LEE
Afterword by HIROKI SUGIHARA

Selection Summary

Chiune Sugihara, a Japanese diplomat in Lithuania in 1940, saved thousands of Jews during the Holocaust by issuing visas to allow for their escape.

Vocabulary Reader

Fly Away, Children
By Lee S. Justice

Nonfiction

❶ Background and Vocabulary

❷ Main Selection

Passage to Freedom
Genre: Nonfiction

❸ Primary Source Link

Instructional Support

Planning and Practice

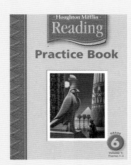

Teacher's Edition

Practice Book

Teacher's Resources

Transparencies

Differentiated Instruction

**Intervention Strategies
for Extra Support**

**Instructional Activities
for Challenge**

**Instructional Strategies for
English Language Learners**

Ready-Made Centers

**Building Vocabulary
Flip Chart**
- center activities
- word skills practice

**Reading in Science and
Social Studies Flip Chart**
- books and center activities
- support for state
  content standards

**Hands-On Literacy Centers
for *Passage to Freedom***
- activities
- manipulatives
- routines

Technology

Audio Selection
Passage to Freedom

Get Set for Reading CD-ROM

Accelerated Reader®

www.eduplace.com
- over 1,000 Online Leveled Books

**HOUGHTON MIFFLIN
Assessment System**
- Test Generator

Leveled Books for Reaching All Learners

Fluency

Increase students' reading fluency using these activities.

● BELOW LEVEL
Display a series of words that share a phonic element. Model reading the words as students repeat after you.

▲ ON LEVEL
Have students read along with the audio CD. Have them choose a passage to practice and then read aloud to a small group.

■ ABOVE LEVEL
Have a student practice reading a passage three or four times until fluent. Then tell the student to record his or her reading as if reading to a friend.

◆ LANGUAGE SUPPORT
Model fluent reading of short passages as students follow in their books. Have students repeat each passage twice after you.

Skills Practice

- Topic, comprehension strategy, and vocabulary linked to main selection
- Lessons in Teacher's Edition, pages 71O–71R

● BELOW LEVEL

Corrie's Secret
by Meish Goldish
illustrated by Dom Lee
Leveled Readers

▲ ON LEVEL

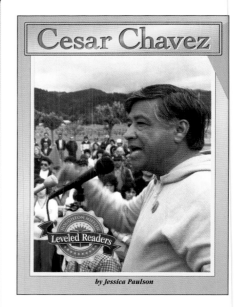

Cesar Chavez
by Jessica Paulson
Leveled Readers

● Below Level Practice

▲ On Level Practice

● Below Level Practice

▲ On Level Practice

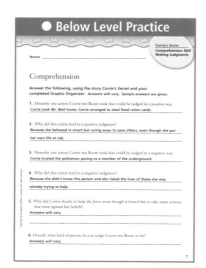

■ ABOVE LEVEL

The Story of
Oskar Schindler
Leveled Readers
by Emma Rose

■ Above Level Practice

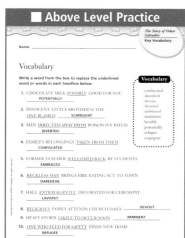

The Story of Oskar Schindler
Key Vocabulary

Name _____

Vocabulary

Write a word from the box to replace the underlined word or words in each headline below.

Vocabulary
confiscated
daredevil
devout
diverted
embraced
imminent
lavishly
potentially
refugee
scapegoat

1. CHOCOLATE MILK _POSSIBLY_ GOOD FOR YOU?
   POTENTIALLY
2. INNOCENT LITTLE BROTHER IS THE _ONE BLAMED_
   SCAPEGOAT
3. MAN _DIRECTED AWAY FROM_ POISON IVY PATCH
   DIVERTED
4. FAMILY'S BELONGINGS _TAKEN FROM THEM_
   CONFISCATED
5. FORMER TEACHER _WELCOMED BACK_ BY STUDENTS
   EMBRACED
6. _RECKLESS MAN_ BRINGS FIRE-EATING ACT TO TOWN
   DAREDEVIL
7. HALL _EXTRAVAGANTLY_ DECORATED FOR CEREMONY
   LAVISHLY
8. _RELIGIOUS_ FAMILY ATTENDS CHURCH DAILY   DEVOUT
9. HEAVY STORM _LIKELY TO OCCUR SOON_   IMMINENT
10. _ONE WHO FLED FOR SAFETY_ FINDS NEW HOME
    REFUGEE

■ Above Level Practice

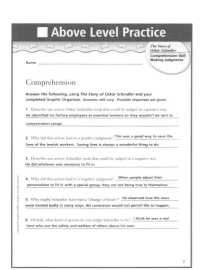

The Story of Oskar Schindler
Comprehension Skill
Making Judgments

Name _____

Comprehension

Answer the following, using *The Story of Oskar Schindler* and your completed Graphic Organizer. Answers will vary. Possible responses are given.

1. Describe one action Oskar Schindler took that could be judged in a positive way.
   He identified his factory employees as essential workers so they wouldn't be sent to concentration camps.

2. Why did this action lead to a positive judgment? This was a good way to save the lives of the Jewish workers. Saving lives is always a wonderful thing to do.

3. Describe one action Schindler took that could be judged in a negative way.
   He did whatever was necessary to fit in.

4. Why did this action lead to a negative judgment? When people adjust their personalities to fit in with a special group, they are not being true to themselves.

5. Why might Schindler have had a "change of heart"? He observed how the Jews were treated badly in many ways. His conscience would not permit this to happen.

6. Overall, what kind of person do you judge Schindler to be? I think he was a real hero who put the safety and welfare of others above his own.

◆ LANGUAGE SUPPORT

Corrie's Important Decision
by Meish Goldish
illustrated by Dom Lee
Leveled Readers

◆ Language Support Practice

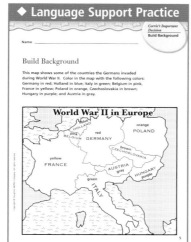

Corrie's Important Decision
Build Background

Name _____

Build Background

This map shows some of the countries the Germans invaded during World War II. Color in the map with the following colors: Germany in red; Holland in blue; Italy in green; Belgium in pink; France in yellow; Poland in orange; Czechoslovakia in brown; Hungary in purple; and Austria in gray.

World War II in Europe

◆ Language Support Practice

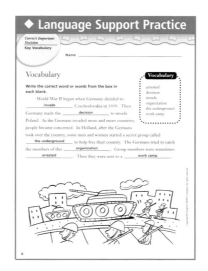

Corrie's Important Decision
Key Vocabulary

Name _____

Vocabulary

Write the correct word or words from the box in each blank.

Vocabulary
arrested
decision
invade
organization
the underground
work camp

World War II began when Germany decided to _invade_ Czechoslovakia in 1939. Then Germany made the _decision_ to invade Poland. As the Germans invaded more and more countries, people became concerned. In Holland, after the Germans took over the country, some men and women started a secret group called _the underground_ to help free their country. The Germans tried to catch the members of this _organization_. Group members were sometimes _arrested_. Then they were sent to a _work camp_.

Leveled Theme Paperbacks

- Extended independent reading in theme-related paperbacks

- Lessons in Teacher's Edition, pages R2–R7

The Little Ships
The Heroic Rescue at Dunkirk in World War II
by LOUISE BORDEN
illustrated by MICHAEL FOREMAN

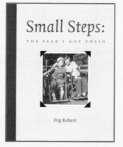

Small Steps:
THE YEAR I GOT POLIO
Peg Kehret

● **BELOW LEVEL**   ▲ **ON LEVEL**

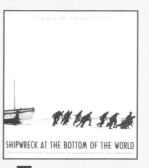

JENNIFER ARMSTRONG

SHIPWRECK AT THE BOTTOM OF THE WORLD

■ **ABOVE LEVEL**

Technology

HOUGHTON MIFFLIN
Online Leveled Books
www.eduplace.com

- over 1,000 Online Leveled Books

Leveled Readers
Audio available

Daily Lesson Plans

 **Technology**
Lesson Planner CD-ROM allows you to customize the chart below to develop your own lesson plans.

T Skill tested on Weekly or Theme Skills Test and/or Integrated Theme Test

DAILY LESSON PLANS

	DAY 1	**DAY 2**
50–60 minutes  **Reading** **Comprehension**   **Leveled Readers** • Fluency Practice • Independent Reading	**Teacher Read Aloud,** 49S–49T *Courage is something everyone has inside them* Background and Vocabulary, 50 **Key Vocabulary,** 51 decision permission superiors diplomat refugees visas government **Vocabulary Reader** **Reading the Selection,** 52–65 **Comprehension Skill,** 52 Making Judgments **T** **Comprehension Strategy,** 52 Evaluate **Leveled Readers**  *Corrie's Secret* *Cesar Chavez* *The Story of Oskar Schindler* *Corrie's Important Decision* Lessons and Leveled Practice, 71O–71R	**Reading the Selection,** 52–65 Comprehension Check, 65 Responding, 66 Think About the Selection **Vocabulary Reader** **Comprehension Skill Preview,** 63 Making Judgments **T** **Leveled Readers** *Corrie's Secret* *Cesar Chavez* *The Story of Oskar Schindler* *Corrie's Important Decision* Lessons and Leveled Practice, 71O–71R
20–30 minutes **Word Work** **Phonics/Decoding** **Vocabulary** **Spelling**	**Phonics/Decoding,** 53 Phonics/Decoding Strategy **Vocabulary,** 52–65 Selection Vocabulary **Spelling,** 71E Long Vowels **T**	**Structural Analysis,** 71C Syllabication **T** **Vocabulary,** 52–65 Selection Vocabulary **Spelling,** 71E Long Vowels Review and Practice **T**
20–30 minutes **Writing and Oral Language** **Writing** **Grammar** **Listening/Speaking/Viewing**	**Writing,** 71K Introducing a Memo **Grammar,** 71I Conjunctions **T** **Daily Language Practice** 1. Grab that piece of burning toost (toast! or toast.) 2. the theam of a book or film is sometimes hard to understand. (The; theme) **Listening/Speaking/Viewing,** 49S–49T, 59 Teacher Read Aloud, Stop and Think	**Writing,** 71K Writing a Memo **Grammar,** 71I Conjunctions Practice **T** **Daily Language Practice** 3. Do you have a favorite quoot from a book. (quote; book?) 4. My hiking pase is fast but I still can't keep up with my brother. (pace; fast,) **Listening/Speaking/Viewing,** 65, 66 Wrapping Up, Responding

Target Skills of the Week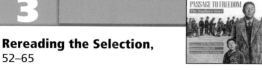

Phonics	Syllabication
Comprehension	Evaluate; Making Judgments
Vocabulary	Dictionary Guide Words
Fluency	Leveled Readers

DAY 3

Rereading the Selection, 52–65

Vocabulary Reader

Comprehension Skill, 71A–71B
Making Judgments **T**

Leveled Readers
Corrie's Secret
Cesar Chavez
*The Story of
Oskar Schindler*
Corrie's Important Decision

Lessons and Leveled Practice, 71O–71R

Phonics Review, 71D
Long Vowels

Vocabulary, 71G
Dictionary Guide Words **T**

Spelling, 71F
Vocabulary: Word Clues; Long Vowels
Practice **T**

Writing, 71L
Capitalization and Punctuation **T**

Grammar, 71J
Compound Sentences **T**

Daily Language Practice
5. Our baseball leeg includes ten teams from all over the city (league; city.)
6. Did you see the colorful patches on the sleve of my coat. (sleeve; coat?)

DAY 4

Reading the Social Studies Link, 68–71
"A Mother's Courage"

Skill: How to Read Primary Sources

Rereading for Genre, 70
Interview

Comprehension Skill Review, 57
Predicting Outcomes

Leveled Readers
Corrie's Secret
Cesar Chavez
*The Story of
Oskar Schindler*
Corrie's Important Decision

Lessons and Leveled Practice, 71O–71R

Phonics/Decoding, 68–71
Apply Phonics/Decoding Strategy to Link

Vocabulary, 71M
Language Center: Building Vocabulary

Spelling, 71F
Long Vowels Game, Proofreading **T**

Writing, 71L
Writing Practice

Grammar, 71J
Compound Sentences Practice **T**

Daily Language Practice
7. my cat likes to rome around the neighborhood at night. (My; roam)
8. We can sit on the rocks and gaz at the setting sun (gaze; sun.)

Listening/Speaking/Viewing, 71
Discuss the Link

DAY 5

Rereading for Fluency, 55

Responding Activities, 66–67

Write from Another Point of View

Cross-Curricular Activities

Information and Study Skills, 71H
Using Reference Sources

Comprehension Skill Review, 61
Fact and Opinion

Leveled Readers
Corrie's Secret
Cesar Chavez
*The Story of
Oskar Schindler*
Corrie's Important Decision

Lessons and Leveled Practice, 71O–71R

Phonics, 71N
Language Center: Newspaper Report

Vocabulary, 71M
Language Center: Vocabulary Game

Spelling, 71F
Test: Long Vowels **T**

Writing, 71L
Sharing Writing

Grammar, 71J, 71M
Combining Sentences
Language Center: Summary with Conjunctions

Daily Language Practice
9. Did you see the royal throon on display at the museum. (throne; museum?)
10. Today I will soke in a pool or I will sit in a cool movie theater. (soak; pool.)

Listening/Speaking/Viewing, 71N
Language Center: Speaking on the Telephone

Managing Flexible Groups

Leveled Instruction and Leveled Practice

	DAY 1	**DAY 2**
WHOLE CLASS	• Teacher Read Aloud (TE pp. 49S–49T) • Building Background, Introducing Vocabulary (TE pp. 50–51) • Comprehension Strategy: Introduce (TE p. 52) • Comprehension Skill: Introduce (TE p. 52) • Purpose Setting (TE p. 53) **After reading first half of *Passage to Freedom*** • Stop and Think (TE p. 59)	**After reading *Passage to Freedom*** • Wrapping Up (TE p. 65) • Comprehension Check (Practice Book p. 33) • Responding: Think About the Selection (TE p. 66) • Comprehension Skill: Preview (TE p. 63)
SMALL GROUPS **Extra Support**	**TEACHER-LED** • Preview vocabulary; support reading with Vocabulary Reader. • Preview *Passage to Freedom* to Stop and Think (TE pp. 52–59). • Support reading with Extra Support/ Intervention notes (TE pp. 53, 56, 57, 58, 62, 64).	**Partner or Individual Work** • Reread first half of *Passage to Freedom* (TE pp. 52–59). • Preview, read second half (TE pp. 60–65). • Comprehension Check (Practice Book p. 33)
Challenge	**Individual Work** • Begin "Rescuers" (Challenge Handbook p. 4). • Extend reading with Challenge Note (TE p. 64).	**Individual Work** • Continue work on activity (Challenge Handbook p. 4).
English Language Learners	**TEACHER-LED** • Preview vocabulary; support reading with Vocabulary Reader. • Preview *Passage to Freedom* to Stop and Think (TE pp. 52–59). • Support reading with English Language Learners notes (TE pp. 50, 55, 63).	**TEACHER-LED** • Review first half of *Passage to Freedom* (TE pp. 52–59). ✔ • Preview, read second half (TE pp. 60–65). • Begin Comprehension Check together (Practice Book p. 33).

Independent Activities

- Get Set for Reading CD-ROM
- Journals: selection notes, questions
- Complete, review Practice Book (pp. 31–35) and Leveled Readers Practice Blackline Masters (TE pp. 71O–71R).
- Assignment Cards (Teachers Resource Blackline Masters, pp. 49–50)
- Leveled Readers (TE pp. 71O–71R), Leveled Theme Paperbacks (TE pp. R2–R7), or book from Leveled Bibliography (TE pp. 23E–23F)

✔ **Opportunity to informally assess oral reading rate**

DAY 3

- Rereading (TE pp. 52–65)
- Comprehension Skill: Main lesson (TE pp. 71A–71B)

TEACHER-LED

- Reread, review Comprehension Check (Practice Book p. 33).
- Preview Leveled Reader: Below Level (TE p. 71O), or read book from Leveled Bibliography (TE pp. 23E–23F). ✔

TEACHER-LED

- Teacher check-in: Assess progress (Challenge Handbook p. 4).
- Preview Leveled Reader: Above Level (TE p. 71Q), or read book from Leveled Bibliography (TE pp. 23E–23F). ✔

Partner or Individual Work

- Complete Comprehension Check (Practice Book p. 33).
- Begin Leveled Reader: Language Support (TE p. 71R), or read book from Leveled Bibliography (TE pp. 23E–23F).

DAY 4

- Reading the Primary Sources Link (TE pp. 68–71): Skill lesson (TE p. 68)
- Rereading the Primary Sources Link: Lesson on Genre (TE p. 70)
- Comprehension Skill: First Comprehension Review lesson (TE p. 57)

Partner or Individual Work

- Reread the Primary Sources Link (TE pp. 68–71).
- Complete Leveled Reader: Below Level (TE p. 71O), or read book from Leveled Bibliography (TE pp. 23E–23F).

Individual Work

- Complete activity (Challenge Handbook p. 4)
- Complete Leveled Reader: Above Level (TE p. 71Q), or read book from Leveled Bibliography (TE pp. 23E–23F).

TEACHER-LED

- Reread the Primary Sources Link (TE pp. 68–71) ✔ and review Link Skill (TE p. 68).
- Complete Leveled Reader: Language Support (TE p. 71R), or read book from Leveled Bibliography (TE pp. 23E–23F). ✔

DAY 5

- Responding: Select from Activities (TE pp. 66–67)
- Information and Study Skills (TE p. 71H)
- Comprehension Skill: Second Comprehension Review lesson (TE p. 61)

TEACHER-LED

- Comprehension Skill: Reteaching lesson (TE p. R10)
- Reread Leveled Theme Paperback: Below Level (TE pp. R2–R3), or read book from Leveled Bibliography (TE pp. 23E–23F). ✔

TEACHER-LED

- Evaluate activity and plan format for sharing (Challenge Handbook p. 4).
- Reread Leveled Theme Paperback: Above Level (TE pp. R6–R7), or read book from Leveled Bibliography (TE pp. 23E–23F). ✔

Partner or Individual Work

- Reread book from Leveled Bibliography (TE pp. 23E–23F).

- Responding activities (TE pp. 66–67)
- Language Center activities (TE pp. 71M–71N)
- **Fluency Practice:** Reread *Passage to Freedom, Hatchet.* ✔
- Activities relating to *Passage to Freedom* at Education Place® www.eduplace.com

Turn the page for more independent activities. ➡

Ready-Made Small Group Activities

 Word Work

Cross Curricular

Building Vocabulary Center Activity 2
● ▲ ■ *I Hereby Declare*

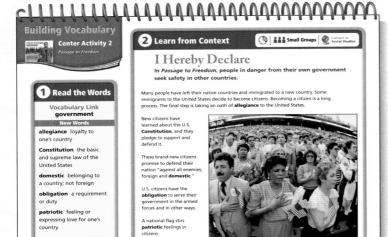

Building Vocabulary
Center Activity 2
Passage to Freedom

2 Learn from Context ⏱ 👥 Small Groups 🔗 Connect to Social Studies

I Hereby Declare
In *Passage to Freedom*, people in danger from their own government seek safety in other countries.

Many people have left their native countries and immigrated to a new country. Some immigrants to the United States decide to become citizens. Becoming a citizen is a long process. The final step is taking an oath of **allegiance** to the United States.

New citizens have learned about the U.S. **Constitution**, and they pledge to support and defend it.

These brand-new citizens promise to defend their nation "against all enemies, foreign and **domestic**."

U.S. citizens have the **obligation** to serve their government in the armed forces and in other ways.

A national flag stirs **patriotic** feelings in citizens.

1 Read the Words

Vocabulary Link
government

New Words
allegiance loyalty to one's country

Constitution the basic and supreme law of the United States

domestic belonging to a country; not foreign

obligation a requirement or duty

patriotic feeling or expressing love for one's country

Syllabication
deceptive, proportion, stupendous

3 Do an Activity ▶

Leveled Activities on side 2

Word Part Cards

full | ness | ous

Key Vocabulary Cards 9–15

decision

Spelling Word Cards 21–40

theme

Reading in Social Studies Independent Book
■ *The Geography of War: The Battle of Salamis*

THE GEOGRAPHY OF WAR
The Battle of Salamis
BY CAROL OTTOLENGHI

Reading in Social Studies Center Activity 2
● ▲ ■ *Interview a Great Leader*

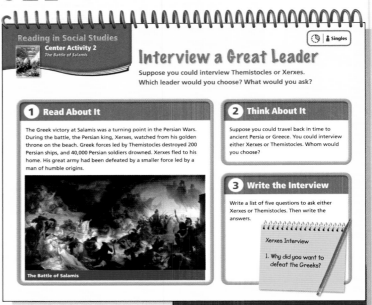

Reading in Social Studies
Center Activity 2
The Battle of Salamis

⏱ 👤 Singles

Interview a Great Leader
Suppose you could interview Themistocles or Xerxes. Which leader would you choose? What would you ask?

1 Read About It
The Greek victory at Salamis was a turning point in the Persian Wars. During the battle, the Persian king, Xerxes, watched from his golden throne on the beach. Greek forces led by Themistocles destroyed 200 Persian ships, and 40,000 Persian soldiers drowned. Xerxes fled to his home. His great army had been defeated by a smaller force led by a man of humble origins.

The Battle of Salamis

2 Think About It
Suppose you could travel back in time to ancient Persia or Greece. You could interview either Xerxes or Themistocles. Whom would you choose?

3 Write the Interview
Write a list of five questions to ask either Xerxes or Themistocles. Then write the answers.

Xerxes Interview
1. Why did you want to defeat the Greeks?

Leveled Activities on side 2

Leveled for ● Below Level, ▲ On Level, ■ Above Level

Reading

Routine Card 2
● ▲ ■ *Partner Reading*

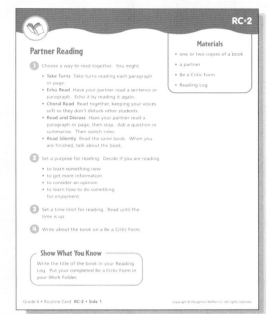

RC·2

Partner Reading

Materials
- one or two copies of a book
- a partner
- Be a Critic Form
- Reading Log

1. Choose a way to read together. You might
   - **Take Turns** Take turns reading each paragraph or page.
   - **Echo Read** Have your partner read a sentence or paragraph. Echo it by reading it again.
   - **Choral Read** Read together, keeping your voices soft so they don't disturb other students.
   - **Read and Discuss** Have your partner read a paragraph or page, then stop. Ask a question or summarize. Then switch roles.
   - **Read Silently** Read the same book. When you are finished, talk about the book.

2. Set a purpose for reading. Decide if you are reading
   - to learn something new
   - to get more information
   - to consider an opinion
   - to learn how to do something for enjoyment

3. Set a time limit for reading. Read until the time is up.

4. Write about the book on a Be a Critic Form.

Show What You Know
Write the title of the book in your Reading Log. Put your completed Be a Critic Form in your Work Folder.

Grade 6 • Routine Card RC-2 • Side 1
Copyright © Houghton Mifflin Co. All rights reserved.

Activity Card 1
▲ ■ *Corrie's Secret*

Passage to Freedom
GRADE 6 THEME 1 WEEK 2
ACTIVITY CARD

1. Corrie's Secret

Who was the real Corrie ten Boom? Research and write a short newspaper article about Corrie's life. Compare details from the story with facts from other sources. Do you think *Corrie's Secret* is a realistic portrayal of Corrie's experience in occupied Holland? Explain.

Writing

Assignment Card 8
● ▲ *Illustration Interpretations*

Assignment Card 8 Passage to Freedom
Illustration Interpretations
Visual Literacy

In a selection that tells about actual events, such as *Passage to Freedom*, the illustrator usually tries to represent these events realistically. Look at the illustrations in *Passage to Freedom* with a partner and discuss what the illustrator has shown in each. Then write a caption for each illustration, explaining what it shows. Use as few words as you can. (You can use the photograph captions in Get Set to Read, pages 50–51, as models.)

© by Houghton Mifflin Co.
Theme 1: Courage

Challenge Card 1–3
■ *Rescuers*

THEME 1/*Passage to Freedom*

1. Rescuers

Goal: Write a short biography of a courageous person in Nazi-occupied territory. Focus on the impact this person had on the lives of others.

Choose Your Hero
Mr. Sugihara's decision to disobey his government and give visas to Jewish refugees made him a hero. List other people you might write about. Some, like Raoul Wallenberg, worked alone. Others, like the Danes who helped save Jews in Denmark, worked together. Ask your teacher for possible resources.

TIPS
- State the reasons for your Roll of Honor choice.
- Use adjectives to describe the actions or qualities of your subject.

Research
Find out about the person you have chosen.
- Learn about the risks he or she took to save others.
- Look for background information on the country where this person lived during World War II. Make your biography more specific.
- Find a photo of your subject, if possible.

Roll of Honor
Using your biographical information, write a paragraph about the person you have chosen. Your biography will be part of a class Roll of Honor. Begin with the statement, "I choose _____ for the Roll of Honor because he or she _____." Work with others to decide how the Roll of Honor will be presented and displayed.

Gr. 6, Challenge Card 1–3
© Houghton Mifflin Co.

Multiple Tiers of Intervention

Core Program Instruction

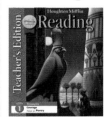

- research-based
- systematic
- assessment-driven

Group Support

Daily lessons and activities for differentiated instruction

Intervention Strategies for Extra Support, pages 24–33

Instructional Activities for Challenge, pages 4–5

Instructional Strategies for English Learners, pages 28–37

Intervention Program
Proven efficacy for struggling readers

Soar to Success

For these materials and more, see **Small Group Independent Activities Kit.**

Oral Language and Fluency

OBJECTIVE
- Listen in order to make judgments.

Building Background

Tell students that you are going to read aloud an essay written by a young person about her courageous family and their journey from Vietnam to the United States.

- Help students locate Vietnam on a map of the world.

- Invite students whose families have come to the United States from other countries to talk about their experiences.

Fluency Modeling

Explain that as you read aloud, you will be modeling fluent oral reading. Ask students to listen carefully to your phrasing and your expression, or tone of voice and emphasis.

COMPREHENSION SKILL

Making Judgments

Explain that

- readers can form judgments, or opinions, about the actions of people in a selection;

- judgments are made based on personal values as well as on selection details.

Purpose Setting Read the selection aloud, asking students to decide whether or not they agree with the writer's ideas as they listen. Then use the Guiding Comprehension questions to assess students' understanding. Reread the selection for clarification as needed.

Teacher Read Aloud

Courage Is Something Everyone Has Inside Them
by Son Ca Lam

INTRODUCTION

How would you remember someone you had loved and lost? Would you write a song, or build a building? Some people are remembered with memorial parks, and others, with statues.

Max Warburg's parents chose a special way to memorialize their son, who died in 1991 of leukemia. They didn't build a park, or make a statue. Instead, they created a program that helps sixth graders in Boston schools learn the meaning of courage and how they can be courageous in their own lives. Students read, write and learn about themselves as part of this "Max Warburg Courage Curriculum." Each year, the best student essays about courage in their own lives are published in book form. The essay that follows is one of the winners.

❶

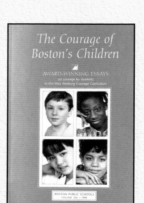

Courage is something everyone has inside them. Courage doesn't mean being a hero or risking your life for someone. The story of my family's courage started in Vietnam. My father joined the military to fight in the Vietnam War against the Communists for our freedom. Unfortunately, we lost. My father and many others were captured by the Communists and kept as prisoners for more than ten years. They had to work hard in the fields from sunrise to sunset and they had very little to eat. Some died from the work and lack of food. My mother and sister had to walk many miles through the swamp to visit **❷** him and to bring him food. When my father was released he had to go to the police station every week so that the officials could check that he had not left the country. My sister could not attend a good school because of our family's record.

❸ My family realized that they would need to escape to America. Finally they found someone who could help them but there was not enough money for all of them to go. My father decided that he would stay back. My family had to hide in the forest for a day and a night. There were men, women and children trying to escape in the darkness of night. At that time my mother was pregnant. Nobody wanted to be left behind; they were running for their lives. They dared not make any sounds. While running, my sister lost her slippers and then had to run barefooted through the woods. Next they reached a small boat and sailed in it for twelve hours. They had reached the shore of Thailand and they went into a refugee camp. From there, they went to the Philippines, where I was born.

❹ Three months later, we came to America. It was very hard for my mother and sister because they didn't know anything and they couldn't speak English. I was too young to know anything about this. My mother went to work to support us. My sister was fourteen; she registered at the middle school for seventh grade. She couldn't understand what the teacher said in class and there wasn't anyone who could speak Vietnamese to her. She would run home to my mother saying that she didn't want to go back to school and that it was too hard for her. My mother would always soothe her. It wasn't until six months later that my father was able to come to America.

Now everyone was away from danger, but not away from the burdens and hardships. After school, my sister would have to baby-sit for my brother and myself. It was hard for everyone in my family, especially for my sister who has now graduated from college. I think my family had a lot of courage to have gone through all this hardship. I would like to thank my parents for working hard to support us and to my sister for taking such good care of us.

CRITICAL THINKING
Guiding Comprehension

❶ **MAKING JUDGMENTS** Do you agree with Son Ca's definition of courage? Why or why not? (Sample answer: yes, because not only heroes show courage.)

❷ **MAKING JUDGMENTS** Do you think the treatment of Son Ca's family by the Communists in Vietnam was fair? Explain. (Sample answer: no, because her father was kept a prisoner and her sister was not allowed to attend a good school)

❸ **MAKING JUDGMENTS** Do you agree that fleeing to America was the best solution for the family? Why or why not? (Sample answers: yes, because life was hard in Vietnam; no, because escape was too dangerous.)

❹ **MAKING JUDGMENTS** What do you think Son Ca means when she says her mother and sister didn't know anything? (Sample answer: They did not know anything about the language and customs of their new country.)

Discussion Options

Personal Response Ask students whether they agree that Son Ca's family showed courage and to give examples from the selection.

⭐ **Connecting/Comparing** Ask students to compare how Son Ca's family survived with how Brian survives in *Hatchet*.

English Language Learners

Support Comprehension

Invite volunteers to share experiences in which they or someone they know had to show courage. Work with students to create a list of everyday situations that might require people to show courage.

Teacher Read Aloud **49T**

Background and Vocabulary

Key Concept: The Role of a Diplomat

Remind students that this theme is about individuals who show courage. Explain that they will now read a true story about a diplomat who must decide between saving lives and obeying government orders. Use "Album for a Hero" on Anthology pages 50–51 to build background and introduce key vocabulary.

- Have students read aloud "Album for a Hero."

- Discuss with students the Nazi persecution of Jewish people and other groups before and during World War II. Explain that some of these people fled to escape this persecution.

Vocabulary Preview

The Vocabulary Reader can be used to preteach or reinforce the key vocabulary.

Vocabulary Reader

HOUGHTON MIFFLIN
Vocabulary Readers
Fly Away, Children
By Lee S. Justice

Get Set to Read

Background and Vocabulary

Album for a Hero

PASSAGE TO FREEDOM
The Sugihara Story

Passage to Freedom

Genre **Nonfiction**

Key Vocabulary
diplomat
government
refugees
superiors
visas

Vocabulary Reader
Fly Away, Children
By Lee S. Justice

e • **Glossary**

During World War II, many people had to leave their countries and become **refugees** — people fleeing the dangers of war. One escape route was the small country of Lithuania, as you will see in the story *Passage to Freedom*. The narrator's father, Chiune Sugihara, could use his powerful job to move people from Lithuania to safety.

Sugihara was a **diplomat** — someone chosen to represent his or her **government** in another country. A diplomat carries out his or her **superiors'** orders.

Kaunas, Lithuania, is the small town where Sugihara and his family lived in 1940.

50

English Language Learners

Supporting Comprehension

Beginning/Preproduction Have students listen to the article. Then have them point out the diplomat and the refugees in the photographs. Ask, Which photograph shows the diplomat's family? Which photo shows the town where they lived?

Early Production and Speech Emergence Have students repeat the Key Vocabulary words after you. Use the photographs on page 51 to help students understand the meaning of *diplomat, refugees,* and *visas*. Ask, What is one decision you made yesterday? How would you ask permission to leave the classroom?

Intermediate and Advanced Fluency In small groups, have students discuss the information in the article. Ask, How did the diplomat, Mr. Sugihara, save so many lives?

Introducing Vocabulary

Chiune Sugihara (*above*) risked the lives of his wife, Yukiko, and his children (*pictured top, right*) to save the lives of thousands of Jews. He issued **visas** — official written permission to enter and travel in another country — to Jewish refugees from Poland. The refugees (*right*) would line the gates outside of Sugihara's home hoping for freedom.

This is the official stamp that was applied to each visa.

51

Key Vocabulary

These words support the Key Concept and appear in the selection.

decision a choice that involves judgment

diplomat one who is appointed to represent his or her government in its relations with other governments

government the body or organization that manages a nation

permission necessary approval to do something

refugees people who flee their homes in order to escape harm

superiors those who have higher rank and more authority

visas documents that give people permission to travel to a specific country

e • Glossary
e • WordGame

See Vocabulary notes on pages 52, 56, 58, and 62 for additional words to preview.

Transparency 1–10

The Job Interview

Ms. Franklin: Tell me, Miss Chew, why do you want to become a **diplomat**?

Miss Chew: I feel it would be an honor to be a representative of our **government** in another country.

Ms. Franklin: I see that you have worked for the federal government for six years. May I have your **permission** to contact your **superiors** to ask about your work?

Miss Chew: Yes, you may contact my former bosses. Now I have a question. In this job, would I have the chance to talk with **refugees** who want **visas**? I am very interested in helping people who are trying to escape wartime dangers.

Ms. Franklin: Yes, but you know you cannot grant permission to visit the United States to everyone who wants it.

Miss Chew: I know that government workers must follow the rules and laws of our country. But I think I can do that and still be very helpful to people.

Ms. Franklin: You have a good attitude, Miss Chew. I think you are a fine candidate for this job. But I will write to tell you of my **decision** soon.

TRANSPARENCY 1–10
TEACHER'S EDITION PAGE 51

ANNOTATED VERSION

COURAGE Passage to Freedom
Key Vocabulary

Practice Book page 31

Passage to Freedom
Key Vocabulary

Name _____

The Official Word

Read the word in each box below from *Passage to Freedom*. Then write a word from the list that is related in meaning. Use a dictionary if necessary.

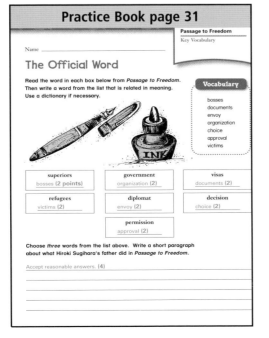

Vocabulary
bosses
documents
envoy
organization
choice
approval
victims

superiors	government	visas
bosses (2 points)	organization (2)	documents (2)

refugees	diplomat	decision
victims (2)	envoy (2)	choice (2)

permission
approval (2)

Choose *three* words from the list above. Write a short paragraph about what Hiroki Sugihara's father did in *Passage to Freedom*.

Accept reasonable answers. (4)

_____
_____
_____

Display Transparency 1–10.

- Model how to figure out the meaning of the word *diplomat* from the context.
- Ask students to use their decoding skills and sentence clues to figure out each remaining Key Vocabulary word. Have students explain how they figured out each word.
- Ask students to look for these words as they read and to use them as they discuss how the diplomat in the story helps save the refugees.

Practice/Homework Assign **Practice Book** page 31.

Introducing Vocabulary 51

COMPREHENSION STRATEGY
Evaluate

Teacher Modeling Explain that good readers evaluate, or form opinions, about what they read. Ask a student to read aloud the Strategy Focus and the first two paragraphs on page 53. Then model evaluating whether this is an effective way for the author to introduce Mr. Sugihara.

Think Aloud *The author starts the story with Mr. Sugihara giving money to a needy child. I think the author did a good job because this beginning shows us right away that Mr. Sugihara is a compassionate person.*

✓ **Test Prep** Tell students that the Evaluate strategy will help them on tests. Remind them to ask themselves, What do I like about this passage? Why?

COMPREHENSION SKILL
Making Judgments

Introduce the Graphic Organizer. Tell students that a Judgments Chart will help them make judgments. Explain that as they read, students will complete **Practice Book** page 32.

- Display **Transparency 1–11.** Have students reread Anthology page 53.
- Fill in the first row. Remind students to fill in the chart as they read.

Vocabulary

diplomat one who is appointed to represent his or her government in its relations with other governments

Selection 2

PASSAGE TO FREEDOM
The Sugihara Story

Written by KEN MOCHIZUKI
Illustrated by DOM LEE
Afterword by HIROKI SUGIHARA

Strategy Focus

Hiroki Sugihara and his family face a difficult problem involving thousands of lives. As you read, **evaluate** how well you think the author captures the difficulty of the family's decision.

52

Transparency 1–11

Judgments Chart

	Facts from the Selection	Own Values and Experiences	Judgment
What kind of person is Mr. Sugihara?	He sees a sad, needy child in a store who doesn't have enough money to buy what he wants, and he gives the child some money.	I think people should do what they can to help those in need.	Mr. Sugihara has done a good thing and has shown himself to be a compassionate person.
Is Mr. Sugihara's decision right or wrong?	First Mr. Sugihara says he will only write a few visas. After talking with the refugees, although his government refuses permission, he says he will issue visas to everyone. When his wife offers to help, he writes the visas alone for safety's sake.	I think a person should do what he or she knows to be right, but not involve others in the process.	Mr. Sugihara's values are excellent. He decides to give the refugees visas and not to listen to his government.
What kind of a person is Hiroki's mother?	Hiroki's mother says they must think about the people outside before themselves. She massages her husband's arm; she encourages him when he is too tired to write.	I think that to be unselfish, you have to think of others in big and small ways.	Hiroki's mother is a good person because she puts the well-being of others ahead of her own.

TRANSPARENCY 1–11
TEACHER'S EDITION PAGES 52 AND 71A

COURAGE *Passage to Freedom*
Graphic Organizer Judgments Chart

ANNOTATED VERSION

Practice Book page 32

Name _____

Passage to Freedom
Graphic Organizer
Judgments Chart

Judgments Chart

	Facts from the Selection	Own Values and Experiences	Judgment
What kind of person is Mr. Sugihara?	He sees a sad, needy child in a store who doesn't have enough money to buy what he wants, and he gives the child some money. (2 points)	I think people should do what they can to help those in need. (2)	Mr. Sugihara has done a good thing and has shown himself to be a compassionate person. (2)
Is Mr. Sugihara's decision right or wrong?	First Mr. Sugihara says he will only write a few visas. After talking with the refugees, although his goverment refuses permission, he says he will issue visas to everyone. When his wife offers to help, he writes the visas alone for safety's sake. (2)	I think a person should do what he or she knows to be right, but not involve others in the process. (2)	Mr. Sugihara's values are excellent. He decides to give the refugees visas and not to listen to his government. (2)
What kind of a person is Hiroki's mother?	Hiroki's mother says they must think about the people outside before themselves. She massages her husband's arm; she encourages him when he is too tired to write. (2)	I think that to be unselfish, you have to think of others in big and small ways. (2)	Hiroki's mother is a good person because she puts the well-being of others ahead of her own. (2)

T here is a saying that the eyes tell everything about a person.

At a store, my father saw a young Jewish boy who didn't have enough money to buy what he wanted. So my father gave the boy some of his. That boy looked into my father's eyes and, to thank him, invited my father to his home.

That is when my family and I went to a Hanukkah celebration for the first time. I was five years old.

In 1940, my father was a diplomat, representing the country of Japan. Our family lived in a small town in the small country called Lithuania. There was my father and mother, my Auntie Setsuko, my younger brother Chiaki, and my three-month-old baby brother, Haruki. My father worked in his office downstairs.

53

Extra Support/Intervention

Selection Preview

pages 53–55 Hiroki Sugihara lives with his family in Lithuania. His father is a Japanese diplomat stationed there. When war breaks out nearby, desperate refugees appear outside the Sugiharas' home.

pages 56–58 The refugees have come for visas so that they can escape the Nazis. Hiroki's father wants to help them, but his superiors deny his request to issue visas.

pages 59–61 The family agrees that Mr. Sugihara should help the refugees. How do you think their support makes Mr. Sugihara feel?

pages 62–64 Mr. Sugihara writes many visas. Then he is forced to leave Lithuania. When will he stop writing visas?

Purpose Setting

- Have students read to learn more about the role of a diplomat in a foreign country.

- Have students preview the selection, looking at the illustrations. Ask them to predict what problem Mr. Sugihara faces. Why does it involve thousands of lives?

- As they read, ask students to explain their reactions. What is their opinion about how the author tells this story?

- Encourage students to think about whether what Mr. Sugihara does is right. Remind them to support their judgments with details from the selection and their own experience.

- You may want to preview with students the Responding questions on Anthology page 66.

Journal ▶ Have students evaluate the story as they read, noting what they think the author did well and what he might have done differently.

STRATEGY REVIEW

Phonics/Decoding

Remind students to use the Phonics/Decoding Strategy as they read.

Modeling Write this sentence from *Passage to Freedom* on the board. Point to *absolutely*: *Still, my father wrote the visas until we absolutely had to move out of our home.*

Think Aloud *To figure out this word, I'll look for familiar word parts. I see the Vowel/Consonant/e pattern in the letters* lute. *I think this syllable is pronounced* loot. *I see the suffix* -ly, *which I know is pronounced* lee. *I'll try breaking the first two syllables between the two consonants:* AB-suh-LOOT-lee. *That word sounds right, and it makes sense in the sentence.*

CRITICAL THINKING
Guiding Comprehension

❶ WRITER'S CRAFT Why do you think the author used Hiroki's voice to tell this story? (Sample answers: to make the story seem more personal; to bring readers closer to the action)

❷ DRAWING CONCLUSIONS How would you describe Hiroki's life in Lithuania before war broke out? (Sample answers: happy, peaceful, normal)

❸ AUTHOR'S VIEWPOINT Why does the author change the mood of the selection when the war begins? (to illustrate the fear and uncertainty of the refugees)

❹ NOTING DETAILS What does Hiroki find mysterious about the people at the gate? (their heavy clothing on a warm day; Although far from home, they do not have suitcases.)

❶   In the mornings, birds sang in the trees. We played with girls and boys from the neighborhood at a huge park near our home. Houses and churches around us were hundreds of years old. In our room, Chiaki and I played with toy German soldiers, tanks, and planes. Little did we know that the real
❷ soldiers were coming our way.

    Then one early morning in late July, my life changed forever.
❸   My mother and Auntie Setsuko woke Chiaki and me up, telling us to get dressed quickly. My father ran upstairs from his office.

    "There are a lot of people outside," my mother said. "We don't know what is going to happen."

54

ASSIGNMENT CARD 7

The "Big Picture"

Writer's Craft

Sometimes an author describes a specific action or event in order to give clues about a general situation that has caused that event. For example, the author says, *My little brother Haruki cried often because we were running out of milk.* This tells you that the situation in the country at that time was making it difficult for the family to get food. Listed below are sentences from the selection. Read each one write down what the sentence tells you about the general situation behind it.

Page 56: Little did we know that the real soldiers were coming our way.

Page 65: Still, my father wrote the visas until we absolutely had to move out of our home.

Page 66: But he fell asleep as soon as he settled into his seat.

Theme 1: Courage

Teacher's Resource BLM page 50

Fluency Practice

Rereading for Fluency Have students choose a favorite part of the selection to reread to a partner, or suggest they read aloud from page 54. Encourage students to read expressively.

In the living room, my parents told my brother and me not to let anybody see us looking through the window. So, I parted the curtains a tiny bit. Outside, I saw hundreds of people crowded around the gate in front of our house.

The grown-ups shouted in Polish, a language I did not understand. Then I saw the children. They stared at our house through the iron bars of the gate. Some of them were my age. Like the grown-ups, their eyes were red from not having slept for days. They wore heavy winter coats — some wore more than one coat, even though it was warm outside. These children looked as though they had dressed in a hurry. But if they came from somewhere else, where were their suitcases? **4**

55

English Language Learners

Supporting Comprehension

Students unfamiliar with Jewish holidays may not know that Hanukkah, "The Festival of Lights," is celebrated in December. Jewish families gather together to eat special food, light candles, and exchange gifts. The celebration lasts eight days.

CRITICAL THINKING
Guiding Comprehension

⑤ WRITER'S CRAFT What does the author's use of Hiroki's point of view add to the story? (Knowing what Hiroki is seeing, hearing, and feeling brings readers closer to the events.)

⑥ TOPIC, MAIN IDEA, AND SUPPORTING DETAILS Why will visas help the refugees escape the Nazis? (Visas will allow them to travel to Japan.)

COMPREHENSION STRATEGY
Evaluate

Teacher/Student Modeling Help students to model using the Evaluate strategy to decide whether the author has done a good job. Use these prompts:

- What details show that Mr. Sugihara wanted to help the refugees?
- What details show that he didn't want to disobey his superiors?
- Was he worried about his family?

Vocabulary

refugees people who flee their homes in order to escape harm

visas documents that give people permission to travel to a specific country

permission necessary approval to do something

government the body or organization that manages a nation

decision a choice that involves judgment

"What do they want?" I asked my mother.

"They have come to ask for your father's help," she replied. "Unless we help, they may be killed or taken away by some bad men."

Some of the children held on tightly to the hands of their fathers, some clung to their mothers. One little girl sat on the ground, crying.

I felt like crying, too. "Father," I said, "please help them."

⑤ My father stood quietly next to me, but I knew he saw the children. Then some of the men in the crowd began climbing over the fence. Borislav and Gudje, two young men who worked for my father, tried to keep the crowd calm.

My father walked outside. Peering through the curtains, I saw him standing on the steps. Borislav translated what my father said: He asked the crowd to choose five people to come inside and talk.

My father met downstairs with the five men. My father could speak Japanese, Chinese, Russian, German, French, and English. At this meeting, everyone spoke Russian.

I couldn't help but stare out the window and watch the crowd, while downstairs, for two hours, my father listened to frightening stories. These people were refugees — people who ran away from their homes because, if they stayed, they would be killed. They were Jews from Poland, escaping from the Nazi soldiers who had taken over their country.

The five men had heard my father could give them visas — official written permission to travel through another country. The hundreds of Jewish refugees outside hoped to travel east through the Soviet Union and end up in Japan. Once **⑥** in Japan, they could go to another country. Was it true? the men asked. Could my father issue these visas? If he did not, the Nazis would soon catch up with them.

My father answered that he could issue a few, but not hundreds. To do that, he would have to ask for permission from his government in Japan.

That night, the crowd stayed outside our house. Exhausted from the day's excitement, I slept soundly. But it was one of the worst nights of my father's life. He had to make a decision. If he helped these people, would he put our family in danger? If the Nazis found out, what would they do?

But if he did not help these people, they could all die.

My mother listened to the bed squeak as my father tossed and turned all night.

The next day, my father said he was going to ask his government about the visas. My mother agreed it was the right thing to do. My father sent his message

56

Extra Support/Intervention

Strategy Modeling: Phonics/Decoding

Model the strategy for *frightening*.

I see the word fright. *It ends in the same three consonants as* light. *I think it is pronounced* fryt. *I also see the familiar endings* -en *and* -ing. *I'll try blending these sounds together:* FRYT-uhn-ihng. *That doesn't sound quite right. I'll try* FRYT-nihng. *That sounds right. It also makes sense in the sentence.*

frightening

FRYT-nihng

by cable. Gudje took my father's written message down to the telegraph office.

I watched the crowd as they waited for the Japanese government's reply. The five representatives came into our house several times that day to ask if an answer had been received. Any time the gate opened, the crowd tried to charge inside.

Finally, the answer came from the Japanese government. It was "no." My father could not issue that many visas to Japan. For the next two days, he thought about what to do.

Hundreds more Jewish refugees joined the crowd. My father sent a second message to his government, and again the answer was "no." We still couldn't go outside. My little brother Haruki cried often because we were running out of milk.

57

Extra Support/Intervention

Strategy Modeling: Evaluate

Use this example to model the strategy.

On page 56, instead of having Hiroki say that his father could not get to sleep, the author has him say My mother listened to the bed squeak as my father tossed and turned all night. *That vivid description tells me how troubled Mr. Sugihara was. I think the author is doing a good job.*

Predicting Outcomes

Review

- Remind students that they can use story events and their own knowledge to predict what will happen to characters after the story is finished.

Practice

- Have partners predict what will happen to Mr. Sugihara after his family moves to Berlin.

- Have them list details from the selection that help them predict what may happen to him. They should complete a chart like the one below. (Sample answers are shown.)

Details	Predictions
helped Jewish refugees	may help other refugees
disobeyed his own government	may be punished by his own government
consulted with his family about issuing visas	may consult with his family about other big decisions

Apply

- Have students predict what will happen to Hiroki in Berlin. (may feel excited and nervous; may learn to speak German)

- Ask them to identify the details that helped make these predictions. Have them complete a chart like the one above.

Review Skill Trace	
Teach	p. 115A
Reteach	p. R14
▶ Review	p. 57; Theme 2, p. 175; Theme 3, p. 281

CRITICAL THINKING
Guiding Comprehension

7 **MAKING INFERENCES** Why do you think Mr. Sugihara takes time to explain the refugees' situation to his son? (He wants Hiroki to understand the importance of helping them.)

8 **CAUSE AND EFFECT** What will happen to the refugees if Mr. Sugihara does not help them? (They will probably be captured by the Nazis and may be killed.)

I grew tired of staying indoors. I asked my father constantly, "Why are these people here? What do they want? Why do they have to be here? Who are they?"

My father always took the time to explain everything to me. He said the refugees needed his help, that they needed permission from him to go to another part of the world where they would be safe.

"I cannot help these people yet," he calmly told me. "But when the time comes, I will help them all that I can."

My father cabled his superiors yet a third time, and I knew the answer by the look in his eyes. That night, he said to my mother, "I have to do something. I may have to disobey my government, but if I don't, I will be disobeying God."

The next morning, he brought the family together and asked what he should do. This was the first time he ever asked all of us to help him with anything.

58

Vocabulary

superiors those who have higher rank and more authority

disobey to not do what one is told to do

patiently in a way that shows a willingness to wait a long time without becoming irritated

embraced hugged

Extra Support/Intervention

REACHING ALL LEARNERS

Review (pages 53–58)

Before students who need Extra Support join the whole class for Stop and Think, have them

- review their predictions/purpose
- take turns modeling Evaluate and other strategies they used
- add to **Transparency 1–11**
- check and revise their Judgments Chart on **Practice Book** page 32, and use it to summarize

My mother and Auntie Setsuko had already made up their minds. They said we had to think about the people outside before we thought about ourselves. And that is what my parents had always told me — that I must think as if I were in someone else's place. If I were one of those children out there, what would I want someone to do for me?

I said to my father, "If we don't help them, won't they die?"

With the entire family in agreement, I could tell a huge weight was lifted off my father's shoulders. His voice was firm as he told us, "I will start helping these people."

Outside, the crowd went quiet as my father spoke, with Borislav translating.

"I will issue visas to each and every one of you to the last. So, please wait patiently."

The crowd stood frozen for a second. Then the refugees burst into cheers. Grown-ups embraced each other, and some reached to the sky. Fathers and mothers hugged their children. I was especially glad for the children.

8

59

ASSIGNMENT CARD 6

Literature Discussion

Discuss the following questions and questions of your own with a group of your classmates:

- What traits do you think a diplomat needs? Which of these has Chiune Sugihara demonstrated?

- Do you think Chiune Sugihara has done the right thing so far? Why or why not?

- What do you think Mr. Sugihara will do now? Why?

- How would you feel if you were in Hiroki Sugihara's place? Why?

Theme 1: Courage

Stop and Think

Critical Thinking Questions

1. **MAKING INFERENCES** Why does Mr. Sugihara worry that he may put his family in danger by helping the refugees? (Nazis will be angry if they find out; they may hurt his family.)

2. **PROBLEM SOLVING** Why does Mr. Sugihara ask his family to help him decide what to do? (He wants to be sure of their support before doing something so risky.)

Strategies in Action

Have students discuss strategies, including Evaluate, that they used while reading.

Discussion Options

You may want to bring the entire class together to do one or more of the activities below.

- **Review Predictions/Purpose** Encourage students to discuss their opinions and judgments about what Mr. Sugihara does.

- **Share Group Discussions** Have students share their literature discussions.

- **Summarize** Ask students to use their Judgments Charts to help them summarize the selection so far.

Monitoring Student Progress

If . . .	Then . . .
students have successfully completed the Extra Support activities on page 58,	have them read the rest of the selection cooperatively or independently.

Reading the Selection 59

CRITICAL THINKING
Guiding Comprehension

9 TEXT ORGANIZATION Why do you think the author and the publisher decided to include a picture but no words on these pages? (to emphasize how happy the people were to find out that they would all be given visas and the chance to stay alive)

10 MAKING INFERENCES How do you think the Sugihara family felt at this moment? (proud that they had made the right decision; happy for the refugees; worried about what might happen when the Nazis arrive)

COMPREHENSION STRATEGY
Evaluate

Student Modeling Have students model using the Evaluate strategy to decide how well the author explains why Mr. Sugihara decided to help the refugees. Offer these prompts if students need help.

- What does Mr. Sugihara's family say when he asks them to help him make this decision?

- What is Mr. Sugihara's reaction to his family's decision? What details show his reaction?

- What details does the author include to show that this was a difficult decision?

60

ASSIGNMENT CARD 8
Illustration Interpretations

Visual Literacy

In a selection that tells about actual events, such as *Passage to Freedom*, the illustrator usually tries to represent these events realistically. Look at the illustrations in *Passage to Freedom* with a partner and discuss what the illustrator has shown in each. Then write a caption for each illustration, explaining what it shows. Use as few words as you can. (You can use the photograph captions in Get Set to Read, pages 50-51, as models.)

Theme 1: Courage

Teacher's Resource BLM page 50

61

Fact and Opinion

Review

- An opinion tells what someone thinks or how someone feels.
- A fact can be proven.

Practice

- Have students read the second and third sentences on page 59.
- Ask, Is the author describing a fact or opinion? Why? (opinion, because his mother and aunt tell what they believe)
- Have students skim pages 56–59 and identify facts. (Sample answers: Sugihara cabled his government three times; government refused each request.)

Apply

- Have small groups identify facts and opinions in the selection.
- Have groups record facts and opinions in a chart like the one shown.

Facts	Opinions
Chioki and I played with the other children in our toy car. (page 62)	Then one early morning in late July, my life changed forever. (page 54)

Review Skill Trace	
Teach	Theme 2, p. 163A
Reteach	Theme 2, p. R8
▶ Review	p. 61

CRITICAL THINKING
Guiding Comprehension

11 MAKING JUDGMENTS In your opinion, how well does Mr. Sugihara fulfill his promise to the refugees? (very well; issues many more visas than he had promised)

12 NOTING DETAILS How do the other members of the Sugihara family help the refugees? (Hiroki's mother counts people waiting in line, massages her husband's tired arm, and encourages him to continue; Hiroki plays with the children.)

13 WRITER'S CRAFT Does the author do a good job of showing the feelings of family members during this period? Give examples to support your opinion. (Sample answer: yes, shows father is tired and worried—eyes red, arm sore; shows mother wants to help—massages arm, watches crowd)

My father opened the garage door and the crowd tried to rush in. To keep order, Borislav handed out cards with numbers. My father wrote out each visa by hand. After he finished each one, he looked into the eyes of the person receiving the visa and said, "Good luck."

Refugees camped out at our favorite park, waiting to see my father. I was finally able to go outside.

Chiaki and I played with the other children in our toy car. They pushed as we rode, and they rode as we pushed. We chased each other around the big trees. We did not speak the same language, but that didn't stop us.

11 For about a month, there was always a line leading to the garage. Every day, from early in the morning till late at night, my father tried to write three hundred visas. He watered down the ink to make it last. Gudje and a young Jewish man helped out by stamping my father's name on the visas.

12 My mother offered to help write the visas, but my father insisted he be the only one, so no one else could get into trouble. So my mother watched the crowd and told my father how many were still in line.

One day, my father pressed down so hard on his fountain pen, the tip broke off. During that month, I only saw him late at night. His eyes were always red and he could hardly talk. While he slept, my mother massaged his arm, stiff and cramped from writing all day.

62

Extra Support/Intervention

Strategy Modeling: Evaluate

Use this example to model the strategy.

On page 62, the author uses the phrase by hand *to emphasize that Mr. Sugihara writes each visa carefully. He also describes how Mr. Sugihara looks into the eyes of each person and wishes him or her well. These details help me understand why Mr. Sugihara is a good diplomat. I think the author describes him very effectively.*

Vocabulary

reassigned ordered out of one job or position and into another

Soon my father grew so tired, he wanted to quit writing the visas. But my mother encouraged him to continue. "Many people are still waiting," she said. "Let's issue some more visas and save as many lives as we can."

While the Germans approached from the west, the Soviets came from the east and took over Lithuania. They ordered my father to leave. So did the Japanese government, which reassigned him to Germany. Still, my father wrote the visas until we absolutely had to move out of our home. We stayed at a hotel for two days, where my father still wrote visas for the many refugees who followed him there.

Then it was time to leave Lithuania. Refugees who had slept at the train station crowded around my father. Some refugee men surrounded my father to protect him. He now just issued permission papers — blank pieces of paper with his signature.

As the train pulled away, refugees ran alongside. My father still handed permission papers out the window. As the train picked up speed, he threw

63

13

English Language Learners

Supporting Comprehension

Reread the line on page 62: *We did not speak the same language, but that didn't stop us.* Ask students what this line means to them. Also ask them to describe activities or situations they are familiar with in which language isn't important, such as a soccer game at the park.

Making Judgments

Teach

- Explain to students that they should use selection details as well as their own opinions to make judgments about whether something is right or wrong.

- Remind students that they need to have evidence that supports their judgments.

Practice

- Have a volunteer read aloud from the second paragraph on page 63 through the first full paragraph on page 64. Ask, Did Mr. Sugihara do the right thing when he kept writing visas even after he was reassigned?

- Have students support their judgments. They should list selection details as well as their own opinions.

Apply

- Ask, Should Mr. Sugihara have disobeyed his government?

- Have students discuss what else they think Mr. Sugihara should have done in that situation. (Sample answers: travel to Japan to talk to his bosses; seek other ways to save the refugees)

- Have students share their judgments with the class. Encourage them to support their judgments with details from the selection.

Target Skill Trace	
Teach	p. 49S, p. 52, p. 63; p. 71A
Reteach	p. R10
Review	pp. M32–M33; Theme 2, p. 149; Theme 3, p. 305; Theme 5, p. 465

Guiding Comprehension

14 **WRITER'S CRAFT** Why do you think the author includes the refugees' words as he describes the Sugiharas' departure? (to show how much the refugees appreciated what Mr. Sugihara did; to show that Mr. Sugihara heard their appreciation)

15 **PREDICTING OUTCOMES** Do you think Mr. Sugihara was punished for issuing the visas? What makes you think this? (Sample answers: yes, because his superiors would have punished him for disobeying; no, because the author would have included this fact)

14 them out to waiting hands. The people in the front of the crowd looked into my father's eyes and cried, "We will never forget you! We will see you again!"

I gazed out the train window, watching Lithuania and the crowd of refugees fade away. I wondered if we would ever see them again.

"Where are we going?" I asked my father.

"We are going to Berlin," he replied.

Chiaki and I became very excited about going to the big city. I had so many questions for my father. But he fell asleep as soon as he settled into his seat. My mother and Auntie Setsuko looked really tired, too.

Back then, I did not fully understand what the three of them had done, or why it was so important.

15 I do now.

64

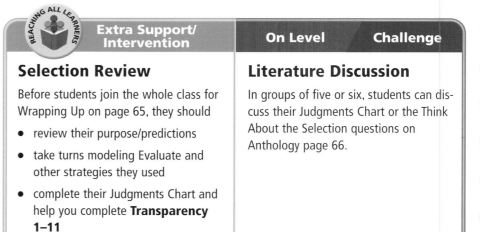

Extra Support/ Intervention

Selection Review

Before students join the whole class for Wrapping Up on page 65, they should

- review their purpose/predictions

- take turns modeling Evaluate and other strategies they used

- complete their Judgments Chart and help you complete **Transparency 1–11**

- summarize the whole selection

On Level **Challenge**

Literature Discussion

In groups of five or six, students can discuss their Judgments Chart or the Think About the Selection questions on Anthology page 66.

READ & COMPREHEND

ABOUT THE AUTHOR

Ken Mochizuki

Hometown: Seattle, Washington

Roots: Grandparents born in Japan

How he got the story: By spending hours on the phone as Sugihara's son recalled what happened 50 years ago

What he thinks of Sugihara: "I consider Chiune Sugihara as one of my personal heroes."

Mochizuki's motto: Believe in what you can do, not in what someone says you can't.

ABOUT THE ILLUSTRATOR

Dom Lee

Roots: Born and raised in Seoul, Korea, but currently lives in Plainsboro, New Jersey

How he makes his art: First he puts handmade beeswax on paper, then scratches out images, and finally adds oil paint and colored pencil to complete the illustration.

Teamwork: Dom Lee and Ken Mochizuki have worked together on two previous children's books, *Baseball Saved Us* and *Heroes*.

 Internet

To find out more about Ken Mochizuki and Dom Lee, visit Education Place. **www.eduplace.com/kids**

Practice Book page 33

Passage to Freedom
Comprehension Check

Name _____

Award for a Hero

Complete the fact sheet below about Chiune Sugihara. Then on a separate sheet of paper design an award that honors Mr. Sugihara.

FACT SHEET

Who Chiune Sugihara was:	the Japanese consul to Lithuania (**1 point**)
Where he was from:	Japan (1)
Where he was working at the beginning of World War II:	in a small town in Lithuania (1)
What his job was:	to represent the Japanese government in Lithuania (1)
Why people needed his help:	to give the refugees visas—written permission to travel east through another country (1)
What conflict he faced:	The Japanese government refused to allow Sugihara to issue visas to the refugees, but Sugihara knew the refugees would probably die if they didn't escape to the east. (1)
What decision he made:	to write visas for as many refugees as he could, and to go against the wishes of his government (1)
Why he is remembered:	He saved thousands of lives by writing the visas and had the courage to do the right thing. (1)

Wrapping Up

Critical Thinking Questions

1. **MAKING INFERENCES** Why do some of the refugees protect Mr. Sugihara as he gets on the train? (They are grateful for his help; they want to make sure the crowd does not hurt him.)

2. **STORY STRUCTURE** Is the setting of this story important? Why or why not? (yes, because the story describes a specific time and place in history)

Strategies in Action

Have students take turns modeling the Evaluate strategy and other strategies they found helpful.

Discussion Options

Bring the entire class together to do one or more of the activities below.

Review Predictions/Purpose Ask students to discuss the opinions and judgments they formed while reading.

Share Group Discussions Have students share their literature discussions.

Summarize Help students use their completed Judgments Chart to summarize the selection.

Comprehension Check

Use **Practice Book** page 33 to assess students' comprehension of the selection.

Monitoring Student Progress

If . . .	Then . . .
students score 6 or below on **Practice Book** page 33,	help them find places in the text that show Mr. Sugihara's heroism.

Reading the Selection **65**

Responding

Think About the Selection

Have students discuss or write their answers. Sample answers are provided; accept reasonable responses that are supported with evidence from the story.

1. DRAWING CONCLUSIONS If Mr. Sugihara wrote visas, he would be disobeying orders and possibly putting his family in danger. If he did not, the refugees would probably be killed.

2. MAKING JUDGMENTS yes, because the boy was needy and it wasn't much money; no, because people should earn the money they get

3. MAKING INFERENCES The narrator saw that they were sad and frightened, and he noticed that some of them were his same age.

4. NOTING DETAILS He listened carefully to what the refugees had to say and to what they wanted. He explained what he could and could not do. Then he requested permission from his superiors to issue visas.

5. CONNECTING TO PERSONAL EXPERIENCES Answers will vary.

6. CONNECTING TO PERSONAL EXPERIENCES Many games that children play do not require much talking. People can communicate with signs and gestures when they don't speak the same language.

7. Connecting/Comparing Brian is courageous because he overcomes his fear and survives. Mr. Sugihara is courageous because he puts others' safety ahead of his own. Both show courage and choose to do the right things.

Responding
Responding

Think About the Selection

1. Why do you think Sugihara's decision to write visas for the refugees was a difficult one? Explain.

2. Do you think Sugihara did the right thing, giving his money to the boy at the store? Why or why not?

3. Why did the narrator feel especially sorry for the children of the refugees?

4. Give examples of how Sugihara used his diplomatic skills in talking to the refugees and communicating with his government.

5. At that time, the narrator didn't fully understand the importance of what his parents had done. Give an example of an event or person in your life that you understand better now than when you were younger.

6. Why didn't the Sugihara children and the children of the refugees need to speak the same language to play with each other?

7. **Connecting/Comparing** Compare Brian's courage in *Hatchet* with Sugihara's courage. How was each courageous in his own way? Explain.

Expressing

Write from Another Point of View

Think of how a Polish refugee may have felt standing outside the Sugiharas' house. Write a few paragraphs expressing the refugee's feelings both while awaiting Mr. Sugihara's decision and after learning that he would grant the visas.

Tips

- To write from the point of view of a refugee, think about what it would be like to *be* that refugee.
- Reread the selection to find clues about how the refugees felt.

66

English Language Learners

Supporting Comprehension

Beginning/Preproduction Go back through the selection with students. Pause at the illustrations to review Key Vocabulary.

Early Production and Speech Emergence Have partners draw pictures of story events and use them to discuss the selection.

Intermediate and Advanced Fluency Have mixed groups reread the last three lines of the selection and summarize the significance of what Mr. Sugihara did. Help them with vocabulary as needed.

Social Studies

Measure Distances

Using a world map, trace the route that the refugees followed as they escaped their homeland. Use the scale on the map to measure the distances between major locations. Make a chart listing each of these distances and the total distance.

Bonus Figure out how the total distance the refugees traveled compares to the distance from the west coast to the east coast of the United States.

Art

Exploring Color

Dom Lee uses a brown color palette in his illustrations for *Passage to Freedom*. This monochromatic color scheme — using different shades of one color — suggests a certain mood. Choose a color scheme that suggests a certain mood for you. Draw, paint, or describe a scene, using shades of those colors to create that mood.

Internet

E-mail a Friend

What did you find most interesting about *Passage to Freedom*? Is there anything you wondered about? Send an e-mail to a friend. Tell your friend all about the story.

67

Additional Responses

Personal Response Invite students to share their personal responses to the selection.

Journal ▸ Ask students to write in their journals about their reactions to *Passage to Freedom*.

Selection Connections Remind students to add to **Practice Book** page 9.

Extra Support/ Intervention

Brainstorming

- Have students study the illustrations on page 57 and pages 60–61.
- Ask them to brainstorm words and phrases that describe the refugees' feelings both before and after learning that Mr. Sugihara would grant them visas.

Practice Book page 9

Launching the Theme
Selection Connections

Name _____

Courage

The characters in this theme show courage in dangerous or challenging situations. After reading each selection, complete the chart below to show what you learned about the characters.

	Hatchet	Passage to Freedom
What challenge does the main character face?	Brian has to survive in the wilderness and build a fire with only a hatchet as a tool. (2.5 points)	Mr. Sugihara has to decide whether to obey his superiors or help save the lives of hundreds of refugees. (2.5)
Where does the challenge take place?	in the wilderness, in modern times (2.5)	in Lithuania, during World War II (2.5)
In what ways does the main character show courage?	Brian learns to cope with being alone in the wilderness. He learns to build a fire from sparks. (2.5)	Mr. Sugihara disobeys his superiors and puts his own job at risk to help the refugees. (2.5)
What do you think the character learns from his or her experience?	Brian learns that he can make a fire from wood scrapings and a spark, and that he can handle difficult situations by himself. (2.5)	Mr. Sugihara learns that sometimes one must follow one's conscience instead of obeying orders. (2.5)

End-of-Selection Assessment

Selection Test Use the test on page 111 in the **Teacher's Resource Blackline Masters** to assess selection comprehension and vocabulary.

Student Self-Assessment Have students assess their reading with additional questions such as these.

- What parts of the selection were easy for me? Why?
- What strategies helped me understand the selection?
- What new words or expressions did I learn?
- Would I like to read more stories about courage of this kind?

Responding 67

Primary Sources Link

Skill: How to Read Primary Sources

- **Introduce** "A Mother's Courage" by Tammy Zambo.

- **Explain** that the author interviewed a woman who hid from the Nazis during World War II. Read the introduction aloud. Review any unfamiliar place names and note the dates.

- **Discuss** the Skill Lesson on page 68. Tell students that primary sources can help them understand what it felt like to be alive at a certain time or under specific conditions.

- **Model** reading the first question and Monique's answer on page 69. Tell students that Monique's story will show them what it was like to be a child in this situation.

- **Set a purpose** for reading. Have students use the title, map, photographs, and captions to form questions about the link. Suggest that they search for answers to these questions as they read. Remind them to use the Evaluate strategy to form an opinion about how effectively Monique Goodrich describes her experiences.

Vocabulary

authorities elected or appointed officials

pantry room near a kitchen used to store food

courtyard a paved space between homes or other buildings; sometimes the buildings themselves as well

---

Primary Sources

Link

Genre

Primary Sources

Skill: How to Read Primary Sources

A primary source is a document or firsthand account from a period of history.

❶ First read the **title** and **introduction**. Ask yourself:

What event does this passage describe?

What special insights might this source offer?

What can I learn from this source?

❷ Look for information that only a person who lived through the event could know about.

❸ Pay special attention to **details**.

A Mother's
Courage

by Tammy Zambo

*M*onique Goodrich (*above, right, with her brother, Michel, in 1942*), who lives in Bradford, Massachusetts, was born Monique Jackson in 1937 in Paris, France. When the Germans invaded Europe in World War II, many Jewish families tried to leave or hide. Some couples, like Monique's parents, Hélène and Charles Jackson, sent their children to live with non-Jewish families until it was safe to be reunited. In this interview, Monique tells what it was like to be a hidden child during the war.

68

English Language Learners

Supporting Comprehension

Before students read the interview, read the introduction aloud and make sure students understand who Monique Goodrich is and what happened to her. Then explain the interview format. Point out that the answers are in the first person and that the speaker is Monique Goodrich.

What do you remember before the war?

    For me there is no "before," because in my earliest recollection, I was in the Pyrenees Mountains and it was already the war.

    When the Germans invaded France in 1940 and were on their way to Paris, the authorities said, "Get out," to the women and children. My mother had a friend who suggested that we go into this little town in the Pyrenees called Saint-Laurent-de-Neste.

How did your parents know when they needed to hide you?

    Someone came to my parents and said that we children should be hidden. Also, the head of the police, Monsieur Couquebert, was my mother's friend, and a help to us. He had told my mother that if the authorities came for my father, he would tell her ahead of time. (At first, the authorities arrested Jewish men only.) We had this old house with a room like a pantry, with thick walls, and my father hid there if anybody came to the house. But I was very young, and I would point and call, "Daddy, Daddy, Daddy." It became very dangerous.

    So they hid me. First it was in the same courtyard, at a neighbor's, Madame Caseau. At night I would go to sleep at her house with their daughter, Renée, who was eighteen or nineteen.

    Then my mother took me to stay with a sister of Madame Caseau who had a farm in a place called Labastide. People would come to Labastide by bicycle, but the road was so steep they couldn't take the bicycles down to the town, so they would leave them at our place.

Were you ever in danger there?

    By then, the Germans were all over France. They would come down the steep hill and park their bicycles, and I would get very scared. I lumped the Germans and the police in the same category, and I would sit by the fireplace on a stool and just shake.

    After a while, my mother was told that she should hide us under another name and in a different area where she wouldn't know where

Monsieur Couquebert, pictured with (clockwise, from upper right) his wife and two daughters, as well as Michel, Monique, and Monique's mother.

Extra Support/Intervention

Sequence of Events

Some students may benefit from listing the events in chronological order. Suggest that students construct a sequence chart and add events to it as they read.

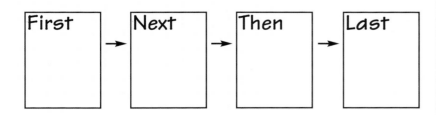

| First | → | Next | → | Then | → | Last |

Interview

Teach

- In an interview, a writer asks a person questions and records his or her answers.
- An interview includes many of the same elements as a nonfiction article.
- It includes information about real people, places, and things.
- It includes main ideas, supporting details, and opinions as well as facts.

Practice/Apply

- Ask, What information did you learn about real people other than Monique's family? (Sample answer: that a policeman, Monsieur Couquebert, helped the family)

- Ask, What is the main idea of this interview? (Sample answer: Children who were hidden during World War II experienced things like this.)

- Ask, What facts does Monique tell? What opinions does she state? (Sample answers: facts: Germans invaded France in 1940; in 1943 the Red Cross placed Monique and her brothers in a home; opinion: Her mother was brave.)

- Discuss how this interview is different from a newspaper article. (Sample answer: A news article wouldn't tell as much about Monique's experience.)

Vocabulary

subsisted stayed alive

ruckus loud, angry protest

internment camp wartime prison for civilians

---

we were. So in 1943, the Red Cross placed me, my brother, and my cousins Louis and Simon in a home. The homeowners didn't give us enough to eat. About the only thing we subsisted on was bread, and water and vinegar to drink. We were so hungry, we used to go in the fields and pick wild turnips.

One day my mother dreamt that we were starving, and she woke my father and said, "We've got to go get the children, because I'm afraid." So she went to the headquarters of the Red Cross, and she insisted that they tell her where we were. She raised such a ruckus that they told her, and she came and was absolutely horrified. I was glad to be with my parents again, but it was very scary getting back to Saint-Laurent-de-Neste, as it was not safe to be on the roads.

Was your family in danger after you reunited?

They did come for my father one night. Monsieur Couquebert sent his wife to tell my mother that my father should not be there that night. As head of police, he himself had to come and knock at the door with the authorities. He had to make believe, and he sent the men through the house. My father was in a barn across the street watching the whole thing. But after that the Jewish refugees in Saint-Laurent-de-Neste had to leave the Pyrenees.

Monique and her family were sheltered in this house in Saint-Laurent-de-Neste, France.

70

How did they leave?

The men decided to go to Spain first. For the children and wives, it was more difficult. Many refugees, including my mother's sister Raymonde, her husband, Jacques, and their son, Marcel, hired a guide who delivered them to the Nazis. When they got on the bridge at Chaum, France, the Germans were waiting for them. When they said, "Halt!" they saw my uncle move and they shot him and killed him. They took the others to Drancy, which was an internment camp in France, and from there they ended up in Auschwitz. My cousins Louis and Simon also perished there.

What was your life like after your father left?

A few times the Nazis came, and then it wasn't safe for my mother to be there. The townspeople would come and tell her, "Hélène, leave." So she put the two of us in a stroller — my brother was two and I was six — and started walking, and she took a little bit of food with her. She would stop at night and knock at a farm and ask if she could stay. They were afraid to let her in, so they told her she could stay in the barn, but she'd have to leave before dawn. She walked like that for about two days. Then Renée came and told her that it was safe to come back.

My mother had a tremendous amount of courage. I always say I owe my life to her more than once. She stood by what she thought she needed to do, and she saved our lives.

After the war ended in 1945, Monique's father was reunited with the family, and they all returned to Paris. In 1950, when Monique was thirteen, her family moved to the United States.

Monique's uncle (far left), Jacques Kadinski, was shot while fleeing France for Spain. His son, Marcel, and wife, Raymonde, died in Auschwitz. At right are Monique with her parents, Charles and Hélène Jackson.

71

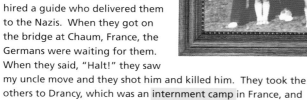

Challenge

World War II Research

Have students use electronic or print encyclopedias, other reference sources, or the Internet to find out more about World War II in Europe and how it affected various groups. Ask them to share the information with the class.

Wrapping Up

Critical Thinking Questions

Have students answer these questions about the interview. Students should support their answers with information from the text.

1. **CAUSE AND EFFECT** What helped Monique and her parents survive? (help from many sources, including friends, the Red Cross, and the local head of police)

2. **NOTING DETAILS** What did Monique's mother do to make sure that her children would survive? (Sample answer: sent the children to live with non-Jewish families under new names and in another part of France)

3. **SEQUENCE OF EVENTS** What happened to Monique's aunt Raymonde and cousin Marcel after her uncle Jacques was shot by the Nazis? (They were captured and sent to an internment camp.)

4. **MAKING INFERENCES** Why do you think Monique Goodrich speaks more of events than of personal feelings? (Sample answer: The feelings are too painful to mention.)

5. **Connecting/Comparing** How are the stories of the Sugihara family and Monique's family alike? (Both did courageous things to avert tragedy in World War II. The Sugiharas helped people like Monique's family.)

OBJECTIVES

- Discuss what it means to make a judgment.
- Make judgments about a character's actions based on story details and personal experience and values.
- Learn academic language: *judgment*.

Preview; Teach	p. 49S, p. 52, p. 63; p. 71A
Reteach	p. R10
Review	pp. M32–M33; Theme 2, p. 149; Theme 3, p. 305; Theme 5, p. 465
See	*Extra Support Handbook*, pp. 26–27; pp. 32–33

Transparency 1–11

Judgments Chart

	Facts from the Selection	Own Values and Experiences	Judgment
What kind of person is Mr. Sugihara?	He sees a sad, needy child in a store who doesn't have enough money to buy what he wants, and he gives the child some money.	I think people should do what they can to help those in need.	Mr. Sugihara has done a good thing and has shown himself to be a compassionate person.
Is Mr. Sugihara's decision right or wrong?	First Mr. Sugihara says he will only write a few visas. After talking with the refugees, although his government refuses permission, he says he will issue visas to everyone. When his wife offers to help, he writes the visas alone for safety's sake.	I think a person should do what he or she knows to be right, but not involve others in the process.	Mr. Sugihara's values are excellent. He decides to give the refugees visas and not to listen to his government.
What kind of a person is Hiroki's mother?	Hiroki's mother says they must think about the people outside before themselves. She massages her husband's arm; she encourages him when he is too tired to write.	I think that to be unselfish, you have to think of others in big and small ways.	Hiroki's mother is a good person because she puts the well-being of others ahead of her own.

TRANSPARENCY 1–11
TEACHER'S EDITION PAGES 52 AND 71A

Practice Book page 32

Name

Passage to Freedom
Graphic Organizer
Judgments Chart

Judgments Chart

	Facts from the Selection	Own Values and Experiences	Judgment
What kind of person is Mr. Sugihara?	He sees a sad, needy child in a store who doesn't have enough money to buy what he wants, and he gives the child some money. (2 points)	I think people should do what they can to help those in need. (2)	Mr. Sugihara has done a good thing and has shown himself to be a compassionate person. (2)
Is Mr. Sugihara's decision right or wrong?	First Mr. Sugihara says he will only write a few visas. After talking with the refugees, although his government refuses permission, he says he will issue visas to everyone. When his wife offers to help, he writes the visas alone for safety's sake. (2)	I think a person should do what he or she knows to be right, but not involve others in the process. (2)	Mr. Sugihara's values are excellent. He decides to give the refugees visas and not to listen to his government. (2)
What kind of a person is Hiroki's mother?	Hiroki's mother says they must think about the people outside before themselves. She massages her husband's arm; she encourages him when he is too tired to write. (2)	I think that to be unselfish, you have to think of others in big and small ways. (2)	Hiroki's mother is a good person because she puts the well-being of others ahead of her own. (2)

TARGET SKILL COMPREHENSION: Making Judgments

❶ Teach

Review making judgments in *Passage to Freedom*. Complete the Graphic Organizer on **Transparency 1–11** with students. (Sample answers are shown.) Have students refer to the selection and to **Practice Book** page 32. Discuss these points.

- Good judgments are based on the facts or details in a selection.
- Good judgments are based on a reader's values and experience.
- Different readers can form different judgments.

Model making a judgment about a character's actions. Tell students that they can frame, or focus on, a fact that will help them make a judgment about a character's actions. Have students reread paragraph 6 on page 56. Then think aloud.

Think Aloud
Mr. Sugihara faces the crowd and asks to speak to five people who can explain what they want. I can use this action, along with my own values, to make a judgment about Mr. Sugihara. I think he is a kind person because he wants to see if he can help these people. I also think he is calm and sensible because he has thought of a method for finding out what they want.

❷ Guided Practice

Have students make judgments about a character's actions. Have students reread "A Mother's Courage" on pages 68–71. Display the chart below. Complete the first column. Ask partners to complete the chart. (Sample answers are shown.)

What Kind of Person Was Monique's Mother?		
Her Action	Own Values and Experiences	Judgment
She moved the family to a distant small town.	You have to be smart in order to think ahead to avoid danger.	Monique's mother was smart.
She sent her children to live with other families.	Sending your children away is hard for a parent.	She was strong and courageous.
She spent days walking with the children in the countryside.	It takes determination to walk for so long with two small children.	She was a very determined person.

❸ Apply

Assign Practice Book pages 34–35. Also have students apply this skill as they read their **Leveled Readers** for this week. You may also select books from the Leveled Bibliography for this theme (pages 23E–23F).

Test Prep Discuss test questions that ask students to write their own answer. Explain that these questions may ask students to make judgments about a reading passage based on their own values and experiences. Emphasize that a sound judgment is one supported by details from the passage.

Leveled Readers and Leveled Practice

Students at all levels apply the comprehension skill as they read their Leveled Readers. See lessons on pages 71O–71R.

● BELOW LEVEL — Corrie's Secret
▲ ON LEVEL — Cesar Chavez · by Jessica Paulson
■ ABOVE LEVEL — The Story of Oskar Schindler · by Emma Ross
◆ LANGUAGE SUPPORT — Corrie's Important Decision

Reading Traits

As students develop the ability to make judgments, they are learning to "read beyond the lines" of a selection. This comprehension skill supports the reading trait **Critiquing for Evaluation.**

Practice Book page 34

Passage to Freedom
Comprehension Skill
Making Judgments

Name _____

Judge for Yourself

Read the passage. Then answer the questions on page 35.

A South African Hero

In 1918, Nelson Mandela was born into a royal African family in South Africa. He was raised to be a chief, but instead chose to become a lawyer. He hoped to help blacks win equal rights in South Africa. At the time, the country was ruled by a white minority that discriminated against blacks. This policy was later called *apartheid*.

In the 1940s, Mandela earned his law degree. He helped set up the first black law firm in South Africa. He also joined the African National Congress (ANC), a group that worked to end apartheid. Mandela soon became a top official in the ANC and a leader of nonviolent protests.

The government cracked down on the ANC, however, and responded to peaceful protests with violence. In 1960, Mandela decided to abandon nonviolence and support armed struggle against apartheid. "The government left us no other choice," he said. Arrested several times for his work, he was tried for treason in 1963. At his trial, Mandela declared, "I have cherished the ideal of a democratic and free society. . . . It is an ideal which I hope to live for and to achieve. But if needs be, it is an ideal for which I am prepared to die."

Mandela was sentenced to life in prison and spent the next twenty-seven years behind bars. The struggle for equal rights in South Africa continued, however, and people around the world called for an end to apartheid. The government offered to free Mandela in exchange for his cooperation, but he refused. Finally, in 1990, the government released him from prison. He later won the Nobel Peace Prize and became South Africa's first black president. As president, Mandela called for peace and harmony in South Africa and tried to ensure equal rights for all South Africans.

Practice Book page 35

Passage to Freedom
Comprehension Skill
Making Judgments

Name _____

Judge for Yourself *continued*

Answer these questions about the passage on page 34.

1. What was important to Nelson Mandela as a young man?
   He valued equal rights for blacks in South Africa. **(2 points)**

2. What facts from the passage reveal his values as a young man?
   He chose to become a lawyer to help blacks win equal rights. He became a top official in the ANC and worked to end apartheid. **(2)**

3. Circle three words you would use to describe Nelson Mandela. *Sample answers shown.*
   (selfless)   (compassionate)   uninspired
   powerless   alienated   (determined)

4. Write each word you circled below. Then tell why you made that judgment about Mandela's character. Use facts from the passage to support your judgment.

Word	Reasons for Judgment
selfless (1)	He was willing to go to prison and even to die for equal rights. (2)
compassionate (1)	He believed that every person should have equal rights and that apartheid should end. (2)
determined (1)	Even after 27 years in jail, he held to his beliefs. (2)

5. How have your own experiences and beliefs helped you make a judgment about Nelson Mandela's character and actions?
   Sample answer: I have seen other people sacrifice for their beliefs. This shows that a person is selfless and determined. (2)

Monitoring Student Progress

If . . .	Then . . .
students score 11 or below on **Practice Book** page 35,	use the Reteaching lesson on Teacher's Edition page R10.
students have successfully met the lesson objectives,	have them do the Challenge/Extension activities on Teacher's Edition page R11.

OBJECTIVES

- Read words that have two or more syllables.
- Use the Phonics/Decoding Strategy to decode longer words.
- Learn academic language: *consonant, syllable, short vowel, long vowel*

Target Skill Trace

Teach	p. 71C
Reteach	p. R18
Review	pp. M34–M35
See	*Handbook for English Language Learners,* p. 29; *Extra Support Handbook,* pp. 24–25; pp. 28–29

Practice Book page 36

Name _____

Sugihara Syllables

Write each underlined word on the line below. Add slashes between the syllables of each word. Then write another sentence using the word correctly.

1. My father was a Japanese diplomat working in Lithuania.
   dip/lo/mat (**1 point**) Example: I would like to become a diplomat for the United States and live abroad. (2)

2. Hundreds of refugees gathered outside our house.
   hun/dreds (1) Example: I have hundreds of sports cards in my collection. (2)

3. They needed visas to leave the country.
   vi/sas (1) Example: Visas allow people to move from one country to another. (2)

4. My father replied that he would help each one of the refugees.
   re/plied (1) Example: When my brother asked a favor, I replied yes. (2)

5. My life changed forever because of my father's action.
   for/ev/er (1) Example: Endangered species are gone forever. (2)

Monitoring Student Progress

If...	Then...
students score 11 or below on **Practice Book** page 36,	use the Reteaching lesson on Teacher's Edition page R18.

STRUCTURAL ANALYSIS/ VOCABULARY: Syllabication

❶ Teach

Discuss the VCCV syllable pattern. Explain that a syllable is a word part that has one sound. Write *He wrote visas from <u>morning</u> to night.*

- Write *V* under the *o* and the *i* of *morning.* Write *C* under the *r* and the *n.* Point to the VCCV pattern.

- Explain that many words with this pattern divide between the consonants. Tell students that the first syllable is closed, so the word begins with a short vowel sound: MOR-nihng.

- Explain that when two or more consonants blend to stand for a single sound, the consonants stay together: an-NOTH-er.

Discuss the VCV syllable pattern. Write *The <u>refugee</u> was upset.*

- Write *V* under the *e* and the *u* of *refugee.* Write *C* under the *f.* Point to the VCV pattern.

- Explain that to decode a word with this pattern, students should first try dividing it after the consonant and pronouncing the syllable with a short vowel sound: REHF-yoo-jee.

- If that doesn't sound like a familiar word, they should divide the word after the vowel and use a long vowel sound.

Model the Phonics/Decoding Strategy. Write *A young Jewish boy stared in the <u>window</u>.* Point to *window.* Write *V* under the *i* and the *o* and *C* under the *n* and the *d.* Model dividing this word.

Think Aloud *This word has the VCCV pattern. I know most words with this pattern divide between the two consonants. I can divide this word between the letters n and d. That makes the first syllable closed, so the vowel has a short sound: WIHN-doh. That sounds right, and it makes sense.*

❷ Guided Practice

Have students divide words into syllables. Display the words below. Have students identify and circle the syllables in each word. Ask partners to discuss their work.

father	refused	morning
diplomat	permission	during

❸ Apply

Assign Practice Book page 36.

PHONICS REVIEW: Long Vowels

OBJECTIVES
- Read words that have a long vowel sound.
- Use the Phonics/Decoding Strategy to decode longer words.

❶ Teach

Review long vowels. Explain the following.

- In most words, long vowel sounds are spelled with the Vowel/Consonant/e pattern (*bike, rode*) or with two vowels written together (*feat, eat*).

- In some words, the long vowel sound is spelled with the vowel alone (*fight, able, try*).

Model the Phonics/Decoding Strategy. Write *But if they came from somewhere else, where were their suitcases?* Then model how to decode *suitcases*.

Think Aloud *Are there long vowels in this word? I will try dividing it between the two consonants that come together,* t *and* c*. In the first syllable I see the vowels* ui *together. They must stand for the* /o͞o/ *sound, as in* soot*. In the next syllable I see the Vowel/Consonant/e pattern, so the vowel probably is long* a, kay*. The whole word is* SOOT-kay-suhz*. That makes sense.*

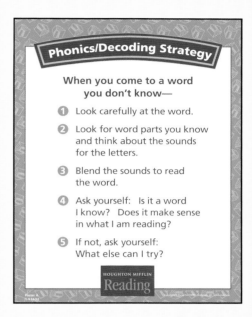

Phonics/Decoding Strategy

When you come to a word you don't know—

❶ Look carefully at the word.

❷ Look for word parts you know and think about the sounds for the letters.

❸ Blend the sounds to read the word.

❹ Ask yourself: Is it a word I know? Does it make sense in what I am reading?

❺ If not, ask yourself: What else can I try?

HOUGHTON MIFFLIN
Reading

❷ Guided Practice

Help students decode words with long vowels. Display the sentences below. Have partners circle the letter or letters that stand for the long vowel sound in each underlined word, pronounce the word, and check to see if it makes sense.

1. Some men began <u>climbing</u> over the fence.
2. They were <u>escaping</u> Nazi soldiers.
3. The entire family was in <u>agreement</u>.
4. They ran <u>alongside</u> the train.

❸ Apply

Have students decode words with long vowels. Ask students to find these words from *Passage to Freedom*, decode them, and discuss their meanings.

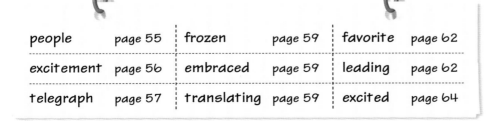

people	page 55	frozen	page 59	favorite	page 62
excitement	page 56	embraced	page 59	leading	page 62
telegraph	page 57	translating	page 59	excited	page 64

SPELLING: Long Vowels

OBJECTIVES

- Write Spelling Words with long vowel patterns.
- Learn academic language: *long vowel*, *silent* e.

SPELLING WORDS

Basic

theme	strain
quote	fade*
gaze*	league
pace	soak
preach	grease
strive	throne
trait	fume
mute	file
sleeve	toast
roam	brake

Review	Challenge
greet	microphone
boast	emphasize
brain	refugee*
code	pertain
squeak*	coax

*Forms of these words appear in the literature.

Extra Support/ Intervention

Basic Word List You may want to use only the left column of Basic Words with students who need extra support.

Challenge

Challenge Word Practice Ask students to write an equation like the following for each Challenge Word: cone – ne + ax = (coax) Have classmates solve the equations.

DAY 1 INSTRUCTION

Long Vowels

Pretest Use the Day 5 Test sentences.

Teach Write these column heads on the board: /ā/, /ē/, /ī/, /ō/, /ū/. Ask students to name the sound each symbol represents.

- Write *fade*, *theme*, *file*, *throne*, and *fume*, each under the symbol for its vowel sound. Have students repeat each word. Underline the long vowel and silent *e* in each word. Explain that a long vowel sound can be spelled with the Vowel/Consonant/*e* pattern.

- Repeat the process with *trait*, *preach*, *sleeve*, and *soak*, underlining *ai*, *ea*, *ee*, and *oa*. Explain that a long vowel sound can also be spelled with two vowels together.

- Say each remaining Basic Word and ask the class to identify the long vowel sound. Write the word in the appropriate column.

Practice/Homework Assign **Practice Book** page 281.

Practice Book page 281

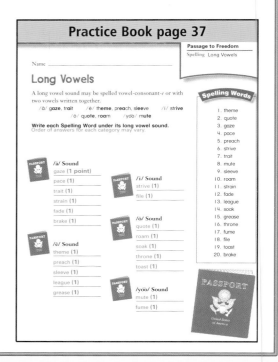

Take-Home Word List

DAY 2 REVIEW & PRACTICE

Reviewing the Principle

Go over the spelling patterns of long vowels with students.

Practice/Homework Assign **Practice Book** page 37.

Practice Book page 37

DAY 3 VOCABULARY

Word Clues

Write the Basic Words on the board.

- Dictate each clue below and tell students to write the Basic Word that fits each one.
  - a chair for a ruler (*throne*)
  - a synonym for wander (*roam*)
  - an arm cover (*sleeve*)
  - unable to speak (*mute*)
  - a device used to stop a wheel (*brake*)
  - an organizer for papers (*file*)
- Have students use each Basic Word from the board orally in a sentence.

Practice/Homework For spelling practice, assign **Practice Book** page 38.

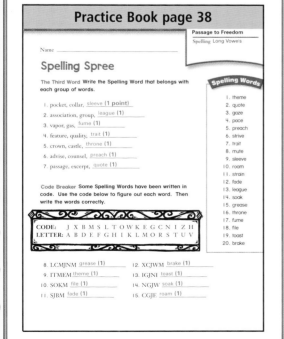

DAY 4 PROOFREADING

Game: Long Vowel Bingo

Have students form groups of 4: 3 players and 1 caller. Each player will need a game card divided into 4 rows of 4 squares each (a grid of 16 squares). In a corner of each square they should randomly write either *VC*e (for Vowel/Consonant/*e*) or *VV* (for two vowels together). Enough space should be left in each box for students to write an additional word.

- To play, the caller reads a Spelling Word, and players write it in an appropriate square, according to how the long vowel sound in the word is spelled.
- The winner is the first player to write 4 correctly spelled words in a row across, down, or diagonally.

Practice/Homework For proofreading and writing practice, assign **Practice Book** page 39.

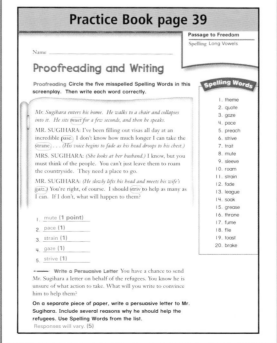

DAY 5 ASSESSMENT

Spelling Test

Say each underlined word, read the sentence, and then repeat the word. Have students write only the underlined word.

Basic Words

1. Greed was the **theme** of the story.
2. They each read a **quote** by Lincoln.
3. We like to **gaze** at paintings.
4. Amy walks at a slow **pace**.
5. Dad tries not to **preach** to me.
6. He will **strive** to do his best.
7. Friendliness is a **trait** I admire.
8. Jay was **mute** with fear.
9. She tore her **sleeve**.
10. Deer **roam** throughout the forest.
11. He had to **strain** to finish the race.
12. The colors are starting to **fade**.
13. Jill plays in a baseball **league**.
14. Please **soak** that dirty pan in hot water.
15. Try to clean the **grease** off the oven.
16. The king sat on his **throne**.
17. Do you smell the **fume** from the fireplace?
18. Her paper is in the **file**.
19. They had **toast** with jam for breakfast.
20. The **brake** on each wheel helps stop the bike.

Challenge Words

21. The **microphone** is too low.
22. These books **emphasize** writing skills.
23. The **refugee** fled across the border.
24. Does the question **pertain** to me?
25. We will **coax** him to join us.

Transparency 1–12

Dictionary Guide Words

Ⓐ **transitive / transport**

translate To express in another language.

disguise / disk jockey
Ⓑ **diffusion / dilemma**
directional / disagree
dinnertime / direction

sold / solo: sometime, soldiers, solemn, soft, solid

virus / vitamins: volcano, visual, violin, vital, visa

Ⓒ **land / lantern:** language, lane, large, laugh, ladder, lance

enclosure / endless: ending, encourage, enemy, emotional, endear

TRANSPARENCY 1–12
TEACHER'S EDITION PAGE 71G

COURAGE Passage to Freedom
Vocabulary Skill Dictionary Guide Words
ANNOTATED VERSION

Monitoring Student Progress

If . . .	Then . . .
students score 11 or below on **Practice Book** page 40,	have them work in small groups to correct the items they missed.

VOCABULARY: Dictionary Guide Words

❶ Teach

Introduce alphabetical order and guide words. Discuss the following points about using a dictionary.

- The words listed in a dictionary are called entry words.
- These words are arranged in alphabetical order.
- Guide words usually appear at the top of a dictionary page and help in locating entry words.

Display Transparency 1–12. Show only the first pair of guide words and the sample entry for *translate.* Ⓐ Emphasize these points.

- The first guide word, *transitive,* is the first entry on the page.
- The second guide word, *transport,* is the last entry on the page.
- *Translate* is one entry on the page that falls in alphabetical order between the entries for *transitive* and *transport.*

Model how to use guide words. Uncover the four pairs of guide words on the transparency. Ⓑ Model how to locate the entry word *diplomat.*

Think Aloud *The entry word* diplomat *must be on a page with guide words that start with the letters* di. *I see four pairs of guide words that start with* di, *so I have to look at the third letter in each word. Now I see that* diplomat *would come after* dinnertime *but before* direction. *So* diplomat *must be on the page that has this pair of guide words at the top.*

❷ Guided Practice

Give students practice using guide words. Show the bottom of the transparency. Ⓒ For each pair of guide words, ask students to identify and circle which of the listed entry words would appear on that page.

❸ Apply

Assign Practice Book page 40.

Practice Book page 40

Passage to Freedom
Vocabulary Skill Dictionary: Alphabetical Order and Guide Words

Name _____

Word-Order Sets

For each set of words, decide which two would be the guide words if all three words were on a dictionary page. On each "page," write the guide words in the correct order on the first line, and the other word on the line below.

office	ceiling	gown	refugees	emergency
offer	celery	government	refuse	embody
offside	celebration	gourmet	refrigerator	embraced

offer **(1 point)** / offside (1)
office (1)

ceiling (1) / celery (1)
celebration (1)

refrigerator (1) / refuse (1)
refugees (1)

gourmet (1) / gown (1)
government (1)

embody (1) / emergency (1)
embraced (1)

STUDY SKILL:
Using Reference Sources

OBJECTIVES

- Use print or electronic resources to locate information.
- Find cross-referenced information in an encyclopedia.

❶ Teach

Introduce print resources.

- An encyclopedia is a set of books containing articles about a variety of topics that are listed alphabetically.

- An atlas is a book of maps.

- A dictionary gives definitions and pronunciations of words that are listed alphabetically.

- A thesaurus gives synonyms and antonyms for words.

- An almanac contains up-to-date information about topics, such as the population of a state.

Introduce electronic resources.

- Electronic versions of dictionaries, encyclopedias, atlases, and thesauruses are widely available.

- Locate information on the Internet by using a search engine to do a keyword search. Type in a topic name and receive a list of related Web sites. Visit any of those sites by clicking on them.

Model how to find cross-referenced information.

- Show the *W* volume of an encyclopedia.

- Explain that you want to find out more about World War II. Turn to the pages containing the article about this topic. Point out cross listings, or related topics, at the end of the article.

- Demonstrate how to use the appropriate volumes to find the information about these related topics.

❷ Practice/Apply

Give students practice using reference sources.

- Have partners use sources to answer these questions below.

- Have students record the answers and the sources they used.

Where is Lithuania?

What does <u>consulate</u> mean?

What are two synonyms for <u>help</u>?

What does the Lithuanian flag look like?

GRAMMAR: Longer Sentences

OBJECTIVES

- Identify conjunctions and the words or sentences they join.
- Identify compound sentences.
- Proofread and correct sentences with grammar and spelling errors.
- Combine choppy sentences into compound sentences to improve writing.
- Learn academic language: *conjunctions, compound sentences.*

DAY 1 INSTRUCTION

Conjunctions

Teach Go over these rules:

– The words *and, or,* and *but* are conjunctions.

– A conjunction may be used to join words in a sentence.

– A conjunction may be used to join sentences.

– Use *and* to add information, *or* to give a choice, and *but* to show contrast.

- Display the sentences at the top of **Transparency 1–14.** Point out the conjunction in each sentence. Ask students whether each conjunction joins words or sentences.

- Have students find sentences with *and, or,* or *but* in *Passage to Freedom* and identify whether the conjunction joins words or sentences.

Daily Language Practice

Have students correct Sentences 1 and 2 on **Transparency 1–13.**

DAY 2 PRACTICE

Independent Work

Practice/Homework Assign **Practice Book** page 41.

Daily Language Practice

Have students correct Sentences 3 and 4 on **Transparency 1–13.**

Transparency 1–13
Daily Language Practice

COURAGE Passage to Freedom
Grammar Skill Conjunctions
Spelling Skill Long Vowels

ANNOTATED VERSION

Correct two sentences each day.

1. Grab that piece of burning toost
   Grab that piece of burning toast! (or toast.)

2. the theam of a book or film is sometimes hard to understand.
   The theme of a book or film is sometimes hard to understand.

3. Do you have a favorite quoot from a book.
   Do you have a favorite quote from a book?

4. My hiking pase is fast but I still can't keep up with my brother.
   My hiking pace is fast, but I still can't keep up with my brother.

5. Our baseball leeg includes ten teams from all over the city
   Our baseball league includes ten teams from all over the city.

6. Did you see the colorful patches on the sleve of my coat?
   Did you see the colorful patches on the sleeve of my coat?

7. my cat likes to rome around the neighborhood at night.
   My cat likes to roam around the neighborhood at night.

8. We can sit on the rocks and gaz at the setting sun
   We can sit on the rocks and gaze at the setting sun.

9. Did you see the royal throon on display at the museum.
   Did you see the royal throne on display at the museum?

10. Today I will soke in a pool or I will sit in a cool movie theater.
    Today I will soak in a pool, or I will sit in a cool movie theater.

TRANSPARENCY 1–13
TEACHER'S EDITION PAGE 711

Monitoring Student Progress

If . . .	Then . . .
students score 7 or below on **Practice Book** page 41 or 42,	use the Reteaching lessons on Teacher's Edition pages R26 and R27.

Transparency 1–14
Conjunctions

COURAGE Passage to Freedom
Grammar Skill Conjunctions

ANNOTATED VERSION

The refugees must flee or face death.
A possible escape route leads through the Soviet Union and Japan.
Chiune Sugihara can write out a few visas, but he cannot issue hundreds.

Sentence	Conjunction	Words or Sentences Joined
The refugees must flee or face death.	or	*Or* joins the words *must flee, face death.*
A possible escape route leads through the Soviet Union and Japan.	and	*And* joins the words *Soviet Union, Japan.*
Chiune Sugihara can write out a few visas, but he cannot issue hundreds.	but	*But* joins the sentences *Chiune Sugihara can write out a few visas. He cannot issue hundreds.*

TRANSPARENCY 1–14
TEACHER'S EDITION PAGE 711

Practice Book page 41

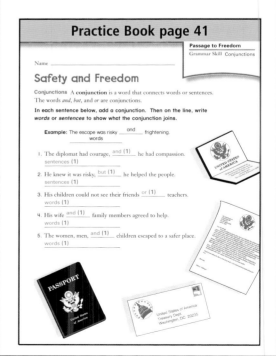

Passage to Freedom
Grammar Skill Conjunctions

Name _____

Safety and Freedom

Conjunctions A **conjunction** is a word that connects words or sentences. The words *and, but,* and *or* are conjunctions.

In each sentence below, add a conjunction. Then on the line, write words or sentences to show what the conjunction joins.

Example: The escape was risky ___and___ frightening.
                                                  words

1. The diplomat had courage, _and (1)_ he had compassion.
   sentences (1)

2. He knew it was risky, _but (1)_ he helped the people.
   sentences (1)

3. His children could not see their friends _or (1)_ teachers.
   words (1)

4. His wife _and (1)_ family members agreed to help.
   words (1)

5. The women, men, _and (1)_ children escaped to a safer place.
   words (1)

DAY 3 INSTRUCTION

Compound Sentences

Teach Go over these rules:

- If two sentences are related, they can be combined to make one compound sentence.

- Use a comma and the conjunction *and, but,* or *or* to combine the sentences.

- Display **Transparency 1–15.** Point out that the first sentence at the top is a compound sentence; it contains two complete sentences joined by *but.* Note that the next sentence is not a compound sentence; *and* does not join two sentences.

- Have students read the remaining two sentences and tell whether each is a compound sentence.

- Ask students to find additional compound sentences in *Hatchet* or *Passage to Freedom.*

Daily Language Practice
Have students correct Sentences 5 and 6 on **Transparency 1–13.**

Transparency 1–15

Compound Sentences

Mr. Sugihara has become very weary, but he writes visa after visa nonetheless. *compound sentence*

Mrs. Sugihara watches the crowd and informs her husband of the number of refugees in line.

The Germans are approaching Lithuania from the west, and the Russians are marching toward it from the east. *compound sentence*

The Sugiharas may be ordered out of the country or even sent to jail. *not a compound sentence*

Compound Sentences	Conjunction	Sentences Joined
Mr. Sugihara has become very weary, but he writes visa after visa nonetheless.	but	Mr. Sugihara has become very weary. / He writes visa after visa nonetheless.
The Germans are approaching Lithuania from the west, and the Russians are marching toward it from the east.	and	The Germans are approaching Lithuania from the west. / The Russians are marching toward it from the east.

TRANSPARENCY 1–15
TEACHER'S EDITION PAGE 71J

COURAGE / Passage to Freedom
Grammar Skill / Compound Sentences
ANNOTATED VERSION

DAY 4 PRACTICE

Independent Work

Practice/Homework Assign **Practice Book** page 42.

Daily Language Practice
Have students correct Sentences 7 and 8 on **Transparency 1–13.**

Practice Book page 42

Passage to Freedom
Grammar Skill Compound Sentences

Name _____

Should We Run, or Should We Hide?

Compound Sentences A **compound sentence** is two simple sentences joined by a comma and a conjunction (*and, but,* or *or*).

Add a comma followed by *and, but,* or *or* to combine the simple sentences below into compound sentences. Conjunctions used will vary.

Example: Our escape was dangerous. We made it safely.
Our escape was dangerous, but we made it safely.

1. World War II brought many hardships. People showed great courage.
World War II brought many hardships, but people showed great courage. **(2 points)**

2. Have you read any books about that war? Did you see any movies about it?
Have you read any books about that war, or did you see any movies about it? **(2)**

3. Bombs fell in many places. They did not fall in America.
Bombs fell in many places, but they did not fall in America. **(2)**

4. My great-grandfather was in the Navy. He showed me his uniform.
My great-grandfather was in the Navy, and he showed me his uniform. **(2)**

5. Our town built a war memorial in the park. My class went to see it.
Our town built a war memorial in the park, and my class went to see it. **(2)**

DAY 5 IMPROVING WRITING

Combining Sentences

Teach Tell students that they can make their writing more interesting by combining choppy sentences into compound sentences.

- Model this example:
  - Years ago, Hiroki Sugihara did not understand his father's actions. He does now.
  - *Improved:* Years ago, Hiroki Sugihara did not understand his father's actions, <u>but</u> he does now.

- Have students review their own writing to see if they can improve it by combining choppy sentences into compound sentences.

Practice/Homework Assign **Practice Book** page 43.

Daily Language Practice
Have students correct Sentences 9 and 10 on **Transparency 1–13.**

Practice Book page 43

Passage to Freedom
Grammar Skill Combining Sentences: Compound Sentences

Name _____

I Can Speak Italian, but I Can't Speak Japanese

Combining Sentences: Compound Sentences Sometimes combining short, choppy sentences into longer sentences makes your writing more interesting. Use a comma and *and, but,* or *or* to combine sentences.

Lee has written a letter to Aunt Lucy. Revise the letter by combining simple sentences to make compound sentences. Insert your marks on, above, and below the line, as shown in the example. The last sentence will not change. (1 point each)

, or
Tomorrow I'd like to go to the zoo. I'd like to visit Mel.

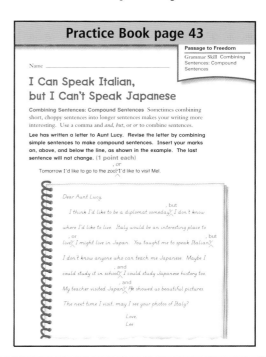

Dear Aunt Lucy,
, but
I think I'd like to be a diplomat someday. I don't know where I'd like to live. Italy would be an interesting place to
, or
live. I might live in Japan. You taught me to speak Italian, but
I don't know anyone who can teach me Japanese. Maybe I
, and
could study it in school. I could study Japanese history too.
, and
My teacher visited Japan. He showed us beautiful pictures.

The next time I visit, may I see your photos of Italy?
Love,
Lee

WRITING: Memo

OBJECTIVES

- Identify characteristics of a good memo.
- Write a memo.
- Capitalize and punctuate sentences correctly.

Writing Traits

Conventions As you teach the lesson on Day 3, emphasize the importance of conventions. Discuss these points.

- Using correct capitalization, punctuation, spelling, and usage make it easier for others to read what you have written.
- Paying attention to conventions is part of making your ideas clear.

DAY 1 ACTIVITY

Introducing the Format

Define memos.

- A memo is a message sent from one person to others in the same company, group, or organization.
- It is less formal, and usually less personal, than a letter.
- It does not include a greeting, closing, or signature.

Start students thinking about memos.

- Ask volunteers to suggest topics for school memos. List them on the board. (Possible answers: special event, project update, schedule change)
- Then have students name the people who might receive a memo about each topic.
- Discuss the usefulness of memos. (Everyone receives the same information. You have a written record.)

DAY 2 INSTRUCTION

Discussing the Model

Display Transparency 1–16. Ask:

- Who will read the memo? (students, teachers, and parents)
- Who wrote it? (Principal Knight)
- When was the memo written? (December 1, 2005)
- What is the subject of the memo? (December schedule of events)
- What four headings are used in this memo? (To; From; Date; Subject)
- How do these headings help the reader? (easy to find information quickly)
- What information is given in the body of the memo? (date, time, and place of three events; schedule for bake sales)
- What does Principal Knight ask people to do? (call if they want to bake or need information)

Display Transparency 1–17 and discuss the guidelines.

Have students write a memo.

- Assign **Practice Book** page 44.
- Provide support as needed.

Transparency 1–16

Writing a Memo

TRANSPARENCY 1-16
TEACHER'S EDITION PAGE 71K

COURAGE Passage to Freedom
Writing Skill Writing a Memo
ANNOTATED VERSION

Title		M e m o r a n d u m
Headings	**To:**	All students, teachers, and parents
	From:	Principal Knight
	Date:	December 1, 2005
	Subject:	December schedule of events
Body of Message (no greeting)		The schedule of evening holiday events during December is as follows:
		Monday, Dec. 4: choral concert
		Wednesday, Dec. 6: band concert
		Wednesday, Dec. 13: all-school holiday program
		All three events are free and begin at 7:00 P.M. in the cafeteria.
		The Parent-Teacher-Student group will host a bake sale beginning one hour before each event. The students are preparing their programs with great enthusiasm and look forward to presenting these enjoyable holiday programs. We urge you to support their efforts and get into the holiday spirit by attending these three events.
(request for action)		If you would like to bake something for one of these events, or need more information, call the school office at 555-1111.
(no closing or signature)		

Transparency 1–17

Guidelines for Writing a Memo

TRANSPARENCY 1-17
TEACHER'S EDITION PAGE 71K

COURAGE Passage to Freedom
Writing Skill Memo
ANNOTATED VERSION

- Use these four headings: *To, From, Date,* and *Subject.* Each heading should be followed by a colon.
- Write the following information after each heading.

> **To:** [the name of the person or group who will read the memo]
> **From:** [your name]
> **Date:** [the date when you wrote the memo]
> **Subject:** [a few words that describe what the body of your memo is about]

- Don't include a greeting or a signature.
- In the body of the memo, explain why you are writing the memo.
- Keep your memo brief but include all the important information.
- Write in clear, direct language.
- Use a formal, businesslike tone and correct grammar and punctuation.

Practice Book page 44

Passage to Freedom
Writing Skill Memo

Name _____

Writing a Memo

Chiune Sugihara was a diplomat in Lithuania in 1940. He probably wrote different forms of business communication, such as letters, reports, and memos. A memo is a brief, informal message that is sent from one person to others in the same company, group, or organization.

Imagine that you are Mr. Sugihara. Plan and organize a memo to your superiors in the Japanese government about the plight of the Jewish refugees from Poland. Follow these steps: (10 points)

1. Name the person or persons to whom you are writing the memo.
2. Tell who is writing the memo.
3. Write the date.
4. Identify the subject of the memo.
5. Write the body of the memo. Begin by stating your reason for writing. Use clear, direct language and a business-like tone. Be brief but include all the important information. If you want a response, end by asking a question or by requesting that a specific action be taken.

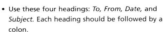

To: _____
From: _____
Date: _____
Subject: _____

_____
_____
_____

Copy your memo on a separate sheet of paper and exchange it with a classmate. Then, using the format above, write a response memo from the officials in the Japanese government to Chiune Sugihara in which you deny him permission to grant visas to the Polish refugees.

DAY 3 INSTRUCTION

Improving Writing: Capitalization and Punctuation

Review capitalization.

- All sentences begin with a capital letter.

- Proper names are the names of people and places. These also begin with a capital letter.

Review punctuation.

- All sentences end with an end mark.

- Use a period with a statement or a command.

- Use a question mark for a question and an exclamation point for an exclamation.

Display Transparency 1–18.

- Have different volunteers read aloud each paragraph of the memo.

- Have volunteers underline letters that need to be capitalized and write in any missing punctuation.

- See Writing Traits on page 71K.

Assign Practice Book page 45.

DAY 4 ACTIVITY

Writing Practice

Have partners plan a memo.

- Ask partners to list at least one activity they are planning with a group.

- They might list a class activity, such as a field trip or a class science experiment.

- They might list an activity that involves the entire school, such as an election, a bake sale, or a sporting event.

- Ask them to write thoughts they have about how this activity should be held.

- Have them decide who should receive the memo.

Have partners write a memo.

- Display **Transparency 1–17** again.

- Have partners write their memo.

DAY 5 ACTIVITY

Sharing Writing

Consider these options for sharing students' writing.

- Ask students to read a piece of their writing from the Author's Chair.

- Encourage students to mail or deliver their memos.

Portfolio Opportunity

Save students' memos as samples of their writing development.

Transparency 1–18

Capitalizing and Punctuating Sentences

To: Students of Room 6B
From: Mrs. Sanchez
Date: October 14, 2005
Subject: Visiting students

next week several groups of students will visit our classroom each group is from a different country what an exciting opportunity this is for us why are these students coming to our school the answer is simple since these students are experiencing our country, they wanted to experience an American school too

on Monday, five students from south korea will visit us in the morning the next day, three students from lithuania will visit during the afternoon on thursday, several students from france will spend the morning with us

I was excited to learn that our class will host these groups this is a wonderful opportunity to meet students from around the world don't you agree

Next week several groups of students will visit our classroom. Each group is from a different country. What an exciting opportunity this is for us! Why are these students coming to our school? The answer is simple. Since these students are experiencing our country, they wanted to experience an American school too.

On Monday, five students from South Korea will visit us in the morning. The next day, three students from Lithuania will visit during the afternoon. On Thursday, several students from France will spend the morning with us.

I was excited to learn that our class will host these groups. This is a wonderful opportunity to meet students from around the world! Don't you agree?

Practice Book page 45

Passage to Freedom
Writing Skill Improving Your Writing

Name _____

Capitalizing and Punctuating Sentences

To communicate effectively, a writer must write sentences correctly. When you write, remember to begin all sentences with a capital letter and to capitalize the names of people and places. Also, remember to end sentences with a period, a question mark, or an exclamation mark.

Proofread the following memo. Look for errors in capitalizing and punctuating sentences. Use these proofreading marks to add the necessary capital letters and end punctuation. (1 point each)

⊙ Add a period.   ∧ Add an exclamation mark.
≡ Make a capital letter.   ? Add a question mark.

To: Mrs. Masue Okimoto, Office Manager

From: Mr. Kenji Hamano

Date: August 28, 1940

Subject: Request for Office Supplies

my assistant boris Lavhas informed me that we need to restock some

office supplies will you kindly send the items listed below

1. two hundred visas and permission forms

2. one dozen fountain pens

3. two dozen bottles of ink

please ship these supplies to my office in lithuania immediately

thank you for your prompt action in this matter

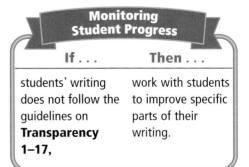

Monitoring Student Progress

If . . .	Then . . .
students' writing does not follow the guidelines on **Transparency 1–17,**	work with students to improve specific parts of their writing.

Language Center

LANGUAGE CENTER

VOCABULARY

Adverb Challenge

👥 Pairs	🕐 20 minutes
Objective	Identify adverbs that describe actions.
Materials	Activity Master 1–2, page R33

The author of *Passage to Freedom* uses the adverbs *quickly, tightly, quietly,* and *calmly* to describe how people act. Think of other adverbs that would help describe actions in dramatic parts of the story.

Work with a partner. Use Activity Master 1–2. Follow these steps:

- Ask questions about key parts of the story.
- Phrase your questions so that they begin with "How."
- Answer your questions in just one word, an adverb ending in -*ly*.
- Answer each question with as many adverbs as possible.

GRAMMAR

Summary with Conjunctions

🧍 Singles	🕐 20 minutes
Objective	Write compound sentences using conjunctions.

Write a summary of *Passage to Freedom*. When you have finished, reread your summary and identify any compound sentences you may have written and the conjunctions that you used to join them. Revise your summary so that it includes at least four compound sentences, each joined by a conjunction.

Guidelines for Compound Sentences
- A compound sentence is formed by joining together two complete sentences.
- The conjunctions <u>and</u>, <u>but</u>, and <u>or</u> can join complete sentences to make compound sentences.
- Use a comma when you join two complete sentences with a conjunction.

VOCABULARY

Vocabulary Groupings

👥 Pairs	🕐 20 minutes
Objective	Create groupings of vocabulary words.

Work with a partner to put the Key Vocabulary in *Passage to Freedom* into groups.

- List the Key Vocabulary words on a sheet of paper.
- Think of groupings that include at least two of the words.
- Think of as many groupings as you can, using each word at least once.

"Words That Name People"
diplomat
refugees
superiors

Consider copying and laminating these activities for use in centers.

LISTENING/SPEAKING

Speaking on the Telephone

Pairs	🕐 30 minutes
Objective	Role-play telephone conversations.

If Mr. Sugihara were living today, he might telephone his superiors instead of sending a cable. Read the guidelines for placing a phone call. Then, take turns with a partner role-playing a caller and a person answering. Role-play these situations:

- calling a store to find out its hours
- calling the dentist's office to check the time of an appointment
- taking a message from a person calling for an older family member
- answering a call that is a wrong number

Guidelines for Telephone Calling
- Start by saying "hello" and identifying yourself.
- Ask for the person you wish to speak to.
- Speak clearly and explain the purpose of your call.
- Listen carefully to the other person's response.
- If you are calling to get information, be ready with paper and pencil to write the information down.
- Say "thank you" before saying "goodbye."

PHONICS/SPELLING

Newspaper Report

👤 Singles	🕐 30 minutes
Objective	Write sentences using words with long vowels.

Imagine that you are a newspaper reporter assigned to cover Mr. Sugihara's story.

- Write a brief article that includes the major details of the selection.
- In the article, use each of the following long vowel sounds in different words: *a, e, i, o,* and *u.*
- Remember, the long vowel sounds can be spelled with either one or two vowels.
- Underline each long vowel sound in the article.

● BELOW LEVEL

Corrie's Secret

Summary *This is a true story about Corrie ten Boom and her family, who successfully saved Jews in Nazi-occupied Holland. Corrie takes great risks to hide Jews in her home, even building a secret hiding place. In 1944, Corrie is caught and arrested. In prison, she learns that the Jews hiding in her home have escaped to safety.*

Vocabulary

Introduce the Key Vocabulary and ask students to complete the BLM.

the underground secret association set up to resist or overthrow a government, *p. 11*

organization group or association, *p. 12*

labor camp place where people are confined and forced to do work against their will, *p. 22*

concentration camp place where people who have committed no crime are held against their will, *p. 22*

Building Background and Vocabulary

Explain as needed that in the spring of 1940, under the leadership of Nazi leader Adolf Hitler, German forces invaded and conquered Belgium, Luxembourg, and the Netherlands. The rights of all citizens were eroded and the rights of Jews were entirely stripped away during the Nazi occupation. Guide students through the text, using some of the vocabulary from the story.

Comprehension Skill: Making Judgments

Have students read the Strategy Focus on the book flap. Remind students to use the strategy and to make judgments about the characters as they read the book. (See the Leveled Readers Teacher's Guide for **Vocabulary and Comprehension Practice Masters.**)

Responding

Have partners discuss how to answer the questions on the inside back cover.

Think About the Selection Sample answers:

1. because of her religious beliefs
2. by providing hiding places for Jews during the Nazi occupation
3. Answers will vary.
4. Answers will vary.

Making Connections Answers will vary.

Building Fluency

Model Read aloud page 9, showing how the voice can indicate conflicting emotions like compassion and fear.

Practice Ask partners to read aloud the passage on page 4. Have them work on inserting two conflicting emotions into their reading.

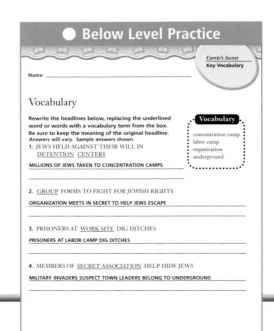

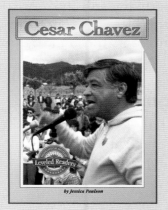

Cesar Chavez

Summary *Cesar Chavez's life was marked by hardships of migrant farm work. As an immigrant he also faced racial prejudice. Chavez organized migrant farm workers and fought to improve their working conditions.*

Vocabulary

Introduce the Key Vocabulary and ask students to complete the BLM.

optimistic having a positive attitude, *p. 3*

prosperous flourishing, *p. 4*

bankrupt unable to pay debts, *p. 4*

segregated separated from the rest of society, *p. 8*

chafed became annoyed, *p. 8*

superiors* those who have higher rank and more authority, *p. 8*

representing speaking for others, *p. 11*

boycotts protests against a product, *p. 12*

appalled filled with alarm or dismay, *p. 13*

*Forms of these words are Anthology Key Vocabulary words.

▲ ON LEVEL

Building Background and Vocabulary

Ask students what they know about labor unions, strikes, and boycotts. Lead a brief discussion about the purpose of labor unions and some of the ways they achieve their objectives. Guide students through the text, using some of the vocabulary from the story.

Comprehension Skill: Making Judgments

Have students read the Strategy Focus on the book flap. Remind students to use the strategy and to make judgments about the characters as they read the book. (See the Leveled Readers Teacher's Guide for **Vocabulary and Comprehension Practice Masters.**)

Responding

Have partners discuss how to answer the questions on the inside back cover.

Think About the Selection Sample answers:

1. Chavez's family had firsthand experience of the hardships migrant farm workers suffered.
2. He wanted to speak English so he could complain about unfair conditions.
3. It helped workers receive a fair contract and be paid better wages.
4. Answers will vary.

Making Connections Answers will vary.

Building Fluency

Model Read aloud page 4 to show how voice modification happens when spoken words appear in quotation marks.

Practice Ask students to find and read aloud other examples of quoted text, as on pages 7 and 12.

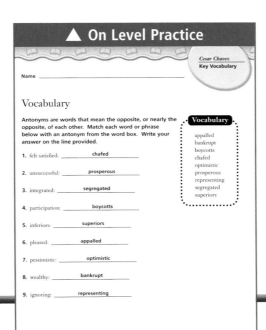

▲ On Level Practice

Cesar Chavez
Key Vocabulary

Name _____

Vocabulary

Antonyms are words that mean the opposite, or nearly the opposite, of each other. Match each word or phrase below with an antonym from the word box. Write your answer on the line provided.

Vocabulary
appalled
bankrupt
boycotts
chafed
optimistic
prosperous
representing
segregated
superiors

1. felt satisfied: _____ chafed
2. unsuccessful: _____ prosperous
3. integrated: _____ segregated
4. participation: _____ boycotts
5. inferiors: _____ superiors
6. pleased: _____ appalled
7. pessimistic: _____ optimistic
8. wealthy: _____ bankrupt
9. ignoring: _____ representing

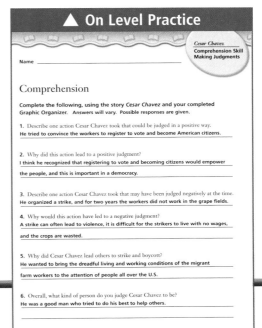

▲ On Level Practice

Cesar Chavez
Comprehension Skill
Making Judgments

Name _____

Comprehension

Complete the following, using the story *Cesar Chavez* and your completed Graphic Organizer. Answers will vary. Possible responses are given.

1. Describe one action Cesar Chavez took that could be judged in a positive way.
He tried to convince the workers to register to vote and become American citizens.

2. Why did this action lead to a positive judgment?
I think he recognized that registering to vote and becoming citizens would empower the people, and this is important in a democracy.

3. Describe one action Cesar Chavez took that may have been judged negatively at the time.
He organized a strike, and for two years the workers did not work in the grape fields.

4. Why would this action have led to a negative judgment?
A strike can often lead to violence, it is difficult for the strikers to live with no wages, and the crops are wasted.

5. Why did Cesar Chavez lead others to strike and boycott?
He wanted to bring the dreadful living and working conditions of the migrant farm workers to the attention of people all over the U.S.

6. Overall, what kind of person do you judge Cesar Chavez to be?
He was a good man who tried to do his best to help others.

The Story of Oskar Schindler

Summary *Oskar Schindler was a successful businessman in Nazi Germany. He deceived the Nazis by protecting Jews. By war's end, Schindler had lost his fortune but was a hero.*

Vocabulary

Introduce the Key Vocabulary and ask students to complete the BLM.

devout religious, *p. 4*

daredevil a reckless person, *p. 4*

scapegoat one who is blamed for others' mistakes, *p. 5*

confiscated taken without permission, *p. 7*

lavishly in a rich way, *p. 10*

diverted misdirected, *p. 12*

imminent likely to happen right away, *p. 13*

potentially with a good chance of happening, *p. 13*

refugee* a person who flees their home in order to escape harm, *p. 15*

embraced readily accepted, *p. 15*

*Forms of these words are Anthology Key Vocabulary words.

■ ABOVE LEVEL

Building Background and Vocabulary

Ask students to share what they know about Nazi Germany and the Holocaust. Be sure students are familiar with the terms "Nazi," "concentration or labor camps," and Jewish "ghettos." Guide students through the text, using some of the vocabulary from the story.

Comprehension Skill: Making Judgments

Have students read the Strategy Focus on the book flap. Remind students to use the strategy and to make judgments about the characters as they read the book. (See the Leveled Readers Teacher's Guide for **Vocabulary and Comprehension Practice Masters.**)

Responding

Have partners discuss how to answer the questions on the inside back cover.

Think About the Selection Sample answers:

1. Germany was defeated in the war, and the Depression caused businesses to close.
2. Possible response: When Schindler agreed, he was thinking about getting rich. He didn't react compassionately until much later.
3. Possible response: Oskar Schindler was charming. He could get what he wanted or needed for himself and his workers from the Germans.
4. Answers will vary.

Making Connections Answers will vary.

Building Fluency

Model Read aloud page 11 to demonstrate the kind of pause and inflection called for by dashes in the text, as opposed to commas or periods.

Practice Ask small groups of students to find and read aloud the other examples of dashes on pages 12, 13, and 14.

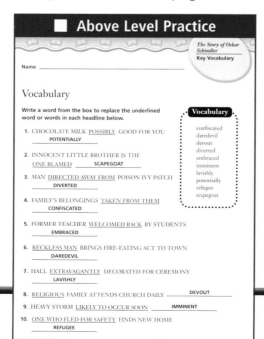

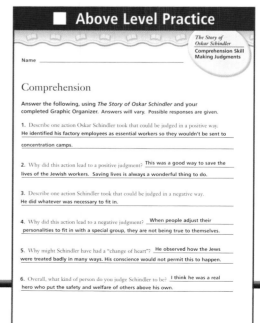

Leveled Readers

Corrie's Important Decision

Summary *Corrie ten Boom lived in Holland during World War II. She became an active member of the Dutch underground, and her efforts saved many Jewish people from the Germans. She and her family were eventually sent to prison and work camps.*

Vocabulary

Introduce the Key Vocabulary and ask students to complete the BLM.

invade to enter by force in order to conquer, *p. 3*

arrested captured and held under authority of law, *p. 6*

the underground a secret organization working against a government in power, *p. 11*

organization persons united for a certain purpose, *p. 12*

decision* a choice that involves judgment, *p. 13*

work camp a place where prisoners are used for forced manual labor, *p. 22*

*Forms of these words are Anthology Key Vocabulary words.

◆ LANGUAGE SUPPORT

Building Background and Vocabulary

Explain that this story takes place during World War II. Ask students to tell facts they know about World War II. Then distribute the **Build Background Practice Master.** Have students find Germany on the map, and show them that in 1939 Germany invaded Czechoslovakia and Poland. Then have them complete the map activity and share their work.

Comprehension Skill: Making Judgments

Have students read the Strategy Focus on the book flap. Remind students to use the strategy and to make judgments as they read the book. (See the Leveled Readers Teacher's Guide for **Build Background, Vocabulary,** and **Graphic Organizer Masters.**)

Responding

Have partners discuss how to answer the questions on the inside back cover.

Think About the Selection Sample answers:

1. They made a lot of rules: Jews had to sew gold stars on their clothing. People had to use ration cards to buy food. Jews were arrested and taken away.

2. The ten Boom family hid Jews in their house. They gave Jews a safe place to stay.

3. Jews stayed in a secret room that had been built in Corrie's house.

4. Answers will vary.

Making Connections Answers will vary.

Building Fluency

Model Have students follow along with page 15 of the recording on the audio CD. Have them listen carefully to the sentences that end with question marks.

Practice Have students read aloud with the recording until they are able to read the text on their own accurately and with expression.

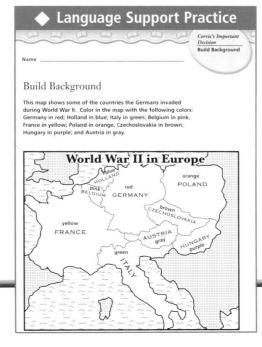

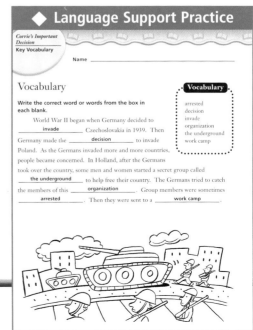

Lesson Overview

Literature

EDWARD MYERS
CLIMB OR DIE

Selection Summary

After a fierce snowstorm causes their family's car to crash, Jake and Danielle must scale Mount Remington in search of the weather station at its peak.

Vocabulary Reader

On Top of The World

1 Background and Vocabulary

Nonfiction

2 Main Selection

Climb or Die
Genre: Fiction

3 Social Studies Link

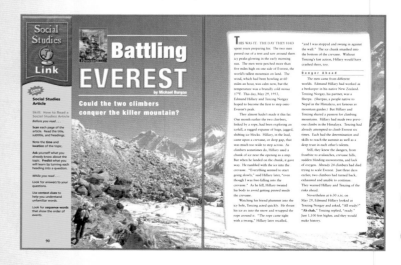

Instructional Support

Planning and Practice

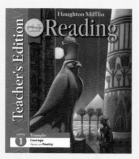

Teacher's Edition

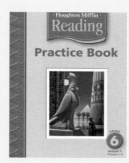

Practice Book

Teacher's Resources

Transparencies

Differentiated Instruction

Intervention Strategies for Extra Support

Instructional Activities for Challenge

Instructional Strategies for English Language Learners

Ready-Made Centers

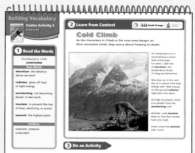

Building Vocabulary Flip Chart
• center activities
• word skills practice

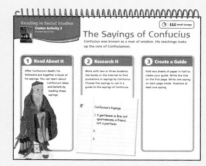

Reading in Science and Social Studies Flip Chart
• books and center activities
• support for state content standards

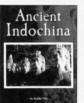

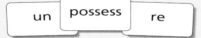

Hands-On Literacy Centers for *Climb or Die*
• activities
• manipulatives
• routines

Technology

Audio Selection
Climb or Die

Get Set for Reading CD-ROM

Accelerated Reader®

www.eduplace.com
• over 1,000 Online Leveled Books

HOUGHTON MIFFLIN
Assessment System
• Test Generator

Leveled Books for Reaching All Learners

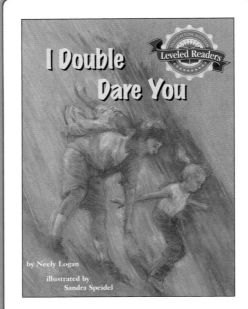

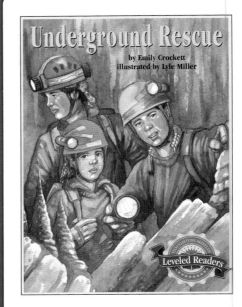

Fluency

Increase students' reading fluency using these activities.

● BELOW LEVEL

Model fluent reading of a passage. Have students discuss where you paused for punctuation. Then practice reading aloud in small groups.

▲ ON LEVEL

Have students read a selection aloud to a partner. Students should alternate passages or pages.

■ ABOVE LEVEL

Have students take turns reading passages aloud in small groups. Ask students to identify the subject and verb of a sentence to help them "chunk" text as they read.

◆ LANGUAGE SUPPORT

Play the audio CD of a passage while students follow along in the book. Then have them listen again and read aloud in unison with the CD.

Skills Practice

- Topic, comprehension strategy, and vocabulary linked to main selection

- Lessons in Teacher's Edition, pages 93O–93R

● BELOW LEVEL

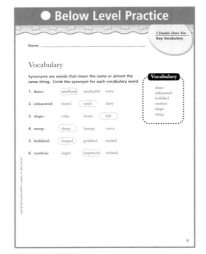

▲ ON LEVEL

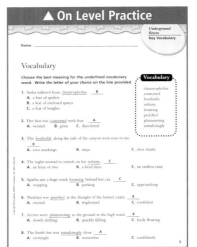

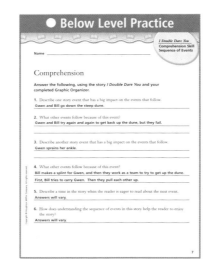

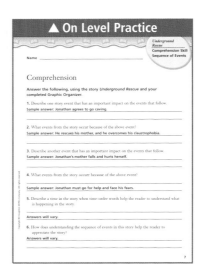

■ ABOVE LEVEL

Hurricane Music
by Ross Weil
illustrated by Andrew Wheatcroft

Leveled Readers

■ Above Level Practice

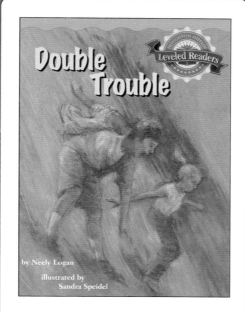

Hurricane Music
Key Vocabulary

Name _____

Vocabulary

Choose the best meaning for each underlined word. Write the letter of your answer on the line provided.

Vocabulary
withstand
manically
ominous
impenetrable
awestruck
surge
paralyzed
boardwalk

1. They were <u>awestruck</u> when the elephants came close to the bus. **B**
   A. scared   B. fascinated   C. wide awake

2. The plastic compound formed an <u>impenetrable</u> cover around the rocket. **A**
   A. solid   B. shiny   C. enclosed

3. The bird's wings flapped <u>manically</u> as it struggled to free itself. **C**
   A. endlessly   B. easily   C. agitatedly

4. The dark clouds that suddenly filled the sky were <u>ominous</u>. **A**
   A. threatening   B. gloomy   C. cheerful

5. Isabelle struggled to <u>withstand</u> the force of the wind. **B**
   A. calculate   B. resist   C. understand

6. A <u>surge</u> of joy rushed over Hadley as she opened her report card. **C**
   A. present   B. feeling   C. onrush

7. Waiting in line for the roller coaster, Daisy became <u>paralyzed</u> with fear. **A**
   A. frozen   B. full   C. mobilized

8. Blake and Jonquil walked along the <u>boardwalk</u> and watched the sun set over the ocean. **B**
   A. highway   B. raised walkway   C. balcony

■ Above Level Practice

Name _____

Hurricane Music
Comprehension Skill
Sequence of Events

Comprehension

Answer the following questions, using the story *Hurricane Music* and your completed Graphic Organizer.

1. Describe one event that had an important impact on the events that followed.
   Sample answer: Elsie's neighbor disappeared in the storm.

2. What details from the story show how important the above event was?
   Sample answer: The boy's mother, Sally, was so worried she had to sit down and put her head in her hands.

3. Describe another event that had an important impact on the events that followed.
   Sample answer: Elsie offered to go find Ben.

4. What details from the story show how important the above event was?
   Sample answer: Sally acted very grateful; Elsie had to summon all her courage to brave the storm.

5. Describe a time in the story when the use of time-order words helped you to understand what was happening.
   Answers will vary.

6. How does understanding the sequence of events help readers to appreciate the story?
   Answers will vary.

◆ LANGUAGE SUPPORT

Double Trouble

Leveled Readers

by Neely Logan

illustrated by
Sandra Speidel

◆ Language Support Practice

Name _____

Double Trouble
Build Background

Build Background

Look at the picture and answer the questions. Answers will vary.

WOW, THAT'S REALLY STEEP!

LET'S GO DOWN TO THE BOTTOM!

1. Why do you think the girl wants to go to the bottom of the dune?

2. What could happen as they go down the dune?

3. What should the boy and girl think about before they make a decision about going to the bottom of the dune?

4. What advice would you give them?

◆ Language Support Practice

Name _____

Double Trouble
Key Vocabulary

Vocabulary

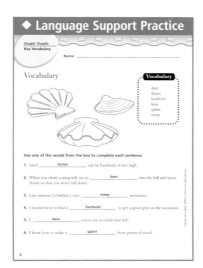

Vocabulary
dare
dunes
foothold
lean
splint
steep

Use one of the words from the box to complete each sentence.

1. Sand ____dunes____ can be hundreds of feet high.

2. When you climb a steep hill, try to ____lean____ into the hill and move slowly so that you won't fall down.

3. Last summer I climbed a very ____steep____ mountain.

4. I learned how to find a ____foothold____ to get a good grip on the mountain.

5. I ____dare____ you to try to climb that hill!

6. I know how to make a ____splint____ from pieces of wood.

Leveled Theme Paperbacks

- Extended independent reading in theme-related paperbacks

- Lessons in Teacher's Edition, pages R2–R7

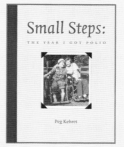

Small Steps:
THE YEAR I GOT POLIO

Peg Kehret

The Little Ships
The Heroic Rescue at Dunkirk in World War II
by LOUISE BORDEN

illustrated by
MICHAEL FOREMAN

● **BELOW LEVEL**   ▲ **ON LEVEL**

SHIPWRECK AT THE BOTTOM OF THE WORLD

■ **ABOVE LEVEL**

Technology

HOUGHTON MIFFLIN
Online Leveled Books
www.eduplace.com

- over 1,000 Online Leveled Books

Leveled Readers
Audio available

Daily Lesson Plans

Technology

Lesson Planner CD-ROM allows you to customize the chart below to develop your own lesson plans.

T Skill tested on Weekly or Theme Skills Test and/or Integrated Theme Test

50–60 minutes

Reading
Comprehension

Leveled Readers
- Fluency Practice
- Independent Reading

20–30 minutes

Word Work
Phonics/Decoding
Vocabulary
Spelling

20–30 minutes

Writing and Oral Language
Writing
Grammar
Listening/Speaking/Viewing

DAY 1

Teacher Read Aloud,
71CC–71DD
Rosie to the Rescue

Background and Vocabulary, 72

Key Vocabulary, 73

belay	foothold	improvising
carabiners	functioned	overcome
desperate	ice ax	pitons
fatigue		

Vocabulary Reader

Reading the Selection, 74–87

Comprehension Skill, 74
Sequence of Events **T**

Comprehension Strategy, 74
Predict/Infer

Leveled Readers
I Double Dare You
Underground Rescue
Hurricane Music
Double Trouble

Lessons and Leveled Practice, 93O–93R

Phonics/Decoding 75
Phonics/Decoding Strategy

Vocabulary, 74–87
Selection Vocabulary

Spelling, 93E
More Vowel Spellings **T**

Writing, 93K
Prewriting a Friendly Letter

Grammar, 93I
Complex Sentences **T**

Daily Language Practice
1. Do you think we can hike all the way to the raveen. (ravine?)
2. Please don't shuve me (shove; me!) or (shove; me.)

Listening/Speaking/Viewing,
71CC–71DD, 81
Teacher Read Aloud, Stop and Think

DAY 2

Reading the Selection,
74–87

Comprehension Check, 87

Responding, 88
Think About the Selection

Vocabulary Reader

Comprehension Skill Preview, 77
Sequence of Events **T**

Leveled Readers
I Double Dare You
Underground Rescue
Hurricane Music
Double Trouble

Lessons and Leveled Practice, 93O–93R

Structural Analysis, 93C
Prefixes *un-* and *re-* **T**

Vocabulary, 74–87
Selection Vocabulary

Spelling, 93E
More Vowel Spellings Review and Practice **T**

Writing, 93K
Drafting a Friendly Letter

Grammar, 93I
Complex Sentences Practice **T**

Daily Language Practice
3. today i will relie on my mother to drive me to school. (Today; I; rely)
4. that song has a pleasint tune. (That; pleasant)

Listening/Speaking/Viewing, 87, 88
Wrapping Up, Responding

Target Skills of the Week

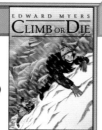

Phonics	Prefixes *un-* and *re-*
Comprehension	Predict/Infer; Sequence of Events
Vocabulary	Parts of a Dictionary Entry
Fluency	Leveled Readers

DAY 3

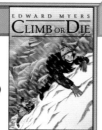

Rereading the Selection, 74–87

Rereading for Writer's Craft, 79
Vivid Verbs

Vocabulary Reader

Comprehension Skill, 93A–93B
Sequence of Events T

Leveled Readers
I Double Dare You
Underground Rescue
Hurricane Music
Double Trouble

Lessons and Leveled Practice, 93O–93R

Phonics Review, 93D
More Vowel Spellings

Vocabulary, 93G
Parts of a Dictionary Entry T

Spelling, 93F
Vocabulary: Context Sentences; More Vowel Spellings Practice T

Writing, 93L
Revising a Friendly Letter
Voice

Grammar, 93J
Fragments and Run-ons T

Daily Language Practice
5. My exercise rootine is thirty minutes on the treadmill (routine; treadmill.)
6. Do you like lether backpacks. (leather; backpacks?)

DAY 4

Reading the Social Studies Link, 90–93
"Battling Everest"

Skill: How to Read a Social Studies Article

Rereading for Genre, 92
Narrative Nonfiction

Comprehension Skill Review, 83
Story Structure

Leveled Readers
I Double Dare You
Underground Rescue
Hurricane Music
Double Trouble

Lessons and Leveled Practice, 93O–93R

Phonics/Decoding 90–93
Apply Phonics/Decoding Strategy to Link

Vocabulary, 93M
Language Center: Building Vocabulary

Spelling, 93F
More Vowel Spellings Game, Proofreading T

Writing, 93L
Proofreading a Friendly Letter

Grammar, 93J
Fragments and Run-ons Practice T

Daily Language Practice
7. have you heard the rhime about the cat and the fiddle? (Have; rhyme)
8. my brother does not denie that he ate the last cookie. (My; deny)

Listening/Speaking/Viewing, 93
Discuss the Link

DAY 5

Rereading for Fluency, 79

Responding Activities, 88–89
Write a Message
Cross-Curricular Activities

Information and Study Skills, 93H
Using Parts of a Book T

Comprehension Skill Review, 85
Noting Details

Leveled Readers
I Double Dare You
Underground Rescue
Hurricane Music
Double Trouble

Lessons and Leveled Practice, 93O–93R

Phonics, 93N
Language Center: Proofreading for a Friend

Vocabulary, 93M
Language Center: Vocabulary Game

Spelling, 93F
Test: More Vowel Spellings T

Writing, 93L
Publishing a Friendly Letter

Grammar, 93J, 93M
Avoiding Run-ons
Language Center: Conversation Fragments

Daily Language Practice
9. The rithim of the music makes me want to dance (rhythm; dance.)
10. When will i get a replie to my last letter? (I; reply)

Listening/Speaking/Viewing, 93N
Language Center: Hold a Literature Discussion

Managing Flexible Groups

Leveled Instruction and Leveled Practice

	DAY 1	**DAY 2**
WHOLE CLASS	• Teacher Read Aloud (TE pp. 71CC–71DD) • Building Background, Introducing Vocabulary (TE pp. 72–73) • Comprehension Strategy: Introduce (TE p. 74) • Comprehension Skill: Introduce (TE p. 74) • Purpose Setting (TE p. 75) **After reading first half of** *Climb or Die* • Stop and Think (TE p. 81)	**After reading** *Climb or Die* • Wrapping Up (TE p. 87) • Comprehension Check (Practice Book p. 48) • Responding: Think About the Selection (TE p. 88) • Comprehension Skill: Preview (TE p. 77)
SMALL GROUPS		
Extra Support	**TEACHER-LED** • Preview vocabulary; support reading with Vocabulary Reader. • Preview *Climb or Die* to Stop and Think (TE pp. 74–81). • Support reading with Extra Support/ Intervention notes (TE pp. 75, 78, 79, 80, 85, 86).	**Partner or Individual Work** • Reread first half of *Climb or Die* (TE pp. 74–81). • Preview, read second half (TE pp. 82–87). • Comprehension Check (Practice Book p. 48)
Challenge	**Individual Work** • Begin "The Summit" (Challenge Handbook p. 6). • Extend reading with Challenge Note (TE p. 86).	**Individual Work** • Continue work on activity (Challenge Handbook p. 6).
English Language Learners	**TEACHER-LED** • Preview vocabulary; support reading with Vocabulary Reader. • Preview *Climb or Die* to Stop and Think (TE pp. 74–81). • Support reading with English Language Learners notes (TE pp. 72, 77, 87).	**TEACHER-LED** • Review first half of *Climb or Die* (TE pp. 74–81). ✔ • Preview, read second half (TE pp. 82–87). • Begin Comprehension Check together (Practice Book p. 48).

Independent Activities

• Get Set for Reading CD-ROM
• Journals: selection notes, questions
• Complete, review Practice Book (pp. 46–50) and Leveled Readers Practice Blackline Masters (TE pp. 93O–93R).
• Assignment Cards (Teacher's Resource Blackline Masters pp. 51–53)
• Leveled Readers (TE pp. 93O–93R), Leveled Theme Paperbacks (TE pp. R2–R7), or book from Leveled Bibliography (TE pp. 23E–23F)

✔ **Opportunity to informally assess oral reading rate**

- Rereading: Lesson on Writer's Craft (TE p. 79)
- Comprehension Skill: Main lesson (TE pp. 93A–93B)

TEACHER-LED

- Reread, review Comprehension Check (Practice Book p. 48).
- Preview Leveled Reader: Below Level (TE p. 93O), or read book from Leveled Bibliography (TE pp. 23E–23F). ✔

TEACHER-LED

- Teacher check-in: Assess progress (Challenge Handbook p. 6).
- Preview Leveled Reader: Above Level (TE p. 93Q), or read book from Leveled Bibliography (TE pp. 23E–23F). ✔

Partner or Individual Work

- Complete Comprehension Check (Practice Book p. 48).
- Begin Leveled Reader: Language Support (TE p. 93R), or read book from Leveled Bibliography (TE pp. 23E–23F).

- Reading the Social Studies Link (TE pp. 90–93): Skill lesson (TE p. 90)
- Rereading the Social Studies Link: Lesson on Genre (TE p. 92)
- Comprehension Skill: First Comprehension Review lesson (TE p. 83)

Partner or Individual Work

- Reread the Social Studies Link (TE pp. 90–93).
- Complete Leveled Reader: Below Level (TE p. 93O), or read book from Leveled Bibliography (TE pp. 23E–23F).

Individual Work

- Complete activity (Challenge Handbook p. 6).
- Complete Leveled Reader: Above Level (TE p. 93Q), or read book from Leveled Bibliography (TE pp. 23E–23F).

TEACHER-LED

- Reread the Social Studies Link (TE pp. 90–93) ✔ and review Link Skill (TE p. 90).
- Complete Leveled Reader: Language Support (TE p. 93R), or read book from Leveled Bibliography (TE pp. 23E–23F). ✔

- Responding: Select from Activities (TE pp. 88–89)
- Information and Study Skills (TE p. 93H)
- Comprehension Skill: Second Comprehension Review lesson (TE p. 85)

TEACHER-LED

- Comprehension Skill: Reteaching lesson (TE p. R12)
- Reread Leveled Theme Paperback: Below Level (TE pp. R2–R3), or read book from Leveled Bibliography (TE pp. 23E–23F). ✔

TEACHER-LED

- Evaluate activity and plan format for sharing (Challenge Handbook p. 6).
- Reread Leveled Theme Paperback: Above Level (TE pp. R6–R7), or read book from Leveled Bibliography (TE pp. 23E–23F). ✔

Partner or Individual Work

- Reread book from Leveled Bibliography (TE pp. 23E–23F).

- Responding activities (TE pp. 88–89)
- Language Center activities (TE pp. 93M–93N)
- **Fluency Practice:** Reread *Climb or Die, Hatchet, Passage to Freedom.* ✔
- Activities relating to *Climb or Die* at Education Place® www.eduplace.com

Turn the page for more independent activities.

FLEXIBLE GROUPS

Climb or Die

Ready-Made Small Group Activities

ⒶⒷⒸ Word Work

Building Vocabulary Center Activity 3
● ▲ ■ *Cold Climb*

Building Vocabulary
Center Activity 3
Climb or Die

2 Learn from Context 🕐 👥 Small Groups | Connect to Science

Cold Climb
As the characters in *Climb or Die* overcome danger on their mountain climb, they worry about freezing to death.

1 Read the Words

Vocabulary Link
overcome

New Words

elevation the distance above sea level

radiates gives off heat or light energy

unrelenting not becoming slower or less harsh

insulate to prevent the loss of heat, electricity, or sound

summit the highest point

Prefixes
unaware, unequal, undecided

Air temperature on a mountaintop is lower than at the base. For every 1,000 feet of **elevation**, the temperature drops 3.5 degrees Fahrenheit.

Mountain air is thin and dry, so it cannot hold heat energy well. Heat energy on the ground **radiates** right back into space.

On high mountains, there is no shelter from the **unrelenting** cold.

Animals' coats **insulate** them so that their bodies hold onto heat.

Snow covers the **summit** year round.

3 Do an Activity

Leveled Activities on side 2

Word Part Cards

un   possess   re

Key Vocabulary Cards 16–25   belay

Spelling Word Cards 41–60   cycle

⚡Cross Curricular⚡ Cross Curricular

Reading in Social Studies Independent Book
■ *Ancient Indochina*

Ancient Indochina

by Susan Tran

Reading in Social Studies Center Activity 3
● ▲ ■ *The Sayings of Confucius*

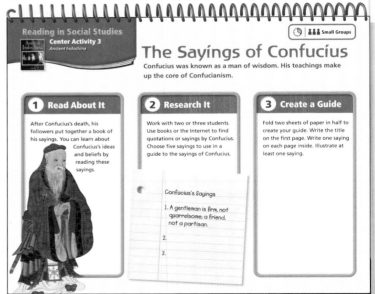

Reading in Social Studies
Center Activity 3
Ancient Indochina

🕐 👥 Small Groups

The Sayings of Confucius
Confucius was known as a man of wisdom. His teachings make up the core of Confucianism.

1 Read About It
After Confucius's death, his followers put together a book of his sayings. You can learn about Confucius's ideas and beliefs by reading these sayings.

2 Research It
Work with two or three students. Use books or the Internet to find quotations or sayings by Confucius. Choose five sayings to use in a guide to the sayings of Confucius.

3 Create a Guide
Fold two sheets of paper in half to create your guide. Write the title on the first page. Write one saying on each page inside. Illustrate at least one saying.

Confucius's Sayings

1. A gentleman is firm, not quarrelsome; a friend, not a partisan.
2.
3.

Leveled Activities on side 2

Leveled for ● Below Level, ▲ On Level, ■ Above Level

Reading

Routine Card 3
● ▲ ■ *Respond to a Story*

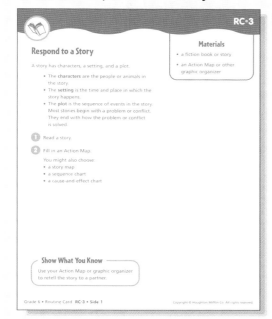

RC·3

Respond to a Story

A story has characters, a setting, and a plot.

- The **characters** are the people or animals in the story.
- The **setting** is the time and place in which the story happens.
- The **plot** is the sequence of events in the story. Most stories begin with a problem or conflict. They end with how the problem or conflict is solved.

Materials
- a fiction book or story
- an Action Map or other graphic organizer

① Read a story.

② Fill in an Action Map.
You might also choose:
- a story map
- a sequence chart
- a cause-and-effect chart

Show What You Know
Use your Action Map or graphic organizer to retell the story to a partner.

Grade 6 • Routine Card RC-3 • Side 1　　　　Copyright © Houghton Mifflin Co. All rights reserved

Activity Card 1
● ▲ *I Double Dare You*

Climb or Die　　　GRADE 6　THEME 1　WEEK 3　ACTIVITY CARD

1. *I Double Dare You*

Bill and Gwen are determined to escape a dangerous situation. With a partner, look through the book for times when the characters work together and when they try to act independently. Decide what is the author's message about working together. Work with a partner to create a silent skit that demonstrates cooperation.

Writing

Activity Card 3
● ▲ *Over the Top*

Climb or Die　　　GRADE 6　THEME 1　WEEK 3　ACTIVITY CARD

3. Over the Top

You are writing an entry for a world record book. Your subject is "The World's Highest Mountains." Write a short entry about three of the world's highest peaks and illustrate it with a map. Consider the following questions.

- Where are these mountains located?
- How tall are they?
- Who were the first people to climb them?

Challenge Card 1–6
■ *Resourcefulness*

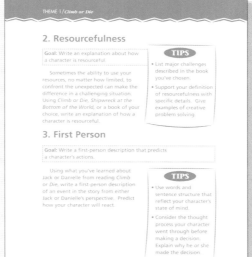

THEME 1/*Climb or Die*

2. Resourcefulness

Goal: Write an explanation about how a character is resourceful.

Sometimes the ability to use your resources, no matter how limited, to confront the unexpected can make the difference in a challenging situation. Using *Climb or Die, Shipwreck at the Bottom of the World*, or a book of your choice, write an explanation of how a character is resourceful.

TIPS
- List major challenges described in the book you've chosen.
- Support your definition of resourcefulness with specific details. Give examples of creative problem solving.

3. First Person

Goal: Write a first-person description that predicts a character's actions.

Using what you've learned about Jack or Danielle from reading *Climb or Die*, write a first-person description of an event in the story from either Jack or Danielle's perspective. Predict how your character will react.

TIPS
- Use words and sentence structure that reflect your character's state of mind.
- Consider the thought process your character went through before making a decision. Explain why he or she made the decision.

Gr. 6 Challenge Card 1-6　　　© Houghton Mifflin Co.

Multiple Tiers of Intervention

Core Program Instruction

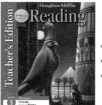

- research-based
- systematic
- assessment-driven

Group Support

Daily lessons and activities for differentiated instruction

Intervention Strategies for Extra Support, pages 34–43

Instructional Activities for Challenge, pages 6–7

Instructional Strategies for English Learners, pages 38–47

Intervention Program
Proven efficacy for struggling readers

Soar to Success

Oral Language and Fluency

Building Background

Tell students that you are going to read aloud a story about a little girl who acts bravely.

• Ask students to recall courageous rescues they have heard about, read about, or seen on television.

Fluency Modeling

Explain that as you read aloud, you will be modeling fluent oral reading. Ask students to listen carefully to your phrasing and your expression, or tone of voice and emphasis.

COMPREHENSION SKILL

Sequence of Events

Explain that

• clue words such as *at first, then, next,* and *finally* show the order in which events happen;

• the clue word *while* shows that two or more events are happening at the same time.

Purpose Setting Read the story aloud, asking students to pay attention to the order of events as they listen. Then use the Guiding Comprehension questions to assess students' understanding. Reread the story for clarification as needed.

Teacher Read Aloud

Rosie to the Rescue
by Fran Hodgkins

❶ Rosie stopped practicing turns on her inline skates when her mother rushed out of the back door of their house. "Rosie!" she called with a frantic look on her face. "We have to get to the Cornell place. The baby fell down the old well!"

❷ When they got to the Cornells' small farm, a crowd of neighbors had already gathered behind a barrier of yellow plastic tape. On the other side, Rosie saw more than a dozen rescuers. One firefighter was on the ground, trying to reach into the well. Two paramedics stood with Mr. and Mrs. Cornell. Being the smallest kid in sixth grade, Rosie easily wormed her way through the grownups to the front of the crowd. As she did, she caught snatches of conversation.

"Didn't they know that old well was there?"

"Guess not. That's the one that dried up on Joe Stebbings back in the fifties. You'd have thought he would have capped it off."

"That poor baby!"

The firefighter who had been on the ground stood up. He shook his head, and Mrs. Cornell wailed. Rosie suddenly realized that all the adults were too big to reach the trapped baby—but she wasn't! She ducked under the yellow tape and ran to a firefighter wearing a black helmet. Rosie spoke quickly, before her nerve failed. "I can fit. Let me try."

The firefighter looked doubtful, and then Mom suddenly appeared. Rosie's heart sank. To her surprise, her mother said, "Let her try. She's strong, and the baby knows her." Rosie stared at her mother, who nodded and said softly, "It's what neighbors do."

The firefighter yelled, "We've got a volunteer!" Suddenly, Rosie felt herself being fitted into a safety harness. "We'll hold the ropes tight," the firefighter in the black helmet said. "We won't let you get stuck, too."

Heart pounding, Rosie nodded. Strong hands gripped her ankles, and ropes tugged on the harness as she wriggled head-first into the old well.

❸ The walls of the hole pressed tight against her shoulders. The air tasted of dirt and metal and salt. In the darkness somewhere ahead she could hear the baby sniffling. "It's okay, Jonathan. It's Rosie. Remember me? We met at your mom's farm stand. We played ball."

"Ball? Ball?" the little boy said.

Rosie reached out and touched his chubby arm. He screamed with fright. "It's okay! It's okay!" she said. "Come on with me, we'll go see Mommy."

"Ma-ma?"

"That's right, Mama." As she spoke, Rosie felt the little boy's arms. They were both above his head. His little pot belly had stuck in the narrowing hole and prevented him from sliding down any further.

Rosie stretched as far as she could to get a solid hold on the child. She grasped the back of his dirt-covered overalls tightly with her left hand, and gathered the front of the overalls into her right hand. She turned her head as much as she could and called, "Pull!"

The rescuers tugged hard on her ankles and the ropes. Rosie felt the strain throughout her body. She shut her eyes. Hang on to him, she thought. Don't let go, no matter what.

❹ Suddenly they were back above ground in the dazzling light. The Cornells rushed in, crying with relief as the paramedic handed them their baby. Rosie looked up at the firefighters and, with surprise, noticed they looked like they were about to cry, too.

Except the first firefighter Rosie had talked to. With a huge smile, he took off his black helmet and put it on Rosie's head.

CRITICAL THINKING
Guiding Comprehension

❶ **SEQUENCE OF EVENTS** What is Rosie doing at the beginning of the story? (She is using her in-line skates.)

❷ **SEQUENCE OF EVENTS** What were the firefighters trying to do when Rosie and her mother arrived at the farm? (rescue a baby from a well)

❸ **SEQUENCE OF EVENTS** What events happen once Rosie is lowered into the well? (She speaks to Jonathan, touches him, reassures him, gets a solid hold on his overalls, and turns her head and calls "Pull!")

❹ **SEQUENCE OF EVENTS** How does the word *Suddenly* in the sentence, *Suddenly they were back above ground in the dazzling light*, show a change of event from the paragaph just before it? (Sample answer: The word *Suddenly* signals that the action has moved from inside the well to above ground.)

Discussion Options

Personal Response Ask students what they would say in a letter to Rosie about her brave rescue of the baby.

⭐ **Connecting/Comparing** Ask students to explain why this story belongs in the same theme as *Hatchet* and *Passage to Freedom*.

 English Language Learners

Language Development

Point out that the word *well* has more than one meaning. *Well* can be used as an adjective, an adverb, or a noun. Write the following examples on the board: *I do not feel well. The soccer team played well. The baby fell into the well.* Read each sentence with students, guiding them to understand each meaning of *well*. Then ask students to use *well* in sentences of their own.

Background and Vocabulary

Key Concept: Mountain Climbing

Remind students that this theme is about people who show courage in the face of challenges. Ask, How dangerous is mountain climbing? Does it require courage? Then discuss how mountain climbing might be more dangerous in winter. Use "Equipped to Climb" on Anthology pages 72–73 to build background and introduce key vocabulary.

- Have a volunteer read aloud "Equipped to Climb."

- Discuss the photographs and captions. Have students tell why they think each piece of equipment shown is useful for snow and ice climbing.

Vocabulary Preview

The Vocabulary Reader can be used to preteach or reinforce the key vocabulary.

Vocabulary Reader

On Top of The World

by Dixie Lee Petrokis

EDWARD MYERS
CLIMB OR DIE

Climb or Die

Genre Fiction

Key Vocabulary

belay
carabiner
desperate
foothold
ice ax
improvising
overcome
piton

Vocabulary Reader

On Top of The World

by Dixie Lee Petrokis

e ● Glossary

72

EQUIPPED TO CLIMB

Mountain climbers in winter must **overcome** the dangers of snow and ice. Special ice-climbing tools have been developed to make their climbing safer. In *Climb or Die*, the characters find themselves in a **desperate** situation where **improvising** their tools is the only solution.

A firm and secure **foothold** is always important for any type of climbing. Crampons, or iron spikes attached to boots, prevent slipping while climbing.

REACHING ALL LEARNERS

English Language Learners

Supporting Comprehension

Beginning/Preproduction Have students listen to the article. Ask students to study the photographs on pages 72–73 and draw a picture of a steep mountain. Then ask them to draw a person climbing the mountain.

Early Production and Speech Emergence Have students repeat the Key Vocabulary words after you. Use the photographs to help students understand the meaning of *foothold, belay, piton, carabiner,* and *ice ax*. Discuss examples of problems students have overcome. Ask, What might make someone feel fatigued? desperate?

Intermediate and Advanced Fluency In small groups have students read the article. Then ask them to discuss the tools they would need for mountain climbing. Ask, What would you use if you didn't have an ice ax or a rope?

Climbers **belay** each other with a rope that is attached (or anchored) to the ice or rock.

A **piton** (*top, above*), is a metal spike hammered into rock or ice as support for mountain climbing.
A **carabiner** is a metal ring used to attach a rope to the piton.

An **ice ax** is used to support the upper body as the climber steps upward.

73

Introducing Vocabulary

Key Vocabulary

These words support the Key Concept and appear in the selection.

belay to secure with a rope for mountain climbing

carabiners oval rings that attach a rope to a piton for mountain climbing

desperate feeling full of despair, hopeless

fatigue extreme tiredness

foothold a place that gives firm support for a foot while climbing

functioned filled a particular purpose or role

ice ax an ax used by mountain climbers to cut steps in ice

improvising making something from available materials

overcome to conquer

pitons metal spikes used in mountain climbing, with eyes or rings at one end to which a carabiner can be attached

 e • Glossary
e • WordGame

See Vocabulary notes on pages 76, 78, 80, 82, and 84 for additional words to preview.

Transparency 1–19

Climbing Words

Newsflash: Young Climber Rescued!

Climber Megan Chin was rescued today after being stranded on a cliff face for several hours. The young climber had apparently lost her <u>foothold</u> while ice-climbing with a friend. The force of her fall pulled out an improperly placed <u>piton</u>, causing her to slip even further. Her partner had stayed below on <u>belay</u>. He was holding a rope secured to the mountain at one end and Megan at the other. He watched in horror as Megan fell. Luckily her <u>carabiners</u> held, and the rope stopped her at the next piton. Fighting to <u>overcome</u> <u>fatigue</u> and <u>desperate</u> fear, Megan started <u>improvising</u>. With her <u>ice ax</u>, she managed to pull herself sideways to a piece of rock, which <u>functioned</u> as a ledge, where she waited until rescuers could get to her. Although park officials praised Megan's quick thinking, they issued a strong warning against climbing without proper experience and the right equipment.

TRANSPARENCY 1–19
TEACHER'S EDITION PAGE 73

ANNOTATED VERSION

COURAGE *Climb or Die*
Key Vocabulary

Practice Book page 46

Climb or Die
Key Vocabulary

Name _____

Complete the Climb

Complete each sentence about mountain climbing with the correct word from the list.

1. Metal spikes with a hole at the end through which you pass a rope are called <u>pitons</u> (1)

2. Metal rings you use to attach rope to pitons are called <u>carabiners</u> (1)

3. To cut into the ice and support your upper body while climbing, you might use an <u>ice ax</u> (1)

4. In order to remain steady on your feet, it is important to find a secure <u>foothold</u> (1)

5. If you and another climber are helping each other climb up the mountain while attached to the same rope, you are on <u>belay</u> (1)

6. Do not push yourself too hard, or you may experience extreme <u>fatigue</u> (1)

7. If you get lost and feel nearly hopeless that help will arrive, you feel <u>desperate</u> (1)

8. If you don't have the proper equipment, you might look for other tools you have and try <u>improvising</u> (1)

9. If you climb cautiously and with safety in mind, you will never have to face an obstacle you won't be able to <u>overcome</u> (1)

10. Safe climbers have always <u>functioned</u> (1) as role models for others.

Vocabulary

carabiners
pitons
foothold
desperate
improvising
belay
ice ax
overcome
functioned
fatigue

Display Transparency 1–19.

- Model how to figure out *foothold*.
- Have students figure out each remaining Key Vocabulary word.
- Ask students to look for these words as they read and to use them to discuss wilderness survival.

Practice/Homework Assign **Practice Book** page 46.

Introducing Vocabulary 73

TARGET SKILL
COMPREHENSION STRATEGY
Predict/Infer

Teacher Modeling Ask a student to read aloud the Strategy Focus. Explain that the way to make a good prediction or inference is to think of a possibility based on text clues and personal experiences. Ask a student to read aloud the introduction. Then model the strategy.

Think Aloud *From the title, the cover, and the introduction, I predict that their climb will be dangerous. Will they make it? Danielle has climbing experience and Jake has a good imagination. I predict they will find clever ways to overcome obstacles.*

Test Prep Tell students to use the Predict/Infer strategy before reading each test passage. Suggest that they use the title and any illustrations to predict whether the passage is fiction or nonfiction. Then they should predict what will happen or what they will learn.

TARGET SKILL
COMPREHENSION SKILL
Sequence of Events

Introduce the Graphic Organizer. Tell students that an Event Chart can help them to understand the sequence of events. Explain that as they read, students will fill out the Event Chart on **Practice Book** page 47.

- Display **Transparency 1–20.** Have students read Anthology page 75.
- Model completing the first box. Tell students to complete the other boxes as they read. Monitor students' work as needed.

Selection 3

EDWARD MYERS
CLIMB OR DIE

Strategy Focus

Danielle and Jake must climb to a weather station near the top of a mountain if they hope to survive. Will they make it? As you read the selection, stop from time to time to **predict** what will happen next.

74

Transparency 1–20

COURAGE Climb or Die
Graphic Organizer Event Chart
ANNOTATED VERSION

Event Chart

1. **Page 75** At first Danielle hits the rock with Dad's hammer. Then she
   turns the hammer around and uses its claw like an ice ax.

2. **Page 77** The hammers work. Next, Jake and Danielle
   start to climb up the icy trench.

3. **Page 78** Danielle gets to the top of the trench first. Then she
   turns to help Jake reach the top.

4. **Pages 80–81** Jake and Danielle are happy to be at the top. Then they realize
   they can't see a weather station anywhere.

5. **Page 82** Crying, Jake and Danielle hug each other. Then Danielle pushes Jake away. Suddenly, Jake realizes that she is
   trying to show him something.

6. **Page 84** Through the clouds, they see
   the weather station on a ridge above them.

7. **Pages 84–85** Danielle is getting weaker. When they finally knock on the weather station door,
   no one answers it.

8. **Page 86** Jake improvises by banging on the door with the hammer. As a result, a man finally opens the door.

Practice Book page 47

Climb or Die
Graphic Organizer Event Chart
Name _____

Event Chart

1. **Page 75** At first Danielle hits the rock with Dad's hammer. Then she
   turns the hammer around and uses its claw like an ice ax. (1)

2. **Page 77** The hammers work. Next, Jake and Danielle
   start to climb up the icy trench. (1)

3. **Page 78** Danielle gets to the top of the trench first. Then she
   turns to help Jake reach the top. (1)

4. **Pages 80–81** Jake and Danielle are happy to be at the top. Then they realize
   they can't see a weather station anywhere. (1)

5. **Page 82** Crying, Jake and Danielle hug each other. Then Danielle pushes Jake away. Suddenly, Jake realizes that she is
   trying to show him something. (1)

6. **Page 84** Through the clouds, they see
   the weather station on a ridge above them. (1)

7. **Pages 84–85** Danielle is getting weaker. When they finally knock on the weather station door,
   no one answers it. (1)

8. **Page 86** Jake improvises by banging on the door with the hammer. As a result, a man finally opens the door. (1)

The Darcy family trip to their cabin in the mountains turns to disaster when their car crashes in a blizzard. To find help, Jake and Danielle must leave behind their injured parents and their dog, Flash. Their only hope for rescue is to reach a manned weather station at the top of Mount Remington. With Danielle's climbing experience at Camp Mountain Mastery and Jake's imagination, the two attempt the final icy cliff. Their only equipment is two hammers, two screwdrivers, and a nylon dog leash.

DANIELLE was bashing at the rock with Dad's hammer. With each blow, chips of icy snow flew like sparks. Some of the chips sprayed toward Jake; a few even struck his face. He held out his hand, motioning for her to stop. Before he could speak, however, something caught his attention.

Danielle wasn't bashing at the rock just to let off her frustration. She was experimenting. She was trying to figure something out.

The hammer came down once, twice, three times.

Chips flew outward.

Then, without saying a word, Danielle turned the hammer around. She continued to grip its metal shaft by the rubber-clad handle, but now she struck at the icy granite with the claw, not with the head. The claw was the side you used for pulling nails out — a curved, pointed piece of forged steel.

"What are you doing?" Jake asked.

Danielle replied, "Improvising."

Jake watched in puzzlement. Then, suddenly, he understood. "An ice ax?"

75

Extra Support/Intervention

Selection Preview

pages 74–77 Danielle tries to use ordinary tools in place of real mountain-climbing equipment. Do you think they will work?

pages 78–79 Jake and Danielle climb the trench, an icy cliff. How might they help each other?

pages 80–83 Jake and Danielle reach the top of Mount Remington, but there is no weather station in sight. Danielle is angry because Jake told her the weather station would be there.

pages 84–86 They find the weather station. They reach it and pound on the door.

Purpose Setting

- Have students read to find out whether Danielle and Jake will reach the top of the mountain.

- Ask students to predict how Danielle's climbing experience and Jake's imagination will help them.

- Tell students that they should read to confirm or revise their predictions as the story unfolds.

- Remind students to pay attention to sequence of events as they read.

- You may want to preview with students the Responding questions on Anthology page 88.

Journal ▸ Students can use their journals to record their original predictions, make changes, and add new predictions.

STRATEGY REVIEW

Phonics/Decoding

Remind students to use the Phonics/ Decoding Strategy as they read.

Modeling Write this sentence from *Climb or Die* on the board: *"It's more like what climbers use for what they call <u>vertical</u> ice."* Point to *vertical*.

Think Aloud *I'll try sounding out the first syllable, VUHR. How do I pronounce t-i? I'll try a short i, tih. I recognize the ending -al. When I blend the sounds, I get VUHR-tih-kuhl. I know this word. It makes sense in the sentence.*

CRITICAL THINKING
Guiding Comprehension

❶ NOTING DETAILS What details show that Jake likes Danielle's plan? (Jake feels a surge of hope and delight, and he hands his hammer to her at once.)

❷ DRAWING CONCLUSIONS Does Danielle think of herself as someone who usually comes up with inventions and other new ideas? How do you know? (no, because she is surprised she thought of this plan)

❸ MAKING INFERENCES What does climbing help the characters discover about themselves? (Danielle can't believe her ideas worked so well, and Jake seems surprised by his ability to keep climbing.)

76

Vocabulary

ice ax an ax used by mountain climbers to cut steps in ice

functioned filled a particular purpose or role

pitons metal spikes used in mountain climbing, with eyes or rings at one end to which a carabiner can be attached

carabiners oval rings that attach a rope to a piton for mountain climbing

improvising making something from available materials

overcome to conquer

ASSIGNMENT CARD 11
Say It Again

Dialogue and Narration

With a partner, read both the passages listed below. Then choose one of the passages to rewrite. If you choose the narration passage, rewrite it as dialogue. If you choose the dialogue passage, rewrite it as narration. Remember to keep the characters' thoughts and feelings the same in your scene as they are in the original.

Page 77: The author uses **narration** to tell what Danielle is thinking and feeling. Narration does not show the words spoken by characters. Instead, it tells about characters' actions, thoughts, or feelings.

Page 82: The author uses **dialogue** to show how angry Danielle is and how sorry Jake is. Dialogue is conversation between two or more characters. The characters' words are in quotation marks and there are phrases like *he said* or *she said*.

Share your scene with a partner. Discuss anything that was challenging.

Theme 1: Courage

Teacher's Resource BLM page 52

"You got it." Danielle struck the slab several times with the hammer's claw. Instead of scattering lots of chips, it sent fewer of them outward and mostly sideways; otherwise the metal dug deep into the crust. "The claw cuts in much more steeply than a regular ice ax would," she told Jake. "It's more like what climbers use for what they call vertical ice. It's not very sharp." She pulled the hammer back with her right hand, then stroked the claw with the fingers of her right. "But like you said — beggars can't be choosers."

Jake felt a surge of hope and delight. "You think it'll work?"

"There's only one way to find out." She reached out to Jake. "Here," she said. "I'll need your hammer, too."

He handed it over at once.

1

The hammers worked, Danielle told herself. Just as the screwdrivers functioned as crude pitons and the loops of nylon leash served as crude carabiners, the hammers worked well as crude ice axes. She couldn't quite believe it, but they worked just fine.

Something else she couldn't believe: Danielle herself had thought up half the system. Not Jake. Danielle. Even though Jake suggested the general idea of improvising hardware, Danielle was the one who figured out most of the specifics. First the fake carabiners, now the fake ice axes. And the system worked!

2

No wonder Jake got such a kick out of doing this, she told herself. It wasn't just coming up with a new idea. It was getting in a jam, then finding a way out. It was a great feeling — a feeling much like what she'd felt at Mountain Mastery when, stuck high on a cliff, Danielle had taken a chance, pulled herself out of danger, and discovered strength she hadn't even known she had.

Somehow he'd done it, Jake thought. He'd fallen, yet he'd pulled himself up. He'd kept going. He'd overcome the pain, the fear, the doubt that he could continue. Despite dropping two or three feet and slamming into the cliff, despite banging his shoulder and his face, he hadn't given up. Here he was now, heading up all over again.

3

77

English Language Learners

Language Development

Explain these idioms on page 77.

- Read aloud *beggars can't be choosers* in the first paragraph. Remind students that beggars have to ask for things they need because they can't buy them. Ask, Why can't beggars be choosers?

- Read aloud *It was getting in a jam* in the second-to-last paragraph. If possible, bring in a jar of jam to help students understand how the word *jam* can mean a situation from which it is difficult to escape or free oneself.

Sequence of Events

Teach

- Tell students that authors sometimes refer to past events to give readers more information. Explain that this is called a time shift.

- Read aloud the second-to-last paragraph on page 77.

- Ask, What past event is the author telling you about? (when Danielle was stuck on a cliff at Mountain Mastery)

- Ask, What do you learn from this time shift? (She's overcome danger before.)

Practice

- Have students identify a time shift on page 82. (*He'd seen it on TV;* that was something Jake did before the story started.)

- Discuss what readers learn from this shift. (They climbed the mountain because of what Jake saw on TV.)

Apply

- Have partners find other examples of time shifts in the selection. (Sample answers: paragraph 6, page 77; paragraph 5, page 80)

Target Skill Trace	
Preview; Teach	p. 71CC, p. 74, p. 77; p. 93A
Reteaching	p. R12
Review	pp. M32–M33; p. 101; Theme 5, p. 461

READ & COMPREHEND

Climb or Die

CRITICAL THINKING
Guiding Comprehension

4 **NOTING DETAILS** What details show that Jake and Danielle are gaining a better understanding of one another? (Jake understands for the first time why Danielle likes sports so much, and Danielle understands why Jake likes being inventive.)

5 **MAKING INFERENCES** What does Jake mean when he says Danielle likes sports not because she likes coming out ahead of others but because she likes coming out ahead of herself? (Danielle values challenging herself more than competing with others.)

COMPREHENSION STRATEGY
Predict/Infer

Teacher/Student Modeling Discuss with students the clue on page 78 that can help them infer that Jake and Danielle need to hurry. (From the sentence *He glanced at his watch* and the words *Three-thirty,* the reader can infer that they don't have much time left.)

After you discuss the strategy, ask students to make predictions about what Danielle and Jake will see at the top of the trench.

Vocabulary

belay to secure with a rope, in mountain climbing

foothold a place that gives firm support for a foot while climbing

fatigue extreme tiredness

coaxed gently urged or eased

4
5
For the first time, Jake started to understand why Danielle liked sports so much. Not because of winning — coming out ahead of everyone else. Instead, because of coming out ahead of *himself.*

He glanced at his watch. Three-thirty.

Now the biggest challenge rose right before them.

"Belay on?" Danielle called down to Jake.

"On belay," he shouted back.

"Climbing."

"Climb."

Climbing that icy trench was the hardest work Danielle had ever done. With a hammer in each hand, she struck out with the right one till it caught securely, then flexed her biceps to pull her body upward while she kicked at the slab with her boots, struggling to find some kind of foothold. Then she struck out with the left hammer and, kicking once again, pulled herself still higher. More often than not, her feet skittered around, helplessly at first. Two or three efforts let her find rough spots for the boot soles to catch on; the slab's angle was sufficiently gradual that she could get by with risky footholds. Somehow she kept going.

Danielle proceeded by exerting most of her weight on the hammers. Sometimes she felt the claws slipping, and once or twice she almost lost control. Yet she managed to keep her grip anyway. She pulled herself upward a few inches at a time. Panting, gasping, and fighting the fatigue that left her close to passing out, Danielle managed to fumble up the trench all the way to the top.

Then it was Jake's turn. Danielle didn't even stop to rest. She tied a length of Flash's nylon leash onto one of the two hammers and lowered it to Jake. After Jake untied it, Danielle pulled up the leash, tied on the second hammer, and lowered it as well. Then she assumed the belay position, told Jake what to do, and coaxed him all the way up.

The snowstorm had eased again. Snow still sifted down from above but so much more thinly now that it might as well have stopped altogether. Danielle could see the snow-covered rocks around them, the clouds massing around the mountain, and even some of the land visible below the clouds.

78

Extra Support/Intervention

Strategy Modeling: Phonics/Decoding

Model the strategy for *sufficiently* on page 78.

To figure out this word, I'll try dividing the first two syllables between the two fs. *I know that the letters* ci *can make the /sh/ sound. I also know how to pronounce the suffix* -ly. *I'll try blending all these sounds together,* suh-FIH-shehnt-lee. *That sounds right, and it makes sense in the sentence.*

sufficiently
suh-FIH-shehnt-lee

79

Vivid Verbs

Teach

- Remind students that authors use vivid verbs to give readers a clear, exciting picture of the story action.

- Write on the board *her feet skittered around, helplessly at first* from page 78.

- Explain that a vivid verb, such as *skittered*, makes the sentence exciting and gives the reader more information.

Practice/Apply

- Have partners find and list other examples of vivid verbs that describe Danielle's climb. (Sample answers: *struck, flexed, kicked*)

- Have them read their lists aloud and record the words on the board.

 Fluency Practice

Rereading for Fluency Have students choose a favorite passage from *Climb or Die* to reread to a partner, or suggest they read the first two paragraphs after the break on page 78. Encourage students to read with feeling and expression.

Extra Support/Intervention

Strategy Modeling: Predict/Infer

Use this example to model the strategy.

On page 78 I see that after Danielle makes the dangerous climb to the top of the trench, she immediately turns to help her brother. I can infer from this that she cares for her brother a great deal. I predict that if they encounter more obstacles, Danielle will help her brother overcome them.

CRITICAL THINKING
Guiding Comprehension

❻ WRITER'S CRAFT Why does the author tell us that Danielle abruptly stops caring about the view? (to show she suddenly realizes the weather station isn't there)

❼ MAKING INFERENCES Why does Danielle say, *"We're dead"*? (She can't see the weather station and is worried she and Jake could die if they don't find shelter.)

She could see that they were on a mountain; she could also see the contours of that particular peak. But where she expected to see the cliff above her, she saw only a low mound of snowy granite rising off to the left. Mount Remington didn't keep going higher, higher, and higher. On the contrary: it seemed to be leveling off.

Danielle felt the angle of the slope underfoot starting to ease. The mountain felt less and less steep. With each step the ground seemed more nearly level. Soon Danielle and Jake couldn't even keep going on all fours — they had to stand upright. Thick mist streaked around them, so they couldn't see much of the terrain, but within a few minutes they weren't climbing at all; they were just walking over an uneven but relatively flat surface.

"Danielle," said Jake, badly winded. "Danielle —" He stopped, leaned over, coughed, then stood upright again, heaving for breath. "I think we — I think this is —"

"The top!" Danielle exclaimed. She wanted to say more but couldn't. She wanted to shout, to scream for joy, to thank her brother for teaming up to do what they'd done — but she couldn't. She could scarcely breathe, much less talk. All she could say was, "The — *top!*"

The snowfall had stopped. Great clouds massed below them, around them, almost everywhere but above them. They were so high up now that the only vistas Danielle could remember like this were what she'd seen from airplanes. Danielle suddenly understood what people meant by a breathtaking view.

❻ Then, abruptly, she didn't care about the view at all. She didn't care if it was beautiful or ugly. She started looking around in a different, almost desperate way.

Something was wrong. Something about the view. Something that wasn't what she saw but was what she *didn't* see.

There was no weather station in sight.

Together Jake and Danielle worked their way over the jumble of rocks. They walked about fifteen or twenty feet ahead to where the flat place they'd reached began curving downward again. Clouds swept all around them. They couldn't see very far — perhaps a few dozen yards down the mountain. But that was just the problem. They were looking down the mountain. Down the mountain's far side.

80

Extra Support/Intervention

Review (pages 74–81)
Before students who need extra support join the whole class for Stop and Think on page 81, they should

- review their predictions/purpose
- take turns modeling Predict/Infer and other strategies they used
- help you add to **Transparency 1–20**
- check and revise their Event Chart on **Practice Book** page 47, and use it to summarize the first half of the story

Vocabulary

contours outlines, or shapes of something

terrain the type of land in an area

desperate feeling full of despair, hopeless

intently with extreme concentration

Danielle turned, took twenty paces to the right, then turned again and worked her way to Jake's left. She peered over the edge and saw nothing but rock and snow vanishing into the clouds below. The sight chilled her more than the wind needling at her.

Danielle watched her brother doing what she herself had just finished doing, except that Jake went farther and peered still more intently over the edge. They must have missed something, she told herself. They hadn't looked hard enough.

Yet she couldn't see anything like what they were looking for. There was nothing at all like a weather station.

They were at the summit.

Alone.

"We're dead," Danielle moaned. "Jake — we're dead."

7

Stop and Think

Critical Thinking Questions

1. **DRAWING CONCLUSIONS** Why do you think Danielle and Jake can't locate the weather station? (Maybe they climbed up the wrong part of the mountain during the blizzard.)

2. **MAKING JUDGMENTS** What do you think Danielle and Jake should do next? (Sample answer: They should plan a new way to get help.)

Strategies in Action

Have students take turns modeling Predict/Infer and other strategies they used.

Discussion Options

You may want to bring the entire class together to do one or more of the activities below.

- **Review Predictions/Purpose** Discuss with students which predictions about Jake and Danielle's climb were accurate and which ones needed to be revised. Record any changes and new predictions.

- **Share Group Discussions** Have students share their literature discussions.

- **Summarize** Have students use their Event Chart to summarize the story so far.

ASSIGNMENT CARD 10

Literature Discussion

Discuss your own questions and the following questions with a group of classmates:

- Have you ever taken a chance and realized you were capable of more than you expected? Describe that experience.

- How does the author show that Danielle and Jake are in a life-threatening situation?

- What clues show you that these characters are resourceful, inventive, and determined?

- What would you do if you faced the problem described at the end of this section? Why?

Theme 1: Courage

Teacher's Resource BLM page 51

Monitoring Student Progress

If . . .	Then . . .
students have successfully completed the Extra Support activities on page 80,	have them read the rest of the story cooperatively or independently.

Guiding Comprehension

8 **MAKING INFERENCES** What does the author mean by *That push hurt worst of all*? (When Danielle pushes Jake away, it confirms his fear that he's let her down.)

9 **NOTING DETAILS** What details show that Danielle is no longer afraid and angry? (The way she shakes Jake changes—she's trying to get his attention.)

Jake stumbled over to her. He had begun to shake and now shook so hard he couldn't stop. He couldn't believe all their efforts had come to this. He couldn't believe his plan hadn't worked. There was supposed to be a weather station up here. He'd seen it on TV. It had to be here. Yet the place around them looked as desolate as the moon. So Jake stood staring at his sister, at how miserable she looked with her gloved hands up against her mouth while she cried, and he felt hollow and terrible inside. "Danielle," he said. "I'm sorry —" A moment later he started crying, too. He reached out to embrace her.

They held each other a long time. He wanted to reassure Danielle, to suggest a new idea that would save them after all, but he couldn't think of anything. All he could think about was the cold. What would it feel like, freezing to death? How long would it take? Would it be peaceful, as some people said it was? Peaceful! What a joke! How could it be peaceful? Even if Jake went numb and didn't feel the pain of his fingers and toes turning to ice, of his blood thickening to slush, then surely he'd still think every last second about how he'd let down Mom, Dad, and Danielle —

8   She was pushing him away. That push hurt worst of all, and tears filled Jake's eyes so fast that his vision went blurry.

"This is *your* fault!" she screamed.

"Danielle, I'm sorry —"

"*Your* fault!"

"Listen —"

"You and your stupid weather station!"

"Danielle, listen —"

She took him by the shoulders and shook him.

"I'm sorry," Jake shouted back. "I'm sorry, I'm sorry, I'm sorry!"

9   She shook him harder and harder. She shook him so hard that Danielle almost knocked him over. But then, gradually at first, the way she shook him started to change. She wasn't punishing him now — she was trying to get his attention. Puzzled at first, Jake soon understood what his sister was doing. He pulled back from her. He wiped his eyes with the back of his glove.

"*Look!*" she cried. "Just look!"

Danielle was pointing into the clouds sweeping past from left to right.

"What is it?"

"Over there!"

82

Vocabulary

desolate having few or no inhabitants; deserted

reassure restore confidence in

83

Story Structure

Review

- Remind students that characters are who the story is about and setting is where the story takes place.

- Remind students that the plot is the events in a story and includes a problem that the characters resolve.

- Draw a story map on the board, and discuss story structure using *Hatchet* as an example.

Story Map for Hatchet
Setting Canadian wilderness
Character Brian
Plot Problem needs fire to survive
        Resolution ignites birch bark
        with sparks from hatchet

Practice/Apply

- Have partners start story maps for *Climb or Die*. (Setting: Mount Remington; Characters: Danielle, Jake; Problem: must climb mountain to find help)

- They can identify and record the new problem Jake and Danielle face once they reach what appears to be the summit. (There's no weather station.)

- Partners can identify and record the solution. (Find the true summit.)

Review Skill Trace	
Teach	Theme 3, p. 319A
Reteach	Theme 3, p. R12
▶ Review	p. 83; Theme 6, p. 623

ASSIGNMENT CARD 12

Super Similes

Writer's Craft: Similes

A simile is a comparison of two or more things, using the word *like* or *as*. Reread the first paragraph on page 82. Find the sentence *Yet the place around them looked as desolate as the moon*. The simile *as desolate as the moon* helps readers picture the mountain top as a rocky, empty place, with no people, plants, or animals.

Write three similes of your own to describe Jake and Danielle's situation. You and your classmates may help each other by first brainstorming possible comparisons for the following: the feeling of being lost and cold; the sound of the hammer hitting the ice; the feel of falling snow; the view from the mountain top. You may also choose to describe a different scene. Share your similes with your classmates.

Theme 1: Courage

Teacher's Resource BLM page 52

CRITICAL THINKING
Guiding Comprehension

10 MAKING INFERENCES Why is it important for Jake and Danielle to make it to the weather station quickly? (because Danielle is rapidly losing body heat)

11 DRAWING CONCLUSIONS Why does Danielle think *Someone* had *to be up here*? (She's desperate to convince herself that someone is at the station, even though it looks deserted.)

TARGET SKILL

COMPREHENSION STRATEGY
Predict/Infer

Student Modeling After students finish reading page 85, ask them to model making predictions about what Jake will do next. If necessary, offer these prompts.

- What has Jake just realized about the music? What might he do as a result?

- What objects does Jake have in his pack that you know about? Which of these things might he be trying to find?

Vocabulary

textures the appearance and feel of surfaces

ridge long, narrow strip of high land

drifts masses of snow

vacant empty

rummaged searched thoroughly

Jake leaned this way and that to get a better look. At first all he saw was the soft gray-white nothingness of the clouds. Then, looking more closely, he realized that what he saw wasn't just the clouds; it was also the clouds shifting, parting, and revealing something beyond. First just textures, then shapes. Some sort of low horizontal box. Some vertical lines. He couldn't tell what it was. Something inside the clouds?

At that moment the clouds shifted and whatever he'd been seeing took on more detail. Walls. Windows. A metal roof. Some sort of shed next to the main structure. A big antenna poking up from the shed. A satellite dish mounted on the roof. The longer he looked, the more he saw. And he saw something else, too: a stony ridge that connected Danielle and Jake's summit to another summit, a pile of massive boulders topped by these ghostly buildings.

"The weather station!" Jake exclaimed.

"We're on a false summit," Danielle said. "That's the real summit over there."

Without another word they rushed over to the edge, and, scrambling as fast as possible without tumbling headfirst, they climbed down toward the ridge connecting where they were to where they wanted to be.

10 Danielle was shaking hard by the time she and Jake worked their way over to the weather station. Her hands shook, her knees shook, her whole body shook. She was shaking from excitement but mostly from the cold. Danielle couldn't remember having ever felt so cold. She almost felt as if she were bleeding to death, except that her blood was heat, and all the heat was leaking from her body. In a few minutes the heat would be gone.

Danielle and Jake staggered the last few feet up the slope to the weather station. Drifts lay piled on the far side of the buildings, drifts so deep that Danielle had to wallow to get anywhere. She lost her balance several times trying to push through. Twice she fell over and ended up with a faceful of snow. Yet somehow she managed, and Jake did, too, and they made it all the way to the biggest of the buildings.

"Where's the door?" Danielle asked.

"Maybe this way," Jake answered, and they worked their way around to the right.

84

Danielle started pounding on the door the moment she reached it. Her hands felt so numb, however, that she couldn't even make a fist. She wasn't really pounding, she was slapping. Then Jake started in, too, striking the door as hard as he could.

They both stopped and fell silent.

All they heard was the whistle of the wind and the fluttering noise it made against the weather station.

"Maybe nobody's home," Jake said.

"Don't be ridiculous," Danielle told him, but his words chilled her even more than the cold. Was it possible? Could they have come all the way here only to reach a vacant building?

She glanced around. There was a relatively flat, open area right next to the building — the sort of area someone might use to park a truck up here — but no truck in sight. Danielle saw no vehicles at all. On the other side of this area, though, was a shedlike structure, and she decided that must be a garage. But she didn't really care. She knew someone was up here. Someone *had* to be up here.

Danielle started pounding again.

Jake interrupted her: "Listen!"

She held off. She waited.

Just then she heard something. "Music!" Danielle exclaimed. Some kind of jazz.

At once she went back to pounding. "Open!" she yelled. "Open up! Please! We need help!"

Jake pounded, too.

Then they stopped, waited, listened.

Nothing happened.

Danielle could feel her excitement vanish in a moment's time. Surely they wouldn't climb all day only to discover that no one could hear them!`

Before she could start pounding again, though, Jake said, "Wait — maybe the music's too loud." He took off his pack, pulled it open, and rummaged around inside. When he couldn't find what he wanted, he dumped everything out onto the snow.

"What are you doing?" Danielle asked.

11

Extra Support/Intervention

Strategy Modeling: Predict/Infer

Use this example to model the strategy.

No one is answering Jake and Danielle's knocks, but they hear music playing inside the station. There must be people inside, but Jake and Danielle need to knock louder in order for them to hear. I predict that Jake will find something in the backpack that he can use to make a louder knock.

Comprehension Review

Noting Details

Review

- Tell students that details show what characters see, hear, and feel.

- Write on the board the words from pages 84–85 that describe what the characters feel physically. *(cold, numbness, fatigue)*

Practice/Apply

- Have students find details from pages 84–85 to complete a T-chart like the one below. (Sample answers are shown.)

What They See	What They Hear
gray-white clouds, walls, windows, metal roof, shed, big antenna, satellite dish, stony ridge	whistle of the wind, jazz music

- Ask students what they can infer from these details about the characters' emotions. (Sample answer: frustrated that they are stuck in the cold; hopeful that someone is at the station)

Review Skill Trace	
Teach	p. 47A
Reteach	p. R8
▶ Review	p. 85; Theme 2, p. 173; Theme 3, p. 279; Theme 4, p. 393; Theme 5, p. 503

CRITICAL THINKING
Guiding Comprehension

12 **COMPARE AND CONTRAST** In what ways is Jake's idea similar to Danielle's earlier idea that helped them climb? (Both involve improvising with the hammer.)

13 **TEXT ORGANIZATION** How can you tell that *Climb or Die* is part of a longer story? (Sample answers: because the story ends abruptly; because *"Trick or treat!"* seems out of context; because so much happened before the selection began, particularly the car crash and the injury of their parents)

12 Jake picked up Dad's biggest hammer. He said, "Improvising." At once he started banging on the door — banging so hard that each blow dented the metal.

The music stopped a few moments later.

Danielle could almost imagine that she heard a voice.

Then Jake said, "Okay, get ready."

"Ready?" Danielle asked, unsure of what he meant. Watching, she saw Jake reach down to his empty pack. Just then Danielle saw what he was going to do, but she understood too late to stop him.

13 As the door swung open, revealing two startled men on the other side, Jake held out his empty pack like a Halloween bag.

"Trick or treat!"

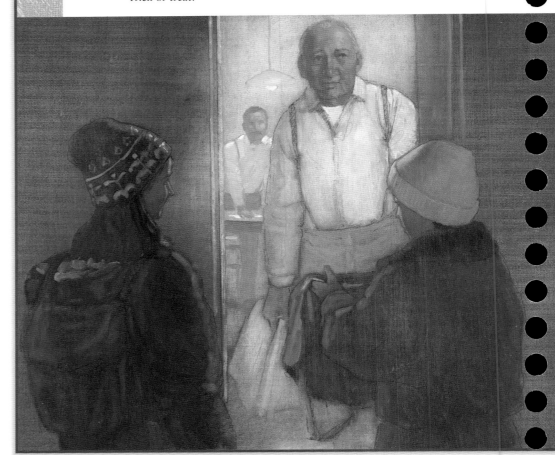

Extra Support/ Intervention

Selection Review

Before students join the whole class for Wrapping Up on page 87, they should

- review their predictions/purpose
- take turns modeling Predict/Infer and other strategies they used
- complete their Event Chart on **Practice Book** page 47 and help you complete **Transparency 1–20**
- summarize the whole selection

On Level **Challenge**

Literature Discussion

In mixed-ability groups of five or six, students can discuss the story using questions of their own or questions in Think About the Selection on Anthology page 88.

ABOUT THE AUTHOR

EDWARD MYERS

Ed Myers loves the outdoors — especially hiking and mountain climbing. Although no one should copy the characters in *Climb or Die*, Ed Myers has successfully tested all the climbing techniques himself. He lives in New Jersey with his wife Edith and two children.

ABOUT THE ILLUSTRATOR

BILL FARNSWORTH

"Draw what you see all the time and talk to illustrators. You have to be a sponge and take in all the information you can," Bill Farnsworth advises. Several times a year, he visits schools to talk with children about what he does as an illustrator. He also enjoys playing tennis, gardening, and cooking in his Sarasota, Florida, home.

 Internet

To find out more about Edward Myers and Bill Farnsworth, visit Education Place. **www.eduplace.com/kids**

87

Wrapping Up

Critical Thinking Questions

1. **FANTASY AND REALISM** Is *Climb or Die* a realistic story? Why or why not? (Sample answer: It's realistic because Jake and Danielle quarrel like real brothers and sisters do and face difficulties on the climb that could happen in real life.)

2. **DRAWING CONCLUSIONS** What do Jake's actions at the very end of the story show about him? (Sample answer: He is mischievous and playful, even during hard times.)

Strategies in Action

Have students take turns modeling Predict/Infer and other strategies they used while reading.

Discussion Options

Bring the entire class together to do one or more of the activities below.

Review Predictions/Purpose Discuss students' predictions. Which were confirmed? Which did they have to revise?

Share Group Discussions Have students share their questions and group discussions.

Summarize Ask students to use their Event Charts to summarize the story.

Comprehension Check

Use **Practice Book** page 48 to assess students' comprehension of the selection.

English Language Learners

Supporting Comprehension

Jake's decision to say *"Trick or treat!"* may be confusing to some English language learners.

- First, ask volunteers to explain what children do and say on Halloween.

- Then work with students to brainstorm why Jake might have said this. (Sample answers: He was happy to see the men; he was relieved to reach safety.)

Practice Book page 48

Climb or Die
Comprehension Check

Name _____

Interview with the Ice Climbers

Complete the interview below by writing the answers Danielle and Jake would give to tell about their experience.

Q: Jake, why did you and your sister climb Mount Remington in the first place?

A: Danielle and I had to get help for our parents after our car crashed in a blizzard. I had seen a weather station on Mt. Remington on TV, so we decided to go there for help. (1 point)

Q: Danielle, how did you and your brother manage to climb without proper equipment?

A: We improvised. We used hammers as ice axes, screwdrivers as pitons, and a nylon leash as a carabiner. (1)

Q: What happened when you reached the top of the trench?

A: We were happy at first because we thought we were at the top. Then we suddenly got scared when we realized we couldn't see the weather station anywhere. (1)

Q: Jake, how did you and your sister feel at that moment?

A: I felt guilty for having been wrong about the weather station. Danielle was angry at me for the same reason. We were both scared of freezing to death. (1)

Q: What happened next that raised your spirits?

A: We realized we were on a false summit when we saw the weather station on a ridge above us. (1)

Q: What happened when you finally got to the weather station?

A: We banged on the door, but nobody answered. At first we thought no one was there, but then we heard faint music coming from inside. (1)

Monitoring Student Progress

If...	Then...
students score 4 or below on **Practice Book** page 48,	help them find places in the text that tell what Danielle and Jake had to do to reach the top.

Responding

Think About the Selection

Have students discuss or write their answers. Sample answers are provided; accept reasonable responses.

1. MAKING JUDGMENTS Sample answers: yes, because I'd do anything to help them; no, because there must be an easier way to find help

2. CONNECTING TO PERSONAL EXPERIENCES Answers will vary.

3. CAUSE AND EFFECT The station is isolated and difficult to reach, especially for two unaccompanied children.

4. WRITER'S CRAFT By shifting the focus between the two characters, the author is able to show exactly what each thinks and feels.

5. MAKING INFERENCES It shows that Jake cares about his sister and feels badly that she's upset by his mistake.

6. DRAWING CONCLUSIONS Danielle learns that she enjoys coming up with new ideas and solving problems. Jake learns that it feels good to push himself beyond what he thinks he can do.

7. Connecting/Comparing All characters use the tools they have in order to make what they need. They survive because they have creative ideas and refuse to give up, even if something doesn't work on the first try.

Responding

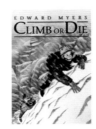

THINK ABOUT THE SELECTION

1. If you were Jake or Danielle, would you try to climb Mount Remington to get help for your parents? Explain.

2. Danielle's interest in climbing increases as she learns more about it. Give an example from your own life of something that interested you as you learned more about it.

3. Why are the people in the weather station surprised to see Jake and Danielle?

4. Why do you think the author chose to alternate the focus in the selection between Danielle and Jake?

5. When they reach the false summit, Danielle pushes Jake away and his feelings are hurt. What does this tell you about Jake?

6. What do you think Jake and Danielle learn from each other?

7. **Connecting/Comparing** Compare how Jake and Danielle improvise their tools with how Brian uses his hatchet. What qualities help them to survive? Explain.

Informing

WRITE A MESSAGE

Suppose that when Danielle and Jake reach the weather station, they find it empty. Write a message they might leave at the weather station. Explain their situation and tell what they plan to do next.

Tips
- State the message very clearly. Remember, the information it contains might lead to the characters' rescue.
- Include the date, the time, and the characters' names.

88

English Language Learners

Supporting Comprehension

Beginning/Preproduction Ask students to make drawings of Danielle and Jake climbing the mountain.

Early Production and Speech Emergence Have students make captioned drawings or a cartoon of Danielle and Jake climbing, reaching the top, and arriving at the weather station.

Intermediate and Advanced Fluency Have students discuss what Danielle and Jake learned on this climb.

READ & COMPREHEND

Vocabulary

DESIGN A CLIMBING CATALOG

Make a catalog of mountaineering tools climbers use. Start with tools from the story such as an ice ax and carabiners. Draw items that you cannot find pictures of. Then label and describe each picture.

Bonus Give an oral report about your catalog. Explain how and why each item is used in climbing.

Listening and Speaking

GIVE A DRAMATIC READING

With a small group, give a dramatic reading of part of the selection. Begin on page 82, at the paragraph that starts with "Jake stumbled over to her." Read through to the end of the selection. One person can read Danielle's lines, while another reads Jake's lines. Other group members can take turns reading the narrator's parts.

Tips

- Read more slowly than usual, and include pauses. Make sure that your audience can hear you.
- You do not need to move or make gestures, but do read with expression.

COMPLETE A WEB CROSSWORD PUZZLE

How much do you learn about the sport of climbing from reading *Climb or Die*? Find out by completing a crossword puzzle that can be printed from Education Place.

www.eduplace.com/kids

89

Additional Responses

Personal Response Invite students to share their personal responses to the selection.

Journal ▸ Have students write in their journals about a time they accomplished something difficult.

Selection Connections Remind students to add to **Practice Book** page 10.

Extra Support/ Intervention

Brainstorming Details

Have students brainstorm and list what information Jake and Danielle might include in the message. (their names and ages; how they came to be on the mountain; where their parents are; what they plan to do next)

Practice Book page 10

Name

Launching the Theme
Selection Connections

Courage continued

	Climb or Die	The True Confessions of Charlotte Doyle
What challenge does the main character face?	Danielle and Jake must climb a steep, icy mountain without the right climbing tools. (2.5)	Charlotte must climb to the top of the royal yard to prove she is fit to be a sailor. (2.5)
Where does the challenge take place?	on a snowy mountain in modern times (2.5)	on a sailing ship in the 1800s (2.5)
In what ways does the main character show courage?	Danielle and Jake bravely complete the climb, using only the tools they have. (2.5)	Charlotte completes the climb even though she is terrified. (2.5)
What do you think the character learns from his or her experience?	Danielle and Jake learn that they are resourceful and stronger than they thought. (2.5)	Charlotte learns that she can climb to the top of the royal yard without falling or getting sick. (2.5)

What have you learned about courage in this theme?
Sample answer: Sometimes people surprise themselves with strength they didn't know they had. (2)

Monitoring Student Progress

End-of-Selection Assessment

Selection Test Use the test on page 113 in the **Teacher's Resource Blackline Masters** to assess selection comprehension and vocabulary.

Student Self-Assessment Have students assess their reading with additional questions such as the following:

- What parts of the story were difficult or easy for me to understand? Why?
- What strategies helped me read and understand difficult passages?
- What new words did I learn?
- Would I like to find out more about what happens to Danielle and Jake? Why or why not?

Responding 89

Social Studies Link

Skill: How to Read a Social Studies Article

- **Introduce** "Battling Everest," a nonfiction article from *National Geographic World* magazine. Tell students that a nonfiction social studies article differs from a made-up story like *Climb or Die* because a nonfiction article contains only facts about real people and places.

- **Discuss** the Skill Lesson on Anthology page 90.

- **Model** scanning the article. Use the title, subtitle, headings, and photographs to tell what the article is about. Note the time and location of the topic.

- **Ask** what students already know about the topic. Have them predict what they will learn by turning headings into questions.

- **Set a purpose** for reading. Have students read the article. Tell them to note how the problems were solved or handled. Encourage them to complete a Problem/Solution chart like the one shown below. (Sample answers are shown.)

Problem	Solution
had to cross a river	built a bridge
Edmund Hillary fell into a crevasse.	Tenzing Norgay stopped the fall with his ice ax.
lack of oxygen	They carried oxygen tanks.

Social Studies Link

Battling EVEREST
by Michael Burgan

Could the two climbers conquer the killer mountain?

Social Studies Article

Skill: How to Read a Social Studies Article

Before you read . . .

Scan each page of the article. Read the title, subtitle, and headings.

Note the **time** and **location** of the topic.

Ask yourself what you already know about the topic. **Predict** what you will learn by turning each heading into a question.

While you read . . .

Look for answers to your questions.

Use **context clues** to help you understand unfamiliar words.

Look for **sequence words** that show the order of events.

90

THIS WAS IT: THE DAY THEY HAD spent years preparing for. The two men peered out of a tent and saw around them icy peaks glowing in the early morning sun. The men were perched more than five miles high on one side of Everest, the world's tallest mountain on land. The wind, which had been howling at 60 miles an hour, was calm now, but the temperature was a brutally cold *minus* 17°F. This day, May 29, 1953, Edmund Hillary and Tenzing Norgay hoped to become the first to step onto Everest's peak.

They almost hadn't made it this far. One month earlier the two climbers, linked by a rope, had been exploring an icefall, a rugged expanse of huge, jagged, shifting ice blocks. Hillary, in the lead, came upon a crevasse, or deep gap, that was much too wide to step across. As climbers sometimes do, Hillary used a chunk of ice near the opening as a step. But when he landed on the chunk, it gave way. He tumbled with the ice into the crevasse. "Everything seemed to start going slowly," said Hillary later, "even though I was free-falling into the crevasse." As he fell, Hillary twisted his body to avoid getting pinned inside the crevasse.

Watching his friend plummet into the icy hole, Tenzing acted quickly. He thrust his ice ax into the snow and wrapped the rope around it. "The rope came tight with a twang," Hillary later recalled,

"and I was stopped and swung in against the wall." The ice chunk smashed into the bottom of the crevasse. Without Tenzing's fast action, Hillary would have crashed there, too.

Danger Ahead

The men came from different worlds. Edmund Hillary had worked as a beekeeper in his native New Zealand. Tenzing Norgay, his partner, was a Sherpa. (Sherpas, a people native to Nepal in the Himalaya, are famous as mountain guides.) But Hillary and Tenzing shared a passion for climbing mountains. Hillary had made two previous climbs in the Himalaya. Tenzing had already attempted to climb Everest six times. Each had the determination and skills to reach the summit as well as a deep trust in each other's talents.

Still, they knew the dangers, from frostbite to avalanches, crevasse falls, sudden blinding snowstorms, and lack of oxygen. Already 24 climbers had died trying to scale Everest. Just three days earlier, two climbers had turned back, exhausted and unable to continue. They warned Hillary and Tenzing of the risks ahead.

Nevertheless at 6:30 A.M. on May 29, Edmund Hillary looked at Tenzing Norgay and asked, "All ready?" "**Ah chah,**" Tenzing replied, "ready." Just 1,100 feet higher, and they would make history.

Extra Support/Intervention

Geography

Have students locate Mount Everest on a map. Then tell them the following:

- Mount Everest is the highest mountain on land in the world. Its peak is more than five and a half miles above sea level.

- It is part of a range of mountains called the Himalayas, which extends through India, Tibet, Nepal, and other countries in south central Asia.

Narrative Nonfiction

Teach

- Explain that "Battling Everest" is a piece of narrative nonfiction.
- It tells about real people, places, and events.
- It tells an interesting story with a problem and a resolution.

Practice/Apply

- Have partners list real people, places, and events mentioned in the link. (Sample answer: People: Tenzing Norgay and Edmund Hillary; Places: Mount Everest; Events: Hillary's plummet into an icy hole, the successful climb)
- Have partners list the problem and how it was solved. (getting past the death zone; by skill and determination)

Vocabulary

hovering floating directly above

glaciers large masses of ice slowly moving over a mountain or through a valley

treacherous dangerous

painstakingly very carefully

Months of Struggle

Their quest to reach the top of Everest had begun more than two months earlier on March 10, 1953. Sir John Hunt, a British army colonel, led a team of 14 climbers, 36 Sherpa guides, and 350 porters carrying tons of supplies.

Tenzing Norgay and Edmund Hillary celebrate the first ascent of Everest over cups of tea.

Hillary, Tenzing, and the other team members set out from Kathmandu, the capital of Nepal. At first they walked along colorful hillsides dotted with small farmhouses. As they climbed higher, the landscape changed. Steep cliffs lined a rushing river. To cross it, the climbers made a rickety bridge of rocks and bamboo. Heavy rains and swarms of hornets tormented them. Progress was slow.

Moving eastward, the party finally saw Everest in the distance as if it were hovering in the sky. The climbers set up a base camp at an elevation above 12,000 feet. From there they would move higher up into the mountains, setting up new camps along the way.

The team spent a few weeks at the base camp to prepare the route upward by cutting steps in the snow. One day Hillary led a small team to explore the Khumbu Icefall, "one of the most awful and utterly forbidding scenes ever observed by man," according to George Mallory, a climber who had died in the region. Hillary and his team came up against a field of tilting, shifting giant blocks of ice pushed, pulled, and swept by glaciers and avalanches.

He guided the team through the treacherous terrain as it shifted and split into crevasses. Avalanches continually threatened to bury the team in boulders of ice. But Hillary found a route through the icefall and set up camp at 19,400 feet.

Along the route, the men named some of the more difficult spots. One they called "Hillary's Horror." Another was "Atom Bomb" for the explosive noises of shifting ice. It was at Atom Bomb that Hillary's fall into a crevasse had almost ended his climb — and his life.

That close call was only a memory now, as Hillary and Tenzing started their final climb. Once again a rope linked them. Tenzing took the lead first, then Hillary went ahead. They hiked along a ridge only a few feet wide. The soft snow made the going tough. Discouraged by the difficulty, they considered turning back. Hillary finally said to himself, "Forget it! This is Everest."

92

English Language Learners

Supporting Comprehension

- Ask students why they think Mount Everest is called *the killer mountain*. Encourage students to share anything they know about it.
- Then go through the article with students and point out the four headings.
- Pair English language learners with English-proficient partners and have them read the article together. Suggest that they read one section at a time, pausing to talk about the main ideas.

Further on the snow became more solid, allowing Hillary to cut steps into it. Still the climbers were cautious. To their right were cornices, or twisted ridges of snow. Just beyond them was an 8,000-foot drop. To their left ran a rocky ledge. Painstakingly the two men — the only members of the team to make it this far — continued up the mountain.

The Death Zone

Each man wore eight layers of clothing and three pairs of gloves. Each carried a 40-pound oxygen tank on his back. At high elevations the air is "thin," meaning it contains less oxygen. But climbers need **extra** oxygen to survive, especially at 25,000 feet, an elevation some call the beginning of "the Death Zone."

As he chipped at the snow, Hillary worried about their oxygen supply. Would they have enough? Now it was even harder to breathe because ice was forming in their oxygen tubes. Hillary and Tenzing had to keep clearing out the tubes to breathe well enough to continue their climb. Nothing, they hoped, would stop them. Yet, as Hillary later said, "We didn't know if it was humanly possible to reach the top of Everest."

The two climbers now came upon a rock wall 40 feet high. They no longer had the strength to climb straight up. Instead Hillary climbed between the rock and a nearby cornice, using his crampons, or spikes on his boots, to help him. Once he reached the top of the wall, Hillary

pulled Tenzing up. Then they went back to cutting steps in the snow.

To the Top

The hours passed. Both men were slowing down. Their conquest, Hillary later said, was turning into a "grim struggle." Then the ridge they were climbing peaked, and they were on the top of Everest!

The two men hugged and shook hands. Hillary snapped some photographs. Tenzing buried candy and biscuits in the snow as presents to the gods that Sherpas believe live on Everest. After 15 minutes, the two men left the peak and its majestic view — a sight no human being had ever seen before. They had reached the roof of the world.

Hillary took this photograph of Tenzing holding a flag at the top of Everest.

Wrapping Up

Critical Thinking Questions

Ask students to use the selection to answer these questions.

1. **COMPARE AND CONTRAST** How were Edmund Hillary and Tenzing Norgay alike and different? (Both were experienced, passionate climbers; however, Edmund Hillary was from New Zealand, while Tenzing Norgay was a Sherpa from Nepal.)

2. **NOTING DETAILS** What dangers did the two men face? (freezing cold weather, avalanches, icefalls, crevasses, frostbite, lack of oxygen, exhaustion)

3. **MAKING INFERENCES** Why do you think the two men were willing to risk their lives to make the climb? (Sample answer: They both loved climbing; it was a chance to make history.)

4. **DRAWING CONCLUSIONS** Why does the author say the men finally *reached the roof of the world*? (Sample answer: Everest's peak is the world's highest point on land.)

5. **Connecting/Comparing** Compare the children's climb in *Climb or Die* to Hillary's and Norgay's famous climb. (*Climb or Die* is fiction about children with little experience or equipment who climb to find help; "Battling Everest" is about real, experienced climbers climbing to reach a goal. Both sets of climbers had to face harsh weather and treacherous terrain.)

REACHING ALL LEARNERS

Challenge

Author's Viewpoint

- Have students work in a group to identify the author's opinion of Edmund Hillary and Tenzing Norgay. (The author is impressed by their accomplishments.)

- Have students identify words and phrases that led them to reach this conclusion. (Sample answer: *determination and skills; deep trust in each other's talents; "grim struggle"*)

- Students may want to read another book or article about Hillary and Norgay and compare its author's viewpoint with the one in this article.

OBJECTIVES

- Identify order of story events.
- Identify words that signal sequence or simultaneous events and verbs that signal events that happened in the past.
- Identify when an author shifts from the present action to past events.

Target Skill Trace

Preview; Teach	p. 71CC, p. 74, p. 77; p. 93A
Reteach	p. R12
Review	pp. M32–M33; p. 101; Theme 5, p. 461
See	*Extra Support Handbook,* pp. 36–37; pp. 42–43

Transparency 1–20

Event Chart

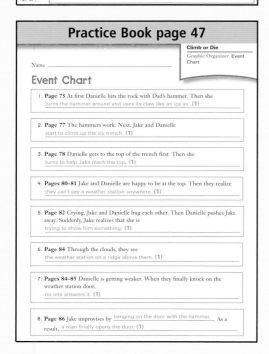

COURAGE *Climb or Die*
Graphic Organizer Event Chart

1. **Page 75** At first Danielle hits the rock with Dad's hammer. Then she
   turns the hammer around and uses its claw like an ice ax.

2. **Page 77** The hammers work. Next, Jake and Danielle
   start to climb up the icy trench.

3. **Page 78** Danielle gets to the top of the trench first. Then she
   turns to help Jake reach the top.

4. **Pages 80–81** Jake and Danielle are happy to be at the top. Then they realize
   they can't see a weather station anywhere.

5. **Page 82** Crying, Jake and Danielle hug each other. Then Danielle pushes Jake away. Suddenly, Jake realizes that she is
   trying to show him something.

6. **Page 84** Through the clouds, they see
   the weather station on a ridge above them.

7. **Pages 84–85** Danielle is getting weaker. When they finally knock on the weather station door,
   no one answers it.

8. **Page 86** Jake improvises by banging on the door with the hammer. As a result, a man finally opens the door.

TRANSPARENCY 1–20
TEACHER'S EDITION PAGES 74 AND 93A

Practice Book page 47

Climb or Die
Graphic Organizer Event Chart

Name _____

Event Chart

1. **Page 75** At first Danielle hits the rock with Dad's hammer. Then she
   turns the hammer around and uses its claw like an ice ax. **(1)**

2. **Page 77** The hammers work. Next, Jake and Danielle
   start to climb up the icy trench. **(1)**

3. **Page 78** Danielle gets to the top of the trench first. Then she
   turns to help Jake reach the top. **(1)**

4. **Pages 80–81** Jake and Danielle are happy to be at the top. Then they realize
   they can't see a weather station anywhere. **(1)**

5. **Page 82** Crying, Jake and Danielle hug each other. Then Danielle pushes Jake away. Suddenly, Jake realizes that she is
   trying to show him something. **(1)**

6. **Page 84** Through the clouds, they see
   the weather station on a ridge above them. **(1)**

7. **Pages 84–85** Danielle is getting weaker. When they finally knock on the weather station door,
   no one answers it. **(1)**

8. **Page 86** Jake improvises by banging on the door with the hammer. As a result, a man finally opens the door. **(1)**

COMPREHENSION: Sequence of Events

❶ Teach

Review the sequence of events in *Climb or Die*. Complete the Graphic Organizer on **Transparency 1–20** with students. (Sample answers are shown.) Students can refer to the selection and **Practice Book** page 47.

- Emphasize that the main story events are told in time order.
- Point out words that signal sequential order (*then, next*) and words that signal events happening at the same time (*while*).

Model using signal words to identify time shifts. Explain that authors can shift from present events to past events to give readers more information. Have a student read aloud the fourth full paragraph on page 80. Then think aloud.

Think Aloud *The words* had stopped *in the first sentence mean that the snow stopped falling before the event in the second sentence took place. The snow stopped and now Danielle is looking down at more clouds below them, as if they were in an airplane. The verb phrase* had stopped *shows what happened before so I can understand what is happening right now.*

❷ Guided Practice

Have students identify time shifts. Have partners reread pages 81 and 82 to find examples of actions that happened in the past, signaled by the word *had*. Have them record their answers on time lines like the ones shown below. (Sample answers are shown.)

(a) Page 81 : ". . . had just finished doing . . . "

FIRST	THEN
Danielle peered over the edge.	Jake peered over the edge while Danielle watched.

(b) Page 82 : ". . . had begun to shake . . . "

FIRST	THEN
Jake began to shake.	Jake shook so hard he couldn't stop.

❸ Apply

Assign Practice Book pages 49–50. Also have students apply this skill as they read their **Leveled Readers** for this week. You may also select books from the Leveled Bibliography for this theme (pages 23E–23F).

Test Prep Remind students that when answering test questions about sequence of events, they should scan the passage for time-order words such as *first, next, last, then, now, tomorrow,* and *yesterday.*

Leveled Readers and Leveled Practice

Students at all levels apply the comprehension skill as they read their Leveled Readers. See lessons on pages 930–93R.

● BELOW LEVEL   ▲ ON LEVEL   ■ ABOVE LEVEL   ◆ LANGUAGE SUPPORT

Reading Traits

Teaching students how to identify sequence of events is one way of encouraging them to "read the lines" of a selection. This comprehension skill supports the reading trait **Establishing Comprehension.**

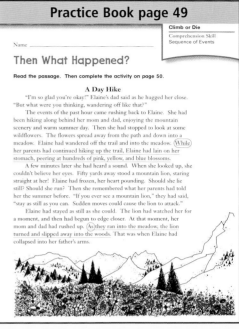

Practice Book page 49

Climb or Die
Comprehension Skill
Sequence of Events

Name _____

Then What Happened?

Read the passage. Then complete the activity on page 50.

A Day Hike

"I'm so glad you're okay!" Elaine's dad said as he hugged her close. "But what were you thinking, wandering off like that?"

The events of the past hour came rushing back to Elaine. She had been hiking along behind her mom and dad, enjoying the mountain scenery and warm summer day. Then she had stopped to look at some wildflowers. The flowers spread away from the path and down into a meadow. Elaine had wandered off the trail and into the meadow. While her parents had continued hiking up the trail, Elaine had lain on her stomach, peering at hundreds of pink, yellow, and blue blossoms.

A few minutes later she had heard a sound. When she looked up, she couldn't believe her eyes. Fifty yards away stood a mountain lion, staring straight at her! Elaine had frozen, her heart pounding. Should she lie still? Should she run? Then she remembered what her parents had told her the summer before. "If you ever see a mountain lion," they had said, "stay as still as you can. Sudden moves could cause the lion to attack."

Elaine had stayed as still as she could. The lion had watched her for a moment, and then had begun to edge closer. At that moment, her mom and dad had rushed up. As they ran into the meadow, the lion turned and slipped away into the woods. That was when Elaine had collapsed into her father's arms.

Practice Book page 50

Climb or Die
Comprehension Skill
Sequence of Events

Name _____

Then What Happened? continued

Complete the sequence chart to show the order of events in the passage on page 49. Begin the chart with an event that happened the year before the events described in the passage.

| Last summer, Elaine's parents tell her to stay still if she ever sees a mountain lion. (2 points) |
| The next summer, Elaine goes hiking in the mountains with her parents. (2) |
| She wanders into a meadow to look at wildflowers while her parents hike up the trail. (2) |
| Elaine sees a mountain lion fifty yards away. (2) |
| She remembers her parents' advice and lies very still. (2) |
| Her parents return and the mountain lion slips away. (2) |
| Elaine's father hugs her. (2) |

Now go back to the passage and underline the sentences that tell where two different events happened at the same time. Circle the sequence words that helped you to figure this out. (4 points)

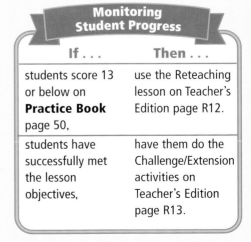

Monitoring Student Progress

If . . .	Then . . .
students score 13 or below on **Practice Book** page 50,	use the Reteaching lesson on Teacher's Edition page R12.
students have successfully met the lesson objectives,	have them do the Challenge/Extension activities on Teacher's Edition page R13.

OBJECTIVES

- Read words that have prefixes *un-* and *re-*.
- Use the Phonics/Decoding Strategy to decode longer words.
- Learn academic language: *prefix, word part, base word.*

Target Skill Trace

Teach	p. 93C
Reteach	p. R20
Review	pp. M34–M35
See	*Handbook for English Language Learners*, p. 39; *Extra Support Handbook*, pp. 34–35; pp. 38–39

Practice Book page 51

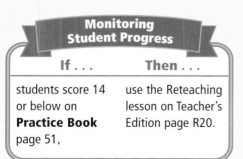

Climb or Die
Structural Analysis Prefixes *un-* and *re-*

Name _____

Prefix Clues

Underline the word in each sentence that has the prefix *un-* or *re-*. Then write a meaning for the word on the line below the sentence.

Prefix	Meaning
un-	not
re-	again, back, backward

1. The hikers agreed to <u>reassemble</u> at the summit. (1 point)
   assemble, or meet together, again (1)
2. Some of them were <u>unprepared</u> for such a long hike. (1)
   not prepared (1)
3. They <u>reconsidered</u> their plan and turned back. (1)
   considered, or thought about, again (1)
4. Jake felt <u>unsteady</u> on the narrow ledge. (1)
   not steady (1)
5. He had <u>renewed</u> energy after eating a banana. (1)
   made new again (1)
6. Danielle <u>rearranged</u> the contents of her bag, looking for the map. (1)
   arranged again, or in a different way (1)
7. Only when the bag was completely <u>unpacked</u> did she find the map. (1)
   not packed (1)
8. When they <u>reexamined</u> the map, they saw that they did not have far to go. (1)
   examined, or looked carefully at, again (1)
9. Since the day was clear, they had an <u>unobscured</u> view of the valley. (1)
   not hidden, clear (1)
10. Despite the <u>unusually</u> warm weather, it was cold on the summit. (1)
    not what is usual or expected (1)

Monitoring Student Progress

If . . .	Then . . .
students score 14 or below on **Practice Book** page 51,	use the Reteaching lesson on Teacher's Edition page R20.

STRUCTURAL ANALYSIS/ VOCABULARY: Prefixes

❶ Teach

Discuss the prefix *un-*. Write *Danielle and Jake were walking over an <u>uneven</u> but flat surface.*

- Circle the prefix *un-* in *uneven*. Underline the base word *even*.
- Explain that a prefix is a word part that comes before a base word and changes its meaning.
- Tell students that the prefix *un-* means "not." Explain that *uneven* means "not even."
- Have students give examples of other words with the prefix *un-* and discuss their meanings. (*unable, unwilling, undone*)

Discuss the prefix *re-*. Write *He wanted to <u>reassure</u> Danielle.*

- Circle *re-* in *reassure*. Underline the base word *sure*.
- Explain that the prefix *re-* means "again" or "back." Ask students to give the meaning of *reassure*. (*assure again*)
- Have students give examples of other words with the prefix *re-* and discuss their meanings. (*revisit, resend, repay, redo*)

Model the Phonics/Decoding Strategy. Write *Danielle was <u>unsure</u> of what Jake meant.* Then model decoding *unsure*.

Think Aloud *I see the familiar prefix* un-. *When I cover it up, I see a base word,* sure. *When I combine the two parts, I get* unsure. *I know* un- *means "not" so this word must mean "not sure." This makes sense in the sentence. Danielle doesn't understand what Jake has said.*

❷ Guided Practice

Have students use the prefixes *un-* and *re-*. Display the phrases below. Have partners circle the prefix in each underlined word, decode the word, and discuss the meaning. Have volunteers model at the board.

<u>untied</u> the hammer	<u>rediscovered</u> her strength
<u>rechecked</u> her belay position	the <u>unopened</u> door

❸ Apply

Assign Practice Book page 51.

PHONICS REVIEW: More Vowel Spellings

❶ Teach

Review less common spellings for the short and long vowel sounds. Explain the following.

- The letters *ea* can stand for the /ĕ/ sound or the /ē/ sound.
- The letter *y* can stand for the /ī/ sound or the /ĭ/ sound.
- The letter pattern *o-consonant-e* can stand for the /ŭ/ sound.
- The letters *ine* can stand for the /ēn/ sound.

Model the Phonics/Decoding Strategy. Write *Climbing the mountain was a mental as well as a* <u>*physical*</u> *challenge*. Model how to decode *physical*.

Think Aloud *First, I know that* ph *often stands for the /f/ sound. I know that* y *can sometimes have the /ī/ sound. I'll try pronouncing the first part* FY. *When I blend it with the rest of the letters, I get* FY-sihk-uhl. *That doesn't sound right. I know that* y *can also have the /ĭ/ sound. I'll try* FIHS-ihk-uhl *or* FIHZ-ihk-uhl. *That last way sounds right. It also makes sense.*

❷ Guided Practice

Help students identify less common vowel spellings. Display the sentences below. Ask students to circle the letters that stand for /ē/, /ī/, /ĭ/, /ĕ/, or /ŭ/ in each underlined word, pronounce the word, and check to see if it makes sense in the sentence. Call on individuals to model at the board.

1. Danielle and Jake improvised a climbing <u>routine</u>.
2. They <u>sweated</u> a lot during the climb.
3. Jake grabbed the hammer with his <u>gloved</u> hand.
4. Danielle heard the <u>rhythms</u> of jazz music.

❸ Apply

Have students identify less common vowel spellings. Ask students to decode and discuss these words from *Climb or Die*.

nylon	page 77	system	page 77	heading	page 77
something	page 77	overcome	page 77	breathtaking	page 80

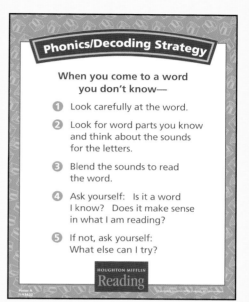

Phonics/Decoding Strategy

When you come to a word you don't know—

❶ Look carefully at the word.

❷ Look for word parts you know and think about the sounds for the letters.

❸ Blend the sounds to read the word.

❹ Ask yourself: Is it a word I know? Does it make sense in what I am reading?

❺ If not, ask yourself: What else can I try?

HOUGHTON MIFFLIN
Reading

SPELLING: More Vowel Spellings

OBJECTIVES

- Write Spelling Words with less common spelling patterns for long and short vowel sounds.
- Learn academic language: *long* e, *long* i, *short* e, *short* i, *short* u.

SPELLING WORDS

Basic

cycle	sponge
sweat	apply
rhythm	threat
rely	myth
pleasant	deny
routine	leather
cleanse	rhyme
shove	thread
reply*	meadow
meant*	ravine

Review	Challenge
breath*	endeavor
measure	oxygen
typical	nylon*
deaf	realm
crystal	trampoline

Forms of these words appear in the literature.

Extra Support/Intervention

Basic Word List You may want to use only the left column of Basic Words with students who need extra support.

Challenge

Challenge Word Practice Have students write a clue for each Challenge Word and exchange papers with a partner. Partners write the Challenge Word that fits each clue.

DAY 1 INSTRUCTION

More Vowel Spellings

Pretest Use the Day 5 Test sentences.

Teach Write five column headings on the board: /ē/ (routine), /ī/ (cycle), /ĕ/ (sweat), /ĭ/ (rhythm), /ŭ/ (shove). Ask students to identify the sound each symbol represents.

- Have students repeat each word. Underline *ine* in *routine*, *y* in *cycle*, *ea* in *sweat*, *y* in *rhythm*, *ove* in *shove*. Explain the less common spelling pattern in each word:

  /ē/ = *i*-consonant-*e (routine)*

  /ī/ = *y (cycle)*

  /ĕ/ = *ea (sweat)*

  /ĭ/ = *y (rhythm)*

  /ŭ/ = *o*-consonant-*e (shove)*

- Have students say each remaining Basic Word and identify the column it belongs in. Write the word in that column.

Practice/Homework Assign **Practice Book** page 283.

Practice Book page 283

DAY 2 REVIEW & PRACTICE

Reviewing the Principle

Go over the less common vowel spellings with students.

Practice/Homework Assign **Practice Book** page 52.

Practice Book page 52

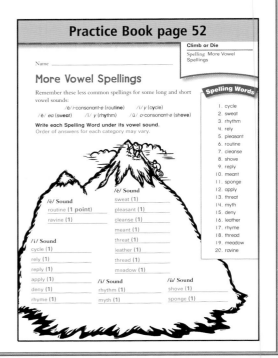

Take-Home Word List

DAY 3 VOCABULARY

Context Sentences

Write the Basic Words on the board.

- Read each context sentence and have students write the word that completes it.

  – Use a _____ to soak up that water. (*sponge*)

  – Are your shoes made of real _____? (*leather*)

  – Did he ever _____ to your e-mail? (*reply*)

  – I mended the shirt with a needle and _____. (*thread*)

  – They read a _____ about a horse with wings. (*myth*)

- Have students use each Basic Word from the board orally in a sentence.

Practice/Homework For spelling practice, assign **Practice Book** page 53.

Practice Book page 53

Climb or Die
Spelling More Vowel Spellings

Name _____

Spelling Spree

Word Changes Write a Spelling Word to fit each clue.

1. Drop two letters from *really* to write a word meaning "to depend."
2. Change a letter in *moth* to write a synonym for *legend.*
3. Drop a consonant from *shovel* to write a word meaning "to push."
4. Replace a consonant in *great* with two letters to write a synonym for *danger.*
5. Change a letter in *repay* to write a synonym for *respond.*
6. Replace two letters in *circle* with one to write a shorthand word for riding a bike.
7. Add a consonant to *peasant* to write a word meaning "enjoyable."
8. Replace a consonant in *leader* with two letters to write a word that names a clothing material.

1. rely **(1 point)**   5. reply **(1)**
2. myth **(1)**   6. cycle **(1)**
3. shove **(1)**   7. pleasant **(1)**
4. threat **(1)**   8. leather **(1)**

Word Addition Write a Spelling Word by adding the beginning of the first word to the end of the second word.

9. throne + bread = thread **(1)**
10. deal + funny = deny **(1)**
11. approach + fly = apply **(1)**
12. swing + defeat = sweat **(1)**
13. rat + thyme = rhyme **(1)**
14. spoke + range = sponge **(1)**

Spelling Words
1. cycle
2. sweat
3. rhythm
4. rely
5. pleasant
6. routine
7. cleanse
8. shove
9. reply
10. meant
11. sponge
12. apply
13. threat
14. myth
15. deny
16. leather
17. rhyme
18. thread
19. meadow
20. ravine

DAY 4 PROOFREADING

Game: Reach the Top

Divide the class into small groups. Have each group make a game board on which the final space is the top of a snowy mountain. They will also need twenty-five 3″ × 5″ word cards, each with a Basic or Review Word on one side and its definition on the other, as well as game markers and a spinner.

- Students place the cards face-down in a pile.
- A player picks up the top card, reads the definition aloud, and spells the word that fits it.
- If the spelling is correct, the player spins the spinner and moves the number of spaces shown.
- Players take turns until one "reaches the top."

Practice/Homework For proofreading and writing practice, assign **Practice Book** page 54.

Practice Book page 54

Climb or Die
Spelling More Vowel Spellings

Name _____

Proofreading and Writing

Proofreading Circle the six misspelled Spelling Words in this travel poster. Then write each word correctly.

You Need a Vacation!

Get away from the daily routeen and head for the mountains! You will clenz your body and your mind with a week of restful hiking and climbing. Follow well-marked trails to a pleasant meddow. Test your climbing skills as you explore a scenic ravene. Delight in the beauty and rythm of nature. You'll discover that the mountains are the place you were ment to be!

1. routine **(1 point)**   4. ravine **(1)**
2. cleanse **(1)**   5. rhythm **(1)**
3. meadow **(1)**   6. meant **(1)**

Spelling Words
1. cycle
2. sweat
3. rhythm
4. rely
5. pleasant
6. routine
7. cleanse
8. shove
9. reply
10. meant
11. sponge
12. apply
13. threat
14. myth
15. deny
16. leather
17. rhyme
18. thread
19. meadow
20. ravine

Write a Comparison and Contrast How does the portrayal of hiking and climbing in the poster above compare with the experience that Danielle and Jake had in the selection? Is one more realistic than the other? Is there anything missing from both accounts?

On a separate piece of paper, write a paragraph in which you compare and contrast the two descriptions. Use Spelling Words from the list. Responses will vary. **(6)**

DAY 5 ASSESSMENT

Spelling Test

Say each underlined word, read the sentence, and then repeat the word. Have students write only the underlined word.

Basic Words

1. How fast can you **cycle** to the store?
2. I **sweat** when I ride fast.
3. Listen to the **rhythm** of the drums.
4. You can **rely** on me whenever you need help.
5. That singer has a **pleasant** voice.
6. What is your daily **routine**?
7. Always **cleanse** a cut to kill the germs.
8. Do not **shove** anyone in line.
9. I will **reply** to your letter.
10. We **meant** to call you earlier.
11. Wash the car with soap and a **sponge**.
12. I will **apply** for that job.
13. The rain was a **threat** to our picnic.
14. We read a Roman **myth** in class.
15. I will not **deny** what I said.
16. The bag is made of soft **leather**.
17. That poem does not **rhyme**.
18. Sew it with strong **thread**.
19. The cows are grazing in the **meadow**.
20. The **ravine** beside the road was deep.

Challenge Words

21. She will **endeavor** to get good grades.
22. People need **oxygen** to live.
23. The tent was made of **nylon**.
24. The king ruled over his **realm**.
25. We jumped on the **trampoline**.

- Understand the types of information that can be found in a dictionary entry.
- Identify the parts of a dictionary entry.
- Learn academic language: *entry word, pronunciation, part of speech, definition, adjectival, adverbial, sample sentence, sample phrase.*

Target Skill Trace

Teach	p. 93G
Review	pp. M36–M37
Extend	Challenge/Extension Activities, p. R21
See	*Handbook for English Language Learners,* p. 43

Transparency 1–21

Parts of a Dictionary Entry

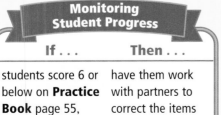

A entry word   pronunciation   part of speech

adjectival forms   **se•cure**   (sĭ kyŏŏr´)   *adj.*
se•cur•er, se•cur•est. 1. Free from danger or
attack: *a secure fortress.* 2. Firmly fastened:
definition   *The rope is secure.* **—se•cure´ly** *adv.*

sample sentence   adverbial form

con•trol (kən trōl´) *v.* **con•trolled, con•troll•ing, con•trols.**
1. To exercise authority or influence over; direct: *The principal
controls the school.* **2.** To adjust to or regulate: *This valve
controls the water in the shower.* **—con•trol•la•ble** *adj.*

em•brace (ĕm brās´) *v.* **em•braced, em•brac•ing,
em•brac•es.** To clasp or hold close with the arms, usually in a
sign of affection; hug: *embrace a child.*

sta•tion (stā´ shən) *n.* **1.** A place or location where a person
or thing stands or is assigned to stand; a post: *a guard station.*
2. An establishment set up for the purpose of study or
observation: *a weather station.*

ver•ti•cal (vûr´ tĭ kəl) *adj.* Being or situated at right angles
to the horizon; directly upright.

B 1. Write the entry word for *embrace.* Draw a line between
the syllables. em | brace
2. Look at the entry for *vertical.* Write the abbreviation
for the part of speech of the entry word. adj.
3. Write the first definition of *control.*
To exercise authority or influence over; direct.
4. Write the sample phrase given for the second definition
of *station.* a weather station

Monitoring Student Progress

If . . .	Then . . .
students score 6 or below on **Practice Book** page 55,	have them work with partners to correct the items they missed.

 VOCABULARY: Parts of a Dictionary Entry

❶ Teach

Introduce parts of a dictionary entry. Dictionary entries have different parts, and each part gives different information.

Display Transparency 1–21. Show only the first entry at the top. **A** Point to each part of the entry as you explain the following:

- The entry word comes at the beginning of the entry and shows the word divided into syllables.
- The pronunciation shows how the word is pronounced.
- The part of speech identifies the word as a noun (*n.*), pronoun (*pron.*), adjective (*adj.*), or adverb (*adv.*).
- The definition gives the meaning of the word. Some entries have several numbered definitions.
- The adjectival and adverbial forms show how the word changes as an adjective or adverb. The various forms of verbs are shown.
- The sample sentence or phrase gives the word in context.

Model how to use a dictionary entry. Write *With a hammer in each hand, she struck out with the right one till it caught <u>securely</u>.* Model how to find the correct definition of *securely.*

Think Aloud
From the end of the entry, I learn that this word is the adverbial form of secure. The first definition, "free from danger or attack," doesn't make sense here. The second definition, "firmly fastened," does make sense since the sentence refers to a hammer striking into ice.

❷ Guided Practice

Give students practice in using dictionary entries. Display the entire transparency. Have partners complete Exercises 1–4. **B**

❸ Apply

Assign Practice Book page 55.

Practice Book page 55

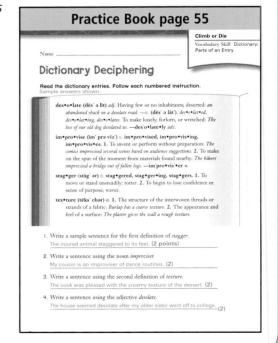

Climb or Die

Vocabulary Skill Dictionary: Parts of an Entry

Name _____

Dictionary Deciphering

Read the dictionary entries. Follow each numbered instruction.
Sample answers shown.

des•o•late (dĕs´ ə lĭt) *adj.* Having few or no inhabitants; deserted: *an
abandoned shack on a desolate road.* —*v.* (dĕs´ ə lāt´). *des•o•lat•ed,
des•o•lat•ing, des•o•lates.* To make lonely, forlorn, or wretched: *The
loss of our old dog desolated us.* —**des•o•late•ly** *adv.*

im•pro•vise (ĭm´ prə vīz´) *v.* **im•pro•vised, im•pro•vis•ing,
im•pro•vis•es.** 1. To invent or perform without preparation: *The
comics improvised several scenes based on audience suggestions.* 2. To make
on the spur of the moment from materials found nearby: *The hikers
improvised a bridge out of fallen logs.* —**im•pro•vis•er** *n.*

stag•ger (stăg´ ər) *v.* **stag•gered, stag•ger•ing, stag•gers.** 1. To
move or stand unsteadily; totter. 2. To begin to lose confidence or
sense of purpose; waver.

tex•ture (tĕks´ chər) *n.* 1. The structure of the interwoven threads or
strands of a fabric: *Burlap has a coarse texture.* 2. The appearance and
feel of a surface: *The plaster gives the wall a rough texture.*

1. Write a sample sentence for the first definition of *stagger.*
   The injured animal staggered to its feet. **(2 points)**
2. Write a sentence using the noun *improviser.*
   My cousin is an improviser of dance routines. **(2)**
3. Write a sentence using the second definition of *texture.*
   The cook was pleased with the creamy texture of the dessert. **(2)**
4. Write a sentence using the adjective *desolate.*
   The house seemed desolate after my older sister went off to college. **(2)**

STUDY SKILL: Using Parts of a Book

❶ Teach

Explain that most books are organized in similar ways.

- Tell students that knowing how a book is organized will help them find information quickly and easily.

- Display a nonfiction book that contains a glossary and an index. Use this to illustrate each part of a book as you discuss the points below.

Discuss each part of a book.

- The title page is usually the first page. It shows the names of the author, the illustrator, and the publisher.

- The copyright page usually follows the title page. It tells when the book was published and whether it has been revised.

- The table of contents lists the chapters of the book and indicates the page number on which each chapter begins.

- A glossary defines important words that appear in the book.

- The index is at the end of a book. It lists topics alphabetically and shows the page numbers where information can be found.

Display Transparency 1–22, and model how to use an index.

Think Aloud *I'd like to see what this book has to say about George Leigh-Mallory, the famous climber who disappeared while trying to reach Mount Everest's summit. I skim the index until I come to* Leigh-Mallory. *I see that the entry says* See Mallory, George, *so I look for the entry that reads* Mallory, George. *I notice that I can find information about George Mallory on pages 33–34 and 37–39. I also see a cross-listing,* search for remains, *that directs me to more information about Mallory on pages 152–153.*

❷ Practice/Apply

Give students practice in using parts of a book.

- Have students use the transparency to answer these questions. Where would you look to find information about Mount Everest's height? (page 23) about Tenzing Norgay? (42–43, 46, 48, 51–52, 148) about Edmund Hillary? (46–52)

- Have partners find a book about mountain climbing, Mount Everest, George Mallory, or a related topic. Ask them to find three interesting pieces of information. Then have them model how they used the parts of the book to help them find this information.

Transparency 1–22

Use Parts of a Book

COURAGE Climb or Die
Information and Study Skills
Use Parts of a Book
ANNOTATED VERSION

TRANSPARENCY 1–22
TEACHER'S EDITION PAGE 93H

INFORMATION & STUDY SKILLS

Climb or Die

GRAMMAR: More About Sentences

OBJECTIVES

- Identify complex sentences.
- Identify and correct fragments and run-on sentences.
- Proofread and correct sentences with grammar and spelling errors.
- Correct run-on sentences to improve writing.
- Learn academic language: *clause, independent clause, subordinate clause, subordinating conjunction, complex sentence, sentence fragment, run-on sentence.*

DAY 1 — INSTRUCTION

Complex Sentences

Teach Go over these rules:

- A clause contains both a subject and a predicate. An independent clause can stand by itself as a sentence. A subordinate clause cannot stand by itself.

- The subordinating conjunction that begins a subordinate clause makes one part of the sentence subordinate to the other part.

- A complex sentence has at least one subordinate clause and an independent clause.

- Display **Transparency 1–24.** Note that Item 1's sentences are combined in a compound sentence (2) and a complex sentence (3).

- Ask volunteers to write *simple, compound,* or *complex* and the conjunction, if any, for each remaining sentence.

Daily Language Practice
Have students correct Sentences 1 and 2 on **Transparency 1–23.**

DAY 2 — PRACTICE

Independent Work

Practice/Homework Assign **Practice Book** page 56.

Daily Language Practice
Have students correct Sentences 3 and 4 on **Transparency 1–23.**

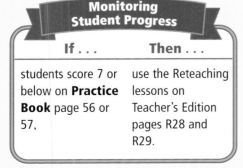

Transparency 1–23
Daily Language Practice

Correct two sentences each day.

1. Do you think we can hike all the way to the raeven.
   Do you think we can hike all the way to the ravine?

2. Please don't shuve me.
   Please don't shove me! (or Please don't shove me.)

3. today i will relie on my mother to drive me to school.
   Today I will rely on my mother to drive me to school.

4. that song has a pleasint tune.
   That song has a pleasant tune.

5. My exercise rootine is thirty minutes on the treadmill
   My exercise routine is thirty minutes on the treadmill.

6. Do you like lether backpacks.
   Do you like leather backpacks?

7. have you heard the rhime about the cat and the fiddle?
   Have you heard the rhyme about the cat and the fiddle?

8. my brother does not denie that he ate the last cookie.
   My brother does not deny that he ate the last cookie.

9. The rithim of the music makes me want to dance
   The rhythm of the music makes me want to dance.

10. When will i get a replie to my last letter?
    When will I get a reply to my last letter?

Monitoring Student Progress

If . . .	Then . . .
students score 7 or below on **Practice Book** page 56 or 57,	use the Reteaching lessons on Teacher's Edition pages R28 and R29.

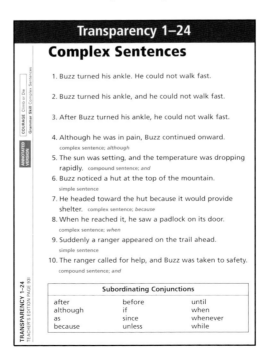

Transparency 1–24
Complex Sentences

1. Buzz turned his ankle. He could not walk fast.

2. Buzz turned his ankle, and he could not walk fast.

3. After Buzz turned his ankle, he could not walk fast.

4. Although he was in pain, Buzz continued onward.
   complex sentence; *although*

5. The sun was setting, and the temperature was dropping rapidly. compound sentence; *and*

6. Buzz noticed a hut at the top of the mountain.
   simple sentence

7. He headed toward the hut because it would provide shelter. complex sentence; *because*

8. When he reached it, he saw a padlock on its door.
   complex sentence; *when*

9. Suddenly a ranger appeared on the trail ahead.
   simple sentence

10. The ranger called for help, and Buzz was taken to safety.
    compound sentence; *and*

Subordinating Conjunctions

after	before	until
although	if	when
as	since	whenever
because	unless	while

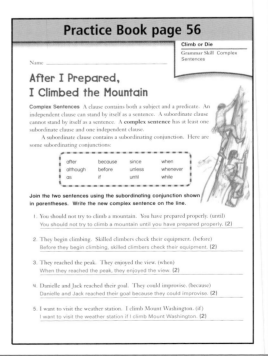

Practice Book page 56

Grammar Skill Complex Sentences

Name _____

After I Prepared, I Climbed the Mountain

Complex Sentences A clause contains both a subject and a predicate. An independent clause can stand by itself as a sentence. A subordinate clause cannot stand by itself as a sentence. A **complex sentence** has at least one subordinate clause and one independent clause.

A subordinate clause contains a subordinating conjunction. Here are some subordinating conjunctions:

after	because	since	when
although	before	unless	whenever
as	if	until	while

Join the two sentences using the subordinating conjunction shown in parentheses. Write the new complex sentence on the line.

1. You should not try to climb a mountain. You have prepared properly. (until)
   You should not try to climb a mountain until you have prepared properly. (2)

2. They begin climbing. Skilled climbers check their equipment. (before)
   Before they begin climbing, skilled climbers check their equipment. (2)

3. They reached the peak. They enjoyed the view. (when)
   When they reached the peak, they enjoyed the view. (2)

4. Danielle and Jack reached their goal. They could improvise. (because)
   Danielle and Jack reached their goal because they could improvise. (2)

5. I want to visit the weather station. I climb Mount Washington. (if)
   I want to visit the weather station if I climb Mount Washington. (2)

DAY 3 INSTRUCTION

Fragments and Run-ons

Teach Go over these definitions and rules:

- A sentence fragment is missing a subject or a predicate. Correct a fragment by adding a subject or a predicate or both.

- A run-on sentence is two or more sentences that are run together into one sentence. Correct a run-on by creating separate sentences, a compound sentence, or a complex sentence.

- Display **Transparency 1–25.** Point out that Item 1 is a run-on sentence and that Item 2 is a fragment. Model how each could be corrected.

- Ask volunteers to correct the remaining fragments and run-on sentences.

Daily Language Practice
Have students correct Sentences 5 and 6 on **Transparency 1–23.**

Transparency 1–25

Correcting Fragments and Run-On Sentences

Answers will vary.

1. A lone hiker gets hurt, he or she may not be able to get help.
   If a lone hiker gets hurt, he or she may not be able to get help.

2. Because hiking alone is dangerous.
   You should hike with a buddy because hiking alone is dangerous.

3. Hiking in the mountains can be thrilling a hiker must prepare properly.
   Hiking in the mountains can be thrilling, but a hiker must prepare properly.

4. People who hike in brand-new boots asking for trouble.
   People who hike in brand-new boots are asking for trouble.

5. When you buy a new pair of boots.
   When you buy a new pair of boots, you should break them in first.

6. You should wear them around town for several weeks, they will become soft and flexible.
   You should wear them around town for several weeks, so they will become soft and flexible.

7. Flexible shoes are more comfortable, they are less likely to cause blisters.
   Flexible shoes are more comfortable, and they are less likely to cause blisters.

8. Hiking downhill more dangerous than hiking uphill.
   Hiking downhill is more dangerous than hiking uphill.

9. You might slip on loose gravel, you might stumble on a tree root.
   You might slip on loose gravel, or you might stumble on a tree root.

10. If you aren't careful.
    If you aren't careful, you might lose your balance.

DAY 4 PRACTICE

Independent Work

Practice/Homework Assign **Practice Book** page 57.

Daily Language Practice
Have students correct Sentences 7 and 8 on **Transparency 1–23.**

Practice Book page 57

Before I Climbed

Correcting Fragments A **sentence fragment** does not express a complete thought. Correct a fragment by adding a subject or a predicate or both.
A **run-on sentence** expresses too many thoughts without correct punctuation. Correct a run-on sentence by creating separate sentences, a compound sentence, or a complex sentence.

Read the following sentence fragments or run-on sentences. Correct the problem, and write a new sentence on the line. There is more than one way to fix each sentence.
Answers will vary.

1. Because the weather can change quickly.
   Bring a warm jacket because the weather can change quickly. **(2 points)**

2. Meteorologists predict the daily weather, they make long-range forecasts.
   Meteorologists predict the daily weather and make long-range forecasts. **(2)**

3. This weather station has recorded the highest wind speeds. And the coldest temperatures in the state.
   This weather station has recorded the highest wind speeds and the coldest temperatures in the state. **(2)**

4. Visitors learn how a barometer works they get a tour of the weather station.
   Visitors learn how a barometer works, and they get a tour of the weather station. **(2)**

5. When the next storm comes.
   When the next storm comes, I will be prepared. **(2)**

DAY 5 IMPROVING WRITING

Avoiding Run-ons

Teach Tell students that a good writer proofreads for and rewrites any run-on sentences.

- Model correcting a run-on sentence:
  - Some hikers wear two pairs of socks to avoid blisters, first they put on a thin pair then they put on a thick pair.
  - *Corrected:* Some hikers wear two pairs of socks to avoid blisters. First, they put on a thin pair, and then they put on a thick pair.

- Have students proofread a piece of their own writing for run-on sentences.

Practice/Homework Assign **Practice Book** page 58.

Daily Language Practice
Have students correct Sentences 9 and 10 on **Transparency 1–23.**

Practice Book page 58

Will It Rain?

Avoiding Run-Ons A **run-on sentence** expresses too many thoughts without correct punctuation. Correct a run-on sentence by creating separate sentences, a compound sentence, or a complex sentence.

A student visited a weather station and wrote the following. Revise it by correcting run-on sentences. You might need to add punctuation, a conjunction, or both. Here are two examples: Answers will vary.

Incorrect: The sky is cloudy I think it will rain.
Correct: The sky is cloudy. I think it will rain.

Incorrect: The sun came out it was still cold.
Correct: The sun came out, **but** it was still cold.

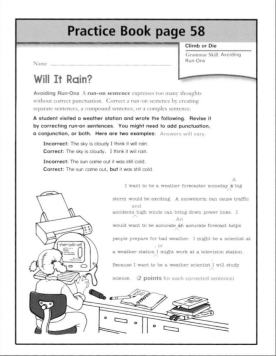

I want to be a weather forecaster someday, a big storm would be exciting. A snowstorm can cause traffic and accidents high winds can bring down power lines. I would want to be accurate an accurate forecast helps people prepare for bad weather. I might be a scientist at a weather station or I might work at a television station. Because I want to be a weather scientist I will study science. **(2 points** for each corrected sentence)

WRITING: Friendly Letter

OBJECTIVES

- Identify the characteristics of a good friendly letter.
- Write a friendly letter.
- Develop an individual voice as a writer.
- Learn academic language: *voice*.

Writing Traits

Word Choice As students draft their letters on Day 2, explain that using exact words will help a reader understand what they are saying. Provide these examples:

Without Exact Words We <u>went</u> down a <u>hill</u>.

With Exact Words We <u>raced</u> down <u>the side of a mountain</u>.

DAY 1 PREWRITING

Introducing the Format

Define friendly letters.

- A friendly letter is a letter that one friend or relative writes to another.
- It shares news, ideas, or special experiences.
- It is usually written in the informal language you would use with a friend.

Start students thinking about writing friendly letters.

- Ask students to list three interesting experiences they have had recently.
- Ask students to list three friends or relatives to whom they might write a letter.
- Have them save their notes.

DAY 2 DRAFTING

Discussing the Model

Display Transparency 1–26. Ask:

- What are the five parts of a friendly letter? (heading, greeting, body, closing, signature)
- Which part tells where the letter was written and the date? (heading)
- Which part tells who will receive the letter? (greeting)
- Where can you find out what the letter is about? (body)
- Which part ends the letter? (closing)
- Which part tells who wrote the letter? (signature)

Display Transparency 1–27, and discuss the guidelines.

Have students draft a friendly letter.

- They can write to a friend or relative.
- Have them use their notes from Day 1.
- Assign **Practice Book** page 59 to help students organize their writing.
- See Writing Traits on this page.
- Provide support as needed.

Transparency 1–26
A Friendly Letter

Heading

1425 Silver Sky Trail
Harmony, CO 80303
October 6, 2004

Greeting
(followed by a comma)

Dear James,

Hi! Thanks for the birthday card. You'll never guess what happened to us last weekend. Our Scout group was hiking in the woods. We were on a trail that we know well, but it was near sunset as we hiked back to the ranger station. All of a sudden we saw a coyote ahead of us. We stopped walking and stayed very quiet! The funny thing was, this coyote just stood there and looked at us. We stared back. Everything was so silent, it was eerie! This went on for a couple of minutes, although it seemed like forever. Then the coyote ran off into the brush. That was the closest I have ever been to a coyote. Have you ever seen a wild animal up close? Write back and tell me what you've been up to.

Body
(personal news)

(invitation to write back)

Closing
(followed by a comma)

Your friend,

Signature

Zack

TRANSPARENCY 1–26
TEACHER'S EDITION PAGE 93K

COURAGE *Climb or Die*
Writing Skill A Friendly Letter
ANNOTATED VERSION

Transparency 1–27
Guidelines for Writing a Friendly Letter

- Include the five parts: a heading, a greeting, a body, a closing, and a signature.
- Use a friendly tone and informal language. Write as if you were talking to the person.
- Tell events or other information. Keep to the point.
- Include exact words that will interest your reader.
- End with a question or comment that encourages your reader to write back soon.

TRANSPARENCY 1–27
TEACHER'S EDITION PAGE 93K

COURAGE *Climb or Die*
Writing Skill Friendly Letter
ANNOTATED VERSION

Practice Book page 59

Climb or Die
Writing Skill Friendly Letter

Name _____

Writing a Friendly Letter

A **friendly letter** is a letter that you write to a friend to share news about what is happening in your life.

Use this page to help you plan and organize a friendly letter. Either write a letter that Jake or Danielle might have written to a friend about climbing to the Mount Remington weather station, or write a letter to a friend of yours in which you share a recent experience or adventure of your own. Follow these steps: (10 points)

1. Write a **heading** (your address and the date) and a **greeting** (*Dear* and the person's name followed by a comma).
2. Write the **body** of your letter below the greeting. Begin by writing something that shows you care about the friend to whom you are writing. At the end of the letter, ask your friend to write back soon.
3. Write an informal **closing** such as *Love* or *Your friend* followed by a comma in the lower right corner. Then sign your name under the closing.

Heading _____

Greeting _____
Body _____

Closing _____
Signature _____

When you finish your friendly letter, copy it onto a clean sheet of paper. If you wrote your letter to a friend, address an envelope and mail it!

Improving Writing: Voice

Explain voice.

- Voice shows a writer's personality.
- Voice shows a writer's feelings about his or her thoughts or experiences.

Display Transparency 1–28.

- Have volunteers read aloud each passage. Ask, Which has more voice? (Passage 2)
- Discuss why Passage 2 has more voice. Ask, Which phrases sound like what the writer uses when speaking? (Sample answers: *What's up?*; *Could you believe*)
- Ask, What phrases in Passage 2 show how the writer felt? (Sample answers: *absolutely the best; so happy; Don't you think that would be fun?*)

Assign Practice Book page 60.

Have students revise their drafts.

- Display **Transparency 1–27** again. Have students use it to revise their letters.
- Have partners hold writing conferences.
- Ask students to revise any parts of their letters that still need work. Have them look for places to make their voice stronger.

Checking for Errors

Have students proofread for errors in grammar, spelling, punctuation, or usage.

- Students can use the proofreading checklist on **Practice Book** page 297 to help them proofread their friendly letters.
- Students can also use the chart of proofreading marks on **Practice Book** page 298.

Sharing Letters

Consider these publishing options.

- Ask students to read their friendly letters or some other piece of writing from the Author's Chair.
- Encourage students to send their letters.

Portfolio Opportunity

Save students' friendly letters as samples of their writing development.

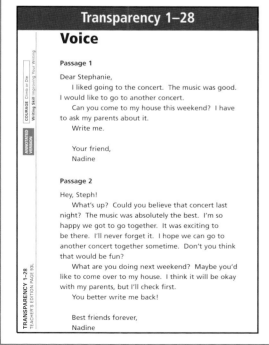

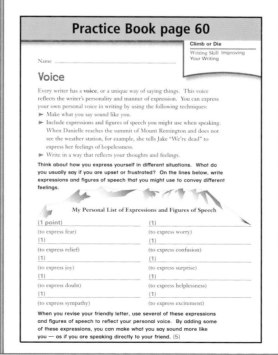

Monitoring Student Progress

If . . .	Then . . .
students' writing does not follow the guidelines on **Transparency 1–27**,	work with students to improve specific parts of their writing.

Language Center

VOCABULARY

Mountain-Climbing Terms

👤 Singles	🕐 30 minutes
Objective	Create a chart of mountain-climbing terms.
Materials	Dictionary, Activity Master 1–3, page R34

In *Climb or Die,* you learned about some of the equipment, techniques, terrain, and hazards associated with mountain climbing. Using Activity Master 1–3, create a chart of the mountain-climbing terms below. Recalling what you learned from the selection, arrange the terms in the appropriate category, and write a brief definition after each word. You may use a dictionary if you need to.

Mountain Climbing Terms		
avalanches	crampons	rappel
belay	glaciers	rope
carabiners	ice axes	summit
cornice	pitons	vertical ice

GRAMMAR

Conversation Fragments

👥 Pairs	🕐 30 minutes
Objective	Correct fragments and run-on sentences.

In dialogues between story characters, as in actual speech, characters often speak in sentence fragments and run-on sentences. To discover how often this is true in *Climb or Die,* work with a partner to follow these steps.

- Find a passage of dialogue in *Climb or Die.*
- Identify any sentence fragments or run-on sentences in the characters' spoken words.
- Rewrite the fragments and run-on sentences as complete sentences.

Danielle replied, "I am improvising."

VOCABULARY

Invent a Story

👥 Pairs	🕐 20 minutes
Objective	Create sentences using Key Vocabulary words.

With a partner, use the Key Vocabulary words to invent a story about mountain climbing. Follow these steps:

- Write a list of all the Key Vocabulary words.
- One partner begins the story by writing until he or she uses one of the Key Vocabulary words. Then the partner stops.
- The other partner writes the next part in the story until he or she uses a different Key Vocabulary word. Then the other partner stops.
- Both partners take turns adding to the story until they have used all of the Key Vocabulary words.

Consider copying and laminating these activities for use in centers.

LISTENING/SPEAKING

Hold a Literature Discussion

👥👥 Groups	⏱ 30 minutes
Objective	Discuss *Climb or Die*.

Discuss *Climb or Die* with a group. You may use the sample discussion questions in the chart below or you may brainstorm others. Here are some guidelines for having a group discussion.

- Stay on the subject.
- Work from questions such as those listed below, that readers might ask about any work of literature.
- State your ideas clearly and briefly.
- Support your ideas with evidence and examples from the selection.
- Respect the ideas and opinions of others, even if you disagree.

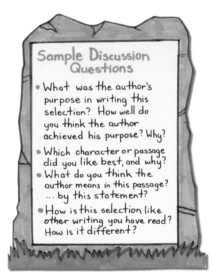

Sample Discussion Questions

- What was the author's purpose in writing this selection? How well do you think the author achieved his purpose? Why?
- Which character or passage did you like best, and why?
- What do you think the author means in this passage? ... by this statement?
- How is this selection like other writing you have read? How is it different?

PHONICS/SPELLING

Proofreading for a Friend

🧍 Singles	⏱ 30 minutes
Objective	Correct vowel spellings.

Your mountain-climbing partner has just written the following journal entry describing your adventure together and has asked you to proofread it.

- Read the journal entry.
- Identify the misspelled words. (Hint: Each misspelling is of a vowel sound.)
- Rewrite the entry, correcting each misspelling.

> Today I climbed a mountain for the first time. I was afraid at the beginning, but I can't denie that the view from the summit was brethtaking. My group crossed a raveen and later a medow. When I learned that these are tipical climbing activities, sumthing happened to make me overcome my fear. The whole experience turned out to be quite plesant.

Proofreading for a Friend
deny; breathtaking; ravine;
meadow; typical; something; overcome

LEVELED READERS

I Double Dare You

Summary *Bill and Gwen are vacationing with their parents at a campground on Lake Michigan. Gwen "double dares" Bill to slide down a steep sand dune. The siblings slide down the dune together and can't climb back up. After many failed attempts to climb the dune, Gwen falls and injures her ankle. At last the children work together and eventually make it up the dune.*

Vocabulary

Introduce the Key Vocabulary and ask students to complete the BLM.

restless impatient, *p. 3*

dune a hill of sand piled up by the wind, *p. 4*

steep rising or falling abruptly, *p. 4*

slope an inclined surface, such as the side of a hill or dune, *p. 6*

exhausted tired out, *p. 12*

hobbled moved with difficulty, *p. 17*

Building Background and Vocabulary

Explain to students that they will be reading about a brother and a sister who are camping with their parents near a beach. Ask students if they have ever tried to walk on sand dunes. Guide students through the text, using some of the vocabulary from the story.

Comprehension Skill: Sequence of Events

Have students read the Strategy Focus on the book flap. Remind students to use the strategy and to think about the sequence of events as they read the book. (See the Leveled Readers Teacher's Guide for **Vocabulary and Comprehension Practice Masters.**)

Responding

Have partners discuss how to answer the questions on the inside back cover.

Think About the Selection Sample answers:

1. Bill probably feels scared but determined to prove himself.
2. They are able to work together to get up the dune.
3. Bill tears his shirt into strips and uses the longest strips to wrap Gwen's ankle in a splint.
4. Answers will vary.

Making Connections Answers will vary.

Building Fluency

Model Read aloud page 6 to show emphasis of an italicized word *(that, I'm)*. Discuss other ways of emphasizing a word or phrase in text (capital letters, exclamation points, underlined words).

Practice Ask pairs of students to choose a sentence from the story and reread it aloud until they have emphasized each different word.

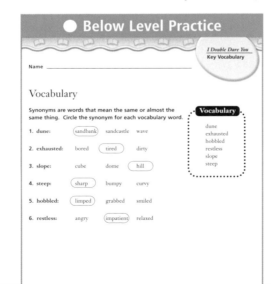

Leveled Readers

Underground Rescue

Summary *Jonathan is claustrophobic, so he's dreading his family's caving adventure. But once inside the cave, he starts to appreciate its beauty. When Mom falls and hurts her leg, Jonathan has to face his fear and crawl out of the cave through a narrow passage. With strength and resourcefulness, he slowly makes it through and rescues his mom.*

Vocabulary

Introduce the Key Vocabulary and ask students to complete the BLM.

looming threatening, *p. 3*

claustrophobic afraid of enclosed spaces, *p. 3*

petrified frozen with fear, *p. 3*

contorted distorted, *p. 11*

footholds* places that give firm support for a foot while climbing, *p. 13*

infinity endless or unlimited space or time, *p. 13*

plummeting falling straight downward, *p. 13*

tantalizingly in a tempting manner, *p. 14*

*Forms of these words are Anthology Key Vocabulary words.

▲ ON LEVEL

Building Background and Vocabulary

Explain to students that this story is about a boy who is claustrophobic, or afraid of being in small spaces. Ask students what they know about caves, rock formations, and the sport of exploring caves. Guide students through the text, using some of the vocabulary from the story.

Comprehension Skill: Sequence of Events

Have students read the Strategy Focus on the book flap. Remind students to use the strategy and to think about the sequence of events as they read the book. (See the Leveled Readers Teacher's Guide for **Vocabulary and Comprehension Practice Masters.**)

Responding

Have partners discuss how to answer the questions on the inside back cover.

Think About the Selection Sample answers:

1. Jonathan has feared enclosed spaces ever since he fell into a pit.
2. In a "live" cave, water seeps in and forms stalactites and stalagmites.
3. Despite his fear of small spaces, he climbs the chimney to get help for his mother.
4. Answers will vary.

Making Connections Answers will vary.

Building Fluency

Model Read aloud page 3 and explain to students that a phrase like *sensed disaster looming* is the technique of foreshadowing. Reread the sentence twice, the first time with dramatic intonation and the second time without.

Practice Ask students to find and read aloud other examples of foreshadowing (pages 6 and 7), once with dramatic intonation and once without.

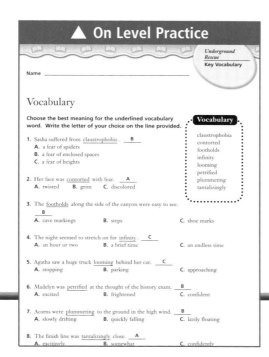

■ ABOVE LEVEL

Hurricane Music

Summary *Elsie, who is terrified of storms, is visiting her grandmother when a hurricane strikes. When Ben, a five-year-old neighbor, is reported missing, Elsie must find him. After battling ferocious winds and driving rain, she finally finds Ben, and the two arrive home safely. Then Elsie, like her grandfather, plays the piano until the storm passes.*

Vocabulary

Introduce the Key Vocabulary and ask students to complete the BLM.

impenetrable solid; impossible to penetrate, *p. 4*

ominous threatening, *p. 5*

withstand resist, endure, *p. 6*

surge increase strongly and suddenly, *p. 7*

paralyzed unable to move, *p. 7*

boardwalk a raised walkway built along a beach, *p. 8*

maniacally hysterically, frenziedly, *p. 12*

awestruck filled with wonder, *p. 13*

Building Background and Vocabulary

Share with students that this story is about a girl who is terrified of storms. Ask students what they know about tropical storms, and what to do to make their homes safe during such emergencies. Guide students through the text, using some of the vocabulary from the story.

Comprehension Skill: Sequence of Events

Have students read the Strategy Focus on the book flap. Remind students to use the strategy and to think about the sequence of events as they read the book. (See the Leveled Readers Teacher's Guide for **Vocabulary and Comprehension Practice Masters.**)

Responding

Have partners discuss how to answer the questions on the inside back cover.

Think About the Selection Sample answers:

1. She doesn't want Elsie to be frightened.
2. She looks for Ben despite her fear of lightning, and she brings him safely home.
3. Yes. Her grandmother tries to hide her own fear to keep Elsie calm. Ben tries to calm and protect Elsie when she is afraid of lightning.
4. Answers will vary.

Making Connections Answers will vary.

Building Fluency

Model Read aloud page 6 to show how ellipses signal readers to let their voices trail off.

Practice Ask partners to find and read aloud other sentences that contain ellipses to practice the appropriate way to end those sentences.

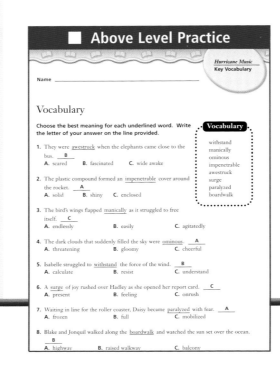

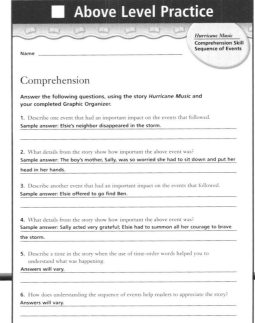

Leveled Readers

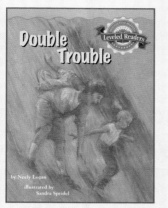

Double Trouble

Summary *Gwen and her brother Bill go camping at Sleeping Bear Dunes near Lake Michigan. Gwen double dares Bill to go down a steep dune. They go down the dune together, but it is too steep for them to get back up. After an accident and many unsuccessful attempts, they find that teamwork gets them back to the top of the dunes.*

Vocabulary

Introduce the Key Vocabulary and ask students to complete the BLM.

dunes hills of windblown sand, *p. 3*

steep very high, *p. 4*

dare to challenge, *p. 6*

foothold* a place that gives firm support for a foot while climbing, *p. 8*

lean to rest one's weight on or against something for support, *p. 8*

splint hard material used to hold a broken bone in place, *p. 14*

*Forms of these words are Anthology Key Vocabulary words.

◆ LANGUAGE SUPPORT

Building Background and Vocabulary

Have students share what they know about camping. Then distribute the **Build Background Practice Master.** Discuss the picture, read the Master aloud, and have students complete it. Invite volunteers to share their responses.

Comprehension Skill: Sequence of Events

Have students read the Strategy Focus on the book flap. Remind students to use the strategy and to notice the sequence of events as they read the book. (See the Leveled Readers Teacher's Guide for **Build Background, Vocabulary,** and **Graphic Organizer Masters.**)

Responding

Have partners discuss how to answer the questions on the inside back cover.

Think About the Selection Sample answers:

1. He feels afraid at first.
2. No, they don't think carefully, because they are too excited about the idea.
3. They try out each other's ideas. Then, when Gwen hurts her leg, they figure out how to pull each other up the dune.
4. Answers will vary.

Making Connections Answers will vary.

Building Fluency

Model Read aloud page 20 as students follow along in their books. Model how emphasis can make the paragraph more exciting and meaningful.

Practice Have partners of equal ability take turns reading aloud the text to each other three times, until they can read it accurately and with emphasis.

◆ **Language Support Practice**

Double Trouble
Build Background

Name _____

Build Background

Look at the picture and answer the questions.
Answers will vary.

WOW, THAT'S REALLY STEEP!

LET'S GO DOWN TO THE BOTTOM!

1. Why do you think the girl wants to go to the bottom of the dune?
_____

2. What could happen as they go down the dune?
_____

3. What should the boy and girl think about before they make a decision about going to the bottom of the dune?
_____

4. What advice would you give them?
_____

◆ **Language Support Practice**

Double Trouble
Key Vocabulary

Name _____

Vocabulary

Vocabulary
dare
dunes
foothold
lean
splint
steep

Use one of the words from the box to complete each sentence.

1. Sand ____dunes____ can be hundreds of feet high.

2. When you climb a steep hill, try to ____lean____ into the hill and move slowly so that you won't fall down.

3. Last summer I climbed a very ____steep____ mountain.

4. I learned how to find a ____foothold____ to get a good grip on the mountain.

5. I ____dare____ you to try to climb that hill!

6. I know how to make a ____splint____ from pieces of wood.

Lesson Overview

Literature

The True Confessions of CHARLOTTE DOYLE

a novel by AVI

Selection Summary

In order to join the crew of the *Seahawk*, thirteen-year-old Charlotte Doyle must climb the tallest mast of the ship as a test of endurance.

Vocabulary Reader

Voyage of the Fram

1 **Background and Vocabulary**

Nonfiction

2 **Main Selection**

The True Confessions of Charlotte Doyle
Genre: Fiction

3 **Social Studies Link**

ALONE Against the SEA

Instructional Support

Planning and Practice

Teacher's Edition

Practice Book

Teacher's Resources

Transparencies

Differentiated Instruction

Intervention Strategies for Extra Support

Instructional Activities for Challenge

Instructional Strategies for English Language Learners

Ready-Made Centers

Building Vocabulary Flip Chart
• center activities
• word skills practice

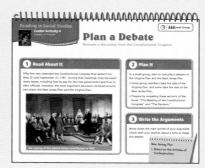

Reading in Science and Social Studies Flip Chart
• books and center activities
• support for state content standards

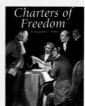

Hands-On Literacy Centers for *The True Confessions of Charlotte Doyle*
• activities
• manipulatives
• routines

Technology

Audio Selection
The True Confessions of Charlotte Doyle

Get Set for Reading CD-ROM

Accelerated Reader®

www.eduplace.com
• over 1,000 Online Leveled Books

HOUGHTON MIFFLIN
Assessment System
• Test Generator

Leveled Books for Reaching All Learners

Fluency

Increase students' reading fluency using these activities.

● BELOW LEVEL

Have students practice reading to a partner, using passages previously modeled. Students should then provide feedback to each other.

▲ ON LEVEL

Have students read a passage with expression. Ask students to discuss the important sentence features that guide expression.

■ ABOVE LEVEL

On the board, display a group of words that have a similar phonic element. Ask students to read the words aloud and identify the similar element.

◆ LANGUAGE SUPPORT

Have students read a passage aloud. Ask them to practice the passage silently, then read it aloud again in small groups.

Skills Practice

- Topic, comprehension strategy, and vocabulary linked to main selection
- Lessons in Teacher's Edition, pages 115O–115R

● BELOW LEVEL

Riding with the Vaqueros by Rebecca Motil, illustrated by Rick Allen

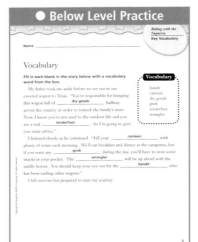

▲ ON LEVEL

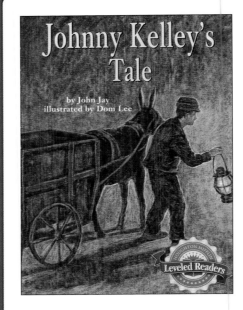

Johnny Kelley's Tale by John Jay, illustrated by Dom Lee

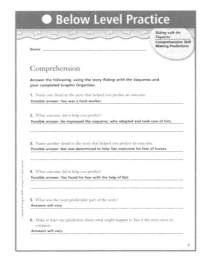

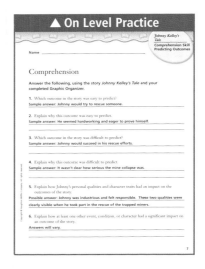

■ ABOVE LEVEL

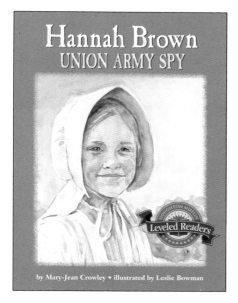

Hannah Brown
UNION ARMY SPY

by Mary-Jean Crowley • illustrated by Leslie Bowman

Leveled Readers

■ Above Level Practice

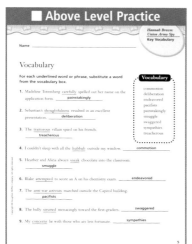

Name _____

Vocabulary

For each underlined word or phrase, substitute a word from the vocabulary box.

Vocabulary
commotion
deliberation
endeavored
pacifists
painstakingly
smuggle
swaggered
sympathies
treacherous

1. Madeline Totenberg carefully spelled out her name on the application form. ___painstakingly___

2. Sebastian's thoughtfulness resulted in an excellent presentation. ___deliberation___

3. The traitorous villain spied on his friends. ___treacherous___

4. I couldn't sleep with all the hubbub outside my window. ___commotion___

5. Heather and Alicia always sneak chocolate into the classroom. ___smuggle___

6. Blake attempted to score an A on his chemistry exam. ___endeavored___

7. The anti-war activists marched outside the Capitol building. ___pacifists___

8. The bully strutted menacingly toward the first-graders. ___swaggered___

9. My concerns lie with those who are less fortunate. ___sympathies___

5

■ Above Level Practice

Name _____

Comprehension

Answer the following, using the story *Hannah Brown: Union Army Spy* and your completed Graphic Organizer.

1. Which outcome in the story was easy to predict?
Possible response: Hannah would be safe from General Early.

2. Explain why this outcome was easy to predict.
Possible response: General Early did not consider young girls, especially Quaker pacifists, to be a threat.

3. Which outcome in the story was difficult to predict?
Possible response: The successful delivery of the coded message to the Quakers.

4. Explain why this outcome was difficult to predict.
Possible response: Because Miss West was in hiding, it could have been difficult to get the warning message to her.

5. Explain how Hannah's personal qualities and character traits influenced your predictions.
Possible response: Hannah was thoughtful and clever. She noticed everything, allowing her to detect suspicion and pass along the coded message.

6. Explain how at least one other event, condition, or character had a significant impact on your predictions about the outcome of the story.
Answers will vary.

7

◆ LANGUAGE SUPPORT

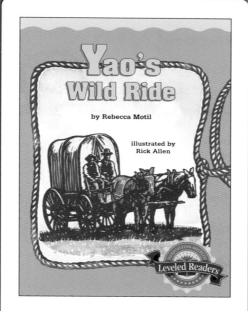

Yao's Wild Ride

by Rebecca Motil

illustrated by Rick Allen

Leveled Readers

◆ Language Support Practice

Name _____

Build Background

saddle
reins
stirrups

Look at the picture and answer these questions.

1. Do you think the boy is afraid of the horse? Why?
Answers will vary.

2. Why could it be difficult and frightening to ride a horse?
Sample answers: Horses are large; they can move fast; it is easy to slide off; there's not much to hold onto; rider sits high off the ground.

3. What can a rider use to stay on a horse?
The saddle, stirrups, saddle horn, and reins can help a rider stay on.

5

◆ Language Support Practice

Name _____

Vocabulary

Fill in each blank with one of the words from the box.

Vocabulary
bandits
cattle
coyote
saddle horn
seasoned
stirrups
vaqueros
wagon

1. A ___coyote___ is like a small wolf and lives in North America.

2. In the Old West, ___bandits___ often robbed travelers.

3. A ___wagon___ is used to carry loads or passengers.

4. The Spanish word for cowboys is ___vaqueros___.

5. Large animals with hoofs that are raised for meat, hides, or dairy products are ___cattle___.

6. A cowboy with a lot of experience could be called ___seasoned___.

7. The raised part at the front of a saddle is called a ___saddle horn___.

8. The loops that a rider steps into to get on a horse are called ___stirrups___.

6

Leveled Theme Paperbacks

- Extended independent reading in theme-related paperbacks
- Lessons in Teacher's Edition, pages R2–R7

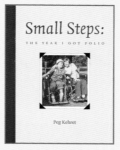

Small Steps:
THE YEAR I GOT POLIO

Peg Kehret

● **BELOW LEVEL**   ▲ **ON LEVEL**

SHIPWRECK AT THE BOTTOM OF THE WORLD

■ **ABOVE LEVEL**

Technology

HOUGHTON MIFFLIN
Online Leveled Books
www.eduplace.com

- over 1,000 Online Leveled Books

Leveled Readers
Audio available

Daily Lesson Plans

 **Technology**
Lesson Planner CD-ROM allows you to customize the chart below to develop your own lesson plans.

T Skill tested on Weekly or Theme Skills Test and/or Integrated Theme Test

Reading
Comprehension

50–60 minutes

Vocabulary Reader

Voyage of the Fram

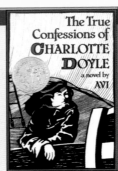

Leveled Readers
- Fluency Practice
- Independent Reading

Word Work

20–30 minutes

Phonics/Decoding
Vocabulary
Spelling

Writing and Oral Language

20–30 minutes

Writing
Grammar
Listening/Speaking/Viewing

DAY 1

Teacher Read Aloud, 93CC–93DD
Storm at Tempest Cove

Background and Vocabulary, 94

Key Vocabulary, 95
ascent	ratlines
endeavored	rigging
entangled	
seasoned	treacherous

Vocabulary Reader

Reading the Selection, 96–109

Comprehension Skill, 96
Predicting Outcomes **T**

Comprehension Strategy, 96
Monitor/Clarify

Leveled Readers

Riding with the Vaqueros
Johnny Kelley's Tale
Hannah Brown,
  Union Army Spy
Yao's Wild Ride

Lessons and Leveled Practice, 115O–115R

Phonics/Decoding, 97
Phonics/Decoding Strategy

Vocabulary, 96–109
Selection Vocabulary

Spelling, 115E
/ou/, /o͞o/, /ô/, and /oi/ **T**

Writing, 115K
Prewriting an Opinion Paragraph

Grammar, 115I
Common/Proper Nouns **T**

Daily Language Practice
1. that tree is beautiful in full blum. (That; bloom.)
2. The yellow rose is finally starting to droup (droop.)

Listening/Speaking/Viewing,
93CC–93DD, 103
Teacher Read Aloud, Stop and Think

DAY 2

Reading the Selection, 96–109

Comprehension Check, 109

Responding, 110
Think About the Selection

Vocabulary Reader

Comprehension Skill Preview, 105
Predicting Outcomes **T**

Leveled Readers
Riding with the Vaqueros
Johnny Kelley's Tale
Hannah Brown,
  Union Army Spy
Yao's Wild Ride

Lessons and Leveled Practice, 115O–115R

Structural Analysis, 115C
Possessives and Contractions **T**

Vocabulary, 96–109
Selection Vocabulary

Spelling, 115E
/ou/, /o͞o/, /ô/, and /oi/ Review and Practice **T**

Writing, 115K
Drafting an Opinion Paragraph

Grammar, 115I
Common/Proper Nouns Practice **T**

Daily Language Practice
3. My baby sister gayle likes to be nauty. (Gayle; naughty.)
4. My friend ben caught a very large troot in the lake. (Ben; trout)

Listening/Speaking/Viewing, 109, 110
Wrapping Up, Responding

Target Skills of the Week

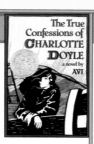

Phonics	Possessives and Contractions
Comprehension	Monitor/Clarify; Predicting Outcomes
Vocabulary	Word Families
Fluency	Leveled Readers

DAY 3

Rereading the Selection, 96–109

Vocabulary Reader

Comprehension Skill, 115A–115B
Predicting Outcomes **T**

Leveled Readers

Riding with the Vaqueros
Johnny Kelley's Tale
Hannah Brown,
 Union Army Spy
Yao's Wild Ride

Lessons and Leveled Practice, 115O–115R

Phonics Review, 115D
The /ou/, /o͞o/, /ô/, and /oi/ Sounds

Vocabulary, 115G
Word Families **T**

Spelling, 115F
Vocabulary: Multiple Meanings Practice **T**

Writing, 115L
Revising an Opinion Paragraph
Combining Sentences **T**

Grammar, 115J
Singular/Plural Nouns **T**

Daily Language Practice
5. A nowne is a person, place, or thing (noun; thing.)
6. The principal is going to appont mr. Suarez to a new job. (appoint; Mr.)

DAY 4

Reading the Social Studies Link, 112–115
"Alone Against the Sea"

Skill: How to Take Notes

Rereading for Visual Literacy, 114
Illustrator's Craft

Comprehension Skill Review, 101
Sequence of Events

Leveled Readers

Riding with the Vaqueros
Johnny Kelley's Tale
Hannah Brown,
 Union Army Spy
Yao's Wild Ride

Lessons and Leveled Practice, 115O–115R

Phonics/Decoding, 112–115
Apply Phonics/Decoding Strategy to Link

Vocabulary, 115M
Language Center: Building Vocabulary

Spelling, 115F
Spelling Game, Proofreading **T**

Writing, 115L
Proofreading an Opinion Paragraph

Grammar, 115J
Singular/Plural Nouns Practice **T**

Daily Language Practice
7. You need fowl weather gear to hike in maine. (foul; Maine.)
8. Most childs like to crooch in small spaces to hide. (children; crouch)

Listening/Speaking/Viewing, 115
Discuss the Link

DAY 5

Rereading for Fluency, 99
Responding Activities, 110–111
Write a Descriptive Paragraph
Cross-Curricular Activities

Information and Study Skills, 115H
Using Graphic Aids **T**

Comprehension Skill Review, 107
Making Generalizations

Leveled Readers
Riding with the Vaqueros
Johnny Kelley's Tale
Hannah Brown,
 Union Army Spy
Yao's Wild Ride

Lessons and Leveled Practice, 115O–115R

Phonics, 115N
Language Center: Complete the Advertisement

Vocabulary, 115M
Language Center: Vocabulary Game

Spelling, 115F
Test: /ou/, /o͞o/, /ô/, and /oi/ **T**

Writing, 115L
Publishing an Opinion Paragraph

Grammar, 115J, 115M
People's Titles
Language Center: Is It Common or Proper?

Daily Language Practice
 9. My parrot phillip likes to squack all day long. (Phillip; squawk)
10. How many boxs of checks can fit in that bank valt? (boxes; vault?)

Listening/Speaking/Viewing, 115N
Language Center: Giving and Listening to Directions

Managing Flexible Groups

Leveled Instruction and Leveled Practice

WHOLE CLASS

DAY 1

- Teacher Read Aloud (TE pp. 93CC–93DD)
- Building Background, Introducing Vocabulary (TE pp. 94–95)
- Comprehension Strategy: Introduce (TE p. 96)
- Comprehension Skill: Introduce (TE p. 96)
- Purpose Setting (TE p. 97)

After reading first half of *The True Confessions of Charlotte Doyle*
- Stop and Think (TE p. 103)

DAY 2

After reading *The True Confessions of Charlotte Doyle*
- Wrapping Up (TE p. 109)
- Comprehension Check (Practice Book p. 63)
- Responding: Think About the Selection (TE p. 110)
- Comprehension Skill: Preview (TE p. 105)

SMALL GROUPS

Extra Support

DAY 1

TEACHER-LED
- Preview vocabulary; support reading with Vocabulary Reader.
- Preview *The True Confessions of Charlotte Doyle* to Stop and Think (TE pp. 96–103).
- Support reading with Extra Support/Intervention notes (TE pp. 97, 100, 102, 104, 106, 108).

DAY 2

Partner or Individual Work
- Reread first half of *The True Confessions of Charlotte Doyle* (TE pp. 96–103).
- Preview, read second half (TE pp. 104–109).
- Comprehension Check (Practice Book p. 63)

Challenge

DAY 1

Individual Work
- Begin "Traveler's Diary" (Challenge Handbook p. 8).
- Extend reading with Challenge Note (TE p. 108).

DAY 2

Individual Work
- Continue work on activity (Challenge Handbook p. 8).

English Language Learners

DAY 1

TEACHER-LED
- Preview vocabulary; support reading with Vocabulary Reader.
- Preview *The True Confessions of Charlotte Doyle* to Stop and Think (TE pp. 96–103).
- Support reading with English Language Learners notes (TE pp. 94, 99, 101, 105).

DAY 2

TEACHER-LED
- Review first half of *The True Confessions of Charlotte Doyle* (TE pp. 96–103). ✔
- Preview, read second half (TE pp. 104–109).
- Begin Comprehension Check together (Practice Book p. 63).

Independent Activities

- Get Set for Reading CD-ROM
- Journals: selection notes, questions
- Complete, review Practice Book (pp. 61–65) and Leveled Readers Practice Blackline Masters (TE pp. 115O–115R).
- Assignment Cards (Teacher's Resource Blackline Masters pp. 54–55)
- Leveled Readers (TE pp. 115O–115R), Leveled Theme Paperbacks (TE pp. R2–R7), or book from Leveled Bibliography (TE pp. 23E–23F)

✔ **Opportunity to informally assess oral reading rate**

DAY 3

- Rereading (TE pp. 96–109)
- Comprehension Skill: Main lesson (TE pp. 115A–115B)

TEACHER-LED

- Reread, review Comprehension Check (Practice Book p. 63).
- Preview Leveled Reader: Below Level (TE p. 115O), or read book from Leveled Bibliography (TE pp. 23E–23F). ✔

TEACHER-LED

- Teacher check-in: Assess progress (Challenge Handbook p. 8).
- Preview Leveled Reader: Above Level (TE p. 115Q), or read book from Leveled Bibliography (TE pp. 23E–23F). ✔

Partner or Individual Work

- Complete Comprehension Check (Practice Book p. 63).
- Begin Leveled Reader: Language Support (TE p. 115R), or read book from Leveled Bibliography (TE pp. 23E–23F).

DAY 4

- Reading the Social Studies Link (TE pp. 112–115): Skill lesson (TE p. 112)
- Rereading the Social Studies Link: Lesson on Visual Literacy (TE p. 114)
- Comprehension Skill: First Comprehension Review lesson (TE p. 101)

Partner or Individual Work

- Reread the Social Studies Link (TE pp. 112–115).
- Complete Leveled Reader: Below Level (TE p. 115O), or read book from Leveled Bibliography (TE pp. 23E–23F).

Individual Work

- Complete activity (Challenge Handbook p. 8).
- Complete Leveled Reader: Above Level (TE p. 115Q), or read book from Leveled Bibliography (TE pp. 23E–23F).

TEACHER-LED

- Reread the Social Studies Link (TE pp. 112–115) ✔ and review Link Skill (TE p. 112).
- Complete Leveled Reader: Language Support (TE p. 115R), or read book from Leveled Bibliography (TE pp. 23E–23F). ✔

DAY 5

- Responding: Select from Activities (TE pp. 110–111)
- Information and Study Skills (TE p. 115H)
- Comprehension Skill: Second Comprehension Review lesson (TE p. 107)

TEACHER-LED

- Comprehension Skill: Reteaching lesson (TE p. R14)
- Reread Leveled Theme Paperback: Below Level (TE pp. R2–R3), or read book from Leveled Bibliography (TE pp. 23E–23F). ✔

TEACHER-LED

- Evaluate activity and plan format for sharing (Challenge Handbook p. 8).
- Reread Leveled Theme Paperback: Above Level (TE pp. R6–R7), or read book from Leveled Bibliography (TE pp. 23E–23F). ✔

Partner or Individual Work

- Reread book from Leveled Bibliography (TE pp. 23E–23F).

- Responding activities (TE pp. 110–111)
- Language Center activities (TE pp. 115M–115N)
- **Fluency Practice:** Reread *The True Confessions of Charlotte Doyle, Hatchet, Passage to Freedom, Climb or Die.* ✔
- Activities relating to *The True Confessions of Charlotte Doyle* at Education Place® www.eduplace.com

Turn the page for more independent activities.

Ready-Made Small Group Activities

Word Work

Cross Curricular

SMALL GROUP ACTIVITIES

Building Vocabulary Center Activity 4
● ▲ ■ *Into the Unknown*

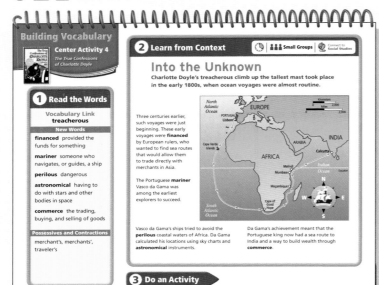

Building Vocabulary
Center Activity 4
The True Confessions of Charlotte Doyle

2 Learn from Context 🕐 ♦♦♦ Small Groups | Connect to Social Studies

Into the Unknown
Charlotte Doyle's treacherous climb up the tallest mast took place in the early 1800s, when ocean voyages were almost routine.

Three centuries earlier, such voyages were just beginning. These early voyages were **financed** by European rulers, who wanted to find sea routes that would allow them to trade directly with merchants in Asia.

The Portuguese **mariner** Vasco da Gama was among the earliest explorers to succeed.

Vasco da Gama's ships tried to avoid the **perilous** coastal waters of Africa. Da Gama calculated his locations using sky charts and **astronomical** instruments.

Da Gama's achievement meant that the Portuguese king now had a sea route to India and a way to build wealth through **commerce**.

1 Read the Words

Vocabulary Link
treacherous

New Words

financed provided the funds for something

mariner someone who navigates, or guides, a ship

perilous dangerous

astronomical having to do with stars and other bodies in space

commerce the trading, buying, and selling of goods

Possessives and Contractions

merchant's, merchants', traveler's

3 Do an Activity

Leveled Activities on side 2

Reading in Social Studies Independent Book
■ *Charters of Freedom*

Charters of Freedom
by Kathleen E. Jones

Reading in Social Studies Center Activity 4
● ▲ ■ *Plan a Debate*

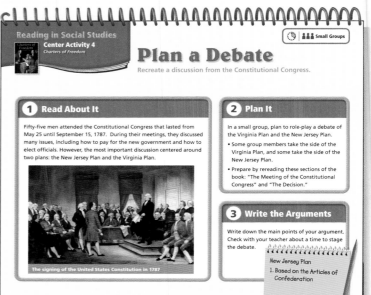

Reading in Social Studies
Center Activity 4
Charters of Freedom

🕐 ♦♦♦ Small Groups

Plan a Debate
Recreate a discussion from the Constitutional Congress.

1 Read About It

Fifty-five men attended the Constitutional Congress that lasted from May 25 until September 15, 1787. During their meetings, they discussed many issues, including how to pay for the new government and how to elect officials. However, the most important discussion centered around two plans: the New Jersey Plan and the Virginia Plan.

The signing of the United States Constitution in 1787

2 Plan It

In a small group, plan to role-play a debate of the Virginia Plan and the New Jersey Plan.

• Some group members take the side of the Virginia Plan, and some take the side of the New Jersey Plan.

• Prepare by rereading these sections of the book: "The Meeting of the Constitutional Congress" and "The Decision."

3 Write the Arguments

Write down the main points of your argument. Check with your teacher about a time to stage the debate.

New Jersey Plan
1. Based on the Articles of Confederation

Leveled Activities on side 2

Letter Cards and Trays

a e i o u

Key Vocabulary Cards 26–32

ascent

Spelling Word Cards 61–79

bloom

Leveled for ● Below Level, ▲ On Level, ■ Above Level

 # Reading

  # Writing

Assignment Card 16
● *Ship Diagram*

Activity Card 2
▲ ■ *Bestseller List?*

Activity Card 3
▲ ■ *Outstanding*

Challenge Card 1–7
■ *Traveler's Diary*

Multiple Tiers of Intervention

Core Program Instruction

- research-based
- systematic
- assessment-driven

Group Support

Daily lessons and activities for differentiated instruction

Intervention Strategies for Extra Support, pages 44–53

Instructional Activities for Challenge, pages 8–9

Instructional Strategies for English Learners, pages 48–57

Intervention Program

Proven efficacy for struggling readers

Soar to Success

Oral Language and Fluency

OBJECTIVE
- Listen to predict outcomes.

Building Background

Tell students that you are going to read aloud a story about a boy in Scotland who helps save two fishing boats during a dangerous storm.

- Discuss with students what life might be like in a small, isolated fishing village.

- Explain that a trawler is a type of fishing boat that drags large nets underwater.

Fluency Modeling

Explain that as you read aloud, you will be modeling fluent oral reading. Ask students to listen carefully to your phrasing and your expression, or tone of voice and emphasis.

COMPREHENSION SKILL

Predicting Outcomes

Explain that predicting outcomes requires

- using details from the story;
- using personal knowledge;
- updating predictions as you read.

Purpose Setting Read the selection aloud, asking students to think about what is going to happen next as they listen. Then use the Guiding Comprehension questions to assess students' understanding. Reread the selection for clarification as needed.

Teacher Read Aloud

Storm at Tempest Cove
by Margaret Underwood

Jamie Morgan stood on the wharf watching the disappearing wakes of the *Sea Witch* and the *Dolphin*, dreaming of the day he would be on board. The fishing trawlers sailed side by side, joined by the net dragged between them to catch the darting silver herring. When the pairs of trawlers grew small in the distance, Jamie headed for school along the empty street.

The Morgans lived in an isolated fishing village on the northeast coast of Scotland. After the trawlers shoved off, the only ones left in the village were women and children and the old men who sat in the sunshine mending fishnets.

1 When Jamie returned home that afternoon his mother had on her "worry" face. He knew she was thinking of the weather.

"We're in for a bad one," Jamie said, voicing her unspoken thoughts. "Black clouds are rolling in from the sea, and the wind is kicking up a gale."

"Aye. I'm thinking of those trawlers bobbing up and down like corks on the water." She sighed.

"Da is the first to spot a storm brewing. He'll be heading for port right now," Jamie assured her.

2 A knock sounded at the door. At that moment, the lights flickered and went out, putting the cottage into twilight gloom. Jamie ran to the door.

It was their neighbor, Gordie Snow. Rain dripped off his slicker and formed a puddle at his feet. "It's bad out there, Mary, but the trawlers are headed for port. Just before the radio quit we got the message that the *Dolphin* suffered a broken rudder and the *Sea Witch* has her in tow."

"Heaven help us! With the power down, the coastline will be in darkness … and now the radio gone!" Jamie's mother shook her head.

Jamie watched Gordie's brow wrinkle into a deep frown. "Now don't be putting a bad face on it, Mary. They're sure to come through this all right."

Jamie wondered if Gordie believed his own words.

Jamie bent into the wind. His macintosh whipped around him, and his sou'wester seemed ready to fly off his head. The gentle waves of the morning were replaced by high walls of water that collapsed on the shore with a roar like thunder. From the supply shack at the dockside, Jamie took flares to fire into the darkness. Their light would help guide the trawlers into the cove.

A steep cliff rose behind the beach, now hidden by the sheets of rain driven by the wind. Jamie knew the flares would be most visible if shot off from the top of the cliff. It would take him forever to backtrack down the beach, then follow the ridge to the top. He would climb the cliffside. He had done it before, but then the wall was not slick and there was not a twenty-knot gale that could tear him from the face of the cliff.

He started to climb, grabbing the gorse growing in the notches. He pulled himself up hand over hand, groping for each slippery foothold. He ignored the plants' prickles that tore into his skin. Shaking from his efforts, he dragged himself over the top.

The first three matches he tried spluttered out. On the fourth try he succeeded in firing off two flares. They rose with a loud swoosh, cutting into the black sky in a bright arc of light. It seemed forever before the answering flares shot up at sea. Jamie fired off two more. A series of answering flares from the trawlers showed they had passed by the entrance to Tempest Cove but then changed course and were now headed into the cove. They were almost home.

❸ Jamie heard voices behind him. He was seized by friendly hands and lifted onto broad shoulders that carried him back to the town hall, where the villagers had gathered. Then followed a feast with cheers to the fishermen and to Jamie Morgan — for his courage and quick thinking that helped save the lives of the men of the village.

CRITICAL THINKING
Guiding Comprehension

❶ PREDICTING OUTCOMES How is Jamie's mother's "worry" face a clue as to what might happen later in the story? (Sample answer: It is a clue that the fishing trawlers she is worrying about will have a problem getting to shore.)

❷ PREDICTING OUTCOMES Why is the loss of electricity at this time so important to the story? (Sample answer: It means there will be no light to guide the fishing trawlers back to safety and no way to contact them by radio. Something else will need to be done to help them.)

❸ PREDICTING OUTCOMES How do you think Jamie would act during another emergency? (Sample answer: He would try to help, because he has done so in the past.)

Discussion Options

Personal Response Ask students to tell whether they found the story exciting and to explain why they feel this way.

⭐ **Connecting/Comparing** Ask students to compare Jamie's actions with those of Danielle and Jake in *Climb or Die*.

English Language Learners

Language Development

Write the following words on the board: *Da*, *slicker*, and *flare*. Point out that *Da* is a word used in Scotland for *Father* or *Dad*, a *slicker* is a type of raincoat, and a *flare* is a bright burning light that is shot into the air as a signal. Ask students to use each word in a sentence.

Background and Vocabulary

Key Concept: Challenges Faced by Sailors

Remind students that this theme is about characters who show courage. Tell them that next they will read about a girl who must overcome a difficult test to become part of a ship's crew in the early 1830s. Use "To Sail a Ship" on pages 94–95 to build background and introduce key vocabulary.

- Ask a student to read aloud "To Sail a Ship."

- Have students identify the dangers involved in climbing a ship's rigging.

- Discuss other challenges faced by sailors of that time.

Vocabulary Preview

The Vocabulary Reader can be used to preteach or reinforce the key vocabulary.

Vocabulary Reader

Voyage of the *Fram*

by Tanner Ottley Gay

Get Set to Read

Background and Vocabulary

To Sail a Ship

The True Confessions of Charlotte Doyle

Genre **Historical Fiction**

Key Vocabulary

entangled

ratlines

rigging

seasoned

treacherous

Vocabulary Reader

Voyage of the *Fram*

e • Glossary

94

What was it like to be on board a sailing ship in the early 1830s? In *The True Confessions of Charlotte Doyle*, a girl finds out what a sailor's life is really like.

On a brig, or two-masted ship, a **seasoned** sailor had to climb the masts or the **rigging** — the ropes that support the masts and sails — to untie the sails so the wind could move the ship. The climb itself was **treacherous**. The sailor might get **entangled** in the **ratlines** and would sometimes even fall. The highest spar, or pole, that supports the top of the highest sail was called the royal yard. It could be as high as 130 feet. During a severe storm at sea, the sails needed to be tied so that they would not be damaged. A sailor's life on a sailing ship provided many challenges.

REACHING ALL LEARNERS

English Language Learners

Supporting Comprehension

Beginning/Preproduction Have students listen to the article. Have students point out the rigging and the ratlines in the illustration. Ask students to show how a sailor might climb up the ratlines.

Early Production and Speech Emergence Have students repeat the Key Vocabulary words after you. Ask them to give examples of treacherous, or dangerous, situations. Ask, Would you like to climb up the ratlines of the ship in the picture? Why or why not?

Intermediate and Advanced Fluency In small groups, have students read the article and discuss some of the dangers a sailor might face working on a sailing ship.

Royal Yard

Rigging

Ratlines

Main Mast

95

Introducing Vocabulary

Key Vocabulary

These words support the Key Concept and appear in the selection.

ascent an upward climb

endeavored attempted

entangled twisted together

ratlines the small ropes, fastened horizontally to ropes supporting a ship's mast, which together form a ladder

rigging the system of ropes, chains, and other gear used to control a ship's sails

seasoned experienced

treacherous marked by unpredictable dangers

 e·Glossary
e·WordGame

See Vocabulary notes on pages 98, 100, 102, 104, 106, and 108 for additional words to preview.

Display Transparency 1–29.

- Model how to figure out the meaning of the word *endeavored* from clues in the first sentence. Remind students that words they can't figure out from sentence clues can be looked up in the dictionary.

- Ask students to use letter sounds and context clues to figure out the meaning of the remaining Key Vocabulary words. Have students explain how they figured out each word.

- Ask students to look for these words as they read and to use them to discuss the challenges sailors faced.

Practice/Homework Assign **Practice Book** page 61.

Transparency 1–29

Sailing Words

Matthew <u>endeavored</u> to prove his courage to the other sailors by climbing to the topmost sail of the ship. However, any <u>ascent</u> to the top of the main mast would be very difficult on this day. A heavy rain was falling that made it difficult to see. Matthew couldn't figure out which part of the <u>rigging</u> to go up. He finally decided to climb the ladder formed by the <u>ratlines</u>. The already <u>treacherous</u> footholds were made more dangerous by the rain on the ropes. Even the most <u>seasoned</u> sailor would have had difficulty climbing in this weather. About halfway up, Matthew got his left leg <u>entangled</u> in a rope. It took several minutes for Matthew to free himself. When he finally reached the top, he was in the clouds. No one from below could see that he had made it.

TRANSPARENCY 1–29
TEACHER'S EDITION PAGE 95

ANNOTATED VERSION | COURAGE *The True Confessions of Charlotte D...* | Key Vocabulary

---

Practice Book page 61

The True Confessions of
Charlotte Doyle
Key Vocabulary

Name _____

A Test of Courage

Use these words to complete the sentences below.

Vocabulary
ascent
entangled
seasoned
endeavored
rigging
ratlines
treacherous

1. Are you a seasoned **(1 point)** _____ sailor, or is this your first voyage?

2. To prove that you will be an able sailor, you must climb to the top of the rigging **(1)** _____.

3. To start your climb, grab one of the ratlines **(1)** _____, the small ropes that form a ladder.

4. As you continue your ascent **(1)** _____ upward, be careful not to become entangled in the ropes.

5. Rain and wind make the climb even more treacherous **(1)** _____ than it usually is.

6. I have endeavored **(1)** _____ to give you guidance, but you must find courage within yourself to make the climb.

Use two vocabulary words in a short description of what it might feel like to make the climb described above.

(2 points)

_____

_____

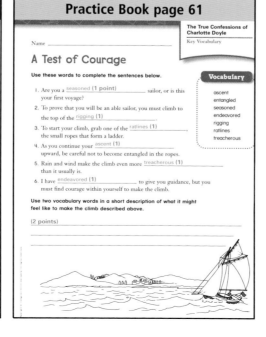

Introducing Vocabulary 95

TARGET SKILL
COMPREHENSION STRATEGY
Monitor/Clarify

Teacher Modeling Ask a student to read aloud the Strategy Focus. Remind students to reread or read ahead to figure out what they don't understand. Ask students to read the introduction on page 99. Then model the strategy.

Think Aloud *I am confused. Why does Charlotte have to climb the tallest mast? I will go back and read the paragraph again. Now I see that climbing the mast is a test. Charlotte must prove she is worthy of being part of the ship's crew.*

✓ **Test Prep** Remind students that many reading tests are timed. Caution them, however, not to rush. In particular, students should take time to monitor and clarify what they are reading.

TARGET SKILL
COMPREHENSION SKILL
Predicting Outcomes

Introduce the Graphic Organizer. Tell students that they will make predictions about what the story characters might do in the future. Explain that as they read, students will fill out the Predictions Chart on **Practice Book** page 62.

- Display **Transparency 1–30.** Have students read Anthology page 99.
- Model how to complete the first section of the Predictions Chart, using details from the story and personal knowledge.
- As students read, have them complete their Predictions Chart. If necessary, monitor students' work.

MEET THE AUTHOR
AVI

How he got that name: His twin sister gave it to him as a baby.

Beating the odds: Avi almost flunked out of school because his writing was so bad. He feels very fortunate to have come as far as he has.

What honed his skill: Avi played a game with his children in which they would give him a subject — "a glass of water" — and he would have to make up a story about it.

Notable books: *The Fighting Ground; Perloo the Bold; Beyond the Western Sea, Books 1 and 2*

MEET THE ILLUSTRATOR
SCOTT MCKOWEN

What he was like as a young boy: Scott McKowen's parents always brought paper and pencils to keep him quiet in restaurants.

How he makes his art: McKowen works in scratchboard, an engraving medium. He carves white lines with a sharp blade onto an all-black board. Then he colors it with a special oil paint.

To discover more about Avi and Scott McKowen, visit Education Place. **www.eduplace.com/kids**

96

Transparency 1–30

Predictions Chart

selection details + personal knowledge + THINKING = prediction

Selection Details page 99	Personal Knowledge
▶ Charlotte must climb the tallest mast to prove her worth. The climb is dangerous. Charlotte is steady, though nervous.	Example: Courageous people will face challenges, despite danger.

Prediction: Example: Charlotte will go through with the test.

Selection Details page 105	Personal Knowledge
▶ Charlotte makes it to just below the top gallant spar. It took her thirty minutes to do what a seasoned sailor could do in two.	Accept reasonable responses.

Prediction: It will take Charlotte a very long time to complete the climb.

Selection Details page 107	Personal Knowledge
▶ Charlotte begins her climb down. She nearly falls because she can't see where to put her feet.	Accept reasonable responses.

Prediction: Charlotte will probably make it down.

Selection Details page 105	Personal Knowledge
▶ Captain Jaggery appears on deck. He is not cheering like everyone else.	Accept reasonable responses.

Prediction: Captain Jaggery will not want Charlotte to become a crew member.

COURAGE *The True Confessions of Charlotte Doyle* Graphic Organizer Predictions Chart
ANNOTATED VERSION
TRANSPARENCY 1–30
TEACHER'S EDITION PAGES 96 AND 115A

Practice Book page 62

The True Confessions of Charlotte Doyle
Graphic Organizer Predictions Chart

Name _____

Predictions Chart

selection details + personal knowledge + THINKING = prediction

Selection Details page 99	Personal Knowledge
▶ Charlotte must climb the tallest mast to prove her worth. The climb is dangerous. Charlotte is steady, though nervous. **(1 point)**	Example: Courageous people will face challenges, despite danger. **(1 point)**

Prediction: Example: Charlotte will go through with the test. **(1)**

Selection Details page 105	Personal Knowledge
▶ Charlotte makes it to just below the top gallant spar. It took her thirty minutes to do what a seasoned sailor could do in two.	Accept reasonable responses. **(1)**

Prediction: It will take Charlotte a very long time to complete the climb. **(1)**

Selection Details page 107	Personal Knowledge
▶ Charlotte begins her climb down. She nearly falls because she can't see where to put her feet. **(1)**	Accept reasonable responses. **(1)**

Prediction: Charlotte will probably make it down. **(1)**

Selection Details page 105	Personal Knowledge
▶ Captain Jaggery appears on deck. He is not cheering like everyone else.	Accept reasonable responses. **(1)**

Prediction: Captain Jaggery will not want Charlotte to become a crew member. **(1)**

Selection 4

The True Confessions of CHARLOTTE DOYLE

a novel by AVI

Strategy Focus

Charlotte Doyle faces the toughest challenge of her life when she joins the ship's crew. As you read, **monitor** how well you understand the selection, and **clarify** parts you don't understand by rereading or reading ahead.

97

Extra Support/Intervention

Selection Preview

pages 97–102 Charlotte can join the ship's crew if she passes the test by climbing to the top of the royal yard. As she looks up at the towering mast, she feels afraid, but she decides to climb.

pages 102–105 The ship begins to sway, and Charlotte's climb becomes much more difficult. Every muscle in her body aches, and she still has a long way to go. How do you think she feels about her decision to climb?

pages 106–107 Charlotte reaches the top. Then she discovers that going back down is even more difficult.

pages 107–109 Will Charlotte reach the deck safely? What do you think is going through the minds of the sailors?

Purpose Setting

- Have students predict whether Charlotte will succeed in climbing the tallest mast of the ship. How will the sailors feel about her by the end of the selection?

- Have students preview the story by looking at the illustrations. Encourage them to reread to clarify what they don't understand about sailing on a ship in the 1830s.

- Have students observe how Charlotte reacts to the challenges she faces. How might she react to challenges if she becomes a crew member?

- You may want to preview with students the Responding questions on Anthology page 110.

Journal ▸ Students can use their journals to describe anything that confuses them and to record details that helped clarify their understanding.

STRATEGY REVIEW

Phonics/Decoding

Remind students to use the Phonics/Decoding Strategy as they read.

Modeling Write this sentence on the board: *"We're agreed," he <u>announced</u>. "Not a one stands in favor of your signing on, Miss Doyle."* Point to *announced*.

Think Aloud *In the middle of this word, I see the familiar vowel pattern* ou, *which makes the /ow/ sound as in the word* out. *I'll try sounding it out:* uh-NOWNST. *It means "gave someone news" or "made known." That sounds right and makes sense in the sentence.*

CRITICAL THINKING
Guiding Comprehension

1 **MAKING INFERENCES** Why do you think Fisk tells Charlotte what might happen if she falls? (He wants to scare her into changing her mind; he wants her to understand the dangers.)

2 **NOTING DETAILS** What details does the author include to show that Charlotte is scared? (Charlotte swallows hard and speaks softly.)

3 **NOTING DETAILS** What details does the author include to show that Fisk isn't sure how he feels about Charlotte's decision to climb? (The look on Fisk's face is a mix of admiration and contempt.)

98

Vocabulary

royal yard the long crossways pole that spreads the topmost sail of the ship

shimmy up to scoot up using arms and legs

shrouds a set of ropes stretched from the top of a mast to the sides of a ship to support the mast

ratlines the small ropes, fastened horizontally to ropes supporting a ship's mast, which together form a ladder

maim to injure or hurt

ASSIGNMENT CARD 16

Ship Diagram

Precise Language

Authors often use special words to make their descriptions as precise as possible. Recognizing these words helps readers understand more clearly what is being described.

- Your teacher will give you a photocopy of the diagram of the ship on page 95, including the labels.

- Turn to page 99 of the story and identify the words the author uses to describe parts of the *Seahawk*. Find these parts on the diagram, adding labels as needed. You may use a dictionary if necessary.

As you read the rest of the story, identify other instances in which the author uses special words to name parts of the *Seahawk*. Add these to the diagram. Then use the diagram to help you summarize Charlotte's trip up and down the main mast.

Theme 1: Courage

Teacher's Resource BLM page 55

The year is 1832 and thirteen-year-old Charlotte Doyle is sailing on the *Seahawk,* a brig bound for America from England. Once on board she finds herself the only passenger and the only girl among a rough crew. When the crew needs a replacement, she boldly offers to join them. Little does she realize that as a test to prove her worth, she must climb the tallest mast of the ship.

"Miss Doyle," he pressed, "you have agreed to climb to the top of the royal yard. Do you know that's the highest sail on the main mast? One hundred and thirty feet up. You can reach it only two ways. You can shimmy up the mast itself. Or you can climb the shrouds, using the ratlines for your ladder."

I nodded as if I fully grasped what he was saying. The truth was I didn't even wish to listen. I just wanted to get past the test.

"And Miss Doyle," he went on, "if you slip and fall you'll be lucky to drop into the sea and drown quickly. No mortal could pluck you out fast enough to save you. Do you understand that?" **❶**

I swallowed hard but nodded. "Yes."

"Because if you're *not* lucky you'll crash to the deck. Fall that way and you'll either maim or kill yourself by breaking your neck. Still certain?"

"Yes," I repeated, though somewhat more softly. **❷**

"I'll give you this," he said with a look that seemed a mix of admiration and contempt, "Zachariah was right. You're as steady a girl as ever I've met." **❸**

99

Rereading for Fluency Have students choose a favorite part of the story to reread to a partner, or suggest that they read page 99. Encourage students to read expressively.

English Language Learners

Supporting Comprehension

- Make sure students understand that the speaker (the *I*) is Charlotte.

- Read the second paragraph aloud. Explain that *fully grasped* means "understood." Ask, What doesn't Charlotte understand?

- Read the third paragraph aloud. Ask, Why will Charlotte be lucky if she drowns quickly?

- Read the last paragraph aloud. Explain that *I'll give you this* means "I'll admit" and that Fisk is praising her a little bit.

CRITICAL THINKING
Guiding Comprehension

4 **MAKING INFERENCES** What does Charlotte mean by thinking, *If I succeeded I'd gain the opportunity of making the climb fifty times a day*? (Climbing the royal yard is part of a sailor's everyday job.)

TARGET SKILL
COMPREHENSION STRATEGY
Monitor/Clarify

Teacher/Student Modeling Have students reread paragraphs 8 and 9 on page 100. Model using the strategy to identify and then clarify confusing parts of the story. Use these prompts:

- Why is Charlotte *fully committed* to the climb? (She can't turn back now; she has already told the crew she will do it.)

- Why does Charlotte think *Not that it mattered*? Does this mean she thinks the climb is not important? (No, it means that she will climb even though she has lost her nerve.)

Vocabulary

quailed shrank back in fear; cowered

escorted went with; accompanied

audacity courage and resolution; boldness

affixed attached

stays heavy ropes used to brace or support a mast or spar

Foley soon returned. "We're agreed," he announced. "Not a one stands in favor of your signing on, Miss Doyle. Not with what you are. We're all agreed to that. But if you climb as high as the royal yard and make it down whole, and if you still want to sign on, you can come as equal. You'll get no more from us, Miss Doyle, but no less either."

Fisk looked at me for my answer.

"I understand," I said.

"All right then," Foley said. "The captain's still in his cabin and not likely to come out till five bells. You can do it now."

"*Now?*" I quailed.

"Now before never."

So it was that the four men escorted me onto the deck. There I found that the rest of the crew had already gathered.

Having fully committed myself, I was overwhelmed by my audacity. The masts had always seemed tall, of course, but never so tall as they did at that moment. When I reached the deck and looked up my courage all but crumbled. My stomach turned. My legs grew weak.

Not that it mattered. Fisk escorted me to the mast as though I were being led to die at the stake. He seemed as grim as I.

To grasp fully what I'd undertaken to do, know again that the height of the mainmast towered one hundred and thirty feet from the deck. This mast was, in fact, three great rounded lengths of wood, trees, in truth, affixed one to the end of the other. Further, it supported four levels of sails, each of which bore a different name. In order, bottom to top, these were called the main yard, topsail, topgallant, and finally royal yard.

4 My task was to climb to the top of the royal yard. And come down. In one piece. If I succeeded I'd gain the opportunity of making the climb fifty times a day.

As if reading my terrified thoughts Fisk inquired gravely, "How will you go, Miss Doyle? Up the mast or

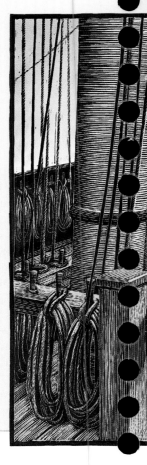

100

Extra Support/Intervention

Strategy Modeling: Monitor/Clarify

Use this example to model the strategy.

What does Foley mean when he says, "Not with what you are"? I'll reread the paragraph. The whole crew voted against Charlotte's becoming a crew member. Why did they do that? I'll reread the beginning of the story. Now I see that Charlotte is the only girl on the ship. That's what Foley means by "what you are."

on the ratlines?"

Once again I looked up. I could not possibly climb the mast directly. The stays and shrouds with their ratlines would serve me better.

"Ratlines," I replied softly.

"Then up you go."

I will confess it, at that moment my nerves failed. I found myself unable to move. With thudding heart I looked frantically around. The members of the crew, arranged in a crescent, were standing like death's own jury.

101

Sequence of Events

Review

- In most stories, events are told in the order in which they happen.

- Sometimes authors may refer to past or future events to give readers more information.

- Authors use time words and phrases to signal when a story event takes place. (Examples: *before, after, next, already, used to, had always*)

Practice

- Have a student read aloud paragraphs 7 and 8 on page 100.

- Ask, What phrase shows that the men were on deck before Charlotte was escorted there? (*had already gathered*)

- Ask, What do the phrases *had always seemed* and *at that moment* show us? (Charlotte had thought about the height of the masts before she stood below them getting ready to climb.)

Apply

- Have small groups of students chart the sequence of events on page 102.

- Have them list the words and phrases that signal the order of events.

Review Skill Trace	
Teach	p. 93A
Reteach	p. R12
▶ Review	p. 101; Theme 5, p. 461

English Language Learners

Language Development

Help students understand the following phrases on pages 100–101:

- "*Not a one stands in favor*" means "no one agrees."

- "*Now before never*" means "if not now, never."

- *My nerves failed* means "I lost my courage."

READ & COMPREHEND

The True Confessions of Charlotte Doyle

Guiding Comprehension

READ & COMPREHEND

❺ **MAKING INFERENCES** Why might Barlow and Ewing want Charlotte to succeed? (Sample answer: They admire her courage.)

❻ **CAUSE AND EFFECT** How did Charlotte's choice of rigging make her climb harder? (Because she chose rigging that did not go all the way to the top, she will have to change to another set of ropes during the climb.)

---

❺ It was Barlow who called out, "A blessing goes with you, Miss Doyle."

To which Ewing added, "And this advice, Miss Doyle. Keep your eyes steady on the ropes. Don't you look down. Or up."

For the first time I sensed that some of them at least wanted me to succeed. The realization gave me courage.

With halting steps and shallow breath, I approached the rail only to pause when I reached it. I could hear a small inner voice crying, "Don't! Don't!"

But it was also then that I heard Dillingham snicker, "She'll not have the stomach."

I reached up, grasped the lowest deadeye, and hauled myself atop the rail. That much I had done before. Now, I maneuvered to the outside so that I would be leaning *into* the rigging and could even rest on it.

Once again I looked at the crew, *down* at them, I should say. They were staring up with blank expressions.

Recollecting Ewing's advice, I shifted my eyes and focused them on the ropes before me. Then, reaching as high as I could into one of the middle shrouds, and grabbing a ratline, I began to climb.

The ratlines were set about sixteen inches one above the other, so that the steps I had to take were wide for me. I needed to pull as much with arms as climb with legs. But line by line I did go up, as if ascending an enormous ladder.

❻ After I had risen some seventeen feet I realized I'd made a great mistake. The rigging stood in sets, each going to a different level of the mast. I could have taken one that stretched directly to the top. Instead, I had chosen a line which went only to the first trestletree, to the top of the lower mast.

For a moment I considered backing down and starting afresh. I stole a quick glance below. The crew's faces were turned up toward me. I understood that they would take the smallest movement down as retreat. I had to continue.

And so I did.

Now I was climbing inside the lank gray-white sails, ascending, as it were, into a bank of dead clouds.

102

Vocabulary

deadeye a flat hardwood disk used to fasten a ship's rigging

maneuvered changed directions or moved in a controlled manner

rigging the system of ropes, chains, and other gear used to control a ship's sails

trestletree one of a pair of horizontal beams set into a mast-head to help spread the shrouds

---

REACHING ALL LEARNERS

Extra Support/Intervention

Review (pages 97–102)

Before students join the whole class for Stop and Think on page 103, they should

- review their purpose/predictions
- take turns modeling Monitor/Clarify and other strategies they used
- add to **Transparency 1–30**
- review their Predictions Chart on **Practice Book** page 62, and use it to summarize

103

Stop and Think

Critical Thinking Questions

1. **CAUSE AND EFFECT** What effect does Dillingham's snicker have on Charlotte? (makes her angry enough to forget her fear; gives her the final push she needs to climb)

2. **MAKING INFERENCES** Why might the sailors have Charlotte take her test while the captain is not watching? (They are afraid he might be angry at their treatment of Charlotte, who is a passenger and a young girl.)

Strategies in Action

Have students take turns modeling Monitor/Clarify and other strategies they used.

Discussion Options

You may want to bring the entire class together to do one or more of the activities below.

- **Review Predictions/Purpose** Discuss predictions about whether Charlotte will succeed. Discuss students' questions about sailing ships.

- **Share Group Discussions** Have students share their literature discussions.

- **Summarize** Ask students to use their Predictions Chart to help them summarize the story so far.

ASSIGNMENT CARD 15

Literature Discussion

Discuss the following questions and questions of your own with a group of your classmates:

- Do you think Charlotte's decision to climb to the top of the royal yard is a good one? Explain why you think as you do.

- How do you think the sailors feel about what Charlotte is doing?

- Why do you think Ewing tells Charlotte not to look up or down? Is this good advice? Why or why not?

- Have you ever faced a challenging situation in which you had to do something to prove yourself? What did you do? How did you feel?

Theme 1: Courage

Teacher's Resource BLM page 54

Monitoring Student Progress

If . . .	Then . . .
students have successfully completed the Extra Support activities on page 102,	have them read the rest of the selection cooperatively or independently.

Reading the Selection 103

CRITICAL THINKING
Guiding Comprehension

❼ DRAWING CONCLUSIONS What can you conclude about the weather from Charlotte's thoughts? (The wind is blowing but not very hard.)

❽ WRITER'S CRAFT Why do you think the author uses three short sentences in a row to describe Charlotte's reaction to the ship's movement? (to speed up the pace; to convey a sense of Charlotte's terror)

❾ NOTING DETAILS What details does the author provide to show you that Charlotte is very high up? (Charlotte thinks the ship looks like a toy and the sailors look like tiny bugs.)

---

❼

Beyond the sails lay the sea, slate-gray and ever rolling. Though the water looked calm, I could feel the slow pitch and roll it caused in the ship. I realized suddenly how much harder this climb would be if the wind were blowing and we were well underway. The mere thought made the palms of my hands grow damp.

Up I continued till I reached the main yard. Here I snatched another glance at the sea, and was startled to see how much bigger it had grown. Indeed, the more I saw of it the *more* there was. In contrast, the *Seahawk* struck me as having suddenly grown smaller. The more I saw of *her*, the *less* she was!

I glanced aloft. To climb higher I now had to edge myself out upon the trestletree and then once again move up the next set of ratlines as I'd done before. But at twice the height!

❽ Wrapping one arm around the mast — even up here it was too big to reach around completely — I grasped one of the stays and edged out. At the same moment the ship dipped, the world seemed to twist and tilt down. My stomach lurched. My heart pounded. My head swam. In spite of myself I closed my eyes. I all but slipped, saving myself only by a sudden grasp of a line before the ship yawed the opposite way. I felt sicker yet. With ever-waning strength I clung on for dearest life. Now the full folly of what I was attempting burst upon me with grotesque reality. It had been not only stupid, but suicidal. I would never come down alive!

And yet I had to climb. This was my restitution.

When the ship was steady again, I grasped the furthest rigging, first with one hand, then the other, and dragged myself higher. I was heading for the topsail, fifteen feet further up.

Pressing myself as close as possible into the rigging, I continued to strain upward, squeezing the ropes so tightly my hands cramped. I even tried curling my toes about the ratlines.

At last I reached the topsail spar, but discovered it was impossible to rest there. The only place to pause was three *times* higher than the distance I'd just come, at the trestletree just below the topgallant spar.

By now every muscle in my body ached. My head felt light, my heart an anvil. My hands were on fire, the soles of my feet raw. Time and again I was forced to halt, pressing my face against the rigging with eyes

104

Vocabulary

folly lack of good sense

restitution the act of making up for loss, damage, or injury

spar a wooden pole used as a yard, mast, or boom on a ship

seasoned experienced

treacherous marked by unpredictable dangers

Extra Support/Intervention

Strategy Modeling: Phonics/Decoding

Model how to decode *attempting.*

I recognize the ending -ing. How do I pronounce the base word? I can pronounce the a /a/ *or* /uh/. *I think the* e *is short. I'll try* a-TEHMPT-ihng. *That doesn't sound quite right. I think it's* uh-TEHMPT-ihng. *That sounds right and makes sense in the sentence.*

attempting

uh-TEHMPT-ihng

---

closed. Then, in spite of what I'd been warned not to do, I opened them and peered down. The *Seahawk* was like a wooden toy. The sea looked greater still.

I made myself glance up. Oh, so far to go! How I forced myself to move I am not sure. But the thought of backing down now was just as frightening. Knowing only that I could not stay still, I crept upward, ratline by ratline, taking what seemed to be forever with each rise until I finally reached the level just below the topgallant spar.

A seasoned sailor would have needed two minutes to reach this point. I had needed thirty!

Though I felt the constant roll of the ship, I had to rest there. What seemed like little movement on deck became, up high, wild swings and turns through treacherous air.

I gagged, forced my stomach down, drew breath, and looked out. Though I didn't think it possible, the ocean appeared to have grown greater yet. And when I looked down, the upturned faces of the crew appeared like so many tiny bugs.

There were twenty-five or so more feet to climb. Once again I grasped the rigging and hauled myself up.

105

English Language Learners

Language Development

Explain these vivid images in the fourth and last paragraphs on page 104:

- The image *the world seemed to twist and tilt* shows how Charlotte saw the sky and the water as she swayed on the mast.
- The images *stomach lurched, heart pounded,* and *head swam* show her feelings of fear and confusion.
- *My head felt light* shows that she is tired, and *my heart an anvil* means her heart is heavy with fear.
- Charlotte's hands are *on fire* because they hurt from climbing.

Predicting Outcomes

Teach

- Explain that readers can predict how a character will behave in different situations.
- Tell students that to make a good prediction they need to combine story details with their personal knowledge and experience.

Practice

- Ask, If Charlotte becomes a crew member, what kind of sailor will she be? (Sample answers: committed, brave, hard-working)
- Ask students what information from the story they used to make this prediction. (Sample answer: She goes through with the climb.)
- Ask students what personal knowledge and experience they used to make this prediction. (Sample answer: Someone who wants a job this badly will be a hard worker.)

Apply

- Have a student read aloud the first paragraph on page 104.
- Have small groups predict what Charlotte might have done if the wind had been blowing hard.
- Have groups explain their predictions to the class.

Target Skill Trace	
Preview; Teach	p. 93CC, p. 96, p. 105; p. 115A
Reteach	p. R14
Review	pp. M32–M33; p. 57; Theme 2, p. 175; Theme 3, p. 281

READ & COMPREHEND

The True Confessions of Charlotte Doyle

CRITICAL THINKING
Guiding Comprehension

10 MAKING INFERENCES Why does Charlotte think that the sea is *eager to swallow me whole*? (She is afraid she will fall.)

11 PREDICTING OUTCOMES Explain what you think Charlotte will do now that she is entangled in the lines. (Answers will vary.)

COMPREHENSION STRATEGY
Monitor/Clarify

Student Modeling Ask students to identify confusing parts of the story and explain what they did to clarify their understanding. Use these prompts:

- Were there any parts of Charlotte's climb that were difficult to understand? If so, what were they?

- What did you do to help clear up your confusion?

106

Vocabulary

gyrations circular or spiraling movements

endeavored attempted

metronome a device with a long arm that provides a steady beat for practicing music

ascent an upward climb

void an empty space

entangled twisted together

Extra Support/Intervention

Strategy Modeling: Monitor/Clarify

Use this example to model the strategy.

In the third paragraph on page 107, I'm not sure what Charlotte means by the metronome motion of the mast, *so I read the previous paragraph. I'm still not sure, so I read ahead. Charlotte describes the Seahawk as turning, tossing, and swaying. I know that the arm of a metronome swings back and forth. The phrase* metronome motion *must mean the mast is swaying back and forth.*

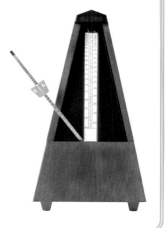

This final climb was torture. With every upward pull the swaying of the ship seemed to increase. Even when not moving myself, I was flying through the air in wild, wide gyrations. The horizon kept shifting, tilting, dropping. I was increasingly dizzy, nauseous, terrified, certain that with every next moment I would slip and fall to death. I paused again and again, my eyes on the rigging inches from my face, gasping and praying as I had never prayed before. My one hope was that, nearer to heaven now, I could make my desperation heard!

Inch by inch I continued up. Half an inch! Quarter inches! But then at last with trembling fingers, I touched the spar of the royal yard. I had reached the top.

Once there I endeavored to rest again. But there the metronome motion of the mast was at its most extreme, the *Seahawk* turning, tossing, swaying as if trying to shake me off — like a dog throwing droplets of water from its back. And when I looked beyond I saw a sea that was infinity itself, ready, eager to swallow me whole.

I had to get back down.

10

As hard as it was to climb up, it was, to my horror, harder returning. On the ascent I could see where I was going. Edging down I had to grope blindly with my feet. Sometimes I tried to look. But when I did the sight of the void below was so sickening, I was forced to close my eyes.

Each groping step downward was a nightmare. Most times my foot found only air. Then, as if to mock my terror, a small breeze at last sprang up. Sails began to fill and snap, puffing in and out, at times smothering me. The tossing of the ship grew — if that were possible — more extreme.

Down I crept, past the topgallant where I paused briefly on the trestletree, then down along the longest stretch, toward the mainyard. It was there I fell.

I was searching with my left foot for the next ratline. When I found a hold and started to put my weight upon it, my foot, slipping on the slick tar surface, shot forward. The suddenness of it made me lose my grip. I tumbled backward, but in such a way that my legs became entangled in the lines. There I hung, *head downward*.

11

I screamed, tried to grab something. But I couldn't. I clutched madly at nothing, till my hand brushed against a dangling rope. I grabbed for it,

---

ASSIGNMENT CARD 17

"Figuratively" Speaking

Figurative Language

The author uses figurative language to help readers understand Charlotte's experiences aboard the Seahawk. Examples:

- **Similes:** phrases that use the word *like* or *as* to compare two unlike things: **The Seahawk was like a wooden toy.** (page 105)

- **Metaphors:** comparisons between two things that do not use the word *like* or *as*: *My head felt light,* **my heart an anvil**. (page 104)

- **Personification:** giving an object human qualities, such as feelings, senses, and actions: *And when I looked beyond, I saw a* **sea** *that was infinity itself,* **ready, eager to swallow me whole.** (page 107)

Write your own descriptions of Charlotte's experiences using all three types of figurative language.

Theme 1: Courage

Teacher's Resource BLM page 55

Making Generalizations

Review

- Explain that generalizations are statements about people or things that are true most of the time.

- Tell students that generalizations often include signal words such as *most, all, few, always, never, generally, often,* and *usually.*

- Write *While climbing up the rigging is difficult, climbing down it is almost always more difficult.* Explain that this is a generalization.

- Remove the word *almost* from the sentence. Ask students how the statement has changed. Explain that the generalization is no longer true because there could be situations when climbing down might be easier.

Practice/Apply

- Have partners or small groups use selection details to make generalizations.

- They can generalize about sailors' attitude toward women, about sailors' strength and stamina, and about the dangers sailors face.

- Have students compare and discuss their generalizations.

Review Skill Trace	
Teach	Theme 3, p. 271A
Reteach	Theme 3, p. R8
▶ Review	p. 107; Theme 2, p. 203; Theme 3, p. 343; Theme 6, p. 579

CRITICAL THINKING
Guiding Comprehension

12 **NOTING DETAILS** What details show that the crew is happy to see Charlotte succeed? (Everyone cheers for her—once when she passes the lowest sail and again when she reaches the deck.)

13 **WRITER'S CRAFT** What words does the author use to show how happy Charlotte is? (*heart swelled with exaltation, joyous heart*)

14 **MAKING INFERENCES** How do you think Captain Jaggery feels when he sees the crew congratulating Charlotte? (Sample answers: angry that the sailors made Charlotte climb; impressed with Charlotte's courage)

missed, and grabbed again. Using all my strength, I levered myself up and, wrapping my arms into the lines, made a veritable knot of myself, mast, and rigging. Oh, how I wept! my entire body shaking and trembling as though it would break apart.

When my breathing became somewhat normal, I managed to untangle first one arm, then my legs. I was free.

I continued down. By the time I reached the mainyard I was numb and whimpering again, tears coursing from my eyes.

I moved to the shrouds I'd climbed, and edged myself past the lowest of the sails.

12 As I emerged from under it, the crew gave out a great "Huzzah!"

108

Vocabulary

veritable real or genuine

exaltation praise

India-rubber rubber made from the milky sap of the rubber tree

Extra Support/ Intervention

Selection Review

Before students join the whole class for Wrapping Up on page 109, they should

- review predictions/purpose
- take turns modeling Monitor/Clarify and other strategies they used
- complete their Predictions Chart and help you complete **Transparency 1–30**
- summarize the whole selection

On Level | **Challenge**

Literature Discussion

In groups of five or six, students can discuss their own questions about the story. Then have students discuss the Responding questions on page 110 of the Anthology.

Oh, how my heart swelled with exaltation!

Finally, when I'd reached close to the very end, Barlow stepped forward, beaming, his arms uplifted. "Jump!" he called. "Jump!"

But now, determined to do it all myself, I shook my head. Indeed, in the end I dropped down on my own two India-rubber legs — and tumbled to the deck.

No sooner did I land than the crew gave me another "Huzzah!" With joyous heart I staggered to my feet. Only then did I see Captain Jaggery push through the knot of men and come to stand before me. ⚓

13

14

109

Practice Book page 63

The True Confessions of
Charlotte Doyle

Comprehension Check

Name _____

A Day on the *Seahawk*

Answer the questions about the setting, characters, and plot of
The True Confessions of Charlotte Doyle.

1. Where is Charlotte when the story begins?
   below deck on the *Seahawk* **(1 point)**

2. What does she have to do to become a member of the crew?
   climb to the top of the royal yard **(1)**

3. Why doesn't Charlotte start over again after she realizes she has begun to climb the wrong set of rigging?
   She doesn't want the crew to think she is retreating. **(1)**

4. After the ship dips, how does Charlotte feel about her decision to climb?
   She worries she will not will make it down alive. **(1)**

5. How long does it take Charlotte to climb to a point on the mast that a seasoned sailor could reach in two minutes?
   thirty minutes **(1)**

6. Why is climbing near the top of the mast more difficult than climbing closer to the bottom?
   The swaying motion of the ship increases at the top of the mast. **(1)**

7. Why is climbing down the rigging more difficult than climbing up?
   Charlotte can't see where she's putting her feet. **(1)**

8. How does the crew react when Charlotte finally returns safely to the deck?
   They cheer for her. **(1)**

Wrapping Up

Critical Thinking Questions

1. **PREDICTING OUTCOMES** Do you think Captain Jaggery will allow Charlotte to become a crew member? Why or why not? (Sample answer: probably not, because he is not as joyous as the other sailors)

2. **MAKING JUDGMENTS** Was it wise for Charlotte to make the climb? Why or why not? (Sample answers; yes, because she needed to pass the test to become a sailor; no, because she could have hurt herself)

Strategies in Action

Invite students to take turns modeling how and where they used Monitor/Clarify and other strategies.

Discussion Options

Bring the entire class together to do one or more of the activities below.

Review Predictions/Purpose Have students discuss what personal qualities helped Charlotte succeed.

Share Group Discussions Have students share their literature discussions.

Summarize Ask students to use their completed Predictions Chart to summarize the selection.

Comprehension Check

Use **Practice Book** page 63 to assess students' comprehension of the selection.

Monitoring Student Progress

If . . .	Then . . .
students score 6 or below on **Practice Book** page 63,	help them find places in the text that tell about the different parts of Charlotte's climb.

Responding

Think About the Selection

Have students discuss or write their answers. Sample answers are provided; accept reasonable responses.

1. **DRAWING CONCLUSIONS** Charlotte lacks experience; they've never had a female crew member.

2. **MAKING INFERENCES** He wants to scare her so she won't try the climb; shows that Fisk worries about others' safety

3. **MAKING JUDGMENTS** yes, because she'd have to do it regularly as a member of the crew

4. **CATEGORIZING AND CLASSIFYING** Sample answer: *determined,* because Charlotte did what she set out to do despite difficulties

5. **WRITER'S CRAFT** effective, because it shows that Charlotte is in danger of being thrown off the *Seahawk*

6. **CONNECTING TO PERSONAL EXPERIENCE** Accept reasonable responses.

7. **Connecting/Comparing** Charlotte climbs to prove she is worthy of becoming a crew member, while Jake and Danielle climb to get help for their family; all show great courage by taking risks and facing danger to achieve their goals.

Responding

Think About the Selection

1. Why do you think none of the crew believe Charlotte is serious about becoming a crew member?

2. Why does Fisk warn Charlotte about the risks of climbing the mast? What does this tell you about Fisk?

3. Do you think that climbing the tallest mast of the ship is a good test of Charlotte's worth as a crew member? Why or why not?

4. Which word best describes Charlotte for you: *determined, steady, terrified,* or some other word? Explain why.

5. From atop the mast, the *Seahawk* was "like a dog throwing droplets of water from its back." How effective is this comparison? Explain.

6. Charlotte feels terrified when she commits herself to a test she isn't sure of passing. Describe a time when you have felt this way.

7. **Connecting/Comparing** Compare Charlotte's reasons for climbing the ship's mast with Jake and Danielle's reasons for climbing Mount Remington. How did they all show courage in their decisions?

Describing

Write a Descriptive Paragraph

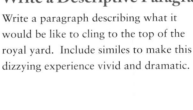

Write a paragraph describing what it would be like to cling to the top of the royal yard. Include similes to make this dizzying experience vivid and dramatic.

Tips

- Remember that a simile uses *like* or *as* to compare things in an unexpected way.
- Arrange your details in spatial order or in order of importance.
- Use strong, exact words.

110

REACHING ALL LEARNERS

English Language Learners

Supporting Comprehension

Beginning/Preproduction Have students draw a picture of the most frightening part of Charlotte's climb.

Early Production and Speech Emergence Have partners draw a sailing ship and label the parts. Then ask them to discuss what Charlotte had to do.

Intermediate and Advanced Fluency Have small groups discuss these questions: Would you have climbed the mast in Charlotte's situation? Why or why not? What else would you need to know to be a good sailor?

Math

Draw a Diagram

With a partner, measure each other's height. Round each number to the nearest foot. If the main mast Charlotte climbed was 130 feet tall, how many times could you be stacked against the height of the mast? How many times could your partner? Draw a diagram to solve the problem.

Internet

Complete a Word Search Puzzle

You've learned a lot of vocabulary related to sailing ships in this selection. Try finding those words in a word search puzzle that can be printed from Education Place. **www.eduplace.com/kids**

111

Hold a Discussion

Form a group with two or three classmates and discuss this topic: Is Charlotte Doyle's climb to the top of the royal yard foolish or courageous? Try to come to a shared conclusion.

Tips

- Listen closely and politely to what others say. Don't let your attention wander.
- Take turns contributing ideas. Give reasons for your opinions.

Additional Responses

Personal Response Invite students to share their personal responses to the selection.

Journal ▶ Have students write in their journals about a time when they faced a challenge and how they dealt with it.

Selection Connections Remind students to add to **Practice Book** page 10.

End-of-Selection Assessment

Selection Test Use the test on page 115 in the **Teacher's Resource Blackline Masters** to assess selection comprehension and vocabulary.

Student Self-Assessment Have students assess their reading with additional questions such as these:

- What parts of the story were easy for me to understand?
- What strategies helped me understand the parts that were difficult for me?
- What new words did I learn?
- Would I like to read more about Charlotte's adventures aboard the *Seahawk?* Why or why not?

REACHING ALL LEARNERS

Extra Support/ Intervention

Brainstorming Similes

Read aloud the simile in the third paragraph on page 107 (*like a dog throwing droplets of water from its back*). Have partners brainstorm a list of other comparisons that could also describe the feeling of clinging to the top of the royal yard.

Practice Book page 10

Launching the Theme
Selection Connections

Name _____

Courage *continued*

	Climb or Die	The True Confessions of Charlotte Doyle
What challenge does the main character face?	Danielle and Jake must climb a steep, icy mountain without the right climbing tools. (2.5)	Charlotte must climb to the top of the royal yard to prove she is fit to be a sailor. (2.5)
Where does the challenge take place?	on a snowy mountain in modern times (2.5)	on a sailing ship in the 1800s (2.5)
In what ways does the main character show courage?	Danielle and Jake bravely complete the climb, using only the tools they have. (2.5)	Charlotte completes the climb even though she is terrified. (2.5)
What do you think the character learns from his or her experience?	Danielle and Jake learn that they are resourceful and stronger than they thought. (2.5)	Charlotte learns that she can climb to the top of the royal yard without falling or getting sick. (2.5)

What have you learned about courage in this theme?

Sample answer: Sometimes people surprise themselves with strength they didn't know they had. (2)

Social Studies Link

Skill: How to Take Notes

- **Introduce** "Alone Against the Sea" from *National Geographic World*.

- **Explain** that taking notes will help students understand and remember what they read.

- **Discuss** the Skill Lesson on Anthology page 112.

- **Model** taking notes on the first three paragraphs on page 113. Write main ideas and important supporting details. Explain that notes should not include minor details. Use this example.

Subaru Takahashi	Start of Journey
–14 years old	–July 22, 1996
–sailed alone across Pacific	–Tokyo Bay, Japan
–faced huge storms	

- **Set a purpose** for reading. Have students read the article and take notes on it. Remind them to use the Monitor/Clarify strategy.

Vocabulary

bailing scooping water out of a boat

navigation deciding what course a boat will take to get from one point to another

boom a long pole that extends from the mast to stretch out the sail

Social Studies Link

Genre

True Experiences

How to Take Notes
As you read . . .

1. Look for the big ideas. Write headings that give the main ideas.

2. Under each heading, jot down supporting details. Keep your notes short.

3. Underline and define key terms in your notes.

ALONE Against the SEA

The Daring Adventure of Subaru Takahashi — the Youngest Person to Sail Across the Pacific Ocean . . . Alone!

112

Lightning flashed, thunder boomed, and heavy rain pounded. A midday storm was exploding far out in the Pacific Ocean. The winds grew stronger and the waves bigger. Subaru Takahashi, then fourteen, of Shirone, in Japan, watched with widening eyes. Soon his 30-foot sailboat was being tossed about like a toy.

Suddenly huge waves began crashing over the side of the boat. As water collected on the deck, Subaru grabbed a cooking pot. Working furiously, he began bailing out the ocean water. Fortunately for him the storm's ferocity lasted only a few hours. Subaru insists today that he was never really worried.

Several weeks earlier, on July 22, 1996, Subaru had begun an ambitious journey from Tokyo Bay, in Japan. Family, friends, and reporters cheered him on. He planned to sail across the world's largest body of water, the mighty Pacific Ocean, alone. He calculated that he could make the crossing — 6,000 miles — and sail into San Francisco Bay within seven weeks.

Aboard the *Advantage*, the sailboat he had rented from a dentist in Tokyo, was a two-month supply of water and food, including rice, noodles, and soup. His boat also was equipped with the most modern radio and navigation equipment.

Nobody who knew Subaru from his earlier childhood was surprised at his voyage. At age nine, he had paddled alone by canoe across nineteen-mile Sado Strait in the Sea of Japan. At age ten he had taken his first sailing lesson in a dinghy, or small boat. And he had not been discouraged when a sail boom hit him in the head and almost knocked him out.

Subaru began to form his plan to cross the Pacific after meeting a Japanese adventurer who had sailed solo around the world without stopping. Six months after the meeting, he began training for his daring journey. After he'd spent 200 hours sailing the *Advantage* in open water, Subaru was ready to go.

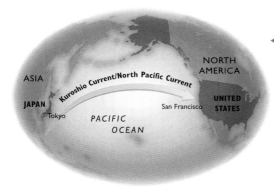

ASIA

Kuroshio Current/North Pacific Current

NORTH AMERICA

JAPAN

Tokyo

San Francisco

UNITED STATES

PACIFIC OCEAN

◄ *Several currents helped Subaru on his journey across the Pacific Ocean. The Kuroshio, or Japan Current, is about sixty miles wide near Japan. Further out it merges with cooler waters and forms the North Pacific Current.*

113

REACHING ALL LEARNERS

English Language Learners

Supporting Comprehension

Read the title aloud. Use the map at the bottom of page 113 to give students an overview of Subaru's trip. Ask them to take notes on what Subaru had to do in order to make this trip as they read. Suggest the headings shown.

Before Trip

During Trip

Arrival

Illustrator's Craft

Teach

- Tell students that artists can show suspense or danger in their illustrations.

- Two methods that illustrators use to do this are by showing a great difference in the size of two objects and by using colors that reflect the mood.

- Have students look at the illustration on page 114.

- Explain that the picture of the large freighter approaching Subaru's small boat illustrates the danger Subaru is in at that moment. Even though the boat is far away, it already looks much bigger than Subaru's boat.

Practice/Apply

- Have partners study the illustrations in *The True Confessions of Charlotte Doyle*.

- Have them describe to each other how the illustrator shows suspense on page 103, when Charlotte is climbing the rigging, and on pages 108–109, when Captain Jaggery appears on deck.

Vocabulary

generator a machine that makes electricity

collision a crash; an event in which two or more things hit each other

As he sailed away from Japan in July, his mother told reporters, "I believe that his strong will to live will bring him back, no matter what." Subaru's parents also believed their son's sailing experiences would teach him things he would never learn in school.

"I was excited when the land disappeared and I reached open ocean," Subaru recalls. "I had confidence I would succeed." Everything went smoothly at first. His occasional companions were whales and dolphins. He used a radio to keep in contact with his parents in Japan. They informed reporters of their son's progress.

To keep from getting bored, Subaru tried fishing. Just as he caught his only fish, a seabird dived and swallowed it. But the bird also swallowed the hook. Despite Subaru's rescue efforts, the bird died. So Subaru hauled it aboard, cooked it, and ate it. He says, "It tasted good."

114

Serious trouble arose on August 11 when an engine died, killing all power to his electric generator. That meant that with five weeks to go, Subaru had no power for the lights, radio, and automatic steering. Knocked out of action, too, was his automatic global positioning system, or GPS. This system picks up signals from satellites and locates a boat's position in the ocean.

Fortunately he had two backup systems that still worked: a hand-held GPS, and a battery-operated radio. But the radio battery failed five days later! Subaru then lost all communication with the outside world. In his last message, he reported that he was 2,790 miles west of San Francisco.

Now Subaru was truly alone. "I began wondering what I had done in my life to deserve such bad luck," he says. "Everything seemed to be going wrong."

One windless day, with his boat at a near standstill, Subaru spotted a large ship on the horizon. As the freighter got closer and closer, Subaru saw it was heading toward his sailboat on a collision course. He frantically waved his arms. Finally someone aboard the ship saw the young sailor in his boat and changed course just in time to avoid disaster.

By the end of August, many people in Japan were convinced Subaru had been lost at sea. They had followed the radio reports of his voyage until

Extra Support/Intervention

Sequence of Events

If students need help following the sequence of events in the article, you may want to create a time line on the board and work with students to place events in chronological order. Explain that graphic aids such as time lines can become a helpful part of their notes.

Subaru Takahashi poses with the Japanese flag shortly after becoming the youngest person to sail solo across the Pacific Ocean. Below, Subaru conducts the final check of his yacht *Advantage* before leaving Tokyo.

the reports stopped abruptly in mid-ocean. But his parents never gave up hope. In anticipation of his arrival, they traveled to San Francisco in September.

They were rewarded on September 13 when Subaru sailed under the Golden Gate Bridge and into San Francisco Bay. "Two days before my arrival, I was so excited I couldn't stop smiling and I couldn't sleep," he recalls. He was soon greeted by his parents and a group of reporters whose news reports made him an instant hero as the youngest person to sail solo across the Pacific Ocean.

As he stepped off the boat, he said, "This is the beginning for me, not the end." He was referring to another goal: sailing solo around the world — just as soon as he can get prepared.

115

Wrapping Up

Critical Thinking Questions

Have students answer these questions about the article. Ask them to support their answers with information from the text.

1. **MAKING JUDGMENTS** Explain what you think was the most dangerous part of Subaru's crossing, and tell why. (Sample answer: when he almost got hit by the freighter, because he had no way to warn the freighter he was there)

2. **DRAWING CONCLUSIONS** What kind of a person is Subaru? How do you know? (Sample answer: He is very determined and likes a challenge. As soon as he had crossed the Pacific Ocean alone, he was thinking about trying to sail around the world alone.)

3. **NOTING DETAILS** How many days did it take Subaru to cross the ocean? How much longer was this than the seven weeks he'd originally calculated? (It took him fifty-four days, which was five days more than he'd originally calculated.)

4. **Connecting/Comparing** How do you think Subaru Takahashi and Charlotte Doyle are alike? How are they different? (Alike: Both are determined to face difficult challenges; both are sailors. Different: Charlotte wants to be part of a crew; Subaru likes to sail alone.)

REACHING ALL LEARNERS

Challenge

Posters Showing Sailing Records

Have students work in small groups to create posters with information about sailing records.

• Suggest that students brainstorm a list of possible records, such as the first recorded crossing, the fastest crossing, and so on.

• Each group should use an encyclopedia, an almanac, and other print reference sources to find out about these records.

• Encourage students to take notes as they research and to use their notes to make their posters.

OBJECTIVES

- Use story details and personal knowledge to make predictions about what will happen in a story.
- Make predictions about how story characters might react in different circumstances.

Target Skill Trace

Preview; Teach	p. 93CC, p. 96, p. 105; p. 115A
Reteach	p. R14
Review	pp. M32–M33; p. 57; Theme 2, p. 175; Theme 3, p. 281
See	*Extra Support Handbook,* pp. 46–47; pp. 52–53

Transparency 1–30

Predictions Chart

selection details + personal knowledge + THINKING = prediction

Selection Details page 99	Personal Knowledge
► Charlotte must climb the tallest mast to prove her worth. The climb is dangerous. Charlotte is steady, though nervous.	Example: Courageous people will face challenges, despite danger.

Prediction: Example: Charlotte will go through with the test.

Selection Details page 105	Personal Knowledge
► Charlotte makes it to just below the top gallant spar. It took her thirty minutes to do what a seasoned sailor could do in two.	Accept reasonable responses.

Prediction: It will take Charlotte a very long time to complete the climb.

Selection Details page 107	Personal Knowledge
► Charlotte begins her climb down. She nearly falls because she can't see where to put her feet.	Accept reasonable responses.

Prediction: Charlotte will probably make it down.

Selection Details page 105	Personal Knowledge
► Captain Jaggery appears on deck. He is not cheering like everyone else.	Accept reasonable responses.

Prediction: Captain Jaggery will not want Charlotte to become a crew member.

TRANSPARENCY 1–30
TEACHER'S EDITION PAGES 96 AND 115A

COURAGE The True Confessions of Charlotte Doyle
Graphic Organizer Predictions Chart
ANNOTATED VERSION

Practice Book page 62

Name _____

The True Confessions of Charlotte Doyle
Graphic Organizer Predictions Chart

Predictions Chart

selection details + personal knowledge + THINKING – prediction

Selection Details page 99	Personal Knowledge
► Charlotte must climb the tallest mast to prove her worth. The climb is dangerous. Charlotte is steady, though nervous. **(1 point)**	Example: Courageous people will face challenges, despite danger. **(1 point)**

Prediction: Example: Charlotte will go through with the test. **(1)**

Selection Details page 105	Personal Knowledge
► Charlotte makes it to just below the top gallant spar. It took her thirty minutes to do what a seasoned sailor could do in two. **(1)**	Accept reasonable responses. **(1)**

Prediction: It will take Charlotte a very long time to complete the climb. **(1)**

Selection Details page 107	Personal Knowledge
► Charlotte begins her climb down. She nearly falls because she can't see where to put her feet.**(1)**	Accept reasonable responses. **(1)**

Prediction: Charlotte will probably make it down. **(1)**

Selection Details page 105	Personal Knowledge
► Captain Jaggery appears on deck. He is not cheering like everyone else.	Accept reasonable responses. **(1)**

Prediction: Captain Jaggery will not want Charlotte to become a crew member. **(1)**

COMPREHENSION: Predicting Outcomes

TARGET SKILL

❶ Teach

Review predicting outcomes in *The True Confessions of Charlotte Doyle.* Complete the Graphic Organizer on **Transparency 1–30** with students. (Sample answers are shown.) Have students refer to the selection and to **Practice Book** page 62.

- Discuss the story details, personal knowledge, and experience students used to make their predictions.
- Review how subsequent story events either confirmed a prediction, made students revise a prediction, or led them to make a new prediction.

Model revising predictions. Remind students that they may need to revise their predictions as they read. Have students read the first paragraph on page 100. Then think aloud.

Think Aloud *The sailors' negative attitude toward Charlotte made me predict that they wouldn't want her to be a crew member even if she made the climb. But when they cheered her on page 108, I changed my prediction. Now I think they might welcome her as a crew member.*

❷ Guided Practice

Have students make predictions about different situations. Display a chart like the one below. Fill in the two situations. Have partners complete the chart. (Sample answers are shown.)

SITUATION	STORY DETAILS	PERSONAL KNOWLEDGE	PREDICTION
A sailor must climb up and tie back the highest sails during a storm. Charlotte and Fisk are the only sailors available.	It took Charlotte thirty minutes to climb as high as an experienced sailor could in two minutes.	In an emergency, doing something quickly is important.	Fisk will climb up to tie the sails alone.
Charlotte must climb to the top of the royal yard again. Will she go up the same way she went before?	Charlotte did not take the most direct route the first time.	A more direct route is usually faster.	She will climb the rigging that runs directly to the top.

❸ Apply

Assign Practice Book pages 64–65. Also have students apply this skill as they read their **Leveled Readers** for this week. You may also select books from the Leveled Bibliography for this theme, pages 23E–23F.

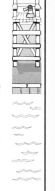 **Test Prep** Test questions about predicting outcomes often ask about events that actually happen in the story. These questions frequently ask students to identify details from the beginning of a story that helped them predict an event that happens later in the story.

Leveled Readers and Leveled Practice

Students at all levels apply the comprehension skill as they read their Leveled Readers. See lessons on pages 115O–115R.

● **BELOW LEVEL**
Riding with the VAQUEROS
by Rebecca Motil
illustrated by Rick Allen

▲ **ON LEVEL**
Johnny Kelley's Tale
by John Jay
illustrated by Doni Lea

■ **ABOVE LEVEL**
Hannah Brown
UNION ARMY SPY
by Mary-Jean Criveley • illustrated by Leslie Bowman

◆ **LANGUAGE SUPPORT**
Yao's Wild Ride
by Rebecca Motil
illustrated by Rick Allen

Reading Traits

As students develop the ability to predict outcomes, they are learning to "read between the lines" of a selection. This comprehension skill supports the reading trait **Realizing Context.**

Practice Book page 64

The True Confessions of Charlotte Doyle
Comprehension Skill
Predicting Outcomes

Name _____

You Guessed It!

Read the story. Then complete the activity on page 65.

The Deep End

Manning flopped around in his bed like a fish. A moment before, he had been sinking to the bottom of a swimming pool. He heard muffled shouts coming from above. He flailed his arms, but it was no use. He just kept sinking. His father's voice roused him from his dream. "Are you ready for your first day of lifeguard training?" Manning groaned.

Rough and Ready Summer Camp was just about the only place around that gave summer jobs to teenagers younger than eighteen. Manning needed money for a backpacking trip to the Rocky Mountains in the fall. He needed to buy a train ticket to Montana. He needed a new backpack and new hiking boots. He needed a job!

He had applied for the position of assistant counselor. He got the job, but was then dismayed to find out that, like all counselors at the camp, he needed to go through lifeguard training. He was a capable swimmer, but he had one discomfort that had been with him all his life: he did not like to be in deep water. In fact, being in water over his head terrified him.

At ten o'clock training began at Taft Pool. The trainer announced that first they would take a swimming test—ten laps of freestyle. "When I blow my whistle, dive in and start swimming," he said. "This is not a race," he added, "it's a test of your endurance."

Manning's heart was pounding. He knew he'd be fine in the shallow water, but what would happen when he reached the deep end? "Swimmers, on your mark!" the trainer called. Manning got into diving position. At the shrill sound of the whistle, he took a deep breath and dove. His body hit the water smoothly, and he fell into an even stroke.

"Just breathe," he told himself as he swam toward the deep end. He concentrated on his stroke. To his relief, he didn't panic as he passed the five-foot marker on the side of the pool. Nor did he panic when he passed the eight-foot marker. By the time he reached the far side of the pool, he was just hitting his best rhythm. He flipped himself around and started back toward the shallow end.

Practice Book page 65

The True Confessions of Charlotte Doyle
Comprehension Skill
Predicting Outcomes

Name _____

You Guessed It! continued

Answer these questions about the passage on page 64.

1. Do you think Manning will successfully complete lifeguard training? Why or why not?
   Yes. He is a capable swimmer and stays calm in the deep water. (2 points)

2. What information in the story might lead you to predict that Manning will not complete the training?
   He is terrified of deep water. He is nervous and doubts his own ability. (2)

3. At which point in the story might you change your prediction?
   I might change my prediction when Manning does not panic in the deep water. (2)

4. What do you think Manning will do with the money he earns as assistant counselor?
   He will buy new camping equipment and a train ticket to Montana. (2)

5. The following statements are generally true in real life. Which statement helps you predict that Manning will most likely succeed in lifeguard training? Circle it.
   A. People often avoid what they fear.
   B. People will often face a difficult challenge to get something they really want. (2)
   C. Good friends help each other through hard times.

Monitoring Student Progress

If . . .	Then . . .
students score 7 or below on **Practice Book** page 65,	use the Reteaching lesson on Teacher's Edition page R14.
students have successfully met the lesson objectives,	have them do the Challenge/Extension activities on Teacher's Edition page R15.

OBJECTIVES

- Read words that are possessives and contractions.
- Use the Phonics/Decoding Strategy to decode longer words.
- Learn academic language: *possessives, singular, plural, contractions, apostrophe.*

Target Skill Trace

Teach	p. 115C
Reteach	p. R22
Review	pp. M34–M35
See	*Handbook for English Language Learners,* p. 49; *Extra Support Handbook,* pp. 44–45; pp. 48–49

Practice Book page 66

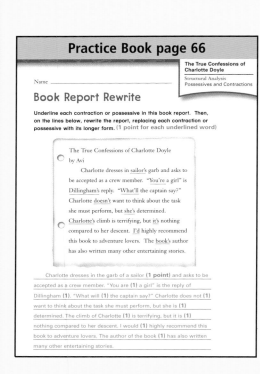

The True Confessions of Charlotte Doyle

Structural Analysis
Possessives and Contractions

Name _____

Book Report Rewrite

Underline each contraction or possessive in this book report. Then, on the lines below, rewrite the report, replacing each contraction or possessive with its longer form. (1 point for each underlined word)

The True Confessions of Charlotte Doyle
by Avi

   Charlotte dresses in sailor's garb and asks to be accepted as a crew member. "You're a girl" is Dillingham's reply. "What'll the captain say?" Charlotte doesn't want to think about the task she must perform, but she's determined.

   Charlotte's climb is terrifying, but it's nothing compared to her descent. I'd highly recommend this book to adventure lovers. The book's author has also written many other entertaining stories.

Charlotte dresses in the garb of a sailor (1 point) and asks to be accepted as a crew member. "You are (1) a girl" is the reply of Dillingham (1). "What will (1) the captain say?" Charlotte does not (1) want to think about the task she must perform, but she is (1) determined. The climb of Charlotte (1) is terrifying, but it is (1) nothing compared to her descent. I would (1) highly recommend this book to adventure lovers. The author of the book (1) has also written many other entertaining stories.

Monitoring Student Progress

If . . .	Then . . .
students score 14 or below on **Practice Book** page 66,	use the Reteaching lesson on Teacher's Edition page R22.

TARGET SKILL

STRUCTURAL ANALYSIS/ VOCABULARY: Possessives and Contractions

❶ Teach

Explain possessives. Write *The crew's faces were turned up toward me.* Circle the *'s* in *crew's faces.* Explain that the *'s* signals possession. Discuss how to form possessive nouns.

- When the noun is singular, add an apostrophe and an -s (*'s*): *the captain's hat.*
- When the noun is plural and ends in -s, add only an apostrophe: *the sailors' jobs.*
- When the noun is plural and does not end in -s, add an apostrophe and an -s (*'s*): *children's toys.*

Explain contractions. Write <u>*You'll* get no more from us.</u>

- Explain that *You'll* is a contraction of the words *You will* and that the apostrophe stands for the missing letters.
- Have students scan Anthology page 99 for other contractions. Work with them to identify the longer form of each one.

Model the Phonics/Decoding Strategy. Write *When <u>she'd</u> reached the deck, <u>Charlotte's</u> legs felt like rubber.* Then model.

> **Think Aloud** *I see an apostrophe in the word* she'd, *so I know this is a contraction. When I read the rest of the sentence, I realize that the longer form is* she had. *I also see the apostrophe in the phrase* Charlotte's legs. *The* 's *helps me know that this phrase refers to legs that belong to Charlotte.*

❷ Guided Practice

Have students use possessives and contractions. Display the sentences and phrases below. Have students write the longer form of each contraction or the meaning of each possessive.

<u>Fisk's</u> hands
the <u>captain's</u> cabin
<u>She'll</u> not have the stomach.

<u>We're</u> agreed.
<u>Don't</u> look down.
the <u>ship's</u> sails

❸ Apply

Assign Practice Book page 66.

PHONICS REVIEW:
The /ou/, /ōō/, /ô/, and /oi/ Sounds

❶ Teach

Review the /ou/, /ōō/, /ô/, and /oi/ sounds. Explain these points:

- The letters *ou* can stand for the /ou/ sound: *round*.
- The letters *oo* can stand for the /ōō/ sound: *smooth*.
- The letters *au*, *aw*, *augh*, and *ough* can stand for the /ô/ sound: *audio*, *paw*, *caught*, and *bought*.
- The letters *oi* and *oy* can stand for the /oi/ sound: *noise* and *boy*.

Model the Phonics/Decoding Strategy. Write *Charlotte could not hear the <u>voices</u> of the crew*. Model decoding *voices*.

Think Aloud   *I know that sometimes words are divided between two vowels. I'll try that here, VOH-ihs-uhz. That doesn't sound right. Now I remember that the letters* oi *can make the /oi/ sound, as in* coin. *I'll try that, VOYS-uhz. That sounds right and makes sense in the sentence.*

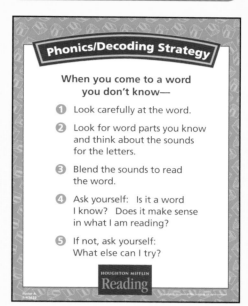

Phonics/Decoding Strategy

When you come to a word you don't know—

❶ Look carefully at the word.

❷ Look for word parts you know and think about the sounds for the letters.

❸ Blend the sounds to read the word.

❹ Ask yourself: Is it a word I know? Does it make sense in what I am reading?

❺ If not, ask yourself: What else can I try?

HOUGHTON MIFFLIN
Reading

❷ Guided Practice

Have students decode words with the /ou/, /ōō/, /ô/, and /oi/ sounds. Display the sentences below. Ask students to circle the vowel combination in each underlined word, pronounce the word, and see if it makes sense in the sentence. Discuss answers.

1. My task was to climb to the top of the <u>royal</u> yard.
2. I was overwhelmed by my <u>audacity</u>.
3. I even felt a little <u>foolish</u> for attempting to climb so high.

❸ Apply

Have students find words with the /ou/, /ōō/, /ô/, and /oi/ sounds. Ask students to find and decode these words from *The True Confessions of Charlotte Doyle* and discuss their meanings.

announced	page 100	caused	page 104	void	page 107
around	page 101	nauseous	page 107	sooner	page 109
outside	page 102	paused	page 107	joyous	page 109

SPELLING: /ou/, /o͞o/, /ô/, and /oi/

OBJECTIVE

- Write Spelling Words that have the /ou/, /o͞o/, /ô/, and /oi/ sounds

SPELLING WORDS

Basic

bloom	mound
stout	groove
droop	foul*
crouch	hoist
annoy	gloom
vault	trout
squawk	noun
avoid	roost
sought	clause
naughty	appoint

Review	Challenge
scoop	bountiful
moist	adjoin
haul*	nauseous*
loose	turquoise
hawk*	heirloom

Forms of these words appear in the literature.

Extra Support/Intervention

Basic Word List You may want to use only the left column of Basic Words with students who need extra support.

Challenge

Challenge Word Practice Have students make puzzles, writing each Challenge Word across, down, or diagonally in a square grid and filling in other letters to complete the grid. Pairs trade papers and circle hidden words.

DAY 1 — INSTRUCTION

/ou/, /o͞o/, /ô/, and /oi/

Pretest Use the Day 5 Test sentences.

Teach Write /ou/, /o͞o/, /ô/, and /oi/ on the board as column heads. Below each head write these Basic Words: /ou/—*stout*; /o͞o/—*bloom*; /ô/—*vault, squawk, sought, naughty*; /oi/—*avoid, annoy.*

- Point to each symbol, say the sound it represents, and have students repeat it.
- Point to the /ou/ column. Say *stout* and have the class repeat it. Underline *ou* and explain that these letters form one pattern that stands for the /ou/ sound.
- Repeat the process for the other words, underlining *oo, au, aw, ough, augh, oi, oy,* and explaining the sounds that they can stand for.
- Say each remaining Basic Word and ask a student to name its vowel sound. Write the word in the appropriate column.

Practice/Homework Assign **Practice Book** page 283.

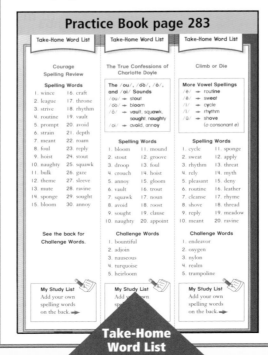

DAY 2 — REVIEW & PRACTICE

Reviewing the Principle

Go over the spelling patterns of /ou/, /o͞o/, /ô/, and /oi/ sounds with students.

Practice/Homework Assign **Practice Book** page 67.

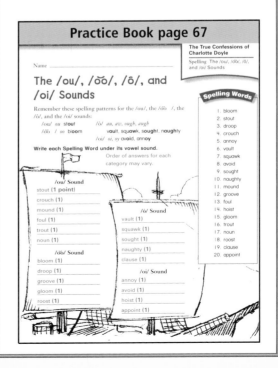

DAY 3 — VOCABULARY

Multiple Meanings

Write *bloom, sprout, vault, mound, hoist,* and *roost* on the board. Tell students that each word can be used as a noun or as a verb.

- Have students write a pair of sentences for each word, using the word as a noun in one sentence and as a verb in the other. Allow students to look up meanings in a dictionary, if necessary.

- Ask students to share their sentence pairs with the class. (Sentences will vary.)

- List the Basic Words on the board. Have students use each word orally in a sentence. (Sentences will vary.)

Practice/Homework For spelling practice, assign **Practice Book** page 68.

Practice Book page 68

Name _____

Spelling Spree

Find a Rhyme Write a Spelling Word that rhymes with the underlined word.

1. If you _____ down, you can see the kangaroo's <u>pouch</u>.
2. The baseball player <u>found</u> his glove near the pitcher's _____.
3. Please <u>pause</u> while I find the _____ in this sentence.
4. I think I can see this bird's _____, if you give me a boost.
5. Every plant in the gardener's room was starting to _____.
6. Don't <u>pout</u> just because you didn't catch a _____ today.

1. crouch **(1 point)**   4. roost **(1)**
2. mound **(1)**   5. bloom **(1)**
3. clause **(1)**   6. trout **(1)**

Word Search Find nine Spelling Words in the Word Search below. Circle each word as you find it, and then write the words in order.

SHOISTERNOUNINGAVOIDAN
SFOULSTEGROOVEDUNVAULTRU
GLOOMDIAPPOINTANAUGHTYARN

7. hoist **(1)**   12. vault **(1)**
8. noun **(1)**   13. gloom **(1)**
9. avoid **(1)**   14. appoint **(1)**
10. foul **(1)**   15. naughty **(1)**
11. groove **(1)**

Spelling Words
1. bloom
2. stout
3. droop
4. crouch
5. annoy
6. vault
7. squawk
8. avoid
9. sought
10. naughty
11. mound
12. groove
13. foul
14. hoist
15. gloom
16. trout
17. noun
18. roost
19. clause
20. appoint

The True Confessions of Charlotte Doyle
Spelling The /ou/, /ô/, /oi/, and /oi/ Sounds

DAY 4 — PROOFREADING

Game: Pick a Pattern

Ask groups of 6 or 8 students to make 8 small spelling-pattern cards: *ou, oo, au, aw, ough, augh, oi, oy*. Give each group a set of letter cards and a Spelling Word list. Have them form 2 teams and follow these steps:

- A member of Team A reads a word from the Spelling Word list.

- The first player on Team B uses letter cards and a selected pattern card to build the word.

- A correctly spelled word earns a point, and that word is crossed off the list. If it is spelled incorrectly, no point is scored, the word is starred on the list, and Team B loses its turn.

- Play continues until all words on the Spelling Word list have been spelled correctly.

- Starred words are replayed after all other words have been spelled.

Practice/Homework For proofreading and writing practice, assign **Practice Book** page 69.

Practice Book page 69

Name _____

Proofreading and Writing

Proofreading Circle the five misspelled Spelling Words in this part of a letter. Then write each word correctly.

Dear Mother,
A most unusual event took place onboard today. Miss Charlotte Doyle, a young woman who sought to join the crew, managed to hoist herself to the top of the royal yard. Many of the crew had expected her to fail, and her success seemed to annoy more than a few of them. One sailor's response was to let his shoulders droop noticeably. Another let loose a rude squawk and said, "She was just lucky." Personally, I think Miss Doyle has a stout heart and will be a valuable addition to the ship.

1. sought **(1 point)**   4. squawk **(1)**
2. annoy **(1)**   5. stout **(1)**
3. droop **(1)**

Spelling Words
1. bloom
2. stout
3. droop
4. crouch
5. annoy
6. vault
7. squawk
8. avoid
9. sought
10. naughty
11. mound
12. groove
13. foul
14. hoist
15. gloom
16. trout
17. noun
18. roost
19. clause
20. appoint

The True Confessions of Charlotte Doyle
Spelling The /ou/, /ô/, /oi/, and /oi/ Sounds

Write a Character Sketch What does Charlotte Doyle's behavior tell you about her? What do you think about her ability to make herself climb to the top of the royal yard?

On a separate piece of paper, write a character sketch in which you describe Charlotte. Use Spelling Words from the list. Responses will vary. (5)

DAY 5 — ASSESSMENT

Spelling Test

Say each underlined word, read the sentence, and then repeat the word. Have students write only the underlined word.

Basic Words

1. What a huge **bloom** that plant has!
2. Use a **stout** rope to pull the cart.
3. Don't let the vine **droop** over the doorway.
4. I must **crouch** to cut the rose.
5. Loud noises **annoy** me and hurt my ears.
6. Our money is safe in the bank **vault**.
7. A sudden **squawk** from the hen startled me.
8. Please **avoid** being late for class.
9. Mom **sought** an answer to my question.
10. Our **naughty** puppy often gets in trouble.
11. Plant the seeds in that **mound** of dirt.
12. The sliding door moves along a **groove**.
13. The **foul** odor came from the dump.
14. Let's **hoist** the sails on the boat.
15. A sad movie can fill me with **gloom**.
16. Nancy caught a **trout** in the lake.
17. A **noun** can name a person or a place.
18. The bird's **roost** was high in a tree.
19. A **clause** is a group of words.
20. Will you **appoint** me team captain?

Challenge Words

21. The farmer had a **bountiful** crop.
22. Does the fence **adjoin** the house?
23. The rough boat ride made Tom feel **nauseous**.
24. My **turquoise** ring fell into the drain!
25. This locket is a family **heirloom**.

OBJECTIVES

- Recognize that words in a word family have similar spellings and related meanings.
- Understand that related words may have different vowel sounds.
- Learn academic language: *word family*.

Target Skill Trace

Teach	p. 115G
Review	pp. M36–M37
Extend	Challenge/Extension Activities p. R23
See	*Handbook for English Language Learners*, p. 53

Monitoring Student Progress

If . . .	Then . . .
students score 6 or below on **Practice Book** page 70,	have them work in small groups to correct the items they missed.

TARGET SKILL

VOCABULARY: Word Families

❶ Teach

Introduce word families. Explain that a word family is a group of words that are related in both spelling and meaning.

- Write *sailor*, *sail*, *sailboat* and *finite*, *infinite*, *infinity*.
- Point out that these are two word families. Emphasize that the groups share the same base word.
- Write and pronounce *personal* and *personality*. Explain that words in a word family can have the same spelling but different vowel sounds.

Model recognizing word families. Write *I realized suddenly how much harder this climb would be if the wind were blowing. This realization gave me courage.* Model thinking about *realized* and *realization*.

Think Aloud *These words don't sound the same:* REE-uh-LYZD *and* REE-uh-li-ZAY-shun. *I know that when an ending is added to a word, the related word that is formed may have a different vowel sound.* Realized *means "understood completely" and* realization *means "the act of realizing." The meanings help me recognize that these words are part of the same family.*

❷ Guided Practice

Give students practice in recognizing word families. Display the words below. Have students match the words that belong to the same word family. Have them look up the words in a dictionary and write their meanings.

admire	inquired
equality	admiration
inquiry	equal

❸ Apply

Assign Practice Book page 70.

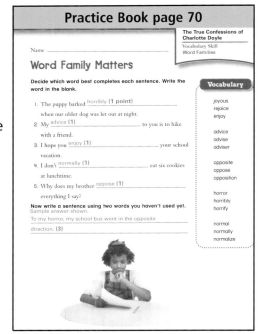

Practice Book page 70

The True Confessions of Charlotte Doyle

Name _____

Vocabulary Skill
Word Families

Word Family Matters

Decide which word best completes each sentence. Write the word in the blank.

1. The puppy barked _horribly_ **(1 point)** when our older dog was let out at night.
2. My _advice_ **(1)** _____ to you is to hike with a friend.
3. I hope you _enjoy_ **(1)** _____ your school vacation.
4. I don't _normally_ **(1)** _____ eat six cookies at lunchtime.
5. Why does my brother _oppose_ **(1)** _____ everything I say?

Now write a sentence using two words you haven't used yet.
Sample answer shown.
To my horror, my school bus went in the opposite direction. **(3)**

Vocabulary

joyous
rejoice
enjoy

advice
advise
adviser

opposite
oppose
opposition

horror
horribly
horrify

normal
normally
normalize

STUDY SKILL:
Using Graphic Aids

OBJECTIVES
- Use a table and a graph to find information.
- Locate sites and interpret information on a map.
- Learn academic language: *map, globe, graph, table, chart.*

❶ Teach

Introduce maps and globes.

- Display a flat map and a globe. Review the purpose of the compass rose, map key, and map scale.

- Explain that political maps show geographical features and political divisions, such as countries, states, and cities. Tell students that a specialized map might show, for example, navigation routes or an area as it was at another time in history.

Display Transparency 1–31 and model finding information in tables.

- Point out the table. Explain that tables, or charts, list information about two or more things.

- Read the title and the headings of the table.

- Model finding information about what Fore-and-Aft rigging did. (It caught the wind full force from behind.)

- Model finding the advantages of square rigging. (It provided the greatest speed on the open seas.)

Use Transparency 1–31 to model finding information in graphs.

- Point out the bar graph. Explain that a bar graph helps readers compare different amounts. Read the title of the graph.

- Model comparing the time it took the ships to cross the Atlantic Ocean.

❷ Practice/Apply

Give students practice in using graphic aids.

- Have students use **Transparency 1–31** to answer these questions: Which type of rigging would be best suited for boats that sailed close to the land? Which rigging could catch wind from more than one direction? Which ship took the most days to cross the Atlantic Ocean?

- Have partners research three seaports on the Atlantic coast of the United States. On a blank map, have them show the location of each seaport.

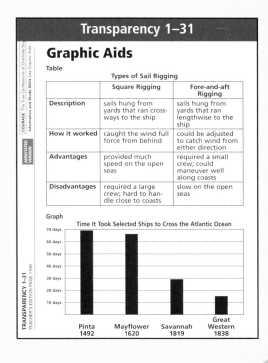

Transparency 1–31

Graphic Aids

Table

Types of Sail Rigging

	Square Rigging	Fore-and-aft Rigging
Description	sails hung from yards that ran crossways to the ship	sails hung from yards that ran lengthwise to the ship
How it worked	caught the wind full force from behind	could be adjusted to catch wind from either direction
Advantages	provided much speed on the open seas	required a small crew; could maneuver well along coasts
Disadvantages	required a large crew; hard to handle close to coasts	slow on the open seas

Graph

Time It Took Selected Ships to Cross the Atlantic Ocean

(bar graph with y-axis labeled 10 days through 70 days; bars for Pinta 1492, Mayflower 1620, Savannah 1819, Great Western 1838)

GRAMMAR: Kinds of Nouns

OBJECTIVES

- Identify common nouns.
- Identify and capitalize proper nouns.
- Identify singular and plural nouns.
- Determine the plural forms of nouns with regular and irregular plurals.
- Proofread and correct sentences with grammar and spelling errors.
- Correctly capitalize and punctuate titles and their abbreviations to improve writing.
- Learn academic language: *common noun, proper noun, singular noun, plural noun.*

DAY 1 — INSTRUCTION

Common/Proper Nouns

Teach Go over the following:

– A common noun names any person, place, thing, or idea.

– A proper noun names a particular person, place, thing, or idea. It is always capitalized. In proper nouns of more than one word, each important word is capitalized.

- Display the sentences at the top of **Transparency 1–33.** Identify each common noun and proper noun.

- Write *Captain Ernest Shackleton* and *ship* in the chart as examples of a proper noun for *leader* and a common noun for *Endurance.*

- Ask volunteers to complete the chart with appropriate common or proper nouns.

Daily Language Practice
Have students correct Sentences 1 and 2 on **Transparency 1–32.**

DAY 2 — PRACTICE

Independent Work

Practice/Homework Assign **Practice Book** page 71.

Daily Language Practice
Have students correct Sentences 3 and 4 on **Transparency 1–32.**

Transparency 1–32

Daily Language Practice

Correct two sentences each day.

1. that tree is beautiful in full blum.
   That tree is beautiful in full bloom.
2. The yellow rose is finally starting to droup
   The yellow rose is finally starting to droop.
3. My baby sister gayle likes to be nauty.
   My baby sister Gayle likes to be naughty.
4. My friend ben caught a very large troot in the lake.
   My friend Ben caught a very large trout in the lake.
5. A nowne is a person, place, or thing
   A noun is a person, place, or thing.
6. The principal is going to appont mr. Suarez to a new job.
   The principal is going to appoint Mr. Suarez to a new job.
7. You need fowl weather gear to hike in maine.
   You need foul weather gear to hike in Maine.
8. Most childs like to crooch in small spaces to hide.
   Most children like to crouch in small spaces to hide.
9. My parrot phillip likes to squack all day long.
   My parrot Phillip likes to squawk all day long.
10. How many boxs of checks can fit in that bank valt?
    How many boxes of checks can fit in that bank vault?

TRANSPARENCY 1–32
TEACHER'S EDITION PAGE 115I

Monitoring Student Progress

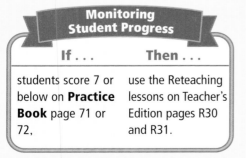

If . . .	Then . . .
students score 7 or below on **Practice Book** page 71 or 72,	use the Reteaching lessons on Teacher's Edition pages R30 and R31.

Transparency 1–33

Common and Proper Nouns

Captain Ernest Shackleton was the leader of an expedition.

He sailed his ship, the *Endurance,* toward the frozen continent of Antarctica.

Common Nouns	Proper Nouns
leader	Captain Ernest Shackleton
ship	*Endurance*
continent	Antarctica
day	Wednesday
state	Answers will vary.
president	Answers will vary.
city	Chicago
ocean	Answers will vary.
country	Answers will vary.
river	Rio Grande
month	Answers will vary.
girl	Answers will vary.

TRANSPARENCY 1–33
TEACHER'S EDITION PAGE 115I

Practice Book page 71

The True Confessions of Charlotte Doyle
Grammar Skill Common and Proper Nouns

Name _____

Charlotte and the Navy

Common and Proper Nouns A **common noun** names a person, a place, a thing, or an idea. A **proper noun** names a particular person, place, thing, or idea. Each important word in a proper noun is capitalized.

Determine which nouns in the following sentences are proper nouns and which are common nouns. List the nouns in the proper columns below the sentences.

Example: New Mexico is a state in the United States.

Proper Nouns	Common Nouns
New Mexico	state
United States	

1. Charlotte Doyle wanted to be a sailor.
2. My big sister joined the U.S. Navy.
3. Her ship is called *The Piedmont.*
4. Last year, she sailed to Hawaii.
5. The crew is sailing in the Atlantic Ocean now.

Proper Nouns	Common Nouns
Charlotte Doyle (1 point)	sailor (1)
U.S. Navy (1)	sister (1)
The Piedmont (1)	ship (1)
Hawaii (1)	year (1)
Atlantic Ocean (1)	crew (1)

Singular/Plural Nouns

Teach Go over the following:

- A singular noun names one person, place, thing, or idea. A plural noun names more than one person, place, thing, or idea.

- Add -s or -es to most singular nouns to form the plural. Use the spelling of the singular noun to decide how to form the plural.

- Some nouns have the same singular and plural forms.

- Some nouns are spelled differently in the plural.

- Display **Transparency 1–34.** Point out the plural nouns in the first sentence. Note the -es and -s.

- Ask volunteers to identify the plural nouns in the rest of the sentences and write each one in the chart beside the rule it illustrates. Have them add more examples.

Daily Language Practice
Have students correct Sentences 5 and 6 on **Transparency 1–32.**

Independent Work

Practice/Homework Assign **Practice Book** page 72.

Daily Language Practice
Have students correct Sentences 7 and 8 on **Transparency 1–32.**

People's Titles

Teach Tell students that a good writer uses correct capitalization and punctuation for people's titles.

- Model correcting improperly written titles:

  - The moderator introduced judge Nuñez and captain Tam.

  - *Corrected:* The moderator introduced <u>Judge</u> Nuñez and <u>Captain</u> Tam.

- Tell students that when titles are abbreviated, they begin with a capital letter and end with a period: Dr., Mr., Mrs., Capt.

- Have students proofread a piece of their own writing for correct capitalization and punctuation of people's titles.

Practice/Homework Assign **Practice Book** page 73.

Daily Language Practice
Have students correct Sentences 9 and 10 on **Transparency 1–32.**

GRAMMAR

The True Confessions of Charlotte Doyle

Transparency 1–34

Singular and Plural Nouns

The house between the churches has two tall chimneys.

One of its balconies faces the ocean, and the other faces the hills and valleys. Children standing on the front balcony can watch fish leap above the waves.

Men and women on the rear balcony can see cows and calves, sheep, fields of tomatoes, and tall silos.

Rules for Forming Plurals of Nouns	Examples
To form the plural of most nouns, add -s.	chimneys hills, waves, cows, fields
To form the plural of a noun ending with x, s, ch, sh, or ss, add -es.	churches
To form the plural of a noun ending with a consonant + y, change the y to i and add -es.	balconies
To form the plural of a noun ending in a vowel + y, add -s.	valleys
In some nouns that end in f or fe, the f changes to a v before -s or -es is added.	calves
In nouns that end in o, the plural may be formed by adding either -s or -es.	tomatoes, silos
Some nouns have plural forms that do not end in -s or -es.	children, men, women
Some nouns have the same singular and plural form.	fish, sheep

Additional examples will vary.

COURAGE The True Confessions of Charlotte Doyle
Grammar Skill Singular and Plural Nouns

TRANSPARENCY 1–34
TEACHER'S EDITION PAGE 115J

Practice Book page 72

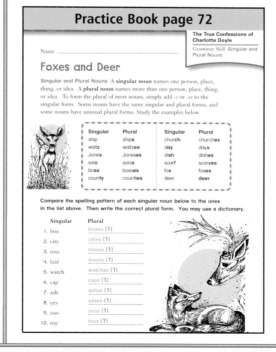

Name _____

Foxes and Deer

Singular and Plural Nouns A **singular noun** names one person, place, thing, or idea. A **plural noun** names more than one person, place, thing, or idea. To form the plural of most nouns, simply add -s or -es to the singular form. Some nouns have the same singular and plural forms, and some nouns have unusual plural forms. Study the examples below.

Singular	Plural	Singular	Plural
ship	ships	church	churches
waltz	waltzes	day	days
Jones	Joneses	dish	dishes
solo	solos	scarf	scarves
boss	bosses	fox	foxes
county	counties	deer	deer

Compare the spelling pattern of each singular noun below to the ones in the list above. Then write the correct plural form. You may use a dictionary.

Singular	Plural
1. box	boxes (1)
2. city	cities (1)
3. toss	tosses (1)
4. leaf	leaves (1)
5. watch	watches (1)
6. cap	caps (1)
7. ash	ashes (1)
8. yes	yeses (1)
9. zoo	zoos (1)
10. toy	toys (1)

The True Confessions of Charlotte Doyle
Grammar Skill Singular and Plural Nouns

Practice Book page 73

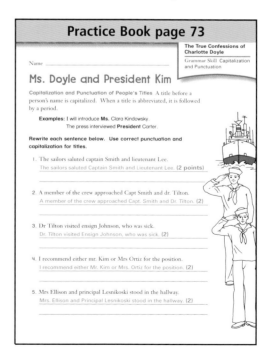

Name _____

Ms. Doyle and President Kim

Capitalization and Punctuation of People's Titles A title before a person's name is capitalized. When a title is abbreviated, it is followed by a period.

Examples: I will introduce **Ms.** Clara Kindowsky.
The press interviewed **President** Carter.

Rewrite each sentence below. Use correct punctuation and capitalization for titles.

1. The sailors saluted captain Smith and lieutenant Lee. **(2 points)**
   The sailors saluted Captain Smith and Lieutenant Lee. (2 points)

2. A member of the crew approached Capt Smith and dr. Tilton.
   A member of the crew approached Capt. Smith and Dr. Tilton. (2)

3. Dr Tilton visited ensign Johnson, who was sick.
   Dr. Tilton visited Ensign Johnson, who was sick. (2)

4. I recommend either mr. Kim or Mrs Ortiz for the position.
   I recommend either Mr. Kim or Mrs. Ortiz for the position. (2)

5. Mrs Ellison and principal Lesnikoski stood in the hallway.
   Mrs. Ellison and Principal Lesnikoski stood in the hallway. (2)

The True Confessions of Charlotte Doyle
Grammar Skill Capitalization and Punctuation

WRITING: Opinion Paragraph

OBJECTIVES

- Identify the characteristics of a good opinion paragraph.
- Write an opinion paragraph.
- Combine sentences with appositives.
- Learn academic language: *opinion*, *appositives*.

Writing Traits

Ideas Emphasize the importance of ideas as students draft on Day 2. Students can ask these questions about their writing.

- What do I want my reader to understand?
- Do I need to add any words or details to help my reader understand this?
- Do I need to delete any words or details?

DAY 1 PREWRITING

Introducing the Format

Define an opinion paragraph.

- An opinion paragraph tells what the writer thinks or feels about a topic.
- It states an opinion in the topic sentence.
- It uses reasons and details to explain the opinion.

Start students thinking about writing an opinion paragraph.

- Display the question shown below.
- Ask students to think about their answer to this question. Have them list their thoughts and feelings.
- Have them save their notes.

> Do you think Charlotte should have been allowed to prove her competence as a sailor by climbing to the top of the yard, or should someone have stopped her from performing this hazardous feat?

DAY 2 DRAFTING

Discussing the Model

Display Transparency 1–35. Ask:

- What is the topic of the paragraph? (young people doing dangerous things)
- What is the writer's opinion about this topic? (Young people should not be allowed to do dangerous things.)
- Where does the writer first state this opinion? (first sentence—the topic sentence)
- What reasons and details explain why the writer thinks this way? (Sample answers: Young people lack experience; parents should keep children safe; takes time away from other important activities)
- How does the writer end the paragraph? (restates the topic sentence)

Display Transparency 1–36, and discuss the guidelines.

Have the students draft an opinion paragraph.

- Have them use their notes from Day 1.
- Assign **Practice Book** page 74 to help students organize their writing.
- See Writing Traits on this page.

Transparency 1–35

Opinion

- Opinion given

  Young people like Subaru Takahashi should not be allowed to attempt dangerous feats such as sailing solo around the world. A young sailor does not have the experience of an older sailor, and is therefore less likely to make the right decisions in an emergency. It is the responsibility of parents to keep their

- Supporting details

  children safe. On many occasions on Subaru's voyage, he faced danger and even death—risks a young person should not have to face, especially alone. Finally, it takes a long time to prepare for such feats, and this preparation takes away from participation at school, in sports, and in other activities that are important to a young person's development. For these

- Summary

  reasons, I believe that young people should be strongly discouraged from pursuing the kind of dangerous ventures Subaru pursued.

COURAGE *The True Confessions of Charlotte Doyle* Writing Skill Opinion

TRANSPARENCY 1–35
TEACHER'S EDITION PAGE 115K

Transparency 1–36

Guidelines for Writing an Opinion Paragraph

- Begin with a topic sentence that clearly states your topic and your opinion about this topic.
- Provide strong reasons that explain, or support, your opinion.
- Give details that explain each reason. Include both facts and examples.
- Tell how you really feel. Let your audience hear your voice.
- Restate your opinion and sum up your ideas in the last sentence.

COURAGE *The True Confessions of Charlotte Doyle* Writing Skill Opinion Paragraph

TRANSPARENCY 1–36
TEACHER'S EDITION PAGE 115K

Practice Book page 74

The True Confessions of Charlotte Doyle
Writing Skill Opinion

Name _____

Writing an Opinion Paragraph

An **opinion** is a strong belief or conclusion that may or may not be supported by facts and reasons. For example, Zachariah in *The True Confessions of Charlotte Doyle* expresses his opinion of Charlotte, saying, "You're as steady a girl as ever I've met." As you read a story, you will form your own opinions about its characters.

As you read *The True Confessions of Charlotte Doyle*, think about this question: Do you think Charlotte should have been allowed to prove her competence as a sailor by climbing to the top of the royal yard, or should someone have stopped her from performing this hazardous feat?

Then use this diagram to record your opinion and to write facts and examples that support it.

Opinion
(3 points)

Facts and Examples (3) | Facts and Examples (3) | Facts and Examples (3)

Using the information you recorded in the diagram, write an opinion paragraph on a separate sheet of paper. In the first sentence, state your opinion in response to the question above. In the body of the paragraph, write two to three reasons why you think and feel the way you do. Support your opinion with facts and examples. Then end your paragraph with a concluding sentence that restates your opinion. (4)

Improving Writing: Combining Sentences

Introduce combining sentences with appositives.

- An appositive is a word or phrase that immediately follows a noun and explains it: *The sailor, a large man, climbed the mast.*

- Appositives are set off by commas.

Display Transparency 1–37.

- Read aloud Passage A, underlining repetitive words or phrases.

- Read aloud Passage B. Point out the appositive phrase. (*Charlotte Doyle, a steady and plucky thirteen year old.*)

- Ask students to combine Passage C into one or two sentences, using appositives.

Assign Practice Book page 75.

Have students revise their drafts.

- Display **Transparency 1–36.** Have students use it to revise their paragraphs.

- Have partners hold writing conferences.

- Ask students to revise any parts of their paragraphs that still need work. Have them look for places to combine sentences.

Checking for Errors

Have students proofread for errors in grammar, spelling, punctuation, or usage.

- Students can use the proofreading checklist on **Practice Book** page 297 to help them proofread their paragraphs.

- Students can also use the chart of proofreading marks on **Practice Book** page 298.

Sharing Paragraphs

Consider these publishing options.

- Ask students to read their paragraphs or some other piece of writing from the Author's Chair.

- Encourage students to post their paragraphs as part of a bulletin board display about *The True Confessions of Charlotte Doyle.*

Portfolio Opportunity

Save students' paragraphs as samples of their writing development.

Transparency 1–37

Combining Sentences with Appositives

Passage A

Charlotte Doyle was the only passenger on the *Seahawk*. Charlotte was thirteen years old. She was the only girl among a rough crew. Charlotte Doyle was steady and plucky.

Passage B

Charlotte Doyle, a steady and plucky thirteen year old, was the only passenger on the *Seahawk* and the only girl among a rough crew.

Passage C

The main mast was tall. It was a thick column made of three logs. The three thick, round logs were affixed end to end. The mast supported four levels of sails.

The tall main mast, a thick column made of three round logs affixed end to end, supported four levels of sails.

TRANSPARENCY 1–37
TEACHER'S EDITION PAGE 115L

Practice Book page 75

The True Confessions of Charlotte Doyle

Writing Skill: Improving Your Writing

Name _____

Combining Sentences with Appositives

One way to improve your writing is to combine two short sentences into one by using an appositive. An **appositive** is a word or group of words that immediately follows a noun and identifies or explains it. Appositives are usually set off from the rest of the sentence by commas. Here is an example of before and after:

Charlotte Doyle was a thirteen-year-old girl. She joined the crew of the *Seahawk.*
Charlotte Doyle, **a thirteen-year-old girl**, joined the crew of the *Seahawk.*

Revise the following sentences from Captain Jaggery's ship's log. Combine each pair of short, choppy sentences into a single sentence with an appositive.

Charlotte Doyle is a young passenger. She wants to work aboard the Seahawk.
Charlotte Doyle, a young passenger, wants to work aboard the *Seahawk.* **(3 points)**

Today two members of the crew described a test of worth that Charlotte had to pass. Zachariah and Foley are the crew members who described the test.
Today Zachariah and Foley, two members of the crew, described a test of worth that Charlotte had to pass. **(3)**

The men asked Charlotte to climb to the top of the royal yard. The royal yard is the tallest mast of the ship.
The men asked Charlotte to climb to the top of the royal yard, the tallest mast of the ship. **(3)**

Ewing gave Charlotte some helpful advice. He is a seasoned sailor.
Ewing, a seasoned sailor, gave Charlotte some helpful advice. **(3)**

Happily, Charlotte passed the test with flying colors. The test was a difficult physical and mental challenge.
Happily, Charlotte passed the test, a difficult physical and mental challenge, with flying colors. **(3)**

Monitoring Student Progress

If . . .	Then . . .
students' writing does not follow the guidelines on **Transparency 1–36,**	work with students to improve specific parts of their writing.

Independent Activities

Language Center

VOCABULARY

Motion Words

👤 Singles	🕐 15 minutes
Objective	Create a word web.

As Charlotte climbs upward, the mast moves in wild *gyrations*. The author uses various words to describe the feeling of motion on shipboard.

- Skim the story to find words related to the motion of the ship and mast.
- Create a word web using these words.
- Think of other movement-related words, and add them to your web.

GRAMMAR

Is It Common or Proper?

👤 Singles	🕐 20 minutes
Objective	Practice using common and proper nouns.

Read Charlotte Doyle's journal entry. Then follow these steps:

- Rewrite the journal entry by substituting a common noun for every underlined proper noun and a proper noun for every underlined common noun. (Make any other changes you need to.)
- Label every noun in your new entry with a *C* for *common* or a *P* for *proper*.

> The crew of the ship made me climb the rigging without the <u>captain's</u> knowledge. I was terrified, but <u>Fisk's</u> words echoed in my head. I was afraid that even if I made it up the mast, I would not have the courage to come down until <u>Tuesday</u>. I'm proud of myself, but more eager than ever to return to my home <u>country</u>.

VOCABULARY

Word-Search Challenge

👥 Pairs	🕐 30 minutes
Objective	Create a word-search puzzle.
Materials	Activity Master 1–4, page R35

Create a word-search puzzle using all the Key Vocabulary words.

- First, look at examples of word-search puzzles for ideas.
- Then, write all the vocabulary words on the Activity Master, one letter in a square. The words may read up, down, left-to-right, right-to-left, or diagonally. Words sharing a common letter may intersect on that letter.
- Fill in the empty squares with random letters.
- Be sure that the finished puzzle takes the shape of a square or rectangle.

When you have completed your puzzle, exchange puzzles with your partner and solve the puzzle you receive.

Consider copying and laminating these activities for use in centers.

LISTENING/SPEAKING

Giving and Listening to Directions

Pairs	**30 minutes**
Objective	Give and listen to oral directions.

Follow the guidelines at the bottom of this column as you plan and practice giving a set of oral directions to a partner. You might give directions for one of the following tasks:

- how to clean your desk
- how to measure your shadow
- how to make something from folded paper
- how to braid yarn
- how to make a sandwich or other simple meal

Guidelines for Giving Directions

1. Think through the steps of your directions before you give them.

2. Plan your directions to fit your purpose and the needs of your audience.

3. Present the steps in order, and use sequence words to signal the beginnings of steps.

4. Give your listeners time to follow each step before continuing.

5. Speak slowly and clearly, keeping your voice helpful and polite.

PHONICS/SPELLING

Complete the Advertisement

Singles	**20 minutes**
Objective	Correctly spell words with the /ou/, /o͞o/, /ô/, and /oi/ sounds

You are writing an advertisement for a shipping company. Follow these steps to complete your task:

- Read and copy the advertisement below.
- Fill in each blank with the correct spelling of the vowel sound in the word.
- Use these spellings: *ou, oo, au, aw, augh, ough, oi,* and *oy.*

Av_____d a Boring Career!

Would you like an unforgettable job? Do traditional occupations ann_____ you? If you have s_____t an exciting career but failed, then j_____n the crew of the ship Seah_____k! She has been app_____nted to sail ar_____nd the world. You will be n_____seous at times, and the weather will often be gl_____my, but if you're interested, see Captain Brown at the dock.

Complete the Advertisement
avoid; annoy; sought; join; Seahawk;
appointed; around; nauseous; gloomy

Riding with the Vaqueros

Summary *Fourteen-year-old Huey Yao is separated from his father while traveling from California to Texas in the late 1800s. Weak from hunger and thirst, Yao is almost trampled by a herd of cattle. A vaquero cowboy named Nat rescues Yao, who overcomes his fear of horses and rides with the vaqueros and their herd to Dodge City. There, Yao and his father are reunited.*

Vocabulary

Introduce the Key Vocabulary and ask students to complete the BLM.

dry goods cloth, clothing, and small useful items (like buttons), *p. 3*

bandit outlaw who lives by robbing, *p. 5*

canteen container for drinking water, *p. 12*

grub food, *p. 13*

wrangler ranch hand who takes care of saddle horses, *p. 16*

tenderfoot someone who is not used to outdoor life, *p. 17*

● BELOW LEVEL

Building Background and Vocabulary

Explain that the story is set in the 1870s, when cowboys herded thousands of cattle north from Texas to towns like Abilene and Dodge City. From there, they were sent by train to slaughterhouses in the Midwest. Ask students to share what they know about cowboys and herding cattle. Guide students through the text, using some of the vocabulary from the story.

Comprehension Skill: Making Predictions

Have students read the Strategy Focus on the book flap. Remind students to use the strategy and to make predictions as they read the book. (See the Leveled Readers Teacher's Guide for **Vocabulary and Comprehension Practice Masters.**)

Responding

Have partners discuss how to answer the questions on the inside back cover.

Think About the Selection Sample answers:

1. so that Yao will escape the three bandits
2. The vaqueros are confident, skillful, and at home in the wild.
3. Answers will vary.
4. Answers will vary. Possible response: Return to Texas and set up the dry-goods store.

Making Connections Answers will vary.

Building Fluency

Model Read aloud page 9 and point out the effects of repeated exclamation points on the listener.

Practice Ask a fluent reader to read aloud page 20 to reinforce the effects of repeated exclamation points.

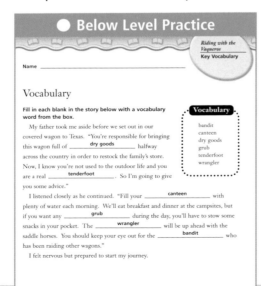

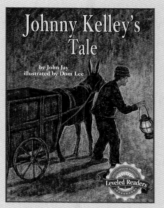

Johnny Kelley's Tale

Summary *Johnny Kelley began working in the coal mines with his father when he was twelve years old. Conditions in the mine are difficult and dangerous. On Johnny's birthday, there is a catastrophic collapse that traps twenty men. Together Johnny and his father lead the rescue crew. Afterward, Johnny's father has a new respect for his son.*

Vocabulary

Introduce the Key Vocabulary and ask students to complete the BLM.

seasoned* experienced, *p. 5*

dwindled became gradually less, *p. 7*

admiration approval, *p. 7*

treacherous* marked by unpredictable dangers, *p. 10*

trepidation fear, *p. 11*

debris wreckage, *p. 14*

maneuvered moved into a desired position, *p. 14*

avalanche a fall or slide of a large mass, *p. 15*

rigging* makeshift construction, *p. 15*

*Forms of these words are Anthology Key Vocabulary words.

▲ ON LEVEL

Building Background and Vocabulary

Explain to students that this story is about a twelve-year-old boy named Johnny who goes to work in the coal mines with his father. Ask students what they know about coal mining and child labor. Guide students through the text, using some of the vocabulary from the story.

Comprehension Skill: Making Predictions

Have students read the Strategy Focus on the book flap. Remind students to use the strategy and to make predictions as they read the book. (See the Leveled Readers Teacher's Guide for **Vocabulary and Comprehension Practice Masters.**)

Responding

Have partners discuss how to answer the questions on the inside back cover.

Think About the Selection Sample answers:

1. He's upset because Johnny quit school to work in the mines.
2. Johnny wants to know if anyone survived. He shows courage by climbing through a small hole to reach the injured men.
3. Johnny feels that his father finally approves of him.
4. Answers will vary.

Making Connections Answers will vary.

Building Fluency

Model Read aloud page 3 to demonstrate how to use the voice to convey complicated emotions, as in this case, resignation.

Practice Ask students to form small groups and read aloud page 7 to experiment with inflection to convey resignation.

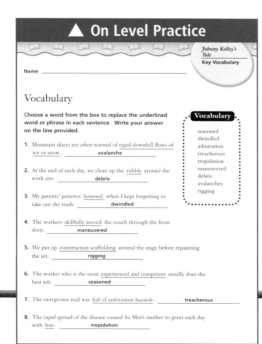

▲ On Level Practice

Johnny Kelley's Tale
Key Vocabulary

Name _____

Vocabulary

Choose a word from the box to replace the underlined word or phrase in each sentence. Write your answer on the line provided.

Vocabulary
seasoned
dwindled
admiration
treacherous
trepidation
maneuvered
debris
avalanches
rigging

1. Mountain skiers are often warned of rapid downhill flows of ice or snow. _____ avalanche

2. At the end of each day, we clean up the rubble around the work site. _____ debris

3. My parents' patience lessened when I kept forgetting to take out the trash. _____ dwindled

4. The workers skillfully moved the couch through the front door. _____ maneuvered

5. We put up construction scaffolding around the stage before repainting the set. _____ rigging

6. The worker who is the most experienced and competent usually does the best job. _____ seasoned

7. The overgrown trail was full of unforeseen hazards. _____ treacherous

8. The rapid spread of the disease caused Su Min's mother to greet each day with fear. _____ trepidation

▲ On Level Practice

Johnny Kelley's Tale
Comprehension Skill
Predicting Outcomes

Name _____

Comprehension

Answer the following, using the story *Johnny Kelley's Tale* and your completed Graphic Organizer.

1. Which outcome in the story was easy to predict?
Sample answer: Johnny would try to rescue someone.

2. Explain why this outcome was easy to predict.
Sample answer: He seemed hardworking and eager to prove himself.

3. Which outcome in the story was difficult to predict?
Sample answer: Johnny would succeed in his rescue efforts.

4. Explain why this outcome was difficult to predict.
Sample answer: It wasn't clear how serious the mine collapse was.

5. Explain how Johnny's personal qualities and character traits had an impact on the outcomes of the story.
Possible answer: Johnny was industrious and felt responsible. These two qualities were clearly visible when he took part in the rescue of the trapped miners.

6. Explain how at least one other event, condition, or character had a significant impact on an outcome of the story.
Answers will vary.

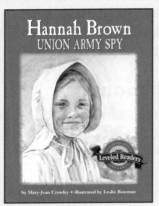
LEVELED READERS

■ ABOVE LEVEL

Hannah Brown UNION ARMY SPY

by Mary-Jean Crowley • illustrated by Leslie Bowman

Hannah Brown: Union Army Spy

Summary *Hannah Brown and her family are living during the American Civil War. When Hannah overhears Confederate troops planning to invade Washington, she delivers a coded warning message that foils the Confederates' plans.*

Vocabulary

Introduce the Key Vocabulary and ask students to complete the BLM.

sympathies feelings of loyalty, allegiance, *p. 4*

smuggle remove secretly, *p. 4*

commotion an agitated disturbance, *p. 4*

swaggered conducted oneself in a superior manner, *p. 5*

pacifists people opposed to war and violence, *p. 7*

treacherous* marked by unpredictable dangers, *p. 9*

painstakingly carefully, *p. 11*

deliberation carefulness, *p. 13*

endeavored* attempted, *p. 14*

*Forms of these words are Anthology Key Vocabulary words.

Building Background and Vocabulary

Explain to students that this story is about a girl named Hannah who is a Quaker living during the time of the American Civil War. Ask students what they know about the Civil War and the Quakers. Guide students through the text, using some of the vocabulary from the story.

Comprehension Skill: Making Predictions

Have students read the Strategy Focus on the book flap. Remind students to use the strategy and to make predictions as they read the book. (See the Leveled Readers Teacher's Guide for **Vocabulary and Comprehension Practice Masters**.)

Responding

Have partners discuss how to answer the questions on the inside back cover.

Think About the Selection Sample answers:

1. They are fighting against slavery.
2. She is a girl, and the daughter of Quakers. They assume she won't be interested.
3. Possible response: Hannah is brave, intelligent, daring, clever, loyal, and careful.
4. Answers will vary.

Making Connections Answers will vary.

Building Fluency

Model Read aloud page 13 to demonstrate ways to manipulate the voice to enhance dialogue between two characters.

Practice Ask partners to practice the dialogue on pages 14 and 15. Encourage them to reread aloud numerous times and then perform for the class.

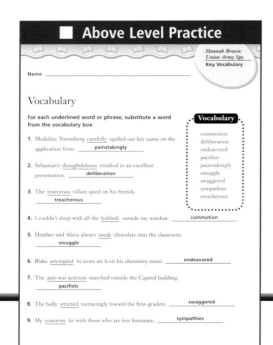

■ **Above Level Practice**

Hannah Brown: Union Army Spy
Key Vocabulary

Name

Vocabulary

For each underlined word or phrase, substitute a word from the vocabulary box.

Vocabulary
commotion
deliberation
endeavored
pacifists
painstakingly
smuggle
swaggered
sympathies
treacherous

1. Madeline Totemberg carefully spelled out her name on the application form. _____ painstakingly

2. Sebastian's thoughtfulness resulted in an excellent presentation. _____ deliberation

3. The traitorous villain spied on his friends. _____ treacherous

4. I couldn't sleep with all the hubbub outside my window. _____ commotion

5. Heather and Alicia always sneak chocolate into the classroom. _____ smuggle

6. Blake attempted to score an A on his chemistry exam. _____ endeavored

7. The anti-war activists marched outside the Capitol building. _____ pacifists

8. The bully strutted menacingly toward the first-graders. _____ swaggered

9. My concerns lie with those who are less fortunate. _____ sympathies

■ **Above Level Practice**

Hannah Brown: Union Army Spy
Comprehension Skill
Predicting Outcomes

Name

Comprehension

Answer the following, using the story *Hannah Brown: Union Army Spy* and your completed Graphic Organizer.

1. Which outcome in the story was easy to predict?
Possible response: Hannah would be safe from General Early.

2. Explain why this outcome was easy to predict.
Possible response: General Early did not consider young girls, especially Quaker pacifists, to be a threat.

3. Which outcome in the story was difficult to predict?
Possible response: The successful delivery of the coded message to the Quakers.

4. Explain why this outcome was difficult to predict.
Possible response: Because Miss West was in hiding, it could have been difficult to get the warning message to her.

5. Explain how Hannah's personal qualities and character traits influenced your predictions.
Possible response: Hannah was thoughtful and clever. She noticed everything, allowing her to detect suspicion and pass along the coded message.

6. Explain how at least one other event, condition, or character had a significant impact on your predictions about the outcome of the story.
Answers will vary.

Yao's Wild Ride
by Rebecca Motil

illustrated by
Rick Allen

Yao's Wild Ride

Summary *Huey Yao becomes separated from his father on a journey to Texas. He travels with a group of* vaqueros *on a cattle drive and, with their help, he learns to overcome his fear of riding horses. Eventually he is reunited with his father.*

Vocabulary

Introduce the Key Vocabulary and ask students to complete the BLM.

wagon a vehicle for carrying loads or passengers, *p. 3*

bandits robbers, *p. 5*

cattle large animals with hooves, raised for meat, hides, or dairy products, *p. 9*

vaqueros Spanish word for cowboys, *p. 13*

seasoned* experienced, *p. 15*

stirrups loops that hang down on either side of the saddle to support the rider's foot, *p. 18*

saddle horn the raised part at the front of a saddle, *p. 19*

coyote an animal similar to a wolf, *p. 20*

*Forms of these words are Anthology Key Vocabulary words.

◆ LANGUAGE SUPPORT

Building Background and Vocabulary

Discuss what students know about the Old West. Tell students that the boy in the story is afraid of horses, but he has to ride them because they are the only form of transportation. Distribute the **Build Background Practice Master** and discuss what students know about horses. Then have them complete the Master.

Comprehension Skill: Predicting Outcomes

Have students read the Strategy Focus on the book flap. Remind students to use the strategy and to predict outcomes as they read the book. (See the Leveled Readers Teacher's Guide for **Build Background, Vocabulary,** and **Graphic Organizer Masters.**)

Responding

Have partners discuss how to answer the questions on the inside back cover.

Think About the Selection Sample answers:

1. Bandits are chasing them.
2. Yao says that his name is Huey Yao, and the vaqueros don't understand that Chinese people say their family names first.
3. He proves to Nat and to himself that he can be brave.
4. Answers will vary.

Making Connections Answers will vary.

Building Fluency

Model Have student follow along in their books as they listen to pages 10–11 of the recording on the audio CD.

Practice Have students read aloud with the recording until they are able to read the text on their own accurately and with expression.

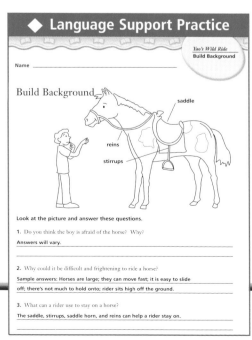

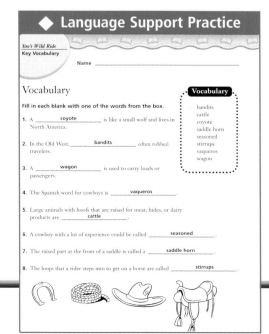

Connecting and Comparing Literature

Check Your Progress

Use these Paired Selections to help students make connections with other theme literature and to wrap up the theme.

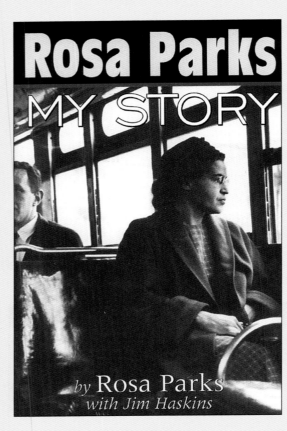

Rosa Parks: My Story
Genre: Nonfiction

Rosa Parks was an African American civil rights activist. Her refusal to give up her seat on a segregated bus sparked the Montgomery Bus Boycott and helped to launch the civil rights movement of the 1950s.

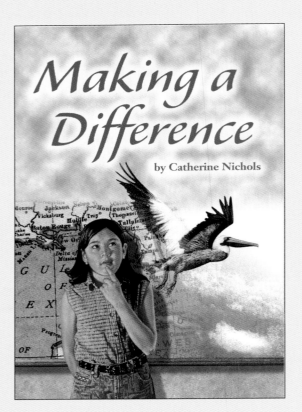

Making a Difference
Genre: Fiction

A young girl named Gloria learns how she can make a difference when she saves a bird trapped in fishing line.

Preparing for Tests

Taking Tests: Strategies

Use this material to prepare for tests, to teach strategies, and to practice test formats.

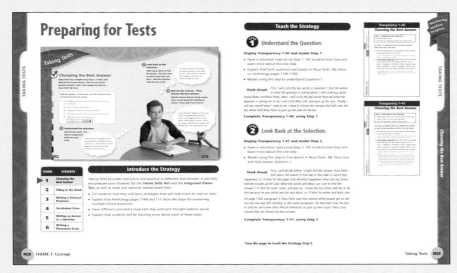

Skill Review

Use these lessons and supporting activities to review tested skills in this theme.

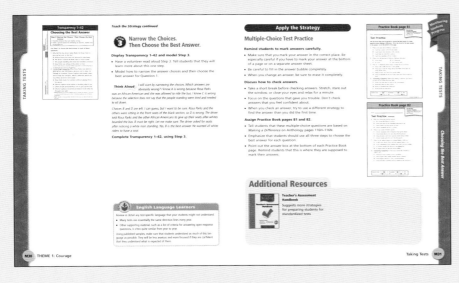

- Independent practice for skills, Level 6.1

- Transparencies
- Strategy Posters
- Blackline Masters

Technology

Audio Selections
Rosa Parks: My Story

Making a Difference

www.eduplace.com
Log on to Education Place® for vocabulary support—
e•Glossary
e•WordGame

Theme Connections

Anthology Literature

Activities to help students think critically

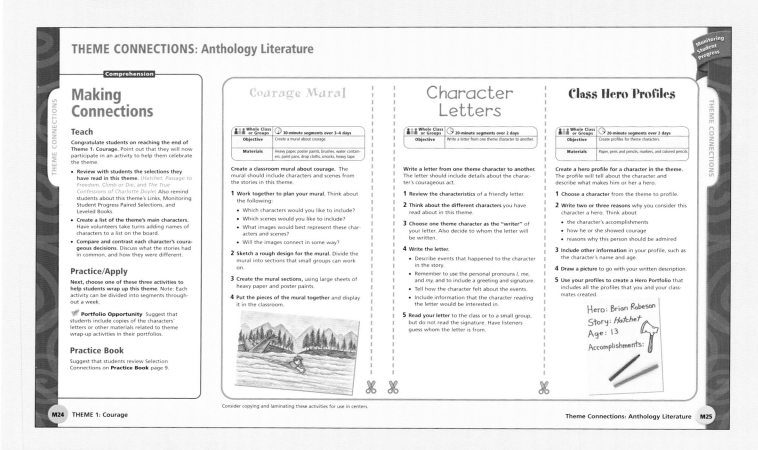

THEME CONNECTIONS: Anthology Literature

Monitoring Student Progress

Comprehension

Making Connections

Teach

Congratulate students on reaching the end of **Theme 1: Courage.** Point out that they will now participate in an activity to help them celebrate the theme.

• Review with students the selections they have read in this theme. (*Hatchet, Passage to Freedom, Climb or Die,* and *The True Confessions of Charlotte Doyle*) Also remind students about this theme's Links, Monitoring Student Progress Paired Selections, and Leveled Books.

• Create a list of the theme's main characters. Have volunteers take turns adding names of characters to a list on the board.

• Compare and contrast each character's courageous decisions. Discuss what the stories had in common, and how they were different.

Practice/Apply

Next, choose one of these three activities to help students wrap up this theme. Note: Each activity can be divided into segments throughout a week.

✔ **Portfolio Opportunity** Suggest that students include copies of the characters' letters or other materials related to theme wrap-up activities in their portfolios.

Practice Book

Suggest that students review Selection Connections on **Practice Book** page 9.

Courage Mural

🧑🧑🧑 Whole Class or Groups	🕑 30-minute segments over 3–4 days
Objective	Create a mural about courage.
Materials	Heavy paper, poster paints, brushes, water containers, paint pans, drop cloths, smocks, heavy tape

Create a classroom mural about courage. The mural should include characters and scenes from the stories in this theme.

1 Work together to plan your mural. Think about the following:

• Which characters would you like to include?
• Which scenes would you like to include?
• What images would best represent these characters and scenes?
• Will the images connect in some way?

2 Sketch a rough design for the mural. Divide the mural into sections that small groups can work on.

3 Create the mural sections, using large sheets of heavy paper and poster paints.

4 Put the pieces of the mural together and display it in the classroom.

Character Letters

🧑🧑🧑 Whole Class or Groups	🕑 20-minute segments over 2 days
Objective	Write a letter from one theme character to another.

Write a letter from one theme character to another. The letter should include details about the character's courageous act.

1 Review the characteristics of a friendly letter.

2 Think about the different characters you have read about in this theme.

3 Choose one theme character as the "writer" of your letter. Also decide to whom the letter will be written.

4 Write the letter.

• Describe events that happened to the character in the story.
• Remember to use the personal pronouns *I, me,* and *my,* and to include a greeting and signature.
• Tell how the character felt about the events.
• Include information that the character *reading* the letter would be interested in.

5 Read your letter to the class or to a small group, but do not read the signature. Have listeners guess whom the letter is from.

Class Hero Profiles

🧑🧑🧑 Whole Class or Groups	🕑 20-minute segments over 2 days
Objective	Create profiles for theme characters.
Materials	Paper, pens and pencils, markers, and colored pencils

Create a hero profile for a character in the theme. The profile will tell about the character and describe what makes him or her a hero.

1 Choose a character from the theme to profile.

2 Write two or three reasons why you consider this character a hero. Think about

• the character's accomplishments
• how he or she showed courage
• reasons why this person should be admired

3 Include other information in your profile, such as the character's name and age.

4 Draw a picture to go with your written description.

5 Use your profiles to create a Hero Portfolio that includes all the profiles that you and your classmates created.

Hero: Brian Robeson
Story: *Hatchet*
Age: 13
Accomplishments:

Consider copying and laminating these activities for use in centers.

Four Main Selections

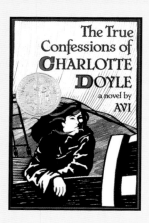

Leveled Books

Activities to help students connect and compare

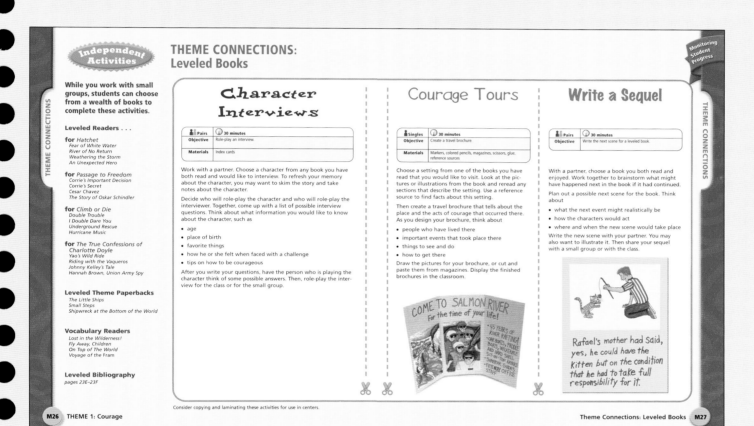

Independent Activities

THEME CONNECTIONS:
Leveled Books

While you work with small groups, students can choose from a wealth of books to complete these activities.

Leveled Readers . . .

for *Hatchet*
Fear of White Water
River of No Return
Weathering the Storm
An Unexpected Hero

for *Passage to Freedom*
Corrie's Important Decision
Corrie's Secret
Cesar Chavez
The Story of Oskar Schindler

for *Climb or Die*
Double Trouble
I Double Dare You
Underground Rescue
Hurricane Music

for *The True Confessions of Charlotte Doyle*
Yao's Wild Ride
Riding with the Vaqueros
Johnny Kelley's Tale
Hannah Brown, Union Army Spy

Leveled Theme Paperbacks
The Little Ships
Small Steps
Shipwreck at the Bottom of the World

Vocabulary Readers
Lost in the Wilderness!
Fly Away, Children
On Top of The World
Voyage of the Fram

Leveled Bibliography
pages 23E–23F

Character Interviews

👥 **Pairs**	🕐 **30 minutes**
Objective	Role-play an interview.
Materials	Index cards

Work with a partner. Choose a character from any book you have both read and would like to interview. To refresh your memory about the character, you may want to skim the story and take notes about the character.

Decide who will role-play the character and who will role-play the interviewer. Together, come up with a list of possible interview questions. Think about what information you would like to know about the character, such as

- age
- place of birth
- favorite things
- how he or she felt when faced with a challenge
- tips on how to be courageous

After you write your questions, have the person who is playing the character think of some possible answers. Then, role-play the interview for the class or for the small group.

Courage Tours

👤 **Singles**	🕐 **30 minutes**
Objective	Create a travel brochure.
Materials	Markers, colored pencils, magazines, scissors, glue, reference sources

Choose a setting from one of the books you have read that you would like to visit. Look at the pictures or illustrations from the book and reread any sections that describe the setting. Use a reference source to find facts about this setting.

Then create a travel brochure that tells about the place and the acts of courage that occurred there. As you design your brochure, think about

- people who have lived there
- important events that took place there
- things to see and do
- how to get there

Draw the pictures for your brochure, or cut and paste them from magazines. Display the finished brochures in the classroom.

Write a Sequel

👥 **Pairs**	🕐 **30 minutes**
Objective	Write the next scene for a leveled book.

With a partner, choose a book you both read and enjoyed. Work together to brainstorm what might have happened next in the book if it had continued.

Plan out a possible next scene for the book. Think about

- what the next event might realistically be
- how the characters would act
- where and when the new scene would take place

Write the new scene with your partner. You may also want to illustrate it. Then share your sequel with a small group or with the class.

Rafael's mother had said, yes, he could have the kitten but on the condition that he had to take full responsibility for it.

Consider copying and laminating these activities for use in centers.

M26   THEME 1: Courage

Theme Connections: Leveled Books   M27

Sixteen Leveled Readers

Three Leveled Theme Paperbacks

Daily Lesson Plans

Technology

Lesson Planner CD-ROM allows you to customize the chart below to develop your own lesson plans.

T Skill tested on Weekly or Theme Skills Test and/or Integrated Theme Test

DAILY LESSON PLANS

50–60 minutes

Connecting and Comparing Literature

CHECK YOUR PROGRESS

Leveled Readers
- Fluency Practice
- Independent Reading

40–60 minutes

Preparing for Tests

TAKING TESTS: Strategies

SKILL REVIEW OPTIONS

Comprehension
Structural Analysis
Vocabulary
Spelling
Grammar
Prompts for Writing

DAY 1

Introducing Paired Selections

Key Vocabulary, M9

civil rights	segregation
activists	reproach
petition	boycott

Reading the Selection, M10–M15
Rosa Parks: My Story

Comprehension Strategy, M10

Predict/Infer **T**

Classroom Management Activities, M6–M7

Leveled Readers
River of No Return
Weathering the Storm
An Unexpected Hero
Fear of White Water

Introduce the Strategy, M28
Choosing the Best Answer

Comprehension, M32–M33
Skill Review Options **T**

Structural Analysis, M34–M35
Skill Review Options **T**

Vocabulary, M36–M37
Skill Review Options **T**

Spelling, M38
Short Vowels **T**

Grammar, M40
Kinds of Sentences **T**

Prompts for Writing, M42
Instructions/Sequence Words and Phrases **T**

DAY 2

Reading the Selection
Rosa Parks: My Story

Connecting and Comparing

Noting Details, M11
Making Judgments, M13, M15

Stop and Think, M16

Classroom Management Activities, M6–M7

Leveled Readers
Corrie's Secret
Cesar Chavez
The Story of Oskar Schindler
Corrie's Important Decision

Step 1: Understand the Question, M29

Comprehension, M32–M33
Skill Review Options **T**

Structural Analysis, M34–M35
Skill Review Options **T**

Vocabulary, M36–M37
Skill Review Options **T**

Spelling, M38
Long Vowels **T**

Grammar, M40
Subjects and Predicates **T**

Prompts for Writing, M42
Memo/Capitalization and Punctuation **T**

Target Skills of the Week

| Phonics |
| Comprehension |
| Vocabulary |
| Fluency |

Monitoring Student Progress

DAY 3

Key Vocabulary, M17
- frantic
- fluttering
- stealthily
- lunged
- biodegradable

Reading the Selection, M18–M22
Making a Difference

Comprehension Strategy, M20
Predict/Infer **T**

Classroom Management Activities, M6–M7

Leveled Readers
I Double Dare You
Underground Rescue
Hurricane Music
Double Trouble

Step 2: Look Back at the Selection, M29

Comprehension, M32–M33
Skill Review Options **T**

Structural Analysis, M34–M35
Skill Review Options **T**

Vocabulary, M36–M37
Skill Review Options **T**

Spelling, M39
More Vowel Spellings **T**

Grammar, M41
Longer Sentences **T**

Prompts for Writing, M43
Friendly Letter/Voice

DAY 4

Reading the Selection
Making a Difference

Connecting and Comparing
Predicting Outcomes, M19
Categorize and Classify, M21

Think and Compare, M23

Theme Connections: Anthology Literature, M24–M25

Classroom Management Activities, M6–M7

Leveled Readers
Riding with the Vaqueros
Johnny Kelley's Tale
Hannah Brown, Union Army Spy
Yao's Wild Ride

Step 3: Narrow the Choices. Then Choose the Best Answer, M30

Comprehension, M32–M33
Skill Review Options **T**

Structural Analysis, M34–M35
Skill Review Options **T**

Vocabulary, M36–M37
Skill Review Options **T**

Spelling, M39
/ou/, /ōō/, /ô/, and /oi/ **T**

Grammar, M41
More About Sentences **T**

Prompts for Writing, M43
Opinion Paragraph/Combining Sentences **T**

DAY 5

Theme Connections: Anthology Literature, M24–M25

Rereading for Fluency, M13, M21

Classroom Management Activities, M6–M7

Leveled Readers

Theme Connections: Leveled Books, M26–M27

Multiple-Choice Test Practice, M31

Comprehension, M32–M33
Skill Review Options **T**

Structural Analysis, M34–M35
Skill Review Options **T**

Vocabulary, M36–M37
Skill Review Options **T**

Spelling Test, M39

Grammar, M41
Kinds of Nouns

Prompts for Writing, M43
Personal Narrative **T**/Varying Sentences

Ready-Made Small Group Activities

 ## Word Work

 ## Cross Curricular

Building Vocabulary Center Activity 5
● ▲ ■ *Carved in Stone*

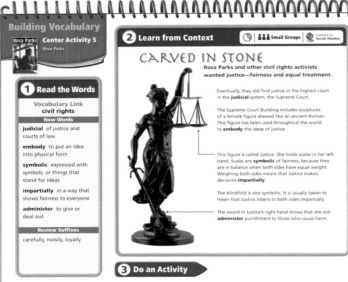

Building Vocabulary
Center Activity 5
Rosa Parks

2 Learn from Context Small Groups · Connect to Social Studies

CARVED IN STONE

Rosa Parks and other civil rights activists wanted justice—fairness and equal treatment.

Eventually, they did find justice in the highest court in the **judicial** system, the Supreme Court.

The Supreme Court Building includes sculptures of a female figure dressed like an ancient Roman. This figure has been used throughout the world to **embody** the ideas of justice.

This figure is called Justice. She holds scales in her left hand. Scales are **symbolic** of fairness, because they are in balance when both sides have equal weight. Weighing both sides means that Justice makes decisions **impartially**.

The blindfold is also symbolic. It is usually taken to mean that Justice listens to both sides impartially.

The sword in Justice's right hand shows that she will **administer** punishment to those who cause harm.

1 Read the Words

Vocabulary Link
civil rights

New Words

judicial of justice and courts of law

embody to put an idea into physical form

symbolic expressed with symbols, or things that stand for ideas

impartially in a way that shows fairness to everyone

administer to give or deal out

Review Suffixes

carefully, noisily, loyally

3 Do an Activity ▶

Leveled Activities on side 2

Game Board 7
● ▲ ■ *Synonym City*

Reading in Social Studies Independent Book
● *Elijah McCoy*

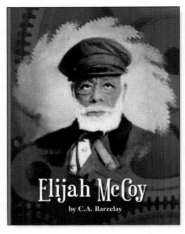

Elijah McCoy
by C.A. Barzelay

Reading in Social Studies Center Activity 5
● ▲ ■ *Be a Playwright*

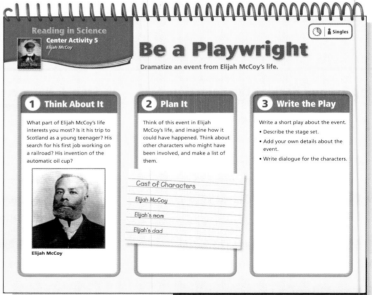

Reading in Science
Center Activity 5
Elijah McCoy

Be a Playwright
Dramatize an event from Elijah McCoy's life.

1 Think About It

What part of Elijah McCoy's life interests you most? Is it his trip to Scotland as a young teenager? His search for his first job working on a railroad? His invention of the automatic oil cup?

Elijah McCoy

2 Plan It

Think of this event in Elijah McCoy's life, and imagine how it could have happened. Think about other characters who might have been involved, and make a list of them.

Cast of Characters
Elijah McCoy
Elijah's mom
Elijah's dad

3 Write the Play

Write a short play about the event.
• Describe the stage set.
• Add your own details about the event.
• Write dialogue for the characters.

Leveled Activities on side 2

Key Vocabulary Cards 33–43

civil rights

Leveled for ● Below Level, ▲ On Level, ■ Above Level

Reading

Writing

Routine Card 1

● ▲ ■ *Independent Reading*

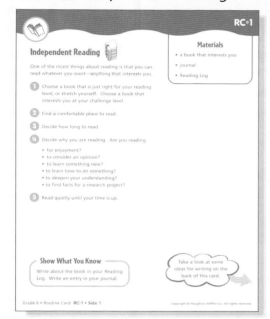

Independent Reading

Materials
- a book that interests you
- journal
- Reading Log

One of the nicest things about reading is that you can read whatever you want—anything that interests you.

1. Choose a book that is just right for your reading level, or stretch yourself. Choose a book that interests you at your challenge level.

2. Find a comfortable place to read.

3. Decide how long to read.

4. Decide why you are reading. Are you reading
   - for enjoyment?
   - to consider an opinion?
   - to learn something new?
   - to learn how to do something?
   - to deepen your understanding?
   - to find facts for a research project?

5. Read quietly until your time is up.

Show What You Know
Write about the book in your Reading Log. Write an entry in your journal.

Take a look at some ideas for writing on the back of this card.

Grade 6 • Routine Card **RC-1** • Side 1   Copyright © Houghton Mifflin Co. All rights reserved.

Routine Card 5

● ▲ ■ *Write a Journal Entry*

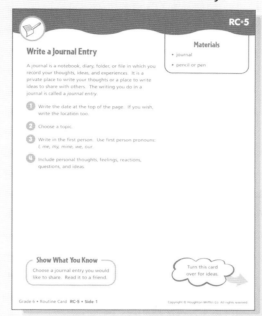

Write a Journal Entry

Materials
- journal
- pencil or pen

A journal is a notebook, diary, folder, or file in which you record your thoughts, ideas, and experiences. It is a private place to write your thoughts or a place to write ideas to share with others. The writing you do in a journal is called a *journal entry*.

1. Write the date at the top of the page. If you wish, write the location too.

2. Choose a topic.

3. Write in the first person. Use first person pronouns: *I, me, my, mine, we, our.*

4. Include personal thoughts, feelings, reactions, questions, and ideas.

Show What You Know
Choose a journal entry you would like to share. Read it to a friend.

Turn this card over for ideas.

Grade 6 • Routine Card **RC-5** • Side 1   Copyright © Houghton Mifflin Co. All rights reserved.

Routine Card 2

● ▲ ■ *Partner Reading*

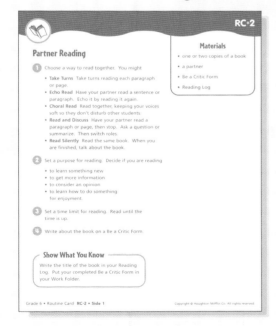

Partner Reading

Materials
- one or two copies of a book
- a partner
- Be a Critic Form
- Reading Log

1. Choose a way to read together. You might
   - **Take Turns** Take turns reading each paragraph or page.
   - **Echo Read** Have your partner read a sentence or paragraph. Echo it by reading it again.
   - **Choral Read** Read together, keeping your voices soft so they don't disturb other students.
   - **Read and Discuss** Have your partner read a paragraph or page, then stop. Ask a question or summarize. Then switch roles.
   - **Read Silently** Read the same book. When you are finished, talk about the book.

2. Set a purpose for reading. Decide if you are reading
   - to learn something new
   - to get more information
   - to consider an opinion
   - to learn how to do something for enjoyment.

3. Set a time limit for reading. Read until the time is up.

4. Write about the book on a Be a Critic Form.

Show What You Know
Write the title of the book in your Reading Log. Put your completed Be a Critic Form in your Work Folder.

Grade 6 • Routine Card **RC-2** • Side 1   Copyright © Houghton Mifflin Co. All rights reserved.

Routine Card 6

● ▲ ■ *Idea Generator*

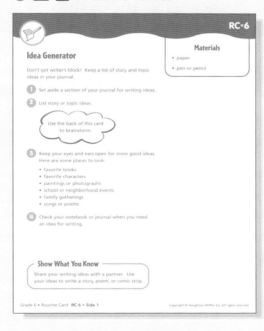

Idea Generator

Materials
- paper
- pen or pencil

Don't get writer's block! Keep a list of story and topic ideas in your journal.

1. Set aside a section of your journal for writing ideas.

2. List story or topic ideas.

Use the back of this card to brainstorm.

3. Keep your eyes and ears open for more good ideas. Here are some places to look.
   - favorite books
   - favorite characters
   - paintings or photographs
   - school or neighborhood events
   - family gatherings
   - songs or poems

4. Check your notebook or journal when you need an idea for writing.

Show What You Know
Share your writing ideas with a partner. Use your ideas to write a story, poem, or comic strip.

Grade 6 • Routine Card **RC-6** • Side 1   Copyright © Houghton Mifflin Co. All rights reserved.

Multiple Tiers of Intervention

Core Program Intervention

- research-based
- systematic
- assessment-driven
- extra support
- English learner support
- reteaching

Intensive Intervention

Proven efficacy for struggling readers

Soar to Success

For these materials and more, see **Small Group Independent Activities Kit.**

Connecting and Comparing Literature

Theme Wrap-Up

Check Your Progress

In this theme you have read about several people with courage, from a thirteen-year-old girl to a Japanese diplomat. Now you will read and compare two new selections, practice your test-taking skills, and review what you've learned throughout the theme.

Look back at pages 23–24. Think about what courage means to Avi and to you. Which characters do you believe have shown the greatest courage so far?

Now read the two selections that follow. Compare the kinds of courage each selection tells about. Think about how difficult, or easy, it seems for these characters to be courageous. How do their courageous actions compare with others in the theme?

116

Read and Compare

Rosa Parks MY STORY
by Rosa Parks with Jim Haskins

In the first selection, learn about Rosa Parks, whose act of defiance sparked the national civil rights movement.

Try these strategies:
Monitor and Clarify
Evaluate

Nonfiction

Making a Difference by Catherine Nichols

Then read a story about a girl who finds the courage to make a speech in front of her class.

Try these strategies:
Predict and Infer
Summarize

Realistic Fiction

Strategies in Action *Remember to use all your reading strategies while you read.*

116 A

Use Paired Selections: Check Your Progress

Have students read page 116. Discuss these questions:

- What do the characters in this theme have in common? How are they different? (They all showed courage in difficult situations; some of them faced life-threatening danger, while others faced difficult but less dangerous situations.)

- Which character would you most like to interview about his or her life? Why? (Answers will vary.)

Have students read page 116A. Ask these questions:

- How might these two selections be similar to other theme selections? How might they be different? (Sample answer: Both characters might show courage but probably in very different situations.)

Strategies in Action Remind students to use the Predict/Infer strategy as they read these paired selections.

M8 THEME 1: Courage

Selection 1

Rosa Parks MY STORY

by Rosa Parks with Jim Haskins

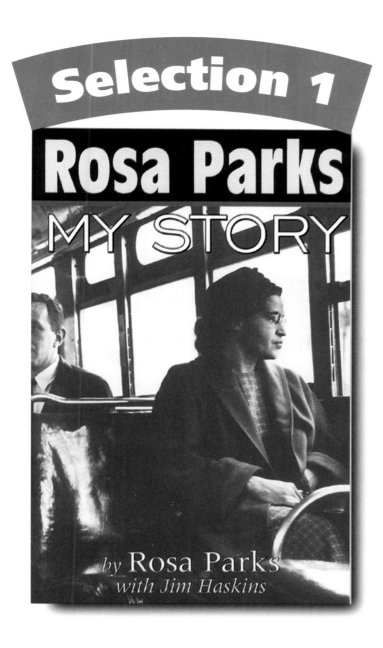

Introducing Vocabulary

Key Vocabulary
These words appear in the selection.

civil rights the rights belonging to all citizens, such as freedom from discrimination

activists people who actively work for social change

petition a document that requests a certain right or benefit

segregation the policy of keeping races separate

reproach blame or disapproval

boycott a protest that involves a refusal to buy from a certain business or person

e • Glossary
e • WordGame

See Vocabulary notes on pages M12 and M14 for additional words to preview.

Have students locate Key Vocabulary words in the story.

- Have volunteers read aloud each sentence containing a Key Vocabulary word.

Display Transparency 1–38.

- Model how to use context clues to determine the meaning of *activists*.

- Then ask students to use context clues to determine the meaning of the remaining underlined words.

Practice/Homework Assign **Practice Book** page 77.

Introduce the Graphic Organizer. Tell students to fill in **Practice Book** page 78 as they read the Paired Selections.

Reading the Paired Selections **M9**

Practice Book page 77

Monitoring Student Progress
Key Vocabulary

Name _____

Words for Change

Write the letter to match each word with its definition.

(1 point)

f boycott	a. people who work hard for a cause they believe in
e petition	b. separating people by race
d reproach	c. the rights belonging to a citizen
a activists	d. disapproval
b segregation	e. a document that requests something
c civil rights	f. a protest that involves refusing to deal with a certain business or person

EQUAL RIGHTS

Write a sentence for each vocabulary word in the spaces provided.
Answers will vary. **(1 point each)**

1. activists: _____

2. petition: _____

3. boycott: _____

4. reproach: _____

5. segregation: _____

6. civil rights: _____

Practice Book page 78

Monitoring Student Progress
Graphic Organizer
Noting Details

Name _____

Making a Difference

After reading each selection, complete the chart below to show what you learned. Wording of answers will vary. Details may vary; sample details are given

	Rosa Parks: My Story	Making a Difference
What challenge does the main character face?	Rosa Parks has to decide whether or not to stand up to the unfair law of segregation. **(2 points)**	Gloria has to give a speech in front of her class, even though she is very afraid to do so. **(2)**
Details that show the main character's courage	1. She does not give up her seat even when the bus driver threatens to have her arrested. **(1)**	1. She frees the bird, even though her sister is frightened by it. **(1)**
	2. She worries that she might be beaten, but she stays seated. **(1)**	2. She gives a speech, even though she is scared. **(1)**

CRITICAL THINKING
Guiding Comprehension

❶ MAKING INFERENCES How does Rosa Parks feel about Claudette Colvin? (Sample answer: approves of her and says she has inherited great pride)

❷ NOTING DETAILS What did activists want the Montgomery bus company to do? (to let blacks sit in the back and whites at the front of the bus and have wherever they met be the dividing line)

TARGET SKILL
COMPREHENSION STRATEGY
Predict/Infer

Teacher Modeling Remind students that they can use their own experience along with clues from the text to make predictions and inferences. Read aloud page 116B and then model the strategy.

Think Aloud *The second paragraph discusses a girl who refused to give up her seat. Knowing that Rosa Parks did not agree with segregation helps me understand why she took an interest in this girl. I predict that Parks will do things herself to fight segregation.*

Vocabulary

civil rights the rights belonging to all citizens, such as freedom from discrimination

activists people who actively work for social change

petition a document that requests a certain right or benefit

segregation the policy of keeping the races separate

Rosa Parks MY STORY
by Rosa Parks, with Jim Haskins

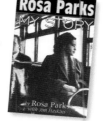

In 1955 Rosa Parks worked in a department store. She was also the secretary for Edgar Nixon, president of the Montgomery National Association for the Advancement of Colored People (NAACP). She, like many other people, took the bus to work. At that time, the buses of Montgomery, Alabama, were segregated, which meant that whites sat in the front part of the bus and African Americans sat in the back. Rosa Parks thought that this law was wrong. What she did on December 1, 1955, sparked the national civil rights movement in the United States.

▲ The "colored" section at the back of the bus (Courtesy of NAACP Public Relations)

Back in the spring of 1955 a teenage girl named Claudette Colvin and an elderly woman refused to give up their seats in the middle section of a bus to white people. When the driver went to get the police, the elderly woman got off the bus, but Claudette refused to leave, saying she had already paid her dime and had no reason to move. When the police came, they dragged her from the bus and arrested her. Now, her name was familiar to me, and it turned out that Claudette Colvin was the great-granddaughter of Mr. Gus Vaughn, the black man with all the children back in Pine Level who refused to work for the white man. His great-granddaughter must have inherited his sense of pride. I took a particular interest in the girl and her case.

116B

REACHING ALL LEARNERS
Challenge

Additional Reading
Students may be interested in reading more of Jim Haskins's work. To learn more about the author, visit Education Place at *www.educationplace.com.*

After Claudette's arrest, a group of activists took a petition to the bus company officials and city officials. The petition asked for more courteous treatment and for no visible signs of segregation. They didn't ask for the end of segregation, just for an understanding that whites would start sitting at the front of the bus and blacks would start sitting at the back, and wherever they met would be the dividing line. I think that petition also asked that black bus drivers be hired. The city officials and the bus company took months to answer that petition, and when they did, every request in it was turned down.

I did not go down with the others to present that petition to the bus company and the city officials, because I didn't feel anything could be accomplished. I had decided that I would not go anywhere with a piece of paper in my hand asking white folks for any favors. I had made that decision myself, as an individual.

Another bus incident involving a woman occurred that summer. I didn't know much about the girl. Her name was Louise Smith, and she was about eighteen years old. They say she paid her fine and didn't protest. Hers certainly wasn't a good case for Mr. Nixon to appeal to a higher court.

116C

Connecting and Comparing

Monitoring Student Progress

Noting Details

- What details in *Rosa Parks: My Story* and in *Passage to Freedom* help you know that they are nonfiction selections? (*Rosa Parks: My Story* tells about a real person, includes photos and captions, and tells facts about a specific time and place; *Passage to Freedom* tells about events that really happened, includes facts about a specific time and place, and has a main character that is a real person.)

- What details help you understand what kind of people Rosa Parks and Mr. Sugihara are? (Sample answers: You can tell that Rosa Parks is involved with civil rights because she works for the NAACP, you can tell she is independent because she says she didn't want any favors from "white folks"; you can tell that Mr. Sugihara is brave because he chooses to help people even though he could get caught, you can tell he cares about his family because he discusses his decision with them.)

Extra Support/Intervention

Selection Preview

pages 116B–116C Rosa Parks is an African American woman who lived in Montgomery, Alabama in the 1950s. At that time, segregation kept the races separate, even on buses. Rosa Parks is interested in the cases of people who refuse to give up their seats to white people. What do you think she might do?

pages 116D–116E One evening after work, Rosa is asked to give up her seat for a white person. She refuses to do this because she is tired of giving in. She is arrested. What do you think will happen to her?

page 116F–116G Rosa's action sparks a city-wide boycott of the bus system, led by Martin Luther King, Jr. Eventually, the Supreme Court rules that Alabama's segregated bus system is unconstitutional.

Guiding Comprehension

3 **NOTING DETAILS** Why does Rosa Parks say, *If I had been paying attention, I wouldn't even have gotten on that bus?* (The bus driver had been mean to her before. If she had been paying attention, she would have avoided him and his bus.)

4 **MAKING JUDGMENTS** Do you think the bus driver acted fairly by telling Rosa Parks he would have her arrested? Why or why not? (Answers will vary.)

5 **PREDICTING OUTCOMES** What do you think will happen next to Rosa Parks when the police arrive? (Answers will vary.)

COMPREHENSION STRATEGY
Predict/Infer

Teacher/Student Modeling After students read page 116E, have them look at the photograph and read the caption. Then have students discuss clues that will help them predict what happens after Rosa Parks is arrested.

Vocabulary

plaintiff a person who files a lawsuit

reproach blame or disapproval

complied followed rules or orders

boycott a protest that involves a refusal to buy from a certain business or person

---

I knew they needed a plaintiff who was beyond reproach, because I was in on the discussions about the possible court cases. But that is not why I refused to give up my bus seat to a white man on Thursday, December 1, 1955. I did not intend to get arrested. If I had been paying attention, I wouldn't even have gotten on that bus.

I was very busy at that particular time. I was getting an NAACP workshop together for the 3rd and 4th of December, and I was trying to get the consent of Mr. H. Council Trenholm at Alabama State to have the Saturday meeting at the college. He did give permission, but I had a hard time getting to him to get permission to use the building. I was also getting the notices in the mail for the election of officers of the Senior Branch of the NAACP, which would be next week.

When I got off from work that evening of December 1, I went to Court Square as usual to catch the Cleveland Avenue bus home. I didn't look to see who was driving when I got on, and by the time I recognized him, I had already paid my fare. It was the same driver who had put me off the bus back in 1943, twelve years earlier. He was still tall and heavy, with red, rough-looking skin. And he was still mean-looking. I didn't know if he had been on that route before — they switched the **3** drivers around sometimes. I do know that most of the time if I saw him on a bus, I wouldn't get on it.

I saw a vacant seat in the middle section of the bus and took it. I didn't even question why there was a vacant seat even though there were quite a few people standing in the back. If I had thought about it at all, I would probably have figured maybe someone saw me get on and did not take the seat but left it vacant for me. There was a man sitting next to the window and two women across the aisle.

The next stop was the Empire Theater, and some whites got on. They filled up the white seats, and one man was left standing. The driver looked back and noticed the man standing. Then he looked back at us. He said, "Let me have those front seats," because they were the front seats of the black section. Didn't anybody move. We just sat right where we were, the four of us. Then he spoke a second time: "Y'all better make it light on yourselves and let me have those seats."

The man in the window seat next to me stood up, and I moved to let him pass by me, and then I looked across the aisle and saw that the two women were also standing. I moved over to the window seat. I could not see how standing up was **4** going to "make it light" for me. The more we gave in and complied, the worse they treated us.

116D

English Language Learners

Supporting Comprehension

Tell students that some words and phrases in the story are sometimes used in the American South. You may want to explain these words and phrases to students: "y'all" (you all), "make it light" (make it easy), and "didn't anybody move" (nobody move).

People always say that I didn't give up my seat because I was tired, but that isn't true. I was not tired physically, or no more tired than I usually was at the end of a working day. I was not old, although some people have an image of me as being old then. I was forty-two. No, the only tired I was, was tired of giving in.

The driver of the bus saw me still sitting there, and he asked was I going to stand up. I said, "No." He said, "Well, I'm going to have you arrested." Then I said, "You may do that." These were the only words we said to each other. I didn't even know his name, which was James Blake, until we were in court together. He got out of the bus and stayed outside for a few minutes, waiting for the police.

5

▼ A "Day of Pilgrimage" protest begins with black Montgomery citizens walking to work, part of their boycott of buses in the wake of the Rosa Parks incident.

116E

Connecting and Comparing

READ & COMPARE

Making Judgments

- Do you agree with the decisions that Rosa Parks and Mr. Sugihara made? Why or why not? (Sample answer: Yes, because they both made decisions that helped people: Rosa Parks's decision to stand up to discrimination sparked the civil rights movement, and Mr. Sugihara's decision to issue visas saved the lives of many Jewish people.)

- Think back to all the characters in this theme. Whose courage did you most admire? Why? (Answers will vary.)

TARGET SKILL

Fluency Practice

Rereading for Fluency Have students choose a favorite part of the story to reread to a partner, or suggest that they reread page 116E. Encourage students to read expressively.

Guiding Comprehension

6 **DRAW CONCLUSIONS** How did Rosa Parks make a difference in the lives of African Americans? (Her actions led to the Montgomery bus boycott, which desegregated the buses. They also helped spark the civil rights movement, which eventually won equal rights for African Americans.)

7 **TEXT ORGANIZATION** How is *Rosa Parks: My Story* organized? How can you tell? (sequence of events; The selection uses words like *next, then,* and *after* to tell what happened.)

As I sat there, I tried not to think about what might happen. I knew that anything was possible. I could be manhandled or beaten. I could be arrested. People have asked me if it occurred to me then that I could be the test case the NAACP had been looking for. I did not think about that at all. In fact if I had let myself think too deeply about what might happen to me, I might have gotten off the bus. But I chose to remain.

◀ Rosa Parks is fingerprinted by D.H. Lackey of the Montgomery Police Department for participating in the bus boycott.

Rev. Martin Luther King, Jr., director of ▶ the segregated bus boycott, brimming with enthusiasm as he outlines boycott strategies to his organizers, including Rosa Parks

116F

Challenge

REACHING ALL LEARNERS

Civil Rights Research

Students may be interested in finding out more about the civil rights movement. Have groups of students choose one aspect of *Rosa Parks: My Story* to research. For example, they may choose to find out more about the Montgomery bus boycott, Dr. Martin Luther King, Jr., or the NAACP. Have students present their findings to the class.

Vocabulary

manhandled treated in a rough manner

THE OUTCOME

After Rosa Parks was arrested for violating the segregation law, the African Americans of Montgomery organized a boycott of the city buses. Rosa Parks attended her trial and was given a suspended sentence. Martin Luther King, Jr., called for an end to the segregation of buses. By the time the United States Supreme Court ruled that segregation on Montgomery buses was unconstitutional, the boycott had lasted nearly a year.

6

7

December 21, 1956: ▼
Rosa Parks sits in the front of a Montgomery city bus as a Supreme Court ruling banning segregation on the city's public transit vehicles takes effect.

116**G**

Connecting and Comparing

Making Judgments

- Which characters in this theme took a risk for something they believed in? Why did they take these risks? (Rosa Parks and Mr. Sugihara; Rosa Parks took a risk because she believed in equal treatment of all races; Mr. Sugihara took a risk because he believed it was important to save people's lives.)

- Which character in this theme do you think took the biggest risk? Why? (Answers will vary.)

Summarize Have students use what they wrote on their Graphic Organizers to summarize *Rosa Parks: My Story.*

READ & COMPARE

Reading the Paired Selections **M15**

Stop and Think

Critical Thinking Questions

1. **AUTHOR'S CRAFT** From what point of view is *Rosa Parks: My Story* written? How does the point of view compare to that of *Passage to Freedom?* (*Rosa Parks: My Story* is told in first person from Rosa's point of view; *Passage to Freedom* is told in first person by Mr. Sugihara's son.)

2. **MAKING INFERENCES** How would you describe Rosa Parks's personality, based on what you learned in the selection? (Sample answer: smart, proud, brave, strong)

3. **MAKING JUDGMENTS** Do you think what Rosa Parks did was brave? Why or why not? (Answers will vary.)

Strategies in Action Have students model how they used Predict/Infer and other strategies to help them understand this selection.

Connecting and Comparing

Compare and Contrast

- Remind students that as they read this selection they will be making judgments about Rosa Parks and other characters.

- Ask volunteers to make one judgment about Rosa Parks based on what they read on page 116. Record answers on the board.

- Have students use **Practice Book** page 79 to compare and contrast their judgments about Rosa Parks with their judgments about Brian in *Hatchet*. Suggest that students focus on the strong and weak points of the two characters.

Practice Book page 79

Monitoring Student Progress

Connecting and Comparing

Name _____

Compare and Contrast Judgments

In *Rosa Parks: My Story*, what beliefs and opinions mattered deeply to Rosa Parks? Choose one quotation to copy into the chart below. Make a judgment about that belief or opinion. In the second block indicate on a scale of 1 (strongly disagree) to 10 (strongly agree) whether you agree with the statement or not. In the third block give at least one reason to support your judgment. Sample answers are provided. Then fill out the next column of the chart using a quotation from another selection in this theme.

	Selection Title: *Rosa Parks: My Story*	Selection Title:
Quotation That States an Opinion or Belief	"I had decided that I would not go anywhere with a piece of paper in my hand asking white folks for favors." (page 116) (2 points)	(2)
Check Scale	Disagree ___10___ Agree (1)	(1) Disagree _____ Agree
Supporting Reason	I agree with Rosa Parks. What she wants is her rights as an American citizen. No one should have to beg for that. (3)	(3)

Extra Support/Intervention

Review Predictions

Have students discuss some of the predictions they made while reading. How did their predictions compare with the events in the selection?

Monitoring Student Progress

If . . .	Then . . .
students had difficulty answering Guiding Comprehension questions,	guide them in reading aloud relevant portions of the text and discussing their answers.

Introducing Vocabulary

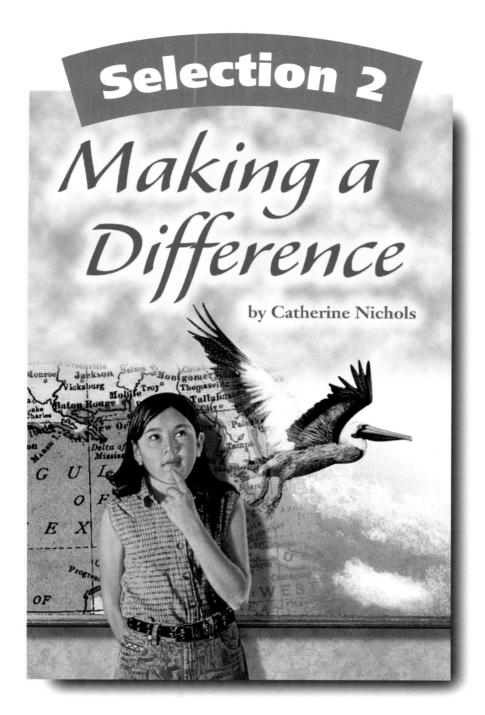

Selection 2

Making a Difference

by Catherine Nichols

READ & COMPARE

Key Vocabulary

These words appear in the selection.

frantic intense and frenzied

fluttering flapping quickly and lightly

stealthily quietly and cautiously

lunged moved forward suddenly

biodegradable able to decompose naturally

e • Glossary
e • WordGame

See Vocabulary notes on pages M18 and M20 for additional words to preview.

Have students locate Key Vocabulary words in the story.

- Have volunteers read aloud each sentence containing a Key Vocabulary word.

Display Transparency 1–39.

- Work with students to fill in the blanks with Key Vocabulary words.

- Ask students to use context clues to determine the correct Key Vocabulary word.

Practice/Homework Assign **Practice Book** page 80.

Transparency 1–39

Key Vocabulary Words

| frantic | fluttering | stealthily |
| lunged | biodegradable | |

My class took a field trip to Lake Johnson last week. Our teacher challenged us to make suggestions that would help the lake's environment.

While we were thinking about this, my friend Holly and I spotted some beautiful orange and yellow butterflies. We moved toward them _stealthily_, careful not to make any unnecessary movements. All of a sudden, Holly tripped on a rock and _lunged_ forward. The butterflies took off, _fluttering_ their wings as they flew away.

Just then, Holly noticed an overturned plastic cup that someone had dropped on the grass. When Holly picked it up, she found a butterfly beating its wings inside. The butterfly was making a _frantic_ attempt to escape, but it had trouble flying because its wings had been damaged from being trapped in the cup.

That's when we realized that plastic cups and other items that are not _biodegradable_ can harm wildlife. Since they do not break down, they can litter the environment for years. Holly and I knew what our suggestion would be—more trash cans!

TRANSPARENCY 1–39
TEACHER'S EDITION PAGE M17

ANNOTATED VERSION

COURAGE *Making a Difference*
Monitoring Student Progress Key Vocabulary

Practice Book page 80

Name _____

Monitoring Student Progress
Key Vocabulary

Outdoor Words

Use the words from the box to complete the sentences below.

Vocabulary
frantic
fluttering
stealthily
lunged
biodegradable

1. "Make sure to throw your cups in the trash can," Mrs. Newsom said. "Plastic is not a _biodegradable (2 points)_ substance."

2. The cat crept _stealthily (2)_ toward the unsuspecting robin.

3. The robin escaped, _fluttering (2)_ its wings as it flew off.

4. Andy _lunged (2)_ forward as he tried to catch a butterfly in his net.

5. A rabbit tangled in a piece of wire hopped back and forth, _frantic (2)_ to get loose.

Use at least two vocabulary words in a short description of what it might be like to spend a day cleaning up a park, lake, or other natural area.

Answers will vary. **(2 points)**

Reading the Paired Selections **M17**

Guiding Comprehension

① NOTING DETAILS Why is Gloria nervous about giving a speech? (She does not like getting up in front of people.)

② PREDICTING OUTCOMES What do you think is causing the noise that Gloria and Elena hear? (Answers will vary.)

Continue the Graphic Organizer

Remind students to fill in their Graphic Organizers as they read *Making a Difference*.

Vocabulary

arepa a food made of cornmeal and cooked on a griddle

mangrove a type of tropical tree

mi cielo an affectionate nickname meaning "my sky"

frantic intense and frenzied

fluttering flapping quickly and lightly

Making a Difference

by Catherine Nichols illustrated by Robert Rodriguez

Gloria ate the last bite of her *arepa*. Her older sister, Elena, lay stretched out beside her on the picnic blanket. Out on Tampa Bay, Gloria could just make out her father in his small boat. She crumpled the wax paper from her sandwich and shoved it into her knapsack. Lunch was over.

Gloria sighed and took a red notebook out of her knapsack. Inside, written in bold letters, was the word *Speech*. Her speech was due tomorrow. "Talk about something that concerns you," her teacher, Ms. Acosta, had said. Gloria had hoped she'd be inspired by being on Mangrove Island, her own special name for her favorite place. But she couldn't even think of a topic. Every time she tried, she saw herself in front of the classroom, and her stomach did a flip-flop. Nothing made her more nervous than the thought of getting **①** up in front of people.

"I was the same way, *mi cielo*," Mami had told her. "The best way to get over it — do it! Get up and speak." Gloria wished she were more like Elena. Elena loved to talk. Giving a speech was nothing to her.

Gloria picked up her pen. She would just write something. Anything. Whatever came to mind. Before she could write a word, **②** a frantic, fluttering noise came from the bushes. Gloria poked her sister. "Elena. Wake up."

Her sister rolled over lazily. "What is it?"

"I heard something," Gloria said. "In the bushes."

116H

Extra Support/Intervention

Selection Preview

pages 116H–116I Gloria and her sister Elena are having a picnic on Mangrove Island. Gloria is nervous about giving a speech the next day in class because she can't think of anything to speak about. The girls hear a noise in the bushes. What do you think it is?

pages 116J–116K The girls discover a bird trapped in fishing line, and they work to free it. A ranger explains that many birds get trapped in fishing line. The next day at school, Gloria volunteers to give her speech first. What do you think she will talk about?

page 116L Gloria gives her speech about the problem she found on Mangrove Island and how she plans to help. She invites her class to join her in cleaning up the island.

Connecting and Comparing

Predicting Outcomes

- All of the selections in this theme are about courage. How do you predict that Gloria will show courage? (Sample answer: She might overcome her fear of giving a speech.)

- How do you predict that this story will be similar to *The True Confessions of Charlotte Doyle?* How do you predict it will be different? (Sample answer: Gloria might overcome her fear the way Charlotte did when she climbed the mast; Gloria will probably not have a physical challenge, as Charlotte did.)

READ & COMPARE

Elena lay back down. "You heard quiet, that's all." She closed her eyes. A loud squawk was followed by more flapping noises. Elena sat up.

"Let's wait for Papi by the shore," Gloria said.

"No, come on," Elena said, scrambling to her feet. "Let's investigate."

116I

English Language Learners

Language Development

For English language learners whose first language is not Spanish, you may want to clarify that this selection mixes Spanish and English words together. Explain that the Spanish words are shown in italics.

Reading the Paired Selections **M19**

Guiding Comprehension

❸ NOTING DETAILS What was wrong with the bird that Gloria and Elena found? (It was tangled in fishing line and couldn't get free.)

❹ MAKING INFERENCES What can you tell about Gloria based on her actions? (Sample answer: She is brave because she saves the bird; she is caring because she is upset at the thought that the bird might have died.)

❺ PROBLEM SOLVING How could Gloria help solve the problem that she discovers on Mangrove Island? (Sample answer: She could try to convince people to help her clean up the island.)

COMPREHENSION STRATEGY

Predict/Infer

Student Modeling After students finish reading page 116K, have them model making predictions about what Gloria will discuss in her speech. If necessary, use this prompt: What do you think the main idea of Gloria's speech will be?

Vocabulary

stealthily quietly and cautiously

lunged moved forward suddenly

niñas girls

biodegradable able to decompose naturally

Gloria followed her older sister, teeth chattering. She was scared — maybe even more scared than she was of giving a speech. But here she went, into the unknown in search of a strange sound. She dodged branches and bushes until they came to a clearing. There, by a mangrove, was a large brownish bird.

"*Mira!*" Gloria cried. "Look! The poor bird's wing is tangled in string."

❸ The bird tried to get free, but the more it struggled, the more tangled it became.

"What do we do?" whispered Gloria.

"Watch me," Elena whispered back, stealthily approaching the bird. Just as she came within a foot or so, the bird lunged. "Ay!" Elena screamed and jumped back.

Gloria noticed that the other end of the string was several feet away, looped around the roots of another mangrove. "Wait," she said.

❹ She crept forward and carefully unwound the plastic string from the roots. The bird stopped struggling, perhaps sensing that she was trying to help it. When the last of the string was off, the bird slipped free. Then it flapped its great wings and flew off.

Papi was waiting for them back at the blanket, a park ranger at his side. "*Niñas*, where have you been? I thought I told you to stay near the blanket."

"Oh, *Papi*, we saved a bird!" Elena cried.

116J

REACHING ALL LEARNERS

Challenge

Is it Biodegradable?

Have students do some research to find out which classroom objects are biodegradable and which are not. Have them make an illustrated two-column list of biodegradable and nonbiodegradable objects in the classroom.

"You girls did well," the ranger said when Elena finished telling what had happened. "In the future, though, you should find a ranger or some other adult to help. Even birds can be dangerous."

"What kind of bird was it?" Gloria asked.

"From what you described, it sounds like a brown pelican," he replied. "This is a nesting area of theirs, though they're not nesting now." He picked up the plastic string they had brought back. "And this is no ordinary string. This is fishing line. Trouble is, this stuff isn't biodegradable." He looked at the girls. "That's a fancy way of saying it doesn't break down. The lines collect and they can do a lot of harm. Hundreds of birds get tangled in them each year, and not all of them are as lucky as your bird. Most die."

"That's terrible!" Gloria cried.

During the car ride back to Ybor City, Gloria sat quietly in the back seat. She remembered how the bird had struggled to free itself. If she hadn't helped, it might have died. Tears pricked her eyes.

"Any volunteers to give the first speech?" Ms. Acosta asked the next day.

Gloria took a deep breath and raised her hand.

"Gloria Perez?" Ms. Acosta looked surprised but pleased. "Go right ahead."

Gloria walked to the front of the class. Her stomach made soft, rumbling noises. Facing the class, she noticed that her hands were trembling. Her throat and mouth felt dry. She remembered the pelican, its wing tangled in the fishing line, and took a deep breath. "I'd like to tell you about something I saw yesterday. . . ."

⑤

116K

Connecting and Comparing

Categorize and Classify

- Which characters or real people in the theme were trying to help make the world a better place? (Rosa Parks, Mr. Sugihara, Gloria)

- Which characters were trying to overcome personal challenges? (Gloria, Brian in *Hatchet,* Jake and Danielle in *Climb or Die,* Charlotte Doyle)

- What are some other categories you could use to classify the selections and characters in the theme? Which selections would go into each category? (Answers will vary. Sample answer: **True Stories:** *Passage to Freedom, Rosa Parks;* **Fictional Stories:** *Hatchet, Climb or Die, The True Confessions of Charlotte Doyle, Making a Difference*)

TARGET SKILL
Fluency Practice

Rereading for Fluency Have students choose a favorite part of the selection to reread to a partner or suggest that they reread a part of the selection silently.

Guiding Comprehension

6 DRAWING CONCLUSIONS How do you think Gloria felt when her classmates came to help clean up Mangrove Island? Why? (proud; She had inspired them to make a difference.)

7 PREDICTING OUTCOMES What do you think Mangrove Island will look like a year after the story ends? Why? (Answers will vary.)

Finish the Graphic Organizer Have students share and discuss their completed Graphic Organizers.

READ & COMPARE

As she spoke, Gloria grew calmer. She told the class about the pelican and about how she and her sister had rescued it. She told them about the fishing line and how dangerous it was. She told them that the ranger said he could always use volunteers to help collect the fishing lines before they hurt wildlife. "I'm going this Saturday to help, and so is my family. I'd like to invite everyone in this class — and Ms. Acosta, too — to come with us. Together, we can make a difference."

Gloria made her way back to her seat. The entire classroom was quiet. The only sound Gloria heard was the *click clack* of her shoes. Back in her seat, she didn't look around. She guessed her speech hadn't gone over well. She guessed that no one cared about pelicans. Then she heard clapping. It grew louder and louder.

That Saturday, Class 5-1, armed with trash bags, piled out of two boats. Under the ranger's direction, they got to work clearing the island of fishing line and other trash. As she worked, Gloria thought about the birds that would now be able to live here safely and raise their families. With just one little speech, she *had* made a big difference.

6

7

116L

Think and Compare

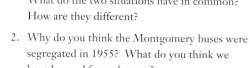

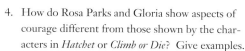

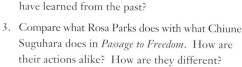

1. Compare Rosa Parks's story with Gloria's story. What do the two situations have in common? How are they different?

2. Why do you think the Montgomery buses were segregated in 1955? What do you think we have learned from the past?

3. Compare what Rosa Parks does with what Chiune Suguhara does in *Passage to Freedom*. How are their actions alike? How are they different?

4. How do Rosa Parks and Gloria show aspects of courage different from those shown by the characters in *Hatchet* or *Climb or Die*? Give examples.

5. Which selection in this theme best fits your own definition of courage? Explain your answer with examples from the selection.

Strategies in Action How did using the reading strategies help you read better during this theme?

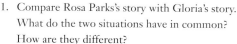

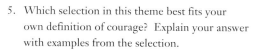

 Reflecting

Write a Journal Entry

Choose a character from the theme. Think of how that character felt when he or she showed courage. Write one or two paragraphs about the experience in a journal entry.

Tips
- Use details from the selection to describe the character's experience.
- Describe events in the order in which they happened.
- Use action verbs.

116M

Extra Support/Intervention

Review Predictions

Have students discuss the predictions they made about the characters and the plot. How do their predictions compare to actual story events?

Think and Compare

Discuss or Write Have students discuss or write their answers. Sample answers are provided; accept reasonable responses.

1. Both characters show courage and stand up for what they believe. Their situations are different. Rosa Parks stands up to an unfair law. Gloria overcomes fear and inspires people to help clean up an island.

2. There were laws that kept African Americans and white people separate in public places. We have learned that these laws were unfair; everyone should be treated equally.

3. They are alike because they both take risks for causes they believe in, put themselves in danger, and help many people. They are different because Mr. Sugihara's actions affected people immediately, while it took time for Rosa Parks's actions to affect large numbers of people.

4. In *Hatchet* and *Climb or Die,* the characters show courage by fighting for their survival in the wilderness. Rosa Parks stood up to racist laws and risked personal danger. Gloria showed courage by overcoming her fear of speaking in front of people.

5. Answers will vary.

Strategies in Action Have students take turns modeling how and where they used Predict/Infer and other strategies.

Monitoring Student Progress

If...	Then...
students had difficulty answering Guiding Comprehension questions,	guide them in reading aloud relevant portions of the text and discussing their answers.

Reading the Paired Selections M23

THEME CONNECTIONS

Comprehension

Making Connections

Teach

Congratulate students on reaching the end of Theme 1: Courage. Point out that they will now participate in an activity to help them celebrate the theme.

- **Review with students the selections they have read in this theme.** (*Hatchet, Passage to Freedom, Climb or Die,* and *The True Confessions of Charlotte Doyle*) Also remind students about this theme's Links, Monitoring Student Progress Paired Selections, and Leveled Books.

- **Create a list of the theme's main characters.** Have volunteers take turns adding names of characters to a list on the board.

- **Compare and contrast each character's courageous decisions.** Discuss what the stories had in common, and how they were different.

Practice/Apply

Next, choose one of these three activities to help students wrap up this theme. Note: Each activity can be divided into segments throughout a week.

📝 **Portfolio Opportunity** Suggest that students include copies of the characters' letters or other materials related to theme wrap-up activities in their portfolios.

Practice Book

Suggest that students review Selection Connections on **Practice Book** page 9.

Courage Mural

👥👥 Whole Class or Groups	🕐 30-minute segments over 3–4 days	
Objective	Create a mural about courage.	
Materials	Heavy paper, poster paints, brushes, water containers, paint pans, drop cloths, smocks, heavy tape	

Create a classroom mural about courage. The mural should include characters and scenes from the stories in this theme.

1 Work together to plan your mural. Think about the following:

- Which characters would you like to include?
- Which scenes would you like to include?
- What images would best represent these characters and scenes?
- Will the images connect in some way?

2 Sketch a rough design for the mural. Divide the mural into sections that small groups can work on.

3 Create the mural sections, using large sheets of heavy paper and poster paints.

4 Put the pieces of the mural together and display it in the classroom.

Consider copying and laminating these activities for use in centers.

Character Letters

Whole Class or Groups	🕐 20-minute segments over 2 days
Objective	Write a letter from one theme character to another.

Write a letter from one theme character to another. The letter should include details about the character's courageous act.

1 **Review the characteristics** of a friendly letter.

2 **Think about the different characters** you have read about in this theme.

3 **Choose one theme character as the "writer"** of your letter. Also decide to whom the letter will be written.

4 **Write the letter.**
- Describe events that happened to the character in the story.
- Remember to use the personal pronouns *I, me,* and *my,* and to include a greeting and signature.
- Tell how the character felt about the events.
- Include information that the character *reading* the letter would be interested in.

5 **Read your letter** to the class or to a small group, but do not read the signature. Have listeners guess whom the letter is from.

Class Hero Profiles

Whole Class or Groups	🕐 20-minute segments over 2 days
Objective	Create profiles for theme characters.
Materials	Paper, pens and pencils, markers, and colored pencils

Create a hero profile for a character in the theme. The profile will tell about the character and describe what makes him or her a hero.

1 **Choose a character** from the theme to profile.

2 **Write two or three reasons** why you consider this character a hero. Think about
- the character's accomplishments
- how he or she showed courage
- reasons why this person should be admired

3 **Include other information** in your profile, such as the character's name and age.

4 **Draw a picture** to go with your written description.

5 **Use your profiles to create a Hero Portfolio** that includes all the profiles that you and your classmates created.

Hero: Brian Robeson
Story: *Hatchet*
Age: 13
Accomplishments:

Independent Activities

THEME CONNECTIONS: Leveled Books

While you work with small groups, students can choose from a wealth of books to complete these activities.

Leveled Readers . . .

for *Hatchet*
Fear of White Water
River of No Return
Weathering the Storm
An Unexpected Hero

for *Passage to Freedom*
Corrie's Important Decision
Corrie's Secret
Cesar Chavez
The Story of Oskar Schindler

for *Climb or Die*
Double Trouble
I Double Dare You
Underground Rescue
Hurricane Music

for *The True Confessions of Charlotte Doyle*
Yao's Wild Ride
Riding with the Vaqueros
Johnny Kelley's Tale
Hannah Brown, Union Army Spy

Leveled Theme Paperbacks

The Little Ships
Small Steps
Shipwreck at the Bottom of the World

Vocabulary Readers

Lost in the Wilderness!
Fly Away, Children
On Top of The World
Voyage of the Fram

Leveled Bibliography

pages 23E–23F

Character Interviews

👥 Pairs	🕐 30 minutes	
Objective	Role-play an interview.	
Materials	Index cards	

Work with a partner. Choose a character from any book you have both read and would like to interview. To refresh your memory about the character, you may want to skim the story and take notes about the character.

Decide who will role-play the character and who will role-play the interviewer. Together, come up with a list of possible interview questions. Think about what information you would like to know about the character, such as

- age
- place of birth
- favorite things
- how he or she felt when faced with a challenge
- tips on how to be courageous

After you write your questions, have the person who is playing the character think of some possible answers. Then, role-play the interview for the class or for the small group.

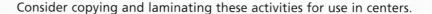

Consider copying and laminating these activities for use in centers.

Courage Tours

👤 Singles	🕐 30 minutes
Objective	Create a travel brochure.
Materials	Markers, colored pencils, magazines, scissors, glue, reference sources

Choose a setting from one of the books you have read that you would like to visit. Look at the pictures or illustrations from the book and reread any sections that describe the setting. Use a reference source to find facts about this setting.

Then create a travel brochure that tells about the place and the acts of courage that occurred there. As you design your brochure, think about

- people who have lived there
- important events that took place there
- things to see and do
- how to get there

Draw the pictures for your brochure, or cut and paste them from magazines. Display the finished brochures in the classroom.

Write a Sequel

👥 Pairs	🕐 30 minutes
Objective	Write the next scene for a leveled book.

With a partner, choose a book you both read and enjoyed. Work together to brainstorm what might have happened next in the book if it had continued.

Plan out a possible next scene for the book. Think about

- what the next event might realistically be
- how the characters would act
- where and when the new scene would take place

Write the new scene with your partner. You may also want to illustrate it. Then share your sequel with a small group or with the class.

Rafael's mother had said, yes, he could have the kitten but on the condition that he had to take full responsibility for it.

Preparing for Tests

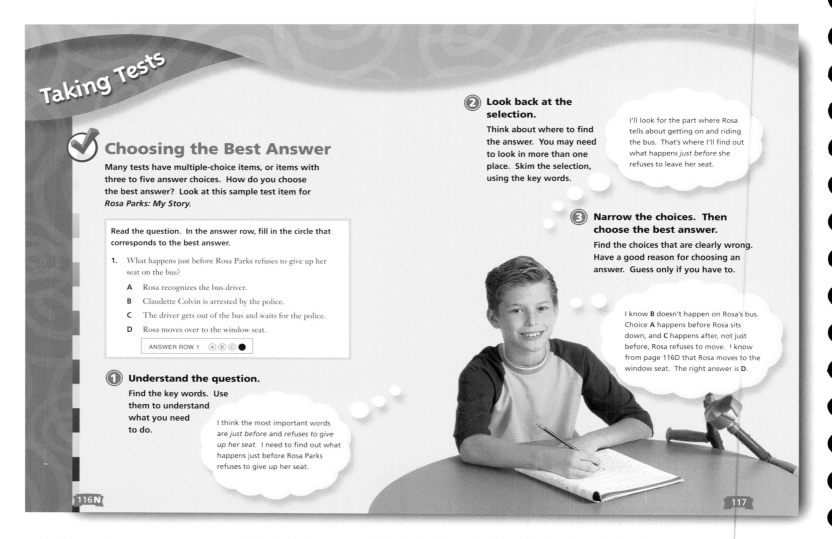

Taking Tests

✓ Choosing the Best Answer

Many tests have multiple-choice items, or items with three to five answer choices. How do you choose the best answer? Look at this sample test item for *Rosa Parks: My Story.*

Read the question. In the answer row, fill in the circle that corresponds to the best answer.

1. What happens just before Rosa Parks refuses to give up her seat on the bus?

   A   Rosa recognizes the bus driver.
   B   Claudette Colvin is arrested by the police.
   C   The driver gets out of the bus and waits for the police.
   D   Rosa moves over to the window seat.

   ANSWER ROW 1   Ⓐ Ⓑ Ⓒ ●

①   Understand the question.

Find the key words. Use them to understand what you need to do.

I think the most important words are just before and refuses to give up her seat. I need to find out what happens just before Rosa Parks refuses to give up her seat.

②   Look back at the selection.

Think about where to find the answer. You may need to look in more than one place. Skim the selection, using the key words.

I'll look for the part where Rosa tells about getting on and riding the bus. That's where I'll find out what happens just before she refuses to leave her seat.

③   Narrow the choices. Then choose the best answer.

Find the choices that are clearly wrong. Have a good reason for choosing an answer. Guess only if you have to.

I know B doesn't happen on Rosa's bus. Choice A happens before Rosa sits down, and C happens after, not just before, Rosa refuses to move. I know from page 116D that Rosa moves to the window seat. The right answer is D.

116N   117

THEME	STRATEGY
► 1	**Choosing the Best Answer**
2	**Filling in the Blank**
3	**Writing a Personal Response**
4	**Vocabulary Items**
5	**Writing an Answer to a Question**
6	**Writing a Persuasive Essay**

Introduce the Strategy

Taking Tests provides instruction and practice in different test formats. It will help you prepare your students for the **Theme Skills Test** and the **Integrated Theme Test,** as well as state and national standardized tests.

- Tell students that they will learn strategies that will help them do well on tests.

- Explain that Anthology pages 116N and 117 show the steps for answering multiple-choice questions.

- Have different volunteers read each step and each thought balloon aloud.

- Explain that students will be learning more about each of these steps.

Teach the Strategy

 Understand the Question.

Display Transparency 1–40 and model Step 1.

- Have a volunteer read aloud Step 1. Tell students that they will learn more about this one step.
- Explain that both questions are based on *Rosa Parks: My Story* on Anthology pages 116B–116G.
- Model using the step to understand Question 1.

Think Aloud *First, I will circle the key words in Question 1 that tell whom or what the question is asking about. I will circle* bus driver James Blake *and* Rosa Parks. *Next, I will circle the key words that tell what the question is asking me to do. I will circle* Why, told, *and* give up her seat. *Finally, I will ask myself what I need to do. I need to choose the answer that tells why the bus driver told Rosa Parks to give up her seat on the bus.*

Complete Transparency 1–40, using Step 1.

 Look Back at the Selection.

Display Transparency 1–41 and model Step 2.

- Have a volunteer read aloud Step 2. Tell students that they will learn more about this one step.
- Model using the step to find details in *Rosa Parks: My Story* that will help answer Question 1.

Think Aloud *First, I will decide where I might find the answer. Rosa Parks tells about the events of that day in the order in which they happened, so I'll look for the pages that tell what happened when the bus driver told her to give up her seat. What key words and ideas can I use to find the answer? I'll skim for* seats, move, *and* give up. *I know the bus driver told her to do this because he was white and she was black, so I'll skim for* white *and* black *also.*

On page 116D, paragraph 5, Rosa Parks says that several white people got on the bus but one was left standing. In the same paragraph, she describes how the driver told her and some other African Americans to give up their seats. These clues should help me choose the best answer.

Complete Transparency 1–41, using Step 2.

Turn the page to teach the Strategy Step 3.

Transparency 1–40

Choosing the Best Answer

Step 1: Understand the Question.
- Find the key words.
- Use them to understand what you need to do.

Use Step 1 to understand each of these questions about *Rosa Parks: My Story*.

1. Why did the bus driver James Blake tell Rosa Parks to give up her seat on the bus?
   Use the Think Aloud on Teacher's Edition page M29 to model using Step 1 to understand this question.
2. **Connecting/Comparing** When Rosa Parks was asked to give up her seat, she made a decision not to obey. In *Passage to Freedom*, Chiune Sugihara also made a decision to help the refugees. What is different about the way these decisions were made?
   - Key words: *Rosa Parks; Chiune Sugihara, different; decisions*
   - What to do: find important details that show differences between these decisions

TRANSPARENCY 1–40
TEACHER'S EDITION PAGE M29

Transparency 1–41

Choosing the Best Answer

Step 2: Look Back at the Selection.
- Think about where to find the answer. You may need to look in more than one place.
- Skim the selection, using the key words.

Use Step 2 to decide where you will find the answer to each of these questions in *Rosa Parks: My Story*.

1. Why did the bus driver James Blake tell Rosa Parks to give up her seat on the bus?
   Use the Think Aloud on Teacher's Edition page M29 to model using Step 2 to decide where to find the answer to this question.
2. **Connecting/Comparing** When Rosa Parks was asked to give up her seat, she made a decision not to obey. In *Passage to Freedom*, Chiune Sugihara also made a decision to help the refugees. What is different about the way these decisions were made?
   - Where to find the answer: Will need to look in more than one place
   - Places in *Passage to Freedom*: pp. 56–57: As the crowd gathers, Mr. Sugihara learns that his government will not help; p. 58: For the third time, the Japanese government refuses to help, so Mr. Sugihara calls his family together; p. 59: With his family's help, Mr. Sugihara makes a decision; Places in *Rosa Parks: My Story*, p. 116D: Rosa explains that she did not plan to get arrested; p. 116E: On her own, Rosa decides that she is willing to be arrested.

TRANSPARENCY 1–41
TEACHER'S EDITION PAGE M29

Transparency 1–42

Choosing the Best Answer

COURAGE
Monitoring Student Progress
Taking Tests Choosing the Best Answer

ANNOTATED VERSION

Step 3: Narrow the Choices. Then Choose the Best Answer.
• Find the choices that are clearly wrong.
• Have a good reason for choosing an answer. Guess only if you have to.

Use Step 3 to choose the best answer to each of these questions.

1. Why did the bus driver James Blake tell Rosa Parks to give up her seat on the bus?
   A African Americans were not allowed to ride buses.
   B The driver wanted all white riders to have a seat.
   C The people standing were tired and needed to sit down.
   D Rosa Parks was sitting in the white section.

   Use the Think Aloud on Teacher's Edition page M30 to model using Step 3 to choose the best answer to this question.

2. **Connecting/Comparing** When Rosa Parks was asked to give up her seat, she made a decision not to obey. In *Passage to Freedom*, Chiune Sugihara also made a decision to help the refugees. What is different about the way these decisions were made?
   A Rosa Parks made her decision without asking others for advice.
   B Chiune Sugihara acted alone in deciding what to do.
   C Other people pressured Rosa not to give up her seat.
   D Chiune Sugihara was given permission to do what he thought was right.

   • **Wrong answers:** B because Sugihara asks his family for advice; C because no one pressured Parks not to obey; D because Sugihara was not given permission
   • **Right answer:** A because Parks decided on her own to refuse to give up her seat

TRANSPARENCY 1–42
TEACHER'S EDITION PAGE M30

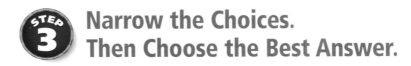

Narrow the Choices. Then Choose the Best Answer.

STEP 3

Display Transparency 1–42 and model Step 3.

• Have a volunteer read aloud Step 3. Tell students that they will learn more about this one step.

• Model how to narrow the answer choices and then choose the best answer for Question 1.

Think Aloud *I will start by narrowing the choices. Which answers are obviously wrong? I know A is wrong because Rosa Parks was an African American and she was allowed to ride the bus. I know C is wrong because the selection does not say that the people standing were tired and needed to sit down.*

Choices B and D are left. I can guess, but I want to be sure. Rosa Parks and the others were sitting in the front seats of the black section, so D is wrong. The driver told Rosa Parks and the other African Americans to give up their seats after whites boarded the bus. B must be right. Let me make sure. The driver asked for seats after noticing a white man standing. Yes, B is the best answer. He wanted all white riders to have a seat.

Complete Transparency 1–42, using Step 3.

English Language Learners

Review in detail any test-specific language that your students might not understand.

• Many tests use essentially the same direction lines every year.

• Other supporting material, such as a list of criteria for answering open-response questions, is often quite similar from year to year.

Using published samples, make sure that students understand as much of this language as possible. They will be less anxious and more focused if they are confident that they understand what is expected of them.

Apply the Strategy

Multiple-Choice Test Practice

Remind students to mark answers carefully.

- Make sure that you mark your answer in the correct place. Be especially careful if you have to mark your answer at the bottom of a page or on a separate answer sheet.

- Be careful to fill in the answer bubble completely.

- When you change an answer, be sure to erase it completely.

Discuss how to check answers.

- Take a short break before checking answers. Stretch, stare out the window, or close your eyes and relax for a minute.

- Focus on the questions that gave you trouble. Don't check answers that you feel confident about.

- When you check an answer, try to use a different strategy to find the answer than you did the first time.

Assign Practice Book pages 81 and 82.

- Tell students that these multiple-choice questions are based on *Making a Difference* on Anthology pages 116H–116N.

- Emphasize that students should use all three steps to choose the best answer for each question.

- Point out the answer box at the bottom of each Practice Book page. Remind students that this is where they are supposed to mark their answers.

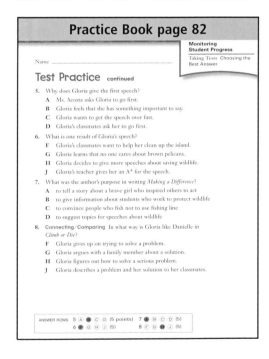

Practice Book page 81

Monitoring Student Progress
Taking Tests Choosing the Best Answer

Name

Test Practice

Use the three steps you've learned to choose the best answer for these questions about *Making a Difference*. Fill in the circle for the best answer in the answer row at the bottom of the page.

1. What is the main idea of *Making a Difference*?
   A A girl has a picnic on her favorite island.
   B A girl inspires her classmates with a speech.
   C A girl helps her sister free a pelican.
   D A girl fears speaking in front of others.

2. Where does the first part of *Making a Difference* take place?
   F on an island   H in a classroom
   G in a boat   J near a picnic table

3. Why do you think the pelican lunges at Elena but not at Gloria?
   A Elena walks loudly but Gloria walks quietly.
   B Elena tries to take the string off the bird while Gloria takes the string off the roots.
   C Elena screams "Ay!" but Gloria speaks softly.
   D Elena accidentally hits the bird with a stick, but Gloria strokes its head.

4. **Connecting/Comparing** Think about *Making a Difference* and *Hatchet*. In what way are Gloria and Brian alike?
   F Both work with others to improve the environment.
   G Both help others by their actions.
   H Both are stranded in the wilderness.
   J Both bravely face their fears.

ANSWER ROWS 1 Ⓐ ● Ⓒ Ⓓ (5 points) 3 Ⓐ ● Ⓒ Ⓓ (5)
             2 ● Ⓖ Ⓗ Ⓙ (5)   4 Ⓕ Ⓖ Ⓗ ● (5)

Continue on page 82.

Practice Book page 82

Monitoring Student Progress
Taking Tests Choosing the Best Answer

Name

Test Practice continued

5. Why does Gloria give the first speech?
   A Ms. Acosta asks Gloria to go first.
   B Gloria feels that she has something important to say.
   C Gloria wants to get the speech over fast.
   D Gloria's classmates ask her to go first.

6. What is one result of Gloria's speech?
   F Gloria's classmates want to help her clean up the island.
   G Gloria learns that no one cares about brown pelicans.
   H Gloria decides to give more speeches about saving wildlife.
   J Gloria's teacher gives her an A+ for the speech.

7. What was the author's purpose in writing *Making a Difference*?
   A to tell a story about a brave girl who inspired others to act
   B to give information about students who work to protect wildlife
   C to convince people who fish not to use fishing line
   D to suggest topics for speeches about wildlife

8. **Connecting/Comparing** In what way is Gloria like Danielle in *Climb or Die*?
   F Gloria gives up on trying to solve a problem.
   G Gloria argues with a family member about a solution.
   H Gloria figures out how to solve a serious problem.
   J Gloria describes a problem and her solution to her classmates.

ANSWER ROWS 5 Ⓐ ● Ⓒ Ⓓ (5 points) 7 ● Ⓑ Ⓒ Ⓓ (5)
             6 ● Ⓖ Ⓗ Ⓙ (5)   8 Ⓕ Ⓖ ● Ⓙ (5)

Additional Resources

Teacher's Assessment Handbook

Suggests more strategies for preparing students for standardized tests

 **SKILL REVIEW:**
Comprehension

Noting Details

Review the purpose of noting details.

• Details can explain story events and characters' feelings.

• Details can help readers understand characters' motives.

Model using details to identify a character's motives.

• Read aloud Anthology page 116J. Think aloud about Gloria's motives for unwinding the string from the roots.

Think Aloud *Gloria feels the bird should be free. She sees that trying to get the string off the bird would be too dangerous. She realizes that if the other end were free, the bird might escape on its own.*

Have students use details to identify a character's motives.

• Have students read the last four paragraphs on Anthology page 116K.

• Ask them to use the details to explain how Gloria feels and why she volunteered to speak first.

Practice Book page 83

Monitoring
Student Progress

Comprehension Skill
Making Judgments

Name _____

What Do You Think?

Read the details below about Rosa Parks and the important actions she took. Then answer the questions.

• Rosa Parks didn't join those who took a petition to the bus company and city officials.
• She didn't want to ask anyone for favors.
• She made decisions herself, as an individual.
• She didn't sit in the bus seat with the intention of getting arrested.
• She remained in the bus seat because she was tired of giving in.

Answers will vary. Sample responses shown.

1. What does her decision not to give up her seat on the bus tell you about Rosa Parks? Make three judgments about Rosa Parks' personality.
She wanted to accomplish things as a result of her own actions rather than
through favors from other people. (2 points)
She is an independent thinker. (2)

She is willing to stand up for things she believes in. (2)

2. Explain why you believe your judgements about Rosa Parks to be true. Use details from the selection.
Rosa Parks thought that the busing situation was unjust. She didn't think that
the way other people were trying to change it made sense. When she found
herself in a situation that could lead to change, she did not back away from it. (6)

Making Judgments

Review making judgments.

• A judgment is an opinion based on story details and a reader's personal experiences and values.

• Good readers try to make sound judgments about a character's actions, personality, and values.

Model making a judgment about a character's actions.

• Recall with students the main events of *Climb or Die.* Then read aloud Anthology page 86.

• Model making a judgment about Jake's personality.

Think Aloud *Despite the dangerous challenges Jake and Danielle face, the first thing he does when the two finally find help is make a joke. I think that Jake has a good sense of humor.*

Have students make judgments about a character's actions.

• Assign **Practice Book** page 83.

Sequence of Events

Review sequence of events.

- The time order in which story events happen is the sequence.

- Words such as *then, after,* and *that* signal sequential order.

- Words such as *while* and *during* signal events happening at the same time.

Model identifying sequence of events.

- Read aloud the last two paragraphs on Anthology page 36 (ending on page 37). Think aloud as you reconstruct the sequence.

Think Aloud *Brian is outside the cave. The word* when *shows that he's thinking about events that have happened previously. The word* now *in the same sentence signals that his thoughts have returned to the present.*

Have students identify sequence of events.

- Ask students to read the end of *Making a Difference* on Anthology page 116L.

- Have partners identify the sequence of events, along with any words that signal time. (as, then, as)

Predicting Outcomes

Review predicting outcomes.

- Readers make predictions about what will happen in a story based on story details and their personal knowledge.

- Readers use subsequent story events to confirm their predictions, revise them, or make new predictions.

Model predicting outcomes in different situations.

- Recall with students the events described in *Hatchet*.

- Make a prediction about how Brian would react to other challenges he might face in the wilderness. Explain the details and personal knowledge on which your prediction is based.

Have students predict outcomes in different situations.

- Assign **Practice Book** page 84.

Practice Book page 84

Monitoring Student Progress
Comprehension Skill
Predicting Outcomes

Name _____

What Would They Do If...?

Read each situation below and answer the questions that follow it. Look in the Anthology if you need help remembering details.

Situation 1: Think about *Making a Difference* on Anthology pages 116H–116L. Imagine that Gloria finds out that a seal at a nearby beach was injured after it swallowed the type of plastic holder that holds six cans of soft-drinks.
Answers will vary. Samples shown.

1. How do you predict Gloria might react?
   Gloria will try to convince her friends and others to clean up the beach. **(2 points)**

2. What story details helped you make this prediction?
   Gloria responded to her encounter with the pelican by giving a speech urging others to help protect wildlife. **(2)**

3. What personal knowledge or experiences helped you with your prediction?
   People who try to protect certain animals usually care about all sorts of wildlife. **(2)**

Situation 2: Think about *Climb or Die* on Anthology pages 74–86. Imagine that Danielle and Jake discover that the men at the weather station cannot help them and that the nearest town is on the other side of Mount Remington.

4. What do you predict Jake and Danielle might do?
   Jake and Danielle will gather useful materials from the weather station and then head off for the town. **(2)**

5. What story details helped you make this prediction?
   Jake and Danielle were resourceful and determined in their efforts to get to the weather station. **(2)**

6. What personal knowledge or experiences helped you with your prediction?
   People like Jake and Danielle do not give up when people they care about need help. **(2)**

Options

SKILL REVIEW:
Structural Analysis/Vocabulary

OBJECTIVES

Students review how to
- decode words with the suffixes *-ful*, *-less*, and *-ly*
- identify syllable patterns within words
- decode words with the prefixes *un-* and *re-*
- decode possessives and contractions

Suffixes

Review the suffixes *-ful*, *-less*, and *-ly*.

- A suffix comes after a base word and adds meaning to it.
- The suffix *-ful* means "full of" or "characterized by."
- The suffix *-less* means "without."
- The suffix *-ly* often means "like" or "in a way that is."

Model decoding a word with *-ful*.

- Display *We heard the <u>delightful</u> news.*

Think Aloud *I recognize the base word* delight. *I see the suffix* -ful, *which means "full of." The word is* delightful, *meaning "full of delight." That makes sense with* news.

Have partners decode words.

- Display *helpless, wonderful, jealously, hurriedly, sorrowful.*
- Have partners take turns decoding the words and explaining their meanings.

Syllabication

Review dividing words into syllables.

- A syllable is a word part containing one vowel sound.
- Words with a VCCV pattern are often divided between the two consonants. Words with a VCV pattern are often divided after the consonant if the first vowel sound is short and before the consonant if the first vowel sound is long.
- When two or more consonants blend to form one sound, the consonants stay together.

Model dividing a word into syllables.

- Display *argument* and model dividing it into syllables.

Think Aloud *I see the VCCV pattern, so I will divide between* r *and* g. *Then I see the VCV pattern. I'll try the long sound, dividing after the vowel* u: AHR-gyoo-muhnt. *That sounds right.*

Have students divide words into syllables.

- Assign **Practice Book** page 85.

Practice Book page 85

Monitoring
Student Progress
Structural Analysis
Syllabication

Name _____

Word Division Decision

Read each sentence. Rewrite each underlined word with slashes to divide the syllables.

1. The <u>pilot</u> kept the little plane on a <u>steady</u> course.
   pi | lot, stead | y **(2 points)**

2. The wind <u>buffeted</u> the plane a bit as it dropped in <u>altitude</u>.
   buf | fet | ed, al | ti | tude **(2)**

3. Annie had <u>taken</u> the seat <u>closest</u> to the window.
   tak | en, clos | est **(2)**

4. She watched as seven brown pelicans <u>glided</u> below with <u>outspread</u> wings.
   glid | ed, out | spread **(2)**

5. The <u>ungainly</u> birds flew in a V <u>formation</u>.
   un | gain | ly, for | ma | tion **(2)**

6. The birds quickly <u>vanished</u> in the <u>distance</u>.
   van | ished, dis | tance **(2)**

7. Annie <u>wondered</u> how far they might <u>travel</u>.
   won | dered, trav | el **(2)**

8. Then she noticed a <u>passenger</u> ship on the <u>horizon</u>.
   pas | sen | ger, ho | ri | zon **(2)**

9. Annie's <u>secret</u> dream was to become a cruise ship <u>captain</u>.
   se | cret, cap | tain **(2)**

Prefixes

Review the prefixes *un-* and *re-*.

- A prefix is added before a base word and adds to its meaning.
- The prefix *un-* means "not."
- The prefix *re-* means "again" or "back."

Model decoding a word with the prefix *re-*.

- Display <u>Remind</u> me to study tonight.
- Model decoding *remind*.

Think Aloud *The first part of the word might be the prefix* re-. *The rest of the word looks like the base word* mind. Re- *means "again" or "back." I think the word is* remind, *meaning "bring to mind again." It makes sense in the sentence.*

Have partners decode words.

- Display *undo, unhappy, unable, recall, unfamiliar, untied, reappear, reexamine.*
- Have partners take turns decoding the words and explaining their meanings.

Possessives and Contractions

Review possessives and contractions.

- To form the possessive of a singular noun or plural noun that does not end in *s*, add *'s: officer's hat, Luis's corner, children's chairs.*
- To form the possessive of a plural noun that ends in *s*, add only an apostrophe: *two weeks' time.*
- In contractions, the apostrophe stands for missing letters: *you are—you're; I will—I'll.*

Model decoding possessives and contractions.

- Display <u>They're</u> buying a <u>boy's</u> jacket.
- Explain that *They're* is the contraction for *They* and *are*, and *boy's* is a possessive indicating that the jacket is for a boy.

Have students decode words.

- Display these phrases: <u>June's</u> prize; <u>she's</u> the winner; the <u>kings'</u> vacation; <u>you're</u> kidding; <u>men's</u> clothing; <u>foxes'</u> tracks.
- Have students decode the underlined words.

 **SKILL REVIEW:**
Vocabulary

OBJECTIVES

Students review how to
- use context to determine meaning
- use dictionary guide words
- use parts of a dictionary entry
- recognize word families

Using Context

Review using context to determine meaning.

- The words and sentences around a word are its *context*.
- A word's meaning can often be inferred from its context.

Model using context to determine meaning.

- Display *Tears filled Jake's eyes so fast that his <u>vision</u> went blurry.*

  Think Aloud *This sentence tells me that Jake is crying and explains what happens as a result of this crying.* Blurry *means "not clear."* With tears in his eyes, Jake can't see clearly. So vision *must mean "ability to see."*

Have students use context to determine meaning.

- Display *To <u>ascend</u> the icy cliff, they had to climb a few slow steps at a time. They looked for a truck but saw no <u>vehicles</u> on the road.*
- Have partners use context to infer the meanings of the under-lined words.

Dictionary Guide Words

Review guide words.

- The words defined in a dictionary are called *entry words*.
- Entry words are listed in the dictionary in alphabetical order.
- The first and last entry words on a dictionary page also appear at the top of the page and are called *guide words*.

Model using guide words.

- Display *disgraceful/dislodge* and *disloyal/dispense*. Tell students that these are the guide words on two dictionary pages.
- Demonstrate how to determine on which page the entry word *dishonest* would appear.

Have students use guide words.

- Display the pairs *combustion/comic; fortify/foul; helm/hence.*
- Have students identify which of these entry words could be found between each pair: *commence, combination, comrade; foster, fortunate, format; helmet, henchman, hemline.*

Parts of a Dictionary Entry

Review the parts of a dictionary entry.

- Display a dictionary entry and review the information provided by each part: entry word, pronunciation, part of speech, definition(s), adjectival and adverbial forms, verb forms, and sample sentences.

- Point out that the most common meaning of a word is listed first.

Model using a dictionary entry.

- Display *A* <u>knot</u> *of reporters waited for the president.*

- Model finding the correct definition of *knot* in a dictionary.

Think Aloud *The entry for* knot *has several meanings. One, "an interlocking thread, cord, or hair," doesn't make sense in the sentence. Other meanings also have to do with string or cord, so they can't be right. One meaning is "a tight cluster of people." That meaning makes sense in the sentence.*

Have students use dictionary entries.

- Assign **Practice Book** page 86.

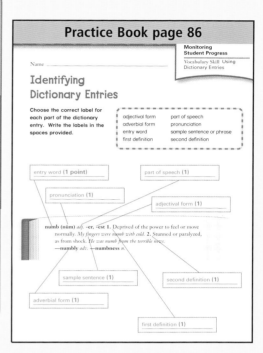

Practice Book page 86

Monitoring Student Progress
Vocabulary Skill Using Dictionary Entries

Name _____

Identifying Dictionary Entries

Choose the correct label for each part of the dictionary entry. Write the labels in the spaces provided.

adjectival form · part of speech
adverbial form · pronunciation
entry word · sample sentence or phrase
first definition · second definition

entry word (1 point) · part of speech (1)
pronunciation (1)
adjectival form (1)

numb (nŭm) *adj.* **-er, -est 1.** Deprived of the power to feel or move normally. *My fingers were numb with cold.* **2.** Stunned or paralyzed, as from shock. *He was numb from the terrible news.* **—numbly** *adv.* **—numbness** *n.*

sample sentence (1) · second definition (1)
adverbial form (1)
first definition (1)

Word Families

Review word families.

- A *word family* is a group of words related in spelling and meaning.

- The members of a word family share a base word or root.

- Words in a family have similar spellings but may have different vowel sounds.

Model identifying word families.

- Display and pronounce *revise* and *revision*.

- Explain that they share the root *vis* but have different vowel sounds for the stressed *i*.

- Display *visual, invisible, vision,* underlining the root *vis*. Explain that it comes from the Latin word meaning "seen." Discuss how all these words relate to seeing.

Have students identify word families.

- Display *invited, noble, human, nobility, invitation, humanity.*

- Have partners match the word family members and pronounce and define each.

Options
SKILL REVIEW: Spelling

OBJECTIVES

Students review

- words with short vowel patterns
- words with long vowel patterns
- words with less common patterns for long and short vowel sounds
- words that have the /ou/, /ōō/, /ô/, and /oi/ sounds

SPELLING WORDS

Basic

wince	craft
league	throne
strive	rhythm
routine	vault
prompt	avoid
strain	depth
meant	roam
foul	reply
hoist	stout
naughty	squawk
bulk	gaze
theme	sleeve
mute	ravine
sponge	sought
bloom	annoy

Challenge

cobweb	endeavor
tepid	oxygen
refugee	nauseous
coax	bountiful
nylon	heirloom

DAY 1 — SHORT VOWELS

Pretest Use the Day 5 sentences.

Review words with short vowels.

- Display *brass*, *else*, *cliff*, *bomb*, and *scrub*.
- Read each word aloud, emphasizing the short vowel sound.
- Underline the letter in each word that spells the short vowel sound.

Have students spell words with short vowels.

- Display and have students copy *w__nce*, *b__lk*, *cr__ft*, *pr__mpt*, and *d__pth*.
- Say *wince*, *bulk*, *craft*, *prompt*, and *depth*. Have students write the correct letter to complete each word.
- Follow the same procedure for the Challenge Words *cobweb* and *tepid*.

Practice/Homework Assign **Practice Book** page 283.

DAY 2 — LONG VOWELS

Review words with long vowel sounds.

- Display *fade* and *trait* and say each word aloud.
- Point out the ways of spelling /ā/: a-consonant-e and *ai*.
- Repeat the procedure for /ē/: *grease*, *theme*, *greet*.
- Repeat for /ī/: *file*.
- Repeat for /ō/: *code*, *toast*.
- Repeat for /ū/: *fume*.

Have students identify words with long vowel sounds.

- Display *throne*, *league*, *mute*, *gaze*, *sleeve*, *roam*, *strain*, *strive*, and *theme*.
- Have students list the words with /ā/ and underline the letters in each that make the long a sound.
- Repeat the procedure for /ē/, /ī/, /ō/, and /ū/.

Practice/Homework Assign **Practice Book** page 87.

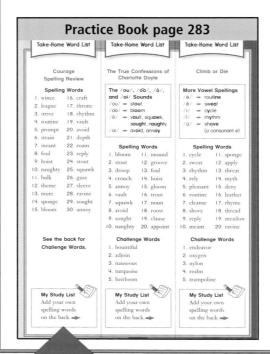

Practice Book page 283

Practice Book page 87

Take-Home Word List

DAY 3 — MORE VOWEL SPELLINGS

Review less common spellings for long and short vowel sounds.

- Display *routine, apply, thread, myth,* and *shove.* Read each word aloud.
- Point out the spelling for /ē/ in *routine:* *i*-consonant-*e.*
- Repeat the procedure for /ī/ in *apply:* *y.*
- Repeat for /ĕ/ in *thread,* /ĭ/ in *myth,* and /ŭ/ in *shove.*

Have students spell words with less common spellings for long and short vowel sounds.

- Display *m__nt, rh__thm, rout____, sp__nge, rav____,* and *repl__.*
- Say aloud *meant, rhythm, routine, sponge, ravine,* and *reply.*
- Have students write each word, adding the correct spellings for the long and short vowel sounds.

Practice/Homework Assign **Practice Book** page 88.

Practice Book page 88

Courage:
Theme 1 Wrap-Up
Spelling Review

Name _____

Spelling Spree

Puzzle Play Write a Spelling Word to fit each clue.

Spelling Words
1. vault
2. theme
3. sleeve
4. squawk
5. meant
6. throne
7. rhythm
8. stout
9. strain
10. hoist
11. sponge
12. bloom
13. naughty
14. annoy
15. gaze

1. a plant's flower — b l o o m (1 point)
2. a muscle injury — s t r a i n (1)
3. screech — s q u a w k (1)
4. a jacket's arm covering — s l e e v e (1)
5. a steady look — g a z e (1)
6. a recurring pattern of sound or movement — r h y t h m (1)
7. disobedient — n a u g h t y (1)

Now write the boxed letters in order. They will spell a mystery word that is a synonym for *courage.*

Mystery Word: b r a v e r y

Word Switch Write a Spelling Word to replace each underlined word or word group in these sentences.

8. The gold coins were kept in a locked storage area for valuables. vault (1)
9. The ruler's chair was inlaid with gems. throne (1)
10. Movers used a crane to haul up the piano to the top floor. hoist (1)
11. We discussed the subject of the book. theme (1)
12. I intended to give her my message, but I forgot. meant (1)
13. The ship was tied to the dock with strong and sturdy ropes. stout (1)
14. The fly's constant buzzing began to irritate me. annoy (1)
15. Please wipe off the table. sponge (1)

DAY 4 — /ou/, /o͞o/, /ô/, AND /oi/

Review words with /ou/, /o͞o/, /ô/, and /oi/.

- Display *mound* and *droop.* Say each word aloud.
- Point out the *ou* spelling for /ou/ and the *oo* spelling for /o͞o/.
- Display *naughty, clause, hawk,* and *sought.* Say each word aloud.
- Point out the various ways of spelling /ô/: *augh, au, aw, ough.*
- Display *annoy* and *hoist.* Say each word aloud.
- Point out the *oy* and *oi* spellings for /oi/.

Have students identify words with /ow/, /o͞o/, /ô/, and /oi/.

- Display *sought, annoy, stout, vault, avoid, squawk, foul, naughty, hoist,* and *bloom.*
- Have students write each word and underline the letters that spell the /ow/, /o͞o/, /ô/, or /oi/ sound.

Practice/Homework Assign **Practice Book** page 89.

Practice Book page 89

Courage:
Theme 1 Wrap-Up
Spelling Review

Name _____

Proofreading and Writing

Proofreading Circle the six misspelled Spelling Words in this letter to the editor. Then write each word correctly.

Spelling Words
1. bulk
2. mute
3. prompt
4. craft
5. league
6. avoid
7. roam
8. ravine
9. reply
10. foul
11. depth
12. wince
13. sought
14. sought
15. strive

As a usual (routine,) I don't write letters to newspapers. (The (bulk) of my writing is reserved for homework!) I must, though, tell the public about a very special person.

Last Saturday, the weather was really (fowle.) Since my baseball (leage) practice was canceled, I decided to test my new hiking rain gear. In the hills town, I slipped and fell into a deep gully. Gushing rainwater swept me along, and I was struck (muete) with terror! Suddenly, a stranger's arms grabbed me and began to hoist me to solid ground. I can never thank that person enough for my rescue. From now on, I will (stryve) to be as courageous aa he is!

1. routine (1)   3. foul (1)   5. mute (1)
2. bulk (1)   4. league (1)   6. strive (1)

Just the Opposite Write the Spelling Word that means almost the opposite of each word or words.

7. to grin — wince (1)   12. confront — avoid (1)
8. stand still — roam (1)   13. quiet — prompt (1)
9. found — sought (1)   14. lack of ability — craft (1)
10. hilltop — ravine (1)   15. to ask — reply (1)
11. width — depth (1)

Write an Interview Script On a separate sheet of paper, write the script of an interview with a real or imagined hero. Use the Spelling Review Words. Responses will vary. (5)

DAY 5 — TEST

Say each underlined word, read the sentence, and then repeat the word. Have students write only the underlined words.

Basic Words

1. Athletes **wince** if they **strain** a muscle.
2. Players in that **league** hit a lot of **foul** balls.
3. Tim **sought** to bother his sister by being **naughty**.
4. What is the **depth** of the **ravine**?
5. Visitors **gaze** at the **throne**.
6. Always **strive** to send a quick **reply**.
7. Do **stout** chickens **squawk** more often?
8. That **routine** will help you add **bulk** to your body.
9. When you **roam**, **avoid** steep canyons.
10. **Hoist** the gold into the **vault**.
11. The author **meant** the story to have an uplifting **theme**.
12. Please **mute** your instrument and follow the **rhythm**.
13. Use a **sponge** to wipe the chocolate off your **sleeve**.
14. Ed learned the **craft** of making a **bloom** into a corsage.
15. You will **annoy** her if you're not **prompt**.

Challenge Words

16. Nell brushed the **cobweb** off the **heirloom**.
17. If you feel **nauseous**, breathe some **oxygen**.
18. Ravindra could not **coax** the twins into the **tepid** water.
19. The official handed the **refugee** a **nylon** jacket.
20. As a reward for our **endeavor**, we received **bountiful** gifts.

SKILL REVIEW: Grammar

OBJECTIVES

Students review how to
- identify the four kinds of sentences
- identify complete and simple subjects and complete and simple predicates
- identify conjunctions and the words or sentences they join
- identify compound sentences
- identify complex sentences
- identify and correct fragments and run-on sentences
- identify common nouns
- identify and capitalize proper nouns
- identify singular and plural nouns

DAY 1 — KINDS OF SENTENCES

Review kinds of sentences and display the examples.

- A declarative sentence makes a statement and ends with a period: *Equality is an important principle.*
- An interrogative sentence asks a question and ends with a question mark: *What sparked the civil rights movement?*
- An imperative sentence gives a command or makes a request. It ends with a period. The subject *you* is understood: *Look at these photographs.*
- An exclamatory sentence shows excitement or strong feeling. It ends with an exclamation point: *What determination the demonstrators showed!*

Have students identify and write kinds of sentences.

- Assign **Practice Book** page 90.

Practice Book page 90

Name _____

Monitoring
Student Progress

Grammar Skill Kinds of
Sentences

Classifying and Rewriting Sentence Types

Write what kind of sentence each is—*declarative, interrogative, imperative,* or *exclamatory.*

1. Why was Rosa Parks arrested? interrogative **(1 point)**
2. She challenged an unfair law. declarative **(1)**
3. How courageous she was! exclamatory **(1)**
4. Make a timeline of the civil rights movement. imperative **(1)**

Read the sentences. Rewrite each as the sentence type indicated in parentheses. Use correct end punctuation.

5. Did Ms. Parks work in Montgomery, Alabama? (declarative)
Ms. Parks worked in Montgomery, Alabama. **(2)**

6. She was determined to eliminate segregation on city buses. (interrogative)
Was she determined to eliminate segregation on city buses? **(2)**

7. You should read this biography of Rosa Parks. (imperative)
Read this biography of Rosa Parks. **(2)**

8. Stories of heroism inspire me. (exclamatory)
Stories of heroism inspire me! **(2)**

DAY 2 — SUBJECTS/PREDICATES

Review subjects and predicates.

- The subject of a sentence tells whom or what the sentence is about.
- The complete subject includes all the words in the subject. The simple subject is the main word or words in the complete subject.
- The predicate tells what the subject does, is, has, or feels.
- The complete predicate includes all the words in the predicate. The simple predicate is the main word or words in the complete predicate. It is always a verb.

Identify subjects and predicates.

- Display *A small plane crashed in the wilderness.*
- Underline the complete subject, *A small plane.* Circle the simple subject, *plane.*
- Draw a vertical line after *plane* to separate the subject and predicate.
- Underline the complete predicate, *crashed in the wilderness.* Circle the simple predicate, *crashed.*

Have students identify subjects and predicates.

- Display *The pilot suffered a heart attack. Only the passenger survived the crash.*
- Have students identify the complete subject and simple subject in each sentence. (*The pilot, pilot; Only the passenger, passenger*)
- Then have students identify the complete predicate and simple predicate in each sentence. (*suffered a heart attack, suffered; survived the crash, survived*)

DAY 3 — LONGER SENTENCES

Review conjunctions and compound sentences.

- The words *and, or,* and *but* are conjunctions.

- A conjunction may be used to join words: *Gloria <u>and</u> Elena are sisters.*

- A conjunction may be used to join sentences: *Elena enjoys soccer, <u>but</u> Gloria dislikes it.*

- Use *and* to add information, *or* to give a choice, and *but* to contrast.

- Two related sentences may be combined into one compound sentence with a comma and the conjunction *and, but,* or *or: Gloria heard a noise, <u>but</u> Elena did not.*

Have students identify conjunctions and write compound sentences.

- Assign **Practice Book** page 91.

Practice Book page 91

Monitoring Student Progress
Grammar Skill Longer Sentences

Name _____

Identifying and Writing Conjunctions and Compound Sentences

Circle each conjunction in the sentences below. After each compound sentence, write *compound sentence.*

1. Birds try to avoid humans, but sometimes they need some human help.
   compound sentence **(2 points)**

2. Sometimes a bird will get entangled in string or wire.
   (1)

3. One helper must calm the bird, and the other must free it from the tangles.
   compound sentence **(1)**

Rewrite each pair of sentences as a compound sentence. Use correct end punctuation. Answers will vary.

4. My brother saw a baby bird. He did not touch it.
   My brother saw a baby bird, but he did not touch it. **(2)**

5. It was in a nest. Its mother was nowhere around.
   It was in a nest, and its mother was nowhere around. **(2)**

6. Soon the mother returned. We were glad we had left the baby bird alone.
   Soon the mother returned, and we were glad we had left the baby bird alone. **(2)**

DAY 4 — MORE SENTENCES

Review complex sentences, fragments, and run-on sentences.

- A clause is a group of words containing a subject and a predicate.

- An independent clause can stand by itself as a sentence. A subordinate clause cannot.

- A subordinate clause can be joined to an independent clause by a subordinating conjunction to form a complex sentence.

- A fragment lacks a subject or a predicate.

- A run-on is two or more sentences run together into one sentence.

Identify complex sentences, fragments, and run-on sentences.

- Display *The children went for help because the car crashed. Unless they reached the weather station. They climbed a mountain it was hard work.*

- Point out the complex sentence (The children went for help because the car crashed.), the subordinate clause (*because the car crashed*), and the subordinating conjunction (because).

- Identify the second group as a fragment and the third as a run-on.

Have students identify complex sentences, fragments, and run-ons.

- Display *The wind is getting stronger the temperature is dropping. If you slip, you'll fall. Unless you tie this rope to your belt.*

- Have students say which is a complex sentence (group 2), a fragment (group 3), and a run-on (group 1).

- Then have students correct the fragment and the run-on.

DAY 5 — KINDS OF NOUNS

Review common, proper, singular, and plural nouns.

- A common noun names any person, place, thing, or idea.

- A proper noun names a particular person, place, thing, or idea. It is always capitalized. In proper nouns of more than one word, each important word is capitalized.

- A singular noun names one person, place, thing, or idea.

- A plural noun names more than one person, place, thing, or idea.

- Add *-s* or *-es* to most singular nouns to form the plural. Use the spelling of the singular noun to decide how to form the plural.

- Some nouns have the same singular and plural forms.

- Some nouns are spelled differently in the plural.

Identify common, proper, singular, and plural nouns.

- Display this list: *woman, Rosa Parks, city, Montgomery.* Identify *woman* and *city* as common nouns and *Rosa Parks* and *Montgomery* as proper nouns.

- Identify *woman* and *city* as singular nouns. Write their plurals (*women, cities*), telling how each is formed. (*Women* is a special plural form; the *y* in *city* is changed to *i* and *-es* is added.)

Have students use common, proper, singular, and plural nouns.

- Have students write a paragraph about a brave person. Ask them to use and underline two of each of the following kinds of nouns: common, proper, singular, and plural.

WRITING

OBJECTIVES

Students review how to

- write instructions
- write a memo
- write a friendly letter
- write an opinion paragraph
- write a personal narrative

Instructions

👤 **Single**	🕐 **30 minutes**
Objective	Write instructions.

Several characters in this theme faced situations in which they had to give or follow directions. Being able to give or follow clear instructions can sometimes mean the difference between life or death.

Choose an event from this theme and write instructions to one or more of the characters, telling the characters how to do something that will be useful to them at that moment. Make sure your instructions

- explain how to do or make something
- are clear, complete, and easy to follow
- present each step in the correct order

Remember to use sequence words and phrases to help readers keep track of the order of steps.

Topic	
Step 1	Details
Step 2	Details
Step 3	Details

Memo

👤 **Single**	🕐 **30 minutes**
Objective	Write a memo.

In *Passage to Freedom,* officials of the Japanese government sent communications to their office in Lithuania. Companies and groups often use memos to communicate news and updates to their staff and members.

Choose an event from this theme involving a group, business, or public agency that might have been involved with the events of that selection. The memo should

- be addressed from one person to another in the same company, group, or organization
- be less formal and less personal than a letter
- *not* include a greeting, closing, or signature
- use the headings *To:, From:, Date:,* and *Subject:*

Remember to capitalize sentences and proper names and to use the appropriate end punctuation at the end of a sentence.

Consider copying and laminating these activities for use in centers.

WRITING

Friendly Letter

👤 Single	🕐 30 minutes
Objective	Write a friendly letter.

When family and friends find out about stirring events like the ones that took place in this theme, they might write letters to show their support and concern.

Write a friendly letter to one of the characters in this theme. Before you write,

- think about the events the character has experienced

In the letter, be sure to

- share news, ideas, or special experiences
- use informal language, as if you were speaking to the character
- include a heading, greeting, body, closing, and signature

Remember to use your own voice while writing to express your personality.

Dear Jake,
I was so impressed to hear that you and Danielle climbed that mountain!

Opinion Paragraph

👤 Single	🕐 45 minutes
Objective	Write an opinion paragraph.

Stories such as *The True Confessions of Charlotte Doyle* portray events that involve controversy. Many of the characters in this theme made decisions or took actions that others might not have agreed with.

Choose an action or decision made by one of the characters in this theme. Write an opinion paragraph expressing your personal feelings and thoughts about that action or choice.

- Tell what the character did or decided.
- Explain what you think or feel about it.
- Give reasons, details, and examples to explain why you think the way you do.

Remember to combine short, choppy sentences into longer sentences by using appositives.

Personal Narrative

👤 Single	🕐 45 minutes
Objective	Write a personal narrative.

When faced with new and challenging situations, people experience different feelings and thoughts. At one time, you have probably faced an unexpected occurrence or made an important decision on your own.

Write a personal narrative about a decision you made or situation you faced that challenged your courage.

- Begin with a question or attention-grabbing statement.
- Use first person in a voice that reflects your personality.
- Arrange the events in the order in which they happened.
- Include specific details and dialogue to bring the story to life.
- Tie up loose ends in a meaningful ending.

Remember to vary your sentence types, using statements, questions, commands, and exclamations.

Assessing Student Progress

Monitoring Student Progress

Preparing for Testing

Throughout the theme, your students have had opportunities to read and think critically, to connect and compare, and to practice and apply new and reviewed skills and reading strategies.

Monitoring Student Progress

For Theme 1, *Courage*, students have read the paired selections—*Rosa Parks: My Story* and *Making a Difference*—and made connections between these and other selections in the theme. They have practiced strategies for answering multiple-choice questions, and they have reviewed all the tested skills taught in this theme, as well as some tested skills taught in earlier themes. Your students are now ready to have their progress formally assessed in both theme assessments and standardized tests.

Testing Options

The **Integrated Theme Test** and the **Weekly Skills Test** are formal group assessments used to evaluate student performance on theme objectives. In addition to administering one or both of these tests, you may wish to assess students' oral reading fluency.

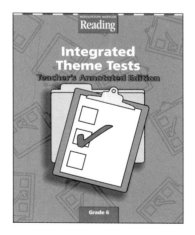

Integrated Theme Test

- Assesses students' progress as readers and writers in a format that reflects instruction
- Integrates reading and writing skills: comprehension strategies and skills, high-frequency words, spelling, grammar, and writing
- Includes authentic literary passages to test students' reading skills in context

Weekly Skills Test

- Assesses students' mastery of discrete reading and language arts skills taught in the week: comprehension skills, high-frequency words, spelling, grammar, writing, and information and study skills
- Consists of individual skill subtests, which can be administered separately
- **Theme Skills Tests** are also available.

Fluency Assessment

Oral reading fluency is a useful measure of a student's development of rapid automatic word recognition. Students who are on level in Grade 6 should be able to read, accurately and with expression, an appropriate level text at the approximate rates shown in the table below.

Early Grade 6	Mid-Grade 6	Late Grade 6
127–153 words correct per minute	140–167 words correct per minute	150–177 words correct per minute

- You can use the **Leveled Reading Passages Assessment Kit** or a **Leveled Reader** from this theme at the appropriate level for each student to assess fluency.

- For some students you may check their oral fluency rate three times during the year. If students are working below level, you might want to check their fluency rate more often. Students can also check their own fluency by timing themselves reading easier text.

- Consider decoding and comprehension, as well as reading rate, when evaluating students' reading development.

- For information on how to select appropriate text, administer fluency checks, and interpret results, see the **Teacher's Assessment Handbook,** pp. 25–28.

Technology

HOUGHTON MIFFLIN Assessment System

- **Instant Test Results** Use scan-and-score answer sheets for instant test results and diagnosis.

- **Prescriptions** Tailor instructions with prescriptions for differentiated instruction.

- **Reports** Generate detailed reports to track performance standards.

- **Testing Options** Include online delivery and plain-paper scanning.

- **Test Generator** Compatible with Houghton Mifflin's ExamView® Test Generator.

Using Multiple Measures

In addition to the tests mentioned on page M44, multiple measures might include the following:

- Observation Checklist from this theme
- Students' personal narrative from the Reading-Writing Workshop
- Other writing, projects, or artwork
- One or more items selected by the student

Student progress is best evaluated through multiple measures. Multiple measures of assessment can be collected in a portfolio. The portfolio provides a record of student progress over time and can be useful when conferencing with the student, parents, or other educators.

Turn the page to continue.

Using Assessment to Plan Instruction

You can use the results of theme assessments to determine individual students' needs for additional skill instruction and to modify instruction during the next theme. For more detail, see the test manuals or the **Teacher's Assessment Handbook**.

This chart shows Theme 1 resources for differentiating additional instruction. As you look ahead to Theme 2, you can plan to use the corresponding Theme 2 resources.

Differentiating Instruction

Assessment Shows	Use These Resources	
Difficulty with Comprehension **Emphasize** Oral comprehension, strategy development, story comprehension, vocabulary development	• Get Set for Reading CD-ROM • Reteaching: Comprehension, *Teacher's Edition,* pp. R8; R10; R12; R14 • Selection Summaries in *Teacher's Resource Blackline Masters,* pp. 21–24	• *Reader's Library Blackline Masters,* pp. 1A–48A • *Extra Support Handbook,* pp. 16–17, 22–23; 26–27, 32–33; 36–37, 42–43; 46–47, 52–53
Difficulty with Word Skills Structural Analysis Phonics Vocabulary **Emphasize** Word skills, phonics, reading for fluency, phonemic awareness	• Get Set for Reading CD-ROM • Reteaching: Structural Analysis, *Teacher's Edition,* pp. R16; R18; R20; R22 • *Extra Support Handbook,* pp. 14–15, 18–19; 24–25, 28–29; 34–35, 38–39; 44–45, 48–49	• *Handbook for English Language Learners,* pp. 18–19, 20, 22–24, 26; 28–29, 30, 32–34, 36; 38–39, 40, 42–44, 46; 48–49, 50, 52–54, 56 • Lexia Quick Phonics Assessment CD-ROM • Lexia Phonics CD-ROM: Intermediate Intervention
Difficulty with Fluency **Emphasize** Reading and rereading of independent level text, vocabulary development	• Leveled Bibliography, *Teacher's Edition,* pp. 23E–23F • Below Level **Theme Paperback** • Below Level **Leveled Readers**	• Leveled Readers: Below Level lesson, *Teacher's Edition,* pp. 47O; 71O; 93O; 115O
Difficulty with Writing **Emphasize** Complete sentences, combining sentences, choosing exact words	• *Handbook for English Language Learners,* pp. 27; 37; 47; 57 • Reteaching: Grammar Skills, *Teachers' Edition,* pp. R24–R31	• Improving Writing, *Teacher's Edition,* pp. 47J, 47L; 49E; 71J, 71L; 93J, 93L; 115J, 115L
Overall High Performance **Emphasize** Independent reading and writing, vocabulary development, critical thinking	• Challenge/Extension Activities: Comprehension, *Teacher's Edition,* pp. R9; R11; R13; R15 • Challenge/Extension Activities: Vocabulary, *Teacher's Edition,* pp. R17; R19; R21; R23 • Reading Assignment Cards, *Teacher's Resource Blackline Masters,* pp. 47–55	• Above Level **Theme Paperback** • Above Level **Leveled Readers** • Leveled Readers: Above Level lesson, *Teacher's Edition,* pp. 47Q; 71Q; 93Q; 115Q • Challenge Activity Masters, *Challenge Handbook,* CH1–1 to CH1–8

POETRY

LESSON OVERVIEW
Focus on Poetry

Literature

POETRY

Vocabulary Reader

1 **Background and Genre Vocabulary**

Nonfiction

◀ **2** **Main Selections**

3 **Write a Poem**

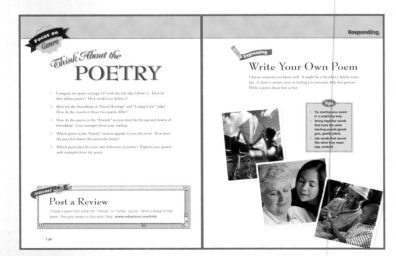

117A

Instructional Support

Planning and Practice

Teacher's Edition

Practice Book

Instruction Transparencies, Blackline Masters, and posters

Ready-Made Centers

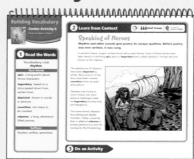

Building Vocabulary Flip Chart
- center activities
- word skills practice

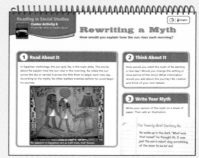

Reading in Science and Social Studies Flip Chart
- books and center activities
- support for state content standards

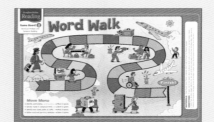

Hands-On Literacy Centers for *Focus on Poetry*
- activities
- manipulatives
- routines

 Technology

 **Audio Selections**
Focus on Poetry

Accelerated Reader®
Practice quiz for the selection

 HOUGHTON MIFFLIN
Online Leveled Books
www.eduplace.com
- over 1,000 Online Leveled Books

Leveled Books for Reaching All Learners

Fluency

Increase students' reading fluency using these activities.

● BELOW LEVEL

Have a student record a reading passage. Ask the student to compare their reading with the audio CD.

▲ ON LEVEL

Ask students to read passages aloud in small groups. Have them identify conjunctions in compound sentences to find the natural breaks in the text.

■ ABOVE LEVEL

Ask a student to read a passage aloud. Suggest other ways the student could use expression and ask the student to read aloud again.

◆ LANGUAGE SUPPORT

Have students work with a partner, reading passages in unison several times.

Skills Practice

- Topic, comprehension strategy, and vocabulary linked to main selection

- Lessons in Teacher's Edition, pages 135O–135R

● BELOW LEVEL

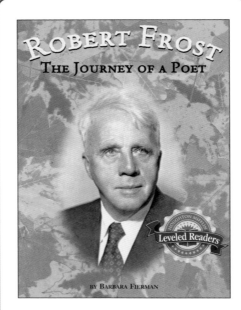

ROBERT FROST
THE JOURNEY OF A POET

BY BARBARA FIERMAN

▲ ON LEVEL

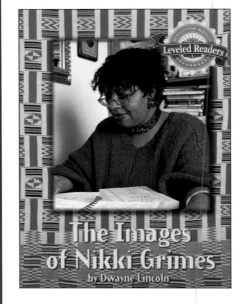

The Images of Nikki Grimes
by Dwayne Lincoln

● **Below Level Practice**

Name

Vocabulary

Read each word in the boxes below. Then write a word from the vocabulary list that is related in meaning.

| refusals | earnings |
| rejections | income |

| affection | countryside |
| fondness | rural |

| clearly | fatherly |
| vividly | paternal |

Vocabulary
fondness
income
paternal
rejections
rural
vividly

Now write a paragraph using any three of the vocabulary words you wrote above.
Answers will vary.

▲ **On Level Practice**

Name

Vocabulary

Under each term in the boxes below, write a word from the vocabulary list that is related in meaning.

| unsettling | ceremonies |
| uncanny | rituals |

| pictures | rough |
| images | calloused |

| disclosing | repeating |
| confiding | recurring |

| inheritance | short poem |
| heritage | haiku |

Vocabulary
calloused
confiding
haiku
heritage
images
rituals
uncanny
recurring

Now write a paragraph using five of the vocabulary words you wrote above.
Answers will vary.

● **Below Level Practice**

Name

Writing

Read the poem that you wrote. What do you need to make it better? Use this page to help you decide. Put a check mark (✔) in the box for each sentence that describes your poem. Then use your evaluation to help you revise your work. Answers will vary.

A Memorable Poem
☐ I have identified the subject of the poem.
☐ The images are clear and strong.
☐ I used creative language.
☐ I painted word pictures for the reader.
☐ The form and structure match the mood and feeling of my poem.
☐ I proofread the work and found no mistakes.

An Average Poem
☐ Some images are not really clear.
☐ I should try another form.
☐ I could try more creative language.
☐ More sensory details would improve the poem.
☐ There are a few mistakes.

Needs More Work
☐ The poem has too few images.
☐ The language is so general that it does not paint word pictures.
☐ The form and structure make no sense.
☐ I have not proofread the poem.

▲ **On Level Practice**

Name

Writing

Read the poem that you wrote. What do you need to make it better? Use this page to help you decide. Put a check mark (✔) in the box for each sentence that describes your poem. Then use this evaluation to help you revise your work. Answers will vary.

A Memorable Poem
☐ My poem has a definite subject.
☐ The images are clear and strong, and may be surprising.
☐ I used precise language in creative ways.
☐ I painted vivid word pictures for the reader.
☐ The sounds, form, and structure match the mood and feeling of my poem.
☐ I proofread the work and found no mistakes.

An Average Poem
☐ The images are predictable or ordinary.
☐ Another form might be more suitable for the content.
☐ My language could be more vivid or creative.
☐ The poem could be improved with additional sensory details.
☐ There are a few mistakes.

Needs More Work
☐ Some images are not really clear.
☐ The language is so general that it does not paint word pictures.
☐ The form and structure have little to do with the content.
☐ I have not proofread the poem.

■ ABOVE LEVEL

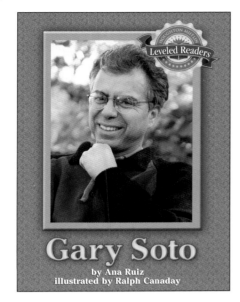

Gary Soto
by Ana Ruiz
illustrated by Ralph Canaday

■ Above Level Practice

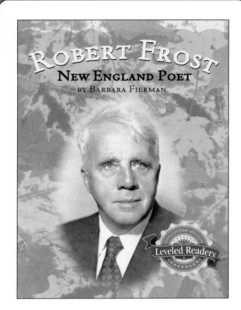

■ Above Level Practice

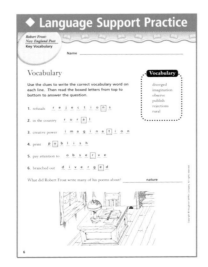

◆ LANGUAGE SUPPORT

ROBERT FROST
NEW ENGLAND POET
BY BARBARA FIERMAN

◆ Language Support Practice

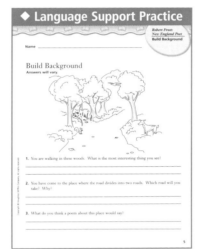

◆ Language Support Practice

Suggestions for Independent Reading

- Recommended trade books for independent reading in the genre

***Very Best (almost)
Friends***
(Candlewick) edited
by Paul Janeczko

Canto Familiar
(Harcourt)
by Gary Soto

Relatively Speaking
(Orchard)
by Ralph Fletcher

***In Daddy's Arms
I Am Tall***
(Lee & Low)
by Javaka Steptoe

Hopscotch Love
(Dial) by Nikki Grimes

Technology

HOUGHTON MIFFLIN
Online Leveled Books
www.eduplace.com

- over 1,000 Online Leveled Books

Leveled Readers
Audio available

Daily Lesson Plans

50–60 minutes

Reading
Comprehension

Leveled Readers
- Fluency Practice
- Independent Reading

20–30 minutes

Word Work
Phonics/Decoding
Vocabulary
Spelling

20–30 minutes

Writing and Oral Language
Writing
Grammar
Listening/Speaking/Viewing

DAY 1

Teacher Read Aloud, 117K–117L
"The Great Figure"

Background and Vocabulary, 118

Genre Vocabulary, 119
figurative language	rhyme
imagery	rhythm
lines	sensory language
repetition	

Vocabulary Reader

Reading the Selection, 120–133

 Comprehension Skill, 120
Understanding Poetry

 Comprehension Strategy, 120
Evaluate

Leveled Readers
Robert Frost: The Journey of a Poet
The Images of Nikki Grimes
Gary Soto
Robert Frost, New England Poet

Lessons and Leveled Practice, 135O–135R

 Phonics/Decoding Longer Words, 121
Phonics/Decoding Strategy

Vocabulary, 120–133
Selection Vocabulary

Spelling, 135E
Consonant Changes

Writing, 135, 135K
Prewriting a Poem

Grammar, 135I
Using Subordinate Clauses

Daily Language Practice
1. Ginny wrote a column about the cleveland bom squad. (Cleveland; bomb)
2. After the column appeared last autum she got a job as a columnist. (autumn,)

Listening/Speaking/Viewing, 117K–117L, 127
Teacher Read Aloud, Stop and Think

DAY 2

Reading the Selections, 120–133

Comprehension Check, 133

Responding, 134
Think About the Selections

Vocabulary Reader

 Comprehension Strategy, 124
Evaluate

Leveled Readers
Robert Frost: The Journey of a Poet
The Images of Nikki Grimes
Gary Soto
Robert Frost, New England Poet

Lessons and Leveled Practice, 135O–135R

 Structural Analysis, 135C
Prefixes and Suffixes un-, re-, -ful, -less, and -ly

Vocabulary, 120–133
Selection Vocabulary

Spelling, 135E
Consonant Changes Review and Practice

Writing, 135K
Drafting a Poem

Grammar, 135I
Using Subordinate Clauses Practice

Daily Language Practice
3. Readers often bombard columnists with letters? (bombard; letters.)
4. Some writers hasen to reply but others let the letters pile up. (hasten; reply,)

Listening/Speaking/Viewing, 133–134
Wrapping Up, Responding

Target Skills of the Week

Phonics	Prefixes and Suffixes *un-*, *re-*, *-ful*, *-less*, and *-ly*
Comprehension	Evaluate; Understanding Poetry
Vocabulary	Connotation
Fluency	Leveled Readers

Focus On Genre

DAY 3

Rereading the Selection

Rereading for Genre, 123
Lyric and Narrative Poetry

Responding, 134
Preparing for Literature Discussion

Vocabulary Reader

Comprehension Skill, 135A–135B
Understanding Poetry

Leveled Readers
Robert Frost: The Journey of a Poet
The Images of Nikki Grimes
Gary Soto
Robert Frost, New England Poet

Lessons and Leveled Practice, 135O–135R

Phonics Review, 135D
Silent Consonants

Vocabulary, 135G
Connotation

Spelling, 135F
Vocabulary: Word Families; Consonant Changes Practice

Writing, 135L
Revising a Poem
Sensory Language

Grammar, 135J
Compound-Complex Sentences

Daily Language Practice
5. Did you notice the desine on the cover of the hymnal. (design; hymnal?)
6. after Marco swept up every crum he gave me a signal and I mopped the floor. (After; crumb,; signal,)

DAY 4

Rereading the Selection

Rereading for Genre, 129
Haiku

Responding, 134
Literature Discussion

Comprehension Skill, 125
Visualizing

Leveled Readers
Robert Frost: The Journey of a Poet
The Images of Nikki Grimes
Gary Soto
Robert Frost, New England Poet

Lessons and Leveled Practice, 135O–135R

Structural Analysis, 135M
Language Center: Word Building Challenge

Vocabulary, 135M
Language Center: Building Vocabulary

Spelling, 135F
Consonant Changes Game, Proofreading

Writing, 135L
Proofreading a Poem

Grammar, 135J
Compound-Complex Sentences Practice

Daily Language Practice
7. Whom did mr Finley designate to inharit his property. (Mr.; inherit; property?)
8. I like that sign because, the musculur person looks like my cousin. (sign,; because; muscular)

Listening/Speaking/Viewing, 134
Literature Discussion

DAY 5

Rereading for Fluency, 129

Rereading for Writer's Craft, 131
The Narrator of a Poem

Responding, 134
Internet Activity

Information and Study Skills, 135H
Specialized Dictionaries

Leveled Readers
Robert Frost: The Journey of a Poet
The Images of Nikki Grimes
Gary Soto
Robert Frost, New England Poet

Lessons and Leveled Practice, 135O–135R

Phonics, 135N
Language Center: Sentence Stumpers

Vocabulary, 135M
Language Center: Vocabulary Game

Spelling, 135F
Test: Consonant Changes

Writing, 135L
Publishing a Poem

Grammar, 135J
Using Commas with Long Sentences

Daily Language Practice
9. Make hayste to repair that wall or it might crumble, and injure someone. (haste; wall,; crumble)
10. Although this song speaks of falling leafs and other lovely autumenal sights. It is difficult to sing and no one wants to include it in our concert. (leaves; autumnal; sights,; it; sing,)

Listening/Speaking/Viewing, 135N
Language Center: Read a Poem Aloud

Managing Flexible Groups

Leveled Instruction and Leveled Practice

		DAY 1	**DAY 2**
WHOLE CLASS		• Teacher Read Aloud (TE pp. 117K–117L) • Building Background, Introducing Vocabulary (TE pp. 118–119) • Comprehension Strategy: Introduce (TE p. 120) • Comprehension Skill: Introduce (TE p. 120) • Purpose Setting (TE p. 121) **After reading "Oranges"** • Stop and Think (TE p. 127)	• Building Background (TE p. 128) • Comprehension Strategy: Reinforce (TE p. 124) **After reading "Family Photo"** • Wrapping Up (TE p. 133) • Comprehension Check (Practice Book p. 95) • Responding: Think About the Selections (TE pp. 134–135)
SMALL GROUPS	**Extra Support**	**TEACHER-LED** • Preview vocabulary; support reading with Vocabulary Reader. • Preview "Good Hotdogs" through "Oranges" to Stop and Think (TE pp. 120–127). • Support reading with Extra Support/ Intervention notes (TE pp. 121, 123, 126, 127, 128, 132).	**Partner or Individual Work** • Reread "Good Hotdogs" through "Oranges" (TE pp. 120–127). • Preview, read "Family Style" through "Family Photo" TE pp. 128–133). • Comprehension Check (Practice Book p. 95)
	Challenge	**Individual Work** • Extend reading with Challenge note (TE p. 125). • See Independent Activities below and Classroom Management (TE pp. 117I–117J).	**Individual Work** • See Independent Activities below and Classroom Management (TE pp. 117I–117J).
	English Language Learners	**TEACHER-LED** • Preview vocabulary; support reading with Vocabulary Reader. • Preview "Good Hotdogs" through "Oranges" to Stop and Think (TE pp. 120–127). • Support reading with English Language Learners notes (TE pp. 118, 129, 135).	**TEACHER-LED** • Review "Good Hotdogs" through "Oranges" (TE pp. 120–127). ✔ • Preview, read "Family Style" through "Family Photo" (TE pp. 128–133). • Begin Comprehension Check together (Practice Book p. 95).

Independent Activities

• Journals: selection notes, questions
• Complete, review Practice Book (pp. 93–97) and Leveled Readers Practice Blackline Masters (TE pp. 135O–135R).
• Leveled Readers (TE pp. 135O–135R) or Suggestions for Independent Reading (TE p. 117F)
• Responding activities (TE pp. 134–135)
• Language Center activities (TE pp. 135M–135N)

✔ Opportunity to informally assess oral reading rate

DAY 3

- Rereading: Lesson on Genre (TE p. 123)
- Comprehension Skill: Main lesson (TE pp. 135A–135B)
- Responding: Preparing for Literature Discussion (TE p. 134, Practice Book p. 96)

TEACHER-LED

- Review Comprehension Check (Practice Book p. 95).
- Preview Leveled Reader: Below Level (TE p. 135O), or read book from Suggestions for Independent Reading (TE p. 117F). ✔

TEACHER-LED

- Preview Leveled Reader: Above Level (TE p. 135Q), or read book from Suggestions for Independent Reading (TE p. 117F). ✔

Partner or Individual Work

- Complete Comprehension Check (Practice Book p. 95).
- Begin Leveled Reader: Language Support (TE p. 135R), or read book from Suggestions for Independent Reading (TE p. 117F).

DAY 4

- Rereading: Lesson on Genre (TE p. 129)
- Rereading: Comprehension Skill lesson (TE p. 125)
- Responding: Literature Discussion (TE p. 134)

Partner or Individual Work

- Complete Leveled Reader: Below Level (TE p. 135O), or read book from Suggestions for Independent Reading (TE p. 117F).

Individual Work

- Complete Leveled Reader: Above Level (TE p. 135Q), or read book from Suggestions for Independent Reading (TE p. 117F).

TEACHER-LED

- Complete Leveled Reader: Language Support (TE p. 135R), or continue book from Suggestions for Independent Reading (TE p. 117F). ✔

DAY 5

- Rereading: Lesson on Writer's Craft (TE p. 131)
- Responding: Select from Activities (TE pp. 134–135)
- Information and Study Skills (TE p. 135H)

TEACHER-LED

- Read or reread book from Suggestions for Independent Reading (TE p. 117F). ✔

TEACHER-LED

- Read or reread book from Suggestions for Independent Reading (TE p. 117F). ✔

Partner or Individual Work

- Read or reread book from Suggestions for Independent Reading (TE p. 117F).

- **Fluency Practice:** Reread any of the poems on pages 120–133. ✔
- Activities relating to these poems at Education Place® www.eduplace.com

Turn the page for more independent activities. ➡

Ready-Made Small Group Activities

Word Work

Cross Curricular

Building Vocabulary Center Activity 6
● ▲ ■ *Speaking of Heroes*

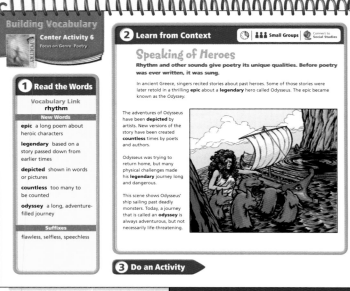

Leveled Activities on side 2

Game Board 6
● ▲ ■ *Word Walk*

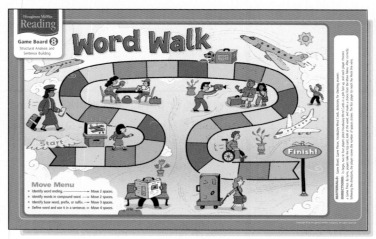

Key Vocabulary Cards 44–49

figurative language

Spelling Word Cards 81–100

autumn

Reading in Social Studies Independent Book
■ *Animal Mummies of Ancient Egypt*

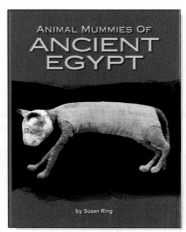

ANIMAL MUMMIES OF
ANCIENT EGYPT

by Susan Ring

Reading in Social Studies Center Activity 6
● ▲ ■ *Rewriting a Myth*

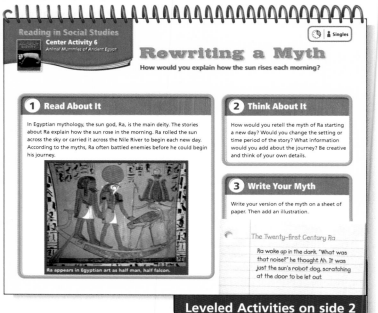

Leveled Activities on side 2

SMALL GROUP ACTIVITIES

Leveled for ● Below Level, ▲ On Level, ■ Above Level

Reading

Writing

Routine Card 2
● ▲ ■ *Partner Reading*

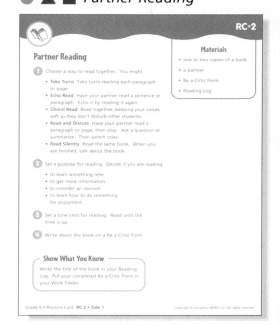

RC•2

Partner Reading

Materials
- one or two copies of a book
- a partner
- Be a Critic Form
- Reading Log

1. Choose a way to read together. You might
   - **Take Turns** Take turns reading each paragraph or page.
   - **Echo Read** Have your partner read a sentence or paragraph. Echo it by reading it again.
   - **Choral Read** Read together, keeping your voices soft so they don't disturb other students.
   - **Read and Discuss** Have your partner read a paragraph or page, then stop. Ask a question or summarize. Then switch roles.
   - **Read Silently** Read the same book. When you are finished, talk about the book.

2. Set a purpose for reading. Decide if you are reading
   - to learn something new
   - to get more information
   - to consider an opinion
   - to learn how to do something for enjoyment.

3. Set a time limit for reading. Read until the time is up.

4. Write about the book on a Be a Critic Form.

Show What You Know
Write the title of the book in your Reading Log. Put your completed Be a Critic Form in your Work Folder.

Grade 6 • Routine Card **RC-2** • Side 1   Copyright © Houghton Mifflin Co. All rights reserved.

Routine Card 7
● ▲ ■ *Publish Your Work*

RC•7

Publish Your Work

Materials
- a favorite piece of your writing
- the ideas on this card

When you publish your work, you share it with other people. There are many ways to publish your work. Here's a menu of ideas.

Make a Book
- Choose heavy paper for your front and back covers.
- Design a cover. Use staples, brads, or yarn to bind your covers and pages into a book.

Join a Writers' Group
- Select a piece of your writing that you like.
- Form a small group.
- Take turns reading your work aloud.

Send Your Work to a Magazine
- Ask a librarian about magazines that look for original poems, short stories, letters, and artwork by young people.
- Introduce yourself in a letter. Ask the editor to publish your work.
- Mail or e-mail your letter and writing to the magazine.

Create a Class Anthology
- Choose a topic for your anthology such as nature poetry, short stories, or letters from pen pals.
- Choose a piece of your own writing that fits into the chosen topic. Illustrate your work.
- Collect all of the writing that will go into the anthology.
- Bind the book and display it in a classroom or library.

Grade 6 • Routine Card **RC-7** • Side 1   Copyright © Houghton Mifflin Co. All rights reserved.

Multiple Tiers of Intervention

Core Program Intervention

- research-based
- systematic
- assessment-driven
- extra support
- English learner support
- reteaching

Intensive Intervention
Proven efficacy for struggling readers

Soar to Success

Routine Card 3
● ▲ ■ *Respond to a Story*

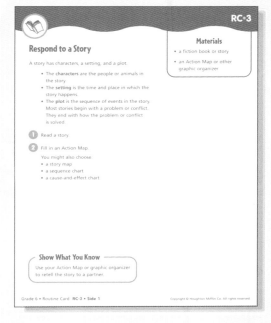

RC•3

Respond to a Story

Materials
- a fiction book or story
- an Action Map or other graphic organizer

A story has characters, a setting, and a plot.
- The **characters** are the people or animals in the story.
- The **setting** is the time and place in which the story happens.
- The **plot** is the sequence of events in the story. Most stories begin with a problem or conflict. They end with how the problem or conflict is solved.

1. Read a story.

2. Fill in an Action Map.
   You might also choose:
   - a story map
   - a sequence chart
   - a cause-and-effect chart

Show What You Know
Use your Action Map or graphic organizer to retell the story to a partner.

Grade 6 • Routine Card **RC-3** • Side 1   Copyright © Houghton Mifflin Co. All rights reserved.

Routine Card 8
● ▲ ■ *Plan and Write a Poem*

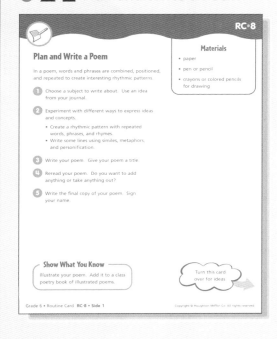

RC•8

Plan and Write a Poem

Materials
- paper
- pen or pencil
- crayons or colored pencils for drawing

In a poem, words and phrases are combined, positioned, and repeated to create interesting rhythmic patterns.

1. Choose a subject to write about. Use an idea from your journal.

2. Experiment with different ways to express ideas and concepts.
   - Create a rhythmic pattern with repeated words, phrases, and rhymes.
   - Write some lines using similes, metaphors, and personification.

3. Write your poem. Give your poem a title.

4. Reread your poem. Do you want to add anything or take anything out?

5. Write the final copy of your poem. Sign your name.

Show What You Know
Illustrate your poem. Add it to a class poetry book of illustrated poems.

Turn this card over for ideas.

Grade 6 • Routine Card **RC-8** • Side 1   Copyright © Houghton Mifflin Co. All rights reserved.

For these materials and more, see **Small Group Independent Activities Kit**.

Oral Language and Fluency

Descriptive Poems

OBJECTIVE

- Listen to identify elements of poetry.

Building Background

Tell students that they will read several poems in this section. They will learn about elements of poetry and try writing a poem of their own. Explain that you will begin by reading aloud two poems.

- Ask students to name a favorite poet or a favorite poem. Invite volunteers to recite a poem they may have memorized.

Fluency Modeling

Explain that as you read aloud, you will be modeling fluent oral reading. Ask students to listen carefully to your phrasing and your expression, or tone of voice and emphasis.

COMPREHENSION SKILL

Understanding Poetry

Ask students how poems differ from stories. (Sample answers: Poems may have verses and stanzas; repeated words or sounds; rhythm, rhyme, and special use of punctuation.)

Purpose Setting Read each poem aloud, asking students to pay attention to images as they listen. Then use the Guiding Comprehension questions to assess students' understanding. Reread each poem for clarification as needed.

The Great Figure
by William Carlos Williams

❶ Among the rain
and lights
I saw the figure 5
in gold
on a red
firetruck
moving
tense
unheeded
❷ to gong clangs
siren howls
and wheels rumbling
through the dark city.

INVENTION

by Billy Collins

3 Tonight the moon is a cracker,
with a bite out of it
floating in the night,

and in a week or so
according to the calendar
it will probably look

like a silver football,
and nine, maybe ten days ago
it reminded me of a thin bright claw.

But eventually —
by the end of the month,
I reckon —

it will waste away
to nothing,
nothing but stars in the sky,

and I will have a few nights
to myself,
4 a little time to rest my jittery pen.

Guiding Comprehension

1 **UNDERSTANDING POETRY** What is the "Great Figure" in the poem by William Carlos Williams? (the figure 5 on the firetruck)

2 **UNDERSTANDING POETRY** What sense words help you hear what the firetruck sounds like? (*gong clangs, siren howls, wheels rumbling*)

3 **UNDERSTANDING POETRY** In the poem "Invention," what things does the poet compare the phases of the moon to? (a cracker; a silver football; a thin, bright claw)

4 **UNDERSTANDING POETRY** After reading his poem, how do you think Billy Collins feels about the moon? (Sample answer: The moon inspires him; when he sees the moon he has to write.)

Discussion Options

Personal Response Have students tell which poem they liked better and to give some reasons why.

⭐ **Connecting/Comparing** Ask students to compare ways in which both poets make their descriptions vivid.

English Language Learners

Language Development

Invite English language learners to share poems that they know in their native languages. Have students listen for rhythm, rhyme, and sound patterns. Then have students explain what the poems they recited are about and why they like them.

Background and Vocabulary

Key Concept: Poetry

Connecting to the Genre Then have a volunteer read aloud the section called What Is Poetry? Tell students that the word *prose,* used in the poem, refers to ordinary writing.

Discuss ways in which poetry differs from prose. Write students' ideas on the board. Be sure the discussion includes these elements of poems:

- Words are arranged in lines and may be grouped in stanzas.
- The sounds of the words and lines suggest meaning and mood.
- Rhyme, rhythm, and repetition may be heard.
- Sensory language appeals to sight, hearing, touch, smell, and taste.
- Poetic language creates word pictures, or images.
- Figurative language includes comparisons such as metaphor, simile, and personification.

Ask students for their ideas about the poet's main point in the poem on page 119. Ask, Why might a poet say that even she does not know what poetry is?

Vocabulary Preview

The Vocabulary Reader can be used to preteach or reinforce the genre vocabulary.

English Language Learners

Supporting Comprehension

Beginning/Preproduction Have students listen as you read aloud the poem on page 119. Then have them illustrate an experience they have had with *the scent of the rose, the light in the sky, the gleam of the fly,* or *the sound of the sea.*

Early Production and Speech Emergence Have students discuss the terms *line, rhyme,* and *repetition.* Have them find examples of these poetic elements in the poem on page 119.

Intermediate and Advanced Fluency Pair students with more proficient English speakers to brainstorm sensory words to describe a rose, the sky, a fly, and the sea. Have students write their words in these categories: look, smell, feel, taste, and sound.

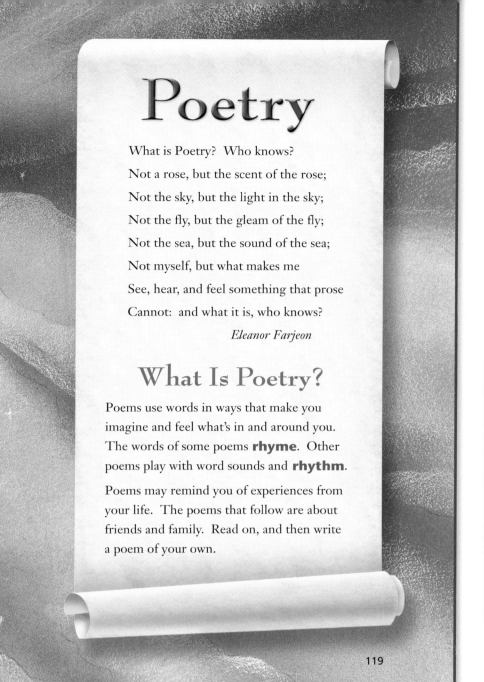

Poetry

What is Poetry? Who knows?

Not a rose, but the scent of the rose;

Not the sky, but the light in the sky;

Not the fly, but the gleam of the fly;

Not the sea, but the sound of the sea;

Not myself, but what makes me

See, hear, and feel something that prose

Cannot: and what it is, who knows?

Eleanor Farjeon

What Is Poetry?

Poems use words in ways that make you imagine and feel what's in and around you. The words of some poems **rhyme**. Other poems play with word sounds and **rhythm**.

Poems may remind you of experiences from your life. The poems that follow are about friends and family. Read on, and then write a poem of your own.

119

Introducing Vocabulary

Genre Vocabulary
These words support the Key Concept.

figurative language words that create vivid pictures by comparing things in unexpected ways

lines rows of words

repetition a repeating pattern of sounds, words, phrases, or lines

rhyme a repeating pattern in the final sounds of words

rhythm a pattern of stressed and unstressed syllables

sensory language words that describe how things look, smell, feel, taste, and sound

e • Glossary
e • WordGame

See Vocabulary notes on pages 122, 124, 126, 130, and 132 for additional words to preview.

Display Transparency F1–1.

- Model reading through the first paragraph and filling in the word *lines*.

- Have students fill in the missing words. Have volunteers explain how they figured out the meaning of each word.

- Ask students to use these words as they discuss poetry.

Practice/Homework Assign **Practice Book** page 93.

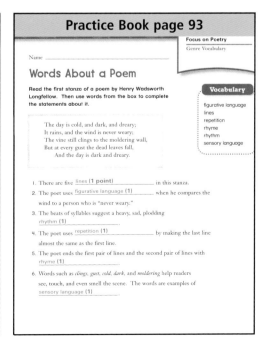

Transparency F1–1

THEME 1 Focus on Poetry
Genre Vocabulary

ANNOTATED VERSION

Genre Vocabulary

| figurative language | imagery | lines | repetition |
| sensory language | rhyme | rhythm | |

What About Poetry?

How does a poem look? Its words are arranged in ___lines___ that may be short, long, or varied.

How does a poem sound? Its ___rhythm___ comes from the beats of spoken words. It may have ___rhyme___, such as *knows* and *rose*, or *sea* and *me*. One kind of ___repetition___ occurs when words that appear at the start of the poem also appear at the end.

How does a poem affect imagination and emotion? A poem may have ___sensory language___ that suggests sound, sight, smell, taste, and touch. Poets use ___figurative language___, such as metaphors, to move beyond literal meanings. Poets use ___imagery___ to make descriptions sharp and colorful.

TRANSPARENCY F1–1
TEACHER'S EDITION PAGE 119

Practice Book page 93

Focus on Poetry
Genre Vocabulary

Name _____

Words About a Poem

Read the first stanza of a poem by Henry Wadsworth Longfellow. Then use words from the box to complete the statements about it.

Vocabulary
figurative language
lines
repetition
rhyme
rhythm
sensory language

The day is cold, and dark, and dreary;
It rains, and the wind is never weary;
The vine still clings to the moldering wall,
But at every gust the dead leaves fall,
    And the day is dark and dreary.

1. There are five ___lines___ (1 point) in this stanza.

2. The poet uses ___figurative language___ (1) when he compares the wind to a person who is "never weary."

3. The beats of syllables suggest a heavy, sad, plodding ___rhythm___ (1).

4. The poet uses ___repetition___ (1) by making the last line almost the same as the first line.

5. The poet ends the first pair of lines and the second pair of lines with ___rhyme___ (1).

6. Words such as *clings, gust, cold, dark,* and *moldering* help readers see, touch, and even smell the scene. The words are examples of ___sensory language___ (1).

COMPREHENSION STRATEGY
Evaluate

Teacher Modeling Tell students that they can evaluate a poem by thinking about how well the poem works. Read aloud "Good Hotdogs" on page 121. Then model the strategy.

Think Aloud *The narrator of the poem is remembering eating hotdogs with a childhood friend. The event was simple, but the memory includes plenty of sharp details—how the friends ran two blocks, exactly what they ordered, and why the hotdogs were so good. The poem includes sensory language—Yellow mustard and onions, Paper for us to hold hot/In our hands; The little burnt tips/Of french fries. The poet has painted a sharp picture of a wonderful memory. I think the poem works well.*

Remind students to use other strategies as well while reading.

COMPREHENSION SKILL
Understanding Poetry

Introduce the Graphic Organizer. Tell students that as they read the poems, they can fill out the Literary Devices in Poetry chart on **Practice Book** page 94.

- Display **Transparency F1–2.** Discuss the list of literary devices in the first column. Fill out the first row.

- Tell students to list at least two poems in each row. Monitor their work.

Contents

120

Transparency F1–2
Literary Devices in Poetry

Sample answers are shown. Students may find other poems and examples.

DEVICE	POEM TITLE	EXAMPLES
Imagery: language that paints sharp pictures *Example: tiny pawprints in the wet sand*	"Good Hot Dogs"	"splash on / . . . Yellow mustard and onions" "little burnt tips / Of french fries"
	"Losing Livie"	"an apple halfway to my mouth" details describing what Livie did to "clean up her own party"
	"Child Rest"	"Her red and yellow flower blossoms, / beadwork complete"
Figurative Language: imaginative comparisons between unlike things *Examples: a voice as calm as moonlight* (simile); *icicles were dripping fangs* (metaphor); *breezes danced playfully* (personification)	"Losing Livie"	"where the wind takes a rest / sometimes"
	"Oranges"	"Fog hanging like old / Coats between the trees"
	"Sundays"	"with cuffs stiff / as the ace of spades" "hands as tough and smooth / as the underside of a tortoise" "as slowly as bread rising, / he rolled up his sleeves"
Rhyme: similar end sounds *Examples: friend/end; pale/detail*	"The Pasture" "My Own Man"	"away/may; young/tongue" "teasing/pleasing"
Repetition: repeated use of words, phrases, or lines *Example: A happy bird/Am I, am I.*	"The Pasture" "Child Rest"	"You come too." "I nap. I sleep. I awake."

TRANSPARENCY F1–2 TEACHER'S EDITION PAGES 120 AND 135A

THEME 1 Focus on Poetry — Graphic Organizer Literary Devices Chart

ANNOTATED VERSION

Practice Book page 94

Focus on Poetry
Graphic Organizer Literary Devices in Poetry

Name _____

Literary Devices in Poetry
Sample answers are shown. Students may find other poems and

Device	Poem Title	Examples
Sensory Language: words that describe how things look, smell, feel, taste, and sound *Example: tiny pawprints in the wet sand* (4 points)	"Good Hotdogs"	"splash on/ . . . yellow mustard and onions" "little burnt tips/ of french fries"
	"Losing Livie"	"an apple halfway to my mouth" details describing what Livie did to "clean up her own party"
	"Child Rest"	"Her red and yellow flower blossoms, beadwork complete"
Figurative Language: imaginative comparisons between unlike things *Examples: a voice as calm as moonlight* (simile); *icicles were dripping fangs* (metaphor); *breezes danced playfully* (personification) (4)	"Losing Livie"	"where the wind takes a rest sometimes"
	"Oranges"	"Fog hanging like old/ Coats between the trees"
	"Sundays"	"with cuffs stiff/ as the ace of spades" "hands as tough and smooth/ as the underside of a tortoise" "as slowly as bread rising,/ he rolled up his sleeves"
Rhyme: similar end sounds *Examples: friend/end; pale/detail* (4)	"The Pasture" "My Own Man"	"away/may; young/tongue" "busy/spicy"
Repetition: repeated use of words, phrases, or lines *Example: A happy bird/Am I, am I.* (4)	"The Pasture" "Family Photo"	"You come too." "One last"

READ & COMPREHEND

Friends

Here are five poems that express the ups and downs of friendship. While you read the poems, think about how you could compare and contrast two of them.

Good Hotdogs

Fifty cents apiece
To eat our lunch
We'd run
Straight from school
Instead of home
Two blocks
Then the store
That smelled like steam
You ordered
Because you had the money
Two hotdogs and two pops for here
Everything on the hotdogs
Except pickle lily

Dash those hotdogs
Into buns and splash on
All that good stuff **❶**
Yellow mustard and onions
And french fries piled on top all
Rolled up in a piece of wax
Paper for us to hold hot
In our hands
Quarters on the counter
Sit down
Good hotdogs
We'd eat
Fast till there was nothing left
But salt and poppy seeds even **❷**
Then little burnt tips
Of french fries
We'd eat
You humming
And me swinging my legs **❸**

— *Sandra Cisneros*

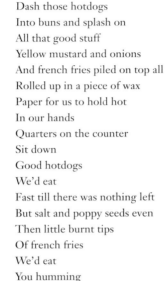

121

Building Background

- Explain that the poems in this section are about different aspects of friendship.

- Have students preview the poems in the section by reading the titles and studying the illustrations.

- Ask, What aspects of friendship do you think these poems portray? Why do you think friendship is a popular topic for poets?

Purpose Setting

Ask students to try reading each poem aloud softly and more than once. Have them think about what makes each a poem and why it is grouped with poems about friendship.

Journal ▸ Students can use their journal to copy phrases or lines that have an emotional impact on them.

STRATEGY REVIEW

Phonics/Decoding

Remind students to use the Phonics/Decoding Strategy as they read.

Extra Support/Intervention

Selection Preview

pages 121–123 The photo on page 122 shows two good friends, like the friends in "Good Hotdogs." The poem "Losing Livie" tells about a farewell party for a friend, set long ago.

pages 124–125 The poems on these pages express contrasting feelings about friendship. What literary device works effectively in both poems?

pages 126–127 The poem "Oranges" tells about the tender and awkward moments that occur on a first date. See if you can discover the special significance that oranges have to the story that the poem tells.

READ & COMPREHEND

Focus on Poetry

CRITICAL THINKING
Guiding Comprehension

1 AUTHOR'S VIEWPOINT In the poem "Good Hotdogs," what is the narrator's attitude toward the time described in the poem? (It was a happy time.)

2 WRITER'S CRAFT What sense words help you smell, taste, and touch the hotdogs? (Sample answers: *steam; splash on; yellow mustard and onions; hot in our hands; salt and poppy seeds*)

3 MAKING INFERENCES Why do you think the poet chose to write about hotdogs? (Hotdogs remind her of good times spent with a friend.)

4 DRAWING CONCLUSIONS In "Losing Livie," what specific examples does the poet use to show what Livie is like? (Sample answer: teased Ray and Hillary, said goodbye to each person separately, helped clean up her own party)

5 MAKING INFERENCES What does the narrator mean by *I'm wondering what kind of friend I am*? (afraid she might not be a good friend because she envies Livie's chance to experience living in another place)

6 MAKING INFERENCES Why does the narrator want to be *on that road to another place*? (Sample answer: Livie is going *out of the dust* to a place where *the wind takes a rest*. This suggests that the narrator's home is in a harsh setting.)

122

Vocabulary

semester half of a school year

REACHING ALL LEARNERS
Extra Support/Intervention

Line Breaks

Help students understand how to read poetry.

- Tell students that instead of pausing after each line of poetry, they should pause at the end of a complete thought.
- Model reading several lines of "Good Hotdogs" and "Losing Livie" aloud so students hear and feel the natural rhythms.
- Have students practice reading aloud these poems.

Losing Livie

Livie Killian moved away.
I didn't want her to go.
We'd been friends since first grade.

The farewell party was
Thursday night
at the Old Rock Schoolhouse.

Livie
had something to tease each of us
    about,
like Ray
sleeping through reading class,
and Hillary,
who on her speed-writing test put
an "even ton" of children
instead of an "even ten."

Livie said good-bye to each of us,
separately.
She gave me a picture she'd made
    of me sitting
in front of a piano,
wearing my straw hat,
an apple halfway to my mouth.

I handed Livie the memory book
    we'd all
filled with our different slants.
I couldn't get the muscles in my
    throat relaxed enough
to tell her how much I'd miss her.

Livie
helped clean up her own party,
wiping spilled lemonade,
gathering sandwich crusts,
sweeping cookie crumbs from the
    floor,
while the rest of us went home
to study for semester reviews.

Now Livie's gone west,
out of the dust,
on her way to California,
where the wind takes a rest
    sometimes.
And I'm wondering what kind of
    friend I am,   **5**
wanting my feet on that road to
    another place,
instead of Livie's.   **6**

from Out of the Dust
— *Karen Hesse*

123

Extra Support/Intervention

Strategy Modeling: Evaluate

Use this example to model the strategy.

"Losing Livie" sounds like a little story about a farewell party, but I think the poet set out to do something more. There's a rhythm to the lines that creates a bittersweet mood for me. When I read the lines, I couldn't get the muscles in my/ throat relaxed enough, *my own throat tightened! Also, the descriptive details help me see the students in that long-ago schoolroom. I think the poet has helped me imagine the scene and feel the mood.*

Focus On Genre

Lyric and Narrative Poetry

Teach

- Poets often distinguish between lyric poems and narrative poems.

- Lyric poems often have a musical quality. The primary purpose of a lyric poem is to express emotions or thoughts.

- The primary purpose of narrative poetry is to tell a story. The story often has a beginning, middle, and an end.

Practice

- Help students identify poems in Poems About Friends on pages 121–127 as lyric or narrative.

- Tell students that people can have different opinions about whether the primary purpose of a poem is to express a thought or emotion or to tell a story.

- Start a T-chart like the one shown below. (Sample answers are shown.)

Lyric Poems	Narrative Poems
"Poem"	"Good Hotdogs"
"The Pasture"	"Losing Livie"
	"Oranges"

Apply

- Have students complete this chart as they read Poems About Family on pages 128–133.

CRITICAL THINKING
Guiding Comprehension

❼ WRITER'S CRAFT Why do you think Langston Hughes chose the title "Poem"? (Sample answer: He wanted to express a deep feeling in just a few words, which is what a poem does.)

❽ DRAWING CONCLUSIONS What time of year is it in "The Pasture"? How can you tell? (It is spring, because a calf has just been born.)

❾ COMPARE AND CONTRAST In what way is the mood of "Poem" different from the mood of "The Pasture"? In what way is each poem about friendship? ("Poem" is sad, as if someone is too grief-stricken to speak. "The Pasture" is hopeful and happy. The first poem is about the loss of friendship; the second is about sharing happy times with a friend.)

COMPREHENSION STRATEGY

Evaluate

Student Modeling Have students model the strategy, using "Poem" and "The Pasture." Use the following prompts:

- Did the author of "Poem" do a good job of conveying his sadness about his friend? Why do you think so?

- Did the author of "The Pasture" do a good job of conveying what it feels like to be friends with someone? Why?

Vocabulary

sha'n't contraction for *shall not*

totters wobbles

---

❼ # Poem

I loved my friend.
He went away from me.
There's nothing more to say.
The poem ends,
Soft as it began —
I loved my friend.

— *Langston Hughes*

124

THE PASTURE

I'm going out to clean the pasture spring;
I'll only stop to rake the leaves away
(And wait to watch the water clear, I may)
I sha'n't be gone long. — You come too.

I'm going out to fetch the little calf
That's standing by the mother. It's so young
It totters when she licks it with her tongue.
I sha'n't be gone long. — You come too.

— Robert Frost

125

Challenge

Word Choice

Discuss some of the word choices poets might make.

- words that create alliteration (the same sounds, usually at the beginning of words), such as "Losing Livie"
- words that create onomatopoeia (a word that imitates the sound being described), such as *humming*
- words that create strong images, such as *Now Livie's gone west/out of the dust*
- words that create figurative comparisons, such as *wanting my feet on that road to another place*

Then ask students to find examples of each in the poems on pages 120–133.

Comprehension

Visualizing

Teach

- Explain that visualizing helps readers use the author's words to create mental pictures while reading.
- Point out that visualizing is especially useful while reading poetry because poets try to paint clear and colorful images with words.

Practice

- Read "The Pasture" aloud while students listen with their eyes closed.
- Ask students to describe exactly what they pictured when they heard the first stanza. (Sample answer: The narrator will be raking the leaves from the surface and edges of the spring, so the water will be disturbed and possibly muddy. The narrator will stand quietly, gazing at the water as the mud settles down.)
- Ask, Why did the poet choose the word *totters* to describe the calf? (to create a word picture of a newborn calf that is still wobbly on its legs, so it can't stand still when its mother pushes against it to lick it)

Apply

- Have students find lines in other poems in this section that suggest images to visualize.
- Have partners practice visualizing as they read these lines to each other.
- Ask students to draw one of their mental pictures. They should use a line from a poem as a caption.

READ & COMPREHEND

Focus on Poetry

Reading the Selection 125

CRITICAL THINKING

Guiding Comprehension

⑩ DRAWING CONCLUSIONS What is the saleslady like? Support your answer with details from the poem. (Sample answer: The saleslady understands that the boy doesn't have enough money but wants to impress the girl. The saleslady is sympathetic and kindhearted. She accepts the orange as payment, along with the nickel, without embarrassing him.)

⑪ MAKING INFERENCES What does this poem tell you about the narrator? (Sample answers: He has a crush on the girl and notices everything about her. He is poor but hopeful and resourceful.)

Oranges

The first time I walked
With a girl, I was twelve,
Cold, and weighted down
With two oranges in my jacket.
December. Frost cracking
Beneath my steps, my breath
Before me, then gone,
As I walked toward
Her house, the one whose

Porch light burned yellow
Night and day, in any weather.
A dog barked at me, until
She came out pulling
At her gloves, face bright
With rouge. I smiled,
Touched her shoulder, and led
Her down the street, across
A used car lot and a line

126

Extra Support/Intervention

Review (pages 121–127)

Before students who need extra support join the whole class for Stop and Think on page 127, have them

- review their purpose
- add to their Literary Devices in Poetry chart on **Practice Book** page 94
- summarize the main idea of each poem

Vocabulary

rouge red makeup

tiered in layered rows

Of newly planted trees,
Until we were breathing
Before a drugstore. We
Entered, the tiny bell
Bringing a saleslady
Down a narrow aisle of goods.
I turned to the candies
Tiered like bleachers,
And asked what she wanted —
Light in her eyes, a smile
Starting at the corners
Of her mouth. I fingered
A nickel in my pocket,
And when she lifted a chocolate
That cost a dime,
I didn't say anything.
I took the nickel from
My pocket, then an orange,
And set them quietly on
The counter. When I looked up,
The lady's eyes met mine,
And held them, knowing
Very well what it was all
About.

10

Outside,
A few cars hissing past,
Fog hanging like old
Coats between the trees.
I took my girl's hand
In mine for two blocks,
Then released it to let
Her unwrap the chocolate.
I peeled my orange
That was so bright against
The gray of December
That, from some distance,
Someone might have thought
I was making a fire in my hands.

11

— *Gary Soto*

127

Critical Thinking Questions

1. **MAKING INFERENCES** Why do you think the poet named his poem "Oranges," after the fruit? (Sample answers: Oranges were important in the story; the boy was poor and used an orange to help pay for the chocolate; the oranges might stand for the two characters, who were two ordinary people.)

2. **DRAWING CONCLUSIONS** In what ways is "The Pasture" different from the other poems? (rhymes; addresses the reader directly—"You"; tells about the present time.)

3. **WRITER'S CRAFT** Why do you think the poet decided to write the poem "Good Hotdogs" with no punctuation? (Sample answers: It allows readers to group lines into different thoughts and find new meanings; it contributes to the jaunty mood.)

4. **EXPRESSING PERSONAL OPINIONS** Choose one image or excerpt with figurative language from the selections in Poems About Friends and explain why you liked it. (Sample answer: I've chosen the second stanza in "The Pasture," which describes the mother licking the calf. The poet's choice of words makes it easy to visualize the scene.)

Strategies in Action

Have students take turns modeling Evaluate and other strategies they used while reading.

Monitoring Student Progress

If . . .	Then . . .
students have successfully completed the Extra Support activities on page 126,	have them read the next group of poems cooperatively or independently.

Extra Support/Intervention

Retelling

Tell students that some poems are about an experience or an event.

- Read aloud parts of "Oranges," and ask students to use their own words to tell what is happening.
- Have partners reread "Oranges" and create a storyboard with captions that can be used to retell the story.

 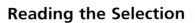
READ & COMPREHEND

Focus on Poetry

Building Background

- Explain that the next group of poems are about families.

- Have students preview the poems in the section by reading the titles and studying the illustrations.

- Ask students to predict what aspects of families and family connections these poems will create a picture of.

Purpose Setting

Have students read to identify what aspect of family life each poem is about.

Journal ▶ Students can write about a special connection that they share with a family member.

CRITICAL THINKING

Guiding Comprehension

 DRAWING CONCLUSIONS Why do you think the poet chose an image of sea gulls for "Family Style"? (They reminded the poet of family members stabbing with chopsticks at a shared platter of fish.)

 MAKING INFERENCES Why do you think the poet chose "Sundays" as the title for a poem about a father? (a special time for the father and son to play together)

Family

Sometimes an image in a poem surprises you. As you read the next six poems about family, pick your favorite image.

Family Style

12 Like hungry sea gulls,
chopsticks fight, trying to snatch
the best piece of fish.

— *Janet Wong*

128

Extra Support/Intervention

Selection Preview

pages 128–129 The poems "Family Style" and "Sundays" are about special times that family members share. Why might someone remember fondly the typical activities of eating together or playing baseball?

pages 130–131 The poem "My Own Man" and the excerpt from Sandburg's longer poem "The People, Yes" are about growing up. Do you think young people benefit from advice about growing up?

pages 132–133 The poems "Child Rest" and "Family Photo" portray memories of precious times spent with family members. Why do you think memories of sharing special occasions are so important to people?

Sundays

For lunch
Dad wore a white shirt
with cuffs stiff
as the ace of spades,
knit pants,
and loafers.

After lunch
we walked to the park
as he rubbed the baseball
with hands as tough and smooth
as the underside of a tortoise.

At the backstop,
as slowly as bread rising,
he rolled up his sleeves
before hitting fly balls
that seemed to skip off the sun
before landing
still warm
in my mitt.

— *Paul B. Janeczko*

129

Haiku

Teach

- Tell students that poets sometimes choose a formal structure for their poems. One such structure originated in Japan and is called haiku (HY-koo).
- Explain that a poem written in the haiku form has seventeen syllables, arranged in three lines of 5, 7, and 5.
- Explain that haiku are often about nature or the seasons.

Practice

- Have students count the syllables in each line of "Family Style."
- Ask whether "Family Style" is about nature. (Sample answers: yes, because of the image of the sea gulls; no, because the subject is really a human family)

Apply

- Have students think of images from nature and list them on the board.
- Have individuals or partners try writing their own haiku, using one of the images from the list.

English Language Learners

Language Development

Help students understand syllable patterns in poems.

- Read aloud "Family Style," tapping out the syllables while students count silently.
- Have partners read aloud other poems in the section and count the syllables they hear.
- Ask partners to choose one poem from the section and record the syllable pattern with marks or symbols.

Fluency Practice

Rereading for Fluency Have students choose a favorite stanza or poem to reread to a partner, or suggest that they reread "Sundays" on page 129. Encourage students to read expressively.

CRITICAL THINKING
Guiding Comprehension

14 **MAKING INFERENCES** What does the title "My Own Man" reveal about the narrator of the poem? (He is what he wants to be, not what others want him to be.)

15 **COMPARE AND CONTRAST** What do you think is Carl Sandburg's main point? Would the narrator of "My Own Man" agree with that point? (Sample answer: Carl Sandburg's poem says that men need many traits to respond to life: be tough and determined but don't forget gentleness. The narrator of "My Own Man" would agree: he is tough when he stands up to name-calling, but he gently prepares supper for his mother.)

14 # My Own Man

When Mom works late I wait with busy
hands, pry soup cans open, spread spicy

mustard on rye with lettuce and tomatoes
sliced so thin the cheese peeks through.

It's my Cheddar Deluxe, which Mom loves
better than anything I cook. The boys next

door say, "How's that look? You fixin' supper
like some girl." I shrug off their teasing

and go on pleasing *me*. I read my books,
choose Jazz *and* Rap, and quiet over

chatter. Blue says, "What's the matter
with that?" And, if I take care of my mom

so what? She takes care of me. "Don't be
no Mama's boy," kids say. Well, tough.
                    I'm made this way.

— *Nikki Grimes*

130

Vocabulary

humdrum dreary, unimaginative

monotony sameness; boredom

amid in the middle of

slack loose; inactive

loam rich soil

From
The People, Yes

A father sees a son nearing manhood.
What shall he tell that son?
"Life is hard; be steel; be a rock."
And this might stand him for the storms
and serve him for humdrum and monotony
and guide him amid sudden betrayals
and tighten him for slack moments.
"Life is a soft loam; be gentle; go easy."
And this too might serve him.
Brutes have been gentled where lashes failed.
The growth of a frail flower in a path up
has sometimes shattered and split a rock.
A tough will counts. So does desire.
So does a rich soft wanting.
Without rich wanting nothing arrives.

— *Carl Sandburg*

15

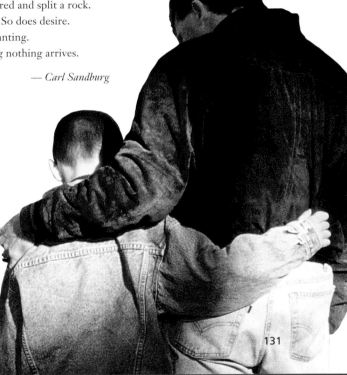

131

The Narrator of a Poem

Teach

- Tell students that the person telling the poem is the narrator.

- Explain that a poem with pronouns such as *I, me, my,* and *ourselves* has a first-person narrator.

- Ask students who the narrator is in the poem "My Own Man." (a boy)

- Point out that the poet, Nikki Grimes, is a woman. Help students to understand that the narrator in a poem is not necessarily the poet. A poet chooses a point of view, just as the author of a story does.

Practice

- Have students find other examples of first-person narrators in the poems on pages 118–133. List titles on the board. ("Good Hotdogs," "Losing Livie," "Poem," "The Pasture," "Oranges," "Sundays," "Child Rest," "Family Photo")

- Ask students which narrators could be the poet and which could not. Have them explain their decisions.

Apply

- Have partners choose two of the poems you listed and write a description of the narration.

- Ask students to use the words *poet* and *narrator* as they write one or two sentences about each example. (Sample answer: The poet Ralph Fletcher wrote "Family Photo" using a first-person narrator who is looking at a family photo.)

CRITICAL THINKING
Guiding Comprehension

16 **WRITER'S CRAFT** What has the poet done in "Child Rest" to help you imagine the scene? What mood has he created? (He has used sensory language—*crispy, salty, smoked, ice water, red and yellow flower blossoms, whistles, hums*—to put the reader in the scene. The poem suggests rest, peace, and comfort.)

17 **WRITER'S CRAFT** What metaphor does the poet use to describe the family in "Family Photo"? What does the metaphor help you understand? (*We're ripples in a pond/ spreading out/ from a stone they threw.* The grandmother and grandfather are at the center of the family because their children have had children.)

Child Rest

Crispy, salty, fry bread, smoked, dried,
    deer meat
And ice water from the nearby spring —
Great grandmother's midday meal.
I nap.

In her lap she takes beeswax, needle,
    beads —
Her red and yellow flower needs an
    afternoon of sewing.
She half whistles, half hums an old song
    for me.
I sleep.

Faithful as a forest doe Kautsa watches
    over me.
Her red and yellow flower blossoms,
    beadwork complete.
Now, continuous humming, tapping of
    her moccasined foot stops . . .
I awake.

— *Phil George*

16

132

Extra Support/Intervention

Review (pages 128–133)

Before students who need extra support join the whole class for Wrapping Up on page 133, have them

- review their predictions/purpose
- complete their Literary Devices in Poetry charts on **Practice Book** page 94
- summarize the main idea of each poem

Vocabulary

fry bread a Native American dish

Family Photo

One last picture
before we head off
in different directions.

One last group shot of
all of us, smirking,
with rabbit ears.

Three generations,
kids on shoulders,
a baby cousin on my lap.

And in the middle
Grandma and Grandpa
who started all this.

We're ripples in a pond
spreading out
from a stone they threw.

17

— *Ralph Fletcher*

133

Critical Thinking Questions

1. **MAKING JUDGMENTS** Which image had a strong impact on you in the poems about family? Why? (Sample answer: Image from "The People, Yes": the poet's use of figurative language to contrast the fragile, beautiful flower with the rough, strong stone makes me think of people who have overcome obstacles in life.)

2. **MAKING GENERALIZATIONS** What ideas are shared by the poems about family? (Sample answers: Family members feel a special connection to one another; the generations take care of each other; experiences with family form lasting memories.)

3. **COMPARING AND CONTRASTING** Which poem about family seems different from the others? Why? (Sample answers: "Family Style" is the only haiku, the shortest poem, and it does not have a first-person narrator. "The People, Yes" is the only poem that's not about a particular family or memory. It's about giving advice to a son.)

Strategies in Action

Have students show how they used the Evaluate strategy with these poems.

Comprehension Check

Use **Practice Book** page 95 to assess students' comprehension of the poems.

Practice Book page 95

Focus on Poetry
Comprehension Check

Name _____

Describing Poetry

Complete each statement about the poem indicated.
Sample answers for both poems are given.
1. In the poem "Child Rest," the poet tells about
a memory of feeling secure and peaceful as a child beside a great grandmother
who is beading .

An example of sensory language in the poem is
"She half whistles, half hums an old song for me" **(4 points)**

2. In "Poem," the poet uses repetition when he says
"I loved my friend" as the first and last lines **(4)**

The poet may have decided to use repetition because
he wanted to emphasize how much he misses his friend **(4)**

3. In the poem "The People, Yes," the poet tells about
opposite pieces of advice that a father might give a son about how to live

An example of figurative language is
"Life is a soft loam" **(4)**

Monitoring Student Progress

If . . .	Then . . .
students score 8 or below on **Practice Book** page 95,	have partners review each poem for details that support the correct answer.

Responding

Think About the Selection

Discuss or Write

1. **COMPARE AND CONTRAST** Sample answer: The poet tries to define poetry with examples of what poetry is not. The paragraphs define poetry by how poems affect the reader's imagination and feelings. My definition is "a kind of writing that is like a song."

2. **COMPARE AND CONTRAST** Sample answer: Both poems describe a friendship in the past. "Good Hotdogs" has a warm, happy mood; "Losing Livie" has a more sorrowful and regretful mood.

3. **MAKING GENERALIZATONS** Sample answer: Friendship includes happiness, sadness, and special memories; Examples: the poems reveal feelings about losing a friend, recall happy memories of a time together, or invite us to join in.

4. **MAKING JUDGMENTS** Answers will vary.

5. **MAKING JUDGMENTS** Answers will vary.

Literature Discussion

To help students prepare for the discussion, assign **Practice Book** page 96. Students may also refer to **Practice Book** page 95.

1. **COMPARE AND CONTRAST** Choose two poems. If you were choosing a photograph to accompany each poem, what would you want the photograph to show? How would it differ from the one now shown? (Answers will vary.)

2. **MAKING JUDGMENTS** Which of these poems do you think would be best to read aloud to an audience? Why? (Answers will vary.)

Focus on Genre

Think About the POETRY

1. Compare the poem on page 119 with the text that follows it. How do they define poetry? How would you define it?

2. How are the friendships in "Good Hotdogs" and "Losing Livie" alike? How do the moods in these two poems differ?

3. How do the poems in the "Friends" section describe the ups and downs of friendship? Give examples from your reading.

4. Which poem in the "Family" section appeals to you the most? How does the poet feel about this particular family?

5. Which poem best fits your own definition of poetry? Explain your answer with examples from the poem.

Internet

Post a Review

Choose a poem from either the "Friends" or "Family" section. Write a review of that poem. Post your review on Education Place. **www.eduplace.com/kids**

134

Practice Book page 96

Focus on Poetry
Literature Discussion

Name _____

Comparing Poems

Choose two poems from this section. Compare and contrast them by answering the questions in the chart. Add questions of your own to the chart too.

	Poem #1 Title: _____	Poem #2 Title: _____
What is the poet's main point?	Answers will vary. (20 points for chart)	
What words in the poem help you imagine and feel?		
Does the poem remind you of something from your own life? Explain.		
What is the mood or tone?		

Which poem did you like more? Why?
Answers will vary. (5)

 **Expressing**

Write Your Own Poem

Choose someone you know well. It might be a friend or a family member. Is there a certain story or feeling you associate with that person? Write a poem about him or her.

Tips

- Try starting your poem in a surprising way.
- String together words that have the same starting sounds (*great grin, gentle joker*).
- Use words that sound like what they mean (*zip, screech*).

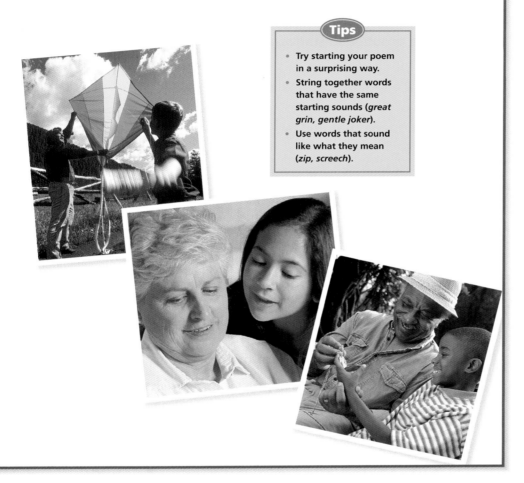

Have students read and briefly discuss the writing assignment on Anthology page 135. Before students begin their own poems, present the writing lesson on pages 135K–135L.

 REACHING ALL LEARNERS

Extra Support/Intervention

Prewriting Support

Help students plan their poems.

- Have students brainstorm memories of special events shared with family and friends. List the ideas on the board.
- Have students choose an idea for their poem and write a main point.
- Have partners play with words to come up with vocabulary associated with their main ideas.

Monitoring Student Progress

End-of-Selection Assessment

Student Self-Assessment Have students assess their reading and writing with questions such as these:

- Which poems were difficult to read? Why?
- Which strategies helped me understand the poems?
- Would I recommend these poems to my friends? Why or why not?

- Identify literary devices used in poetry.
- Understand that poets use varied approaches to the same subject.

Target Skill Trace

Preview; Teach p. 117K, p. 120; p. 135A

Transparency F1–2

Literary Devices in Poetry

Sample answers are shown. Students may find other poems and examples.

DEVICE	POEM TITLE	EXAMPLES
Imagery: language that paints sharp pictures Example: *tiny pawprints in the wet sand*	"Good Hot Dogs" "Losing Livie" "Child Rest"	"splash on / . . . Yellow mustard and onions" "little burnt tips / Of french fries" "an apple halfway to my mouth" details describing what Livie did to "clean up her own party" "Her red and yellow flower blossoms, / beadwork complete"
Figurative Language: imaginative comparisons between unlike things Examples: *a voice as calm as moonlight* (simile); *icicles were dripping fangs* (metaphor); *breezes danced playfully* (personification)	"Losing Livie" "Oranges" "Sundays"	"where the wind takes a rest / sometimes." "Fog hanging like old / Coats between the trees." "with cuffs stiff / as the ace of spades" "hands as tough and smooth / as the underside of a tortoise" "as slowly as bread rising, / he rolled up his sleeves"
Rhyme: similar end sounds Examples: *friend/end; pale/detail*	"The Pasture" "My Own Man"	"away/may; young/tongue" "teasing/pleasing"
Repetition: repeated use of words, phrases, or lines Example: *A happy bird/Am I, am I.*	"The Pasture" "Child Rest"	"You come too." "I nap. I sleep. I awake."

TRANSPARENCY F1–2
TEACHER'S EDITION PAGES 120 AND 135A

THEME 1: Focus on Poetry
Graphic Organizer Literary Devices Chart

ANNOTATED VERSION

Practice Book page 94

Focus on Poetry
Graphic Organizer Literary Devices in Poetry

Name _____

Literary Devices in Poetry

Sample answers are shown. Students may find other poems and

Device	Poem Title	Examples
Sensory Language: words that describe how things look, smell, feel, taste, and sound *Example: tiny pawprints in the wet sand* (4 points)	"Good Hotdogs" "Losing Livie" "Child Rest"	"splash on/ . . . yellow mustard and onions" "little burnt tips/ of french fries" "an apple halfway to my mouth" details describing what Livie did to "clean up her own party" "Her red and yellow flower blossoms, beadwork complete"
Figurative Language: imaginative comparisons between unlike things *Examples: a voice as calm as moonlight* (simile); *icicles were dripping fangs* (metaphor); *breezes danced playfully* (personification) (4)	"Losing Livie" "Oranges" "Sundays"	"where the wind takes a rest sometimes." "Fog hanging like old/ Coats between the trees." "with cuffs stiff/ as the ace of spades" "hands as tough and smooth/ as the underside of a tortoise" "as slowly as bread rising,/ he rolled up his sleeves"
Rhyme: similar end sounds *Examples: friend/end; pale/detail* (4)	"The Pasture" "My Own Man"	"away/may; young/tongue" "busy/spicy"
Repetition: repeated use of words, phrases, or lines *Example: A happy bird/Am I, am I.* (4)	"The Pasture" "Family Photo"	"You come too." "One last"

TARGET SKILL COMPREHENSION: Understanding Poetry

❶ Teach

Review the elements of poetry. Have students give definitions or examples for the terms listed below.

- **lines, stanzas** (Poems are written in rows of words, or lines. Lines may be grouped in stanzas.)
- **rhyme, rhythm, repetition** (matching ending sounds, patterns of stressed and unstressed syllables, and repeated words or lines)
- **imagery, sensory language** (language that creates word pictures, and language that appeals to the five senses)
- **metaphor, simile, personification** (types of figurative language; point out likenesses between things not usually compared)

Complete the Graphic Organizer on Transparency F1–2 with students. (Sample answers are shown.) Have students refer to the poems and to **Practice Book** page 94. Have students share their examples. Discuss the effects of each device.

Discuss poems about people. Discuss these categories:

- poems that tell a personal story
- poems that create a memorable image
- poems that express a state of mind or belief

Model thinking about the poet's approach to the subject. Direct students to reread "The People, Yes" on page 131.

Think Aloud *This is the kind of poem that expresses a belief or state of mind. Why do I think that? I find two opposing ideas—life is hard, and life is soft. The father offers advice about each view of life and ends by stressing that a young person needs a "tough will" but also a "rich soft wanting."*

❷ Guided Practice

Have students examine a poem. Ask students to reread the poem "Sundays" on page 129.

- What is the subject of this poem? (a boy's memory of his father)
- Does this poem mainly tell a story, create a memorable image, or express a belief? (create a memorable image)
- How are the lines arranged? (short lines in three stanzas)
- List the two similes in the poem. (Sample answers: *stiff as the ace of spades; tough and smooth as the underside of a tortoise*)

---

❸ Apply

Assign Practice Book page 97. Students can also think about poets' work as they read their **Leveled Readers** for this week. You may also suggest a book from the Books for Independent Reading on the Lesson Overview (page 117D).

✔️ **Test Prep** Reading tests will sometimes include poetry. Students may be asked to identify literary devices commonly found in poems.

Leveled Readers

Students at all levels build their understanding of a poet's work as they read their Leveled Readers. See lessons on pages 135O–135R.

● **BELOW LEVEL** ▲ **ON LEVEL** ■ **ABOVE LEVEL** ◆ **LANGUAGE SUPPORT**

Reading Traits

Teaching students to think about genre is one way of encouraging them to "read the lines" of a selection. This comprehension skill supports the reading trait **Decoding Conventions.**

Practice Book page 97

Focus on Poetry
Comprehension Skill
Understanding Poetry

Name _____

What Makes a Good Poem?

Reread the poem "Oranges" on pages 126–127. Fill in the blanks below to complete a summary of the story that the poem tells.

The narrator is a twelve-year-old boy who describes a time in December when he goes on his <u>first date</u> **(1 point)** with a girl. After he meets her at her house, they both walk to a <u>drugstore</u> **(1)**. He brings her to the <u>candies</u> **(1)** and tells her to pick what she wants. She picks a chocolate that costs a <u>dime</u> **(1)** and he has only a <u>nickel</u> **(1)**. The boy then places the nickel and an orange from his pocket on the counter. Fortunately, the saleslady understands that the boy wants to <u>impress</u> **(1)** the girl but doesn't have the <u>money</u> **(1)**. After that, the boy and the girl walk <u>hand in hand</u> **(1)**.

Answer these questions. Include quotations from the poem. Sample answers given below. Try to use names of literary devices too.

1. How does the poet make the time of year come alive?
   <u>Sample answer: uses imagery and sensory language: hearing the "frost cracking beneath my steps," seeing "breath before me, then gone," and "the gray of December."</u> **(4 points)**

2. How does the poet show the narrator's feelings about the girl?
   <u>Sample answer: The author shows what the narrator does when he's with her. "I smiled, touched her shoulder"; "I took my girl's hand/ in mine for two blocks"</u> **(4)**

3. What is a particularly vivid image in the poem?
   <u>Sample answers: "A few cars hissing past,/ Fog hanging like old/ coats between the trees"</u> **(4)**

Monitoring Student Progress

If . . .	Then . . .
students score 14 or below on **Practice Book** page 97,	have them work with partners to correct the items they missed.

STRUCTURAL ANALYSIS/ VOCABULARY: Prefixes and Suffixes

TARGET SKILL

❶ Teach

Review prefixes and suffixes. Have students identify the prefix or suffix in each word below. Then ask them to compare and contrast meanings.

- *unwrap, rewrap* (The prefix *un-* means "not" or "the opposite of"; *to unwrap* means "to take off the wrapping"; the prefix *re-* means "again"; *to rewrap* means "to wrap something again.")
- *careful, careless* (The suffix *-ful* means "full of"; *careful* means "full of care"; the suffix *-less* means "without"; *careless* means "without care.")
- *hungrily* (The suffix *-ly* means "in a way that is"; *hungrily* means "in a hungry way.")

Model the Phonics/Decoding Strategy Write *A poet searches* <u>ceaselessly</u> *for the perfect word.* Point to the underlined word.

Think Aloud *When I look at the parts of this word, I see that it is made up of a base word and the suffixes -less and -ly. I recognize the base word* cease. *I know how to pronounce it, and I know it means "stop." Adding the suffix -less to* cease *makes a word that means "without stopping" and adding -ly makes a word that means "in a way that is without stopping." That makes sense in the sentence.*

❷ Guided Practice

Have students decode words with prefixes and suffixes. Display the phrases below. Ask partners to write the underlined words, circle each prefix or suffix, and discuss what the word means. Discuss word meanings as a class.

1. <u>faithful</u> as a forest doe
2. the <u>restless</u> wind
3. <u>unrolled</u> his shirt sleeves
4. study for semester <u>reviews</u>

❸ Apply

Assign Practice Book page 98.

Practice Book page 98

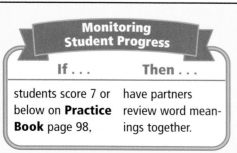

Focus on Poetry
Structural Analysis Prefixes and Suffixes

Name

Prefixes and Suffixes

The words in the box have the prefixes *re-* and *un-* and the suffixes *-less, -ful,* and *-ly.* Find the word that matches each clue. Write it in the letter spaces.

| reunited | priceless | unaware | carelessly | plentiful |
| completely | unknown | fearfully | breathless | retelling |

1. in a total way: c o m p l e t [e] l y (1 point)
2. without taking in air: b r e a t h l e s s (1)
3. not seeing or feeling something: u n [a] w a r e (1)
4. explaining again: r e t e l l i [n] g (1)
5. like a treasure: p r i c e l e s [s] (1)
6. more than enough: p l e n t i f [u] l (1)
7. together again: [r] e u n i t e d (1)
8. not at all bravely: f e a r f u l [l] y (1)
9. not familiar: u n [k] n o w n (1)
10. in a sloppy way: c a r e l e s s l y (1)

Write the boxed letters in order on the spaces below to complete the quotation.

An ancient Greek once wrote, "Painting is silent poetry, and poetry painting

t h a t s p e a k s ."

Monitoring Student Progress

If . . .	Then . . .
students score 7 or below on **Practice Book** page 98,	have partners review word meanings together.

PHONICS REVIEW: Silent Consonants

OBJECTIVES

- Decode words with silent consonants.
- Apply the Phonics/Decoding Strategy.

Focus On Genre

❶ Teach

Review spelling patterns with silent consonants. Remind students that in certain consonant combinations, one or more of the consonants may be silent.

- Write c*limb*, *autumn*, *listen*, *sign*, *scene*, and *through*.
- Point to the underlined letters as you say the words.
- Have students identify the silent consonants. (*b* in *climb*; *n* in *autumn*; *t* in *listen*, *g* in *sign*, *c* in *scene*, *gh* in *through*)

Model the Phonics/Decoding Strategy. Write *My feet are* *number* *than my fingers.* Point to the underlined word.

Think Aloud *I know the word* NUHM-bur, *but it doesn't make sense in the sentence. This might be a word in which the* b *of* mb *is silent. I'll say* NUHM-ur. *Yes, this word is made of the base word* numb—"without feeling"—*and the ending* -er.

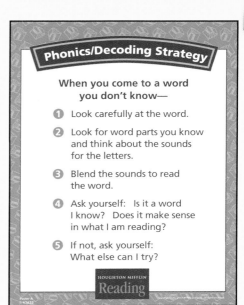

Phonics/Decoding Strategy

When you come to a word you don't know—

1. Look carefully at the word.
2. Look for word parts you know and think about the sounds for the letters.
3. Blend the sounds to read the word.
4. Ask yourself: Is it a word I know? Does it make sense in what I am reading?
5. If not, ask yourself: What else can I try?

HOUGHTON MIFFLIN
Reading

❷ Guided Practice

Help students decode words with silent consonants. Display the phrases with underlined consonant combinations as shown. Have students read the phrases aloud and discuss meaning and pronunciation. Have them copy the words with silent letters and underline the silent letter or letters. Discuss students' work.

> ran strai**gh**t home for spa**gh**etti (strai*gh*t, spa*gh*etti)
> scrambled after la**mb**s (la*mb*s)
> to fas**t**en with pas**t**e (fas*t*en)
> sole**mn**ly sang from the hy**mn**al (sole*mn*ly)
> a forei**gn** dignitary (forei*gn*)
> a fas**c**inating but **sc**ary **sc**ene (fas*c*inating, s*c*ene)

❸ Apply

Have students find words with silent consonants. Direct small groups to scan the poems on pages 119–133 for words with the consonant combinations *sc*, *gh*, and *mb*, list all the different words they find, and underline those with at least one silent letter.

SPELLING: Consonant Changes

OBJECTIVE

- Write Spelling Words that are related in spelling and meaning in which a silent letter in one word is sounded in the other word.

SPELLING WORDS

Basic

autumn	haste
autumnal	hasten
muscle*	column
muscular	columnist
crumb*	heir
crumble	inherit
sign	hymn
signal	hymnal
bomb	design
bombard	designate

Review	Challenge
soft*	doubt
soften	dubious
limb	condemn
limber	condemnation

Forms of these words appear in the literature.

REACHING ALL LEARNERS

Extra Support/Intervention

Basic Word List You may want to use only the left column of Basic Words with students who need extra support.

Challenge

Challenge Word Practice Have students write four tongue twisters, using at least one Challenge Word in each sentence.

DAY 1 INSTRUCTION

Silent to Sounded

Pretest Use the Day 5 Test sentences.

Teach Write *muscle* and *muscular*.

- Ask these questions.

  What is the meaning of each word? (*muscle:* body tissue that contracts and relaxes to cause movement; *muscular:* having well-developed muscles)

  How are the meanings related? (Both have to do with the same part of the body.)

  What is similar about their spellings? (first four letters the same)

  Which letter is silent in one word and pronounced in the other? (c)

- Explain that the spelling of a word with a silent consonant may be remembered by thinking of a word related in meaning in which the consonant is sounded.

- Write the remaining Basic Words. Discuss the meaning, spelling, and pronunciation of each pair.

Practice/Homework Assign **Practice Book** page 293.

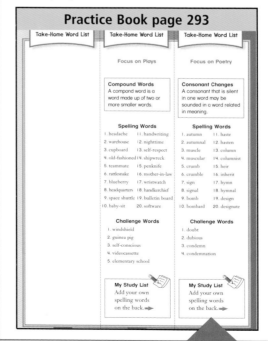

Practice Book page 293

DAY 2 REVIEW & PRACTICE

Reviewing the Principle

Go over the principle that the spelling of a word with a silent consonant may sometimes be remembered by thinking of a word related in meaning in which the consonant is pronounced.

Practice/Homework Assign **Practice Book** page 99.

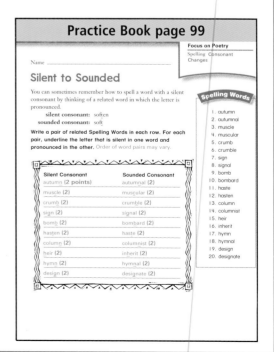

Practice Book page 99

Take-Home Word List

DAY 3 — VOCABULARY

Word Families

- Explain that many of the Spelling Word pairs belong to larger families of related words. For example, *signature* is part of the same family as *sign/signal*.

- Have groups list as many words as they can that belong to the same word family as each pair of words below.

  muscle/muscular (muscled, muscling, muscly, musculature)

  crumb/crumble (crumbly, crumblier, crumbliest)

  sign/signal, design/designate (signature, designer, resign, resignation, consignment, assign, assignment, insignia, signify, significant, significance)

  bomb/bombard (bombardier, bombastic)

  haste/hasten (hasty, hastily)

  heir/inherit (inheritance, heiress, heirloom, heritage, heredity)

Practice/Homework For spelling practice, assign **Practice Book** page 100.

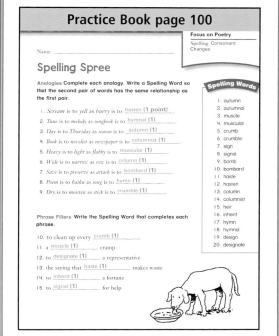

Practice Book page 100

Focus on Poetry
Spelling Consonant Changes

Name _____

Spelling Spree

Analogies Complete each analogy. Write a Spelling Word so that the second pair of words has the same relationship as the first pair.

1. *Scream* is to *yell* as *hurry* is to __hasten (1 point)__
2. *Tune* is to *melody* as *songbook* is to __hymnal (1)__
3. *Day* is to *Thursday* as *season* is to __autumn (1)__
4. *Book* is to *novelist* as *newspaper* is to __columnist (1)__
5. *Heavy* is to *light* as *flabby* is to __muscular (1)__
6. *Wide* is to *narrow* as *row* is to __column (1)__
7. *Save* is to *preserve* as *attack* is to __bombard (1)__
8. *Poem* is to *haiku* as *song* is to __hymn (1)__
9. *Dry* is to *moisten* as *stick* is to __crumble (1)__

Phrase Fillers Write the Spelling Word that completes each phrase.

10. to clean up every __crumb (1)__
11. a __muscle (1)__ cramp
12. to __designate (1)__ a representative
13. the saying that __haste (1)__ makes waste
14. to __inherit (1)__ a fortune
15. to __signal (1)__ for help

Spelling Words
1. autumn
2. autumnal
3. muscle
4. muscular
5. crumb
6. crumble
7. sign
8. signal
9. bomb
10. bombard
11. haste
12. hasten
13. column
14. columnist
15. heir
16. inherit
17. hymn
18. hymnal
19. design
20. designate

DAY 4 — PROOFREADING

Game: What's the Letter?

Have pairs or small groups write each Spelling Word with a silent consonant on ten cards, one word per card, drawing a short line in place of the silent consonant. Each group also draws a ladder with five rungs. Tell students to stack the word cards face-down.

- Player 1 turns over a card and names the missing consonant.

- If correct, that player names the related Spelling Word in which the consonant is sounded and spells that word. If correct again, Player 1 moves his or her marker one square. If incorrect, Player 1 does not move. Used cards are put aside.

- Players take turns until someone reaches the top rung.

- If all cards are used before anyone wins, players shuffle and reuse them.

Practice/Homework For proofreading and writing practice, assign **Practice Book** page 101.

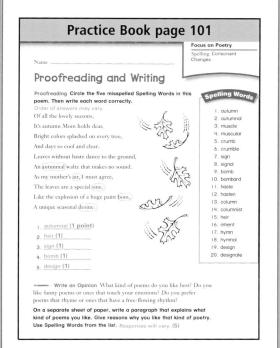

Practice Book page 101

Focus on Poetry
Spelling Consonant Changes

Name _____

Proofreading and Writing

Proofreading Circle the five misspelled Spelling Words in this poem. Then write each word correctly. Order of answers may vary.

Of all the lovely seasons,
It's autumn Mom holds dear,
Bright colors splashed on every tree,
And days so cool and clear.
Leaves without haste dance to the ground,
An ~autumnal~ waltz that makes no sound.
As my mother's ~air~, I must agree,
The leaves are a special ~sine~,
Like the explosion of a huge paint ~bom~,
A unique seasonal ~desine~.

1. __autumnal (1 point)__
2. __heir (1)__
3. __sign (1)__
4. __bomb (1)__
5. __design (1)__

Spelling Words
1. autumn
2. autumnal
3. muscle
4. muscular
5. crumb
6. crumble
7. sign
8. signal
9. bomb
10. bombard
11. haste
12. hasten
13. column
14. columnist
15. heir
16. inherit
17. hymn
18. hymnal
19. design
20. designate

Write an Opinion What kind of poems do you like best? Do you like funny poems or ones that touch your emotions? Do you prefer poems that rhyme or ones that have a free-flowing rhythm?

On a separate sheet of paper, write a paragraph that explains what kind of poems you like. Give reasons why you like that kind of poetry. Use Spelling Words from the list. Responses will vary. (5)

DAY 5 — ASSESSMENT

Spelling Test

Say each underlined word, read the sentence, and then repeat the word. Have students write only the underlined word.

Basic Words

1. Winter follows **autumn**.
2. An **autumnal** chore is raking leaves.
3. He put ice on the sore **muscle**.
4. The **muscular** man lifts weights.
5. Each ant carried a **crumb**.
6. I **crumble** crackers in my soup.
7. He hung up the OPEN **sign**.
8. The flashing light was a **signal**.
9. The officer defused the **bomb**.
10. Will he **bombard** you with questions?
11. In his **haste,** he forgot his keys.
12. We must **hasten** to catch the bus.
13. My uncle writes a **column**.
14. I disagree with that **columnist**.
15. Her grandson is her only **heir**.
16. Who will **inherit** the old house?
17. Everyone sang the **hymn**.
18. Put a **hymnal** on each chair.
19. Did he **design** the stage set?
20. Can you **designate** a leader?

Challenge Words

21. Do you **doubt** his excuse?
22. His alibi was **dubious**.
23. We **condemn** that plan.
24. The mayor issued a strong **condemnation** of the crime.

Practice Book page 102

Focus on Poetry
Vocabulary Skill Connotation

Name _____

Negatives to Positives

Susie Plotkin thinks Artie is a great reporter, but the job recommendation she wrote for him doesn't sound very positive. Fix her letter by replacing each underlined word with one that has either a positive or a neutral connotation. Write the new word on the line that has the same number. Next to each word, write *positive* or *neutral* to describe the connotation of your new word.
Suggest that students use a thesaurus and a dictionary. Answers will vary.
Sample answers shown.

Artie Shaw is an <u>obsessive</u> worker who never leaves a job unfinished. His <u>nosiness</u> can sometimes get him into <u>impossible</u> situations, but he always manages to <u>barge</u> through any doors that are <u>slammed</u> in his face. His <u>cutthroat</u> style guarantees that he always finishes first. Thanks to Artie's <u>relentless</u> reporting skills, he has <u>stolen</u> many <u>lurid</u> stories from under the noses of other writers on our staff. Needless to say, his coworkers <u>resent</u> him. If you ask me, they all wish they had his <u>devious</u> talent for news gathering. What else can I say about Artie? I'm sure you'll find him a very <u>odd</u> employee, and I mean that in the best possible way.

1. attentive (positive) **(1 point)**
2. curiosity (neutral) **(1)**
3. challenging (neutral) **(1)**
4. go (neutral) **(1)**
5. shut (neutral) **(1)**
6. ambitious (positive) **(1)**
7. determined (positive) **(1)**
8. taken (neutral) **(1)**
9. exciting (positive) **(1)**
10. envy, admire (neutral, positive) **(1)**
11. clever (positive) **(1)**
12. unique (special/positive) **(1)**

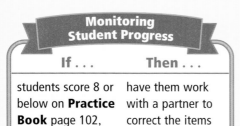

English Language Learners

Language Development

Review thesaurus entries for *strong* and for *hungry*. Discuss how the synonyms differ in degree.

Monitoring Student Progress

If . . .	Then . . .
students score 8 or below on **Practice Book** page 102,	have them work with a partner to correct the items they missed.

VOCABULARY SKILLS: Connotation

❶ Teach

Explain connotations. Tell students that words may suggest, or connote, feelings and associations that go beyond dictionary definitions. Write *One last group shot of/ all of us, smirking,* from "Family Photo" on page 133.

- Ask students to mime *smirking*.
- Discuss why the poet chose the word *smirking*, instead of a more neutral or positive word, such as *smiling*.
- Explain that *smirking* has a less favorable connotation than *smiling*; a smirk is a smile of self-satisfaction and is often rude.
- Emphasize that all careful writers, and especially poets, choose a word for its connotation as well as its literal meanings.

Model thinking about connotation. Write this line from "The People, Yes," page 131: *A <u>tough</u> will counts.* Point to *tough*.

Think Aloud *What is the connotation of* tough *in this line? The poet could have chosen a more neutral word, such as* firm. *He could also have chosen a word with a negative connotation, such as* stubborn. *The word* tough *suggests strength, and that is probably why the poet chose it.*

❷ Guided Practice

Give students practice in understanding connotations. Have partners review this list of phrases and discuss how positive, negative, or neutral each underlined word is. Discuss answers as a class.

1. Jon always does his work <u>hastily/quickly/promptly</u>.
2. Maya is <u>frugal/thrifty/stingy</u> with her earnings.
3. I detect the <u>odor/fragrance/scent</u> of perfume.
4. Damon worked <u>doggedly/steadily/diligently</u> toward his goal.
5. The business owner is <u>clever/slick/shrewd</u>.

❸ Apply

Assign Practice Book page 102.

STUDY SKILL:
Specialized Dictionaries

OBJECTIVES

- Understand that some dictionaries have specialized information arranged alphabetically.
- Use a rhyming dictionary, a biographical dictionary, and a geographic dictionary to find specific information.

Focus On Genre

❶ Teach

Introduce three kinds of specialized dictionary.

- Rhyming dictionaries are used by poets and songwriters looking for words that rhyme.

- Biographical dictionaries are used by researchers who want to check spellings of names and basic facts about famous people, past and present.

- Geographic dictionaries, also called gazetteers, can be used to check spellings of place names and basic facts.

Display and discuss Transparency F1–3.

- Rhyming dictionaries have words alphabetically arranged by the ending sounds, rather than spellings.

- The information in biographical dictionaries is brief. Entries are organized alphabetically by last name and often by category.

- Geographic dictionaries give brief information about cities, states and provinces, countries, rivers, and other features, sometimes with pronunciation. Entries are listed alphabetically.

Model using the sample dictionary entries on the transparency to answer questions.

- What are two good words to rhyme with *basketball?* (Sample answer: *fall, enthrall*)

- What is a well-known work by Amy Lowell? (What's O'Clock)

- Where are the mountains called the Sierra Morena? (in southern Spain)

❷ Practice/Apply

Have students use specialized dictionaries to answer these questions.

- What are five words that rhyme with *lost?*
- What are three rhymes for *forever?*
- What year did the poet Emily Dickinson die?
- Where was the American poet Langston Hughes born?
- Where is Lake Louise?
- In what part of the world is Tegucigalpa? How is the name pronounced?

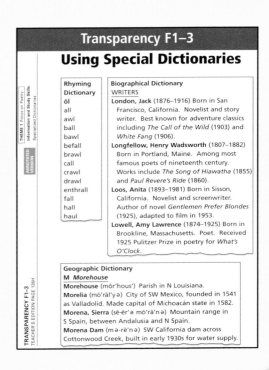

Transparency F1–3
Using Special Dictionaries

Rhyming Dictionary	Biographical Dictionary
ôl	WRITERS
all	**London, Jack** (1876–1916) Born in San Francisco, California. Novelist and story writer. Best known for adventure classics including *The Call of the Wild* (1903) and *White Fang* (1906).
awl	
ball	
bawl	
befall	**Longfellow, Henry Wadsworth** (1807–1882) Born in Portland, Maine. Among most famous poets of nineteenth century. Works include *The Song of Hiawatha* (1855) and *Paul Revere's Ride* (1860).
brawl	
call	
crawl	
drawl	**Loos, Anita** (1893–1981) Born in Sisson, California. Novelist and screenwriter. Author of novel *Gentlemen Prefer Blondes* (1925), adapted to film in 1953.
enthrall	
fall	
hall	**Lowell, Amy Lawrence** (1874–1925) Born in Brookline, Massachusetts. Poet. Received 1925 Pulitzer Prize in poetry for *What's O'Clock*.
haul	

Geographic Dictionary
M *Morehouse*
Morehouse (môr'hous') Parish in N Louisiana.
Morelia (mō'rāl'yə) City of SW Mexico, founded in 1541 as Valladolid. Made capital of Michoacán state in 1582.
Morena, Sierra (sē-ĕr'ə mō'rā'nə) Mountain range in S Spain, between Andalusia and N Spain.
Morena Dam (mə-rē'nə) SW California dam across Cottonwood Creek, built in early 1930s for water supply.

GRAMMAR: More Complex Sentences

GRAMMAR

OBJECTIVES

- Transform compound sentences to form complex sentences, using appropriate subordinating conjunctions.
- Combine sentences to form compound-complex sentences.
- Proofread and correct sentences with grammar, spelling, capitalization, and punctuation errors.

DAY 1 · INSTRUCTION

Using Subordinate Clauses

Teach Remind students that a complex sentence is two simple sentences joined by a subordinating conjunction, such as *before* or *when*.

- Display **Transparency F1–5.** Ask students how the example compound sentence was changed to form the second and third sentences. (by using a subordinate clause) Ask a student to identify the subordinating conjunction. (*after*)

- Point out the comma that sets off a subordinate clause at the beginning of a sentence.

- Explain that using complex sentences from time to time can improve sentence fluency.

- Ask volunteers to change Sentences 1–3 to complex sentences, using the subordinating conjunction in parentheses.

Daily Language Practice
Have students correct Sentences 1 and 2 on **Transparency F1–4.**

DAY 2 · PRACTICE

Independent Work

Practice/Homework Assign **Practice Book** page 103.

Daily Language Practice
Have students correct Sentences 3 and 4 on **Transparency F1–4.**

Transparency F1–4
Daily Language Practice

Correct two sentences each day.

1. Ginny wrote a column about the cleveland bom squad. Ginny wrote a column about the Cleveland bomb squad.
2. After the column appeared last autum she got a job as a columnist. After the column appeared last autumn, Ginny got a job as a columnist.
3. Readers often bombard columnists with letters? Readers often bombard columnists with letters.
4. Some writers hasen to reply but others let the letters pile up. Some writers hasten to reply, but others let the letters pile up.
5. Did you notice the desine on the cover of the hymnal. Did you notice the design on the cover of the hymnal?
6. after Marco swept up every crum he gave me a signal and I mopped the floor. After Marco swept up every crumb, he gave me a signal, and I mopped the floor.
7. Whom did mr Finley designate to inharit his property. Whom did Mr. Finley designate to inherit his property?
8. I like that sign because, the musculur person looks like my cousin. I like that sign, because the muscular person looks like my cousin.
9. Make hayste to repair that wall or it might crumble, and injure someone. Make haste to repair that wall, or it might crumble and injure someone.
10. Although this song speaks of falling leafs and other lovely autumenal sights. It is difficult to sing and no one wants to include it in our concert. Although this song speaks of falling leaves and other lovely autumnal sights, it is difficult to sing, and no one wants to include it in our concert.

Monitoring Student Progress

If . . .	Then . . .
students score 7 or below on **Practice Book** page 103,	have them work in pairs to correct their mistakes.

Transparency F1–5
Using Subordinate Clauses

Richie ate his tuna sandwich, and he ate his apple.
After Richie ate his tuna sandwich, he ate his apple.
Richie ate his tuna sandwich after he ate his apple.

1. My mother works late during the week, and I prepare dinner for her and me. (when)
When my mother works late during the week, I prepare dinner for her and me.

2. I took a nap on the couch, and I ate fry bread and roast corn. (before)
Before I took a nap on the couch, I ate fry bread and roast corn.

3. Grandmother prepared lunch, and she worked on her beadwork. (after)
After Grandmother prepared lunch, she worked on her beadwork.

Practice Book page 103

Focus on Poetry
Grammar Skill: Using Subordinate Clauses

Name

Apple Season

Using Subordinate Clauses Compound sentences can be changed into complex sentences, using subordinating conjunctions.

Rewrite each sentence as a complex sentence, using a subordinating conjunction from the box. Use each conjunction once. Use commas correctly. Answers may vary. Sample answers are given.

after	as	before	when	while

1. The apples in Grandma Wallace's orchard ripen, and everyone in the family helps pick them.
When the apples in Grandma Wallace's orchard ripen, everyone in the family helps pick them. (2 points)

2. The apples have been picked, and they must be washed.
After the apples have been picked, they must be washed. (2)

3. Dad spreads newspaper on the floor, and the grandchildren begin peeling the apples.
Before the grandchildren begin peeling the apples, Dad spreads newspaper on the floor. (2)

4. Dad cuts each apple into pieces, and he also removes the core with its seeds.
As Dad cuts each apple into pieces, he also removes the core with its seeds. (2)

5. The apples simmer slowly in a big pot, and Grandma occasionally stirs them.
While the apples simmer slowly in a big pot, Grandma occasionally stirs them. (2)

135I   THEME 1: Focus on Poetry

DAY 3 INSTRUCTION

Compound-Complex Sentences

Teach Display **Transparency F1–6.**

- Use the first two example sentences to review compound and complex sentences and conjunctions.

- Point out that the third example sentence includes both a compound sentence and a complex sentence. Explain that this is a **compound-complex sentence.**

- Explain that using this type of sentence can improve sentence fluency but using too many could make writing seem wordy.

- Point out the use of commas.

- Ask volunteers to combine Sentences 1–3 into compound-complex sentences. For Sentence 2, point out that *Then* gets dropped and no comma is used. Note that the subordinate clause could have been put at the beginning instead.

Daily Language Practice
Have students correct Sentences 5 and 6 on **Transparency F1–4.**

Transparency F1–6

Compound-Complex Sentences

My parents come home from work at 5:30, and my father cooks dinner.
My father cooks dinner, and my mother cleans up the house.
When my parents come home from work at 5:30, my father cooks dinner, and my mother cleans up the house.

1. Jared is always late for soccer practice. The coach made him sit on the bench during yesterday's game, and Jared may have to sit out the next game, too. (because)
Because Jared is always late for soccer practice, the coach made him sit on the bench during yesterday's game, and Jared may have to sit out the next game, too.

2. Lupe must help her sister clean up the house, and her brother Eduardo must mow the lawn. Then they can go to the movies. (before)
Lupe must help her sister clean up the house, and her brother Eduardo must mow the lawn before they can go to the movies.

3. Artie started to speak. He was afraid everyone would be bored, but no one in the audience moved a muscle. (when)
When Artie started to speak, he was afraid everyone would be bored, but no one in the audience moved a muscle.

DAY 4 PRACTICE

Independent Work

Practice/Homework Assign **Practice Book** page 104.

Daily Language Practice
Have students correct Sentences 7 and 8 on **Transparency F1–4.**

Practice Book page 104

Focus on Poetry
Grammar Skill Compound-Complex Sentences

Name

Farewell to a Friend

Compound-Complex Sentences A compound sentence and a subordinate clause can be combined to form a compound-complex sentence.

Rewrite each pair of sentences as a compound-complex sentence, using a subordinating conjunction from the box. Use each conjunction once. Use commas correctly. (Answers may vary. Sample answers are given.)

| although | while | because | before | when |

1. My best friend Jamie told us she was moving. I felt very sad, and we both cried.
When my best friend Jamie told us she was moving, I felt very sad, and we both cried. **(2 points)**

2. Jamie's father has a new job. Her family will move to Idaho, and they plan to leave soon.
Because Jamie's father has a new job, her family will move to Idaho, and they plan to leave soon. **(2)**

3. Jamie leaves next month. Our class will make a memory poster, and Jerome will write a funny poem for her.
Before Jamie leaves next month, our class will make a memory poster, and Jerome will write a funny poem for her. **(2)**

4. We will miss Jamie. We hope she will be happy in her new school, and we want her to write to us.
Although we will miss Jamie, we hope she will be happy in her new school, and we want her to write to us. **(2)**

5. We still have some time. She and I will go to some movies, and she will sleep over at my house.
While we still have some time, she and I will go to some movies, and she will sleep over at my house. **(2)**

DAY 5 IMPROVING WRITING

Using Commas with Long Sentences

Teach Write these sentences. Have students tell where to add commas.

Some students go right home after school but others head for a snack shop. (before *but*)

Before you take the picture I want to comb my hair. (after *picture*)

Although my father wants to give me good advice, he doesn't always know what to say or he says it at the wrong time. (before *or*)

- Suggest that students review a piece of their writing to see if they can improve the sentence fluency by rewriting some sentences to include subordinate clauses. Have them proofread for correct comma placement.

Practice/Homework Assign **Practice Book** page 105.

Daily Language Practice
Have students correct Sentences 9 and 10 on **Transparency F1–4.**

Practice Book page 105

Focus on Poetry
Grammar Skills Using Commas with Long Sentences

Name

Poetry in Motion

Using Commas with Long Sentences Use a comma before the conjunction to separate the two parts of a compound sentence. Use a comma after a subordinate clause when the clause begins a sentence. A comma is usually not used before a subordinate clause at the end of a sentence.

Use proofreading marks to correct the ten errors in punctuation and capitalization in this journal entry.
1 point for each correction
Example: before I walked, to the gym I went to my poetry class.

Proofreading Marks
¶ Indent
∧ Add
✂ Delete
≡ Capital letter
/ Small letter
⊙ Add Period
∨ Add Comma
∨∨ Add Quotes
∽ Transpose

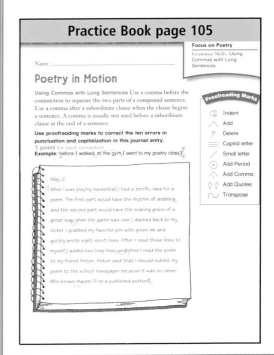

May 2.
While I was playing basketball, I had a terrific idea for a poem. The first part would have the rhythm of dribbling, and the second part would have the soaring grace of a great leap when the game was over. I dashed back to my locker. I grabbed my favorite pen with green ink and quickly wrote eight short lines. After I read those lines to myself, I added two long lines, and then I read the poem to my friend Anton. Anton said that I should submit my poem to the school newspaper because it was so clever. Who knows, maybe I'll be a published author?

WRITING: Poem

OBJECTIVES

- Write a poem about a person.
- Include literary devices found in poetry.
- Use exact details and sensory language.

DAY 1 — PREWRITING

Introducing the Format

Review elements of a poem about a person.

- Show the person in action by recounting a short personal story.
- Describe the person's appearance, gestures, speaking style; consider using dialogue.
- Focus on your feelings about the person.
- Include the special features of poetry—imagery, figurative language, rhythm, possibly repetition and rhyme.

Start students thinking about their own poem.

- Ask, What special events have you shared with friends or family?
- Ask, Who would be an interesting subject for your poem?
- Have students make and save their lists of possible subjects.

DAY 2 — DRAFTING

Discussing the Model

Have students reread "Child Rest" on Anthology page 132. Ask:

- Who is the subject of the poem? (the narrator's great grandmother)
- How does the poet help readers imagine the person? (with details about her traditional Native American midday meal, beading materials in her lap, sounds of an old song, tapping of her moccasined foot)
- How does the narrator feel about the person? (loving, cared for, protected)
- What is an example of figurative language? (the simile, "faithful as a forest doe")
- What other literary devices do you notice? (rhythm, repetition, imagery)

Display Transparency F1–7 and discuss the guidelines.

Have students draft a poem about a person.

- They can use their prewriting notes from Day 1 to choose a subject.
- Assign **Practice Book** page 106 to help students organize their writing.

Transparency F1–7

Guidelines for Writing a Poem About a Person

Follow these guidelines when you write a poem about a person.
- Use exact details, strong images, and sensory language to portray the person. Stamp out vagueness!
- Listen for the sounds of your words. Choose words with sounds that contribute to your meaning. Decide whether to use rhyme, repetition, or both.
- Listen for the rhythm of your lines. Aim for a smooth or bouncy rhythm, for example. Arrange the lines in an interesting way.
- Use punctuation to suit the poem. Try out different sentence lengths, sentences of dialogue, or phrases that stand alone.

THEME 1 Focus on Poetry
Writing Skill Guidelines for Writing a Poem About a Person

ANNOTATED VERSION

TRANSPARENCY F1–7
TEACHER'S EDITION PAGES 135K AND 135L

Practice Book page 106

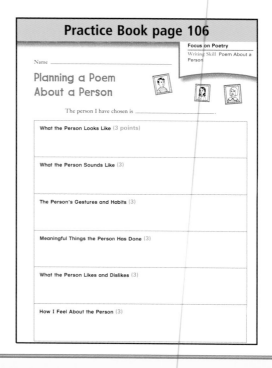

Focus on Poetry
Writing Skill Poem About a Person

Name _____

Planning a Poem About a Person

The person I have chosen is _____

| What the Person Looks Like (3 points) |
| What the Person Sounds Like (3) |
| The Person's Gestures and Habits (3) |
| Meaningful Things the Person Has Done (3) |
| What the Person Likes and Dislikes (3) |
| How I Feel About the Person (3) |

Writing Traits

Word Choice As students revise on Day 3, remind them that a poet chooses sensory words with precisely the right connotation and sound. Discuss these examples.

Vague: Dad awakened, his head <u>shooting</u> bright red spikes of hair.

Precise: Dad awakened, his head <u>sprouting</u> bright red spikes of hair.

DAY 3 REVISING

Improving Writing: Sensory Language

Review sensory language.

- Poets use words that appeal to the senses: sight, hearing, taste, touch, and smell.
- Sensory language draws readers into the experience of the poem.

Display Transparency F1–8.

- Read each sentence. Have students imagine the person described and identify the sense that could be appealed to.
- Discuss sensory language to use in a replacement sentence.
- Rewrite the first sentence and direct partners to complete Items 2–5.
- Have students compare their sentences.

Assign Practice Book page 107.

Have students review their drafts.

- Display **Transparency F1–7** again. Have students use it to revise their poems.
- Have partners hold writing conferences.
- Ask students to read their poems aloud and to revise the parts that still need work, adding sensory words.
- See Writing Traits on the preceding page.

Transparency F1–8

Sensory Language

Sample answers are shown.

1. Keisha wore a bright sweater.
   Keisha glowed in a yellow and orange sweater.

2. Uncle Joe has an unusual laugh.
   Uncle Joe has a bellowing laugh.

3. My brother makes a tasty salsa!
   My brother's tongue-tingling salsa brings tears to the eyes.

4. Great-aunt May always uses a strong perfume.
   Great-aunt May lives inside a cloud of lilac perfume.

5. Grandpa has a bald head.
   Grandpa's head is shiny-smooth on top.

TRANSPARENCY F1–8
TEACHER'S EDITION PAGES 135K AND 135L

THEME 1 Focus on Poetry **Writing Skill** Improving Your Writing

ANNOTATED VERSION

DAY 4 PROOFREADING

Checking for Errors

Have students proofread for errors in grammar, spelling, and usage.

- Remind them that punctuation in poetry can break the rules, but poets still make careful decisions about how to use commas, end marks, and other punctuation.
- Students can use the proofreading checklist on **Practice Book** page 297 to help them proofread their poem.
- Students can also use the chart of proofreading marks on **Practice Book** page 298.

Practice Book page 107

Focus on Poetry
Writing Skill Improving Your Writing

Name _____

Sensory Language

Identify the sensory language in this passage.
Write the words and phrases on the chart in the correct space.

The Creative Chef

I could tell by the smoky odor and sizzling hiss that my brother Paul had invaded the kitchen. I walked in. A pot was spilling over with thick red sauce. On the counter was a pan heaped with drooping slices of eggplant. Paul smiled weakly. "Hi," he said. "I call this dish Eggplant Madness. It will be ready in an hour. I bet you can't wait to try some." Then he raced to the pot and stirred furiously. "Don't worry, I threw away the burned part. Here, taste this sauce."

I'm a sport. I took the spoon Paul offered and slid the warm, smooth sauce into my mouth. I recognized a zingy garlic flavor and a tinge of sweet basil. Believe it or not, I was starting to look forward to Eggplant Madness.

Sight	spilling over with thick red sauce; heaped with drooping slices; smiled weakly; raced; stirred furiously (3 points)
Hearing	sizzling hiss (1)
Taste	zingy garlic flavor; tinge of sweet basil (1)
Smell	smoky odor (1)
Touch	slid the warm, smooth sauce (1)

Write a sentence of your own that could belong in "The Creative Chef." Use sensory language. (3)

DAY 5 PUBLISHING

Sharing Poetry

Consider these publishing options.

- Ask students to read their poem or some other piece of writing from the Author's Chair.
- Have students contribute their poem, with an actual or imagined photograph, to a group photo-poetry album.

Portfolio Opportunity

📁 Save students' poems as samples of their writing development.

Monitoring Student Progress

If . . .	Then . . .
students' writing does not follow the guidelines on **Transparency F1–7,**	have them reread the poem aloud several times to listen for words or lines to improve.

Independent Activities

Language Center

VOCABULARY

Building Vocabulary

👥👥👥 Groups	🕐 20 minutes
Objective	Brainstorm words that are related to *memory*.

Create a group word web that shows words related to *memory*. Start with the web below. Then follow these steps.

- Discuss what the word *memory* means.
- Check a dictionary or a thesaurus for ideas.
- Compare your group's web with those of other groups and add new words to your web.

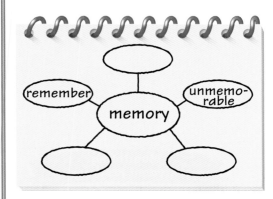

PHONICS/SPELLING

Sentence Stumpers

👤 Singles	🕐 20 minutes
Objective	Write sentences that have related spelling word pairs.

Working with your partner, read the list of Spelling Words and choose five pairs of words.

- Working individually, write five sentences using a word pair in each. Leave a blank space where each word would go.
- Exchange papers with your partner. Decide which word pair belongs in the sentence and write the words in the blanks.
- Return the papers and check the spelling of the answers.

VOCABULARY

What's My Connotation?

👥👥👥 Groups	🕐 20 minutes
Objective	Play a connotation game.
Materials	Activity Master 1–5, page R36, and scissors

Play a game to determine the connotation of a word.

- Cut out the sentence cards on Activity Master 1–5.
- Shuffle the cards and place them face-down in a pile. Have one student choose the top card and read the sentence twice using a different word choice in the blank each time.
- After both sentences have been read, group members decide which words give *positive*, *negative*, or *neutral* connotations.
- Explain your choices.

Consider copying and laminating these activities for use in centers.

LISTENING/SPEAKING

Read a Poem Aloud

👥 Pairs	🕐 30 minutes
Objective	Read a poem aloud.

The best way to appreciate the sounds and rhythm of a poem is to read it aloud. Choose a poem that is not in the Anthology to read aloud to the class.

- Read the poem aloud to yourself first. Note the rhyme, rhythm, punctuation, pacing, and tone of the poem.

- Decide where it is best to pause or not to pause in order to convey the sense of the poem.

- Use your voice to dramatize the meaning of the poem.

- Practice reading your poem aloud with a partner several times before you read it to the class. Listen to your partner's comments about your reading.

STRUCTURAL ANALYSIS

Word Building Challenge

👥 Groups	🕐 20 minutes
Objective	Build words using base words, prefixes, and suffixes.
Materials	Index cards cut in half or small pieces of paper

See who can build the most words from base words, prefixes, and suffixes.

- Copy the base words, prefixes, and suffixes listed below onto cards.

- Display the prefix and suffix cards.

- Have one player choose a base word and try different combinations of prefixes and suffixes to form new words.

- Have a recorder write down all of the words that are made.

- Continue until all of the base word cards have been used.

Prefixes	Base Words		Suffixes
	blame	rest	
re	do	roll	ful
un	faith	separate	less
	friend	slow	ly
	harm	sorrow	
	peace	wrap	
	joy	write	

 joy ful ly

Leveled Readers

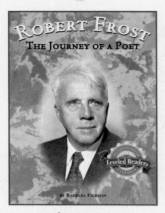

Robert Frost: The Journey of a Poet

Summary *Robert Frost gained an appreciation for language from his father, a journalist, and his mother, who shared with him poems and stories. When Robert's father died, his mother moved the family to New England, where the change in seasons inspired his writing. Eventually, Frost had his first book of poetry published. He went on to win the Pulitzer Prize four times, and he is one of America's best-loved poets.*

Vocabulary

Introduce the Key Vocabulary and ask students to complete the BLM.

fondness a strong preference, *p. 5*

vividly presented in a clear and striking manner, *p. 6*

paternal related through one's father, *p. 7*

income money received for goods or services, *p. 11*

rejections notifications of not being accepted, *p. 12*

rural characteristic of the country, *p. 12*

● BELOW LEVEL

Building Background and Vocabulary

Tell students they will be reading a biography of Robert Frost. Ask students to share the names of any poets they know, or describe any poems that are familiar to them. Guide students through the text, using some of the vocabulary from the story.

Writing Skill: Writing a Poem

Have students read the Strategy Focus on the book flap. Remind students to use the strategy and to think about the elements of poetry as they read the book. (See the Leveled Readers Teacher's Guide for **Vocabulary and Comprehension Practice Masters.**)

Responding

Have partners discuss how to answer the questions on the inside back cover.

Think About the Selection Sample answers:

1. Possible response: He enjoyed exploring San Francisco with his father.
2. He experienced the four seasons and spent more time observing nature.
3. when his poem was published in the school paper
4. Answers will vary.

Making Connections Answers will vary.

Building Fluency

Model Read aloud page 3. Discuss the effects of ending a page with a question or sentence that starts with *But* (grab the reader's attention, encourage the desire to turn the page).

Practice Ask students to find and read aloud the other pages in which the last sentence begins with *But* (pages 7 and 12).

The Images of Nikki Grimes

Summary *Poet Nikki Grimes determined from an early age that she would become a writer. She also vowed to write poems and books that include African American characters and culture. Because she moved often while growing up, friendships and other relationships are also important topics in her poems.*

Vocabulary

Introduce the Key Vocabulary and ask students to complete the BLM.

uncanny strange, eerie, *p. 3*

recurring happening again or repeatedly, *p. 4*

images likenesses of living things, places, or objects, *p. 7*

calloused roughened, *p. 7*

confiding sharing secrets, *p. 9*

rituals ceremonies or rites used in worship, *p. 10*

heritage customs passed down through generations, *p. 11*

haiku a Japanese verse form of five, seven, and five syllables, *p. 13*

▲ ON LEVEL

Building Background and Vocabulary

Tell students they will be reading a biography of the poet Nikki Grimes. Ask what might inspire poets and what skills they must have to be successful. Guide students through the text, using some of the vocabulary from the story.

Writing Skill: Writing a Poem

Have students read the Strategy Focus on the book flap. Remind students to use the strategy and to think about the elements of poetry as they read the book. (See the Leveled Readers Teacher's Guide for **Vocabulary and Comprehension Practice Masters.**)

Responding

Have partners discuss how to answer the questions on the inside back cover.

Think About the Selection Sample answers:

1. She grew up in New York City. The city and its sights and sounds form the background for most of her poems.
2. Images bring things to life by using one or more of the five senses.
3. Growing up, she never found any books or poems about children like her, so she decided to write some herself.
4. Answers will vary.

Making Connections Answers will vary.

Building Fluency

Model Read aloud page 6. Point out the slashes that separate the lines of poetry in the text.

Practice Have six volunteers stand before the class and read aloud the poetry lines on pages 7, 9, 11, 12, 13, and 14.

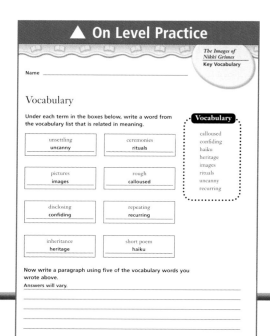

Leveled Readers

■ ABOVE LEVEL

Gary Soto
by Ana Ruiz
illustrated by Ralph Canaday

Gary Soto

Summary *Poet and author Gary Soto is the grandson of immigrants from Mexico. He writes mostly about Mexican Americans and about everyday life, finding poetry in the ordinary.*

Vocabulary

Introduce the Key Vocabulary and ask students to complete the BLM.

heritage customs passed down through generations, *p. 3*

Chicano a Mexican American, *p. 3*

anthology a collection of literary pieces, *p. 6*

alienated isolated from society, *p. 6*

obsessed excessively preoccupied with something, *p. 6*

eminent distinguished, *p. 8*

critique a critical review, *p. 9*

free verse poem of unrhymed lines, usually with no fixed rhythm, *p. 12*

resonate to bring forth a shared emotion, *p. 12*

Building Background and Vocabulary

Lead a discussion about poets. Consider what might inspire them and what skills they must have to be successful. Guide students through the text, using some of the vocabulary from the story.

Writing Skill: Writing a Poem

Have students read the Strategy Focus on the book flap. Remind students to use the strategy and to think about the elements of poetry as they read the book. (See the Leveled Readers Teacher's Guide for **Vocabulary and Comprehension Practice Masters.**)

Responding

Have partners discuss how to answer the questions on the inside back cover.

Think About the Selection Sample answers:

1. He earned money by selling copper to a junkyard, picking fruit, and washing cars.

2. in college, when he discovered an anthology of poems about everyday life

3. Answers will vary. Example: Everyone's life can be the subject of good poetry.

4. Answers will vary.

Making Connections Answers will vary.

Building Fluency

Model Read aloud the first paragraph of page 13. Ask students what they think the author means by *his magical knack for transforming ordinary things into meaningful details, images, and metaphors.*

Practice Ask students to find and read aloud examples of this *transformation* from the poems mentioned in the text (example: page 10, *holding an orange in winter . . .*).

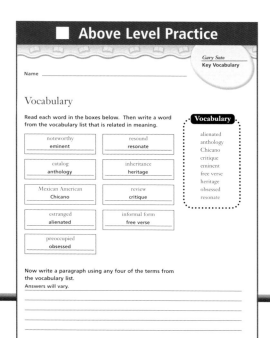

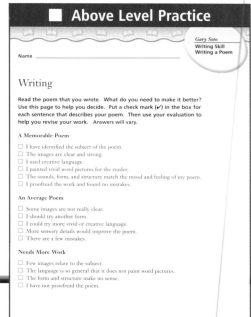

◆ LANGUAGE SUPPORT

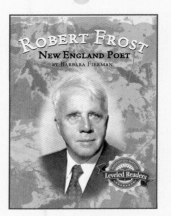

Robert Frost: New England Poet

Summary *The poet Robert Frost was born in 1874 in San Francisco. When he was ten, his family moved to New England. He taught school and wrote poetry whenever he had time. Many of his poems are about his observations of nature. Frost moved to England to write his first full book of poetry. After returning to the United States, Robert Frost won four Pulitzer Prizes.*

Vocabulary

Introduce the Key Vocabulary and ask students to complete the BLM.

observe to see and pay attention to, *p. 4*

imagination creative power; originality, *p. 5*

rejections refusals to accept or consider, *p. 12*

rural relating to the country or life in the country, *p. 12*

publish to print and offer for public sale, *p. 13*

diverged went in different directions; branched out, *p. 16*

Building Background and Vocabulary

Explain that this story is about the poet Robert Frost. Distribute the **Build Background Practice Master** and point out the picture. Read the directions and questions aloud, and have partners complete the Master. Then share and discuss responses. (See the Leveled Readers Teacher's Guide for **Build Background and Vocabulary Masters**.)

Reading Strategy: Evaluate

Have students read the Strategy Focus on the book flap. Remind students to use the strategy as they read the book.

Responding

Have partners discuss how to answer the questions on the inside back cover.

Think About the Selection Sample answers:

1. in San Francisco, California
2. He was able to write down what he observed, and what he imagined.
3. Frost was a determined person, and he believed his poetry was good.
4. Answers will vary.

Making Connections Answers will vary.

Building Fluency

Model Read aloud page 16 as students follow along in their books. Point out how the poem looks different from the other sentences on the page. Read the poem again as students listen carefully to the rhythm.

Practice Have partners practice reading the poem several times, trying out different rhythms and pacing. Have volunteers read the poem aloud.

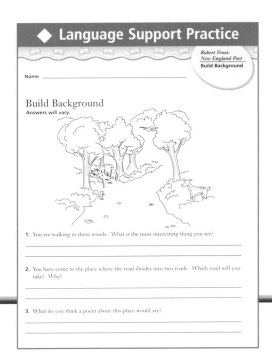

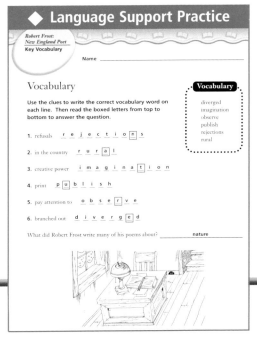

Resources for Theme 1

Contents

Leveled Theme Paperbacks

The Little Ships: The Heroic Rescue at Dunkirk in World War II

Summary *This fictional narrative in free verse is based on a historic event: the evacuation of British and French soldiers from Dunkirk in May and June of 1940. The episode is recounted from the viewpoint of a fictional participant, the young daughter of a British fisherman.*

Preparing to Read

Building Background Have students briefly tell what they know about the start of World War II. Use a map to point out Western Europe, drawing students' attention to England, France, the English Channel, Dunkirk, and Dover. Read aloud the introduction, or have students read it aloud. Remind students to use their reading strategies as they read the book.

Developing Vocabulary The context will offer meanings for most terms about boats and ships. Preview with students the meanings of the Vocabulary words listed at the left for the two suggested segments of the book, pages 1–14 and pages 15–30.

Previewing the Text

The Little Ships may be read in its entirety. If broken into two segments, the first segment ends on page 14, with the line "by the wild mess of an army on the run." To preview each segment, students may give their ideas about the mood and content of the illustration on each spread.

Supporting the Reading

pages 1–14

- Why does the author begin the book with the foreword by Christopher Dreyer? (The foreword gives background that explains how the author gained insight into the historical event.)

- On page 4, the narrator says, *But now their talk was about the trouble at Dunkirk.* When is now? (The time is May 1940, when British and French soldiers were trapped across the Channel.)

- Why does the narrator want to participate in the rescue? (She feels she is as able as any of the men, and she wants to help her father. She has a strong desire to rescue the stranded soldiers, especially since one of them may be her brother.)

- How did you figure out possible meanings for the words *towropes,* on page 9, and *minesweeper,* on page 14? (Students should note the two words that make up each compound as they tell how the meaning of each helped them to understand the meaning of the compound word.)

Vocabulary

motley, p. 8: made up of an odd assortment

convoy, p. 8: a group of ships traveling together

armada, p. 8: a big fleet of warships

wakes, p. 9: the visible tracks of waves and foam behind boats or ships

half-swamped, p. 22: filled with water nearly to the point of sinking

pages 15–30

- What do you think is likely to happen next? Why do you think so? (Students' predictions should incorporate information from the text. They may predict that the narrator will or will not find her brother or that the narrator will have to face danger.)

- The author decided to tell this story using a form of poetry called free verse. What lines suggest the nonstop action of the rescuers? (Answers will vary. One possibility, from page 16: "We were all there rowing/ and carrying/ and paddling/ and ferrying…")

- The narrator says, *I had to pretend that my arms didn't ache.* Why does she have to pretend? (She has a life-or-death job to do. This is not the time or place for complaining.)

- Was the evacuation of Dunkirk a victory? Give reasons for your judgment. (Answers will vary. Students should include information from the text to justify their reasoning.)

- Recount the most important events in the *heroic rescue at Dunkirk in World War II.* (Toward the end of May 1940, British and French soldiers were trapped across the English Channel in Dunkirk. German troops were closing in. Fishermen and other everyday people in England banded together to create a fleet of rescue ships. Along with the British navy, these little boats brought hundreds of thousands of soldiers home to safety.)

- Why does the author end the book with a passage from Winston Churchill's speech to Parliament? (Churchill's speech reflects the inspiration the British felt after their success at Dunkirk.)

Responding

Have students summarize the main events of the book. Then ask them to scan the text again for examples of *repetition*—repeated words or phrases. Suggest that they read aloud examples, and discuss how repetition conveys mood and meaning.

English Language Learners

Discuss the idiomatic meaning of the phrase *my father's daughter* in the sentence *Fishermen on the beach said I was my father's daughter* (page 5). Help students understand that this means that the girl and her father are alike. What similarities do students notice between the two?

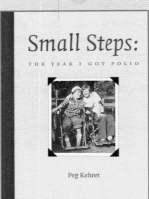

Small Steps: The Year I Got Polio

Summary *This autobiographical account focuses on an ordeal that changed the author's life. In 1949, at the age of twelve, she contracted polio and spent seven months in an ultimately successful attempt to recover the use of her muscles.*

Vocabulary

paralysis, p. 9: inability to move a part of the body

spasms, p. 13: sudden, involuntary contractions of a muscle

isolation, p. 17: separation from others

jubilantly, p. 60: with great joy

compassion, p. 84: an awareness of the suffering of another, with the desire to relieve it

mobility, p. 105: the ability to move

camaraderie, p. 132: warm feelings among friends

vaccinations, p. 172: inoculations with a vaccine to help fight off a disease

---

▲ ON LEVEL

Preparing to Read

Building Background Read the prologue with students and briefly discuss what they know about polio. Ask students what the author might mean when she says she is using *fictional techniques* to tell a true story. Remind students to use their reading strategies as they read the book.

Developing Vocabulary The context will offer meanings for most terms about polio and its treatment. Preview with students the meanings of the Vocabulary words listed at the left for the three suggested segments of the book: pages 9–59, pages 60–118, and pages 119–174.

Previewing the Text

Small Steps may by read in its entirety or broken into three reading segments: the prologue through chapter 6, pages 9–59; chapters 7–12, pages 60–118; and chapter 8 through the epilogue, pages 119–174. To preview the book, students may read through the chapter headings in the table of contents, discussing the definitions of the medical terms. They may also preview the photographs on pages 87–90.

Supporting the Reading

pages 9–59

- When do Peg's symptoms first appear? (On a Wednesday early in September 1949, she develops a sore throat and a headache. Two days later, she has a fever and aching muscles.)

- What is an isolation ward, and why is Peg put there? (An isolation ward is a place in the hospital where patients with contagious diseases are kept isolated, or separated, from people who might catch the disease. Peg has a highly contagious virus, so no one is allowed into her private room except the doctors and nurses, who wear masks.)

- How does the author convey her reaction to her paralysis? (Answers will vary. Students should point to the author's word choice and narrative development as ways of conveying emotions such as terror, panic, and helplessness.)

pages 60–118

- Why does the author describe her first movement after paralysis by saying, *It was Christmas and my birthday and the Fourth of July, all at the same time.* (The author wants to convey her intense excitement and joy at being able to move again.)

- How does Peg react to getting mail from her classmates? (Their concerns seem unimportant to her, and she realizes that facing death has changed her forever.)

- What is the rehabilitation that the Sheltering Arms provides? (The rehabilitation mainly consists of physical and activity-related therapy, but the hospital is also homelike, which may aid in her recovery.)

- Summarize Peg's experience so far in the rehabilitation hospital. (Peg forms close friendships with the other girls. Comparing herself to them, she realizes that her parents' attention makes her privileged. She gets physical therapy and the Sister Kenny treatments. She learns to use a wheelchair, and her muscle strength grows. But on a visit home, she realizes that she is not strong enough to leave the hospital.)

pages 119–174

- What details reveal the generosity of Peg's parents? (They make Peg's roommates feel like members of the family. They distribute goodies. Peg's mother helps convince her to give up her childhood possessions so that the hospitalized children can have toys and books.)

- What is the elation that the author describes on page 161? (It is the great joy she feels about going home permanently.)

- On page 170, the author writes, *I knew that in many ways, I was stronger than when I left.* What does she mean? (Her battle against polio has left her with weaker muscles but a stronger spirit.)

Responding

Have students tell how they were able to follow the author's account of events and emotions. They may give examples of their use of the Monitor/Clarify strategy to improve their understanding. Students may then share their reactions to the book. For example, ask whether the author has indeed shown that *feelings are the most important part of any story.* Finally, have students summarize the author's message.

English Language Learners

The author personifies polio, calling it an enemy and using the language of war to describe it. Discuss these words from the epilogue: *victory, vanquished, strike, battle, weapon.* Have students find earlier examples of words that fit in the same category.

THEME PAPERBACKS

THEME PAPERBACKS

Shipwreck at the Bottom of the World: The Extraordinary True Story of Shackleton and the Endurance

Summary *This nonfiction book tells the story of Antarctic explorer Sir Ernest Shackleton and his crew. Readers learn about the conditions the men faced from January 1915, when the ship was trapped in the ice, to August 1916, when all were rescued.*

Vocabulary

alpine, p. 12: relating to high mountains

floes, p. 17: flat masses of floating ice

gale, p. 39: a very strong wind

dire, p. 51: having dreadful consequences; desperate

salvage, p. 55: to rescue a ship's cargo

monotony, p. 69: tiresome sameness

skipper, p. 74: the captain of a ship

foundering, p. 86: sinking below the water

■ ABOVE LEVEL

Preparing to Read

Building Background Briefly discuss what students know about winter and summer conditions in Antarctica. Then have a volunteer read aloud "Just Imagine" on page 1. What do students think their greatest problem would be if they were stranded in Antarctica? Remind them to use their reading strategies as they read the book.

Developing Vocabulary The context will offer meanings for most terms about weather, ice, and navigation. Preview with students the meanings of the Vocabulary words listed at the left for the two suggested segments of the book, pages 1–71 and pages 72–126.

Previewing the Text

Shipwreck at the Bottom of the World may be read in its entirety or in two segments: chapters 1–10, pages 1–71; and chapter 11 through the epilogue, pages 72–126. Point out the photo, diagrams, and maps in the front matter, reminding students to refer to these while reading.

Supporting the Reading

pages 1–71

- Why does the author begin the book with the sentence *Just imagine yourself in the most hostile place on Earth?* (The author wants to convey from the start the harsh conditions.)

- What is Shackleton's purpose in Antarctica? (He wants to be the first explorer to cross the continent and to learn about its interior, satisfy his hunger for exploration, and win honor for England.)

- What is life like for the men from January through mid-October 1915? (They are trapped on the ship by pack ice. They hunt when they can and try to stay warm. They wait for the pack ice to drift north as it will allow the ship to break free.)

- When and why does Shackleton decide to break up Ocean Camp and move on? (In late December, the floe on which they are living is decaying. The ice pack seems to be moving east, but Shackleton wants to head for Paulet Island.)

- What is the mutiny that Shackleton prevents? (McNeish, a crew member, refuses to do any more hauling of the heavy lifeboats across the pack ice. Shackleton persuades McNeish and the crew to obey him.)

pages 72–126

- What words on pages 72 and 73 relate to determining one's position in the open ocean, and how did you figure out their meaning? (Students may note how they use the context to understand *latitude, parallel, longitude, meridian, coordinates, horizon, sextant, chronometer, compass, nautical table,* and *occultation.*)

- What is the voyage to Elephant Island like? (The men row the *Endurance's* three lifeboats. They make many attempts but are forced back into the pack ice. Dehydrated, frostbitten, wet, and exhausted, they see the island but must row for days before reaching it.)

- Why do the men split up? (Shackleton, Worsley, and four others sail the *James Caird* 800 miles to South Georgia Island to get help. The other crew members stay on Elephant Island.)

- What happens between the time the *James Caird* sets out for South Georgia Island and the Norwegian whaling captain sees Shackleton? (Worsley's navigation is successful. After sailing for over two weeks, the men survive a hurricane and land on the island, but on the wrong coast. Shackleton, Worsley, and two others set off to cross South Georgia Island on foot across glaciers and mountains. At last they reach the whaling station.)

- Why does the author end the story with the crewman's comment to Shackleton, *We knew you'd come back?* (Answers will vary. Students may note that the author wants to show the crew's respect for Shackleton or Shackleton's devotion to his crew.)

Responding

Have students tell how they were able to follow events and understand the technical information in the story. They may give examples of how they used the Monitor/Clarify Strategy. Students may then share their reactions to the book. Finally, they should summarize the key ideas.

Bonus Have students reread passages describing extremely arduous conditions and visualize the scenes. Tell them to select one scene to illustrate with a drawing, a map, or a diagram.

English Language Learners

List these words from the book: *treacherous, perilous, disastrous.* Point out the shared suffix, *–ous,* which usually identifies an adjective. Have students pair each adjective with a noun to make a phrase about Shackleton's extraordinary story.

Noting Details

OBJECTIVES

- Identify important ideas made known through details.
- Use details to explain a character's feelings.
- Use details to visualize events.

Target Skill Trace

- Noting Details, pp. 47A–47B

Teach

Write the following sentence on the board:

> This place has textbooks, a teacher, students, desks, chairs, chalk, a bulletin board, and a globe.

Encourage students to ask themselves, What place usually has textbooks, a teacher, a chalkboard, and so on? Ask students to identify the place and to discuss how they figured it out.

After students have responded, point out that they chose some important details and put them together to reach their answer. Remind students that instead of saying something directly like "Brian felt sorry for himself," the author gives details that readers can use to discover this information for themselves.

Take students through the process. Have students reread page 30, paragraphs 2 and 3, from *The smell was one of rot* to *a noise coming from his throat.* Model identifying and putting together details that show how Brian feels.

Think Aloud *I think that Brian is terrified. He smells something that makes him think of cobwebs, old death, the bear, and monsters. Something slithers near his feet. I know that snakes slither. Maybe Brian thinks of snakes, too. If I add up the details—being alone in the dark, in a strange place with these sounds and smells—I am pretty sure that Brian feels very scared.*

Help students put the strategy you have modeled in their own words. For example:

To find important details I could ask myself:

1. *How do I think this character is feeling?*

2. *What details gave me this idea?*

3. *Do these details add up?*

Practice

Have students work with a partner or in a small group to locate important details that could help explain one of Brian's feelings or actions listed below. Suggest that they note these details on a word web.

- discouragement: Skim pages 33-34
- persistence: Skim pages 37 (bottom)– 40 (bottom)
- successful: Skim pages 40 (bottom)– 43 (top)

Encourage partners and groups to share their thinking with the rest of the class.

Apply

As they read their **Leveled Readers** for the week, have students keep track of when they note details. Remind them to identify important ideas as they note details.

Monitoring Student Progress

If . . .	Then . . .
students need more practice with noting details,	suggest that they apply the Noting Details strategy to another story.

CHALLENGE/EXTENSION: Noting Details

Explore Animal Defenses

Porcupine quills, which Brian pulls out of his leg, are a good example of an animal defense. In times of danger, a porcupine defends itself with its quills.

Make a chart that shows other defenses—usual or unusual—that different animals use in times of danger. List details that describe each animal's defense and why it is effective. Focus on animals that live in your area.

CHALLENGE

Create Plans for Survival

Lost in the Canadian wilds, Brian Robeson faces a very uncertain future. Develop a survival plan for Brian by showing on a chart what Brian could do in the short term to find food, shelter, warmth, and protection.

Also suggest what Brian might do over the long term to make his rescue more likely. For example, is there a way he could signal would-be rescuers? List your ideas on a chart. Then present your chart to the class.

Write an Explanation with Details

Fire became a friend to Brian in the wilderness. In a paragraph, explain why Brian would call fire a friend. State your main idea clearly and support it with good details, reasons, and examples.

RETEACHING

Making Judgments

Teach

Ask students to recall TV shows set in courtrooms. Have students discuss what a judge usually does to examine a case before reaching a judgment. Use a word web such as the following:

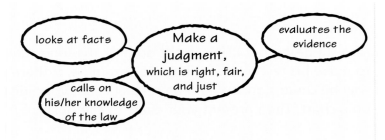

looks at facts

Make a judgment, which is right, fair, and just

evaluates the evidence

calls on his/her knowledge of the law

Engage students in a discussion about the importance of using each strategy to making a good judgment. Remind students that they, too, make judgments about the people and events they read about. Explain that they do this by thinking carefully about the situation in a story, looking carefully at what happens and why, and thinking about what they know is fair, right, or just.

Have students reread from page 58, paragraph 2, to page 59. Model the process of making a judgment about the text.

Think Aloud *As I read this passage, I realize that the refugees are desperate. Mr. Sugihara is careful to ask permission from his government. When it is denied, he thinks about what it would be like to be a refugee, discusses the problem with his family, and then makes his choice.*

Using what I now know about what happened to so many Jews in Europe during World War II, and looking at the facts the author presented, I can make the judgment that Mr. Sugihara acted responsibly and made a wise decision.

Practice

Help students list the main aspects of the situation that Mr. Sugihara must consider before he decides what to do. Ask students to suggest what Mr. Sugihara might be thinking as he evaluates his situation. Have students discuss whether they think Mr. Sugihara makes the right decision.

Help students put the strategy in their own words. For example:

To determine whether I have made a valid judgment about characters and events, I could ask myself:

1. *Is my judgment supported by evidence in the text?*

2. *Is my judgment supported by what I already know?*

3. *Am I being objective?*

Apply

As they read their **Leveled Readers** for the week, have students keep track of when they make judgments. Remind them to use story details and their own knowledge as they make judgments.

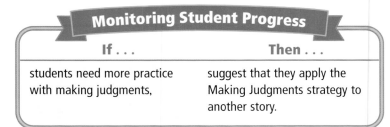

Monitoring Student Progress

If . . .	Then . . .
students need more practice with making judgments,	suggest that they apply the Making Judgments strategy to another story.

CHALLENGE/EXTENSION:
Making Judgments

CHALLENGE

 Around the World Escape

The Jews who gathered outside Mr. Sugihara's office had come to Lithuania from Poland. They hoped to travel to Japan and then make their way to the United States. Use a classroom globe or map to plot an escape route for these refugees, beginning in Poland and ending in Japan. Draw a map of the route, listing the countries and bodies of water the refugees would cross. Also, show the scale of miles to calculate the approximate distances of each leg of the journey.

 Debate the Issue

When Mr. Sugihara takes up his new position in Germany, his new supervisor will question him about why he issued the visas when he was told not to. With a partner, create dialogue for the debate that ensues between Mr. Sugihara and his new boss. Have Mr. Sugihara argue that he did the right thing to save the lives of the refugees; have his boss argue that Mr. Sugihara should have followed orders. If you would like, share your dialogue with the class.

 Write a Thank-You Note

Imagine that you are one of the refugees who received a visa from Mr. Sugihara. Write a thank-you note to the diplomat, explaining how his courage made a difference in your life. Tell about what happened after you left Lithuania for Japan. Include as many details as possible.

Sequence of Events

<table>
<tr><td>

OBJECTIVES

- Identify the sequence of events in a story.
- Recognize words that signal sequence.
- Use verb tense to determine the order of events.

Target Skill Trace

- Sequence of Events, pp. 93A–93B

</td></tr>
</table>

Teach

Have students think about what happens on a typical weekend. Ask them to name three or four events in the order in which they normally occur. Suggest that students use time-order words, such as *first, next, then,* and *last* to list these events. Write the time-order words students use.

Have students think about *Climb or Die* and list some important events that happen up to page 81, as Danielle and Jake climb Mount Remington. Write the following major events from the story on the board and have students copy them on index cards:

> Danielle and Jake reach the summit.
>
> Danielle and Jake do not see the
>
> weather station.
>
> Danielle and Jake use hammers
>
> as ice axes.
>
> Danielle and Jake begin to argue.

Model how you might organize these events in the sequence in which they occur. As you model, write the words *First, Next, Then,* and *Finally* next to the events to show their order.

Think Aloud *When the story first opens, Danielle and Jake are climbing up Mount Remington, using the hammers as ice axes. So I'll write* First *next to that event. Of course, I know earlier events happened in the story—such as the car crash and blizzard—but they're not part of the story I've read. With a great deal of effort, Danielle and Jake manage to reach the top. That's the second main event, so I'll write* Next *beside it. The next thing that happens is they don't see the weather station. So I'll write* Then *next to it. That's such a big disappointment that they start to argue. That's the last thing that happens up to page 81. So I'll write* Finally *next to it.*

Practice

Ask students to recall the main events they read from page 82 to the end of the story. Have them jot down at least four main events, each on an index card.

Next, have students arrange the events in the sequence in which they occur. Suggest that they write the words *first, next, then,* and *finally* to show the order of events. When students finish, help them express the process in their own words.

1. Read the story and try to remember the order of events that happen.
2. Look for time-order words, such as *now, then, when,* and *afterward,* that show sequence.
3. Try to picture the events as they happened.
4. Go back and reread the story if you aren't sure of the sequence.

Apply

As they read their **Leveled Readers** for the week, have students keep track of sequence of events. Remind them to identify and use time-order words as they note the sequence of events.

Monitoring Student Progress

If . . .	Then . . .
students need more practice with sequence of events,	suggest that they look for time-order words in other stories they read.

CHALLENGE/EXTENSION:
Sequence of Events

 ## An Eye on the Storm

Think about storms you have experienced, such as blizzards, hurricanes, thunderstorms, hailstorms, or even tornadoes. Prepare notes on index cards that describe in sequence what you experienced during one storm. Focus on details about the storm and how it affected you directly. Draw pictures that illustrate the storm. Share your experiences and illustrations of the storm with a partner or with the whole class.

 ## Write a Personal Narrative

Improvising can be an important skill in everyday life, often enabling us to solve problems or accomplish goals in unexpected ways. Recall a real-life situation in which you had to improvise. Write a short narrative, using time-order words to indicate sequence, describing the problem you faced and how you solved it.

CHALLENGE

 ## Explore Cooperation

Create a chart that lists ways in which people in communities and neighborhoods cooperate with one another to improve the health and well-being of the neighborhood. List at least five examples on your chart. Choose one of your examples and write in order the steps that would have to be taken to make this improvement a reality. Include illustrations if you like.

Predicting Outcomes

OBJECTIVES

- Use story details combined with personal knowledge to make predictions about the text.
- Confirm or revise a prediction, or make a new one based on story developments.

Target Skill Trace

- Predicting Outcomes, pp. 115A–115B

Teach

Ask students to think of times when they predicted what would happen in a movie or TV story. Help students see that predictions are not wild guesses.

Point out that to make a prediction about what will happen in a story readers have to

- look at the details and clues that the author includes
- think about their own knowledge and life experiences
- put details and their own experiences together

Have students reread page 99. Model how to predict which choice Charlotte might make. As you model, add details to the graphic organizer.

Selection Details	+ Personal Knowledge and Thinking	= Prediction
• mast—130' high	hard to shimmy	not enough information yet
• mast— has great round trunk	Shrouds and ratlines have resting places.	Charlotte will climb the shrouds and ratlines.
• shrouds and ratlines		

Think Aloud *As I read page 99, I note that Charlotte must choose to climb to the top of the main mast by shimmying up the main mast or climbing the shrouds and ratlines. The story tells me that the main mast is a great rounded tree trunk about 130 feet high. I know from my own experience*

of climbing trees that it would be almost impossible to shimmy up such a great distance, especially for someone who hadn't practiced. From pictures I have seen of sailing ships, I know that the shrouds and ratlines are attached to smaller masts and spars that hold the sails. If she chooses this route, Charlotte will be able to rest on her way up. Therefore, I predict she will climb the shrouds and ratlines.

Remind students that as more information becomes available, they should check their predictions and make any needed changes.

Practice

Ask students to think about how Charlotte managed to climb. Encourage them to suggest some personal character traits that she showed. Then have them predict how Charlotte might respond to other dangerous situations that could arise during the voyage to America. For example, students can predict what Charlotte might do if the *Seahawk* were damaged in a storm and needed to have a shroud repaired.

Suggest that students make a prediction and give reasons for it. Encourage students to share the prediction-making process they used with the whole group.

Apply

As they read their **Leveled Readers** for the week, have students keep track of the outcomes they predict. Remind them to use story clues and personal knowledge as they predict outcomes.

Monitoring Student Progress

If . . .	Then . . .
students need more practice with predicting outcomes,	suggest that they use story clues and personal knowledge to make predictions.

CHALLENGE/EXTENSION:
Predicting Outcomes

 ## Explore Heights

Charlotte has to climb 130 feet to reach the top of the *Seahawk*'s main mast. Predict what buildings and objects might be the same height as the mast. Check your predictions by using graph paper to show the heights of the objects and buildings. Represent the main mast by drawing items to scale (one square on the graph paper might equal five feet). Represent the height of a student in the group as well as familiar objects and buildings, such as the school, a flag pole, and a nearby tree.

 ## Write a News Story

Recall a time when, like Charlotte, you faced a difficult or dangerous task. For example, you might think about a time when you tried to do something for the first time. Write a short news story about the event, including information on *Who, What, Where, When, Why,* and *How.* Write the end to your story on a separate paper. Have your partner read your story and predict how it will turn out. Use the ending your partner wrote for his or her story to check your predictions.

CHALLENGE

 ## What's Next for Charlotte?

With a partner, work together to predict what will happen when Captain Jaggery confronts Charlotte after her climb. Write dialogue for both Charlotte and Captain Jaggery. After rehearsing the scene, partners can perform it for the class.

RETEACHING

Suffixes *-ful*, *-less*, and *-ly*

OBJECTIVES

- Decode words with the suffixes *-ful*, *-less*, and *-ly*.
- Identify the meaning of words with the suffixes *-ful*, *-less*, and *-ly*.

Target Skill Trace

- Suffixes *-ful*, *-less*, and *-ly*, p. 47C

Teach

Put the following on the board:

Lead students to identify how the underlined words are the same and how they are different. Review the concepts <u>base</u> <u>word</u> and <u>suffix</u>. Circle the suffix(es) in each underlined word. Remind students that knowing that words have suffixes can help them decode those words more quickly.

Have students reread page 40, paragraph 5 ("Maybe not enough …"). Then use the Think Aloud to model how to decode the word <u>briefly</u> in the last sentence.

Think Aloud *I can't read this word right away, so I'll look at it carefully for a part I know, like a base word, and cover the rest of the word. I know* brief. *Now I'm going to look at the other part of this word. I know the suffix* -ly. *I can read* brief *and I can read* -ly. *When I read the parts together, I get the word* briefly. *I can read the rest of this phrase now:* many sparks that found life and took briefly, but they all died.

Practice

Remind students of the following tips for decoding words with suffixes:

- A suffix always appears after the base word.
- A suffix is usually a syllable.
- A suffix has the same pronunciation in different words.

Help students practice identifying visual patterns of words with suffixes. Display the following word pairs: *deep / deeply, slight / slightly, worth / worthless, care / careless, doubt / doubtful, hand / handful.*

Read each pair of words aloud with students and discuss the meanings. Repeat the process with student-supplied words ending in *-ly*, *-less*, or *-ful*.

Students can refer to the **Phonics/Decoding Strategy Poster** for more tips.

Apply

Write these sentences on the board or a chart.

1. Lost in the woods, Brian faces dreadful problems.
2. He thinks his situation is hopeless.
3. Eventually, he is able to make a fire.
4. Hopefully, his situation will now improve.

Ask students to read the sentences aloud. Have students underline the words with suffixes, circle the suffixes, and define each word. Ask students to model the strategy for reading words with suffixes.

Monitoring Student Progress

If . . .	Then . . .
students need more practice with suffixes *-ful*, *-less*, and *-ly*,	repeat the Practice activity, using words with suffixes from another story.

CHALLENGE/EXTENSION:
Vocabulary

Using Context

Read the following sentences from the story: *His fingers <u>gingerly</u> touched a group of needles that had been driven ... into the fleshy part of his calf.* (p. 32) *Just touching the needles made the pain more <u>intense</u>.* (p. 33) *It was <u>painstaking</u> work, slow work, and he stayed with it for over two hours.* (p.39)

The words and sentences that surround an unfamiliar word often contain clues about the word's meaning. Use sentence context and your own prior knowledge to figure out the meaning of the underlined words. Record your thought process on a chart and then use a dictionary to confirm the meanings of the words.

Unfamiliar Word	Its Meaning	How I used Context and What I Know to Figure out the Meaning

---

CHALLENGE

Vocabulary Expansion

Gary Paulsen names various animals, plants, and stones that are found in the Canadian wilderness where Brian's plane crashes. Make three columns and label them *Animals, Plants,* and *Stones.* List words from the story that relate to each category. For example:

Animals: porcupine, quills
Plants: raspberries, twigs, birches, bark, limbs
Stones: granite, sandstone, cave, boulder

With a partner, discuss the features of the items you each listed. Together, suggest other items for each category, especially items that might be found in a northern setting.

Syllabication

OBJECTIVES

- Read long or unfamiliar words with two or more syllables.
- Use syllabication to decode long words.

Target Skill Trace

- Syllabication, p. 71C

Teach

Remind students that long words can be divided into smaller parts called *syllables*. Each syllable has one vowel sound. Breaking words into syllables is another strategy for figuring out a long or unfamiliar word.

Display the following chart and discuss the generalizations and examples.

1. Divide between two consonants most of the time.	un•der•stand
2. When a consonant is between two vowels, divide after the first consonant.	man•y
3. When a syllable ends in a vowel, the vowel sound is usually long.	ref•u•gee
4. When a syllable ends in a consonant, the vowel sound is short.	dip•lo•mat
5. Consonant blends and consonant digraphs are not divided.	stamp•ing
6. A prefix or suffix is also a syllable.	ex•cite cel•e•bra•tion

Next, read page 63, paragraph 2, sentence 4 with students. Then use the following Think Aloud to model how to break the word *absolutely* into syllables.

Think Aloud *I know the first small part is* ab-. *The break is between two consonants,* b *and* s. *I can cover the first small part,* ab-, *and look for the next small part,* -so-. *Now I can read* abso-. *There's a suffix here,* -ly, *which I know. That leaves one syllable with the VCVe pattern:* lute. *That probably sounds like* / loot /. *When I blend the smaller parts together, I get* absolutely. *I check, and it makes sense in the sentence.*

Practice

Help students break two or three of these story words into syllables. *rep / re / sent / ing, ex / haust / ed, ap / proached, per / mis / sion, trans / late, sig / na / ture, dis / o / bey / ing.* Jot the whole word and its syllables in this format:

rep

rep re

rep re sent

rep re sent ing

representing

Have students read down each row rhythmically and as quickly as possible. They can clap hands with each syllable.

Apply

Have students break the following story words into syllables using the technique they use in the Practice exercise: *rep / re / sent / a / tives, down / stairs, gov / ern / ment.* Encourage students to write sentences in which they use these words.

Monitoring Student Progress

If . . .	Then . . .
students need more practice with syllabication,	suggest that they apply the technique they just practiced and applied to long words in other stories.

CHALLENGE/EXTENSION: Vocabulary

Syllabication

Identify words of two or more syllables from a story you read in this theme. These might include compound words, words with double letters, or words beginning with a vowel sound. Write at least twenty words containing two or more syllables on lined paper.

Then exchange papers with a classmate, and divide the words into syllables. After you are done, return the words to your partner. Each partner should check that the syllabication is accurate. Encourage students to use the dictionary to check their work.

Vocabulary Expansion

Copy the following events from the story *Passage to Freedom* on a sheet of paper:

- Hiroki peeks out the window and sees the crowd shouting in Polish.
- Hiroki asks his father to help the crying children outside his house.
- The first reply comes from the Japanese government. The answer is *no*.

- The author's father calls the whole family together to make a decision.
- The author's father tells the crowd that he will issue visas to all of them.

Use this sample format to record your feelings about story events: When I read about _____ I felt _____ because _____ .

CHALLENGE

Synonym Contest

The following words are from *Passage to Freedom*: *neighborhood, children, crying, frightening, exhausted, messages, constantly.* Work in pairs and use a dictionary or thesaurus to find synonyms for each of the words. Write each word and its synonym on a sheet of paper.

Then form groups of four to play a guessing game with your synonyms. One team should read a synonym, while the other team tries to guess the word from the list. The teams can continue until all the words have been identified.

RETEACHING: Structural Analysis/Vocabulary Skills

Prefixes *un-* and *re-*

> ### OBJECTIVES
> - Decode words with the prefix *un-* or *re-*.
> - Identify the meaning of words with the prefixes *un-* and *re-*.
>
> ### Target Skill Trace
> - Prefixes *un-* and *re-*, p. 93C

Teach

Write the following on the board:

> Jake <u>untied</u> the rope on the hammer.
>
> Later Danielle <u>retied</u> the rope.

Ask students to read the sentences and note what is similar about both underlined words. (Both words are formed with the base word *tied*.)

Ask students to note what is different about the structure of the two words. (*untied* has the prefix *un-; retied* has the prefix *-re*) Explain that *un-* and *re-* are prefixes, or word parts, added to the front of a base word. Remind students that knowing when words have prefixes can help them decode those words more quickly.

Write this sentence on the chalkboard: *Danielle looked unhappy when the storm clouds reappeared.* Use the Think Aloud to model decoding words with prefixes for the words *unhappy* and *reappeared*.

Think Aloud *I read,* Danielle looked _____. *If I didn't recognize the next word, I would look carefully for a part I know, like a base word, and cover the rest of the word. I know* happy. *Now I'm going to look at the other part of this word. I know the prefix* un-; *it means "not." I can read* happy *and I can read* un-. *When I read the parts together, I get the word* unhappy. *I check, and it makes sense in the sentence.*

Repeat the process with the word *reappeared* in the same sentence. Review the meaning of *re-.* (again)

Practice

Remind students that the following tips can help them decode words with the prefixes *un-* and *re-*.

- A prefix always appears before the base word.
- A prefix is usually a syllable.
- A prefix has the same pronunciation in different words.

Help students practice identifying visual patterns of words with prefixes. Display the following word pairs: *easy / uneasy, move / remove, finished / unfinished, changed / unchanged, discover / rediscover.*

Read each pair of words aloud with students and discuss their meanings. Repeat the process with student-supplied words starting with the prefix *un-* or *re-*.

Students can refer to the **Phonics/Decoding Strategy Poster** for more tips.

Apply

Write the following sentences on the board.

> 1. Danielle had to relearn skills from Mountain Mastery.
> 2. Despite the difficulty, Jake and Danielle were unafraid.
> 3. After reaching the false summit, Jake and Danielle had to retackle the real one.
> 4. Luckily, they reached the weather station unharmed.

Ask students to underline the words with prefixes, circle the prefix, and define each word. Have students model the strategy for reading words with prefixes.

> ### Monitoring Student Progress
>
> | If ... | Then ... |
> | --- | --- |
> | students need more practice with prefixes *un-* and *re-*, | repeat the Practice activity, using words with prefixes from other stories. |

CHALLENGE/EXTENSION:
Vocabulary

Suffix Word Search

Use dictionaries to list as many words as possible that include the suffixes -ful, -ly, and -er. Then use a piece of graph paper to create a word search using at least ten of the words. Write the words so that one letter of the word is in each square. Words may be written left-to-right, top-to-bottom, or diagonally top-to-bottom. Fill in the remaining empty squares with any letters you choose.

When you are finished, exchange papers and use a colored pen or marker to identify the words you find in your partner's word puzzle. Check off each word on the list as you find it in the puzzle.

Vocabulary Expansion

Look through the story and make a list of words and phrases related to climbing and mountaineering. After you have found as many words as possible, write a short rhyming poem about climbing or mountaineering using your words and some of the words and phrases from the following list: *hammer, ice ax, vertical ice, carabiners, pitons, climbing, dropping, belay, on belay, icy, foothold, peak, steep, slope, summit, ridge*.

CHALLENGE

Prefix Spelling Bee

Form two groups with the same number of players on each. An additional student can be the moderator. Write words containing the prefixes *un-* and *re-* on index cards. Then pile the cards in a stack. The moderator chooses cards and asks alternating teams to spell the words. For additional challenge, players should define the word after they spell it correctly.

RETEACHING

Possessives and Contractions

OBJECTIVES

- Identify contractions.
- Identify possessive nouns.
- Decode words with apostrophes.

Target Skill Trace

- Possessives and Contractions, p. 115C

Teach

Display the following sentences: *Climbing up the ship's main mast <u>was not</u> an easy task. Climbing up the ship's main mast <u>wasn't</u> an easy task.*

Have students identify the word(s) in each sentence that are different. Then review these concepts:

1. *Wasn't* is a contraction. It is a combination of two words, *was* and *not*.

2. The apostrophe (') takes the place of one or more letters.

3. A contraction has the same meaning as the two words that were combined.

4. To understand the meaning of a contraction, readers need to know the letters that the apostrophe replaces.

Have students identify another word in the model sentence that isn't a contraction. (ship's) Underline the *'s*. Explain that this ending makes *ship* a possessive noun—a noun that shows ownership. *Ship's mast* is a short way of saying "the mast that belongs to the ship."

Display the following sentence:

Charlotte hasn't fallen yet, and she's reached the top of the mast.

Use a Think Aloud to model identifying contractions and possessives.

> **Think Aloud** *I see two contractions. The first (point to hasn't) is a short way of saying "has not." The two words, has and not, were combined, and an apostrophe takes the place of the o in "not." (Repeat the process with she's.) Finally, I see the word ship's. The 's on ship signals ownership. The mast belongs to the ship.*

Practice

Display the following contractions and possessives: *we're, she'll, don't, I'd, ship's captain, crew's cheers.* Work with students to identify the two words making up each contraction and the ownership indicated by each possessive.

Apply

Have students read these sentences taken from the selection, underline the words with apostrophes, and identify them as contractions or possessives.

1. *"<u>You're</u> a girl as steady as ever <u>I've</u> met."* contraction

2. *The crew stood like <u>death's</u> own jury.* possessive

3. *Recollecting <u>Ewing's</u> advice, I shifted my eyes.* possessive

4. *"<u>She'll</u> not have the stomach."* contraction

Monitoring Student Progress

If . . .	Then . . .
students need more practice with possessives and contractions,	suggest that they identify contractions and possessives in other reading material.

CHALLENGE/EXTENSION: Vocabulary

Possessives

Make a list of your classmates' names on a sheet of paper. Beside each person's name, write something the person is wearing, an object the person owns, or a positive characteristic of that person. Here is an example: Carl's red shirt, Teresa's markers, the teacher's smile.

Be sure to use apostrophe *s* to indicate possession.

Contraction Word Wheel

Make two circles out of construction paper, one about 2 inches larger than the other. Attach the two circles with a brad, so that the smaller circle is on top of the larger circle. Write words on outside rims of the circles as if they were spokes on a wheel. The words for the inner circle include the following: *she, he, we, they, I, you,* and *it.* The words for the outer circle are *will, am, are, would,* and *is.*

Work with a partner to line up a word on the inner circle with a word on the outer circle. Take turns saying the words aloud, writing the two words in contraction form, and then saying aloud the contraction that is made from those two words. Remember that not all word pairs can be made into a contraction.

CHALLENGE

Vocabulary Expansion

Nautical is a word that refers to sailing, sailors, and the sea. Find nautical words and terms in the story *The True Confessions of Charlotte Doyle.* Make a dictionary of nautical words and terms. Using a glossary, dictionary, or encyclopedia, look up the meaning of each word or phrase.

Write each word and its definition on a separate piece of paper. Under the definition, illustrate the word. Put the finished pages into alphabetical order and bind them into a book.

RETEACHING: Grammar Skills

Kinds of Sentences

OBJECTIVES

- Identify the four kinds of sentences.
- Punctuate sentences appropriately.

Target Skill Trace

- Kinds of Sentences, p. 47I

Teach

Refer students to the illustration on pages 32–33 that show Brian confronting the porcupine.

Ask students to suggest the following:

- a *statement* about the picture; for example, *Brian sees a low, dark form slithering in the shelter.*
- a *question* that Brian might be asking himself; for example, *What is that?*
- a *command* that Brian might give to the dark shape in his shelter; for example, *Get out of here!*
- an *exclamation* Brian might utter when he realizes he has been hurt; for example, *Ow! Those quills hurt!*

Write the students' responses on the board and label each sentence type as you describe it. (A statement tells something; a question asks something; a command gives an order or makes a strong request; an exclamation shows strong feeling.) Point out the appropriate end marks.

Have students read the four sample sentences aloud. Have them discuss how their voices change when they read different kinds of sentences. For example, a high tone of voice usually ends a question, whereas a lower tone and higher volume usually indicates an exclamation.

Practice

Have students write each sentence type and its punctuation on a separate index card. Read the following passage based on the story. Pause after each sentence, and ask students to raise the index card that names the type of sentence you have just read.

As Brian slept alone in the darkness of the shelter, he dreamed about his father. What was his father trying to say? (statement; question)

"Dad, Dad," Brian shouted, "I can't hear you!" (exclamation)

His father faded, and Terry stepped out from a foggy place. He kept pointing from the flame to some type of lighter. (statement)

"Look at this!" he gestured. (command)

Apply

Have students revisit *Hatchet*. Encourage students to work in pairs to find one example of each sentence type from the selection. Ask students to write their own example of each sentence type.

Monitoring Student Progress

If . . .	Then . . .
students need more practice identifying kinds of sentences,	revisit another selection, and repeat the Practice and Apply activities.

Subjects and Predicates

OBJECTIVES

- Identify simple subjects and predicates.
- Identify complete subjects and predicates.
- Write complete subjects and predicates.

Target Skill Trace

- Subjects and Predicates, p. 47J

Teach

Write this sentence on the board: *The boy worked hard.*

Ask students, *What or whom is this sentence about?* Discuss their responses. Help students understand that *boy* is the subject of this sentence. Underline it.

Then ask, What does the subject do, have, or feel? Discuss student responses. Help students understand that *worked* is the predicate of this sentence. It is the main word or group of words in the predicate. Draw a double line under it. Remind students that a sentence needs both a subject and predicate to express a complete thought.

Then write this sentence on the board: *The tired boy worked very hard.*

Help students determine all the words that are part of the complete subject (The tired boy) and all the words that are part of the complete predicate (worked very hard).

Lead students to understand the following concepts: The main word in the subject is the *simple subject* (boy). The main word in the predicate is the *simple predicate* (worked). The *complete subject* contains all the words in the subject part of the sentence. The *complete predicate* contains all the words in the predicate part of the sentence.

Practice

Write the following on the board:

> touched the quills gingerly
>
> small and dry twigs glowed

Have students discuss whether each line is a complete sentence. If it is not, ask them what it needs. Have students supply any missing parts to make complete sentences. Write their responses on the board, and read the completed sentences together.

Apply

Have students in small groups fold a piece of paper lengthwise and mark the left column *Complete Subject* and the right column *Complete Predicate*.

Tell one student in each group to write a complete subject or predicate and pass the paper left. The receiver completes the sentence and passes the paper left. Repeat the process.

After five minutes, have students take turns reading a favorite sentence.

Monitoring Student Progress

If . . .	Then . . .
students need more practice with subjects and predicates,	extend the Practice or Apply activities, using a specific topic for the subjects and predicates.

Conjunctions

OBJECTIVES

- Identify the conjunctions *and, but,* and *or.*
- Identify sentences that contain the conjunctions *and, but,* or *or.*

Target Skill Trace

- Conjunctions, p. 71I

Teach

Display the following sentences:

1. They chose five people to come inside and talk.
2. Father cabled his government, but he received no answer.
3. Father had to choose helping or turning the people away.

Explain that the words *and, or,* and *but* are called *conjunctions.* Conjunctions are used to join words or groups of words in a sentence. Work with students to identify the conjunction in each sentence above. Help them identify the words each conjunction joins. (*and* joins the two verbs *come* and *talk; but* joins the two sentences; *or* joins *helping* and *turning*)

Display the following sentences:

4. Mr. Sugihara brought his family together.
5. Mr. Sugihara asked them what he should do.
6. Mr. Sugihara brought his family together and asked what he should do.

Ask students to identify what words are the same in sentences 4 and 5. (Mr. Sugihara) Explain that sentences 4 and 5 say two things about the same person. Use sentence 6 to discuss how the conjunction *and* works. Here, it joins two groups of words that tell what Mr. Sugihara did.

Practice

Have students write the conjunctions *and, but,* and *or* on a separate index card. Then call on a student to find and read aloud a story sentence that contains one of these conjunctions.

Ask students to raise the index card that shows the conjunction that was read aloud. Continue until students have identified all three conjunctions as often as necessary. Look especially at the following: *and,* pp. 56, 58; *but,* pp. 58, 62; *or,* p. 64.

Apply

Ask pairs of students to copy some of the sentences that were identified in the Practice activity. Have them circle the conjunction in each sentence and underline the words that are joined by the conjunction. Bring students together to share and compare their sentences.

Monitoring Student Progress

If . . .	Then . . .
students need more practice with conjunctions,	suggest that they identify sentences with conjunctions in other stories they read.

Compound Sentences

Teach

Display this compound sentence:

> Helping the refugees was dangerous, but Mr. Sugihara did it.

Explain that a compound sentence consists of two complete thoughts. Each complete thought has a subject and a predicate. Ask students to identify the conjunction that joins the two simple sentences above. (but) Remind students that they can use the conjunctions *and, but,* or *or* to join related ideas.

Write the following pairs of sentences on the board:

1. Hiroki's father wanted to help. His mother agreed.
2. Hiroki wanted to go out to play. His father said no.
3. Hiroki's father must write the visas. Many people would die.

For pair 1, point out that both sentences are related but are very short. Help students think of a way to express both of these ideas in one sentence, using the word *and*. Remind students to place a comma before the conjunction in all compound sentences. (Hiroki's father wanted to help, and his mother agreed.)

For pair 2, point out that the ideas are related, but the two sentences are short and choppy. Help students combine ideas into one sentence, using the word *but* to connect ideas. (Hiroki wanted to go out to play, but his father said no.)

For pair 3, help students combine the two ideas into one sentence, using the word *or* to connect them. (Hiroki's father must write the visas, or many people would die.)

Practice

Display these sentence pairs and conjunctions:

1. It was warm outside. The children wore coats. (but)
2. Mr. Sugihara could give them visas. He could refuse. (or)
3. The answer came from Japan. It was "no." (and)

Help students combine each pair of sentences into one sentence. Remind students to use a comma before a conjunction that joins two complete thoughts.

Apply

Ask students to write three compound sentences that tell about events in *Passage to Freedom*. Suggest that they circle each conjunction they use. Remind students when to use a comma.

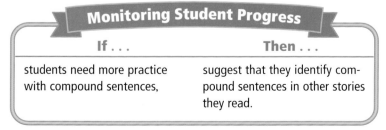

Monitoring Student Progress	
If . . .	Then . . .
students need more practice with compound sentences,	suggest that they identify compound sentences in other stories they read.

Complex Sentences

OBJECTIVES

- Identify complex sentences.
- Identify an independent clause.
- Identify a subordinate clause.

Target Skill Trace

- Complex Sentences, p. 93I

Teach

Display this sentence on the board:

Danielle and Jake reached the summit, and they found the weather station.

Review that the sentence above is a compound sentence. It is formed from two simple sentences connected with a conjunction. Remind students that each part of a compound sentence has a subject and predicate and states one complete idea.

Each simple sentence in a compound sentence is called an *independent clause* because it can stand alone. Point out the independent clauses in the example. Review *clause* and define it as "a group of words that has a subject and a verb."

Write the following on the board: *because they were on a false summit*

Point out that this is a *subordinate clause* because even though the clause has a subject and predicate, it is not a complete thought.

Display this sentence:

They had to climb higher because they were on a false summit.

Tell students that the sentence above is a *complex sentence*. It is complex because it includes an independent clause and at least one subordinate clause.

Ask students to read the sentence you just displayed for them aloud with you. Underline the part of the sentence that is the subordinate clause. (because they were on a false summit) Point out that subordinate clauses often begin with the words *since, although, if, when, while,* or *because*. Also point out that when the subordinate clause begins the sentence, it is followed by a comma.

Rewrite this sentence so that the subordinate clause comes first. (Because they were on a false summit, they had to climb higher.) Point out the use of the comma.

Practice

Have students each write a subordinate clause on one index card and an independent clause to go with it on another index card. Ask students to read the independent clause alone first. Then have them combine the independent and subordinate clause into one complex sentence.

Apply

Ask students to work in pairs to find examples of complex sentences in the story.

Monitoring Student Progress

If . . .	Then . . .
students need more practice with complex sentences,	suggest that they look for complex sentences in other stories they read.

Correcting Fragments and Run-on Sentences

OBJECTIVES

- Identify sentence fragments.
- Identify run-on sentences.
- Correct sentence fragments.
- Correct run-on sentences.

Target Skill Trace

- Correcting Fragments and Run-on Sentences, p. 93J

Teach

Write the following words on the board, and ask students if either is a complete sentence. Have them explain their reasoning.

> During a blizzard, Jake and Danielle.
>
> Finally reached the summit.

Point out that the first group of words has no verb or predicate, and the second group of words needs a subject. Neither group expresses a complete thought. Explain that when a group of words has a subject or a predicate missing, it is called a *sentence fragment*.

Have students look at the first sentence fragment again. Ask: What is missing, the subject or the predicate?

Encourage students to suggest a predicate to complete the sentence. Write a corrected version of the sentence on the board. Help students think of ways to correct the second fragment.

Briefly review the *run-on sentence*. Display this text: *Danielle lost her balance several times, twice she fell over.* Explain that there are too many ideas in this group of words and nothing to keep them separate. Model how to correct a run-on sentence; for example: *Danielle lost her balance several times. Twice she fell over.*

Help students correct the following:

> He banged the door hard, each blow dented the metal. Jake thought no one was home, the thought sent a chill through Danielle.

Practice

Display the following:

> 1. The Darcy family took a trip to their cabin in the mountains, on the road they had a bad car crash.
> 2. Parents badly injured.
> 3. At camp, Danielle learned about mountain climbing she knew how to climb to the summit.
> 4. Had no real mountain climbing equipment at hand.

Ask a student to read each group of words aloud and decide which are run-on sentences (1 and 3) and which are fragments. (2 and 4) Help students correct the sentences.

Apply

Have students exchange drafts of their current writing with a partner. Ask each student to look for fragments and run-on sentences and suggest to his or her partner ways to correct them.

Monitoring Student Progress

If . . .	Then . . .
students need more practice correcting fragments and run-on sentences,	suggest that they continue to share their writing, looking for fragments and run-on sentences.

Common/Proper Nouns

OBJECTIVE

● Identify common and proper nouns.

Target Skill Trace

● Common and Proper Nouns, p. 115I

Teach

Develop a chart with these headings: *Things, Places, People.* Encourage students to supply general, not specific, words for each category; for example, *dog,* not *Scruffy.*

Remind students that *nouns* name a person, place, or thing. Nouns that don't name a particular person, place, or thing, such as *brother, town, hat,* are called *common nouns.*

Write the following sentences on the board:

> A young girl crossed the ocean on a tiny ship. Charlotte Doyle crossed the Atlantic Ocean on the Seahawk.

Point out that the nouns in the first sentence do not name any particular *girl, ocean,* or *ship. Girl, ocean,* and *ship* are general names. *Girl, ocean,* and *ship* are all common nouns.

Have students look at the second sentence and note that the nouns do name a particular girl—*Charlotte Doyle,* a particular ocean—*the Atlantic,* and a particular ship—*the Seahawk.* Explain that a noun that names a particular person, place, or thing is a *proper noun.* Point out that proper nouns always begin with a capital letter.

Practice

Write two columns on the board with the headings *Common Noun* and *Proper Noun.*

Have students scan page 99 for common and proper nouns. Ask students to find nouns, identify their types, and write them in the appropriate column.

Apply

Ask students to work in pairs to find more examples of common nouns and proper nouns in earlier stories in the theme.

Monitoring Student Progress

If . . .	Then . . .
students need more practice with common and proper nouns,	suggest that they repeat the Practice activity using another story.

Singular and Plural Nouns

OBJECTIVES

- Identify singular and plural nouns.
- Determine the regular or irregular plural forms of nouns.

Target Skill Trace

- Singular and Plural Nouns, p. 115J

Teach

Remind students that a *noun* names a person, place, or thing. Then write these sentences on the board, and ask students to comment on the difference between the nouns *sailor* and *sailors*:

> Charlotte became a <u>sailor</u> on the Seahawk. The other <u>sailors</u> were men.

Explain that *sailor* is a *singular noun* because it names one person, whereas *sailors* is a *plural noun* because it names more than one. Ask students how they can tell *sailors* is a plural noun. (It has the -s ending; the -s ending is used to make most nouns plural.)

Display the following nouns and have students tell whether they are singular or plural: *ships, mainmast, ratlines, shrouds, deck, rigging, sails.*

Point out that some singular nouns add *-es,* not just *-s,* to form their plurals. Explain that nouns that end in *s, x, ch,* or *sh* usually add *-es* to form their plurals. As examples, write the following words on the board, and have students suggest the spelling of their plurals: *glass* (glasses), *box* (boxes), *bush* (bushes), and *ditch* (ditches).

Also explain that singular nouns that end in a consonant and *y* form their plurals by changing the *y* to *i* and adding *-es.* As an example, write the words *pony, hobby,* and *lady* on the board, and have students write their plurals. (ponies, hobbies, ladies)

Finally, explain that a few singular nouns change their spellings in irregular ways to form the plurals. Have students name some familiar singular nouns and their plural forms; for example, *child, children; woman, women; tooth, teeth;* and *mouse, mice.*

Practice

On the board, write the following singular nouns. Ask students to write their plural forms. Have students tell how they know whether to add *-s* or *-es: fox, lunch, eyelash, lock, body, wave, sky, day, loss, gas, sandwich.* foxes, lunches, eyelashes, locks, bodies, waves, skies, days, losses, gases, sandwiches

Apply

Have students work in pairs to find examples of singular and plural nouns in the story. For each singular noun, have them tell how to form its plural. For each plural, have them identify its singular form.

Monitoring Student Progress

If . . .	Then . . .
students need more practice with singular and plural nouns,	extend the Apply activity to other stories they read.

Name _____

Sentence Type Challenge

Write a declarative, interrogative, imperative, and exclamatory sentence for each situation.

Brian and the brushing sound in the shelter	Declarative sentence _____ _____ Interrogative sentence _____ _____ Imperative sentence _____ _____ Exclamatory sentence _____ _____
Brian's dream	Declarative sentence _____ _____ Interrogative sentence _____ _____ Imperative sentence _____ _____ Exclamatory sentence _____ _____

Theme 1: **Courage**

Adverb Challenge

Ask questions about key parts of the story.

Story part	Key story part: _____ Our question: _____ _____ Adverbs with -*ly:* _____ Number of adverbs: _____
Story part	Key story part: _____ Our question: _____ _____ Adverbs with -*ly:* _____ Number of adverbs: _____
Story part	Key story part: _____ Our question: _____ _____ Adverbs with -*ly:* _____ Number of adverbs: _____
Story part	Key story part: _____ Our question: _____ _____ Adverbs with -*ly:* _____ Number of adverbs: _____

Total number of adverbs in -*ly:* _____

Theme 1: **Courage**

Name _____

Mountain-Climbing Terms

Write mountain-climbing terms from *Climb or Die* in the appropriate column.

Equipment	Techniques	Terrain/Hazards

Theme 1: **Courage**

Name _____

Word-Search Challenge

Use the Key Vocabulary words to create a word-search puzzle.

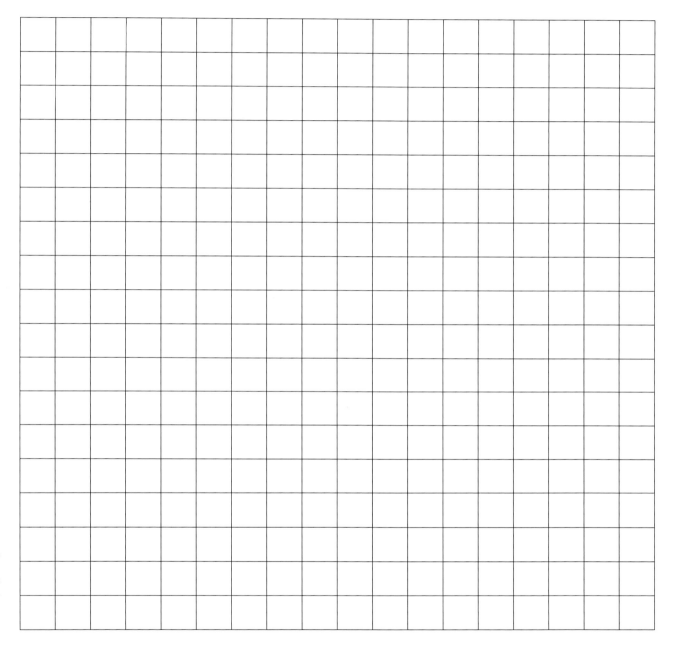

Theme 1: **Courage**

Consider copying and laminating this game for use in centers.

What's My Connotation?

Cut out the sentence cards. Decide whether each word has a positive, a negative, or a neutral connotation.

I _____ loose change.	save	hoard
The _____ gentleman sat next to me.	old	elderly
You always do your homework _____.	hurriedly	swiftly
We were _____ because of the rain.	tardy	late
That woman is _____ with her money.	thrifty	stingy
His bedroom is always _____.	spotless	clean
That paint color makes the wall look _____.	dull	dingy
Losing the game made her feel _____.	miserable	sad
I feel really _____ after running that race.	tired	frazzled
The smallest puppy is the _____ one.	frail	weak

Theme 1: **Focus on Poetry**

Consider copying and laminating these game pieces for use in centers.

Writer _____   Listener _____

Writing Conference

What Should I Say?

In a writing conference, a writer reads a draft to a partner or a small group. A listener can help the writer by discussing the draft and asking questions such as these.

If you're thinking . . .

- I don't understand when things happened.
- What does this part have to do with the main part of the story?
- This doesn't sound like you.

You could say . . .

- Could you add time clues, such as *first, then,* or *after?*
- Is that part about _____ really important? Could you leave it out?
- How did you feel when that happened?

More Questions a Listener Might Ask

Read these questions before you listen. Take notes on the other side of this paper. Then discuss your thoughts with the writer.

1. What do you like about the writer's personal narrative?

2. What experience is the writer telling about? Retell what you heard.

3. What details make the writer's experience clear?

4. Are there places where the writer needs to tell more? or tell less? Give examples.

Theme 1: **Courage**

TECHNOLOGY RESOURCES

American Melody
P.O. Box 270
Guilford, CT 06437
800-220-5557
www.americanmelody.com

Audio Bookshelf
174 Prescott Hill Road
Northport, ME 04849
800-234-1713
www.audiobookshelf.com

Baker & Taylor
100 Business Center Drive
Pittsburgh, PA 15205
800-775-2600
www.btal.com

BDD Audio/Random House
400 Hohn Road
Westminster, MD 21157
800-733-3000

Big Kids Productions
1606 Dywer Ave.
Austin, TX 78704
800-477-7811
www.bigkidsvideo.com

Books on Tape
P.O. Box 25122
Santa Ana, CA 92799
800-541-5525
www.booksontape.com

Broderbund Company
1 Martha's Way
Hiawatha, IA 52233
www.broderbund.com

Filmic Archives
The Cinema Center
Botsford, CT 06404
800-366-1920
www.filmicarchives.com

Great White Dog Picture Company
10 Toon Lane
Lee, NH 03824
800-397-7641
www.greatwhitedog.com

HarperAudio
10 E. 53rd St.
New York, NY 10022
800-242-7737
www.harperaudio.com

Houghton Mifflin Company
222 Berkeley St.
Boston, MA 02116
800-225-3362

Informed Democracy
P.O. Box 67
Santa Cruz, CA 95063
800-827-0949

JEF Films
143 Hickory Hill Circle
Osterville, MA 02655
508-428-7198

Kimbo Educational
P.O. Box 477
Long Branch, NJ 07740
800-631-2187
www.kimboed.com

Library Video Co.
P.O. Box 580
Wynnewood, PA 19096
800-843-3620
www.libraryvideo.com

Listening Library
P.O. Box 25122
Santa Ana, CA 92799
800-541-5525
www.listeninglibrary.com

Live Oak Media
P.O. Box 652
Pine Plains, NY 12567
800-788-1121
www.liveoakmedia.com

Media Basics
Lighthouse Square
P.O. Box 449
Guilford, CT 06437
800-542-2505
www.mediabasicsvideo.com

Microsoft Corp.
One Microsoft Way
Redmond, WA 98052
800-426-9400
www.microsoft.com

National Geographic School Publishing
P.O. Box 10597
Des Moines, IA 50340
800-368-2728
www.nationalgeographic.com

New Kid Home Video
P.O. Box 10443
Beverly Hills, CA 90213
800-309-2392
www.NewKidhomevideo.com

Puffin Books
345 Hudson Street
New York, NY 10014
800-233-7364

Rainbow Educational Media
4540 Preslyn Drive
Raleigh, NC 27616
800-331-4047
www.rainbowedumedia.com

Recorded Books
270 Skipjack Road
Prince Frederick, MD 20678
800-638-1304
www.recordedbooks.com

Sony Wonder
Dist. by Professional Media Service
19122 S. Vermont Ave.
Gardena, CA 90248
800-223-7672
www.sonywonder.com

Spoken Arts
195 South White Rock Road
Holmes, NY 12531
800-326-4090
www.spokenartsmedia.com

SRA Media
220 E. Danieldale Rd.
DeSoto, TX 75115
800-843-8855
www.sra4kids.com

SVE & Churchill Media
6677 North Northwest Highway
Chicago, IL 60631
800-829-1900
www.svemedia.com

Tom Snyder Productions
80 Coolidge Hill Road
Watertown, MA 02472
800-342-0236
www.tomsnyder.com

Troll Communications
100 Corporate Drive
Mahwah, NJ 07430
800-526-5289
www.troll.com

Weston Woods
143 Main St.
Norwalk, CT 06851-1318
800-243-5020
www.scholastic.com/westonwoods

PRONUNCIATION GUIDE

In this book some unfamiliar or hard-to-pronounce words are followed by respellings to help you say the words correctly. Use the key below to find examples of various sounds and their respellings. Note that in the respelled word, the syllable in capital letters is the one receiving the most stress.

Dictionary letter or mark	Respelled as	Example	Respelled word
ă (pat)	a	basket	BAS-kiht
ā (pay)	ay	came	kaym
âr (care)	air	share	shair
ä (father)	ah	barter	BAHR-tur
ch (church)	ch	channel	CHAN-uhl
ĕ (pet)	eh	test	tehst
ē (bee)	ee	heap	heep
g (gag)	g	goulash	GOO-lahsh
ĭ (pit)	ih	liver	LIHV-ur
ī (pie, by)	y	alive	uh-LYV
	eye	island	EYE-luhnd
îr (hear)	eer	year	yeer
j (judge)	j	germ	jurm
k (kick, cat, pique)	k	liquid	LIHK-wihd
ŏ (pot)	ah	otter	AHT-ur
ō (toe)	oh	solo	SOH-loh
ô (caught, paw)	aw	always	AWL-wayz
ôr (for)	or	normal	NOR-muhl
oi (noise)	oy	boiling	BOYL-ihng
ŏŏ (took)	u	pull, wool	pul, wul
ōō (boot)	oo	bruise	brooz
ou (out)	ow	pound	pownd
s (sauce)	s	center	SEHN-tur
sh (ship, dish)	sh	chagrin	shuh-GRIHN
ŭ (cut)	uh	flood	fluhd
ûr (urge, term, firm, word, heard)	ur	earth	urth
		bird	burd
z (zebra, xylem)	z	cows	kowz
zh (vision, pleasure, garage)	zh	decision	dih-SIHZH-uhn
ə (about)	uh	around	uh-ROWND
(item)	uh	broken	BROH-kuhn
(edible)	uh	pencil	PEHN-suhl
(gallop)	uh	connect	kuh-NEHKT
(circus)	uh	focus	FOH-kuhs
ər (butter)	ur	liter	LEE-tur

Glossary

This glossary contains meanings and pronunciations for some of the words in this book. The Full Pronunciation Key shows how to pronounce each consonant and vowel in a special spelling. At the bottom of the glossary pages is a shortened form of the full key.

Full Pronunciation Key

Consonant Sounds

b	**b**i**b**, ca**bb**age	kw	**ch**oir, **qu**ick	t	**t**igh**t**, stopp**ed**
ch	**ch**ur**ch**, sti**tch**	l	li**d**, nee**d**le, ta**ll**	th	**b**a**th**, **th**in
d	**d**ee**d**, mail**ed**, pu**dd**le	m	a**m**, **m**an, du**mb**	th	**b**a**th**e, **th**is
f	**f**ast, **f**i**f**e, o**ff**, **ph**rase, rough	n	**n**o, su**dd**en	v	ca**v**e, **v**al**v**e, **v**ine
g	**g**a**g**, **g**et, fin**g**er	ng	thi**ng**, i**nk**	w	**w**ith, **w**olf
h	**h**at, **wh**o	p	**p**o**p**, ha**pp**y	y	**y**es, **y**olk, on**i**on
hw	**wh**ich, **wh**ere	r	**r**oa**r**, **rh**yme	z	**r**o**s**e, **s**i**z**e, **x**ylophone, **z**ebra
j	**j**u**dg**e, **g**em	s	mi**ss**, **s**au**c**e, **s**cene, **s**ee	zh	gara**g**e, plea**s**ure, vi**s**ion
k	**c**at, **k**ick, s**ch**ool	sh	**di**sh**, **sh**ip, **s**ugar, ti**ss**ue		

Vowel Sounds

ă	p**a**t, l**au**gh	ŏ	h**o**rrible, p**o**t	ŭ	c**u**t, fl**oo**d, r**ou**gh, s**o**me
ā	**a**pe, **ai**d, p**ay**	ō	g**o**, r**ow**, t**oe**, th**ou**gh	û	c**i**rcle, f**u**r, h**ea**rd, t**e**rm, t**u**rn, **u**rge, w**o**rd
â	**ai**r, c**a**re, w**ea**r	ô	**a**ll, c**au**ght, f**o**r, p**aw**		
ä	f**a**ther, k**o**ala, y**a**rd	oi	b**oy**, n**oi**se, **oi**l	yoo	c**u**re
ĕ	p**e**t, pl**ea**sure, **a**ny	ou	c**ow**, **ou**t	yoo	**a**b**u**se, **u**se
ē	b**e**, b**ee**, **ea**sy, p**ia**no	oo	f**u**ll, b**oo**k, w**o**lf	ə	**a**go, sil**e**nt, penc**i**l, lem**o**n, circ**u**s
ĭ	**i**f, p**i**t, b**u**sy	oo	b**oo**t, r**u**de, fr**ui**t, fl**ew**		
ī	r**i**de, b**y**, p**ie**, h**igh**				
î	d**ea**r, d**ee**r, f**ie**rce, m**e**re				

Stress Marks

Primary Stress ´: bi·ol·o·gy [bī **ŏl**´ə jē]
Secondary Stress ´: bi·o·log·i·cal [bī´ ə **lŏj**´ ĭ kəl]

Pronunciation key and definitions © 1998 by Houghton Mifflin Company. Adapted and reprinted by permission from *The American Heritage Children's Dictionary.*

A

a·ban·doned (ə **băn**´ dənd) *adj.* Permanently left behind; deserted. *A colony of squirrels is living in the abandoned house.*

ab·stract (ăb **străkt**´, **ăb**´ străkt´) *adj.* Not representing a recognizable image. *People enjoy abstract art for its colors and forms.*

ac·ces·si·ble (ăk **sĕs**´ ə bəl) *adj.* Affordable; easy to get. *The silver bowls are very expensive, but the stainless steel ones are accessible to most customers.*

ac·com·plish (ə **kŏm**´ plĭsh) *v.* To succeed in doing something. *Her education will help her accomplish great things.*

ac·count·ant (ə **koun**´ tənt) *n.* Someone trained to keep the financial records of a business. *The accountant figured out how much money the company owed in taxes.*

ac·count·ing (ə **kount**´ ĭng) *n.* A detailed narrative; a record of events. *For several days, the newspaper gave a detailed accounting of destruction from the hurricane.*

a·dorn (ə **dôrn**´) *v.* To decorate. *The Hawaiians adorned their visitors with garlands of beautiful flowers.*

aer·o·nau·tics (âr´ ə **nô**´ tĭks) *n.* The design and construction of aircraft. *The person in charge of our rocket experiments has vast knowledge of aeronautics.*

af·ter·deck (**ăf**´ tər dĕk´) *n.* The part of a ship's deck near the rear. *The passengers stood on the afterdeck, watching the island disappear.*

a·nal·y·sis (ə **năl**´ ĭ sĭs) *n., pl.* **analyses** (ə **năl**´ ĭ sēs) The separation of a substance into its parts in order to study each part. *A high-powered microscope was used for an analysis of the virus.*

ap·pli·cant (**ăp**´ lĭ kənt) *n.* A person who requests employment or acceptance. *There were six applicants for the shipping clerk job.*

as·cent (ə **sĕnt**´) *n.* An upward climb. *The ascent to the mountain's summit took two days.*

as·tro·naut (**ăs**´ trə nôt´) *n.* A person trained to fly in a spacecraft. *Sally Ride was the first American female astronaut in space.*

astronaut

at·ten·tion (ə **tĕn**´ shən) *n.* Close or careful observing or listening. *The tour guide asked the group to give her their full attention.*

a·vi·a·tion (ā´ vē ā´ shən, ăv´ ē ā´ shən) *n.* The operation of aircraft. *The history of aviation goes back to the days of hot air balloons.*

aviation
French speakers in the nineteenth century created a word for the operation of aircraft from the Latin word *avis*, which means "bird."

awk·ward (**ŏk**´ wərd) *adj.* Uncomfortable. *Roger felt awkward when he realized that everyone else had worn nice clothes to the party.*

ōō b**oo**t / ou **out** / ŭ c**u**t / û f**u**r / hw **wh**ich / th **th**in / th **th**is / zh vi**s**ion / ə **a**go, silent, pencil, lemon, circus

---

B

bartering
Our modern meaning for the word *barter* comes from the old French word *barater,* which means both "to exchange" and "to deceive."

bar·ter·ing (**bär**´ tər ĭng) *n.* The trading of goods without the exchange of money. *By clever bartering, the milkmaid got two geese in exchange for the butter.*

be·lay (bĭ **lā**´) *v.* To secure by means of a rope, in mountain climbing. *To protect themselves, the mountain climbers will belay as they climb. —adj.* Secured by a rope. *He waited in the belay position while the others caught up with him.*

brag (brăg) *v.* To boast. *Nella bragged that she was the best basketball player in her class.*

brisk·ly (**brĭsk**´ lē) *adv.* Quickly, energetically. *The pilot strode briskly through the airport to the plane.*

bulk·head (**bŭlk**´ hĕd´) *n.* One of the walls that divides the cabin of a ship into compartments. *A sailing chart was pinned on the bulkhead by the cabin door.*

buoy

buoy (**boo**´ ē, boi) *n.* An anchored float, often with a bell or light, used on a lake or ocean to mark safe passage or to warn of danger. *Swimmers are told not to swim beyond the harbor buoy.*

C

can·vas (**kăn**´ vəs) *n.* The stiff, heavy fabric on which an artist paints. *Before painting, Emma stretched the canvas tightly over a wooden frame.*

car·a·bi·ner (kăr´ ə **bē**´ nər) *n.* In mountain climbing, an oval ring that attaches to a piton. *The carabiners allow ropes to run freely through them.*

car·a·van (**kăr**´ ə văn´) *n.* A file of vehicles or pack animals traveling together. *Twenty camels led the caravan of spice traders across the desert.*

cause·way (**kôz**´ wā´) *n.* A raised roadway across water or marshland. *The farmers built causeways crossing the fields that flooded in the spring.*

cer·ti·fy (**sûr**´ tə fī´) *v., pl.* **certifies** Official recognition of a particular skill or function. *Medical technicians are certified to provide help in an emergency.*

cheap (chēp) *adj.* Costing very little. *Because she had very little money, Randi bought a cheap rubber ball instead of a real baseball.*

com·mon room (**kŏm**´ ən room) *n.* A large room where people gather to eat or share other activities. *The storyteller drew a crowd in the common room after dinner.*

ă r**a**t / ā p**ay** / â c**a**re / ä f**a**ther / ĕ p**e**t / ē b**e** / ĭ p**i**t / ī p**ie** / î f**ie**rce / ŏ p**o**t / ō g**o** / ô p**aw**, for / oi **oi**l / ōō b**oo**k

---

D

com·mute (kə **myoot**´) *v.* To travel back and forth regularly. *My aunt and uncle commute from Gilroy to Sunnyvale every day.*

con·cep·tu·al (kən **sĕp**´ choo əl) *adj.* Having to do with ideas. *A conceptual artist uses a variety of media to communicate an idea.*

con·di·tion·ing (kən **dĭsh**´ ə nĭng) *adj.* Contributing to the process of becoming physically fit. *The track coach stressed the importance of conditioning drills.*

con·quered (**kŏng**´ kərd) *adj.* Defeated in battle. *The conquered peoples gave up their treasures to their victorious enemy.*

con·sol·ing (kən **sōl**´ ĭng) *adj.* Comforting. *Marcia's father gave her a consoling hug after she wrecked her bike.*

con·ver·sa·tion (kŏn´ vər **sā**´ shən) *n.* A spoken sharing of thoughts between two or more people. *Alexa knows so much about sports that our conversations are always interesting.*

crafts·man (**krăfts**´ mən) *n., pl.* **craftsmen** A skilled worker. *The work of colonial craftsmen is highly valued today.*

crus·ta·cean (krŭ **stā**´ shən) *n.* One of a large group of hardshelled animals that have jointed parts and live mostly in the water. *The lobster is a well-known crustacean.*

day·dream (**dā**´ drēm´) *v.* To think in a dreamy way, often about things one wishes would come true. *Because Cho was daydreaming, he did not hear my question.*

de·ci·sion (dĭ **sĭzh**´ ən) *n.* A choice that involves judgment. *Alex's decision was to quit the team.*

dem·on·strate (**dĕm**´ ən strāt´) *v.* To show clearly. *Mike demonstrates that he has what it takes to become a great pitcher.*

de·pot (**dē**´ pō, **dĕp**´ ō) *n.* A railroad station. *Brent arrived at the depot just as the train from Baltimore was pulling in.*

depot

der·e·lict (**dĕr**´ ə lĭkt´) *n.* A piece of property, usually a ship at sea, that has been deserted by its owner. *A derelict was blown in by the storm and smashed on the rocks.*

des·o·late (**dĕs**´ ə lĭt, **dĕz**´ ə lĭt) *adj.* Having few or no inhabitants; deserted. *The car ran out of gas on a desolate stretch of highway.*

des·per·ate (**dĕs**´ pər ĭt) *adj.* Feeling full of despair, hopeless. *The girl made a desperate plea for someone to save the cat.*

de·ter·mi·na·tion (dĭ tûr´ mə **nā**´ shən) *n.* The firm intention to accomplish a goal. *The combination of talent and determination enabled Alf to win a medal.*

ōō b**oo**t / ou **out** / ŭ c**u**t / û f**u**r / hw **wh**ich / th **th**in / th **th**is / zh vi**s**ion / ə **a**go, silent, pencil, lemon, circus

Glossary continued

dip·lo·mat (**dip**´ lə mát´) *n.* One who is appointed to represent his or her government in its relations with other governments. *Rachel's mother was sent as a diplomat to Brazil.*

dis·ap·pear·ance (dis´ ə **pir**´ əns) *n.* The state of having vanished. *Lydia was saddened by the disappearance of her pet mouse.*

dis·count (**dis**´ kount, dis **kount**´) *v.* To doubt the truth of something or regard it as a wild exaggeration. *Reference books discount myths about dragons and sea serpents.*

dis·cour·aged (di **skŭr**´ ijd, di **skŭr**´ ijd) *adj.* Disheartened; in a low mood because of a disappointment. *Having never won a baseball game, Nathan felt very discouraged.*

do·main (dō **mān**´) *n.* The territory ruled by a government. *Spain was included in the domain of ancient Rome.*

du·ra·ble (**door**´ ə bəl, **dyoor**´ ə bəl) *adj.* Sturdy and long-lasting. *Stone fences are more durable than wooden fences.*

dy·nas·ty (**dī**´ nə stē) *n., pl.* **dynasties** A line of rulers from one family. *China's ancient Ming dynasty held power for about 300 years.*

erosion

E

em·pire (**ěm**´ pīr) *n.* A large area made up of many territories under one government. *The ancient Roman empire once included parts of Great Britain.*

en·cour·age (ĕn **kŭr**´ ij, ĕn **kŭr**´ ij) *v.* To give support or confidence. *Effective coaches encourage their players during a game.*

en·deav·or (ĕn **dĕv**´ ər) *v.* To attempt. *She endeavored to keep her balance on the rocking deck of the ship.*

en·dur·ance (ĕn **door**´ əns, ĕn **dyoor**´ əns) *n.* The ability to keep going without giving in to stress or tiredness. *A marathon runner must have exceptional endurance.*

en·gi·neer (ĕn´ jə **nîr**´) *n.* A person specially trained to design and build machines and systems. *The engineers designed a complex landing system for the spacecraft.*

en·tan·gled (ĕn **tăng**´ gəld) *adj.* Twisted together. *The kitten's paws became entangled in the yarn.*

en·tou·rage (ŏn´ tŏŏ **räzh**´) *n.* A group of followers. *The queen's entourage included both servants and people of high rank.*

e·ro·sion (i **rō**´ zhən) *n.* All the natural processes that wear away earth and rock. *The erosion of the hillside was caused by heavy rains and wind.*

ă rat / ā **pay** / â care / ä father / ĕ **pet** / ē be / ĭ **pit** / ī **pie** / î **fierce** / ŏ **pot** / ō go / ô **paw**, **for** / oi **oil** / ŏŏ **book**

646

ev·i·dence (**ĕv**´ ĭ dəns) *n.* The data used to draw a conclusion. *Scientists studying dinosaurs look at the evidence found in prehistoric bones.*

ex·ca·va·tion (ĕk´ skə **vā**´ shən) *n.* The process of finding something by digging for it. *A later excavation of the site turned up more fossils.*

ex·clude (ĭk **sklood**´) *v.* To keep someone or something out. *The boys angered the girls by excluding them from the basketball game.*

ex·hi·bi·tion (ĕk´ sə **bish**´ ən) *n.* A show of an artist's work. *A traveling exhibition of Winslow Homer's work has come to our museum.*

ex·press (ĭk **sprĕs**´) *v.* To put into words; to communicate. *Toddlers express their feelings through words, noises, and actions.*

ex·tinct (ĭk **stingkt**´) *adj.* No longer living on the earth; having died out. *The passenger pigeon became extinct at the beginning of the twentieth century.*

ex·trav·a·gance (ĭk **străv**´ ə gəns) *n.* Careless, wasteful spending on luxuries. *Luke's extravagance put him deeply into debt.*

F

fa·tigue (fə **tēg**´) *n.* Extreme tiredness. *Her fatigue was so great she wanted to sleep for days.*

fig·u·rine (fig´ yə **rēn**´) *n.* A small molded or sculpted figure. *China figurines of children and dogs were lined up on the windowsill.*

flour·ish·ing (**flûr**´ ish ing, **flŭr**´ ish ing) *adj.* Growing energetically. *After the railroad was built, Greensville became a flourishing community.*

foot·hold (**fŏŏt**´ hōld´) *n.* A place that gives firm support for a foot while climbing. *The crumbling ledge could not provide a safe foothold.*

fos·sil (**fŏs**´ əl) *n.* The hardened skeleton or other remains of a creature of prehistoric times. *Dinosaur fossils have been found in many parts of the world.*

frus·tra·tion (frŭ **strā**´ shən) *n.* The discouragement and irritation that comes from not being able to achieve one's goal. *She felt frustration at not being able to solve the math problem.*

func·tion (**fŭngk**´ shən) *v.* To fill a particular purpose or role. *The knife functioned as a screwdriver to take the screws out of the clock.*

excavation
For ancient Latin speakers, *excavare* meant to hollow something out. Thus, an excavation is the hollowing out of a space by digging. The English word *cave* is from the same Latin verb.

flourishing
The Latin verb *florere*, meaning "to flower," is the origin of both *flourish* and *flower*.

fossil
Our word *fossil* came from the Latin adjective *fossilis*, meaning "dug up."

ŏŏ **boot** / ou **out** / ŭ cut / û **fur** / hw **which** / th **thin** / th **this** / zh **vision** / ə **ago**, silent, pencil, lemon, circus

647

humble
Humble has its origins in the Latin word *humus*, meaning "ground."

G

ge·lat·i·nous (jə **lăt**´ n əs) *adj.* Like gelatin; thick and slow to flow. *Tapioca pudding has a lumpy, gelatinous texture.*

ge·ol·o·gist (jē **ŏl**´ ə jĭst) *n.* A scientist who studies the earth's crust and the rocks it is made of. *Rocks can tell geologists a lot about how the earth changed in a particular place.*

goods (gŏŏdz) *n.* Items for sale. *The small store sold fabric, boots, farm tools, and other useful goods.*

gov·ern·ment (**gŭv**´ ərn mənt) *n.* The body or organization that manages a nation. *Our government sent representatives to Australia to discuss trade regulations.*

H

hatch·et (**hăch**´ it) *n.* A small, short-handled ax, to be used with only one hand. *A hatchet is useful for cutting firewood.*

hearth (härth) *n.* The floor of a fireplace, which usually extends into a room. *Julia sat by the wide brick hearth and warmed her hands.*

hov·er (**hŭv**´ ər, **hŏv**´ ər) *v.* To remain close by. *Helicopters hovered above the freeways so reporters could check the traffic conditions.*

hatchet

hum·ble (**hŭm**´ bəl) *adj.* Not rich or important. *The humble workers could not afford luxury items.*

hy·per·re·al·ist·ic (hī´ pər rē´ ə **lis**´ tik) *adj.* Extremely real-looking. *Many hyperrealistic paintings look exactly like photographs.*

hy·poth·e·sis (hī **pŏth**´ ĭ sĭs´) *n., pl.* **hypotheses** (hī **pŏth**´ ĭ sēz´) A scientific suggestion based on what is known so far. *Ideas remain hypotheses until evidence proves that they are true.*

I

ice ax (īs ăks) *n.* An ax used by mountain climbers to cut into the ice. *Jennifer hacked at the cliff with her ice ax.*

im·pro·vise (**im**´ prə vīz´) *v.* To make something from available materials. *When it began to rain, the hikers improvised a tent out of plastic garbage bags.*

in·quir·y (in **kwīr**´ ē, **in**´ kwə rē) *n., pl.* **inquiries** A request for information. *The park ranger received many inquiries about campsites.*

in·spi·ra·tion (in´ spə **rā**´ shən) *n.* A positive example that encourages others to attempt to reach their goals. *Her success in college is an inspiration to her younger sisters.*

ă rat / ā **pay** / â care / ä father / ĕ **pet** / ē be / ĭ **pit** / ī **pie** / î **fierce** / ŏ **pot** / ō go / ô **paw**, **for** / oi **oil** / ŏŏ **book**

648

in·ter·fer·ing (in´ tər **fir**´ ing) *adj.* Intruding in the business of other people; meddling. *Kara did not ask why her brother was crying, because she didn't want to seem to be interfering.*

in·ter·pret (in **tûr**´ prĭt) *v.* To determine or explain the meaning of something. *She interpreted the lab data to draw conclusions about the experiment.*

in·tri·cate (**in**´ trĭ kit) *adj.* Complicated; made up of many details. *The bracelet has an intricate design.*

J

jour·nal (**jûr**´ nəl) *n.* A personal record of events; a diary. *Angela wrote about her vacation in her journal.*

K

kay·ak (**kī**´ ăk´) *n.* A lightweight canoe, propelled by a double-bladed paddle, with a small opening for one or two people. *The girls paddled the kayak across the bay.*

kin·dling (**kind**´ ling) *n.* Small pieces of wood or other material used for starting fires. *A big log won't catch fire unless kindling is burning below it.*

L

lab·o·ra·to·ry (**lăb**´ rə tôr´ ē, **lăb**´ rə tôr´ ē) *n., pl.* **laboratories** A room or building equipped for scientific research or experiments. *She works in a laboratory where blood cells are analyzed.*

la·bor·er (**lā**´ bər ər) *n.* A worker who does tasks that do not require special skills. *The managers of the mines hired many laborers.*

ledg·er (**lĕj**´ ər) *n.* A book in which financial records are kept. *The ledgers show how much the business has paid its employees.*

M

main·land (**mān**´ lănd´, **mān**´ lənd) *n.* The large land mass of a country or continent that does not include its islands. *Hawaiians refer to the rest of the United States as the mainland.*

make·shift (**māk**´ shift´) *adj.* Used as a substitute for something. *The pioneer mother used a bureau drawer as a makeshift crib for the new baby.*

man·age (**măn**´ ij) *v.* To succeed in doing something with difficulty. *Rolf managed to finish the race even though he turned his ankle near the end.*

kayak

ŏŏ **boot** / ou **out** / ŭ cut / û **fur** / hw **which** / th **thin** / th **this** / zh **vision** / ə **ago**, silent, pencil, lemon, circus

649

ma·neu·ver (mə nōō´ vér, mə nyōō´ vər) *n.* A controlled change in the movement or direction of a vehicle. *Beginning drivers practice maneuvers for getting into tight parking spaces.*

mas·sive (măs´ ĭv) *adj.* Large and solid. *Redwoods are massive trees.*

me·nag·er·ie (mə năj´ ə rē, mə năzh´ ə rē) *n.* A collection of wild animals. *The veterinarian attended to a menagerie of wounded animals at the wildlife shelter.*

me·thod·i·cal·ly (mə thŏd´ ĭ kə lē, mə thŏd´ ĭk lē) *adv.* In a careful, orderly way. *She methodically searched through her books for the facts she needed.*

me·tic·u·lous (mĭ tĭk´ yə ləs) *adj.* Extremely careful and exact. *His meticulous lettering made the poster easy to read.*

me·trop·o·lis (mĭ trŏp´ ə lĭs) *n.* A major city; a center of culture. *Being a transportation center has made Chicago a great metropolis.*

mon·i·tor (mŏn´ ĭ tər) *v.* To supervise; to keep watch over. *The fire chief monitored the rescue operation.*

N

nav·i·ga·tion (năv´ ĭ gā´ shən) *n.* The practice of planning and controlling the course of a craft. *The captain's skill at navigation brought the ship safely through the storm.*

nav·i·ga·tor (năv´ ĭ gā´ tər) *n.* Someone who plans, records, and controls the course of a ship or plane. *The navigator plotted a course across the Pacific Ocean.*

no·mad·ic (nō măd´ ĭk) *adj.* Moving from place to place. *Nomadic shepherds often move their sheep to new grazing lands.*

no·tice (nō´ tĭs) *v.* To become aware of. *People will notice the colorful balloons tied to the stair railing.*

O

o·a·sis (ō ā´ sĭs) *n., pl.* **oases** (ō ā´ sēz) A green spot in a desert, where water can be found. *The travelers rested at the oasis and watered their camels at its spring.*

ob·sta·cle (ŏb´ stə kəl) *n.* Something that makes it difficult to continue. *His sisters' loud music and his lack of privacy were obstacles to serious studying.*

o·cean·og·ra·pher (ō´ shə nŏg´ rə fər) *n.* A scientist who specializes in the study of the sea. *Both oceanographers are interested in undersea volcanoes.*

---

meticulous
Perhaps Latin speakers of long ago lived in fear of making mistakes, for this adjective comes from the Latin word *meticulosus*, meaning "fearful."

metropolis
The ancient Greeks combined their words for *mother* and *city* to form *metropolis*, a word they used to describe the first settlement in a colony.

navigation, navigator
The Latin word *navis*, meaning "ship," and the word *agere*, meaning "to drive," were combined to form the Latin verb *navigare*, "to navigate."

---

op·ti·cal·ly (ŏp´ tĭk ə lē, ŏp´ tĭk lē) *adv.* Having to do with vision. *As I stared at the painting, the colors blended optically into a vivid swirl.*

o·ver·come (ō´ vər kŭm´) *v.* To conquer. *She has overcome her fear of heights.*

P

pains·tak·ing (pānz´ tā´ kĭng) *adj.* Requiring great and careful effort. *Repairing watches is painstaking work.*

pa·le·on·tol·o·gist (pā´ lē ŏn tŏl´ ə jĭst) *n.* A scientist who studies prehistoric life. *A paleontologist compares the bones of dinosaurs to those of modern animals.*

pal·ette (păl´ ĭt) *n.* A board on which an artist mixes colors. *Austin squeezed dabs of white and blue paint onto his palette.*

per·mis·sion (pər mĭsh´ ən) *n.* Necessary approval to do something. *The travelers need official permission to cross the border.*

per·mit·ted (pər mĭt´ əd) *adj.* Allowed. *Swimming is permitted from sunrise to sunset at Howe's Beach.* — *n.* A person who is allowed to do something. *Only permitteds can go past the gate.*

phase (fāz) *n.* One of the changes in appearance that the moon or a planet goes through each month. *The moon looks like a half circle in one of its phases.*

phys·ics (fĭz´ ĭks) *n.* The science of matter and energy and of how they relate to one another. *You can use simple physics to predict how soon a falling object will hit the ground.*

pi·ton (pē´ tŏn´) *n.* A metal spike, used in mountain climbing, with an eye or ring at one end. *The mountain climber's standard gear includes pitons.*

pix·el (pĭk´ səl, pĭk sĕl´) *n.* One of the tiny elements that make up an image on a TV or computer screen. *In computer drawing programs, widths of lines are measured in pixels.*

por·trait (pôr´ trĭt, pôr´ trāt) *n.* A drawing, painting, or photograph of a person. *A portrait of the first mayor of Centervale hangs in the lobby of the town hall.*

port (pôrt) *n.* The left side of a ship as one faces forward. *A small rowboat pulled up on the port side of the ship.*

pre·vi·ous (prē´ vē əs) *adj.* Occurring before something else in time or order. *The professor had explained the rule in a previous lecture.*

pri·mar·y (prī´ mĕr´ ē, prī´ mə rē) *adj.* Main; basic. *The club's primary purpose is to welcome new students.*

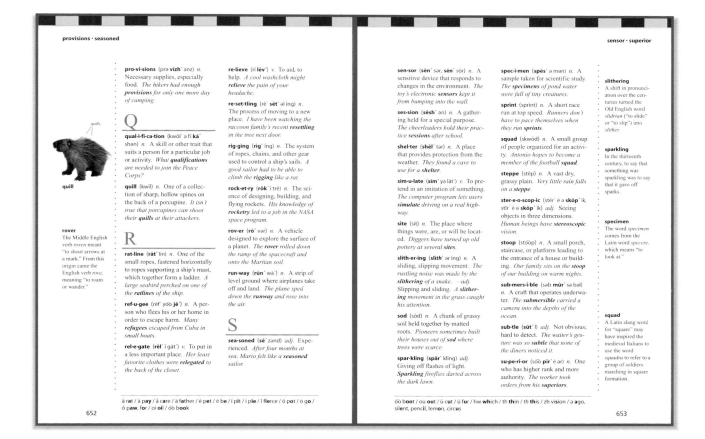

palette

palette
In Old French, *pale* was the word for a shovel or spade. A palette, then, was a small shovel.

pixel
The word *pixel* was created around 1969 by combining the word *pix* (short for *pictures*) and the first syllable of the word *elements*.

---

pro·vi·sions (prə vĭzh´ ənz) *n.* Necessary supplies, especially food. *The hikers had enough provisions for only one more day of camping.*

Q

qual·i·fi·ca·tion (kwŏl´ ə fĭ kā´ shən) *n.* A skill or other trait that suits a person for a particular job or activity. *What qualifications are needed to join the Peace Corps?*

quill (kwĭl) *n.* One of a collection of sharp, hollow spines on the back of a porcupine. *It isn't true that porcupines can shoot their quills at their attackers.*

R

rat·line (răt´ lĭn) *n.* One of the small ropes, fastened horizontally to ropes supporting a ship's mast, which together form a ladder. *A large seabird perched on one of the ratlines of the ship.*

ref·u·gee (rĕf´ yŏŏ jē´) *n.* A person who flees his or her home in order to escape harm. *Many refugees escaped from Cuba in small boats.*

rel·e·gate (rĕl´ ĭ gāt´) *v.* To put in a less important place. *Her least favorite clothes were relegated to the back of the closet.*

re·lieve (rĭ lēv´) *v.* To aid, to help. *A cool washcloth might relieve the pain of your headache.*

re·set·tling (rē´ sĕt´ əl ĭng) *n.* The process of moving to a new place. *I have been watching the raccoon family's recent resettling in the tree next door.*

rig·ging (rĭg´ ĭng) *n.* The system of ropes, chains, and other gear used to control a ship's sails. *A good sailor had to be able to climb the rigging like a rat.*

rock·et·ry (rŏk´ ĭ trē) *n.* The science of designing, building, and flying rockets. *His knowledge of rocketry led to a job in the NASA space program.*

rov·er (rō´ vər) *n.* A vehicle designed to explore the surface of a planet. *The rover rolled down the ramp of the spacecraft and onto the Martian soil.*

run·way (rŭn´ wā´) *n.* A strip of level ground where airplanes take off and land. *The plane sped down the runway and rose into the air.*

S

sea·soned (sē´ zənd) *adj.* Experienced. *After four months at sea, Mario felt like a seasoned sailor.*

quill

rover
The Middle English verb *roven* meant "to shoot arrows at a mark." From this origin came the English verb *rove*, meaning "to roam or wander."

---

sen·sor (sĕn´ sər, sĕn´ sôr) *n.* A sensitive device that responds to changes in the environment. *The toy's electronic sensors kept it from bumping into the wall.*

ses·sion (sĕsh´ ən) *n.* A gathering held for a special purpose. *The cheerleaders hold their practice sessions after school.*

shel·ter (shĕl´ tər) *n.* A place that provides protection from the weather. *They found a cave to use for a shelter.*

sim·u·late (sĭm´ yə lāt´) *v.* To pretend in an imitation of something. *The computer program lets users simulate driving on a real highway.*

site (sīt) *n.* The place where things were, are, or will be located. *Diggers have turned up old pottery at several sites.*

slith·er·ing (slĭth´ ər ĭng) *n.* A sliding, slipping movement. *The rustling noise was made by the slithering of a snake.* — *adj.* Slipping and sliding. *A slithering movement in the grass caught his attention.*

sod (sŏd) *n.* A chunk of grassy soil held together by matted roots. *Pioneers sometimes built their houses out of sod when trees were scarce.*

spar·kling (spär´ klĭng) *adj.* Giving off flashes of light. *Sparkling fireflies darted across the dark lawn.*

spec·i·men (spĕs´ ə mən) *n.* A sample taken for scientific study. *The specimens of pond water were full of tiny creatures.*

sprint (sprint) *n.* A short race run at top speed. *Runners don't have to pace themselves when they run sprints.*

squad (skwŏd) *n.* A small group of people organized for an activity. *Antonio hopes to become a member of the football squad.*

steppe (stĕp) *n.* A vast dry, grassy plain. *Very little rain falls on a steppe.*

ster·e·o·scop·ic (stĕr´ ē ə skŏp´ ĭk, stĭr´ ē ə skŏp´ ĭk) *adj.* Seeing objects in three dimensions. *Human beings have stereoscopic vision.*

stoop (stŏŏp) *n.* A small porch, staircase, or platform leading to the entrance of a house or building. *Our family sits on the stoop of our building on warm nights.*

sub·mers·i·ble (səb mûr´ sə bəl) *n.* A craft that operates underwater. *The submersible carried a camera into the depths of the ocean.*

sub·tle (sŭt´ l) *adj.* Not obvious; hard to detect. *The waiter's gesture was so subtle that none of the diners noticed it.*

su·pe·ri·or (sŏŏ pîr´ ē ər) *n.* One who has higher rank and more authority. *The worker took orders from his superiors.*

slithering
A shift in pronunciation over the centuries turned the Old English word *slidrian* ("to slide" or "to slip") into *slither*.

sparkling
In the thirteenth century, to say that something was sparkling was to say that it gave off sparks.

specimen
The word *specimen* comes from the Latin word *specere*, which means "to look at."

squad
A Latin slang word for "square" may have inspired the medieval Italians to use the word *squadra* to refer to a group of soldiers marching in square formation.

Glossary **G3**

tentacle

treacherous
This adjective comes from the Old French verb *trichier,* meaning "to trick." If something is treacherous, or marked by unpredictable dangers, it may also be said to be tricky.

sur·viv·al (sər **vī**´ vəl) *n.* The preservation of one's life; the continuing of life. *An injury lessens an animal's chance of* ***survival.***

sus·pi·cious (sə **spĭsh**´ əs) *adj.* Having the feeling that something unusual or wrong is going on. *The long silence in the children's room made their mother* ***suspicious.***

T

tax·i (**tăk**´ sē) *v.* To move slowly on the ground before taking off or after landing. *The plane* ***taxied*** *to a halt at the end of the runway.*

ten·ta·cle (**tĕn**´ tə kəl) *n.* One of the long, elastic, narrow limbs of an animal, used to feel, grasp, or move. *An octopus uses its* ***tentacles*** *to hold its prey.*

ter·rain (tə **rān**´) *n.* The physical features of an area of land. *The rugged* ***terrain*** *of the desert discourages travelers.*

ter·ri·fy (**tĕr**´ ə fī´) *v.* To frighten. *The howls of the mountain lion* ***terrified*** *the camper.*

the·o·ry (**thē**´ ə rē, **thîr**´ ē) *n., pl.* **theories** An idea that is based on evidence but that cannot be stated as fact. *In the 1860s, Joseph Lister published his* ***theory*** *that unseen germs cause infections.*

trans·mis·sion (trăns **mĭsh**´ ən, trănz **mĭsh**´ ən) *n.* A message sent by radio. *The tornado interrupted the* ***transmission*** *from the research station.*

treach·er·ous (**trĕch**´ ər əs) *adj.* Marked by unpredictable dangers. *A narrow ledge provided a* ***treacherous*** *path up the mountainside.*

trib·ute (**trĭb**´ yōōt) *n.* A gift given to those in power by people who have been defeated or who want protection. *Each year* ***tributes*** *of gold and spices were sent to the capital city from all over the kingdom.*

trin·ket (**trĭng**´ kĭt) *n.* A small item of little value. *For her son's sixth birthday party, Ana decorated the room with strings of beads, toy horns, and other* ***trinkets.***

U

un·con·ven·tion·al (ŭn´ kən **vĕn**´ shə nəl) *adj.* Out of the ordinary. *Nowadays, wearing an old-fashioned top hat is* ***unconventional.***

un·du·late (**ŭn**´ jə lāt´, **ŭn**´ dyə lāt´) *v.* To move in a smooth, wavy motion. *Tall grass* ***undulates*** *when a breeze blows over it.*

un·fath·om·a·ble (ŭn **făth**´ ə mə bəl) *adj.* Impossible to measure. *In mid-ocean the sea floor lies at* ***unfathomable*** *depths.*

ă rat / ā pay / â care / ä father / ĕ pet / ē be / ĭ pit / ī pie / î fierce / ŏ pot / ō go / ô paw, for / oi oil / ŏŏ book

ur·gen·cy (**ûr**´ jən sē) *n., pl.* **urgencies** The need to do something quickly. *When Vikash asked for a ride to the hospital, there was a sense of* ***urgency*** *to his voice.*

V

vi·cin·i·ty (vĭ **sĭn**´ ĭ tē) *n., pl.* **vicinities** The region within close range of a particular place. *The middle school is in the* ***vicinity*** *of Lincoln Park.*

vil·lage (**vĭl**´ ĭj) *n.* A small settlement. *There are thirty houses in the mountain* ***village.***

vi·sa (**vē**´ zə) *n., pl.* **visas** A document that gives a person approval to travel through a specific country. *Most tourists need* ***visas*** *as well as passports to travel through Russia.*

vis·i·bil·i·ty (vĭz´ ə **bĭl**´ ĭ tē) *n., pl.* **visibilities** The greatest distance over which it is possible to see. *When the fog rolled in,* ***visibility*** *was limited to a few yards.*

vol·un·teer (vŏl´ ən **tîr**´) *n.* A person who freely offers to do something. *Our clubhouse was built by* ***volunteers.***

W

ware (wâr) *n.* An item for sale. *The rug merchants displayed their* ***wares*** *at the street fair.*

village

visa

ōō boot / ou out / ŭ cut / û fur / hw which / th thin / *th* this / zh vision / ə ago, silent, pencil, lemon, circus

Acknowledgments

Main Literature Selections

Selection from *The Adventures of Sojourner: The Mission to Mars That Thrilled the World,* by Susi Trautmann Wunsch. Copyright © 1998 by Susi Trautmann Wunsch. Reprinted by permission of the publisher, Mikaya Press Inc.

Selection from *Amelia Earhart: First Lady of Flight,* by Jan Parr. Copyright © 1997 by Jan Parr. Reprinted by permission of Franklin Watts, a division of Grolier Publishing.

Selection from *Beneath Blue Waters: Meetings with Remarkable Deep-Sea Creatures,* by Deborah Kovacs and Kate Madin, principal photographs by Larry Madin. Copyright © 1996 by Deborah Kovacs and Kate Madin. Reprinted by permission of Viking Children's Books, a division of Penguin Putnam Inc.

Selections from *The Buried City of Pompeii,* a Hyperion/Madison Press Book by Shelley Tanaka, diagrams by Jack McMaster. Copyright © 1997 by Madison Press Limited. Reprinted by permission of Madison Press Limited.

"The Challenge" from *Local News,* by Gary Soto. Copyright © 1993 by Gary Soto. Reprinted with permission of Harcourt Inc.

Selection from *Chuck Close Up Close,* by Jan Greenberg and Sandra Jordan. Copyright © 1998 by Jan Greenberg and Sandra Jordan. Reprinted by permission of Dorling Kindersley Publishing, Inc.

Selection from *Climb or Die,* by Edward Myers. Copyright © 1996 by Edward Myers. Reprinted by permission of Hyperion Books for Children.

Selection from *Dinosaur Ghosts: The Mystery of Coelophysis,* by J. Lynett Gillette, illustrated by Doug Henderson. Text copyright © 1997 by J. Lynett Gillette. Illustrations copyright © 1997 by Douglas Henderson. Reprinted by permission of Dial Books for Young Readers, a division of Penguin Putnam Inc.

Excerpt from *Eugenie Clark: Adventures of a Shark Scientist,* by Ellen R. Butts and Joyce R. Schwartz. Copyright © 2000 by Ellen R. Butts and Joyce R. Schwartz. Reprinted by permission of Linnet Book, an imprint of The Shoe String Press, Inc., North Haven, CT.

"Franklin R. Chang-Diaz" from *Standing Tall: The Stories of Ten Hispanic Americans,* by Argentina Palacios. Copyright © 1994 by Argentina Palacios. Reproduced by permission of Scholastic Inc.

The Girl Who Married the Moon: Tales from Native North America. Text copyright © 1994 by Joseph Bruchac and Gayle Ross. Published by BridgeWater Books, an imprint and trademark of Troll Communications, LLC. Reprinted by permission of Troll Communications LLC.

Selection from *The Great Pyramid,* by Elizabeth Mann, illustrations by Laura Lo Turco. Copyright © Mikaya Press. Reprinted by permission of Mikaya Press.

Selection from *The Great Wall,* by Elizabeth Mann, with illustrations by Alan Witschonke. Copyright © 1997 Mikaya Press. Original illustrations copyright © by Alan Witschonke. Reprinted by permission of Mikaya Press Inc.

Selection from *Hatchet,* by Gary Paulsen. Jacket painting by Neil Waldman. Copyright © 1987 by Gary Paulsen. Jacket copyright © 1987 by Bradbury Press. Reprinted by permission of Simon & Schuster Books for Young Readers, an imprint of Simon & Schuster Children's Publishing Division.

Selection from *The Ink-Keeper's Apprentice,* by Allen Say. Text copyright © 1979 by Allen Say. Reprinted by permission of Houghton Mifflin Company. All rights reserved.

"Jerry Pinkney: My Story," published in the book *Talking with Artists* © 1992, compiled and edited by Pat Cummings, published by Bradbury Press, a division of Macmillan Publishing Company. Copyright © 1992 by Jerry Pinkney. Reprinted by permission of the author and the Sheldon Fogelman Agency, Inc. The watercolor painting "Boy with a Wagon" by Jerry Pinkney. Copyright © 1946 by Jerry Pinkney. Reprinted by permission of the author and the Sheldon Fogelman Agency, Inc. The illustration from *Black Cowboy, Wild Horses: A True Story,* by Julius Lester, illustrated by Jerry Pinkney. Illustration copyright © 1998 by Jerry Pinkney. Reprinted by permission of Dial Books for Young Readers, a division of Penguin Young Readers Group, a member of Penguin Group (USA) Inc. The illustration from *Aesop's Fables,* illustrated by Jerry Pinkney, published by Sea Star Books, a division of North-South Books Inc. Copyright © 2000 by Jerry Pinkney. Reprinted by permission of the publisher. Cover and one-page spread from *The Adventures of Spider,* by Joyce Cooper Arkhurst, illustrated by Jerry Pinkney. Text copyright © 1964 by Joyce Cooper Arkhurst. Illustration copyright © 1964 by Barker/Black Studio, Inc. Reprinted by permission of Little, Brown and Company, (Inc.). All rights reserved.

Selection from *A Kind of Grace,* by Jackie Joyner-Kersee. Copyright © 1997 by Jackie Joyner-Kersee. Reprinted by permission of Warner Books Inc.

Selection from *Last Summer with Maizon,* by Jacqueline Woodson. Copyright © 1990 by Jacqueline Woodson. Reprinted by permission of Random House Children's Books, a division of Random House Inc.

"The Lord of the Nile" from *Egyptian Myths,* by Jacqueline Morley, published by Peter Bedrick Books. Copyright © 1999 by Jacqueline Morley. Reprinted by permission of The McGraw-Hill Companies.

Selection from *Lost Temple of the Aztecs,* by Shelley Tanaka, illustrated by Greg Ruhl. Copyright © 1998 by The Madison Press Ltd. Illustrations © by Greg Ruhl. Reprinted by permission of Hyperion Books for Children.

"The Night of the Pomegranate" from *Some of the Kinder Planets,* by Tim Wynne-Jones, published by Orchard Books, an imprint of Scholastic Inc. Copyright © 1993 by Tim Wynne-Jones. Reprinted by permission of Scholastic Inc., and Groundwood Books/Douglas & McIntyre Ltd., Toronto, Canada.

"Out There" from *Rogue Wave and Other Red-Blooded Sea Stories,* by Theodore Taylor. Copyright © 1996 by Theodore Taylor. Reprinted by permission of Harcourt Inc.

Passage to Freedom, by Ken Mochizuki, illustrated by Dom Lee. Text copyright © 1997 by Ken Mochizuki. Illustrations copyright © 1997 by Dom Lee. Reprinted by permission of Lee & Low Books, Inc.

Selection from *Rosa Parks: My Story,* by Rosa Parks with Jim Haskins. Copyright © 1992 by Rosa Parks. Published by arrangement with Dial Books for Young Readers, a member of Penguin Putnam Inc.

Selection from *The Royal Kingdoms of Ghana, Mali, and Songhay,* by Patricia and Fredrick McKissack. Copyright © 1994 by Patricia and Fredrick McKissack. Reprinted by permission of Henry Holt and Company, LLC.

Selection from *The True Confessions of Charlotte Doyle,* by Avi. Copyright © 1990 by Avi. Reprinted by permission of Orchard Books, New York.

Selection from *Under the Royal Palms,* by Alma Flor Ada. Copyright © 1998 by Alma Flor Ada. Reprinted with the permission of Atheneum Books for Young Readers, an imprint of Simon & Schuster Children's Publishing Division. Cover photograph copyright © 1998 by Alma Flor Ada. Photograph used with permission of the Author and Bookstop Literary Agency. All rights reserved.

Selection from *The View from Saturday,* by E.L. Konigsburg. Text copyright © 1996 E.L. Konigsburg. Jacket illustration copyright © 1996 E.L. Konigsburg. Reprinted by permission of Atheneum Books for Young Readers, an imprint of Simon & Schuster Children's Publishing Division.

Selection from *Where the Red Fern Grows,* by Wilson Rawls. Copyright © 1961 by Sophie S. Rawls, Trustee, or successor Trustee(s) of the Rawls Trust, dated July 31, 1991. Copyright © 1961 by the Curtis Publishing Company. Reprinted by permission of Dell Publishing, a division of Random House, Inc.

"Wolfgang Amadeus Mozart" from *Lives of the Musicians: Good Times, Bad Times (and What the Neighbors Thought),* by Kathleen Krull. Copyright © 1993 by Kathleen Krull. Reprinted by permission of Harcourt, Inc.

Selection from *Yolonda's Genius,* by Carol Fenner. Copyright © 1996 by Carol Fenner. Reprinted with the permission of Margaret K. McElderry Books, an imprint of Simon & Schuster Children's Publishing Division.

Focus Selections

"Arachne the Spinner" from *Greek Myths,* by Geraldine McCaughrean, illustrated by Emma Chichester Clark. Copyright © 1992 by Geraldine McCaughrean. Illustrations copyright © 1992 by Emma Chichester Clark. Reprinted by permission of Margaret K. McElderry Books, an imprint of Simon & Schuster Children's Publishing Division.

"A Better Mousetrap," by Colleen Neuman. Copyright © 1993 by Colleen Neuman. Reprinted by permission of Baker's Plays, Quincy, MA.

"Child Rest," by Phil George from *Whispering Wind,* edited by Terry Allen. Copyright © 1972 by The Institute of American Indian Arts. Reprinted by permission of Doubleday, a division of Random House, Inc.

Excerpt from *"A Commencement Speech"* by Katherine Ortega. Copyright © by Katherine Ortega. Reprinted by permission of the author.

Selection from *The Diary of Anne Frank,* by Frances Goodrich and Albert Hackett. Copyright © 1954, 1956 as an unpublished work. Copyright © 1956 by Albert Hackett, Frances Goodrich Hackett, and Otto Frank. Reprinted by permission of Random House Inc.

"Family Photo" from *Relatively Speaking,* by Ralph Fletcher. Text copyright © 1999 by Ralph Fletcher. Reprinted by permission of Orchard Books, New York.

"Family Style" from *Good Luck Gold and Other Poems,* by Janet S. Wong. Copyright © 1994 by Janet S. Wong. Reprinted with permission of Margaret K. McElderry Books, an imprint of Simon & Schuster Children's Publishing Division.

Focus on Speeches opening page: Illustration is from *The Gettysburg Address,* illustrated by Michael McCurdy. Illustration copyright © 1995 by Michael McCurdy. Reprinted by permission of Houghton Mifflin Company. All rights reserved.

"Good Hotdogs" from *My Wicked Wicked Ways.* Copyright © 1987 by Sandra Cisneros. Published by Third Woman Press and in hardcover by Alfred A. Knopf. Reprinted by permission of Third Woman Press and Susan Bergholz Literary Services, New York. All rights reserved.

"Guitar Solo" from *The Bronze Cauldron,* by Geraldine McCaughrean, illustrated by Bee Willey. Text copyright © 1997 by Geraldine McCaughrean. Illustrations copyright © 1997 by Bee Willey. Reprinted with the permission of Margaret K. McElderry Books, an imprint of Simon & Schuster Children's Publishing Division.

"How Music Was Fetched Out of Heaven" from *The Golden Hoard,* by Geraldine McCaughrean, illustrated by Bee Willey. Text copyright © 1995 by Geraldine McCaughrean. Illustrations copyright © 1995 by Bee Willey. Reprinted with the permission of Margaret K. McElderry Books, an imprint of Simon & Schuster Children's Publishing Division.

Excerpt from the speech *"I Have a Dream"* by Martin Luther King, Jr. Copyright © 1963 by Martin Luther King, Jr. Copyright © renewed 1991 by Coretta Scott King. Reprinted by permission of the Heirs to the Estate of Martin Luther King, Jr. c/o Writers House Inc., as agent for the proprietor.

"Losing Livie" from *Out of the Dust,* by Karen Hesse. Published by Scholastic Press, a division of Scholastic Inc. Copyright © 1997 by Karen Hesse. Jacket illustration copyright © 1997 by Scholastic Inc. Reprinted by permission of Scholastic Inc. Jacket photograph courtesy of the Library of Congress Prints and Photographs division, Farm Security Administration Collection.

"My Own Man" from *My Man Blue,* by Nikki Grimes. Copyright © 1999 by Nikki Grimes. Reprinted by permission of Dial Books for Young Readers, a division of Penguin Putnam, Inc.

Excerpt from the speech *"On Accepting the Newbery Medal"* by Jerry Spinelli. Copyright © 1991 by Jerry Spinelli. Reprinted by permission of the American Library Association.

"Oranges" from *New and Selected Poems,* by Gary Soto. Copyright © 1995 by Gary Soto. Published by Chronicle Books, San Francisco. Reprinted by permission of the publisher.

"The Pasture" from *The Poetry of Robert Frost,* edited by Edward Connery Lathem. Copyright 1944 by Robert Frost. Copyright 1916, © 1969 by Henry Holt and Company, LLC. Reprinted by permission of Henry Holt and Company, LLC.

Selection from *"The People, Yes"* from *Rainbows Are Made: Poems by Carl Sandburg.* Copyright © 1982 by The Carl Sandburg Family Trust. Reprinted by permission of Harcourt Inc.

"Poem" from *Collected Poems,* by Langston Hughes. Copyright © 1994 by the Estate of Langston Hughes. Reprinted by permission of Alfred Knopf Inc.

"Poetry," by Eleanor Farjeon from *Poems for Children.* Copyright 1938 by Eleanor Farjeon. Copyright © renewed 1966 by Gervase Farjeon. Reprinted by permission of Harold Ober Associates Incorporated.

"A Story of Courage, Bravery, Strength and Heroism. . ." by Shao Lee. Copyright © 1995 by Shao Lee. Reprinted by permission of The Asian Pages.

"Sundays" from *Brickyard Summer,* by Paul B. Janeczko (Orchard Books). Copyright © 1989 by Paul B. Janeczko. Reprinted by permission of the author.

Links and Theme Openers

"Alone Against the Sea" from the April 1997 issue of *National Geographic World.* Copyright © 1997 by the National Geographic Society. Reprinted by permission of the publisher.

Selection from *Ancient Romans at a Glance,* by Dr. Sarah McNeill. Copyright © 1998 by Macdonald Young Books. Reprinted by permission of NTC/Contemporary Publishing Group, Inc.

"Barnstorming Bessie Coleman," by Sylvia Whitman from *Cobblestone* February 1997 issue: "Tuskegee Airmen." Copyright © 1997 by Cobblestone Publishing Company. All rights reserved. Reprinted by permission of the publisher.

"Battling Everest" from the January 1999 issue of *National Geographic World.* Copyright © 1999 by the National Geographic Society. Reprinted by permission of the publisher.

"Brazilian Moon Tale," by Jane Yolen was first published in *What Rhymes with Moon?* published by Philomel Books. Copyright © 1993 by Jane Yolen. Reprinted by permission of Curtis Brown, Ltd.

"Build and Launch a Paper Rocket" was adapted from *NASA's Rockets: Physical Science Teacher's Guide with Activities*.

"Courage in the News" from an article entitled "Boy Wonder" published in the October 4, 1991 issue of the *St. Louis Post-Dispatch*. Copyright © by the *St. Louis Post-Dispatch*. Reprinted by permission of the publisher.

"Daily Life in Ancient Greece" from *Ancient Greece*, by Robert Nicholson. Text copyright © 1994 by Two-Can Publishing Ltd. Reprinted by permission of Chelsea House Publishers.

"Different Strokes," by Samantha Bonar, from *American Girl*, May/June 1999 issue. Copyright © 1999 by Pleasant Company. Artwork © Alexandra Nechita. Reprinted by permission of Alexandra Nechita and Pleasant Company.

"Doctor Dinosaur," by Carolyn Duckworth. Copyright © 1997 by Carolyn Duckworth. Reprinted by permission of the author.

"Half Moon," by Federico García Lorca from *Obras Completas* (Galaxia Gutenberg, 1996 edition). Translation by W.S. Merwin copyright © Herederos de Federico García Lorca and W.S. Merwin. All rights reserved. For information regarding rights and permissions, contact lorca@artslaw.co.uk or William Peter Kosmas, Esq., 8 Franklin Square, London W14 9UU, England. Translation reprinted by permission of New Directions Publishing Corp.

"Help Wanted: Group Seek Kid Volunteers to Change the World, No Experience Necessary" by Anna Prokos, from the December 1997 issue of 3-2-1 *Contact* magazine. Copyright © 1997 by Children's Television Workshop. Reprinted by permission of Children's Television Workshop.

"Home-Grown Butterflies" from the May 1998 issue of *Ranger Rick* magazine with the permission of the National Wildlife Federation. Copyright © 1998 by the National Wildlife Federation.

"How to Be a Good Sport" from *Current Health 1*®, Vol. 22, No. 4, December 1998. Copyright © 1998 by Weekly Reader Corporation. All rights reserved. Reprinted by permission of the publisher.

"Little Brother, Big Idea," by Ethan Herberman, from *Current Science* magazine, December 1998. Copyright © 1998 by the Weekly Reader Corporation. Reprinted by permission of the publisher.

"Moon" from *Sky Songs*, by Myra Cohn Livingston (Holiday House, New York). Copyright © 1984 by Myra Cohn Livingston. Reprinted by permission of Marian Reiner.

"A Poem for Langston Hughes" from *The Selected Poems of Nikki Giovanni*, by Nikki Giovanni. Copyright © 1996 by Nikki Giovanni. Reprinted by permission of HarperCollins Publishers.

"Poetic Power" by Ariel Eason, Julia Perez-Axzell and Rebecca Owen. Copyright © 1996 by New Moon Publishing. Reprinted with permission from *New Moon® The Magazine for Girls and Their Dreams*, New Moon Publishing, Duluth, MN.

"Puppy Love" adapted from *American Girl*, Vol. 3, No. 2. Copyright © 1995 by Pleasant Company. Reprinted by permission of Pleasant Company.

"Raising Royal Treasures" from the November 13, 1998 issue of *Time for Kids*. Copyright © 1998 by Time Inc. Reprinted by permission of the publisher.

"A Real Jazzy Kid" from the March 1994 issue of *U.S. Kids* magazine. Copyright © 1994 by Children's Better Health Institute, Benjamin Franklin Literary & Medical Society, Inc., Indianapolis, IN. Reprinted by permission.

"Sharks Under Ice" from the February 1999 issue of *National Geographic World*. Copyright © 1999 by the National Geographic Society. Reprinted by permission of the publisher.

"Summer Full Moon," by James Kirkup. Copyright © 1992 by James Kirkup. Reprinted by permission of the author.

"Sylvia Earle" from "Exploring the Deep" in the Winter 1999 issue of *Time for Kids*. Copyright © 1999 by Time Inc. Reprinted by permission of the publisher.

"Winter Moon" from *Collected Poems*, by Langston Hughes. Copyright © 1994 by the Estate of Langston Hughes. Reprinted by permission of Alfred A. Knopf, a division of Random House, Inc.

"Youth" from *Collected Poems*, by Langston Hughes. Copyright © 1994 by the Estate of Langston Hughes. Reprinted by permission of Alfred A. Knopf, a division of Random House Inc.

Special thanks to the following teachers whose students' compositions appear as Student Writing Models:

Writing Models

Cindy Cheatwood, Florida; Diana Davis, North Carolina; Kathy Driscoll, Massachusetts; Linda Evers, Florida; Heidi Driscoll, Michigan; Eileen Hoffman, Massachusetts; Julia Kraftsow, Florida; Bonnie Lewison, Florida; Kanetha McCord, Michigan

Credits

Index

Boldface page references indicate formal strategy and skill instruction.

Extra Support/Intervention. *See* Reaching All Learners.

Fact and opinion. *See* Comprehension skills.

Fiction. *See* Literary genres; Selections in Anthology.

Fiction/nonfiction, distinguishing, *46, 90*

Figurative language. *See* Writer's craft.

Fluency
assessing, *BTS19–20, 39, 55, 79, 99, M45, 129*
independent reading, *37, 59, 81, 103, 127, R2–R3, R4–R5, R6–R7*
leveled activities for, *24C, 49K, 71U, 93U, 117C*
modeling, *25G, 47O–47R, 49S, 71O–71R, 71CC, 93CC, 93O–93R, 115O–115R, 117K, 135O–135R*
oral reading, *33, 37, 39, 99, 101, 105, 117I, 117J, 121, 129*
practice for, *39, 47O–47R, 55, 71O–71R, 79, 93O–93R, 99, 115O–115R, M13, M21, 129, 135O–135R*
See also Rereading.

Gender diversity. *See* Literary analysis.

Generalizations, making. *See* Comprehension skills.

Genre. *See* Literary genres.

Get Set to Read
"Album for a Hero," *50–51*
"Equipped to Climb," *72–73*
"In the Wild," *26–27*
"To Sail a Ship," *94–95*

Glossary in Student Anthology, *G1–G5*

Grammar and usage
sentence, parts of a
clauses, ***93I–93J, 135I–135J, M40, M41, R28***
compound subjects and predicates, ***47J, M40, R25***
simple and complete predicates, ***47I–47J, M40, R25***
simple and complete subjects, ***47I–47J, M40, R25***
sentence structure
complex, ***93I–93J, 135I, M41, R28***
compound, ***71I–71J, 71M, 135I, M41, R27***
compound-complex, ***135I, M41, R28***
sentences, types of
declarative, ***47I–47J, 47M, M40, R24***
exclamatory, ***47I–47J, 47M, M40, R24***
imperative, ***47I–47J, 47M, M40, R24***

interrogative, ***47I–47J,*** *47M,* ***M40, R24***
speech, parts of. *See* Speech, parts of.
spelling connection. *See* Lessons, specific, grammar.
usage
sentence fragments, ***93I–93J,*** *93M, M41, R29*
run-on sentences, ***93I–93J,*** *M41, R29*

Graphic information, interpreting
captions, *68,* ***115H***
charts, ***115H***
diagrams, *98*
globe, ***115H,*** *R11*
graphs, ***115H***
maps, *67, 68,* ***115H,*** *91, R11*
photographs, *68–69*
tables, ***115H***

Graphic organizers
cause-and-effect chain, *41, 49B*
charts, *45*
cooperation chart, *R13*
details chart, *28, 29, 36, 42, 43, 47A*
diagram, *111*
event chart, *74, 75, 80, 81, 86, 87, 93A*
fact and opinion chart, *61*
flow chart, *115O*
judgments chart, *52, 58, 64, 65, 71A*
literary devices in poetry chart, *120, 126, 132*
prediction chart, *95B, 95C, 96, 102, 105, 108, 109, 115A*
problem-solution chart, *90, 93*
story map, *83*
timeline, *93A*

Graphophonemic/graphophonic cues. *See* Phonics.

Guided comprehension. *See* Critical thinking.

Handwriting, *49G*

Home-Community Connection. *See* Home/Community Connections book.

Home-School Connection. *See* Home/Community Connections book.

Homework. *See* Home/Community Connections book.

Illustrator's craft
characterization, *60*
mood, *67, 114, R2*
picture details, *60*
suspense and danger, *114*

Illustrators of Anthology selections
Farnsworth, Bill, *87*

Lee, Dom, *65*
McKowen, Scott, *96*
Rodriguez, Robert, *M18*
Steirnagle, Michael, *28*

Independent and recreational reading
suggestions for, *23E–23F, 47B, 47O–47R, 71B, 71O–71R, 93B, 93O–93R, 115B, 115O–115R, 135B, 135O–135R, R2–R3, R4–R5, R6–R7*
See also Reading modes; Ready-Made Small Group Activities.

Independent writing
suggestions for, *47L, 71L, 93L, 115L, 135L*
See also Language Center; Ready-Made Small Group Activities; Teacher's Resource Blackline Masters.

Individual needs, meeting. *See* Reaching All Learners.

Inferences, making
about writer's craft, *122, 124, 127, 128*
about characters' actions and feelings, *34, 36, 42, 58, 59, 60, 62, 65, 66, 71, 76, 78, 80, 82, 88, 93, 98, 100, 102, 106, 108, 110, M10, M16, M20, 122, 126, 130*
See also Comprehension skills: cause and effect; Comprehension skills: generalizations, making.

Inflected forms. *See* Structural analysis.

Information skills
graphic aids: graphs, tables, captions, and charts, using, ***115H***
index, using, ***93H***
interviewing, *47*
parts of a book, using, ***93H***
primary sources, how to read, ***68–71***
print and electronic card catalogs, using, ***47H***
print and electronic reference sources, using, *71,* ***71H,*** *115, 117J,* ***135G***
synthesizing, *45, 60*
See also Reference and study skills.

Interviewing. *See* Speaking.

Journal, *28, 29, 45, 52, 53, 67, 75, 89, 97, 111, 121*

Judgments, making. *See* Comprehension skills.

Knowledge, activating prior. *See* Background, building.

Language and usage. *See* Grammar and usage.

program materials. *See* Teaching and management.

small groups. *See* Ready-Made Small Group Activities.

Managing flexible groups. *See* Lesson plans.

Maps, using. *See* Graphic information, interpreting.

Mathematics activities. *See* Cross-curricular activities.

Meaning, constructing from text. *See* Comprehension skills; Decoding; Language concepts and skills; Phonics; Strategies, reading.

Mechanics, language
capitalization
first word of sentence, ***71L, M42***
people's titles, ***115J, M42***
proper nouns, ***115I–115J***
proofreading, *47L, 49F, 71L, 93L, 115J*
punctuation
apostrophe in possessives and contractions, ***115C***
appositives, using commas with, *115L*
exclamation point, *47I, 47J,* ***71L,*** *M42, R24*
period, *47I, 47J,* ***71L,*** *M42, R24*
proofreading, *47J, 49F, 71L, 115J*
question mark, *47I, 47J,* ***71L,*** *M42*

Media
and advertising, *35*
projects, presenting, *35*
See also Links, content area, media literacy.

Metacognition. *See* Comprehension skills; Modeling, Think Aloud; Strategies, reading.

Modeling
student, *32, 36, 37, 38, 42, 43, 56, 58, 59, 60, 64, 65, 80, 81, 84, 87, 93C, 93D, 93H, 100, 106, 109, M12, M20, 124, 127*
teacher, *28, 29, 33, 41, 47A, 47C, 47D, 47G, 47H, 51, 52, 53, 56, 57, 62, 68, 71A, 71C, 71D, 71G, 71H, 73, 74, 75, 78, 90, 93A, 93C, 93D, 93G, 93H, 93J, 95, 96, 97, 100, 104, 106, 112, 115A, 115C, 115G, 115H, M10, M12, M20, M23, M29, M30, M32, M33, M34, M35, M36, M37, 119, 120, 123, 135A, 135C, 135D, 135G, 135H, R16, R18, R20, R22*
Think Aloud, *28, 29, 33, 47A, 47C, 47D, 47G, 47H, 52, 53, 71A, 71C, 71D, 71G, 74, 75, 78, 93A, 93C, 93D, 93G, 93H, 96, 97, 115A, 115C, 115G, M10, M29, M30, M32, M33, M34, M35, M36, M37, 120, 135A, 135C, 135D, 135G*
writing, *47S–49H*

Monitoring comprehension. *See* Strategies, reading.

Morphemes. *See* Decoding skills.

Morphology. *See* Decoding skills; Phonics.

Multi-age classroom. *See* Combination classroom.

Multicultural activities/information
adapting to a new culture, *49S–49T*
Hillary and Norgay's Mount Everest climb, *93*
persecution of Jews by Nazis, *50, 68, 69*

Narrative text, *28–43, 74–87, 97–109, M18–M22*

National Test Correlation. *See* Assessment, planning for.

Newsletters. *See* Home/Community Connection book; Teacher's Resource Blackline Masters.

Nonfiction. *See* Expository text; Literary genres; Selections in Anthology.

Notes, taking, *31, 47,* ***112–115,*** *M26*

Oral composition. *See* Speaking.

Oral language development. *See* Listening; Speaking.

Oral presentations. *See* Speaking.

Oral reading. *See* Reading modes; Rereading.

Oral reading fluency. *See* Fluency.

Oral summary. *See* Summarizing.

Paired learning. *See* Classroom management, partners.

Parent involvement. *See* Home/Community Connections book.

Parts of a book. *See* Reference and study skills.

Peer conferences. *See* Reading-Writing Workshop: conferencing.

Peer evaluation. *See* Cooperative learning activities; Reading-Writing Workshop, conferencing.

Peer interaction. *See* Cooperative learning activities.

Personal response. *See* Responding to literature.

Phonics
connect to spelling and writing, *47D, 71D, 93D, 115D, 135D*
patterns
CV pattern, ***71D***

long vowel CVC final *e, 53,* ***71D***
short vowel CVC, ***47D,*** *71C*
VCCV pattern, *47C, 71C*
vowel(s)
ea as short vowel, ***93D***
final *y* sounded as long *e, 47C*
final *y* sounded as long or short *i,* ***93D***
igh, *56*
o-consonant-*e,* as short *u, 93D*
/ou/, /oo/, /ô/, and /oi/ sounds, ***115D***
short vowels, ***47D***
ui, *71D*
silent consonants, *135D, 135E*
See also Decoding skills; Spelling.

Picture clues, *60, 114, R2*

Plot. *See* Story elements.

Poems in Anthology
"Child Rest" by Phil George, *132*
"Family Photo" by Ralph Fletcher, *133*
"Family Style" by Janet Wong, *128*
"Good Hotdogs" by Sandra Cisneros, *121–122*
"Losing Livie" by Karen Hesse, *123*
"My Own Man" by Nikki Grimes, *130*
"Oranges" by Gary Soto, *126–127*
"The Pasture" by Robert Frost, *125*
"Poem" by Langston Hughes, *124*
"Poetry" by Eleanor Farjeon, *119*
"The People, Yes," from the poem by Carl Sandburg, *131*
"Sundays" by Paul Janeczko, *129*

Predicting outcomes. *See* Comprehension skills.

Predictions, making and checking
checking, *42, 64, 86, 108, 132*
from previewing, *53, 74*
review, *43, 65, 87, 109, M16, M23, 133*
while reading, *57, 78, 108*

Prefixes. *See* Structural analysis.

Previewing
author, illustrator, cover, title, *28, 68, 69, 74, 90, 95B, 112, 121*
extra support for, *42, 64, 86, 108, M11, M18, 132*
illustrations, *49J, 69, 114, 121, 128*
text, *29, 53, 59, 75, 96, 97, 103, 128, R2, R4, R6*

Prewriting. *See* Reading-Writing Workshop, steps of; Writing skills.

Prior knowledge. *See* Background, building.

Problem solving. *See* Comprehension skills.

Process writing. *See* Reading-Writing Workshop, steps of; Writing skills.

Pronunciation Guide, *R41*

Proofreading. *See* Reading-Writing Workshop, steps of; Writing skills, proofreading skills.

Study skills. *See* Reference and study skills; Skills links.

Study strategies. *See* Reference and study skills.

Suffixes. *See* Structural analysis.

Summarizing
oral summaries, *32, 36, 38, 42, 43, 59, 64, 80, 81, 86, 87, 93, 102, 108, R2, R4, R6*

Syntactic cues. *See* Structural analysis.

Syntax. *See* Decoding, context clues.

Teacher Read Alouds
essay
    "Courage Is Something Everyone Has Inside Them" by Son Ca Lam, *49S–49T*
    "Rosie to the Rescue" by Fran Hodgkins, *71CC–71DD*
    "Run, Kate Shelley, Run" by Julia Pferdehirt, *93CC–93DD*
story
    "Jamison Way, The" by Kitty Colton, *25G–25H*
    "Mummy Mystery, A" by Andrew Clements, *BTS6–BTS19*
    "Rescuer from Lime Rock, The" by Stephen Currier, *25G–25H*

Teaching across the curriculum. *See* Content areas, reading in the; Cross-curricular activities; Links, content area.

Teaching and management
managing assessment, *23K–23L*
managing instruction, *23G–23H*
managing program materials, *22A–23A, 49Q–49R, 72C–72D, 94C–94D*
parent conferences. *See* Home/Community Connections book.
special needs of students, meeting. *See* Reaching All Learners.
See also Classroom Management Handbook.

Technology resources
address list, *R38*
Internet, *28, 45, 65, 87, 89, 96, 111*
www.eduplace.com, *28, 45, 65, 87, 89, 96, 111*

Test Prep, *28, 47B, 52, 71B, 74, 93B, 96, 115B, 135B*

Tests, Taking
Choosing the Best Answer, *M29–M31*

Text organization and structure
chapter headings, *R2, R4, R6*
diagrams and maps, *91, R6*
epilogue, *R4*
headings, *90, 92*
interview format, *68–71*
introduction, *28, 68, 74, 95B, R2*
newspaper format, *46–47*
photographs and captions, *46, 47, 49N, 69, 72, 90, 112*

preface, *R4*
subtitle, *90*
See also Comprehension skills.

Theme, Launching the, *23M–23P*

Theme paperbacks. *See* Leveled Theme Paperbacks.

Theme Skills Overview, *23G–23H*

Think Aloud. *See* Modeling.

Thinking
creatively. *See* Creative thinking.
critically. *See* Critical thinking.

Topic, main idea and details. *See* Comprehension skills.

Topics, selecting. *See* Reading-Writing Workshop, steps of, prewriting; Research activities.

Usage. *See* Grammar and usage.

Viewing
art, *67*
illustrations. *See* Picture clues.
illustrator's craft, **114**
purpose
    to determine illustrator's craft, *67, 114*

Visual literacy
illustrator's craft, **114**

Visualizing, *33, 98, 117I,* **125,** *R7*

Vocabulary, building
animals, plants, stones of Canada, **R17**
definitions, *71F*
easily confused words, *47M*
feeling words, *R19*
genre vocabulary (poetry), *119*
idioms, *77, 87*
motion words, *115M*
mountaineering and climbing words, *93M, R21*
nautical words, *R23*
parts of an entry, **93G**
specialized/technical vocabulary, *R4*
synonyms, *135G, R19*
See also Language concepts and skills, Ready-Made Small Group Activities, word work.

Vocabulary Readers
Fly Away, Children, 50
Lost in the Wilderness!, 26
On Top of The World, 72
Paul Laurence Dunbar, Poet, 118
Voyage of the Fram, 94

Vocabulary, selection
key words, *26, 27, 30, 32, 34, 38, 40, 47M, 50, 51, 52, 56, 59, 62, 68, 70, 71M, 73, 76, 78,*

80, 82, 84, 90, 92, 93M, 95, 98, 100, 102, 104, 106, 108, 114, 115M, M9, M10, M12, M14, M17, M18, M20, 119, 122, 124, 126, 130, 132, R2, R4, R6
See also Context clues; Daily Language Practice; Decoding skills.

Vocabulary skills
association, *135G*
classifying, *47F*
compound words. *See* Structural analysis.
context, using, **47G,** *93F*
connotation, **135G**
dictionary, using, *29,* **71G,** *81,* **93G,** *115G, R19, R21*
multiple meanings, *115F*
sense words, *45*
signal words for generalizations, *107*
signal words for sequence, *77, 90, 93A, 101, 115P*
while reading, *26, 27, 30, 32, 34, 38, 40, 50, 51, 52, 56, 59, 62, 68, 70, 73, 75, 76, 78, 80, 82, 84, 90, 92, 95, 98, 100, 102, 104, 106, 108, 114, R2, R4, R6, R8*
word families related by meaning, **115G,** *135E, 135F, M37*
word webs. *See* Graphic organizers, word web.
See also Dictionary skills; Vocabulary, building; Vocabulary, selection.

Vowels. *See* Phonics; Spelling.

Word analysis. *See* Structural analysis; Vocabulary, building.

Word work activities. *See* Ready-Made Small Group Activities, word work.

Writer's craft
alliteration, *125*
characterization, *47A, 62, 71A, 76, 80*
comparisons, *125*
descriptive language, *84, 105, 108*
details, *47, 47A, 62, 104*
dialogue, *64, 76*
figurative language, *40, 43, 83, 107, 117J*
imagery, *32, 34, 40, 105, 125, 135A*
indirect explanation, *54*
literary devices chart, *120*
metaphor, *118, 132, 135A*
mood, *54, 104*
narration, *76*
narrator of a poem, **131**
onomatopoeia, *125*
personification, *118, 135A*
point of view, *54, 56, 88*
    first-person, *M16*
precise language, *98*